P9-DXH-330
03540754

"A Country Nourished on Self-Doubt"

Documents in Canadian History,
1867–1980

OKANAGAN COLLEGE
LIBRARY
BRITISH COLUMBIA

"A Country Nourished on Self-Doubt"

Documents in Canadian History,
1867–1980

edited by Thomas Thorner

broadview press

Canadian Cataloguing in Publication Data

Main entry under title:
    "A country nourished on self-doubt": documents in Canadian history,
    1867–1980

Includes bibliographical references.

ISBN 1-55111-151-9

1. Canada -- History -- Sources.   I. Thorner, Thomas.

FC18.C68 1998   971   C97-932411-4
F1026.C69 1998

Copyright © 1998, the authors

All rights reserved. The use of any part of this publication reproduced, transmitted in any form or by any means, electronic, mechanical, photocopying, recording, or otherwise, or stored in a retrieval system, without prior written consent of the publisher — or in the case of photocopying, a licence from CANCOPY (Canadian Copyright Licensing Agency), 6 Adelaide Street East, Suite 900, Toronto, Ontario M5C 1H6 — is an infringement of the copyright law.

broadview press   broadview press
P.O. Box 1243   3576 California Road
Peterborough, Ontario   Orchard Park, NY
K9J 7H5   Canada   14127   USA

B.R.A.D. Book Representation   Bruce Watson,
& Distribution Ltd.   St. Clair Press
244a, London Road   P.O. Box 287
Hadleigh, Essex   Rozelle, NSW
SS7 2DE United Kingdon   2039 Australia

printed in Canada

Contents

Acknowledgements

A project of this size was not without its problems. Support arrived from several sources. Kwantlen University College provided me with the services of a work study student, Bettie Ann Moroz, who for one semester scanned several early chapter prototypes. My colleagues Frank Abbott and Thor Frohn-Nielsen never wavered in their support for this project and adopted the early drafts without reservation as required readings for their courses. Thor, in particular, assisted by revising all and writing some of the chapter introductions. My debt to him is rather significant. Frank Leonard of Douglas College proved to be my best sounding board and source for alternative ideas. On various occasions when total termination of this project loomed large, Frank always managed to persuade me that the book had merit. Comments and suggestions from students at Kwantlen University College who read the various drafts of these readings also made this a better text. With this volume and its pre-Confederation counterpart astute editorial assistance was provided by Eileen Eckert. Finally to Val, Emily and Julia a heartfelt thanks for putting up with still another project.

Introduction

a country nourished on self-doubt
where from the reverse image of detractors
an opposite nation is talked into existence
that doesn't resemble any other one
a cross-breed plant that survives the winter
         Al Purdy, "A Walk on Wellington Street", 1968

O urs is a history of self-doubt. From the moment of Confederation Canada has often been threatened by disintegration. Part of this problem stems from the fact that neither cultural symbols, a shared heritage, nor even a common language united Canadians when the nation emerged in 1867. Because much of the nation's growth in the years that followed could be attributed to immigrants who often retained their hyphenated ethnic status and never felt totally at home here, ambiguity about the significance of Canada or what it meant to be a Canadian was hardly surprising. The sheer problem of communication over vast distances and distinct regional economies also promoted disunity. By the 1880s Canada had already lost much of its lustre. Political tensions and economic depression caused many to doubt whether the nation could or should continue to exist. In Quebec separatist emotions had grown more pronounced, and the Nova Scotia legislature had endorsed a resolution favouring secession. Young Canadians by the thousands expressed their discontent with their feet when they left for better opportunities south of the border. After Macdonald's "national policy" had failed to generate prosperity or unite the country, the country's leading intellectual, Goldwin Smith, asked: What justifies Canada's existence? He concluded that Canada could not be considered a nation because it had failed to mould competing cultures and regions into a single community. In his mind Canada was nothing but an artificial entity totally at odds with the natural geographical and economic factors operating in North America.

The twentieth century, however, saw some Canadians beginning to celebrate the cultural diversity that Smith found so abhorrent. Particularly in contrast to the American "melting pot," they put forth the idea of the cultural mosaic as the very foundation of Canada's strength and identity. But as articulated by W.D. Scott in Chapter 4, most Canadians remained doubtful whether building a nation with the discontented and dispossessed of the world was sound practice. Canada's immigration policies of the period between the two world wars could hardly be characterized as promoting cultural diversity and tolerance. Instead, many immigrants found the pressure to conform just as pronounced as it was in the United States.

But the gravest doubts about Canada in the mid-twentieth century focused upon foreign relations, not domestic affairs. While it had taken several decades of the new century for Canada to finally cut most of the vestiges of British control, the Second World War saw a nervous Canada give up much of its military independence in return for American protection. The school texts of the period proudly proclaimed our growth from colony to nation, but based upon American economic and cultural domination, critics increasingly characterized Canada's status as having shifted from a British colony to an American satellite. In 1965 the philosopher George Grant went so far as to announce Canada's death as a sovereign nation.

More recently the challenges to Canadian sovereignty came from within as demonstrated by the F.L.Q. crisis and the rise of the Parti Québécois. When the separatists came to power as the government of Quebec in 1976 and remained a viable political entity throughout the 1980s and '90s many wondered if Canada would indeed survive.

Yet Purdy's poem also alludes to positive aspects: a "nourishing" self-doubt, a nation that "doesn't resemble any others," and a "cross-breed plant" that survives the winter. Canadians have remained profoundly uncertain of who they were and their place in the world. Many other nations have regarded this modesty as comfortably non-threatening, especially in comparison to the crass boosterism of the Americans, and as such viewed Canada as an ideal candidate for international peacekeeping assignments. It is also a rather strange quirk of history that Canada's inhibited national consciousness is now taken by many outsiders as a sign of our maturity in an increasingly post-national world.

What follows is a volume that attempts to bring together compelling excerpts of divergent eyewitness accounts of specific topics in post-Confederation Canadian history. The fascination of primary sources lies in their personal perspective and the immediacy of experience they convey. However lacking in objective insight they may be, they were written by people at or close to the source of the events they describe.

Many collections of Canadian readings on the market today reprint articles from academic journals as models of scholarship. Although such articles may certainly be of great value, they naturally tend to be written with a scholarly audience in mind. Coupled with standard survey texts, the near-total reliance upon secondary sources has had wide-ranging consequences. A student registering for a course on the Victorian novel would, no doubt, expect to read Victorian novels, not simply digest what secondary sources had to say about them. Even if the raw materials were as dense, drab and dull as the popular perception of Canadian history makes them out to be, bypassing them would be disturbing. But primary sources are far from dull. What historians usually find most enjoyable about the craft is research — the labyrinthine quest in primary sources for answers about the past. In the same way, readers of this book are encouraged to analyze the arguments and information in the sources for themselves.

This is still very much a book aimed at those largely unfamiliar with the subject. In order to make available the greatest possible amount of original material that is interesting and important, some less pertinent passages have been deleted. Exercising even a minimal shaping hand will sacrifice some dimensions of the past, but even if the occasional reader feels uncomfortable that the integrity of some documents has been violated, one hopes that in the interest of engaging a wider readership and lifting the veil of boredom from Canadian history, the end will have justified the means.

Editors of document collections such as this must also be sensitive to the criticism that reproducing historical documents such as these perpetuates negative images, particularly about ethnic groups, and as such constitutes hate literature. Without a doubt many documents written by ethnocentric Anglo Canadians form part of a literature written to justify assimilation and domination. But it hardly follows that reprinting these inaccuracies constitutes disseminating hate literature. Instead these documents may provide a means of exposing those falsehoods, of demonstrating the basis of intolerance, and of understanding that prejudice is commonplace. In some respects these documents may be used to confront the current complacency or smugness of Canadians who assume that especially compared to the United States, ours has been a kinder, gentler history and therefore lacks a foundation for bigotry and racism.

1

"Our Hands Are Poor But Our Heads Are Rich"

The Treaty Process

DOCUMENT

A) The Treaties of Canada with the Indians, 1880
Alexander Morris

Graphic scenes of confrontation from Oka in Quebec to Gustafsen Lake in British Columbia remind Canadians that all is not well between the federal government and Canada's First Nations. Much of the problem stems from the absence of treaties, as in British Columbia, or from disputes over the exact terms of what had been promised in the treaties. Today treaties have an importance for Native people that many other Canadians find hard to understand. For that reason the process is worth analyzing. What did Natives concede? Who controlled the negotiation process? Were one culture's concepts successfully transmitted to the other? Many Natives categorically state that treaty-making constituted sanctioned robbery and therefore has neither legitimacy nor validity. The Manitoba Indian Brotherhood, for example, called treaties "legal fraud in a very sophisticated manner committed upon unsophisticated, unsuspecting, illiterate, uninformed natives." Others argue that the federal government dealt generously and fairly with Canada's native people, crafting treaties under conditions appropriate to the time.

The federal government's negotiator, Alexander Morris (1826–1889), enjoyed solid connections to Prime Minister John A. Macdonald. After all, Morris articled in law under Macdonald. He was called to the bar in 1851 and soon established a large and lucrative commercial practice in Montreal. Ten years later he entered politics, and joined Macdonald's cabinet in 1869. Morris devoted himself to the notion of a united Canada, and predicted a transcontinental railway service some thirty years before it actually occurred. Financial, political, and health problems forced his resignation in 1872, but Macdonald appointed him Chief Justice of the Manitoba Court of Queen's Bench, and later Lieutenant Governor of Manitoba, positions he tackled with eagerness. Although he worked particularly hard to create a regular postal service, laws governing the alcohol trade, and a police force for the North West Territories, treaty-making gave him his greatest satisfaction. Acting on behalf of the Federal government, Morris created four major treaties with indigenous prairie people, spanning a large part of the modern prairie provinces.

Morris loved the pomp and circumstance of the treaty process: he thrived on being the Queen's representative with the prestige the role accorded him. Just the same, he wanted fair treaties with people whom he believed had inherent title to the land, and he often disagreed with Ottawa's lack of generosity toward Natives. His most intricate and delicate agreement, Number Three, required almost three years of protracted diplomatic negotiations before the Ojibway of the Lake of the Woods area in northwestern Ontario came to terms. "The North-West Angle Treaty," as it was called, became the template for subsequent agreements.

His mandate ended in 1876, but Alexander Morris should be known for more than only numbered treaties on the Canadian prairies. He also founded the University of Manitoba and introduced responsible government to that province. Those contributions may have won him the respect and affection of many Manitobans, but not the Métis whose land he failed to preserve in perpetuity. They showed their wrath in 1878 by foiling his electoral bid for a seat in Parliament. Morris eventually moved back to Ontario and won a seat in the provincial legislature from which he championed federalism over provincial rights until his death in 1889.

The lives of the Natives with whom Morris spoke remain unrecorded.

Among the others mentioned in Morris's account, Simon James Dawson (1818–1902), MP for Algoma, was appointed Commissioner to negotiate the terms of settlement. His fame in Canadian history rests more with his work as surveyor of the "Dawson Route" from Lake Superior to the Red River than with his efforts at treaty making.

James McKay (1828–1879) had been a fur trader and then a member of the Manitoba Legislative Council. Morris commented that this "remarkable man, the son of an Orkneyman by an Indian mother ... possessed large influence over Indian tribes, which he always used for the benefit and the advantage of the government." McKay acted as both interpreter and negotiator. He read out the text of the treaty in Ojibway to the Native audience.

Joseph Alfred Norbert Provencher (1843–1887) served as another Commissioner. This Quebec-born lawyer held a variety of posts in the federal civil service.

A) The Treaties of Canada with the Indians, 1880
Alexander Morris

NORTH-WEST ANGLE, October 1, 1873

... His Excellency [Alexander Morris] then said — "I told you I was to make the treaty on the part of our Great Mother the Queen, and I feel it will be for your good and your children's. I should have been very sorry if you had shut my mouth, if I had had to go home without opening my mouth. I should not have been a true friend of yours if I had not asked you to open my mouth. We are all children of the same Great Spirit and are subject to the same Queen. I want to settle all matters both of the past and the present, so that the white and red man will always be friends. I will give you lands for farms, and also reserves for your own use. I have authority to make reserves such as I have described, not exceeding in all a square mile for every family of five or thereabouts. It may be a long time before the other lands are wanted, and in the meantime you will be permitted to fish and hunt over them. I will also establish schools whenever any band asks for them, so that your children may have the learning of the white man. I will also give you a sum of money for yourselves and every one of your wives and children for this year. I will give you ten dollars per head of the population, and for every other year five dollars a-head. But to the chief men, not exceeding two to each band, we will give twenty dollars a-year for ever. I will give to each of you this year a present of goods and provisions to take you home, and I am sure you will be satisfied."

After consultation amongst themselves, the Councillors went to have a talk about the matter and will meet the Governor [Morris] tomorrow morning, when it is expected the bargain will be concluded. Of course the Indians will make some other demands.

Immediately after the adjournment as above, the Governor presented an ox to the people in camp; and the way it disappeared would have astonished the natives of any other land. Half-an-hour after it was led into encampment, it was cut up and boiling in fifty pots.

THIRD DAY.

Proceedings were opened at eleven o'clock by the Governor announcing that he was ready to hear what the Chiefs had to say. The Fort Francis Chief acted as spokesman, assisted by another Chief, Powhassan.

MA-WE-DO-PE-NAIS — "I now lay down before you the opinions of those you have seen before. We think it a great thing, to meet you here. What we have heard yesterday, and as you represented yourself, you said the Queen sent you here, the way we understood you as a representative of the Queen. All this is our property where you have come. We have understood you yesterday that Her Majesty has given you the same power and authority as *she* has, to act in this business; you said the Queen gave you her goodness, her charitableness in your hands. This is what we think, that the Great Spirit has planted us on this ground where we are, as you were where you came from. We think where we are is our property. I will tell you what he said to us when he planted us here; the rules that we should follow — us Indians — He has given us rules that we should follow to govern us rightly. We have understood you that you have opened your charitable heart to us like a person taking off his garments and throwing them to all of us here. Now, first of all, I have a few words to address to this gentleman (Mr. Dawson). When he understood rightly what was my meaning yesterday, he threw himself on your help. I think I have a right to follow him to where he flew when I spoke to him on the subject yesterday. We will follow up the subject from the point we took it up. I want to answer what we heard from you yesterday, in regard to the money that you have promised us yesterday to each individual. I want to talk about the rules that we had laid down before. It is four years back since we have made these rules. The rules laid down are the rules that they wish to follow — a council that has been agreed upon by all the Indians. I do not wish that I should be required to say twice what I am now going to lay down. We ask fifteen dollars for all that you see, and for the children that are to be born in future. This year only we ask for fifteen dollars; years after ten dollars; our Chiefs fifty dollars per year for every year, and other demands of large amounts in writing, say $125,000 yearly."

ANOTHER CHIEF — "I take my standing point from here. Our councillors have in council come to this conclusion, that they should have twenty dollars each; our warriors, fifteen dollars; our population, fifteen dollars. We have now laid down the conclusion of our councils by our decisions. We tell you our wishes are not divided. We are all of one mind." (Paper put in before the Governor for these demands.)

CHIEF — "I now let you know the opinions of us here. We would not wish that anyone should smile at our affairs, as we think our country is a large matter to us. If you grant us what is written on that paper, then we will talk about the reserves; we have decided in council for the benefit of those that will be born hereafter. If you do so the treaty will be finished, I believe."

GOVERNOR — "I quite agree that this is no matter to smile at. I think that the decision of to-day is one that affects yourselves and your children after, but you must recollect that this is the third time of negotiating. If we do not shake hands and make our Treaty to-day, I do not know when it will be done, as the Queen's Government will think you do not wish to treat with her. You told me that you understood that I represented the Queen's Government to you and that I opened my heart to you, but you must recollect that if *you* are a council there is another great council that governs a great Dominion, and they hold their councils the same as you hold yours. I wish to tell you that I am a servant of the Queen. I cannot do my own will; I must do hers. I can only give you what she tells me to give you. I am sorry to see that your hands were very wide open when you gave me this paper. I thought what I promised you was just, kind and fair between the Queen and you. It is now three years we have been trying to settle this matter. If we do not succeed to-day I shall go away feeling sorry for you and for your children that you could not see what was good for you and for them. I am ready to do what I promised you yesterday. My hand is open and you ought to take me by the hand and say, "yes, we accept of your offer." I have not the power to do what you ask of me. I ask you once more to think what you are doing, and of those you have left at home, and also of those that may be born yet, and I ask you not to turn your backs on what is offered to you, and you ought to see by what the Queen is offering you that she loves her red subjects as much as her white. I think you are forgetting one thing, that what I offer you is to be while the water flows and the sun rises. You know that in the United States they only pay the Indian for twenty years, and you come here today and ask for ever more than they get for twenty years. Is that just? I think you ought to accept my offer, and make a treaty with me as I ask you to do. I only ask you to think for yourselves, and for your families, and for your children and children's children, and I know that if you do that you will shake hands with me to-day."

CHIEF — "I lay before you our opinions. Our hands are poor but our heads are rich, and it is riches that we ask so that we may be able to support our families as long as the sun rises and the water runs."

GOVERNOR — "I am very sorry; you know it takes two to make a bargain; you are agreed on the one side, and I for the Queen's Government on the other. I have to go away and report that I have to go without making terms with you. I doubt if the Commissioners will be sent again to assemble this nation. I have only one word more to say; I speak to the Chief and to the head men to recollect those behind them, and those they have left at home, and not to go away without accepting such liberal terms and without some clothing."

CHIEF — "My terms I am going to lay down before you; the decision of our Chiefs; ever since we came to a decision you push it back. *The sound of the rustling of the gold is under my feet where I stand;* we have a rich country; it is the Great Spirit who gave us this; where we stand upon is the Indians' property, and belongs to them. If you grant us our requests you will not go back without making the treaty."

ANOTHER CHIEF — "We understood yesterday that the Queen had given you the power to act upon, that you could do what you pleased, and that the riches of the Queen she had filled your head and body with, and you had only to throw them round about; but it seems it is not so, but that you have only half the power that she has, and that she has only half filled your head."

GOVERNOR — "I do not like to be misunderstood. I did not say yesterday that the Queen had given me all the power; what I told you was that I was sent here to represent the Queen's Government, and to tell you what the Queen was willing to do for you. You can understand very well; for instance, one of your great chiefs asks a brave to deliver a message, he represents you, and that is how I stand with the Queen's Government."

CHIEF — "It is your charitableness that you spoke of yesterday — Her Majesty's charitableness that was given you. It is our chiefs, our young men, our children and great grandchildren, and those that are to be born, that I represent here, and it is for them I ask for terms. The white man has robbed us of our riches, and we don't wish to give them up again without getting something in their place."

GOVERNOR — "For your children, grandchildren, and children unborn, I am sorry that you will not accept of my terms. I shall go home sorry, but it is your own doing; I must simply go back and report the fact that you refuse to make a treaty with me."

CHIEF — "You see all our chiefs before you here as one mind, we have one mind and one mouth. It is the decision of all of us; if you grant us our demands you will not go back sorrowful; we would not refuse to make a treaty if you would grant us our demands."

GOVERNOR — "I have told you already that I cannot grant your demands; I have not the power to do so. I have made you a liberal offer, and it is for you to accept or refuse it as you please."

CHIEF — "Our chiefs have the same opinion; they will not change their decision."

GOVERNOR — "Then the Council is at an end."

CHIEF (of Lac Seule) — "I understand the matter that he asks; if he puts a question to me as well as to others, I say so as well as the rest. We are the first that were planted here; we would ask you to assist us with every kind of implement to use for our benefit, to enable us to perform our work; a little of everything and money. We would borrow your cattle; we ask you this for our support; I will find whereon to feed them. The waters out of which you sometimes take food for yourselves, we will lend you in return. If I should try to stop you — it is not in my power to do so; even the Hudson's Bay Company — that is a small power — I cannot gain my point with it. If you give what I ask, the time may come when I will ask you to lend me one of your daughters and one of our sons to live with us; and in return I will lend you one of my daughters and of my sons for you to teach what is good, and after they have learned, to teach us. If you grant us what I ask, although I do not know you, I will shake hands with you. This is all I have to say."

GOVERNOR — "I have heard and I have learned something. I have learned that you are not all of one mind. I know that your interests are not the same — that some of you live in the north far away from the river; and some live on the river, and that you have got large sums of money for wood that you have cut and sold to the steamboats; but the men in the north have not this advantage. What the Chief has said is reasonable; and should you want goods I mean to ask you what amount you would have in goods, so that you would not have to pay the traders' prices for them. I wish you were all of the same mind as the Chief who has just spoken. He wants his children to be taught. He is right. He wants to get cattle to help him to raise grain for his children. It would be a good thing for you all to be of his mind, and then you would not go away without making this treaty with me."

BLACKSTONE (Shebandowan) — "I am going to lay down before you the minds of those who are here. I do not wish to interfere with the decisions of those who are before you, or yet with your decisions. The people at the height of land where the waters came down from Shebandowan to Fort

Francis, are those who have appointed me to lay before you our decision. We are going back to hold a Council."

MR. DAWSON — "I would ask the Chief who has just spoken, did the band at Shebandowan — did Rat McKay, authorize him to speak for them? Ke-ha-ke-ge-nen is Blackstone's own Chief; and I am perfectly willing to think that he authorized him. What I have to say is that the Indians may not be deceived by representations made to them, and that the two bands met me at Shebandowan and said they were perfectly willing to enter into a treaty."

GOVERNOR — "I think the nation will do well to do what the Chief has said. I think he has spoken sincerely, and it is right for them to withdraw and hold a Council among themselves."

Blackstone here handed in a paper which he alleged gave him authority as Chief, but which proved to be an official acknowledgement of the receipt of a letter by the Indian Department at Ottawa.

The Governor here agreed with the Council that it would be well for the Chiefs to have another meeting amongst themselves. It was a most important day for them and for their children, and His Excellency would be glad to meet them again.

The Council broke up at this point, and it was extremely doubtful whether an agreement could be come to or not. The Rainy River Indians were careless about the treaty, because they could get plenty of money for cutting wood for the boats, but the northern and eastern bands were anxious for one. The Governor decided that he would make a treaty with those bands that were willing to accept his terms, leaving out the few disaffected ones. A Council was held by the Indians in the evening, at which Hon. James McKay, Pierre Léveillée, Charles Nolin, and Mr. Genton were present by invitation of the Chiefs. After a very lengthy and exhaustive discussion, it was decided to accept the Governor's terms, and the final meeting was announced for Friday morning. Punctually at the appointed time proceedings were opened by the Fort Francis Chiefs announcing to His Excellency that they were all of one mind, and would accept his terms, with a few modifications. The discussion of these terms occupied five hours, and met every possible contingency so fully that it would be impossible to do justice to the negotiators otherwise than by giving a full report of the speeches on both sides; but want of space compels us to lay it over until next week.

The treaty was finally closed on Friday afternoon, and signed on Saturday; after which a large quantity of provisions, ammunition and other goods were distributed.

When the council broke up last (Thursday) night, 3rd October, it looked very improbable that an understanding could be arrived at, but the firmness of the Governor, and the prospect that he would make a treaty with such of the bands as were willing to accept his terms, to the exclusion of the others, led them to reconsider their demands. The Hon. James McKay, and Messrs. Nolin, Genton, and Léveillée were invited in to their council, and after a most exhaustive discussion of the circumstance in which they were placed, it was resolved to accept the Governor's terms, with some modifications. Word was sent to this effect, and at eleven o'clock on Friday, conference was again held with His Excellency.

The Fort Francis Chief opened negotiations by saying: — "We present our compliments to you, and now we would tell you something. You have mentioned our councillors, warriors and messengers — every Chief you see has his councillors, warriors and messengers."

GOVERNOR — "I was not aware what names they gave me — they gave their chief men. I spoke of the subordinates of the head Chiefs; I believe the head Chiefs have three subordinates — I mean the head Chief and three of his head men."

CHIEF — "I am going to tell you the decision of all before you. I want to see your power and learn the most liberal terms that you can give us."

GOVERNOR — "I am glad to meet the Chiefs, and I hope it will be the last time of our meeting. I hope we are going to understand one-another to-day. And that I can go back and report that I left my Indian friends contented, and that I have put into their hands the means of providing for themselves and their families at home; and now I will give you my last words. When I held out my hands to you at first, I intended to do what was just and right, and what I had the power to do *at once*, — not to go backwards and forwards, but at once to do what I believe is just and right to you. I was very much pleased yesterday with the words of the Chief of Lac Seul. I was glad to hear that he had commenced to farm and to raise things for himself and family, and I was glad to hear him ask me to hold out my hand. I think we should do everything to help you by giving you the means to grow some food, so that if it is a bad year for fishing and hunting you may have something for your children at home. If you had not asked it the Government would have done it all the same, although I had not said so before. I can say this, that when a band settles down and actually commences to farm on their lands, the Government will agree to give two hoes, one spade, one scythe, and one axe for every family actually settled; one plough for every ten families; five harrows for every twenty families; and a yoke of oxen, a bull and four cows for every band; and enough barley, wheat and oats to plant the land they have actually broken up. This is to enable them to cultivate their land, and it is to be given them on their commencing to do so, once for all. There is one thing that I have thought over, and I think it is a wise thing to do. That is to give you ammunition, and twine for making nets, to the extent of $1,500 per year, for the whole nation, so that you can have the means of procuring food. — Now, I will mention the last thing that I can do. I think that the sum I have offered you to be paid after this year for every man, woman and child now, and for years to come, is right and is the proper sum. I will not make any change in that, but we are anxious to show you that we have a great desire to understand you — that we wish to do the utmost in our power to make you contented, so that the white and the red man will always be friends. This year, instead of ten dollars we will give you twelve dollars, to be paid you at once as soon as we sign the treaty. This is the best I can do for you. I wish you to understand we do not come here as traders, but as representing the Crown, and to do what we believe is just and right. We have asked in that spirit, and I hope you will meet me in that spirit and shake hands with me [to]day and make a treaty for ever. I have no more to say."

CHIEF — "I wish to ask some points that I have not properly understood. We understand that our children are to have two dollars extra. Will the two dollars be paid to our principal men as well? And these things that are promised will they commence at once and will we see it year after year?"

GOVERNOR — "I thought I had spoken fully as to everything, but I will speak again. The ammunition and twine will be got at once for you, *this year*, and that will be for every year. The Commissioner will see that you get this at once; with regard to the things to help you to farm, you must recollect, in a very few days the river will be frozen up here and we have not got these things here now. But arrangements will be made next year to get these things for those who are farming, it cannot be done before as you can see yourselves very well. Some are farming, and I hope you will all do so."

CHIEF — "One thing I did not say that is most necessary — we want a cross-cut saw, a whip saw, grindstone and files."

GOVERNOR — "We will do that, and I think we ought to give a box of common tools to each Chief of a Band."

CHIEF — "Depending upon the words you have told us, and stretched out your hands in a friendly way, I depend upon that. One thing more we demand — a suit of clothes to all of us."

GOVERNOR — "With regard to clothing, suits will be given to the Chiefs and head men, and as to the other Indians there is a quantity of goods and provisions here that will be given them at the close of the treaty. The coats of the Chiefs will be given every three years."

CHIEF — "Once more; powder and shot will not go off without guns. We ask for guns."

GOVERNOR — "I have shown every disposition to meet your view, but what I have promised is as far as I can go."

CHIEF — "My friends, listen to what I am going to say, and you, my brothers. We present you now with our best and our strongest compliments. We ask you not to reject some of our children who have gone out of our place; they are scattered all over, a good tasted meat hath drawn them away, and we wish to draw them all here and be contented with us."

GOVERNOR — "If your children come and live here, of course they will become part of the population, and be as yourselves."

CHIEF — "I hope you will grant the request that I am going to lay before you. I do not mean those that get paid on the other side of the line, but some poor Indians who may happen to fall in our road. If you will accept of these little matters, the treaty will be at an end. I would not like that one of my children should not eat with me, and receive the food that you are going to give me."

GOVERNOR — "I am dealing with British Indians and not American Indians; after the treaty is closed we will have a list of the names of any children of British Indians that may come in during two years and be ranked with them; but we must have a limit somewhere."

CHIEF — "I should not feel happy if I was not to mess with some of my children that are around me — those children that we call the Half-breed — those that have been born of our women of Indian blood. We wish that they should be counted with us, and have their share of what you have promised. We wish you to accept our demands. It is the Half-breeds that are actually living amongst us — those that are married to our women."

GOVERNOR — "I am sent here to treat with the Indians. In Red River, where I came from, and where there is a great body of Half-breeds, they must be either white or Indian. If Indians, they get treaty money; if the

Half-breeds call themselves white, they get land. All I can do is to refer the matter to the government at Ottawa, and to recommend what you wish to be granted."

CHIEF — "I hope you will not drop the question; we have understood you to say that you came here as a friend, and represented your charitableness, and we depend upon your kindness. You must remember that our hearts and our brains are like paper; we never forget. There is one thing that we want to know. If you should get into trouble with the nations, I do not wish to walk out and expose my young men to aid you in any of your wars."

GOVERNOR — "The English never call the Indians out of their country to fight their battles. You are living here and the Queen expects you to live at peace with the white men and your red brothers, and with other nations."

ANOTHER CHIEF — "I ask you a question — I see your roads here passing through the country, and some of your boats — useful articles that you use for yourself. Bye and bye we shall see things that run swiftly, that go by fire-carriages — and we ask you that us Indians may not have to pay their passage on these things, but can go free."

GOVERNOR — "I think the best thing I can do is to become an Indian. I cannot promise you to pass on the railroad free, for it may be a long time before we get one; and I cannot promise you any more than other people."

CHIEF — "I must address myself to my friend here, as he is the one that has the Public Works."

MR. DAWSON — "I am always happy to do anything I can for you. I have always given you a passage on the boats when I could. I will act as I have done though I can give no positive promise for the future."

CHIEF — "We must have the privilege of travelling about the country where it is vacant."

MR. MCKAY — "Of course, I told them so."

CHIEF — "Should we discover any metal that was of use, could we have the privilege of putting our own price on it?"

GOVERNOR — "If any important minerals are discovered on any of their reserves the minerals will be sold for their benefit with their consent, but not on any other land that discoveries may take place upon; as regards other discoveries, of course, the Indian is like any other man. He can sell his information if he can find a purchaser."

CHIEF — "It will be as well while we are here that everything should be understood properly between us. All of us — those behind us — wish to have their reserves marked out, which they will point out, when the time comes. There is not one tribe here who has not laid it out."

COMMISSIONER PROVENCHER (the Governor being temporarily absent) — "As soon as it is convenient to the Government to send surveyors to lay out the reserves they will do so, and they will try to suit every particular band in this respect."

CHIEF — "We do not want anybody to mark out our reserves, we have already marked them out."

COMMISSIONER — "There will be another undertaking between the officers of the Government and the Indians among themselves for the selection of the land; they will have enough of good farming land, they may be sure of that."

CHIEF — "Of course, if there is any particular part wanted by the public works they can shift us. I understand that; but if we have any gardens through the country, do you wish that the poor man should throw it right away?"

COMMISSIONER — "Of course not."

CHIEF — "These are matters that are the wind-up. I begin now to see how I value the proceedings. I have come to this point, and all that are taking part in this treaty and yourself. I would wish to have all your names in writing handed over to us. I would not find it to my convenience to have a stranger here to transact our business between me and you. It is a white man who does not understand our language that is taking it down. I would like a man that understands our language and our ways. We would ask your Excellency as a favor to appoint him for us."

GOVERNOR — "I have a very good feeling to Mr. C. Nolin, he has been a good man here; but the appointment of an Agent rests with the authorities at Ottawa and I will bring your representation to them, and I am quite sure it will meet with the respect due to it."

CHIEF — "As regards the fire water, I do not like it and I do not wish any house to be built to have it sold. Perhaps at times if I should be unwell I might take [a] drop just for medicine; and shall anyone insist on bringing it where we are, I should break the treaty."

GOVERNOR — "I meant to have spoken of that myself, I meant to put it in the treaty. He speaks good about it. The Queen and her Parliament in Ottawa have passed a law prohibiting the use of it in this territory, and if any shall be brought in for the use of you as medicine it can only come in by my permission."

CHIEF — "Why we keep you so long is that it is our wish that everything should be properly understood between us."

GOVERNOR — "That is why I am here. It is my pleasure, and I want when we once shake hands that it should be forever."

CHIEF — "That is the principal article. If it was in my midst the fire water would have spoiled my happiness, and I wish it to be left far way from where I am. All the promises that you have made me, the little promises and the money you have promised, when it comes to me year after year — should I see that there is anything wanting, through the negligence of the people that have to see after these things, I trust it will be in my power to put them in prison."

GOVERNOR — "The ear of the Queen's Government will always be open to hear the complaints of her Indian people, and she will deal with her servants that do not do their duty in a proper manner."

CHIEF — "Now you have promised to give us all your names. I want a copy of the treaty that will not be rubbed off, on parchment."

GOVERNOR — "In the mean time I will give you a copy on paper, and as soon as I get back I will get you a copy on parchment."

CHIEF — "I do not wish to be treated as they were at Red River — that provisions should be stopped as it is there. Whenever we meet and have a council I wish that provisions should be given to us. We cannot speak without eating."

GOVERNOR — "You are mistaken. When they are brought together at Red River for their payments they get provisions."

CHIEF — "We wish the provisions to come from Red River."

GOVERNOR — "If the Great Spirit sends the grasshopper and there is no wheat grown in Red River, we cannot give it to you."

CHIEF — "You have come before us with a smiling face, you have shown us great charity — you have promised the good things; you have given us your best compliments and wishes, not only for once but for ever; let there now for ever be peace and friendship between us. It is the wish of all that where our reserves are peace should reign, that nothing shall be there that will disturb peace. Now, I will want nothing to be there that will disturb peace, and will put every one that carries arms, — such as murderers and thieves — outside, so that nothing will be there to disturb our peace."

GOVERNOR — "The Queen will have policemen to preserve order, and murderers and men guilty of crime will be punished in this country just the same as she punishes them herself."

CHIEF — "To speak about the Hudson's Bay Company. If it happens that they have surveyed where I have taken my reserve, if I see any of their signs I will put them on one side."

GOVERNOR — "When the reserves are given you, you will have your rights. The Hudson's Bay Company have their rights, and the Queen will do justice between you."

CHIEF OF FORT FRANCIS — "Why I say this is, where I have chosen for my reserve I see signs that the H. B. Co. has surveyed. I do not hate them. I only wish they should take their reserves on one side. Where their shop stands now is my property; I think it is three years now since they have had it on it."

GOVERNOR — "I do not know about that matter; it will be inquired into. I am taking notes of all these things and am putting them on paper."

CHIEF — "I will tell you one thing. You understand me now, that I have taken your hand firmly and in friendship. I repeat twice that you have done so, that these promises that you have made, and the treaty to be concluded, let it be as you promise, as long as the sun rises over our head and as long as the water runs. One thing I find, that deranges a little my kettle. In this river, where food used to be plentiful for our subsistence, I perceive it is getting scarce. We wish that the river should be left as it was formed from the beginning — that nothing be broken."

GOVERNOR — "This is a subject that I cannot promise."

MR. DAWSON — "Anything that we are likely to do at present will not interfere with the fishing, but no one can tell what the future may require, and we cannot enter into any engagement."

CHIEF — "We wish the Government would assist us in getting a few boards for some of us who are intending to put up houses this fall, from the mill at Fort Francis."

GOVERNOR — "The mill is a private enterprise, and we have no power to give you boards from that."

CHIEF — "I will now show you a medal that was given to those who made a treaty at Red River by the Commissioner. *He* said it was silver, but *I* do not think it is. I should be ashamed to carry it on my breast over my heart. I think it would disgrace the Queen, my mother, to wear her image on so base a metal as this. [Here the Chief held up the medal and struck it with the back of his knife. The result was anything but the 'true ring,' and made every man ashamed of the pettimeanness that had been practised.]

Let the medals you give us be of silver — medals that shall be worthy of the high position our Mother the Queen occupies."

GOVERNOR — "I will tell them at Ottawa *what* you have said, and *how* you have said it."

CHIEF — "I wish you to understand you owe the treaty much to the Half-breeds."

GOVERNOR — "I know it. I sent some of them to talk with you, and I am proud that all the Half-breeds from Manitoba, who are here, gave their Governor their cordial support."

The business of the treaty having now been completed, Chief, Ma-we-do-pe-nais, who, with Powhassan, had with wonderful tact carried on the negotiations, stepped up to the Governor and said:—

"Now you see me stand before you all; what has been done here to-day has been done openly before the Great Spirit, and before the nation, and I hope that I may never hear any one say that this treaty has been done secretly; and now, in closing this Council, I take off my glove, and in giving you my hand, I deliver over my birth-right and lands; and in taking your hand, I hold fast all the promises you have made, and I hope they will last as long as the sun goes round and the water flows, as you have said."

The Governor then took his hand and said:

"I accept your hand and with it the lands, and will keep all my promises, in the firm belief that the treaty now to be signed will bind the red man and the white together as friends for ever."

A copy of the treaty was then prepared and duly signed, after which a large amount of presents, consisting of pork, flour, clothing, blankets, twine, powder and shot, etc., were distributed to the several bands represented on the ground.

On Saturday, Mr. Pether, Local Superintendent of Indian Affairs at Fort Francis, and Mr. Graham of the Government Works, began to pay the treaty money — an employment that kept them busy far into the night. Some of the Chiefs received as much as one hundred and seventy dollars for themselves and families.

As soon as the money was distributed the shops of the H. B. Co., and other resident traders were visited, as well as the tents of numerous private traders, who had been attracted thither by the prospect of doing a good business. And while these shops did a great trade — the H. B. Co. alone taking in $4,000 in thirty hours — it was a noticeable fact that many took home with them nearly all their money. When urged to buy goods there, a frequent reply was: "If we spend all our money here and go home and want debt, we will be told to get our debt where we spent our money." "Debt" is used by them instead of the word "credit." Many others deposited money with white men and Half-breeds on whose honor they could depend, to be called for and spent at Fort Garry when "the ground froze."

One very wonderful thing that forced itself on the attention of every one was the perfect order that prevailed throughout the camp, and which more particularly marked proceedings in the council. Whether the demands put forward were granted by the Governor or not, there was no petulance, no ill-feeling, evinced; but everything was done with a calm dignity that was pleasing to behold, and which might be copied with advantage by more pretentious deliberative assemblies.

On Sunday afternoon, the Governor presented an ox to the nation, and after it had been eaten a grand dance was indulged in. Monday morning the river Indians took passage on the steamer for Fort Francis, and others left in their canoes for their winter quarters.

The Governor and party left on Monday morning, the troops, under command of Captain McDonald, who had conducted themselves with the greatest propriety, and had contributed, by the moral effect of their presence, much to the success of the negotiation, having marched to Fort Garry on Saturday morning.

THE NORTH-WEST ANGLE TREATY, NUMBER THREE.

ARTICLES OF A TREATY made and concluded this third day of October, in the year of our Lord one thousand eight hundred and seventy-three, between Her Most Gracious Majesty the Queen of Great Britain and Ireland, by her Commissioners, the Hon. Alexander Morris, Lieutenant-Governor of the Province of Manitoba and the North-West Territories; Joseph Albert Norbert Provencher, and Simon James Dawson, of the one part; and the Saulteaux tribe of the Ojibbeway Indians, inhabitants of the country within the limits hereinafter defined and described, by their Chiefs, chosen and named as hereinafter mentioned, of the other part;

Whereas the Indians inhabiting the said country have, pursuant to an appointment made by the said Commissioners, been convened at a meeting at the North-West angle of the Lake of the Woods, to deliberate upon certain matters of interest to Her Most Gracious Majesty, of the one part, and the said Indians of the other;

And whereas the said Indians have been notified and informed by Her Majesty's said Commissioners, that it is the desire of Her Majesty to open up for settlement, immigration, and such other purposes as to Her Majesty may seem meet, a tract of country bounded and described as hereinafter mentioned, and to obtain the consent thereto of her Indian subjects inhabiting the said tract, and to make a treaty and arrange with them, so that there may be peace and good will between them and Her Majesty, and that they may know and be assured of what allowance they are to count upon and receive from Her Majesty's bounty and benevolence:

And whereas, the Indians of the said tract, duly convened in Council, as aforesaid, and being requested by Her Majesty's said Commissioners to name certain Chiefs and head men, who should be authorized on their behalf to conduct such negotiations, and sign any treaty to be founded thereon, and to become responsible to Her Majesty for the faithful performance by their respective bands of such obligations as shall be assumed by them, the said Indians have thereupon named the following persons for that purpose, that is to say Kee-tak-pay-pi-nais (Rainy River), Kitihi-gay-lake (Rainy River), Note-na-qua-hung (North-West Angle), Mawe-do-pe-nais (Rainy River), Pow-wa-sang (North-West Angle), Canda-com-igo-wi-ninie (North-West Angle), Pa-pa-ska-gin (Rainy River), May-no-wah-tau-ways-kung (North-West Angle), Kitchi-ne-ka-be-han (Rainy River), Sah-katch-eway (Lake Seul), Muka-day-wah-sin (Kettle Falls), Me-kie-sies (Rainy Lake, Fort Francis), Oos-con-na-geist (Rainy Lake), Wah-shis-kince (Eagle Lake), Rah-kie-y-ash (Flower Lake), Go-bay (Rainy Lake), Ka-me-ti-ash (White Fish Lake), Nee-sho-tal (Rainy River), Kee-gee-go-kay (Rainy River), Sha-sha-gance (Shoal Lake), Shah-win-na-bi-nais (Shoal Lake), Ay-ash-a-wash (Buffalo Point), Pay-ah-be-wash (White Fish Bay), Rah-tay-tay-pa-o-cutch (Lake of the Woods).

And thereupon in open council the different bands having presented their Chiefs to the said Commissioners as the Chiefs and head men for the purposes aforesaid of the respective bands of Indians inhabiting the said district hereinafter described.

And whereas the said Commissioners then and there received and acknowledged the persons so presented as Chiefs and head men for the purposes aforesaid of the respective bands of Indians inhabiting the said district hereinafter described;

And whereas the said Commissioners have proceeded to negotiate a treaty with the said Indians, and the same has been finally agreed upon and concluded as follows, that is to say:

The Saulteaux tribe of the Ojibbeway Indians, and all other the Indians inhabiting the district hereinafter described and defined, do hereby cede, release, surrender, and yield up to the Government of the Dominion of Canada, for Her Majesty the Queen and her successors forever, all their rights, titles and privileges whatsoever to the lands included within the following limits, that is to say:

Commencing at a point on the Pigeon River route where the international boundary line between the territories of Great Britain and the United States intersects the height of land separating the waters running to Lake Superior from those flowing to Lake Winnipeg, thence northerly, westerly and easterly, along the height of land aforesaid, following its sinuosities, whatever their course may be, to the point at which the said height of land meets the summit of the watershed from which the streams flow to Lake Nepigon, thence northerly and westerly, or whatever may be its course along the ridge separating the waters of the Nepigon and the Winnipeg to the height of land dividing the waters of the Albany and the Winnipeg, thence westerly and north-westerly along the height of land dividing the waters flowing to Hudson's Bay by the Albany or other rivers from those running to English River and the Winn[i]peg to a point on the said height of land bearing north forty-five degrees east from Fort Alexander at the mouth of the Winnipeg; thence south forty-five degrees west to Fort Alexander at the mouth of the Winnipeg; thence southerly along the eastern bank of the Winnipeg to the mouth of White Mouth River; thence southerly by the line described as in that part forming the eastern boundary of the tract surrendered by the Chippewa and Swampy Cree tribes of Indians to Her Majesty on the third of August, one thousand eight hundred and seventy-one, namely, by White Mouth River to White Mouth Lake and thence on a line having the general bearing of White Mouth River to the forty-ninth parallel of north latitude; thence by the forty-ninth parallel of north latitude to the Lake of the Woods, and from thence by the international boundary line to the place of beginning.

The tract comprised within the lines above described embracing an area of fifty-five thousand square miles, be the same more or less.

To have and to hold the same to Her Majesty the Queen and her successors forever.

And Her Majesty the Queen hereby agrees and undertakes to lay aside reserves for farming lands, due respect being had to lands at present cultivated by the said Indians, and also to lay aside and reserve for the benefit of the said Indians, to be administered and dealt with for them by Her Majesty's Government of the Dominion of Canada, in such a manner as shall seem best, other reserves of land in the said territory hereby ceded, which said reserves shall be selected and set aside where it shall be deemed most convenient and advantageous for each band or bands of Indians, by the officers of the said Government appointed for that purpose, and such selection shall be so made after conference with the Indians: Provided, however, that such reserve whether for farming or other purposes shall in nowise exceed in all one square mile for each family of five, or in that proportion for larger or smaller families, and such selection shall be made if possible during the course of next summer or as soon thereafter as may be found practicable, it being understood, however, that if at the time of any such selection of any reserves as aforesaid, there are any settlers within the bounds of the lands reserved by any band, Her Majesty reserves the right to deal with such settlers as she shall deem just, so as not to diminish the extent of land allotted to Indians; and provided also that the aforesaid reserves of lands or any interest or right therein or appurtenant thereto, may be sold, leased or otherwise disposed of by the said Government for the use and benefit of the said Indians, with the consent of the Indians entitled thereto first had and obtained.

And with a view to show the satisfaction of Her Majesty with the behavior and good conduct of her Indians, she hereby through her Commissioners, makes them a present of twelve dollars for each man, woman and child belonging to the bands here represented, in extinguishment of all claims heretofore preferred.

And further, Her Majesty agrees to maintain schools for instruction in such reserves hereby made as to her Government of her Dominion of Canada may seem advisable, whenever the Indians of the reserve shall desire it.

Her Majesty further agrees with her said Indians, that within the boundary of Indian reserves, until otherwise determined by the Government of the Dominion of Canada, no intoxicating liquor shall be allowed to be introduced or sold, and all laws now in force, or hereafter to be enacted to preserve her Indian subjects inhabiting the reserves, or living elsewhere within her North-West Territories, from the evil influence of the use of intoxicating liquors shall be strictly enforced.

Her Majesty further agrees with her said Indians, that they, the said Indians, shall have right to pursue their avocations of hunting and fishing throughout the tract surrendered as hereinbefore described, subject to such regulations as may from time to time be made by her Government of her Dominion of Canada, and saving and excepting such tracts as may from time to time be required or taken up for settlement, mining, lumbering or other purposes, by her said Government of the Dominion of Canada, or by any of the subjects thereof duly authorized therefore by the said Government.

It is further agreed between Her Majesty and her said Indians that such sections of the reserves above indicated as may at any time be required for public works or buildings, of what nature soever, may be appropriated for that purpose by Her Majesty's Government of the Dominion of Canada, due compensation being made for the value of any improvements thereon.

And further, that Her Majesty's Commissioners shall, as soon as possible, after the execution of this treaty, cause to be taken an accurate census of all the Indians inhabiting the tract above described, distributing them in families, and shall in every year ensuing the date hereof at some period in each year, to be duly notified to the Indians, and at a place or places to be appointed for that purpose within the territory ceded, pay to each Indian person the sum of five dollars per head yearly.

It is further agreed between Her Majesty and the said Indians, that the sum of fifteen hundred dollars per annum shall be yearly and every year expended by Her Majesty in the purchase of ammunition, and twine for nets for the use of the said Indians.

It is further agreed between Her Majesty and the said Indians, that the following articles shall be supplied to any band of the said Indians who are now actually cultivating the soil, or who shall hereafter commence to cultivate the land, that is to say — two hoes for every family actually cultivating; also one spade per family as aforesaid; one plough for every ten families as aforesaid; five harrows for every twenty families as aforesaid; one scythe for every family as aforesaid, and also one axe and one cross-cut saw, one hand saw, one pit saw, the necessary files, one grindstone, one auger for each band, and also for each Chief for the use of his band, one chest of ordinary carpenter's tools; also for each band, enough of wheat, barley, potatoes and oats to plant the land actually broken up for cultivation by such band; also for each band, one yoke of oxen, one bull and four cows; all the aforesaid articles to be given once for all for the encouragement of the practice of agriculture among the Indians.

It is further agreed between Her Majesty and the said Indians, that each Chief, duly recognized as such, shall receive an annual salary of twenty-five dollars per annum, and each subordinate officer, not exceeding three for each band, shall receive fifteen dollars per annum; and each such Chief and subordinate officer as aforesaid shall also receive, once in every three years, a suitable suit of clothing; and each Chief shall receive, in recognition of the closing of the treaty, a suitable flag and medal.

And the undersigned Chiefs, on their own behalf and on behalf of all other Indians inhabiting the tract within ceded, do hereby solemnly promise and engage to strictly observe this treaty, and also to conduct and behave themselves as good and loyal subjects of Her Majesty the Queen. They promise and engage that they will, in all respects obey and abide by the law; that they will maintain peace and good order between each other, and also between themselves and other tribes of Indians, and between themselves and others of Her Majesty's subjects, whether Indians or whites, now inhabiting or hereafter to inhabit any part of the said ceded tract; and that they will not molest the person or property of any inhabitant of such ceded tract, or the property of Her Majesty the Queen, or interfere with or trouble any person passing or travelling through the said tract or any part thereof; and that they will aid and assist the officers of Her Majesty in bringing to justice and punishment any Indian offending against the stipulations of this treaty, or infringing the laws in force in the country so ceded.

In witness whereof, Her Majesty's said Commissioners and the said Indian Chiefs have hereunto subscribed and set their hands, at the north-west angle of the Lake of the Woods, this day and year herein first above-named ...

Signed by the Chiefs within named in presence of the following witnesses, the same having been first read and explained by the Honorable James McKay ...

2

"Not an Ordinary Criminal"

The Execution of Louis Riel

DOCUMENTS

A) Memorandum Respecting the Case of The Queen v. Riel, November 25, 1885
   Alexander Campbell, Minister of Justice

B) Speech, Champ de Mars, Montreal, November 22, 1885
   Honoré Mercier

C) House of Commons Debates, March 16, 1886
   Wilfrid Laurier

D) House of Commons Debates , March 11, 1886
   Joseph Adolphe Chapleau, M.P.

E) Reminiscences of the North West Rebellions, 1886
   Charles A. Boulton

Well over one hundred years after his execution in the Regina police barracks, the enigmatic and controversial Louis Riel still stirs Canadian emotions. Whether it was over a stylized sculpture of him on the Manitoba legislature grounds, or the recent federal declaration of Riel as a national hero, the man, his memory, and his place in Canadian history continue to foment debate, letters to editors, and quiet anguish over what it is to be Canadian. Interpreting his place in the nation's history still occupies interested citizens, historians, nationalists, westerners, Quebecois, Métis, Natives, and students. Riel has, over the intervening years since his death, mutated from traitor, through a "sad, pathetic, and unstable man leading his people on a suicidal crusade," to a brave hero of Canadian minority rights and one of the nation's founding fathers. Perhaps Riel, more than anyone, personifies the dichotomy and ambivalence of modern federal Canada. Perhaps that is why his execution remains virtually as controversial today as it was immediately after the fact.

Debate over the legitimacy of Riel's actions began with the Red River "Rebellion" in 1869–70, and simmered before boiling over again during the Northwest Rebellion of 1885. Ontario, in general, wanted "Riel's head in a sack." Quebec felt more ambivalent. Riel was, after all, French speaking and Catholic: a cultural brother. French Canadians saw him as a champion of minority rights fighting a tyrannical federal government running roughshod over local wishes. Riel was, to many Quebecois, a heroic David struggling against their common Goliath. On the other hand, Quebecers were also law-abiding Canadians who did not accept armed insurrection or flagrantly flouting Canadian law as methods of redressing grievances.

Disagreement over the appropriateness of his execution started well before the moment Riel's neck snapped at the end of the noose at dawn on November 16, 1885. He became, for many, a political martyr to the ideals of individual liberty, justice, and minority rights. Most holding that interpretation believed he had no chance against the monolithic central government and its courts. Nobody who challenged the federal steamroller rumbling across the Canadian prairies emerged unscathed.

Citizens of Ontario, meanwhile, seethed over Riel's actions in 1869–70. To them he was a "half-breed papist" who had stymied federal efforts to annex the Northwest. Although he had acted in conjunction with the local Métis community, Ontario singled out Riel as the leader of the resistance movement and as the chief instigator of the Métis court martial and execution of Thomas Scott, a man one Ontario newspaper called "a pure flower of Ontario youth." When the whole chain of events repeated itself fifteen years later in Saskatchewan, the people of Ontario believed that Riel deserved to twitch at the end of a hangman's rope.

The debate really boiled down to two core issues: were Riel's actions justified, and did he know what he was doing when he waged war against the federal government in 1885? If the prairie situation warranted rebellion, then he could hardly be guilty of treason. If it did not, then he got what he deserved: the mandatory death sentence meted out by the ancient English Statute of Treasons. Compounding this was the question of his sanity. If insane at the time, then he was not responsible for his actions and the state should have pitied, not punished, him. The difference here was in the type of sentence passed: execution versus indefinite incarceration in an asylum. The federal government and its prosecution team believed him sane. Riel agreed, contending throughout his trial that he knew exactly what he was doing during the rebellion. In this he parted company with his defense team, which built its case around his insanity. Pleading sanity to the charges, argued his lawyers, surely proved his insanity.

Sir Alexander Campbell (1822–1892) was perhaps as responsible as anyone for the verdict in Riel's trial and his subsequent execution. Born in England, he was brought to Canada as an infant when his family immigrated in 1823. The family initially settled in Montreal, but eventually made Kingston, Ontario, home. Campbell attended the local grammar school and eventually served a legal apprenticeship under John A. Macdonald, with whom he developed a life-long friendship. He was a successful businessman involved in interests as diverse as railroads, mines, insurance, and western land speculation. Campbell's public career began in 1850 when the people of Kingston elected him alderman. From there he slowly worked his way through the political ranks until, at the time of the Northwest Rebellion, he was Minister of Justice in Macdonald's administration. Campbell was a cool, frugal, conscientious public servant with a deep conservative streak and a narrow legalistic bearing. It was he who refused to allow Riel's trial to proceed in Winnipeg — the closest province to the event and arguably the most appropriate venue. He wrote to Macdonald, insisting that Riel be taken to Regina and tried there under the Northwest Territories Act, by which prisoners were not entitled to mixed Anglophone-Francophone juries. Such a jury, feared Campbell, might bring in a verdict other than guilty, the possibility of which he considered a miscarriage of justice.

Honoré Mercier (1840–1894) was one of the most prominent and eloquent Quebecois during the Riel era, and a great champion of Catholic and French-Canadian rights. Like so many of his Quebec political contemporaries, he rose through the Catholic school system into law, and from there jumped into politics. Mercier, however, also became a journalist along the way. He first sat as a member of the *Parti National* in the House of Commons in 1872, but then shifted to provincial politics, eventually succeeding Henri Joly as leader of the provincial Liberal party in 1883. The provincial Conservatives lost office in 1886, and Mercier became Premier for the next four years. Though innovative and progressive, Mercier's government was dogged by scandal, and it aroused deep resentment among Quebec anglophones. In 1891, and as a direct result of waning confidence in Mercier's administration, the Lieutenant-Governor of Quebec took the unprecedented step of dismissing him and calling an election, which the Liberals resoundingly lost. Riel's death caused Mercier, a consummate orator, to rally all French-Canadians under a common banner denouncing Ottawa, and encouraging the strengthening of Quebec's control of its own destiny within the federal system. He only partially succeeded, as the French-Canadian political landscape was formed of interests far too disparate for a grand alliance.

As Canada's first French-Canadian Prime Minister, Sir Wilfrid Laurier (1841–1919) was well aware of the narrow tightrope bridging the chasm between French and English Canada. It was his life's ambition to successfully walk that high-wire between the two solitudes, and he perhaps came as close as any to accomplishing it. After studying law at McGill, Laurier practiced briefly before turning his attention to federal politics. He won a seat in the House of Commons in 1874, and remained there as a Liberal until 1919. His political and organizational skills plus his deep dedication to the federal cause earned him a place in Alexander MacKenzie's cabinet in 1877. He became Liberal leader in 1887, taking over from Edward Blake, and led the party until his death. Laurier tried hard to unite English and French, treading carefully with each successive piece of legislation lest it alienate one or the other. He immediately recognized the fundamentally divisive potential of the Riel issue, but his personal integrity compelled him to take a strong stance against John A. Macdonald's policy toward the Northwest and the Métis. He did not deny that Riel rebelled, but placed the blame squarely on the Prime Minister's shoulders. He believed that decades of studied federal indifference, ignorance, condescension, and greed ensured that the Métis would eventually have to take a stand: they had no other recourse. Laurier's position proved popular in Quebec, but won him few supporters in the rest of the country — except Manitoba.

Another career politician swept up in the Riel rebellions and their aftermath, Sir Joseph Adolphe Chapleau (1840-1898) was born in Lower Canada. Chapleau eventually became a lawyer and entered public service in 1867 as a Conservative member of the Quebec Legislative Assembly. Chapleau showed himself a headstrong and independent thinker, but clearly gravitated toward the French-Canadian Catholic and nationalist cause — though ironically he married a Protestant woman from a distinguished English army family. He eventually rose to become Premier of Quebec in 1880, and then shifted to federal politics, which he entered in 1883 as a Conservative. Thus French-Canadians tarred him with the same brush they used on John A. Macdonald when Louis Riel died. Many of his constituents urged him to resign from the party that had "[a]ffronted the [French-Canadian] race," but Chapleau stayed on. He even managed to win his and nearby ridings for the Conservatives in the 1887 federal election. The damage was done, however, and Chapleau never regained the political momentum he enjoyed prior to the Northwest Rebellion.

Charles Arkoll Boulton (1841–1899) came from a long line of military men and, not surprisingly, followed in their footsteps. Born in Upper Canada, he went to the colony's premier private boys' school, Upper Canada College, before buying a commission in the Royal Canadian Regiment. He served with the initial survey party that Louis Riel repelled from Red River in 1869. Boulton subsequently tried to raise a force to unseat Riel and his provisional government, but lost his nerve. He was condemned to death after his capture by the Métis, but his captors fortunately commuted the sentence. He returned to civilian life after the Red River resistance, becoming a farmer in the new province of Manitoba. He was in Winnipeg when the Northwest Rebellion broke out fifteen years later and used his army experience to muster a small band known as Boulton's Scouts, which played major roles in the battles of Fish Creek and Batoche. Dogged by financial woes most of his life, Boulton felt deeply frustrated and disillusioned by the lack of compensation for his part in crushing the Métis uprising.

A) Memorandum Respecting the Case of The Queen v. Riel, November 25, 1885
Alexander Campbell, Minister of Justice

The case of Louis Riel, convicted and executed for high treason, has excited unusual attention and interest, not merely in the Dominion of Canada but beyond its limits. Here it has been made the subject of party, religious and national feeling and discussion; and elsewhere it has been regarded by some as a case in which, for the first time in this generation, what is assumed to have been a political crime only, has been punished with death.

The opponents of the Government have asserted that the rebellion was provoked, if not justified, by their maladministration of the affairs of the North-West Territories, and inattention to the just claims of the half-breeds.

With this question, which has been made one of party politics, it is not thought becoming to deal here.

Upon such a charge, when made in a constitutional manner, the Government will be responsible to the representatives of the people, and before them they will be prepared to meet and disprove it.

Appeals to the animosities of race have been made in one of the Provinces, with momentary success. Should these prevail, the future of the country must suffer. Parliament will not meet for some time, and in the interval, unless some action is taken to remove these animosities, they will gain ground, and it will become more difficult to dispel belief in the grounds which are used to provoke them.

It is thought right, therefore, that the true facts of the case, and the considerations which have influenced the Government, should be known, so that those who desire to judge of their conduct impartially may have the information which is essential for that purpose.

It has been asserted that the trial was an unfair one, and before a tribunal not legally constituted; that the crime being one of rebellion and inspired by political motives, the sentence, according to modern custom and sentiment, should not have been carried out; and that the prisoner's state of mind was such as to relieve him from responsibility for his acts.

After the most anxious consideration of each one of these grounds the Government have felt it impossible to give effect to any of them, and have deemed it their duty to let the law take its course.

I am now desired, in a matter of such grave importance and responsibility, to place on record the considerations which have impelled them to this conclusion:

1. As to the jurisdiction of the court and the fairness of the trial.

It should be sufficient to say that the legality of the tribunal by which he was tried has been affirmed by the Privy Council, the highest court in the Empire, and has seemed to them so clear that the eminent counsel who represented the prisoner could not advance arguments against it which were thought even to require an answer ...

Of the competency of the court, which had been affirmed by the full court in Manitoba, the Government saw no reason to entertain doubt; but having regard to the exceptional character of the case, the usual course was departed from in the prisoner's favor, and a respite was granted, to enable him to apply to the ultimate tribunal in England, and thus to take advantage to the very utmost of every right which the law could afford to him.

The fairness of the trial has not been disputed by the prisoner's counsel, nor challenged either before the Court of Appeal in Manitoba or the Privy Council. It has, on the contrary, been admitted, not tacitly alone by this omission, but expressly and publicly ...

The evidence of the prisoner's guilt, both upon written documents signed by himself and by other testimony, was so conclusive that it was not disputed by his counsel. They contended, however, that he was not responsible for his acts, and rested their defense upon the ground of insanity.

The case was left to the jury in a very full charge, and the law, as regards the defense of insanity, clearly stated in a manner to which no exception was taken, either at the trial or in the Court of Queen's Bench of Manitoba, or before the Privy Council.

2. With regard to the sanity of the prisoner and his responsibility in law for his acts, there has been much public discussion.

Here again it should be sufficient to point out that this defense was expressly raised before the jury, the proper tribunal for its discussion; that the propriety of their unanimous verdict was challenged before the full court in Manitoba, when the evidence was discussed at length and the verdict unanimously affirmed. Before the Privy Council no attempt was made to dispute the correctness of this decision.

The learned Chief Justice of Manitoba says in his judgment: "I have carefully read the evidence and it appears to me that the jury could not reasonably have come to any other conclusion than the verdict of guilty. There is not only evidence to support the verdict, but it vastly preponderates."

And again: "I think the evidence upon the question of insanity shows that the prisoner did know that he was acting illegally, and that he was responsible for his acts."

Mr. Justice Taylor's conclusion is: "After a critical examination of the evidence, I find it impossible to come to any other conclusion than that at which the jury arrived. The appellant is, beyond all doubt, a man of inordinate vanity, excitable, irritable, and impatient of contradiction. He seems to have at times acted in an extraordinary manner; to have said many strange things, and to have entertained, or at least professed to entertain, absurd views on religious and political subjects. But it all stops short of establishing such unsoundness of mind as would render him irresponsible, not accountable for his actions. His course of conduct indeed shows, in many ways, that the whole of his apparently extraordinary conduct, his claims to Divine inspiration and the prophetic character, was only part of a cunningly devised scheme to gain, and hold, influence and power over the simple-minded people around him, and to secure personal immunity in the event of his ever being called to account for his actions. He seems to have had in view, while professing to champion the interests of the Métis, the securing of pecuniary advantage for himself" …

Mr. Justice Killam says: "I have read very carefully the report of the charge of the Magistrate, and it appears to have been so clearly put that the jury could have no doubt of their duty in case they thought the prisoner insane when he committed the acts in question. They could not have listened to that charge without understanding fully that to bring in a verdict of guilty was to declare emphatically their disbelief in the insanity of the prisoner."

And again: "In my opinion, the evidence was such that the jury would not have been justified in any other verdict than that which they gave ... I hesitate to add anything to the remarks of my brother Taylor upon the evidence on the question of insanity. I have read over very carefully all the evidence that was laid before the jury, and I could say nothing that would more fully express the opinions I have formed from its perusal than what is expressed by him. I agree with him also in saying that the prisoner has been ably and zealously defended, and that nothing that could assist his case appears to have been left untouched."

The organization and direction of such a movement is in itself irreconcilable with this defense; and the admitted facts appear wholly to displace it. The prisoner, eight months before this rebellion broke out, was living in the United States, where he had become naturalized under their laws, and was occupied as a school teacher. He was solicited to come, it is said, by a deputation of prominent men among the French half-breeds who went to him from the North-West Territories, and, after a conference, requested him to return with them, and assist in obtaining certain rights which they claimed from the Dominion Government, and the redress of certain alleged grievances. He arrived in the Territories in July, 1884, and for a period of eight months was actively engaged in discussing, both publicly and privately, the matters for which he had come, addressing many public meetings upon them in a settlement composed of about six hundred French and a larger number of English half-breeds, together with others. The English half-breeds and other settlers observed his course, and saw reason to fear the outbreak which followed; but the suggestion of insanity never occurred, either to those who dreaded his influence in public matters over his race, and would have been glad to counteract it, or to the many hundreds who unhappily listened to him and were guided by his evil counsels to their ruin.

If, up to the eve of the resort to arms, his sanity was open to question, it is unaccountable that no one, either among his followers or his opponents, should have called public attention to it. If the Government had then attempted to place him under restraint as a lunatic, it is believed that no one would have been found to justify their action, and that those who now assert him to have been irresponsible would have been loud and well warranted in their protest. It may be well also to call attention to the obvious inconsistency of those persons —

not a few — who have urged the alleged maladministration of the affairs of the North-West Territory by the Government as a ground for interfering with the sentence, without ceasing to insist upon the plea of insanity. The prisoner cannot have been entitled to consideration both as the patriotic representative of his race and an irresponsible lunatic. It may be asked, too, if the leader was insane, upon what fair ground those who were persuaded by and followed him could be held responsible; and, if not, who could have been punished for crimes which so unquestionably called for it?

It has been urged, however, that his nature was excitable, and his mental balance uncertain; that as the agitation increased his natural disposition overcame him, and that the resort to violence was the result of over-wrought feelings, ending in insanity for which he cannot fairly be held accountable — that, in short, he was overcome by events not foreseen or intended by him ...

A simple statement of the facts will show that this view is wholly without foundation; that throughout he controlled and created the events, and was the leader, not the follower; and that the resort to armed violence was designed and carried out by him deliberately, and with a premeditation which leaves no room whatever for this plea ...

It may be asserted with confidence that there never has been a rebellion more completely dependent upon one man; that had he at any moment so desired, it would have come to an end; and that had he been removed a day before the outbreak, it would, in all probability, never have occurred. A dispassionate perusal of the whole evidence will leave no room for doubt upon this point, and that this was his own opinion appears by his statement to Father André, to be presently referred to.

Finally, under this head, as regards the mental state of the prisoner, after his trial and before execution, careful enquiry was made into this question by medical experts employed confidentially by the Government for that purpose, and nothing was elicited showing any change in his mental powers or casting any doubt upon his perfect knowledge or his crime, or justifying the idea that he had not such mental capacity as to know the nature and quality of the act for which he was convicted, as to know that the act was wrong, and as to be able to control his own conduct.

3. It has been urged that the prisoner's crime was a political one, inspired by political motives alone; that a rebellion prompted only for the redress of alleged political grievances, differs widely from an ordinary crime, and that however erroneous may be the judgment of its leader, in endeavoring

to redress the supposed wrongs of others, he is entitled, at least, to be regarded as unselfish, and as in his own view, patriotic.

This ground has been most earnestly considered, but the Government has been unable to recognize in the prisoner a political offender only, or to see that upon the evidence there can be any doubt that his motives were mainly selfish. On the contrary, it seems plain that he was willing at any moment, for the sake of gain, to desert his deluded followers, and to abandon his efforts for the redress of their alleged grievances, if, under cover of them, he could have obtained satisfaction for his own personal money demands.

It is believed that many who have espoused his crime and desired to avert from him the sentence which the law pronounced must have been ignorant of this fact, or cannot duly have considered its proper effect, for it seems incredible that anyone knowing it could regard the prisoner as entitled to the character of a patriot, or adopt him as the representative of an honorable race.

It is to be remembered that the prisoner had left this country and gone to the United States, where he had become an American citizen. He was brought here, therefore, avowedly to represent the claims of others, although in his letter of acceptance to the delegates he mentioned his own grievances as enabling him to make common cause with them. It is clear, however, from the evidence of Dr. Willoughby and Mr. Astley, that from the beginning his own demand, which he himself claimed against the Government, was uppermost in his thoughts, and as early as December he attempted to make a direct bargain with the Government for its satisfaction ...

The counsel for the other half-breeds who pleaded guilty also stated in court that Riel had himself procured the request to him to come to this country; and on two occasions in court these learned gentlemen most earnestly and indignantly denounced the prisoner as one who had misled and deceived their clients, and to whom all the misery and ruin which this unhappy rebellion had brought upon them was to be attributed.

But if an unselfish desire could be credited to the prisoner to redress political wrongs even by armed rebellion, it would at least have been necessary to disprove the charge which lies against him, that in his own mind the claims of humanity had no place, but that he was prepared to carry out his designs by bringing upon an unoffending people all the horrors of an Indian rising with the outrages and atrocities which, as he knew full well, must inevitably accompany it. That this cannot be disproved, but that it is beyond all dispute true, the evidence makes plain.

From the beginning, even before Duck Lake, he was found in company with Indians armed, and to the end he availed himself of their assistance ...

It could not be overlooked either, upon an application for executive clemency, that upon the trials of One Arrow, Poundmaker, White Cap and other Indians, it was apparent that they were excited to the acts of rebellion by the prisoner and his emissaries. Many of these Indians so incited and acting with him from the commencement were refugee Sioux from the United States, said to have been concerned in the Minnesota massacre and the Custer affair, and therefore of a most dangerous class.

It is to the credit of the Indian chiefs that their influence was used to prevent barbarity, but by individuals among them several cold-blooded, deliberate murders were committed, for which the perpetrators now lie under sentence of death. These crimes took place during the rebellion, and can be attributed only to the excitement arising out of it.

4. Whether rebellion alone should be punished with death is a question upon which opinions may differ. Treason will probably ever remain what it always has been among civilized nations, the highest of all crimes; but each conviction for that offense must be treated and disposed of by the Executive Government upon its own merits, and with a full consideration of all the attendant circumstances. In this particular instance, it was a second offense and, as on the first occasion, accompanied by bloodshed under the direct and immediate order of the prisoner, and by the atrocity of attempting to incite an Indian warfare, the possible results of which the prisoner could and did thoroughly appreciate. In deciding upon the application for the commutation of the sentence passed upon the prisoner the Government was obliged to keep in view the need of exemplary and deterrent punishment for crimes committed in a country situated in regard to settlement and population as are the North-West Territories; the isolation and defenseless position of the settlers already there; the horrors to which they would be exposed in the event of an Indian outbreak; the effect upon intending settlers of any weakness in the administration of the law; and the consequences which must follow in such a country if it came to be believed that such crimes as Riel's could be committed, without incurring the extreme penalty of the law, by anyone who was either subject to delusions, or could lead people to believe that he was so subject. The crime of the prisoner was no constructive treason; it was accompanied by much bloodshed, inflicted by his own direct orders; and the Government have felt, upon a full and most earnest consideration of the case,

that they would be unworthy of the power with which they are entrusted by the whole people, and would have neglected their plain duty to all classes, had they interfered with the due execution of a sentence pronounced as the result of a just verdict, and sanctioned by a righteous law.

B) Speech, Champ de Mars, Montreal, November 22, 1885
Honoré Mercier

Riel, our brother, is dead, a victim of his devotion to the cause of the Métis whose chief he was, a victim of fanaticism and of betrayal; of the fanaticism of Sir John and of his friends; of the betrayal of three of our own people who, to maintain their cabinet posts, have sold their brother.

Riel died on the scaffold, as the patriots of 1837 died, as brave and Christian men! In surrendering his head to the executioner as did (François) Lorimier, he has given his heart to his country; as Christ he forgave his murderers.

He went up to the scaffold with a firm and sure step; not a muscle of his face trembled; his soul, strengthened by martyrdom, knew not the weakness of agony.

In killing Riel, Sir John has not only struck at the heart of our race but especially at the cause of justice and humanity which, represented in all languages and sanctified by all religious beliefs, demanded mercy for the prisoner of Regina, our poor friend of the North-West.

Riel's last gasp has echoed sorrowfully throughout the entire world; it has reverberated as a piercing cry from the soul of all civilized peoples; and this cry has had the same effect on the Minister and the executioner; both, their hands stained with blood, tried to hide their shame: the one in an Orange Lodge hearing the howls of gratified fanaticism; the other [Macdonald], on the ocean in order not to hear the curses of a whole people in sorrow.

There are about fifty thousand free citizens here [on the Champ de Mars] gathered together under the protecting shield of the constitution, in the name of humanity which cries for vengeance, in the name of all friends of justice which has been trampled under foot, in the name of two million French who are in tears, in order to cast on the Minister in flight a final curse which, reverberating from echo to echo along the banks of our great river, will overtake him as he loses sight of the soil of Canada, which he has soiled through a judicial murder.

As to those who remain; as to the three who represent the province of Quebec in the federal government and who signify nothing but betrayal, let us bow our heads in the face of their shortcoming and let us cry about their sad fate; for the stain of blood they carry on their brow is as indelible as the memory of their cowardice. They will share the fate of their brother Cain; the memory of them will be as detestable as of him; and as the sons of Abel who sought refuge in the desert to avoid meeting again the first brother-killer in the world, our children will turn their heads to avoid seeing the three brother-killers of Canada.

In the face of this crime, in the presence of these failings, what is our duty? We have three things to do: unite to punish the guilty, break the alliance which our deputies made with Orangeism and seek in an alliance more natural and less dangerous, protection of our national interests.

We, united! Oh! how comfortable I feel in speaking these words! Twenty years ago I asked for a union of all the passionate forces of the nation. Twenty years ago I said to my brothers to sacrifice, on the alter of the fatherland in danger, the hatred that was blinding us and the divisions that were destroying us. You replied to this call for unity which came from a patriotic heart, with insults, recriminations, calumnies. It required the national misfortune we deplore, it required the death of one of our own for this cry of unity to be understood.

Today, distracted by grief, we recognize our fault, and faced with the body of Riel we hold out a fraternal hand to one another. Kneeling at the blessed grave, we ask God for pardon and mercy, pardon for our past strife, mercy for our race so grievously attacked. Will this entreaty be heard; will our prayers made in sobs and coming from our souls in despair be granted?

Are there among all the hands clasped in sublime enthusiasm the hands of some traitors? The God who probes the depths of our being, this God alone knows. While waiting till He reveals His secrets to us, till He lifts a corner of the future all of whose mysteries He knows, let us hope and have confidence.

All those who are united in spirit in this day of atonement, are of the same race, speak the same language, kneel at the same altar, the same blood rekindles their heart; these are all brothers! May heaven assure this time that they hear the voice of blood.

Then let us not forget, we who are Liberals, that if the nation is in mourning as a result of the assassination of Riel, our Conservative brothers are in the depths of grief greater than our own. They are shedding tears over Riel as we are, but they are crying also over the downfall and the betrayal of their leaders. Those who were, with reason, so proud of Chapleau and Langevin, those who saw in the eloquence of one and the competence of the other, the preservation of the country, are forced to bow their heads and curse today those they blest yesterday. Gentlemen, respect this great and legitimate grief; and do not belittle it.

This union, gentlemen, which we have organized and which we beg you to bless, in the name of the fatherland you represent, is not a union of race against other races, of religion against other religions.

We do not wish to atone for a crime with another. Grief renders us neither foolish or unjust, and does not destroy the respect we have for our brothers of other nationalities. We know that the Irish, sons of a race persecuted as ours, are with us in the solemn protest we are making; we know that the English, friends of justice, and the Scotch, friends of liberty, sympathize with us in the misfortune which has struck us; we know too that it is betrayal rather than fanaticism that killed Riel ...

It must be avowed that the leaders of the Conservative party are degenerating; but I have confidence that the soldiers of this great party remain stout-hearted, and that there will be among them enough patriotism to induce them to join with us, as one man, in the great national movement which is being organized at this moment.

Let us hope also, gentlemen, that our Canadian clergy whose lofty and noble traditions are written in letters of gold in our historic annals, will not fail us at this conjuncture; and that its powerful co-operation, given with prudence and reserve, will assure the realization of our hopes.

We are not unaware that in the neighbouring province and in all other parts of Canada there are generous hearts ready to devote themselves to the common cause, to the cause of justice and humanity.

Just yesterday, an influential newspaper, the *Globe*, speaking of "the duty of the hour" justifies the demonstrations that the death of Riel has provoked in the province of Quebec, recalls the causes which led to the rebellion in the North West and the readiness of the Ministers, directly after the revolt, to grant the demands of the Métis ... "The people of Ontario should not forget that the French Canadians ask nothing but justice ... The only way to save Canada is in a cordial union, made between the two provinces, to punish the despicable people who are in power."

That is what they say in Ontario; it is not, therefore, a racial war we want; it is not only an exclusive French Canadian party we ask, but a union of all the friends of justice and humanity whose sacred cause has been outraged by the death of Riel.

This death, the crime of our enemies, will become for us a rallying sign and an instrument of salvation.

Our duty, therefore, is to unite and punish the guilty; may this union be consecrated by our people and let us make an oath before God and man, to fight with all our strength and all our soul and with all the resources provided us by the Constitution, the perfidious government of Sir John, the three traitors who have dishonoured our race, and all those who will be wicked enough to seek to imitate or to excuse their crime! ...

C) House of Commons Debates, March 16, 1886
Wilfrid Laurier

... In every instance in which a Government has carried out the extreme penalty of the law, when mercy was suggested instead, the verdict of history has been the same. Sir, in the Province to which I belong, and especially amongst the race to which I belong, the execution of Louis Riel has been universally condemned as being the sacrifice of a life, not to inexorable justice, but to bitter passion and revenge ...

It has been stated by sober-minded people that the execution, even if unjust, of the man who was executed and who is believed to have been insane by those who sympathise with him, does not make this a case for the outburst of feeling which has been made in Quebec on the occasion of Riel's execution. I differ from that view. In our age, in our civilisation, every single human life is valuable and is entitled to protection in the councils of the nation. Not many years ago England sent an expedition and spent millions of her treasure and some of her best blood simply to rescue prisoners whose lives were in the hands of the King of Abyssinia. In the same manner I say that the life of a single subject of Her Majesty here is valuable, and is not to be treated with levity. If there are members in this House who believe that the execution of Riel was not warranted, that under the circumstances of the case it was not judicious, that it was unjust, I say they have a right to arraign the Government for it before this country, and if they arraign the Government for it and the Government have to take their trial upon it, it must be admitted as a consequence that certain parties will feel upon the question more than others. It is not to be supposed that the same causes which influenced public opinion in Lower Canada acted in the same manner with all classes of the community, that the causes which actuated the community at large were identical in all classes of the community. Some there were who believed that the Government had not meted out the same measure of justice to all those that were accused and who took part in the rebellion. Others believed that the state of mind of Riel was such that it was a judicial murder to execute him; but the great mass of the people believed that mercy should have been extended to all the prisoners, Riel included, because the rebellion was the result of the policy followed by the Government against the half-breeds. That was the chief reason which actuated them, and it seems to me it is too late in the day now to seriously attempt to deny that the rebellion was directly the result of the conduct of the Government towards the half-breeds. It is too late in the day to dispute that fact ... The half-breeds ... they sent their friends upon delegations to Ottawa; ... yet the Government never took any action in the matter until the 28th of January, 1885, when the Minister felt his seat shaken by the tempest that was threatening to sweep over the country. But it was then unfortunately too late. When the seeds of discontent have long been germinating, when hearts have long been swelling with long accumulating bitternesses, and when humiliations and disappointments have made men discontented and sullen, a small incident will create a conflagration, just as a spark on the prairie, under certain circumstances, will kindle a widespread and unquenchable fire. Then the Government moved, but it was too late ... I have charged the Government with not only having been negligent in the duty they owed to the half-breeds, but with denying to the half-breeds the rights to which they were entitled. I charge them with, not ignoring only, but actually refusing, of design aforethought, the rights to which the half-breeds were entitled ... In 1879 the First Minister took power to extend the same privileges to the half-breeds of the North-West. It will be seen that the half-breeds of Manitoba were treated as a special class. They were not treated as Indians; they were not treated as whites, but as participating in the rights of both the whites and the Indians. If they had been treated as Indians they would have been sent to their reserves; if they had been treated as whites they would have been granted homesteads; but as I have said they were treated as a special class, participating in both rights of whites and Indians; as whites they were given a homestead of 160 acres on the plot of land of which they happened to be in possession; as Indians, they were given scrip for lands to the extent of 160 acres for each head of their family, and 240 acres for minors. In 1879, as I have said, the Government passed a statute similar to the statute of Manitoba. Did they act upon it? When did they act upon it? When was the first thing done by the

Government of Canada to put in force the Act of 1879? The first thing ever done by the Government of Canada to put in force the Act they themselves had passed was on the 28th January, 1885. Six long years elapsed before they attempted to do that justice to the half-breeds which they had taken power from Parliament to do at the time. During all that time the Government was perfectly immovable ... Sir, if the Government had done their duty by the half-breeds, how is it that the half-breeds so often petitioned the Government to grant them their rights? How is it that they so often deluged the Department with petitions and deputations? ... How is it that these men, in order to obtain the rights which were denied them, have gone through such an ordeal as they have, if the Government did justice by them? Is this not the greatest condemnation that could be pronounced against them? ... The Government had been refusing for years, and at last these men took their lives and liberties in their hands, and at last the Government came down and gave them what they were entitled to. I appeal now to any friend of liberty in this House; I appeal not only to the Liberals who sit beside me, but to any man who has a British heart in his breast, and I ask, when subjects of Her Majesty have been petitioning for years for their rights, and those rights have not only been ignored, but have been denied, and when these men take their lives in their hands and rebel, will anyone in this House say that these men, when they got their rights, should not have saved their heads as well, and that the criminals, if criminals there were in this rebellion, are not those who fought, and bled and died, but the men who sit on those Treasury benches? Sir, rebellion is always an evil, it is always an offence against the positive law of a nation; it is not always a moral crime. The Minister of Militia [Adolphe Caron] in the week that preceded the execution of Riel, stated his sentiments of rebellion in these words: "I hate all rebels; I have no sympathy, good, bad or indifferent with rebellion." Sir, what is hateful — I use the word which the hon. gentleman made use of — what is hateful is not rebellion, but is the despotism which induces that rebellion; what is hateful are not rebels, but the men who, having the enjoyment of power, do not discharge the duties of power; they are the men who, having the power to redress wrongs, refuse to listen to the petitions that are sent to them; they are the men who, when they are asked for a loaf, give a stone ... Where would be the half-breeds to-day if it had not been for this rebellion? Would they have obtained the rights which they now enjoy? I say, Sir, that the Canadian Government stands convicted of having yielded their rights only to rebellion, and not to the just representation of the half-breeds and of having actually forced them into insurrection ... Though, Mr. Speaker, these men were in the wrong; though the rebellion had to be put down, though it was the duty of the Canadian Government to assert its authority and vindicate the law, still, I ask any friend of liberty, if there is not a feeling rising in his heart, stronger than all reasoning to the contrary, that these men were excusable? ... I am a British subject, and I value the proud title as much as anyone in this House. But if it is expected of me that I shall allow fellow countrymen unfriended, undefended, unprotected and unrepresented in this House, to be trampled under foot by this Government, I say that is not what I understand by loyalty, and I would call that slavery. I am a British subject, but my loyalty is not of the lips. If hon. gentlemen opposite will read history, they will find that my ancestors, in all their struggles against the British Crown in the past, never sought anything else than to be treated as British subjects, and as soon as they were treated as British subjects, though they had not forgotten the land of their ancestors, they became amongst the most loyal subjects that England ever had ... But loyalty must be reciprocal. It is not enough for the subject to be loyal to the Crown; the Crown must also be loyal to the subject ... [T]his Government has not done its duty towards the half-breeds. The Government are shocked, and their friends profess to be shocked, because those men claim their rights and demanded them with bullets. Have the Government been loyal to those half-breeds? If they had been loyal to the half-breeds no such trouble would have occurred. But the Government have not been loyal to the laws. If the Government do not respect the law themselves, and if afterwards men, to vindicate their rights, take weapons in their hands and brave the laws, I say the Government are bound to search their consciences and see if they have given occasion for rebellion, and if they have, to give the benefit to the guilty ones. This is what we, in Lower Canada, have been claiming, and this is one of the reasons why we have felt so warmly upon this question. But such is not, however, the doctrine of the Government ... Sir, I am not of those who look upon Louis Riel as a hero. Nature had endowed him with many brilliant qualities, but nature denied him that supreme quality without which all other qualities, however brilliant, are of no avail. Nature denied him a well-balanced mind. At his worst he was a subject fit for an asylum; at his best he was a religious and political monomaniac. But he was not a bad man — do not believe at least that he was the bad man that he has been represented to be in a certain press. It is true that at the trial a most damaging fact was brought against him; it is true that he had offered to accept a bribe from the Government. But justice to his memory requires that all the circumstances connected with that fact should be laid before the House. If he accepted this money, it is evident that in his own confused mind it was not with a view of betraying the cause of his fellow countrymen ... I grant that if that reasoning had been made by a man in his senses, such as an hon. gentleman on the other side, it would be enough to stifle any sympathy we could have for him; but we must make due allowances for the fact that it is proved that if he was not actually insane, no man can deny that upon this subject of politics his mind was not right or sound; and of course in the case of a mind unsound or insane we cannot apply the same tests that we should apply to a reasonable mind — it would be unfair to him. But that he was insane seems to me beyond the possibility of controversy ... But we never knew, until the Minister of Public Works [H.L. Langevin] spoke the other day, what was the true reason of the execution of Riel. We have it now; he has spoken and we know what was the true inwardness of it. The Government had written a pamphlet in order to justify themselves. The utility of that pamphlet is gone; it never had any; not one of the reasons it gave for the execution of Riel was the true reason. It never had any usefulness at all, except, perhaps, as affording to the Government job printing to settle the wavering consciences of some of their followers. But now we know the true reason why Riel was executed, and here it is in the language of the Minister of Public Works:

> We had this before us, we had the fact that Louis Riel had, fifteen years before this, committed an act which was considered at the time one that should have been punished in the most severe way. The prisoner, Louis Riel, at that time was not condemned to a severe punishment; he was allowed to remain out of the country for five years, and he was not brought before a tribunal to be tried, and punished or absolved, for the death of Thomas Scott.

Here is the reason — the death of Thomas Scott ... the death of Scott is the cause of the death of Riel to-day. Why, if the hon. gentleman thinks that the death of Scott was a crime, did he not punish Riel at the time? Scott was executed in the early days of 1870, the Government remained in power until the fall of 1873, yet they never did anything to bring that man to justice, who had committed such a crime as they say now he committed.

1870-71-72-73, almost four full years, passed away, and yet the Government, knowing such a crime as it has been represented here had been committed, never took any step to have the crime punished. What was their reason? The reason was that the Government had promised to condone the offence; the reason was that the Government were not willing to let that man come to trial, but, on the contrary, actually supplied him with money to induce him to leave the country, and, Sir, I ask any man on the other side of the House, if this offence was punishable, why was it not punished then? and if it was not punishable then, why should it be punished now? ... Indeed the Government have convinced all the people here mentioned, the half-breeds, the Indians, the white settlers, that their arm is long and strong, and that they are powerful to punish. Would to heaven that they had taken as much pains to convince them all, the half-breeds, Indians and white settlers, of their desire and their willingness to do them justice, to treat them fairly. Had they taken as much pains to do right, as they have taken to punish wrong, they never would have had any occasion to convince those people that the law cannot be violated with impunity, because the law would never have been violated at all. But today, not to speak of those who have lost their lives, our prisons are full of men who, despairing ever to get justice by peace, sought to obtain it by war, who, despairing of ever being treated like freemen, took their lives in their hands, rather than be treated as slaves. They have suffered a great deal, they are suffering yet, their sacrifices will not be without reward. Their leader is in the grave; they are in durance, but from their prisons they can see that the justice, that liberty which they sought in vain, and for which they fought not in vain, has at last dawned upon their country ... Yes, their country has conquered with their martyrdom. They are in durance today; but the rights for which they were fighting have been acknowledged. We have not the report of the commission yet, but we know that more than two thousand claims so long denied have been at last granted. And more — still more ... This side of the House long fought, but fought in vain, to obtain that measure of justice. It could not come then, but it came after the war; it came as the last conquest of that insurrection. And again I say that their country has conquered with their martyrdom, and if we look at that one fact alone there was cause sufficient, independent of all others, to extend mercy to the one who is dead and to those who live.

D) House of Commons Debates , March 11, 1886
Joseph Adolphe Chapleau, M.P.

On the motion made, before the House of Commons, on the 11th March, 1886, to blame the Government for having allowed the execution of Riel.

... Louis Riel has written with his own hand and with his own deeds the darkest pages in the history of the North-West of this Dominion; he has signed those bloody pages, and sealed them with his blood on the scaffold of Regina on the 16th of November last. The scaffold has spread its hideous shadow over the newly christened town of Regina — christened after the name of our beloved Sovereign; and the virgin soil of the Province of Assiniboia was torn open to receive the dead body of a man who had sown the seeds of discontent, of revolt, and of war and death in a land which should have been reserved for peace, unity, happy tranquility and industry. The solemn sanction which was then given to the law should deter all other men, and deter, I hope, all other evil-disposed and evil-thinking men from imitating his example. Unfortunately, Sir, from the cell of the doomed agitator, from the scaffold, and the grave of the executed criminal, there came the wind of revolt and the poison of national animosity, which pervaded one of the great Provinces of this Dominion, and which threaten even now, perhaps to a larger extent than we believe, the future tranquility and destinies of the Dominion.

Mr. Speaker, if I bring to your recollection these sad events, it is only to show you the unfortunate position in which are placed those who in the Province of Quebec have espoused — some with sincerity and good faith, others with schemes for political supremacy — the cause of rebellion, which, it cannot be denied, has produced in this country one of the most unfortunate periods in our political history.

Mr. Speaker, it is the deep feeling of the danger arising from the present crisis which has animated me during the whole of that period, and which has often driven away from my lips and from my pen words of anger and words of violent rebuke, which would have been justified by the treatment to which I and my hon. colleagues in the Government have been subjected for over three months past. During that time, Sir, we have seen an infuriated and maddened mob tearing to pieces our likenesses, and hanging and burning us in effigy; but this has had upon me no other effect than to make me feel more pity than anger towards the crowd who had been excited against us.

In the city of Montreal, my portrait has been for days exposed in windows, bearing on the forehead a large red stain, to convey the idea that I was the murderer of one of my fellow-countrymen ...

Well, my hon. friend has said the Government had acted badly towards the Half-breeds, and that the insurrection on the Saskatchewan was justifiable — not only excusable, but justifiable, he said. And how, and why? He said the legislation of 1879 concerning the Half-breeds of the North-West was nothing but the completion of the legislation of 1870. But he added: You have taken from 1879 to 1885, the whole of that time, to give justice to those people who were entitled to what you gave them in 1885, under the Act of 1870. I admit, for argument's sake, the delays of the Government have been faulty. But they were only delays. And has the hon. gentleman considered that the responsibility for those delays bears much more heavily on the Government to which he belonged than it does on this Government? No, he forgot that circumstance. If his own Government had not given as an answer to the Half-breeds that they would not be treated otherwise than as white settlers, those delays might perhaps have been avoided and the revolt of 1885 averted.

In that great display of eloquence we had from the hon. gentleman, he declared that the Government had only moved when bullets were coming upon them. But the hon. gentleman was obliged to admit that on 26th January the Government had decided to grant those rights, and to send a commission to see that those rights were granted to the parties entitled to them. He has stated that the Government did not want to give the Half-breeds their rights and do justice to them, and that they only intended to take a census of the Half-breeds who might have been entitled, under treaty rights according to the Acts of 1870 and 1879. He thereby dealt the heaviest blow at the Government, of which he has been a member, and at those who have taken up arms against this Government, in stating that we had had the prudence to think as to who were entitled to the rights according to the Act of 1870. The hon. gentleman was forgetting, that of all those who rebelled and fought on the Saskatchewan, not more than 21 had really a right to claim land under that title. The other Half-breeds, who were acting with Riel, had already obtained land by virtue of the Act of 1870, after the transfer of Manitoba and the North-West Territories to the Government. In that list, it is true, a few names were given among the rebels, but those were probably the greatest proportion of those who had reasons to urge their claims before the Government ...

But let us return to the main issue. Was Riel insane at the time of the insurrection, and is that insanity a reason against the verdict obtained against him, and against the sentence rendered against him? Riel had been put into an asylum, it is true. I was the Minister of the Government at Quebec who signed the papers for his entrance into the asylum at Longue-Pointe. I am at a loss to know, even at this moment, whether the man was insane then or not. I shall state in a few moments why my doubts exist. Previous insanity is not a proof of insanity at a subsequent period. Where shall we take then the evidence of the insanity of Riel if we do not take it at the trial from the verdict of the jury? The insanity of Riel is proven by whom? By the missionaries who were, at that time, in that region? If they had believed that Riel was really insane, as insane as a man is legally, would they not have taken the means, during that time, to have him arrested as a lunatic, and confined as a lunatic? Let us take the testimony of his fellow-countrymen. The first man who said that the Government had hanged an insane man in hanging Riel, was slandering the Métis nation. We have the testimony of those who were with him, and we are told by one member of this House that he might have been insane and yet might have led sane men; that we have seen on some occasions an insane man creating a riot. That might be the case, for a few hours, in a sudden rising, but have we ever seen, and can we say, as sensible men, that a lunatic, that a demented man, from the month of July, 1884, to the month of April or May, 1885, could have acted as he did without anyone protesting against him, where men were placing in his hands their liberties and their lives, and could not perceive, by their daily and nightly communication with him, that he was not in possession of his senses?

We might go further. Take the plan of his campaign? I do not speak of the plan for the organisation of the party of Louis Riel, but the plan of his campaign.

We are supposed to be sane men; we might be acting under delusions, as my hon. friends have been acting under delusions since November last, that this Government would see its last days in consequence of this crisis, but we are supposed to be sane men, and yet did we not, last year, suppose, and do we not now think, that his plan of campaign was not only the work of a sane man but a very cunning man?

The season when the outbreak took place, the 19th March, at the beginning of spring, is a time when the roads are almost impassable, and when, in that country, even ordinary vehicles can hardly be used on those prairies, and the use of cannons and batteries, which Riel probably thought would be brought into the field, would be much more impossible.

Take the plan of his campaign. The Canadian Pacific Railway was not then finished, and Riel knew it as well as we did. He knew it better than the leader of the Opposition did, who was asking at that time what gaps of the railway remained uncompleted, how many miles remained to be constructed, and what were the difficulties to be encountered in building that road? The railway was not completed. Was it not the work of a sane man to choose that time for an insurrection, when that road was not in a condition to use for the conveyance of troops into the North-West? ...

It is useless for my hon. friends on the other side to try to make of this rising, as my hon. friend from Quebec-East (Mr. Laurier) has been trying to make it, an insurrection that might be justified and excused. It is of no use for them to try to make Riel a martyr, as my hon. friend from Maskinongé (Mr. Desaulniers) said he did, or a hero, as my hon. friends opposite have tried to prove him, or even an insane man, as some of my friends on this side have been disposed to think him, giving the benefit of any doubt they had, not to the law, but to that humane tenderness which exists for a man who is condemned to the gallows.

No, Sir, history, in its impartiality, shall not decree him a hero. The *bonum commune*, the interest of the nation was not the motive of his actions. He had dreamed of being a Napoleon, but he was ready and willing to be the chief of a guerilla band, ruling by violence and terror over the region of his exploits, living on plunder and waiting for the accident of a fortunate encounter to secure a heavy ransom with the safety of his own life.

... Riel was not an ordinary criminal, who, under the impulse of strong ruling passions, and for lucre, lust and revenge, committed murder, arson and pillage, with "malice aforethought". Riel has been an unscrupulous agitator, getting up a rebellion against the Sovereign for the sake of personal ambition and profit under the color of redressing public grievances. Riel was a born conspirator, a dreamer of power and wealth, frustrated in his design but not subdued by his former defeat, which had shaken his brains without eradicating the germ of his morbid ambition, he had been patiently watching his opportunity to come to the surface, until that opportunity came to him; fully cognizant of the nature of the insurrection he was planning and preaching; fully aware of the grave consequences of that movement, ready to accept the full responsibility of the loss of his life in the prosecution of his design. He considered the alleged grievances of the Half-breeds more in the light of the opportunities it would give him to resume power in the North-West, than with the view of redressing those wrongs. He had always advocated that the Hudson Bay Company's privileges and government were an usurpation, and, as a consequence, that the Canadian Government, who had acquired from the Hudson Bay Company, were not the legitimate rulers of the North-West and the Half-breeds. He was a convinced, although an extravagant, pretender. He believed in his mission, and to accomplish it, he willfully agreed, with his conscience, to kill or to be killed. He measured the distance between his ambition and the success that could crown it, and he deliberately consented to fill the gap, if necessary, with the corpses of his enemies or even his friends. Devoid of the courage of a soldier, he believed in his own shrewdness as a plotter. He expected success by a surprise, not from a regular battle. He was a willful and dangerous rebel. If rebellion, with the sacrifice of human life, with the aggravating circumstance of having incited to an Indian war, deserves the penalty of death, Riel deserved it as a political offender in the highest degree.

It has been pretended that, in his extravagant career, Riel was not sound in his mind and could not reason, although he accepted the responsibility of his actions. After the most careful examination of all the evidence which came before us, I cannot help saying that Riel, from the moment he left his home in the United States for the avowed purpose of assisting the Half-breeds in their demands for redress of alleged grievances, until the end of the North-West insurrection, has deliberately pursued the object he had in view, namely, to obtain full control of the North-West Half-breeds and Indians. To obtain his object, he aroused in himself, and communicated to others, to an intense degree, a sort of national and religious fever. This was a comparatively easy work with an excitable and credulous people. Having thus subdued the Half-breeds, his next effort was directed towards alienating them from the Government and from their clergy. When he had succeeded in doing this, he sought the alliance of the Indians and of the American sympathisers.

All that, he planned with a great amount of sagacity and with great pain. But the extravagant confidence he showed in his success, the smallness of the means he collected, his absolute impassiveness when reverse came, the unfeigned faith he had in what he called his mission, all point out to the conclusion that he was the prey to exaltation, to hallucination.

Though not insane, in the legal sense of the word, he was, to use a common expression, a "crank," but a crank of the worst kind, knowing well what was good and what was bad, what was wicked and what was kind, what was the value of life and what was death; but his notions of what was right and what was wrong had been distorted and altered by the determination and fixity of his purpose, by an ardent and selfish ambition, leading to injustice and cruelty. He was certainly, and without affectation, convinced that what he did was permitted by divine and moral laws, and that his treason was justifiable ...

In this case the purpose was supreme power, both civil and religious. The redress of grievances on one part, and the desire of personal pecuniary advantages on the other, do not seem to me to have been the principal motors of Riel's actions, though they certainly were important factors in his conduct. But that object, supreme power, was criminal and could not qualify, could not excuse him. It is a wrong theory, and it would be a dangerous doctrine to excuse and leave without punishment crimes committed with the conviction that the act accomplished is one calculated to redress a wrong or to bring good results to the community ...

The crime of Louis Riel had been committed, the criminal had been taken and tried. The trial had been an impartial, a fair trial. A verdict had been rendered against Riel, the only verdict that could be found according to the evidence. Sentence of death had been passed against him. The sentence was a just punishment of the crime committed. It would serve as an example, a warning, a terror to all future criminal impostors; as a remedy against the increasing contagion of cranks. Riel had been pardoned once for the commission of a great crime; a second exercise of the prerogative of royal mercy would have looked as an inducement to treason and homicide. A commutation into life imprisonment would have been a danger to society. The people whom he had deluded, those whose prejudices had been aroused, and those who would have found an interest in working up a continuous excitement in the country, would have found themselves greatly assisted by the prolonged existence of Louis Riel.

The clamor outside was loud, asking for pardon, for commutation of the sentence, but no protest against the correctness of the verdict was made since the decision of Her Majesty's Privy Council. The time fixed for the execution was nearing, when a last appeal was made on behalf of the convict, stating that he was, at that moment, so unsound in mind, so diseased in his brain, that to punish him would be useless cruelty, and request was made that medical men be appointed to go and examine Riel and report upon his sanity or insanity, that is whether he could rightly understand the nature of his crime and the measure of his punishment. That demand was supported by the almost unanimous prayer of the people of one of the Provinces. The Government yielded to that demand, and the enquiry took place. Medical men whose character and respectability are above suspicion, made the examination of the prisoner, and agreed in their conclusions that Riel was an accountable being for his actions and that therefore he could discern right from wrong, he could understand the verdict found against him and measure the severity of the punishment inflicted upon him. And after that report the Executive agreed that the sentence should be carried out against the unfortunate man ...

E) Reminiscences of the North West Rebellions, 1886
Charles A. Boulton

... His career and fate teach lessons which it is worth while for a moment to dwell on. The constitution under which British subjects are governed is of the most liberal character, and affords a legitimate vent for the expression of opinions and the redress of grievances that no other constitution so liberally provides. In 1869, the French half-breeds can fairly claim they had a legitimate right to know what terms were going to be accorded to them in the transfer of the country to Canada, and up to the point of forbidding the entrance of the Hon. Mr. Macdougall [*sic*] into the country, until some guarantee had been provided for the protection of their interests, the agitation that was commenced may be called legitimate. But the moment they took up arms, threatened the peace of the country, and prevented by bodily fear a free expression of the wants of the people in their negotiations with the Canadian Governor or Commissioners, it became rebellion, and any loss of life or property in consequence of this, the rebellious become responsible for.

Riel, however, realizing that the people had a grievance, took advantage of the circumstances to arouse their fears and hostilities, to obtain their support and enable him to usurp authority, not scrupling to take life, that he might occupy the position of autocrat of the country. After the arrival of the Canadian Commissioners, with power to treat with the people, Riel was criminal in every act that he committed. He was going beyond the constitutional privileges which are the great safeguard and protection of the people. In retaining prisoners and keeping them confined in unwholesome prisons, he was cruel; vindictive, and tyrannical. In taking the life of Scott, for no other reason than to make his power felt as dictator and autocrat of the country, he was a murderer. That crime was done at his bidding and for the purpose of advancing his personal ends. The circumstances of the country at the time were such that the Government could not bring him to justice for his crime. The amnesty having once been promised by Archbishop Taché put a different phase upon the circumstances, and Riel escaped the consequences of his act with the moderate punishment of banishment for five years to the United States — a country where he had for some time previously resided and where he was quite satisfied to make his home.

The years go by, and the half-breeds recollect the excitement and the profit they derived from the rebellion of 1869–70, and remember that the benefits of scrip which had been accorded to them at that time were withheld, or rather that the principle of issuing scrip had not yet been extended to the North-West Territory. More than that, the half-breeds who had left the Province of Manitoba, and who had there secured the patents for their lands, and obtained the scrip for themselves and families, now thought that they could claim the same privileges over again as residents of the North-West Territory. In order to obtain the pecuniary advantage of the scrip which the Government issued, they sent for Riel as having the ability to make this demand in such a forcible way that they might have some hope of obtaining it. The secret of the rebellion lies in the fact that the majority of the half-breeds were petitioning for something they were not entitled to, and were not likely to get by constitutional means, but which might be obtained by extreme measures of violence if successful. Riel also formulated a scheme which raised the hopes and ambitions of the half-breeds and Indians. The half-breed reserve in the Province of Manitoba was allotted on the proportion of one-seventh of the lands contained in the Province at that time created, which, upon computation, was found to be 1,400,000 acres, or 240 acres of land to each resident half-breed then born. Riel at once made the bold claim that the principle of one-seventh of the land which had been accorded in the Province of Manitoba should be carried out in the North-West Territory, and held out hopes to the Indians that one-seventh of the land should be theirs also. It was those ambitious ideas that enabled him to exercise a control over the half-breeds and Indians, in leading them to break out into open and murderous rebellion, while Riel hoped to make a big stake for himself in consequence, as he supposed, of the weakness of the Government ...

3

"Hopeless Degradation of the Toiling Masses"

Workers and Industrialization

DOCUMENTS

A) The Labour Question
   The Mail (Toronto), April 25, 1872

B) Preamble and Declaration of Principles of the Knights of Labor, 1883

C) Royal Commission on the Relations of Labor and Capital in Canada, 1889

D) Fourth Annual Report of the Inspector of Factories. Ontario, 1892

E) The Sweating System: The 'People's Press' Reports
   The Daily Mail and Empire (Toronto), October 9, 1897

F) There is a Reason For It
   Industrial Banner (London, Ontario), February, 1897

G) Labour Demands Equal Rights
   Industrial Banner (London, Ontario), October, 1897

H) The Rise of Socialism
   Labour Advocate (Toronto), September 4, 1891

I) The Curse of Chinese Immigration
   Industrial Banner (London, Ontario), October, 1897

Many proud mid-nineteenth-century Canadian artisans faced what they saw as the complete destruction of everything they trained for and believed in; all that gave them a sense of purpose, belonging, and pride. Industrialization, the development of an urban capitalist economy driven by machines, threatened their lifestyles as nothing else. Steam engines worked relentlessly without breaks or complaint, producing far more than men, often to a higher and more uniform quality, using docile and low-paid women and children as operators. Artisans saw themselves becoming expendable as industrialization tolled the death knell of their once proud and independent crafts. Frightened and defensive workers fought back as best they could, often collectively, as they realized that strength comes from numbers.

And yet the new industrial economy quickened the British North American pulse. It created work for thousands. Mass production and economies of scale made a cornucopia of former luxury goods available to the masses. Industrialization and dynamic capitalism also encouraged investment in infrastructures such as canals, roads, and railroads.

The face of the labour movement changed drastically from the early 1870s, when trade unions lacked legal recognition, to the late 1890s. Craft unions initially assumed that by uniting those whose expertise had taken years to develop they could exercise a significant degree of economic control. Although employers welcomed the alternative of cheap labour provided by unskilled women, the members of craft unions resented women's introduction into such occupations as tailoring and shoemaking. Their exclusive nature meant that craft unions only slowly recognized common interests with workers who possessed skills other than their own. Fragmented and isolated, early craft unions emerged mostly in larger industrial towns of the Maritimes, Quebec, and southern Ontario.

Perceived as a landmark by some, the Trade Unions Act passed by John A. Macdonald's government in 1872 gave unions the right to exist, but related legislation still criminalized various activities related to organizing workers. Until the mid-twentieth century employers retained the right to obstruct unions with strikebreakers or blacklists and to sue unions for damages caused by strikes or breaches of contract. Lines formed, and confrontations between workers and owners increased. Canadian workers initially united into the Nine Hour movement of 1872, and Conservative newspapers, such as *The Mail*, responded (Document A). Many craftsmen actually resented collectivist ideas, especially the notion of grouping all working people, regardless of prestige, under the same banner. Organizations like the innovative Knights of Labor argued, however, that capitalism would win unless workers set aside petty differences and built a strong united front. The enemy, they argued, was the free enterprise system, not fellow proletarians. Thus the American-born Knights welcomed all workers — except lawyers, bankers, stockbrokers, and professional gamblers — into their ranks, regardless of skill or gender. It grew to 300 locals by the 1880s, and dominated Canada's first national union organization, the Trades and Labour Congress.

A combination of cynical politicking plus genuine concern over the appalling working conditions in many of Canada's factories led successive provincial and federal governments to investigate the lot of Canadian workers, and the results shocked many. Ontario's Fourth Annual Report of the Inspector of Factories was one example, John A. Macdonald's Royal Commission on Labour and Capital another. It travelled from Cape Breton coal pits, through the cotton mills of New Brunswick, to Toronto and Montreal factories, interviewing over 1800 workers and witnesses on subjects as disparate as child and female labour, sanitation, and safety provisions. Although the Commission reflected Conservative party views, many of its members came from within working-class ranks and included a printer, a carpenter, a journalist, and several builders. This rather unusual Commission enjoyed a unique opportunity to examine and evaluate the new economy, but apart from the implementation of the Labour Day holiday, most of its recommendations came to naught and it had little impact.

Early labour organizations fought on other fronts as well, supporting some of Canada's first independent labour newspapers, such as the radical *Industrial Banner*. Founded by tinsmith Joseph Marks in 1892 in order to attract followers to his Industrial Brotherhood, this newspaper did not reach beyond southwestern Ontario, and quickly died. The *Labour Advocate*, meanwhile, received its funding from both the Knights of Labor and the Toronto Trades and Labour Council. Its first editorial, on December 5, 1890, unequivocally set the tone for subsequent editions and must have raised eyebrows behind mansion walls when it stated: "Realizing that the monopoly of land, capital and the means of exchange and transportation is the cause of poverty of the masses, the *Labour Advocate* will keep steadfastly in view the need of abolishing monopoly in all its forms, and asserting the right of the workers to control for their benefit all the opportunities and requisites for production." Most mainstream penny dailies of the era reflected establishment views but some newspapers, such as the *Daily Mail and Empire*, began courting working-class readers by reconsidering their positions on certain labour issues.

Friction between the narrowly focussed craft unions and the all-encompassing ideology of the Knights of Labor was inevitable. This problem was accentuated by the fact that many Canadian craft unions had affiliated with larger American-based unions who aimed to control the continental labour market. With affiliation came increased bargaining power and organizational expertise as well as a more pragmatic approach to negotiating union goals. The utopian ideals of the Knights of Labor also fell out of favour because craft unionists had always been uncomfortable with organizations that included less skilled or unskilled workers.

To fill the void, wage earners in fishing, logging, and particularly mining formed new unions based upon industries, not skills. Far more radical than craft unionists, militant members of these new unions spread socialist ideas and welcomed confrontation. But neither they nor the craft unions experienced sustained growth. Repeated periods of economic depression saw fragile unions often disappear overnight. Only the sustained economic upswing of the period from 1896 to 1912 witnessed clearly accelerated patterns of union growth, as evident in the federal government's decision to intervene into the country's increasingly acrimonious industrial relations through the formation of a Department of Labour in 1900. In that era of high-paced economic expansion, the concentration of productive power through mergers between financial capital and corporations saw the displacement of family-run businesses by giant joint-stock companies and the development of an increasingly professional industrial management class. The multitude of immigrants that flooded Canada's labour market in the 1890s increased competition for jobs and served to fragment the working class still further along ethnic lines. Thousands of these new immigrants did not speak English, and many came from homelands that lacked any tradition of labour organization. Although some unions went out of their way to accommodate new European immigrants, they did not do the same for Asian newcomers. Racism prevented any working-class solidarity. Well before the 1890s Canadian unions, whether craft- or industry-based, refused to support Oriental labourers in job actions as these workers were perceived as undercutting standards of living. By law the Chinese were even restricted from working underground or in various vocations (such as doctors, lawyers, or teachers) in British Columbia. Under such circumstances it is little wonder that they regularly accepted employment in dangerous, low-paid jobs and as strike breakers.

A) The Labour Question
The Mail *(Toronto), April 25, 1872*

… The merits of the question involved in the nine hours movement is another matter. The refusal of a number of work men to work beyond a limited number of hours a day should be based on some good reason. If nine hours' work exhaust the system, and be as long a working day as is compatible with the preservation of health; if longer hours would reduce workmen to a condition of mere animalism; if the workshops necessarily, or in fact, are charged with noxious gases or impure air, to breathe which more than so many out of the twenty-four impairs the health and debilitates the constitution; if any of these or any similar results would come of making a greater number of hours a day's work, then a case would be made out for a shorter number of hours. To talk of making the length of the working day uniform, in all occupations, is to overlook the differences in the effects of different employments on the health; and is not a whit more sensible than would be a proposal that all men of whatever height should wear clothes of uniform length. There are occupations in which men cannot safely work nine hours a day; among them may be ranked glass blowing, the desiccation of certain kinds of excrementitious matters, and mixing paints. But are there not undoubtedly others at which healthy men can work, without detriment to their frames, ten hours a day? Indeed we believe it will be generally found to be true that ten hours' labour is perfectly consistent with the preservation of health; and that any curtailment of them would be at least as injurious to the workmen as to the employers. Even the same employments are more or less injurious, according to the conditions under which they are followed. Book printers, who do their work in the day, can work longer than printers engaged in the production of morning papers, whose labour must be done in the night.

We take it for granted that, in a normal condition of society, the hours of labour should not be so long as to abridge life or to make it a burthen. There may be states of society in which the lot of the workman is necessarily miserable. But we ought not to find this in new countries, where the gifts and bounties of nature yield as certainly as here in Canada to the labour of man.

The production of wealth is not everything. Man is not a mere physical machine out of which so much labour is to be ground, and which has no further use. His moral and social nature requires cultivation. If this be neglected, society will be the loser ... One of the pleas for a shortening of the hours of labour is the necessity that there is to obtain time for the mental improvement of the workmen. The usual reply is that the cases in which the extra time taken from work would be used for mental improvement are very rare; that, as a rule, it would not be so used; and that if a man be particularly anxious for such improvement he will not allow ten hours' labour to bar his way to knowledge. In this there is much truth; but it is not the whole truth, and it scarcely puts the case fairly. We must take the average workman as he is; and we fear we must admit the probability of the extra hour taken from labour being generally used for some other purpose than mental improvement. But that of itself is no reason why the opportunity should be withheld. And if the manual toil be prolonged so as to exhaust the frame, the desire and the power of mental exertion will be wanting: drowsiness will supervene, and repose appear to be the greatest earthly good ...

The moral right of workmen to combine for the purpose of getting the highest price for their labour is as clear as any right which freemen can exercise; and any old laws that prevent its exercise ought to be repealed. For nearly three centuries British legislation was directed against Trades' Unions. But it failed to put them down; and nearly half a century ago (1826) this policy was abandoned. Since then any combination of men has been at liberty to say for what wages and on what conditions its members would work, and to use persuasion to induce others to act upon their views. That is their right. But they enjoy this liberty on the same condition that others enjoy theirs. Coercion is incompatible with the enjoyment of liberty; and whoever resorts to that forbidden weapon seeks to destroy the conditions on which his own liberty rests. The punishment of this wrong is in the interest of society, to which liberty is as necessary as air and water. While one man has a moral right to refuse to sell his labour at a certain price and on certain terms, another has the same right to accept that price and to waive those terms. For a combination of men to interfere by violence or intimidation to prevent the latter is just as tyrannical as for the legislative authority to interfere to compel the former.

The workmen who value their own liberty should respect that of others. They can hardly be said to do this when they insist on providing against future imaginary evils in the shape of an excess of labour by assuming to abridge the liberty of their employers in restricting the number of apprentices they shall take. This seems to be a remnant of the old system of corporate exclusion, which existed when workmen and capitalists were combined in the same persons. Then the restriction was the conspiracy of a class against the general public; now, when capital and labour have been divorced, it is the conspiracy of labour against capital ... Much has been said, and often truly, of the tyranny of capital over labour; but if this is not the tyranny of labour over capital, of employed over employer, it would be difficult to say what it is. It is by insisting on such things as this that workmen put themselves in the wrong ... Nothing that is not reasonable can succeed in the long run; and every folly of labour is the ground of a victory for capital.

If the mere fact of workmen uniting to raise the rate of wages ought to continue to rank among our laws as a crime, a combination of employers to keep down wages would have to be placed in the same category. The liberty of combination must either be refused or granted both to employers and employed. Justice has not two scales, one for labour and another for capital. Combinations among merchants to keep up the price of particular articles would have to come under the common rule, what ever it might be …

The shortening of the hours of labour has the effect of raising wages in two ways. First, by giving less labour for the same money, unless it can be shown that the shorter hours give as good a result as can be got out of the longer; and second by increasing the competition among employers. A manufacturer employs one hundred hands. By shortening the hours of labour, the hundred men do no more than ninety did before. He wants ten more men, and he finds all his neighbours in the same position. To attract these ten from other shops, he must offer higher wages, and as he cannot pay the increased rate to the ten without paying it to the other ninety, the general wage-rate in that employment goes up. Or if the additional hands cannot be obtained, production is lessened while the cost remains the same; the profits of capital are reduced and the cost of the particular manufacture is raised. In that case, and supposing the reduction of production to be general, there would be a general rise of prices and the workman would have to pay more for almost everything he consumes. He would, in fact, have succeeded in duping himself when he thought he was merely wresting from capital a further share of profit.

The labour question can only be satisfactorily regulated by allowing both parties the greatest liberty; and we are glad to see that a movement has been made by the Minister of Justice to expunge a law which is a disgrace to the statute book, and which the British Parliament repealed nearly half a century ago.

B) Preamble and Declaration of Principles of the Knights of Labor, 1883

The alarming development and aggression of aggregated wealth, which, unless checked, will inevitably lead to the pauperization and hopeless degradation of the toiling masses, renders it imperative, if we desire to enjoy the blessings of life, that a check should be placed upon its power and upon unjust accumulation, and a system adopted which will secure to the laborer the fruits of his toil; and as this much desired object can only be accomplished by the thorough unification of those who earn their bread by the sweat of their brow, we have formed the order of the Knights of Labor, with a view of securing the organization and direction, by co-operative effort, of the power of the industrial classes; and we submit to the world the object sought to be accomplished by our organization, calling on all who believe in securing "the greatest good to the greatest number," to aid and assist us.

1. To bring within the fold of organization every department of productive industry, making knowledge a standpoint for action, and industrial, moral worth, not wealth, the true standard of individual and national greatness.
2. To secure to the toilers a proper share of the wealth that they created; more of the leisure that rightfully belongs to them; more society advantages; more of the benefits, privileges and emoluments of the world; in a word, all those rights and privileges necessary to make them capable of enjoying, appreciating, defending and perpetuating the blessings of good government.
3. To arrive at the true condition of the producing masses in their educational, moral and financial condition, by demanding from the various governments the establishment of bureaus of labor statistics.
4. The establishment of co-operative institutions, productive and initiative.
5. The reserving — of public lands — the heritage of the people — for the actual settler. Not another acre for railroads or corporations.
6. The abrogation of laws that do not bear equally upon capital and labor; the removal of unjust technicalities, delays and discriminations in the administration of justice; and the adopting of measures providing for the health and safety of those engaged in mining, manufacturing and building pursuits.
7. The enactment of laws to compel chartered corporations to pay their employees weekly, in full, for labor performed the preceding week, in the lawful money of the country.
8. The enactment of laws giving mechanics and laborers the first lien on their work for their full wages.
9. The abolishment of the contract system on national, state and municipal roads or corporations.
10. The substitution of arbitration for strikes, whenever and wherever employers and employees are willing to meet on equitable grounds.

11. The prohibition of the employment of children in workshops, mines and factories, before attaining their fourteenth year.

12. To abolish the system of letting out by contract the labor of convicts in our prisons and reformatory institutions.

13. To secure for both sexes equal pay for equal work.

14. The reduction of the hours of labor to eight per day, so that the laborers may have more time for social enjoyment and intellectual improvement, and be able to reap the advantages conferred by the labor-saving machinery which their brains have created.

15. To prevail upon governments to establish a purely national circulating medium, issued directly to the people, without the intervention of any banking corporations, which money shall be a legal tender in payment of all debts, public and private.

C) Royal Commission on the Relations of Labor and Capital in Canada, 1889

Olivier David Benoit, Boot & Shoe Maker, of Montreal, called and sworn.

By Mr. Helbronner:

Q.—Are you a boot and shoe maker? A.—Yes, sir.

Q.—Do you work by the day, or by the piece? A.—By the day.

Q.—Can you tell us if wages in the boot and shoe trade have increased in the past ten years? A.—No; I beg your pardon. They have been lowered, instead of increased. They have been lowered by about 15 to 20 per cent in certain branches.

Q.—Are young people employed in your trade? A.—Yes, a few; but only a few among very young people.

Q.—Are there young people, who are employed in your trade, engaged as apprentices, or to do certain lines of work, and help other workmen? A.—It is only as helps in the factory ...

Q.—They cannot be regarded as boot and shoe apprentices? A.—No; they cannot be so regarded, because there is the machinery. Every one works in his particular branch; and, naturally, if you work in one branch for twenty years you cannot make a boot, nor even a shoe.

Q.—These young people are, therefore, unable to make a pair of boots or shoes after they have done what they call their apprenticeship? A.—They have no apprenticeship at all, and when they leave a factory, they are skillful in only one branch of the trade. Take myself, for example; it is about twelve years since I left the factory, and about twenty years that I am working, and I am able to do only a single branch of my trade.

Q.—There are very few boot and shoemakers to-day, who are able to make a pair of boots or shoes? A.—There are in the factories very few boot and shoe men who can make a boot or shoe; they are so few, indeed, that they can hardly be found at present. In other words, the boot and shoemakers of old times and the boot and shoemakers of our time are not the same men, because the boot and shoe men of the old times could make a shoe or boot, make the uppers, sole it, or make the pattern and put it on the last, and then finish it and put it on the foot, whereas to-day, as a general rule, all the men working in factories, especially the large factories, are able to do only one kind of work, as to set a heel or sew a sole, or set the uppers, because to-day perfected machinery has replaced hand work.

Q.—This means that to-day a perfect machine can make a boot or shoe or a series of machines can make a boot or shoe without the help of work men and only assisted by young people? A.—That is true in a great measure.

Q.—Has the introduction of machinery in the boot and shoe trade, resulted in a lowering of wages? A.—Yes; and that is the reason that I came here, before this Commission, to say that our wages have been lowered, and not only the wages but the work has decreased, inasmuch as to-day one machine most certainly takes the place, on an average, of five or six men.

Q.—Does machinery have, as a result, the lowering of prices in boots and shoes? A.—Well, machinery brought on competition, and competition has been spread and been distributed over hand work, I think, and I am certain that, so far as the goods themselves go, if they have been lowered in price, it is the workmanship that has suffered ...

Pierre Pleau, Machinist, of the city of Montreal, sworn:

By Mr. Helbronner:

Q.—Have you been employed in cotton factories? A.—Yes, sir; for some fifteen or eighteen years.

Q.—At Montreal? A.—In the United States and at Montreal. I have worked in Montreal for four years. I was foreman for four years at the Ste. Anne manufactory ...

Q.—According to your remembrance how many men were employed by the company when you were there? A.—I cannot speak for the whole factory; but I can answer for my department. In my department, at the time that I worked there, I had from 60 to 70 men employed under me.

Q.—How many young women and women were there? A.—On an average during the year, there might be from 34 to 36 young women.

Q.—Were there any children in your department? A.—There were little boys and little girls. Among the 34 or 36 persons whom I have just mentioned, there were small young girls from 13 to 14 years of age.

Q.—Which was the youngest child employed in your department? A.—The youngest child who worked under me was about thirteen years old.

Q.—Were there in the Ste. Anne Mills children younger than this, in the other departments? A.—I have seen such; but they did not work under me.

Q.—What age might they have been? A.—They did not appear to me to be above ten years old.

Q.—At what hour did work begin? A.—In my time, work began at twenty-five minutes past six ...

Q.—At what hour, in ordinary times, did work cease? A.—Work ceased at a quarter past six.

Q.—At what hour had you your dinner? A.—We had three quarters of an hour for dinner, but generally speaking the hands were forced to resume work after a half hour. The engine was set in motion after the half hour, and the speed started immediately after the half hour. ·

Q.—Was there much overtime made? A.—Last winter, that is a year ago last winter, we worked for two months time up to a quarter past seven; but only in my department.

Q.—Did they give you any time to rest in the afternoon? A.—No; no rest. When the girls wanted to eat they were not allowed to go out and I sent out a little girl of twelve or thirteen years, who was employed in changing the work, to get a little lunch and thus they eat while working.

Q.—Has it ever happened that you worked later than a quarter past seven in your department? A.—Yes. We have worked up to nine o'clock at night.

Q.—You have worked up to nine o'clock at night for several days in succession? A.—We have already worked up to three nights in succession during the same week ...

Q.—Did they allow any time for rest when they made you work up till nine o'clock at night? A.—Not more than when we worked up to a quarter past seven.

Q.—If I understand you properly, then, you worked from a quarter to one in the afternoon, until nine o'clock in the evening, without any rest? A.—Yes; without rest; only he came to me, towards three o'clock in the afternoon, and he said to me: "You will notify your men that they will work to-night till nine o'clock."

Q.—Without stopping? A.—Yes; without stopping. I myself gave them a chance. I gave them the privilege of sending out for something to eat. I said to them: "Send one of your sisters, or one of the little girls, to get food, if you have none." When he asked me in the forenoon to tell the hands that we should work at night, I said to the hands at noon: "Bring some lunch with you, we shall have to work till nine o'clock to-night."

Q.—Why did you have to work till nine o'clock at night? A.—I cannot say. It seems to me that a couple of times I heard the manager, and the other foremen, say that they were working also for the other factory — for the Hudon Company below, who were in arrears with their work, and had not enough filling or warp.

Q.—But you were not given time to eat, you had to eat during your work? A.—We had to eat during our work.

Q.—So that the children of whom you speak, who were only thirteen years old, were forced to work from a quarter to one, in the afternoon, till nine o'clock at night, without stopping, and without taking time to eat? A.—Yes; just the same as grown people.

Q.—Did it happen often that you had to work thus until nine o'clock at night? A.—During the time that I was foreman, that happened, generally, every fall, for seven or eight weeks running. We worked every second night ...

Q.—Could you give us some examples of cases where you saw fines imposed? A.—This very evening, I was around among a few neighbours, and I think that I have, on my person, some forty envelopes, in which fines are set down. I could show them to you. I should not wish that the names be known.

Q.—How are wages paid at the present time? A.—At the present time, the wages are paid every fortnight.

Q.—Then, they are the envelopes of the fortnight that you have with you. A.—Yes; these envelopes all belong to the same family. In the last five months,

I believe that there have been docked off over $30.00 for fines. There are fines of $2 on a single pay. I might have others, if I had more time. There is another parcel of envelopes all belonging to the same family ...

Q.—Is there any by-law concerning these fines pasted up in the factory? A.—No; not at all. What they do, is this; they will go and talk to the party, and if that party answers coarsely, they will break out swearing and say: "I will fine you 50 cents," and then they go off.

Q.—Who does that? A.—It is the first foreman ...

Q.—What is, to your knowledge, the highest fine that has been imposed? A.—I believe that it was five dollars.

Q.—All at once? A.—All at once. It was imposed on a boy for having broken a roller.

Q.—Had he broken it voluntarily or maliciously? A.—No; it was an accident.

Q.—How much, to your knowledge, did that boy earn per day? A.—That boy, I believe, earned fifty or fifty-five cents per day. I cannot say exactly what were his wages ...

Q.—Did you ever see these children badly treated in the factory? A.— Once I saw one of these small boys taken by the arm and cuffed, but most generally their money was taken from them and fines were imposed upon them.

Q.—What was, to your knowledge, the highest fine that a boy had to pay during a month? A.—There were small boys who earned twenty-five cents per day, and during the month of four weeks they sometimes had a dollar or seventy-five cents stopped; this was as they were quiet. There were small girls also who paid fines.

Theophile Charron, Journeyman Cigar-maker, aged 14, of Montreal, sworn.

By Mr. Helbronner:
Q.—How old are you? A.—I was 14 on the 10th January last.

Q.—When you call yourself a cigar-maker, you mean that you have served your apprenticeship, do you not? A.—Yes, sir.

Q.—How long? A.—Three years.

Q.—You began working at 11 years ? A.—Yes, sir.

Q.—What wages do you get now? Are you paid by the piece? A.—Yes, sir.

Q.—You receive the same wages as the workingmen? A.—Yes.

Q.—What wages did you get during your apprenticeship? A.—One dollar a week for the first year, $1.50 for the second year, and $2 for the third year. When I worked extra I got more ...

Q.—Did you have any fines to pay during your apprenticeship? A.—Yes, sir.

Q.—Many? A.—A good number.

Q.—Do you remember how many? A.—No.

Q.—Do you remember the most you paid in one week? A.—Twenty-five cents.

Q.—This is the highest you paid? A.—Yes, sir.

Q.—How many hours did you work a day? A.—Sometimes ten hours, other times eight hours. It was just as they wanted it.

Q.—Do you remember why you paid these fines? A.—Sometimes for talking too much; mostly for that.

Q.—You were never kicked? A.—Yes; not kicked so as any harm was done me, but sometimes they would come along, and if we happened to be cutting our leaf wrong, they would give us a crack across the head with the fist.

Q.—Was it usual to beat children like that? A.—Often.

Q.—Were you beaten during the first year of your apprenticeship? A.—Yes, sir.

Q.—That is, you were beaten at eleven years? A.—Yes, sir.

Q.—Have you seen other children beaten? A.—Yes, sir.

Q.—Did you see them beaten worse than yourself? A.—No, sir.

Q.—Do you know of a factory where there is a blackhole? A.—Yes, sir.

Q.—Have you seen children put in that blackhole? A.—Yes, sir.

Q.—How old were these children? A.—I could not tell the age.

Q.—Younger than yourself? A.—No, sir.

Q.—Why were they put into the blackhole? A.—Because they lost time.

Q.—Who put them into the blackhole? A.—The man who kept the press.

Q.—Do you know whether this man wears a constable's medal? A.—Yes, sir.

Q.—Do the children cry out? A.—No, sir.

Q.—Were they taken to the blackhole brutally? A.—No, sir.

Q.—How long did they stop in the hole, as a general thing? A.—Some of them stopped there till seven o'clock.

Q.—When were they put in? A.—In the afternoon.

Q.—Was it seven o'clock in the evening or seven hours of time? A.—Seven o'clock in the evening. They put them in during the afternoon until seven in the evening.

Q.—At what time do the men leave the factory? A.—Generally at five o'clock and sometimes at six.

Q.—Do you mean to say that those children were kept in the blackhole after the men had left the factory? A.—Yes, sir.

Q.—Who let them out? The same that put them in? A.—Yes, sir, I think so, but I never saw him.

Q.—Was this blackhole heated? A.—I don't know, sir.

Q.—In what floor of the factory is this blackhole? A.—In the cellar.

Q.—Is there a furnace in the cellar? A.—Yes, sir.

Q.—Is the blackhole near the furnace? A.—No, sir.

Q.—Is there a window therein? A.—No.

Q.—When children were shut in there, you never heard them cry to get someone to let them out? A.—No, sir.

Q.—At what age did you quit school? A.—At ten years and a half.

Q.—Can you read and write? A.—A little.

Edward Gilfoy, carding room employee in Halifax Cotton Mill, sworn and examined.

By Mr. Heakes:

Q. How long have you worked there? A. Four years.

Q. How old are you now? A. Fifteen ...

Q. Are there any fines imposed in your room? A. Yes; sometimes.

Q. What are those fines imposed for? A. Sometimes about the machinery getting smashed.

Q. And for being late? A. Yes.

Q. Are you ever fined for playing? A. Yes; sometimes.

Q. I suppose boys and girls there will play sometimes? A. Yes.

Q. Are you pretty well treated? A. Yes.

Q. Have you ever seen boys or girls getting whipped? A. Yes.

Q. What for? A. For playing.

By the Chairman:

Q. Who beat them? A. The boss.

Q. Would that be the foreman or the manager? A. The foreman.

Q. Did he whip them very hard? A. No; not very.

Q. Just gave them a slap? A. Yes.

Q. Do you work the same hours as the other witnesses? A. Yes.

Q. Do you find it very hard to work so many hours a day? A. I do sometimes feel it pretty hard.

Q. You are pretty tired at night? A. Yes.

Q. Do you have much time for play? A. No.

Q. What time have they to be there in the morning? A. They have to be there at a quarter past six.

Q. If they are not there exactly on time are they fined? A. Yes.

Q. They do not get any grace? A. No.

Q. What time have they for dinner? A. They have an hour.

Q. Do many of them go home to dinner? A. No; a good many take it with them.

Q. Is there much dust in the spinning room? A. Yes; there is a good deal.

Q. Is there so much that you have to open the windows? A. No; the windows are never opened.

Q. Don't you find it too warm in summer? A. Yes.

Q. Do they work on piece work in the spinning room? A. They have this fortnight.

Q. Do they make more on piece work? A. We don't know yet.

Q. Are they kept busy? A. Yes; pretty busy.

Q. Do they work after six o'clock? A. No; we would not do it. The manager wanted us to do it and he said before he would let the Halifax people have their own way he would send for English spinners, but as long as the steam had gone down he concluded to let us go.

Q. You went? A. Yes.

Q. Is any abusive language used towards those employed in that room? A. Yes; when they are not doing the work quick enough.

Q. Who does this? A. There is an under boss that does it.

Q. Does he swear at them? A. Yes.

Q. Does he cuff any of them? A. He kicks the boys when they are not doing the work.

Q. Have any of them cried on account of being kicked? A. Yes.

Q. Does he ever cuff the little girls? A. No; I never saw him beat the girls.

Q. But you have seen him kick the boys until they have cried? A. Yes.

Q. Do you know if the boys ever complain to the manager about their being kicked? A. No.

Q. You don't know whether they did or did not? A. No ...

Joseph Larkins, biscuit maker, sworn.

By Mr. Heakes:

Q. How old are you? A. I am 11 years.

Q. What is the matter with your hand? A. It got hurt in the machinery.

Q. How? A. It got caught in the rollers.

Q. What rollers? A. The rollers of a cracker machine — a biscuit machine.

Q. How long were you working in the biscuit factory? A. About seven weeks.

Q. Was it part of your work to look after the machinery? A. No; I was taken in as a packer and was then put to work on the machinery.

Q. How much wages did they give you? A. A dollar a week first, and then a dollar and a-quarter.

Q. How much do they give you now? A. Nothing at all.

Q. How long is it since you were hurt? A. Nine weeks Thursday.

Q. And have they not given you anything? A. No; except for the week when I was hurt ...

By Mr. Freed:

Q. How long were you working at the machinery before you were hurt? A. I could not say.

Q. What were you doing at the machinery? A. I was brushing the dough off according as it came through.

By Mr. Kelly:

Q. Are other boys of your age employed in the concern? A. I could not say. There was a boy about the same size.

By Mr. Heakes:

Q. Did you lose any fingers? A. I lost one.

Q. Did you lose any of the joints of the others? A. I think I will lose a second finger ...

D) Fourth Annual Report of the Inspector of Factories. Ontario, 1892

One effect of this depression in manufacturing is towards some relaxation in the working hours of females in some branches. Another effect is, owing to the ease in which older help can be obtained, to do away largely with the employment of children (males between 12 and 14 years of age) in many industries, which has made the Inspector's duty in this respect comparatively light. Though I am of the opinion that should a fair improvement in the demand for manufacturers show itself, the number of children employed would materially increase ...

The following are the weekly working hours of females in some of the principal trades in Toronto, west of Yonge street. Baking powder, 55; bookbinding, 50 to 55; baby carriage trimming, 54; boots and shoes, 49; brooms and brushes, 55; binding and other twine, 48 to 50; caps, 49 to 50½; coffin trimming, 50; corsets, 47 to 50½; clothing, 50 to 57½; cigars, 4½ to 50; envelopes, 53 to 55; electro-typing, 48; fringe and tassels, 54; fancy boxes, 54; furs, 53; hats, straw and felt, 52½; india rubber goods, 50; jute and cotton bags, 49; knitting, 54 to 60; laundries, 55 to 60; millinery goods, 49; overalls, 47½; paper bags and boxes, 49 to 53; printing, 56; rope making, 60; soap, 52; thread spooling, 52½; tobacco, 52; trunks and valises, 52½; ladies' white wear, 50 to 56; window shades, 53; wall papers, 51½; umbrellas, 54.

In some of the above industries two sets of hours are given, that means there are more than one establishment on that class of goods, and their working hours vary. I give the shortest and longest.

In some trades the hours are the same in all the factories. In other cities the hours are about the same, but in the smaller places are somewhat longer. In some of the above mentioned trades males are also employed, and usually their hours are longer, generally ten hours a day. From what I see, read and gather in conversation, from employers and employed, I feel convinced that the tendency is towards shorter hours than at present prevails, where 60 hours a week is the allotment.

Many factories shut down from two to ten weeks in the winter, and others such as those engaged in manufacturing harvesting implements do so, or greatly slacken down in the summer, when the sales for the year are done. Some cotton mills have not made one-half time with full staff in the two previous years; though this year, owing to a number of the principal mills on grey goods coming under the control of one company and thus working to better advantage, the cotton trade has improved. Not long ago I noticed that one company had declared a dividend of seven per cent., and no doubt other companies also have divided profits. I observe that the number of occupations in which females are employed is gradually being enlarged, and it is now not at all uncommon to find them doing work that fifteen or even ten years ago would have been considered as out of harmony with public opinion, for the employer to ask them to do, such work at that time being considered proper for males only. There are various reasons for this to which I need not allude, but I cannot in my own mind justify all the reasons. I frequently meet with persons who think that females should not work in factories, but instead, sufficient wages should be given to fathers and brothers to enable them to keep the girls at home, and thus not go into competition with male labor. But there are many trades in which at least a portion of the work is more suitable for females, and can be better done by them; though in the clothing and other wearing apparel branches of trade, males do in some cases operate the sewing machines and do the ironing of shirts. So it seems that if females are encroaching on the field of labor which was formerly considered as exclusively belonging to males, the latter, on the other hand, are spreading out on the territory devoted to female labor. In mentioning the occupations in which females are employed, I refer only to this Province, particularly to the western district. In other countries, in the old world, females have long been doing most laborious work, much of it under most degrading conditions, which are being slowly improved by legislation.

E) The Sweating System: The 'People's Press' Reports
The Daily Mail and Empire *(Toronto), October 9, 1897*

There is possibly no phase of industrial employment so frequently spoken of and so little understood by those who are fondest of treating of it, as the sweating system. The term itself has something about it which savours of human sacrifice, as the result of brutal oppression, and has been used in this sense to denote all manner of tyranny, and often a condition of depravity. The term "sweating," when properly used, denotes a condition of labour in which a maximum amount of work in a given time is performed for a minimum wage, and in which the ordinary rules of health and comfort are disregarded. It is inseparably associated with contract work, and is intensified by sub-contracting in shops conducted in homes … Although the sweating system exists in a number of occupations, it is the garment-making industry (comprising men's clothing, ladies' cloaks and suits, undergarment, and shirt-making branches) that has given it its real significance. Garments lend themselves readily to such a system of manufacture. Sewing is a branch preeminently suited for the home, and a coat or blouse is as easily manufac-

tured there as in a factory. Merely working at home on some article of manufacture is not in itself so objectionable, it is that the rate of wages paid for
labour is, as a rule, so low when the sweating system has come into vogue
that work from early morn till late at night will scarcely suffice to procure
the necessaries of a bare existence. But even this is not the worst feature of
the evil. The combination of living apartment and factory, and the employment of outsiders therein, constitute the detrimental features which in time
become a menace to the community.

Here is the process in its simplicity and detail. A large wholesale house
will undertake the manufacture of ready-made clothing. A quantity of cloth
is bought at wholesale rates. It is put in the hands of the designer, who designs the styles of clothing for the season's trade. He is usually also the foreman, and controls the letting out of the work to the contractors and other
individuals who may apply. These latter, on learning that the house has a quantity of garments which it wants manufactured, apply to the foreman, who
makes a contract with them to make up so many articles at a stipulated price.

THE SUB-CONTRACTOR

Now the persons stipulating for the contract may do one of two things. They
can, in the first place, take the articles home and work individually or with
the assistance of their families upon them, or they may engage a number of
hands to work for them, and take the garments to a shop, where, with the aid
of the hired help, their manufacture is completed. In the first case, owing to
the fact that one individual has to do nearly all the work upon each garment,
only a very few can be completed in the allotted time, and the amount realized in consequence is very small. In the second case, a large number of garments are manufactured owing, as a rule, to the minute subdivision of labour,
but the contractor desirous of realizing a profit much above the running expense of his shop, pays those in his employ a sum which is frequently below a
living wage. In a large shop there may be engaged in the manufacture of a
single coat no less than 16 different individuals, each of whom works at a special line, and, after completing one stage in the process of manufacture, passes
the garment on to the next, who is skilled in his line, and so on, till the article is completed. But there is frequently another stage. The contractor as a
rule does not have the button-hole making and finishing or "felling" done in
the shop, but sub-contracts this work, or it is returned to the foreman of the
wholesale house, who contracts for that part again. The "felling" and button-

hole making are usually done by women at their homes, and very often by the whole family. Under such an arrangement it is easily seen that, aided by competition, prices and wages must continue to fall and the work-day be lengthened until the limit of human endurance is reached. The limit, it seems, has been touched through the task system, an arrangement in the coat-making branch by which the contractor and the employees engage in a sort of competition, under which the contractor agrees with his employees to solicit work from the warehouses at a figure perhaps refused by another, provided they (the set of hands) are willing to do a certain task for a "day's work" for so much wages, even though it takes two or three days to do the specified "day's work." This set, of course, can work as many hours in a day as it chooses, the only limit being that of endurance.

WHERE THE SWEATING BEGINS

So much for the system as it is. In reading it over it seems to fit so nicely that there appears no objection. All that is needed is the introduction into it of human life, men and women, living human beings with hearts as well as hands, and possibly feelings also, to see the iniquity which not only may be, but usually is, worked at every stage. More than this, if it were possible to accurately do so, instead of the word "home," a description of the home should be given; instead of the term "shop," a description of the place which is spoken of as such, and instead of the simple non-committal "contractor" a portrayal of the man who hires life and blood, and knows as a rule how to buy it at the cheapest rate ...

BUTTON-HOLE WORK

The next shop entered was one in which a man, his wife, two children, and a hired woman were busily engaged making button-holes in cloaks and over-coats. For the large two-inch button-holes they were receiving a dollar a hundred, or one cent each; for the others they got 50, 60, and 75 cents a hundred, according to the size. They had to furnish the thread and silk themselves. The woman who was working said that she received only $1.50 a week, and out of this paid 75 cents a week for a room. She was entirely dependent upon herself, and had been forced to take this wage rather than starve to death. When asked how she could possibly live on 75 cents a week she replied that it would not be long before she would have to give up altogether. The hours were long, from eight in the morning until six every night;

incessant work; no one to talk to, for the Polish Jew who was employing her did not know much of English, and she had scarcely enough to eat. Later on she said that she had been driven to crime to supplement her wages, but she called God to witness that the fact of her working steadily week after week at whatever she could get was evidence enough to prove that she was an unwilling party to it. During the day's rounds similar stories were told by those who brought only condemnation on themselves in the telling both by the oppressor and the oppressed …

The question naturally suggests itself, are such conditions of things inevitable? No one would think of asking, "are they right?" A comparison with methods pursued by other firms [firms not contracting out to home operators] would suggest that even if large profits was the object mostly desired that it could be equally well attained in a right and proper way. With a view to presenting both sides fairly the representative of *The Mail and Empire* visited a large factory in connection with a leading wholesale house in the city, and was given an opportunity to see for himself, and even to inspect the books. Here it was found that men and women were employed making cloaks, but instead of wearing out their lives with a heavy machine all the machines were run by electricity. There was plenty of light, and the air was good. More than that, the employees were not driven without a moment's cessation, but were allowed, if they so desired, to work by the piece, and to receive remuneration according to the amount done. The books showed that the average wage paid operators was $10 a week, and that in some cases it ran as high as $20. The shop was not open to the women till eight in the morning, and was generally closed at six p.m., and all Saturday afternoon. One of the poorest paid operators received $7.60 a week …

A UNION SHOP

A union "back-shop" was also visited. This is a shop where only union men are employed, and where every garment that is manufactured goes out with a union label upon it, which is a guarantee that it has been made in a shop subject to inspection, where proper sanitary conditions have been complied with, and where the hours of labour and rate of wages are such as are considered fair and right. The men were receiving 21 cents per hour for work which was scheduled as first and second-class, and 20 cents per hour for work which was classed as third. There could be no dispute about the rates, as they were in printed form, and both employer and employed had copies of them.

These last two cases are mere instances; they are sufficient, however; in the first place to prove that the evil of sweating need not exist at all; and secondly, that, where it does exist, there are means by which it may be overcome. It need not exist, because right-minded employers who have been paying a proper wage have been able to secure their profits as well; it may be overcome where it does exist, because both in the case of the factory cited, and the union back-shop, it finds no place at all ...

The law in Ontario goes a certain length, but that conditions are such as have been related is sufficient to suggest that it does not go far enough. Almost every article of food is subject to inspection, and the public as well as individuals will some day wake up to the consciousness that it is to their interest to have the clothing which they wear subject to inspection as well. So long, however, as clothes are made in private houses or in shops where the most careful supervision is not exercised, both individual and public health will be in danger ...

The influence of the public as purchasers is one which can be made more effectual than law. It has been found in the United States that quite a number of large manufacturers have been obliged to withdraw work sent to sweating contractors, through the systematic appeals made by unions of the trade upon members of other unions and sympathizers to withhold patronage from dealers handling or keeping such goods on sale. Usually a retail clothier will cease dealing with an objectionable manufacturer rather than incur the opposition of patrons.

VALUE OF THE UNION LABEL

In line with this method the union label has been of service. It is designed to enable people to distinguish and give preference to goods guaranteed to be made under union, fair, and sanitary conditions. Some of the retail tailors in Toronto have already adopted this label. Again the matter of reform is in the hands of the purchaser, and he can not only profit himself, but be instrumental in bringing about a better condition which will be helpful to many others by requesting that when he pays his money, he and not the shopkeeper alone, shall profit, by the price that is paid.

Under the sweating system as it now exists the retailer of ready-made goods has to make a profit out of the wholesale manufacturer, he in turn makes a profit out of the contractor, and in cases where the contract system is abused the foreman makes a profit as well. The contractor again makes a profit out of those in his employ, and in many instances this is almost extortionate, another profit is sometimes made out of the sub contractor who undertakes the button-hole making and "felling," and he again clears a profit from those in his employ. At the bottom of the scale are the hundreds of men and women who are toiling from dawn till sundown, whose lives are being consumed with over-toil and lack of pay, and whose labour is in the last analysis practically the only labour which has added value to the garment from the time it is sewn together till it reaches the consumer's hands. Any reform which tends to bring the actual producer and the actual consumer nearer together and to lessen the number of middlemen who draw profit from a source on which they have not laboured, will not only have a tendency to secure to the man who buys a better article, which in the end must prove a cheaper one, but also bring to the one who labours most a more adequate remuneration and an opportunity for a better and possibly also a nobler life. Surely such an attainment is worthy of any strivings, and individual effort can do most to bring about the desired goal.

F) There is a Reason For It
Industrial Banner *(London, Ontario), February, 1897*

A sermon was recently delivered by a clergyman in this city in which he contrasted the condition of affairs to-day with what existed at the commencement of the century, and among other things he stated that the artizan did not labor as many hours as he used to do. While this is true, it is as well to understand how it has come about. It has been accomplished not because humanity and civilization has advanced so much as because labor was organized. The reduction of the hours of toil has been gained as the price of unceasing conflict and unrelenting determination on the part of the Trades Unions.

They have been resisted and opposed at every turn by capital and the capitalistic class. Every concession gained has been wrung from unwilling hands; and at the present moment the same conflict is being waged for an eight-hour day, and it is being just as resolutely opposed, and by the same class of people as have stood in opposition all along. Therefore, if the mechanic and laborer is working a less number of hours per day now than he was fifty years ago, he can thank the organizations of labor that such is the case. Without organization the capitalist would not hesitate to make him work his twelve or fourteen hours straight. It is a fact, however, that workingmen are working too many hours as it is.

With the multiplication of labor-saving machinery the science of production has advanced with such tremendous strides that one man can now turn out as much material as demanded the skill of twenty men a few short years ago, and hence as a result thousands of unemployed abound in the land.

The only possible chance to place this class at profitable employment is to reduce the hours of toil to keep pace with the increased power of production, and this is what the employing class is resisting, tooth and nail.

It is no virtue for the pulpit to inform the producing classes that they work less hours now than they used to do. Rather let them boldly proclaim the truth, and acknowledge that the conditions under which workingmen and workingwomen now earn a livelihood are more onerous than when they worked twelve hours a day.

The struggle for a bare existence is more bitter at this moment than it ever was before. More workers are out of employment, and their ranks are constantly swelling. Work in the past was at best reasonably sure; not so in the present.

And, pray, who is fighting the battle for shorter hours now — the pulpit, the press, the universities, the employers, or the men of business? Most certainly not. It is the workingman himself, and he is met with opposition on every hand. In the future, we doubt not, when progressive trade unionism has succeeded in still more materially reducing the hours of toil, some preacher will arise and tell the producers how much better off they are than we to-day. If the organizations of labor had never existed, it is safe to say no preacher could take such unction to his soul as to think humanity was advancing, and point to these decreasing hours of toil as a proof.

If workingmen are better off in this respect to-day than formerly, they know whom they have to thank. They are intelligent enough to understand that the working classes must work out their own salvation; that if they have gained concessions in the past it was because they were in a position to demand them and able to enforce the demand. They are not so ignorant as to believe that the leopard will change his spots, or the lion become a lamb. They recognize that the class who have antagonized their legitimate claims for justice in the past will likewise oppose them in the future; that any concession they may gain will be conceded only when the opposing class is powerless to withhold it. In a word, the laborer is becoming aware that only as he becomes organized and intelligent has he any show whatever of securing the least recognition in the community, or any consideration of his rights.

Because the hours of labor have been reduced in the past it would be unsafe to say that humanity was getting better. First recognize how and why they have been reduced, and then ask yourself the question: "Why should men even work eight hours a day when the advanced mechanical skill and productive power of the world is sufficient to feed, clothe, house and provide every luxury requisite to happiness with less than four hours of toil a day?" Is it not a fact easily proved that even at eight hours a day, the worker is just toiling four hours too long?

It is well to recognize that the reason why so many men are in poverty, with no work to do is because they who do the work have to toil so long.

G) Labour Demands Equal Rights
Industrial Banner *(London, Ontario), October, 1897*

How persistently the world sticks to old ideas; how sacred even injustice becomes if sanctioned by age and antiquity. A hundred years ago it was looked upon as treasonable to argue that a mechanic or laborer should have a vote. Workingmen to-day enjoy the privileges of the franchise only because they have forced the concession, after years of bitter struggle, from a class who believed and taught that it was divinely ordained that property should rule; and the same privileged class to-day teach the same doctrine, and enact it whenever possible.

If you doubt this assertion, just ask yourself how it is that so many workingmen are only part citizens, with only a partial and unequal say in the institutions of their own towns and cities.

No man, however intelligent or capable, can sit in the mayor's chair, or even aspire to the dignity of a petty alderman, nor vote on any question involving the expenditure of public money, unless he is possessed of a certain amount of real estate, but must be content to act the role of a partial citizen at best ...

The law requiring property qualifications for the holding of public office is a relic of feudalism and one that is destined to be swept away as have other abuses before it. The number of intelligent men who are ashamed to defend such a system is rapidly growing larger. The artisan class has had to overcome hostility, persecution, ridicule and abuse in the attainment of the ballot, and the same battle is going on to secure the privileges of full citizenship, a battle that will end with the same results — the triumph of justice ...

Every citizen should have equal rights; character should count for more than money, and brains for more than property. The electorate should have the right to nominate whoever they wish for office, and no law enacted for the benefit of a privileged class should have the power to hinder them ...

H) The Rise of Socialism
Labour Advocate *(Toronto), September 4, 1891*

The Trades and Labor Congress for the Dominion began its annual session on Monday last in Quebec ... It is to be hoped that in arranging the programme of measures for which the labor organizations are to be asked to agitate, much more advanced ground will be taken than in the past. It is high time that the workers in Canada felt the impulse of the "new unionism" which has entirely transformed the character of the labor movement in Britain. Canadian workingmen ought surely to be capable of learning, as the workers of other countries have learned, that the thing to be aimed at is not merely a little more wages, or a few hours in the week less work for the men of this or that craft, but the overthrow of the various forms of monopoly and social injustice which keep the worker in an inferior and dependent position. It is folly to expect any material change for the better, either by trying to squeeze a little more out of the employers or clamouring for a few miserable inadequate legislative palliatives which leave the root of social abuses untouched.

If the labor movement is to be anything but a donkey-engine for this or that political party, and a bitter disappointment to those who are sincere in desiring the emancipation of the workers — the efforts of its councils and congress must be directed towards securing thorough going radical reforms in the direction of the national control of industry. They must not be content with labor bureaus, factory and shipping inspection, anti-Chinese laws, or any such wretched makeshifts which the Government throws to the labor organizations from time to time as sops to a hungry and troublesome dog. They should demand nothing less than the abolition of land, money, and transportation monopolies, and the recognition of the right of the worker to all he produces. No one expects, of course, that social revolution of this kind can come suddenly or without long years of agitation. But what we do say is, that no labor reform organization in this day is worthy [of] the name which does not clearly realize and boldly proclaim that the reorganization of the industrial system is the end they have in view, and demand such immediate measures of legislation as tend in that direction.

The address of welcome by Mayor Fortier of Quebec ... should be a warning to labor bodies to avoid the mistake of inviting partizan politicians and capitalistic flunkeys to take part in their proceedings. "Those whom you have invited to join," said this functionary, "magistrate, capitalists, and others, prove that your object is not really against authority or capital." If the Labor Congress does not belie this twaddle by its actions, and show that it is emphatically against capitalism, it might as well dissolve for all the good it will ever accomplish. And for the future, labor organizations in order to avoid being placed in a false position, will do well to avoid seeking the patronage of self-seeking politicians and others whose interests are identified with the existing order of things.

l)   The Curse of Chinese Immigration
Industrial Banner *(London, Ontario), October, 1897*

What It Has Done for Other Countries and What It is Doing for Canada.

In a large measure the people of eastern Canada are blind to the grave menace that Chinese immigration is to the interests of the country. The action of the Dominion Trades and Labor Congress in asking the Dominion Parliament to raise the tax on Chinamen entering Canada from $50 to $500 is a step in the right direction. A great deal of false sympathy is expended on behalf of John [a man from China] by people who have never investigated the question or asked why organized labor seeks to prevent the unrestricted immigration of Chinamen. We are assured that if we wish to make a Christian of John we should welcome him with outstretched arms and try to do him good; but we candidly confess, without any apology, if those are the only terms on which he can be Christianized he had better remain a heathen, for a little while longer at any rate.

Now, as a matter of fact, every country that has suffered through the immigration of the Mongolian race has had sooner or later to take active steps to combat the evil ... We have it on the authority of a prominent clergyman, who made a study of the question as it affected San Francisco, that for every Chinaman converted to Christianity in that city he was confident that, at a very low estimate, twenty Americans went to hell. Children in that city, to his personal knowledge, were in hospitals through the contraction of loathsome vices and diseases as a direct result of their contact with Chinamen. In the Chinese quarters of the city the inhabitants are herded like rats, an ordinary room in many cases having as many as two additional floors placed in it so as to make three with not space for a man to stand upright; and here, packed like sardines in a box, the Chinaman lives, works, eats and sleeps. He can subsist on a few cents a day; and this is the kind of competition that self-respecting white labor is asked to meet.

As more directly affecting Canadians we can state that at the present times the Chinese are increasing in British Columbia to an alarming extent, and they are bringing with them the same vices that have worked such dire effects in San Francisco. They are entering all avenues of trade and are slowly, but surely, displacing white labor on every hand; they are in the mines and canneries, and, in fact, it is hard to find an avocation that sooner or later they do not enter. Even the clergymen in British Columbia are standing shoulder to shoulder with organized labor, as indeed do all classes of the community, for there, where the evil is recognized, no maudlin sentimentality or false sympathy is wasted.

It is not only British Columbia that is threatened but the whole Dominion. Mr. Chinaman does not stand still; once he has secured a footing he gradually works his way, and, once established, it is next to impossible to get rid of him. During the last year the increase of the Chinese in Winnipeg, Manitoba, was over 25 per cent, and even there people are beginning to realize the danger. Here in London, and in points further east, we have them, and though as yet in no great numbers they are increasing. So far they have confined themselves to the laundry business; this is always the first step, but, inevitable as fate, when the time comes they will invade other fields, and when too late the people of the east will realize that the people of the western provinces should have had their support before the evil had gained too great a footing. Australia has had to grapple with this question and they have already done what the Dominion Trades and Labor Congress has asked the Dominion Parliament to do.

Wherever free and slave labor has come into competition, free labor has always inevitably been forced to the wall. Living as he does under the most degrading conditions, subsisting on the outlay of a few cents a day, the Chinaman is in a position to take a situation for a pittance that no self-respecting white man could live on, leave alone support a family. The Chinaman has no desire to be raised to a higher position or plane of life; he has no intention of becoming a citizen; on a miserable pittance he can live and accumulate what will be a fortune when he returns to China. It is because of this that the people of the Pacific province are crying out for relief. It is for this that the Dominion Trades and Labor Congress has asked for an increase of the tax. Canadians cannot, at this time, afford to waste sympathy where it is not needed. Organized labor has been actuated by no narrow or contracted spirit, it has no fight with the Chinaman because he is a Chinaman or foreigner but because of the grave menace which his presence is to the welfare of the country. Shall we stand idly by and see free labor displaced by slave labor, because slave labor means a larger profit for those who employ the Chinese; or shall we insist that Canadian labor shall be protected and stem this tide that threatens such dire calamities to the working classes. Agitate this question everywhere until the government shall be compelled to act and stem the tide of undesirable Mongolian immigration.

We will have more to say on this matter in the future for we believe that if not resolutely encountered now it will have to be faced when it has grown to more alarming proportions. Now is the time to crush the danger, and it cannot be undertaken a moment too soon.

4

"Let Someone Else Have a Taste of Our Good Life"

The Immigrant Experience

DOCUMENTS

A) The Immigration by Races, 1914
   W.D. Scott

B) Beginnings in Canada
   Maria Adamowska

C) Conditions of Life for Women in Canada, 1913
   Georgina Binnie-Clark

"Come to Canada", they said, "and satisfy all your needs!" In 1900 the federal Immigration Branch published and distributed over one million pamphlets, in many different languages, extolling the virtues of the Canadian West to Europeans anxious for a fresh start on a young continent far from the stifling decay, lack of opportunities for economic advancement, and perpetual turmoil of their motherlands. Earlier Canadian immigration policy favoured residents of the British Isles to the virtual exclusion of others, but Prime Minister Wilfrid Laurier and his Minister of the Interior, Clifford Sifton, took the controversial step of inviting immigrants from east and central Europe as well. Sifton argued that a "stalwart peasant in a sheepskin coat with a stout wife" could develop the Northwest as well as, if not better than, newcomers from Great Britain and Ireland.

Waves of immigrants subsequently surged across the Atlantic, funnelled via the CPR through Winnipeg, and spilled out into the prairies. The Canadian west had a population of 300,000 before 1896, which rose to a remarkable 1.5 million by the eve of the First World War in 1914. Nor do numbers alone describe the new west emerging from under the immigrant's plow. The prairies developed a unique multicultural environment unlike any other in the country.

Perhaps Canada did offer better opportunities than their original homelands, but life on the prairies was much harsher than immigrants had been told. Government propaganda pamphlets only described success stories, never failures. They always welcomed without mentioning the expectation of assimilation. They offered friendly invitations, omitting mention of the racism, bigotry, and discrimination that many newcomers often experienced in their new Canadian homes. Pamphlets never commented upon homesickness, loneliness, or any of the myriad other negative emotions so common to new immigrants. Later, the CPR even failed to mention winter or snow in its promotions advertising the Canadian prairies to new immigrants.

W.D. Scott (1861–1925) was superintendent of the Immigration Branch from 1906 to 1923. In that capacity, he developed and implemented immigration policy, and although his 1914 article (Document A) was not an official statement, it reflected and articulated the host society's fears as it nervously watched new immigrants arrive upon Canada's shores.

Maria Adamowska (1890–1961) arrived in Canada in 1899 and wrote a number of poems and articles about her experiences as a Ukrainian immigrant. This material appeared as articles in the *Almanac of the Ukrainian Voice* in 1937 and 1939.

Georgina Binnie-Clark (1871–1955) and her sister arrived in Canada in the summer of 1905 to visit their brother's Saskatchewan homestead. Binnie-Clark decided to stay and, like so many middle-class women with few prospects of marriage in her native England, spent most of her life in Canada — but did not marry. Her training in music and journalism hardly suited life in the prairie environment, but she rose to the occasion and helped her sister run a wheat farm. She became the leading critic of Canada's homestead law, which restricted grants to male applicants. She also published two books recounting her experiences in western Canada.

A) The Immigration by Races, 1914
W.D. Scott

… Compared with other European settlers the British start with the advantage of having the same mother tongue as Canadians; with this exception they are on an equal footing with all others and must be prepared to compete on these terms. Much is said of the preference which Canada should give to persons from the mother country, but there is little sentiment in business, and if an Italian immigrant can do more work than an Englishman, the Italian "gets the job." Fortunately for Canada and for the immigrants there is usually work for both.

Considering the immense number of British immigrants arriving — some 674,000 in the first decade of the century — it speaks well for them and well for the country that so few have failed. Those who do not succeed are the exception. Although the success is of varying degree, it is as a rule according to the energy and tenacity of purpose displayed. There are few British immigrants in Canada who are not in a position much superior to that which they would now be occupying had they remained at home.

For the last twelve fiscal years, 1901–12, the immigration from Great Britain and Ireland amounted to 823,188 in the following proportion: English and Welsh, 601,963; Scottish, 171,897; Irish, 49,328. The largest number in any one year was for the twelve months ending March 31, 1912, when the total reached the immense figure of 138,121, made up of 96,806 English and Welsh, 32,988 Scottish and 8327 Irish.

United States Immigration

The people from the United States most readily adapt themselves to Canadian conditions. The greater portion come from the Northern and Western States, where climatic and agricultural conditions closely resemble those of the Dominion. As they are largely of the agricultural class and come to Canada to take up farming, they know the proper course to adopt immediately upon arrival. United States immigrants may be considered the most desirable for a number of reasons. They understand Canadian conditions so well that their success in the so called dry belt of Alberta has been greater than that of the Canadian born; immediately on arrival they put large tracts under cultivation, and induce the railway companies to provide transportation facilities in the districts where they settle; they use the most recent machinery and labour-saving devices, and are thus an object-lesson, more especially to foreign settlers, who, without this clear proof of the value of improved machinery, would be slow in commencing its use; and, lastly and most important of all, they employ upon their farms large numbers of the immigrants of all races, who yearly arrive without sufficient capital to commence operations at once on their own account, and who must seek employment with others until they have saved enough to begin work on their free homesteads.

Much is spoken and written of the danger that Western Canada may become Americanized. The force of such arguments depends upon what is meant by "Americanized." If it is to be taken to mean the growing up of a sentiment in favour of annexation with the United States, the charge is groundless; if it means that the progressiveness of the American will be copied by the Canadian, the more rapid the Americanization the better. The Western Canadian is never averse to learning, no matter who may be his teacher. Sometimes the American settler finds in turn that in many things he may safely follow the lead of his Canadian neighbour.

When speaking of the possibility of annexation to the United States it is well to remember that probably not more than 50 percent of the immigrants from the United States were born there, and that, in addition to the 10 percent of the immigrants who are Canadians returning to the Dominion, which they left when the conditions were adverse, there are numbers who, while born in the States, are children of Canadian parents, and look upon themselves as really Canadians. Nor must it be forgotten that a considerable portion were born in the British Islands, and, coming again under the same flag, immediately upon arrival look upon themselves as Canadians.

The immigrants from the United States become naturalized at the earliest opportunity, while those who may be repatriated upon a three months' residence are quick to avail themselves of the opportunity. Generally speaking, the Americans are staunch supporters of the Canadian system of government, and are ever ready to point out wherein it is superior to that which they have left. More especially is this true with regard to the Canadian system of judiciary. No warmer advocate of the appointive system of judges exists than the American, who has had experience of the elective system ...

Austro-Hungarians

One of the largest contributors of immigrants to Canada of late years has been Austria-Hungary. The term Austro-Hungarian, however, has no very definite meaning. Such words as English, French, German, Norwegian convey to the mind a class of persons of certain language, type, appearance and peculiarities. Not so with the term Austro-Hungarian. Austria-Hungary is not a country wherein dwells a particular class of people, but is a certain area under two constituted governments, ruled over by one sovereign. The population is made up of a number of races with different languages, religions and social ideals. Divided into a large number of provinces, the country as a whole has an area of 240,942 square miles and a population of about fifty millions. Of these 45 percent are Slavs, 25 percent Germans, 16 percent Magyars; the remainder consist of Roumanians, Croatians, Ruthenians, Ser[b]ians, Poles, Bohemians, Jews and numerous other races. Of the different races the Germans are the most desirable in every respect, their educational standard being much higher, their industry more noticeable, and their ideals more closely approaching those of Canadians than is the case with the other races. The provinces which have contributed most largely to the movement of immigrants to Canada are Galicia and Bukowina. The North Atlantic Trading Company, which will be mentioned later, brought Canada to the attention of the people in these two provinces especially, and the movement once commenced continued through the indirect immigration work carried on by those who were successful in their new homes. The census of 1901 showed 28,407 persons in Canada who had been born in Austria-Hungary, and 18,178 of these were classified as Austro-Hungarians, the balance presumably being of German origin. Since that date the immigration movement has been large, nearly 140,000 arriving in the years 1901–12.

Coming from a country where agriculture is the principal industry, the Galicians and others from Austria-Hungary are fitted in some ways to make suitable settlers in Canada. They have been, however, embarrassed for want of capital. They have, moreover, preferred to settle on lands well covered with timber, and the cost of clearing the land and bringing it under cultivation has been higher than that of cultivating prairie land. In the majority of cases when the $10 entry fee for a homestead was paid and a not very habitable house erected, the head of the family, together with any other members able to act as wage-earners, found it necessary to seek work in order to secure funds to purchase stock and machinery. Employment could generally be secured with farmers in the harvesting season, with threshing outfits during the autumn, and in the bush during the winter. In this way the men have secured some knowledge of the English language, as have also some of the women who have become domestic servants.

The Galicians and other Austro-Hungarians are settled largely in the eastern portion of Manitoba and the northern sections of Saskatchewan and Alberta. They have improved their positions by coming to Canada, but whether or not they are a valuable acquisition to the Dominion is an open question. They are slow to assimilate and adopt Canadian customs, and, after all is said, this should be the final test as to the desirability of any class of immigrants. If they will not aid in forming a people united in customs and ideals, their room should be more acceptable than their company. Time will, no doubt, work wonders in their case, as it has in the case of other nationalities, and eventually it is hoped that they will make good Canadians. The process, however, will be slow.

What has already been said refers to those who have gone upon farms in Canada. Those who have settled in the cities form an entirely different problem. Living as they do in crowded, insanitary and usually filthy quarters, existing upon food and under conditions which a self-respecting Canadian would refuse to tolerate, they enter into unfair competition with the wage-earners of Canada and constitute a source of danger to the national life. Crime is all too common among them, and it is without doubt the city element of this people which has brought about the prejudice which exists against Galicians in the minds of Canadians. Since 1906 no effort has been made by the Canadian government to secure further immigration of this class. But, although all the restrictive regulations mentioned later on are enforced against them, large numbers still arrive, and are likely to arrive for years to come. A flow of any particular class of immigrants is usually difficult to start, but when once commenced it is often just as difficult to check.

The Italians

According to the 1901 census there were then in Canada 6,854 persons born in Italy and 10,834 persons of Italian origin. Between the fiscal years 1901–2 and 1911–12 nearly 62,000 immigrants arrived from Italy. The large majority of the Italians cannot, however, in the true sense be classed as immigrants, for they do not come with the intention of making permanent homes. They are "hewers of wood and drawers of water" who, by living at the lowest possible expense and by working diligently, hope to accumulate sufficient wealth to enable them to live comfortably in "Sunny Italy." They arrive with little that cannot be carried tied up in a handkerchief, and leave with a travelling outfit of about the same dimensions. Stored about their persons, or transmitted already to their native land, is the money they have earned during their sojourn here.

If we except the hand-organ man and the fruit-dealer, practically all are engaged at work as navvies. In every city you see them digging drains; on railway construction from the Atlantic to the Pacific their services are eagerly sought. The Italian is a good navvy. He obeys the orders of the "boss." He is anxious [not] to go on strike, as he counts that any increase in wages would in the short period he intends to remain in the country no more

than reimburse him for the wages lost while the strike was on. At construction work he boards himself, or, if eating at the contractor's boardinghouse,
is likely to be satisfied with whatever fare is furnished. He has no desire to
insist upon exceptionally clean sleeping quarters, and, in a word, is exactly
the class of help which contractors desire for the rough work of railway construction. When times are slack the Italians flock to the cities, and in their
little colonies in Montreal, Toronto, Winnipeg and Vancouver huddle into
their cheap boarding houses and live under appalling conditions, at a rate
so low as almost to shatter belief in the much talked of "increased cost of
living." When work is again available they are shipped off by employment
agents to points at which their services are needed.

They have arrived from their native land with the idea that it is for them
to right their own wrongs in person. Thus, while crimes committed by them
against other than Italians are uncommon, stabbing and shooting affrays are
all too common where men of their own race are the victims. Edward A.
Steiner, in his book *On the Trail of the Immigrant*, writes thus of the Italian
attitude towards crime:

> The worst thing about the Italians is that they have no sense
> of shame or remorse. I have not yet found one of them who
> was sorry for anything except that he had been caught; and
> in his own eyes and in the eyes of his friends he is "unfor-
> tunate" when he is in prison and "lucky" when he comes
> out. "He no bad," his neighbour says. "He good, he just
> caught." And when he comes out he is received as a hero.

Of the Black Hand societies, of which we hear so much in the large
cities of the United States, little as yet has been heard in Canada. That they
exist is admitted by those most familiar with the Italian in the Dominion,
but as their threats are invariably addressed to members of their own race,
information is unlikely to be furnished to the courts, or even to creep into
the press of the country.

That labour is necessary to carry on the large public works throughout
the Dominion is admitted; that, if not on hand, it must be brought to the
country is conceded. We may, however, hold that the help should be secured from such immigrants as are considered desirable, so that the country
may have as its labourers those who intend to become permanent residents.
The Italians are not of this class. They merely save money with which to
return to their native land.

The enforcement of the regulation requiring Italians upon arrival to present their penal certificates has resulted in the rejection of many. A penal certificate is a civil document showing the number of convictions registered against the person to whom it is issued. As each Italian is supposed by the laws of his own country to possess one, the fact that he is without one is taken as evidence that he does not wish it seen, or, in other words, that it shows him to have been convicted of crime. As many have been rejected, either on account of information furnished on the penal certificate or through not possessing a penal certificate, it is evident that many of the Italians attempting to come to Canada (and the same is true of the United States) belong to the criminal class. The government has never encouraged immigration from Italy, except, for a very brief period, in the case of some northern Italians. The large number of arrivals from Italy is accounted for simply by the fact that those emigrating desire work, and that the work awaits them in Canada.

The French

With the population of France at a standstill and the people prosperous, it is not to be expected that any great movement of settlers should take place from that country; nevertheless, since the beginning of the twentieth century there has been a steady flow of emigration to Canada. The number for the years 1901-12 was 17,970. As in 1901 there were only 7,944 persons in Canada who had been born in France, this class of population has more than doubled in the last decade.

The French coming to Canada have settled largely in Quebec, Ontario and the western provinces. There are several very progressive colonies in Saskatchewan. The French are an industrious and thrifty people, and will make a success of agricultural work in the Dominion.

More important than the movement from France is that of "Returned Canadians" from the Eastern States. These people left Quebec when Canada was far from being as prosperous as it now is, and are returning to Canada to take up free homesteads in the prairie provinces, or to secure crown lands in Quebec or Ontario.

The Belgians

The people from Belgium also make excellent settlers. Of these there were 2,280 in 1901, and since that date the arrivals have been 10,184.

The Dutch

The Dutch are as yet slightly represented in the Dominion, there being in 1901 only 385 in Canada who were born in Holland. In the first decade of the present century 4,895 arrived, and a heavier immigration is expected in the future. They make good settlers, and those who have already come have made very rapid material progress.

The Swiss

The Swiss are lightly represented in the immigration returns, only 1,717 having arrived between 1901 and 1912. They also make good settlers.

The Germans

In Canada in 1901 there were only 27,300 persons who had been born in Germany; there were, however, 310,501 of German origin, or almost 6 percent of the total population of the Dominion. In the early days … Canada received considerable German immigration both directly from the Fatherland and indirectly from the German settlements in the United States. The descendants of these settlers form the greater part of the present population of German origin. The immigration from Germany during the years 1901–12 was about 25,000. In addition to the above a considerable portion of the immigration from Austria-Hungary and Russia is of German origin. For the fiscal years 1909–10 and 1910–11 the unnaturalized Germans from the United States numbered 2,378 and 1,123 respectively.

Sturdy, intelligent, honest and industrious, the German makes an ideal farmer, and he is in other walks of life a good citizen. Although he clings to his language he also acquires English, and the younger people especially adopt Canadian customs. They are amongst Canada's best settlers, and it is to be regretted that the laws of Germany prohibit the active immigration propaganda which would enable the Dominion to secure a much larger number than are now arriving.

The Scandinavians

… As of [Icelanders], so of the other Scandinavian races — Swedes, Norwegians, and Danes — nothing but good can be said. The larger part of the immigrants of these races go on the land; but whether they engage in agriculture or take up employment in the cities they prove hard-working, honest, thrifty and intelligent settlers of whom any country might be proud. In addition to those coming direct from the homeland many have been moving for years past from the Western States into Saskatchewan and Alberta, and are there looked upon as amongst the most progressive settlers. They readily acquire the English language, become naturalized at the earliest possible moment, take an interest in the political questions affecting their new homes, and, in a word, "become Canadians." In 1901 there were in Canada 2,075 Danes and 10,256 Norwegians and Swedes. Between 1901–1902 and 1911–12 over 4,700 Danes and over 36,500 Norwegians and Swedes arrived in the Dominion. With the Scandinavian race there is really no question of assimilation. They are sprung largely from the same stock as are the English, and, when they have acquired the language and become acquainted with Canadian customs, they will be as other Canadians. True, the first generation will be distinguished by their accent, but even this disappears in the second generation.

Turks, Armenians and Syrians

Turkey, Armenia and Syria supply some of Canada's most undesirable immigrants. With them assimilation is out of the question and, except rarely, they are not producers. The Italians have their faults; Canadians may not approve of the manner in which the Poles and many other Eastern European races live. But these people are at least workers. If they take money out of the country when they go back to their homes, they leave behind them tasks performed, for which as a rule they have received no more than they have earned. But with the Turks, Syrians and Armenians it is different. They live under conditions which are a menace to the country, and their time is spent in trade and barter. Like the Gypsies, they are quick to avail themselves of naturalization, not that they admire Canada's form of government or take any interest in political events, but merely because of the extra protection which naturalization affords or which they imagine it affords. They are of a wandering nature, and many of them have lived on both sides of the international boundary. It is not uncommon to meet people of these classes who carry with them when travelling naturalization papers from both Canada and the United States. They find them of value in passing from one country to the other. There were 1,571 Turks and Syrians in Canada in 1901, and of these 481 were naturalized. Since that date there have arrived 2,456 Turks, 5,229 Syrians and 1,473 Armenians. Pedlars are no great acquisition to any country, and there are few people in the Dominion who would care to see the day arrive when people of these races might be pointed out as fair samples of Canadian citizens.

Greeks, Macedonians and Bulgarians

The Greeks, Macedonians and Bulgarians are all dwellers in cities when that is possible. If city work is not available they take railway construction work, and, as they can live on very little, they are able to save a large part of their earnings. The Greek is rapidly branching out into two new callings, shoe-polishing and confectionery. Amongst the Macedonians and Bulgarians the highest ambition seems to be to keep small stores where they sell the necessaries of life, even if in a small way, as it gives them a better opportunity to prey upon their countrymen.

The modern Greek, Macedonian and Bulgarian have far from a high sense of truthfulness. The writer has seen squads of forty or fifty examined at the ocean port. Each one gave an address to which he was proceeding, and gravely informed the inspector that the person he was going to join was his brother. Each one gave the same address. When asked if he had any relatives accompanying him, each stated that he had none. When confronted with the statements of others of the party these dissemblers would then change their story and claim to be cousins, brothers-in-law, or to have any other convenient relationship to the one already in the country. A recent case occurred in which a Macedonian naturalized in Canada sent his naturalization papers to a friend in the United States who desired to come to the Dominion. This person, when stopped by an immigration official, demanded entry as a Canadian citizen. The fraud was discovered, the would-be immigrant was fined and deported, and the Macedonian Canadian citizen was fined $250 for aiding and abetting the entry of an undesirable.

Practically all these three classes in the Dominion have arrived since the beginning of the present century, the Greek and Macedonian immigration numbering 3,997 in the first decade and the Bulgarian 4,484 in the same time. Since the 1910 Immigration Act came into force the rejections amongst these classes have been very heavy. None are now admitted if they can be legally kept out.

The Chinese

Chinese immigration has undergone many changes. It was openly encouraged in the early eighties when Chinese labourers were needed in the construction of the Canadian Pacific Railway. In 1886 an agitation carried on by trade unions resulted in the imposing of a head tax of $50 on this class of immigrants. In 1901 this was increased to $100 and in 1904 to $500. In 1901 there were 17,043 persons in Canada who had been born in China. The number of those of Chinese origin was probably somewhat larger. Between 1901 and 1912 upwards of 30,000 entered Canada. Very few of the Chinese arriving in Canada come on their own initiative. Their fares and head tax are paid by "tyees" or contractors, who hold them practically in bondage until they repay the expense entailed in bringing them to Canada, together with an exorbitant profit. They are industrious workers, very thrifty, live well according to their standards, and insist upon receiving the highest rate of remuneration which their services can secure.

The Chinese in Canada may be divided into four classes: merchants, dealing largely in teas, silks, opium and other oriental products; gardeners who devote their attention almost entirely to garden products, and who in British Columbia appear able to make large profits after paying a yearly rental of $25 an acre for their land; restaurant keepers and laundrymen; and, lastly, domestic servants. In the last-mentioned occupation they give excellent satisfaction to their employers, but as their wages have doubled since the imposition of the $500 head tax, it is their proud boast that it is the Canadians and not themselves who are mulcted. For this boast they apparently have good grounds.

Generally speaking the Chinamen are quiet, inoffensive, law-abiding people, if we leave out of account their tendency to gamble and to indulge in opium. Many missions exist for their conversion to Christianity. It is true, however, that while large numbers profess conversion some will admit to their intimate friends that they have done so because, as they say, it is "good for blizness". When gambling they are not averse to deception, but in business transactions they are credited with having a strict sense of honour; many who know them best say that a Chinaman's word is as good as his bond.

The large increase in numbers arriving during 1910–11 is reported to have been caused by the circulation of a report in China that the Canadian government intend raising the head tax to $1,000. Although not popular, the Chinaman may be said to be now the least hated Oriental on the western coast. As the desire of the Chinese is to accumulate wealth to take back to their native land, and as assimilation is out of the question, they cannot be classed as desirable, but, unless the numbers arriving increase very largely, they cannot be said to constitute any great menace to Canada.

The Japanese

The Japanese are, from a Canadian standpoint, the most undesirable of the Orientals. Belonging to an emigrating race, filled with patriotism for their own country, and living within such easy reach of Canada's western coast, they might, if allowed to come, flood the Province of British Columbia and dominate not only the labour market, but, through the investment of capital, the principal industries as well. That they are industrious and capable is admitted by all acquainted with them. They would, however, never become Canadians, and their arrival in large numbers is, therefore, a contingency which should be carefully guarded against. Unlike the other Orientals, they are not content to remain "hewers of wood and drawers of water." Possibly this desire to figure in all walks of life is not unconnected with the dislike which the white races bear towards them. There were about 4,700 Japanese in Canada in 1901. Between 1901 and 1912 about 15,000 entered the Dominion, the heaviest immigration being in 1907–8, when 7,601 arrived. There was a great falling off in the numbers (495) arriving in 1908–9 as compared with 1907–8; this was the result of an arrangement between Canada and Japan, whereby the Japanese coolies arriving in any one year were to be restricted to a certain number. Japan has kept well within the number arranged for. So long as this arrangement remains in force Japanese immigration need cause no anxiety to Canada.

The Hindus

Of the different immigration problems which from time to time have faced the Dominion, that of the influx of Hindus appeared for a time to be possibly the most serious. This movement commenced in 1905. The arrivals up to the close of the fiscal year 1911-12 were 5,203. British Columbia, the nearest province to the Orient and the one possessing the climate most closely resembling that of their native land, was the ultimate destination of these unwelcome comers, and British Columbia was not slow in expressing her disapproval of them. "A White Canada" was her cry. That these immigrants were British subjects; that many had fought for the Empire; that many expressed their willingness to do so again should occasion arise — all this in no way lessened the antipathy of the white race towards them.

True, there were some imperialists who, recognizing in the Hindus subjects of the same sovereign, argued that they were entitled to enter the Dominion as a matter of right, and that any action towards restricting their movements from one part of the British domains to another would endanger the existence of the Empire. But the counsels of the advocates of "A White Canada" finally prevailed, and an order-in-council was passed providing that persons of Asiatic origin, other than Chinese and Japanese, must have in their possession $200 at the time of landing in Canada. This came into force in 1908, and the numbers arriving immediately dropped from 2,623 in that year to almost nothing.

The Hindus who came to Canada were largely from the Punjab and, physically, were a fine set of men. The term Hindu as here applied is a misnomer, denoting as it does a religious sect rather than a race of people. In religion they were divided, some being Hindus, others Buddhists and others Mohammedans. It is doubtful whether with their constitutions, suitable for the country and climate from which they came, they will ever become thoroughly acclimatized in Canada. Pneumonia and pulmonary troubles have already resulted in the death of no small number. Their bodies were disposed of by cremation, the burial method of their own country; possibly this is the only one of their customs which might with advantage be adopted.

Saw-mills and railway construction work afforded employment to the Hindus. While they were able at most times to secure employment, it was at a lower rate than that paid to white men or even to Japanese or Chinese. They were unaccustomed to Canadian methods, and though able to speak a little English were slow to learn more. Their greatest disadvantage, however, is their caste system, which prevents them from eating and sometimes even from working with white men, or even with others of their own race who belong to a different social scale — for this is practically the meaning of caste. Now that the influx is checked the Hindu problem is ended ...

The Jews

Scattered over the face of the earth, a people but not a nation, the Jews seek the land where they may hope to reap a harvest from their labours. Canada, in common with the United States, has proved a loadstone to draw these wanderers from the ends of the earth ...

Efforts at colonization on the land have been made. Two of the most important were at Wapella and Hirsch. Neither has proved a conspicuous success. More recently the Jews have attempted the cultivation of the finer grades of tobacco in the Province of Quebec, and although their efforts are apparently meeting with success it is as yet too soon to predict the final result. They cannot be classed as agriculturalists, and the number who have engaged in this occupation is small compared with those engaged in trade and barter or who take up manufacturing.

The Jews are pre-eminently dwellers in cities. The clothing trade in its various branches provides employment for many; other occupations that attract them are cigar and cigarette making, shoe-repairing, fruit-dealing and vegetable-dealing, and rag and other varieties of peddling.

The increase in the Hebrew population has been very rapid in Canada, rising from 667 in 1881 to 16,131 in 1901; since then the immigration of this race has amounted to over 50,000. According to the census of 1901, of the 16,131 Jews then resident in Canada 13,470 lived in twelve cities. In Montreal, Toronto and Winnipeg the conditions under which some, especially the Russian Jews, live are far from satisfactory, either as respects air-space, ventilation or cleanliness. Sweat-shops have not yet reached in Canada the deplorable condition found in the United States, but the tendency is in that direction, and the Jews are one of the strongest factors in bringing this about. No effort is or ever has been made by the government of Canada to induce Jewish immigrants to come to the Dominion, and the influx has been entirely unsolicited. In their movements to America they are aided largely by their philanthropic societies. These also do useful work amongst their own people by looking after those unable to support themselves …

THE IMMIGRATION POLICY OF CANADA

The immigration policy of the government of Canada at the present time is, and for many years past has been, to encourage the immigration of farmers, farm labourers and domestic servants from countries which are classed as desirable. The list of countries had undergone change from time to time, and at the present includes the United States, the British Isles, France, Belgium, Holland, Switzerland, Germany, Denmark, Norway, Sweden and Iceland.

On the other hand, it is the policy of the government to do all in its power to keep out of the country undesirables, who may be divided into three classes:

1. Those physically, mentally or morally unfit whose exclusion is provided for by the immigration act already quoted.

2. Those belonging to nationalities unlikely to assimilate and who, consequently, prevent the building up of a united nation of people of similar customs and ideals.

3. Those who from their mode of life and occupations are likely to crowd into urban centres and bring about a state of congestion which might result in unemployment and a lowering of the standard of Canadian national life.

While neither the Immigration Act nor the orders-in-council passed thereunder prohibit the landing in Canada of persons belonging to the second and third classes above mentioned, still their entry has been made difficult. Their coming is discouraged in a number of ways. Chinese are subject to a head tax of $500. The number of Japanese coolies has been limited by arrangements between the two countries. Orders-in-council have been passed requiring (1) Asiatic arrivals to have $200 in cash at the time of landing; (2) the production of passports and penal certificates by persons coming from the countries which issue these; (3) the continuous journey of all immigrants from the country of their birth or citizenship on tickets purchased in that country or purchased or prepaid in Canada. All these regulations put obstacles in the way of immigrants from Asia and Southern and Eastern Europe, and, consequently, the numbers coming or likely to come from those countries are correspondingly diminished.

Briefly, this is the immigration policy of the government. In so far as the administration of the restrictive part of the policy is concerned the Immigration department has at all times endeavoured to be both just and humane, bearing in mind, however, that its duty is to Canada and to Canada only, and that while every applicant for admission who is likely to be an acquisition to the country shall be admitted if the law will permit it, on the other hand, every person who is likely to be a detriment to the country must be rejected if the law will allow it.

It may be here stated that until 1903 immigrants, upon arrival in Canada, underwent no medical examination which might result in their rejection through physical or mental unfitness. In 1903, however, a medical examination was commenced, and from that year rejections at the ocean ports have been frequent, both upon medical and civil grounds. The rejections at border points between Canada and the United States commenced in 1908-9. During the fiscal years 1902-12 8,500 rejections were recorded at ocean ports and 51,015 at border stations on the United States boundary. Even with the care exercised in the rejection of undesirables when they apply for admission, a certain percentage enter Canada who prove failures and who are deported. During the years 1902-12 5,626 such deportations were made ...

THE PROBLEM OF FUTURE IMMIGRATION

At the present time there is no large number of persons in Canada whose presence is a menace to the country from a political, moral or economic point of view. The reason for the absence of such a problem is that representatives of undesirable nationalities have as yet come in small number only. Who would care to see Alberta a second Mississippi or Georgia, as far as population is concerned? Who would wish to see the day arrive when British Columbia could be termed the "Second Flowery Kingdom," as might easily happen if the doors were thrown open to the Japanese? Who would not regret to see the ghettos and slums of New York, with her hived population and her reeking sweat-shops, duplicated in Montreal, Toronto and Winnipeg? These are the questions which today confront Canadians, and this is the problem of the future. More important than the drilling of armies, more important than the construction of navies, more important even than the fiscal policy of the country is the question of who shall come to Canada and become part and parcel of the Canadian people.

Fifty years ago the United States was receiving practically the class which is to-day coming to Canada. With the disappearance of free lands the character of the immigration to the United States has changed, and now Southern and Eastern Europe are furnishing most of her new settlers, and a large percentage of her immigrants remain in the cities. The people of the republic are now awake to the danger which this involves, and anti-immigration leagues and similar organizations are being formed to bring the question prominently before the public. Canada, with this object-lesson before her, has no excuse if she allows the same evils to grow. Much has already been done to prevent this. One suggestion for further checks is the introduction of educational tests. It is, for instance, suggested that no one over ten years of age shall be admitted who is unable to speak, read and write either English, Welsh, Gaelic, French, German, Dutch, Danish, Norwegian, Swedish or Icelandic. This would practically confine immigration to the countries where immigration work is now carried on ...

In checking undesirable immigration it must be decided what constitutes an undesirable, and the following definition is put forward for consideration: undesirable immigrants are those who will not assimilate with the Canadian people, or whose presence will tend to bring about a deterioration from a political, moral, social or economic point of view.

B) Beginnings in Canada
Maria Adamowska

... Finally, we sailed into port at Halifax. On the shore, a crowd of people stared at us, some out of curiosity, some out of contempt. Our men, particularly those from Galicia, were dressed like gentlemen for the voyage, but the women and children traveled in their everyday peasant costumes. The older men from Bukovina attracted attention to themselves by their waist-length hair — greased with reeking lard — and by their smelly sheepskin coats. Perhaps that was the reason why the English people stopped their noses and glued their eyes upon us — a strange spectacle, indeed.

In Halifax, we boarded a train and continued on our journey. As we sped across Ontario with its rocks, hills, and tunnels, we were afraid we were coming to the end of the world. The heart of many a man sank to his heels, and the women and children raised such lamentation as defies description.

At last we arrived in Winnipeg. At that time, Winnipeg was very much like any other small farmers' town. From the train we were taken to the immigration home ...

One must remember that times were different then. Nowadays when an immigrant arrives in Canada, he feels more or less at home. Here he can find his own people everywhere and hear his own language. But in those days you had to wander far and wide before you could meet one of your countrymen. No matter what direction you turned, all you could see was the prairie like a vast sea on which wild animals howled and red-skinned Indians roamed. It was not until after our arrival that the mass immigration of Ukrainians to Canada began ...

From Winnipeg, we went to Yorkton, Saskatchewan. There we hired a rig which took us more than thirty miles farther north. At long last, after a miserable trip — we were nearly devoured alive by mosquitoes — we managed to reach our destination, the home of our acquaintances.

Our host, who had emigrated to Canada a year or two before, had written us to boast of the prosperity he had attained in such a short time. He said that he had a home like a mansion, a large cultivated field, and that his wife was dressed like a lady. In short, he depicted Canada as a country of incredible abundance whose borders were braided with sausage like some fantastic land in a fairy tale.

How great was our disenchantment when we approached that mansion of his and an entirely different scene met our eyes! It was actually just a small log cabin, only partly plastered and roofed with sod. Beside the cabin was a garden plot which had been dug with a spade. The man's face was smeared with dirt from ear to ear, and he looked weird, like some unearthly creature. He was grubbing up stumps near the house, and his wife was poking away in the garden. She reminded us of Robinson Crusoe on an uninhabited island. She was suntanned like a gypsy and was dressed in old, torn overalls. A wide-brimmed hat covered her head.

When mother saw this scarecrow, she started crying again. Later on, father reprimanded the man for writing us such nonsense. But his only answer was, "Let someone else have a taste of our good life here." ...

Our troubles and worries were only just beginning. The house was small, and there were eighteen of us jammed within its four walls. What was one to do?

My father had brought some money with him, and with it he bought a cow and, later, a horse. Needless to say, I was the cow-herd ...

Winter was setting in. Dreading the idea of having to spend the season in such cramped quarters, my father dug a cave in a riverbank, covered it with turf, and there was our apartment, all ready to move into. Oh, how fortunate we felt! We would not have traded that root cellar for a royal palace. To this spot, we carried hay in bed sheets on our backs and stacked it. We also dragged firewood on our backs and made other preparations.

Day by day, our provisions ran lower and lower. The older folk were able to put up with hunger, but the famished children howled pitifully, like wolves.

One day I sneaked into our hostess' garden and pulled a turnip. Then I slipped out of the patch and ran as fast as I could into a gorge where I planned to hide myself in the tall grass and enjoy a real treat. Unfortunately, our hostess spied me, grabbed a club, and chased after me with the speed of a demon. To escape, I hid in some tall grass, but this heartless woman searched until she found me. There she stood over me and, as she raised her club, hissed, "You detestable intruder! One blow with this, and you'll be dead like a dog."

Fear of death made me forget about the turnip. It did not matter now how hungry I was: life was still sweet. And the woman was so ferocious that one blow of that club would certainly have meant the end of my life.

With tears in my eyes I began to plead, "Auntie darling, forgive me. I'll never again set my foot in your garden as long as I live."

Spitting at me with disgust the woman said, "Remember! Write that down on your forehead."

And so, for a piddling turnip, I almost paid with my life.

Came winter. Our cow stopped giving milk. Aside from bread, there was nothing to eat at home. Was one to gnaw the walls? One time I happened to notice tears rolling down mother's cheeks as she sipped something from a small pot. We children began to weep with her. "Mother, why are you crying? Won't you let us taste what you're eating?"

Mother divided the gruel among us. She tried to say something, but all she could manage was "My chil—"; further words died on her lips. Only a moan of anguish escaped from her breast. We learned afterwards that, late in the fall, mother had visited the garden of our former host and painstakingly raked the ground for potatoes that had been too small to be worth picking at potato-digging time. She had found a few tiny ones, no larger than hazel nuts. From these potatoes, she had made a gruel that tasted like potato soup, and it was this gruel which we children shared, tears flooding our eyes. Who knows how we would have managed if father had not brought his gun from the old country. With it he went hunting, and we had game all winter.

Before spring arrived, father went to look for a farm. He found one some fifteen miles to the west of us, and we began to build a house. We dug a round pit in the ground about five yards in diameter, just deep enough to scrape the black earth off the top and reach clay underneath. We mixed hay and water with the clay and kneaded it with our bare feet. With this clay, we plastered our house. In the spring, we moved into it. By that time, all our provisions had run out.

And so it was that father left home one day, on foot, prepared to tramp hundreds of miles to find a job. He left us without a piece of bread, to the mercy of fate.

While father was away, mother dug a plot of ground and planted the wheat she had brought from the old country, tied up in a small bundle. Every day, she watered it with her tears.

That done, there was no time to waste; every moment was precious. Mother and I began to clear our land. But since I was hardly strong enough for the job, I helped by grabbing hold of the top of each bush and pulling on it while mother cut the roots with the ax. Next we dug the ground with spades. How well did I do? At best, I had barely enough strength to thrust half the depth of the blade into the ground, no deeper. But that did not excuse me from digging. Where the ground was hard, mother had to correct my work, and thus the two of us cleared and dug close to four acres of land.

We lived on milk. One meal would consist of sweet milk followed by sour milk; the next meal would consist of sour milk followed by sweet milk. We looked like living corpses.

In the beginning of our life in Canada, old and young alike had to work grievously hard, often in the cold and in hunger. The effects of this hard work can now be painfully felt in even the tiniest bones of our bodies ...

Our Rumanian neighbor, who lived a mile from our place, had made himself a small handmill for grinding wheat into flour. In the fall, when our wheat was ripe, mother reaped it very thoroughly, every last head of it, rubbed the kernels out, winnowed the grain, and poured it into a sack. Then she sent me with this grain — about eight pounds of it — to have it ground at our neighbor's mill.

It was the first time I had ever been to his place. As soon as I entered the vestibule of the house, I could see the hand mill in the corner. Now a new problem faced me: I had not the faintest idea how to operate the mill, and there was no one around to show me. I sat down and began to cry. After a while, the neighbor's wife showed up and spoke to me, but I could not understand her so I just kept on crying. I had the feeling that she was scolding me for sneaking into her house. I pointed to the bag of wheat. She understood what I wanted, pointed to the hand mill, and went inside the house, leaving the door open. She sat down at the table, picked up a piece of bread which was as dark as the ground we walked on, dipped it in salt, and munched away at it.

As I watched her, I almost choked with grief. Oh, how strong was my urge to throw myself at her feet and plead for at least one bite of that bread. But, as she obviously was not thinking of me, I got ahold of myself. That piece of bread might well have been the last she had in the house. That experience gave me the most profound shock of my entire life. No one can fully appreciate what I went through unless he has lived through something similar himself.

Continually swallowing my saliva, I kept grinding the wheat until I had finished. Then I ran home with that little bit of flour, joyfully looking forward to the moment when we, too, would have bread.

But my joy quickly evaporated. Mother pondered a moment and said, "This will make two or three loaves of bread, and the flour will be all gone. Not enough to eat and not enough to feast our eyes upon. I'm going to cook cornmeal for you; it will last longer." And so we teased ourselves with cornmeal for some time.

On his way home from the other side of Brandon, where he'd been working, father stopped at Yorkton and bought a fifty-pound sack of flour. He carried it home on his back every inch of the twenty-eight miles. When we saw him coming home, we bounced with excitement and greeted him with joyous laughter mixed with tears. And all this excitement over the prospect of a piece of bread! Father had not earned much money, for he had lost a lot of time job-hunting. Then, at work, he had fallen from a stack onto the tines of a pitchfork and been laid up for a long time. But he had managed to earn something like twenty dollars, enough for flour to last us for a time.

The coming of winter presented new problems. We had nothing to wear on our feet. Something had to be done about that. Mother had brought a couple of woolen sheets from the old country. From these she sewed us footwear that kept our feet warm all winter.

That winter our horse died. We were now left with only one horse and he was just a year-old colt, though he looked like a two-year old. Father made a harness from some ropes, and a sled, and began to break him in.

… Even in winter we had no rest. We had settled in a low-lying area. In the summertime, water lay everywhere, and the croaking of frogs filled the air. And it never rained but poured in those days. Often the downpour continued for two or three weeks without a letup. In the winter, the water in the lakes froze up, the wells — always few in number — dried up, and there was nothing one could do about it. We were concerned not so much about ourselves as about our few head of livestock, which would have no water. We could not let them die; a way had to be found to obtain water for them.

Father found a piece of tin somewhere, shaped it into a trough, built an enclosure out of stones, placed the trough over it, built a fire in the enclosure under the trough, kept the trough filled with snow, and, as the snow melted, collected the water in a tub at the bottom end of the trough. But this was not the best way to water cattle. A cow could drink up a couple of tubs of water at a time and then look around and moo for more.

As a result, we messed around with snow all winter long, until at times the marrow in our bones was chilled. And talk about snow in those days! Mountains of it! Your cattle might be lowing pitifully in the stable, and you could not get to them because heaps of snow blocked your way. It might take a hard morning's work before a tunnel could be dug to the stable, and the cattle fed …

Ours was a life of hard work, misery, and destitution. Things got a little better only after we acquired a yoke of oxen to work with. But when we first got them, we experienced some unhappy and frustrating moments ...

With each day of labor, our poor settlers could see some progress. They now lived in hastily built houses, as everyone was sick and tired of living in damp, smelly root cellars. Although these houses lacked in comfort, there was at least fresh air in them. By now, each settler had dug up a piece of land and owned a few head of cattle and other livestock ...

In the spring, father was able to get some seed wheat. When he finished seeding our tiny, little field, he left home to look for a job again. At home, the family buckled down to clearing, digging, and haying. Mother mowed the hay with a scythe, and we children raked it, carried it home on our backs, and stacked it. We also brought a supply of wood for the winter.

In the meantime, the people from the old country had arrived. This added a touch of brightness to our social life. The newcomers, Mrs. D.F. Stratychuk and Mrs. P. Denys, even helped us to harvest our crop ...

That autumn father's earnings were a little more substantial. He was able to buy another cow and another steer. And he bought me a pair of shoes and material for a skirt. Those shoes meant more to me than any ordinary ones ...

As for their durability, suffice it to say that when one of us girls got married, she handed the shoes down to the younger sister, and the process was repeated until four of us had worn them, each for a few years. And who knows how many more generations those shoes would have survived if it had not been for mother. She got so disgusted with them that she threw them into the stove one day and burned them.

As for my skirt, it was made of the finest quality "silk," the kind used for making overalls. So one can imagine how I looked in that gorgeous costume. But, poor me, I was quite happy with it.

In the wintertime, father used to ask some of his neighbors to give him a hand in threshing his wheat with flails. Once the threshing was done, he had other work to do, such as making a yoke for the oxen and repairing the harrow and the plow, so that everything would be ready for spring work ...

In our neighborhood, there were settlers of other nationalities, mainly Rumanian. One of them put on a wedding for his daughter and invited us to attend. We accepted first because there had not been such an event in the few years that we had been in Canada, and second, out of simple curiosity to see a Rumanian ceremony ...

The town of Canora was founded five miles from our place. Our people were quite happy about that, and they were happy when its first store was opened by a Jewish merchant. For one thing, we were fed up with traveling all that distance to Yorkton to do our shopping. Secondly, with a Jew we could always speak in our own language, for at that time how many of us immigrants could speak English? When we did try, it was only by means of sign language ...

Year by year the cultivated area of our farm grew in size. And when the field got too large to be harvested with sickles, father had to buy a binder. For the first couple of years we used it, we hitched our oxen to it. That was a miserable experience. Cutting grain of medium height posed no problem, but if it was heavy or lying flat and you had to give the binder a little more speed, you could not make the oxen move faster even by lighting a fire under them. They kept to the same slow pace no matter what. The only way to cope with this problem was to buy another horse. A team of horses made harvesting so much easier.

During the long winter evenings, I taught younger children to read in Ukrainian. Among my students were a girl [of] non-Ukrainian descent and an elderly gentleman. There were no schools anywhere around in those days. Children grew up like barbarians ...

We had quite a few books at home. Father had brought a lot of them from the old country, all on serious subjects. Later on, when Ukrainian newspapers began to be published, none of them escaped father's attention. Even if he had to go without food and live on water for a whole week, he found the money for newspaper subscriptions. Since there were several literate people in our community, they used to get together at our home on the long winter evenings, to read the papers and discuss their contents. Many a sunrise found these men, though weary from the previous day's hard toil, going without a wink of sleep to forge a happier lot for themselves and their children.

Those sleepless nights were not spent in vain. In 1904-05, thanks to the efforts of our pioneer fathers, a small but beautiful school was built. Its first teacher was the scholarly and patriotic Ukrainian, the late Joseph Bychynsky ...

As for churches or Ukrainian priests, you could not have found one if you'd searched the country with a fine-tooth comb. Occasionally a priest would stray our way, but he was what we called an "Indian priest," and we could not understand him, nor he us. Our poor settlers consulted among themselves and decided to meet every Sunday and sing at least those parts of the liturgy that were meant to be sung by the cantor. Since our house was large enough, that was where the meetings were held. On Sunday morning, everyone hurried to our house the way one would to church ...

In due course, the Bukovinians built themselves a church in which services were at first conducted by a visiting Russian priest. Often we were invited to attend but we could not understand their service, which was in Rumanian ...

That year Easter came very early. It was the Saturday before Easter, but only here and there was the snow beginning to melt. The day before, a severe blizzard had piled up banks of snow and drifted over all the roads. But there was no power on earth which could have stopped us from carrying out our plans ...

Whatever the course of later events, it must be recognized that, in the beginning, the pioneer priests contributed a great deal to the cultural development of our people here, in what was then a foreign land to them. And for their efforts and troubles, they sought no favors from anyone. They suffered the same woes and miseries as did everyone else. In short, they proved themselves to be true sons of the Ukrainian people ...

In those days, no one dreamed of such luxuries as paint or lime. For whitewashing jobs, people used a kind of ash-gray clay found under the surface of the ground cover in swampy areas. They dug this clay, pressed it into flat cakes, and dried it. Dissolved in water, it was used for whitewashing.

Bitter and unenviable were our beginnings, but by hard work and with God's help, we gradually got established. Not very far from our place a few neighbors pooled their resources and bought a steam threshing outfit in partnership. Father decided it was time, we, too, had our threshing done by a threshing machine ...

In 1908, father traded farms with an Englishman, and our family moved thirty miles farther north, to the Hyas district ...

By moving to Hyas, we had to start all over again and suffer the same hardships as in the beginning. But hope of better times lifted our spirits and gave us courage and strength to face future labors.

Such were the tremendous hardships our people had to endure in the early days of immigration. Since there were as yet no railways, they were compelled to travel hundreds of miles on foot. Toiling in cold and hunger, they cleared the forests, [cleaned] the land of rocks, and converted the inaccesible areas into fertile fields. Many of the pioneers who came here in the prime of their lives are no longer with us. Those who are still with us are stooped with age; tomorrow it will be their turn to leave us for their eternal rest ...

C) Conditions of Life for Women in Canada, 1913
Georgina Binnie-Clark

In the present phase of the development of Canada, the immigration of English women is a matter of vital importance to the Canadian race, and bound to affect Canada in her future career among nations.

To-day the great need of the North-West is the need of the service and the influence of woman. Nevertheless, hitherto in its programme of invitation to the English emigrant, the Canadian department of immigration has offered very little inducement to Englishwomen to emigrate to Canada.

It gives a definite promise of adequately remunerative occupation to those women who are prepared to accept such work as in England we are accustomed to associate with the duties and the position of the domestic servant; further than this it seems afraid to commit itself. The direct consequence is that in the main, the number of English women who emigrate annually to Canada are drawn from the ranks of women employed over here in domestic service, or from those women of the cultured classes who have no choice left, and who accept the alternative of "domestic service" with the grain of bitterness in the heart which does not contribute towards the wisdom of success.

The Canadian department of Immigration has much to learn of the capabilities of the cultured women of Britain; the working gentlewomen of this land have much to learn of the all-round meaning of the term "domestic service" in its relation to Canadian conditions.

It has to be borne in mind that in Canada there are no women of leisure, and that social classification is barred as being baneful to the development, and naturally distasteful to the free and independent spirit of the country. The individual is judged on personal merit as it appears in the light of Canadian opinion; and Canadian opinion so far neither aims to reach lofty height, nor profound depth; its key-note is progress running on the lines of common sense; it has a strong bias towards the liberty of the individual in its intention; in its nature and influence it is wholesome. It is a healthy, strongwilled child of keen intelligence with its eyes fixed, not on the stars, but on the place where the footsteps of To-morrow can catch up with the desire of To-day. Neither fame, name, nor colossal fortune will exempt the individual from this examination under the X-rays of Canadian opinion, nor can the individual be pressed by the accident of circumstance below the just reach of personal force and service ...

No woman should dream of emigrating to Canada unless fortified with the courage of hard work. From their childhood Canadian women are trained to the household work of their own homes, in fact they are born into the enclosure of the beatitude of those who have learned to do things for themselves. A leader of Canadian society would, generally speaking, be highly recommendable as a competent housemaid, a well-trained parlour-maid, and excellent cook, an efficient laundress, and possibly a clever dressmaker, in any household of any country; in the housewife's battle of the daily round and common task, the palm of victory seems to me to be indisputably in the hands of the Canadian woman; yet she is never the bond-slave of her domestic concern, but contrives to combine the roles of Martha and Mary with ease as well as generosity.

What then will be the natural attitude of the Canadian employer towards an English working woman, gentle or simple, accepting a post in her household with the responsibility of domestic service? Firstly and always, she will be unfeignedly glad to see her. Canadian women seldom love their tasks so well that they do not prefer to share them with another; besides, they are naturally sociable and kind-hearted. Secondly, she will be her critic from every point of the daily round — nothing will escape her observation or her intuition in domestic detail. She is generous in her admiration of the intellectual gifts and graces, and has a fine appreciation of the advantages and acquirements of women brought up in an European environment; but she also has scorn for the frequent helplessness of the cultured woman in the duties of the daily round. She will be no mocker of the mistakes of her imported help; on the contrary, she is always rather pleased to teach and to help; but she is by nature entirely frank, and can be merciless to the slightest symptom of martyrdom.

Apart from the obligation of her service, the domestic help will, generally speaking, take her place as a member of the family, in the city or on the farm. From the social point of view the English are looked upon as an acquisition in Canada; the "help" will always take part in such public amusements as occur in the district of her employers, and will usually be included in any invitations which fall to their lot. I spent my first winter in the home of an Englishman who had married a Canadian woman; occasionally she launched out into the — in Canada — rare form of entertainment — a dinner party. Everything was prepared as far as possible beforehand, but in a meal of several courses some small culinary attention is always required before each. The English help was present in her evening gown, and changed the meats and the plates without a tinge of self consciousness, assisted by the English youth, also in orthodox evening dress, who at the time was earning his winter's keep in exchange for such duties as wood-chopping, stable-work, water-hauling, stove attendance, and occasional aid at the washing machine. He, by the way, was the son of an English clergyman, and his brothers were officers in the British army and navy.

What I would endeavour to make quite clear is that the ultimatum of "domestic service" need prevent no woman of refinement from emigrating to Canada. On the contrary, it is an excellent position from which to feel the pulse of the new country, whilst watching for opportunity. The English gentlewoman need never fear to accept service in a Canadian household because of its circumstances; but she does need to consider it most carefully and conscientiously, from the point of her own efficiency to fulfil the tasks of the daily round. These duties are reduced in Canada through the simple manner of living, and also by those many ingenious devices curtailing and facilitating human labour, which naturally occur to the mind of man and woman in a country where human labour is the most expensive item in the market; but, as an English girl, who had turned her back on blanket-washing once remarked to me, "It is not that they expect an extraordinary amount of work of you, but they expect the most ordinary thing to be so extraordinarily well done."

I have dwelt on domestic service as it is the one calling which directly or indirectly concerns all immigrants; but there are openings for all sorts and conditions of women workers in Canada, if only they will resign themselves to accept domestic service until their vision is accustomed to the new environment where opportunity lurks on every side. There is room for school-teachers, stenographers, landscape-gardeners, vegetable and fruit gardeners, trained nurses, dressmakers, milliners, shop assistants, buyers, but efficiency is the watchword in the female labour market of Canada, and they love it stamped with the hall-mark of a certificate. A Canadian journalist was talking over some Englishwomen to me, who as Canadian immigrants had proved failures. She mentioned among others a girl to whom she, with others, had shown help and kindness. She said the girl had come over with the idea to teach dancing and drill. "Where is your diploma?" demanded my friend. "And would you believe it," she added, "that girl expected to come out here and induce Canadians to pay her to teach their children to dance without a diploma!"

I find among Englishwomen, whose experience of the conditions and nature of women should give weight to their judgment, a strong tendency to sympathise with the complaint of the married woman on the prairie. It seems to centre in the lack of congenial society, aggravated by the incessant toil attached to unfamiliar household duties, and the general superstition that comfort and refinement are impossible within severe climatic conditions. Those household duties are difficult, and the bitter side of them seems to be in the fact that the Canadian woman of refinement will get through them so easily and beautifully, that she doesn't appear to work at all; but the woman of average intelligence and resource need not be uncomfortable in Canada. Comfort is a positive instinct with Canadians, but to be comfortable in a country of severe climatic conditions one must get on to that country's lines of comfort. For instance, an open British grate with a scarlet fire from British coal warms the heart; a few home-cut logs in the cheapest of Canadian stoves will warm one's back, even though there be an inch of ice on the window-pane, which for some reason or another the English settler may have omitted to protect with storm-windows. It is the custom to furnish modern and orthodox Canadian houses with a furnace, and, by means of pipe and register, its heat is evenly diffused throughout the building; but in the drawing rooms of the English and of many Canadians there is also an open grate with the heart-warming fire on the hearth "for remembrance."

One view of the complaint I cannot share is that the condition of isolation, now less generally attached to prairie life, owing to the rapid development of the railways, should be so much harder for the woman of refined and cultured tastes and accomplishments, than for her fellow-countrywoman, who has been brought up to all sorts and conditions of domestic work. It is our good fortune to have been born in the era of the intellectual emancipation of woman. Within certain conditions of wealth and early training, every opportunity is now offered to woman for her advance in knowledge and in taste. Are we to possess the royal advantage of life as a weapon, or merely as a defence against the intrusion of the undesired? Is advance in knowledge and taste to mean the fence of exclusion, or the gateway of expansion — hindrance or help? I think if one has really found the courage of life in the wisdom of knowledge and treasures of taste, in which it is our special privilege to be environed in Europe, it will not desert us on the prairie which some have named the wilderness. On the contrary, whether it be in the preparation of those three commonplace meals for hungry toilers, or the Monday morning warfare of the washing machine, the wrestle with the understanding of the nature of a plough in the turning of furrows; whether it be gathering the standing grain into the sheaf with the binder-reaper, or the harder work of gathering the sheaves into stook; if one has truly lived by the inspiration of the ideal in Europe, it stands by with the strength or sweetness of the moment, to overcome the difficulties of the daily round in Canada, in the home or on the land. In the nature of humankind mind is the propeller; the woman of trained hands may know better what to do, but the woman of trained mental power ought to know better how to do without.

During the working months the wife of a Canadian farmer should have breakfast served at six o'clock, five is the better hour, because it will allow for a long rest for man and beast during the mid-day heat. The men are supposed to be on the land for five hours, and to return to the house for a twelve o'clock meal of meat and vegetables, with pie or pudding. The greater part of the household duties can be accomplished in the morning, so that between the mid-day meal and six o'clock supper, which usually consists of cold meat and potatoes, with cakes and preserves, or stewed fruit, there is ample time for rest and recreation. After the evening meal the milk must be set, and the wants of the stock supplied, but by eight o'clock one's time should be one's own again. There will be extra men during the harvest, but as a rule they bring their own rugs and blankets and sleep in a granary, so it is merely a matter of extra cooking. During the thrashing-season there is usually a party of from eighteen to twenty men, and if weather is bad and operations cease, they may be one's guests for several days. They justly expect to be well fed, not only with plenty of beef, but Canadian women have spoilt them with a wide choice of the excellent confectionery for which they are famed. I saw that they had the best of meat and as much as they cared for, with a plentiful supply of stewed fruit, scones, potatoes and bread and butter, but my finest tribute has never scored a higher point than excellent intentions. In winter, work on the land ceases with "freeze-up"; the farmer has little to do beyond cleaning the stable, feeding stock, and hauling his grain to the nearest wheat-market. The small farmer seldom keeps hired men round during the winter, so that his wife will probably be left alone during wheat-hauling days. This fact has to be faced. I have known women who cannot face it.

The true sportswoman will neither be dull nor bored on the prairie; riding, driving, shooting, wolf-hunting, skating, snow-shoeing are within the reach of all. The woman with a business instinct has a fine point of vantage on her husband's farm, because grain is all over the place, and eggs and poultry command a ready sale and good prices in the railway towns; and even in new settlements there are always many bachelors, thankful for the chance of purchasing bread, butter, eggs and household commodities of all kinds. Hog-raising and bacon-curing are also fine sources of wealth on a Canadian farm. Many women have paved the way of husbands through the dark wilderness of bad wheat seasons with contributions from such profitable, although frequently neglected, sources of wealth.

I think none has ever heard of the complaint of a child on the Canadian prairie; it is the happiest nursery in the world. All young things, babies, beasts, birds and buds seem to adore life and each other; and if when school-time comes, mothers are inclined to think wistfully of the attractive training ground of our English public schools — the wheat of the wilderness, the oats and the barley, the pigs and the poultry will also contribute to the realisation of that desire of the heart, if they are given a real chance. In any case the education provided for every child within the Dominion by the Government is sound and thorough, sufficient to insure the state against that bitter reproach of its child prophesied by Emerson in his claim for the national right to mental training; "This which I might do is made hopeless through my want of weapons."

To the sincerely exclusive, and I think everyone has sympathy with sincerity in any form, the entertainment of gossip is seldom available in Canadian farm life, nor can one for obvious reasons find solace in the attraction of charming frocks and luxurious surroundings which avail in Europe. Good gossip, charming frocks, and delightful surroundings *are* among the joys, and within the inspiration of life; but if one feels that they are indispensable to content, that the new life cannot offer sufficient compensation for the surrendered delights of the old, it is not wise to decide that one's years of youth and vigour shall be spent on a Canadian farm. None can tell how immeasurably a woman's help and influence can contribute to a man's welfare amid the stress of his early wrestle with new conditions, but it seems to me that the spirit of true comradeship is an essential condition to the happiness of married people, in the more or less isolated and always active life on the prairie. By a comrade, I mean the one who, visible or invisible, is always at the other end of the load. We are not all endowed with this fine quality of enduring sympathy, and it is still within the wisdom of love to refuse to become a married woman on the prairie ...

5

"Our Rightful Place"
Continentalism, Imperialism, or Nationalism

DOCUMENTS

A) Canada and the Canadian Question, 1891
   Goldwin Smith
B) On Imperial Federation, 1889
   George M. Grant
C) The French Canadian in the British Empire, 1902
   Henri Bourassa
D) Canadian Nationality: A Present-day Plea, 1880
   William Norris

M any British North Americans expressed reservations about Confederation when it occurred in 1867; this skepticism developing into hostility in some quarters by the 1880s. It was a time of profound and anxious soul-searching as the fledgling nation haltingly staggered toward the twentieth century. Macdonald's "National Policy" created neither a sense of national unity nor a sustained prosperity. Separatism in Quebec now percolated with a vigour threatening to boil over, especially in the face of those clamouring for closer British ties. In Nova Scotia, the long simmering anti-Confederationist sentiment in the legislature boiled into a resolution favouring secession. Federally, the Liberals touted free trade with America as the nation's best course through the muddy shoals of early nationhood. Imperialists countered by championing the British Empire as the sole bulwark against total absorption by aggressive Yankees to the south. Fervid Loyalist descendants, ultra-Protestant Orange Order members, many teachers and lawyers, and others clung fiercely to the Union Jack through organizations such as the Imperial Federation League.

The furore over Canada's future reached far beyond the domain of traditional political hacks, journalistic pundits, the socio-political elite, malcontents, and special interest groups. It became, in fact, a popular topic among ordinary Canadians in everyday parlours, shops, and offices. Even writers like Sara Duncan joined the fray with her popular and perceptive novel depicting small-town Ontario, *The Imperialist* (1904). The nation's future was at stake, and that involved everyone.

Born into a prosperous English family, Goldwin Smith (1823–1910) followed a typical trajectory for a bright young man of his class: school at Eton, then on to Oxford to study classics, and finally law. He accepted an appointment as professor of modern history at Oxford in 1858 rather than a call to the bar, but contemporary issues remained his chief interest. Family tragedy cut short this seemingly blissful life, forcing his resignation and departure from England. He taught briefly at Cornell University in New York before moving to Toronto where he settled into married life with his new and very wealthy wife. Smith published hundreds of articles in newspapers, magazines, and journals, and had an opinion on everything from public morality to women's rights. He was anti-Semitic, and his virulent anti-Catholicism buttressed his view that French Canadians were "unprogressive" obstacles to national unity. Even so, Smith earned a reputation as one of Canada's intellectual leaders. He became president of the Ontario Teachers Federation and sat on the board of the University of Toronto. His book, *Canada and the Canadian Question*, remains one of the most challenging critiques of Canada.

Of course, Smith had his critics, none better than the brilliant George M. Grant (1835–1902). Born into a poor Gaelic-speaking Nova Scotian family of Scottish descent, Grant struggled against the odds to gain a graduate degree from the University of Glasgow, after which he put his devout Presbyterianism to work as a missionary in Scottish slums. He returned to Nova Scotia as a preacher in 1861. Unlike Smith, Grant remained optimistic about Canada's future. In his mind, Canada would emerge as one of the most populated and powerful nations, its civic spirit united by a single national church that would overcome traditional linguistic, cultural, and geographical cleavages. Thus it is hardly surprising that he championed Confederation, one of the few Nova Scotians to do so, and found the chronic carping over the material disadvantages of Confederation repugnant and beneath contempt. Membership in the "divinely inspired" British Empire, Grant believed, offered Canada the finest concept of freedom, and he did not see any contradiction between Canada's status as a nation and its participation in the Empire.

Grant taught divinity at Queen's College, and as principal, transformed it into one of Canada's foremost educational institutions. Progressive in many ways, he favoured universal education for women, and supported aboriginal rights.

Henri Bourassa (1868–1952) was the grandson of Louis Joseph Papineau, one of French Canada's greatest 19th-century political reformers. Bourassa entered the House of Commons as a Liberal in 1896. A man of unyielding principles who was ever suspicious of Canada's relationship with Britain, he quit the party after Prime Minister Laurier sent a contingent of Canadians to fight alongside Britain against the Boers. South Africa, he contended, was not Canada's fight. He re-entered the political arena in 1908, this time in the Quebec legislature, but in 1925 shifted back to the federal scene. Bourassa, along with a number of other young compatriots, founded the "Nationalist League" in 1903, using it as a vehicle for French Canadian rights. He is perhaps best known as the influential editor of the newspaper *Le Devoir*, which he founded in 1910. Opposed to most imperialists who viewed French Canadians as, at best, quaint anachronisms, Bourassa saw them as the only true Canadian nationalists.

Historians know little of William Norris except that he was a journalist with political ambitions.

A) Canada and the Canadian Question, 1891
Goldwin Smith

Whether the four blocks of territory constituting the Dominion can for ever be kept by political agencies united among themselves and separate from their Continent, of which geographically, economically, and with the exception of Quebec ethnologically, they are parts, is the Canadian question …

Let those who prophesy to us smooth things take stock of the facts. When one community differs from another in race, language, religion, character, spirit, social structure, aspirations, occupying also a territory apart, it is a separate nation, and is morally certain to pursue a different course, let it designate itself as it can. French Canada may be ultimately absorbed in the English-speaking population of a vast Continent; amalgamate with British Canada so as to form a united nation it apparently never can …

From British as well as from French Canada there is a constant flow of emigration to the richer country, and the great centres of employment. Dakota and the other new States of the American West are full of Canadian farmers; the great American cities are full of Canadian clerks and men of business, who usually make for themselves a good name. It is said that in Chicago there are 25,000. Hundreds of thousands of Canadians have relatives in the United States. Canadians in great numbers — it is believed as many as 40,000 — enlisted in the American army during the civil war ... A young Canadian thinks no more of going to push his fortune in New York or Chicago than a young Scotchman thinks of going to Manchester or London. The same is the case in the higher callings as in the lower: clergymen, those of the Church of England as well as those of other churches, freely accept calls to the other side of the Line. So do professors, teachers, and journalists. The Canadian churches are in full communion with their American sisters, and send delegates to each other's Assemblies. Cadets educated at a Military College to command the Canadian army against the Americans, have gone to practise as Civil Engineers in the United States. The Benevolent and National Societies have branches on both sides of the Line, and hold conventions in common. Even the Orange Order has now its lodges in the United States, where the name of President is substituted in the oath for that of the Queen. American labour organizations ... extend to Canada. The American Science Association met the other day at Toronto. All the reforming and philanthropic movements, such as the Temperance movement, the Women's Rights' movement, and the Labour movements, with their conventions, are continental. Intermarriages between Canadians and Americans are numerous, so numerous as scarcely to be remarked. Americans are the chief owners of Canadian mines, and large owners of Canadian timber limits. The railway system of the continent is one. The winter ports of Canada are those of the United States. Canadian banks trade largely in the American market, and some have branches there. There is almost a currency union, American bank-bills commonly passing at par in Ontario, while those of remote Canadian Provinces pass at par only by special arrangement. American gold passes at par, while silver coin is taken at a small discount: in Winnipeg even the American nickel is part of the common currency. The Dominion bank-bills, though payable in gold, are but half convertible, because what the Canadian banks want is not British but American gold. Canadians go to the American watering-places, while Americans pass the summer on Canadian lakes. Canadians take American periodicals, to which Canadian writers often contribute. They resort for special purchases to New York stores, or even those of the Border cities. Sports are international; so are the Base Ball organisations; and the Toronto "Nine" is recruited in the States. All the New-World phrases and habits are the same on both sides of the Line. The two sections of the English-speaking race on the American continent, in short, are in a state of economic, intellectual, and social fusion, daily becoming more complete. Saving the special connection of a limited circle with the Old Country, Ontario is an American State of the Northern type, cut off from its sisters by a customs line, under a separate government and flag ...

The isolation of the different Canadian markets from each other, and the incompatibility of their interests, add in their case to the evils and absurdities of the protective system. What is meat to one Province is, even on the protectionist hypothesis, poison to another. Ontario was to be forced to manufacture; she has no coal; yet to reconcile Nova Scotia to the tariff a coal duty was imposed; in vain, for Ontario after all continued to import her coal from Pennsylvania. Manitoba and the North-West produced no fruit; yet they were compelled to pay a duty in order to protect the fruit-grower of Ontario 1500 miles away. Hardest of all was the lot of the North-West farmer. His natural market, wherein to buy farm implements, was in the neighbouring cities of the United States, where, moreover, implements were made most suitable to the prairie. But to force him to buy in Eastern Canada 25 per cent was laid on farm implements. As he still bought in the States, the 25 per cent was made 35 per cent ...

Without commercial intercourse or fusion of population, the unity produced by a mere political arrangement can hardly be strong or deep ...

The thread of political connection is wearing thin. This England sees, and the consequence is a recoil which has produced a movement in favour of Imperial Federation. It is proposed not only to arrest the process of gradual emancipation, but to reverse it and to reabsorb the colonies into the unity of the Empire. No definite plan has been propounded, indeed, any demand for a plan is deprecated, and we are adjured to embrace the principle of the scheme and leave the details for future revelation — to which we must answer that the principle of a scheme is its object, and that it is impossible to determine whether the object is practically attainable without a working plan. There is no one in whose eyes the bond between the colonies and the mother country is more precious than it is in mine. Yet I do not hesitate to say that, so far as Canada is concerned, Imperial Federation is a dream. The Canadian people will never part with their self-government. Their tendency is entirely the other way. They have recently ... asserted their fiscal independence, and by instituting a Supreme Court of their own, they have evinced a disposition to withdraw as much as they can of their affairs from the jurisdiction of the Privy Council. Every association, to make it reasonable and lasting, must have some practical object. The practical objects of Imperial Federation would be the maintenance of common armaments and the establishment of a common tariff. But to neither of these, I am persuaded, would Canada ever consent; she would neither contribute to Imperial armaments nor conform to an Imperial tariff. Though her people are brave and hardy, they are not, any more than the people of the United States, military, nor could they be brought to spend their earnings in Asiatic or African wars ... Remember that Canada is only in part British. The commercial and fiscal circumstances of the colony again are as different as possible from those of the mother country ...

Annexation is an ugly word; it seems to convey the idea of force or pressure applied to the smaller State, not of free, equal, and honourable union, like that between England and Scotland. Yet there is no reason why the union of the two sections of the English-speaking people on this Continent should not be as free, as equal, and as honourable as the union of England and Scotland. We should rather say their reunion than their union, for before their unhappy schism they were one people. Nothing but the historical accident of a civil war ending in secession, instead of amnesty, has made them two ...

That a union of Canada with the American Commonwealth, like that into which Scotland entered with England, would in itself be attended with great advantages cannot be questioned, whatever may be the considerations on the other side or the reasons for delay. It would give to the inhabitants of the whole Continent as complete a security for peace and immunity from war taxation as is likely to be attained by any community or group of communities on this side of the Millennium. Canadians almost with one voice say that it would greatly raise the value of property in Canada; in other words, that it would bring with it great increase of prosperity ...

Again, Canadians who heartily accept democracy wish that there should be two experiments in it on this Continent rather than one, and the wish is shared by thoughtful Americans not a few. But we have seen that in reality the two experiments are not being made. Universal suffrage and party government are the same, and their effects are the same in both Republics. Differences there are, such as that between the Presidential and the Cabinet system, of a subordinate kind, yet not unimportant, and such as might make it worthwhile to forego for a time at least the advantages of union, supposing that the dangers and economical evils of separation were not too great, and if the territorial division were not extravagantly at variance with the fiat of Nature. The experiments of political science must be tried with some reference to terrestrial convenience. Besides, those who scan the future without prejudice must see that the political fortunes of the Continent are embarked in the great Republic, and that Canada will best promote her own ultimate interests by contributing without unnecessary delay all that she has in the way of political character and force towards the saving of the main chance and the fulfilment of the common hope. The native American element in which the tradition of self-government resides is hard pressed by the foreign element untrained to self-government, and stands in need of the reinforcement which the entrance of Canada into the Union would bring it ...

In the present case there are, on one side, geography, commerce, identity of race, language, and institutions, which with the mingling of population and constant intercourse of every kind, acting in ever-increasing intensity, have brought about a general fusion, leaving no barriers standing but the political and fiscal lines. On the other side, there is British and Imperial sentiment, which, however, is confined to the British, excluding the French and Irish and other nationalities, and even among the British is livelier as a rule among the cultivated and those whose minds are steeped in history than among those who are working for their bread; while to set against it there is the idea, which can hardly fail to make way, of a great continent with an almost unlimited range of production forming the home of a united people, shutting out war and presenting the field as it would seem for a new and happier development of humanity ...

B) On Imperial Federation, 1889
George M. Grant

Imperial Federation, from a Canadian point of view, means simply the next act in a process of political and historical development that began in 1763, when Canada — with the consent of all parties concerned — was declared to be British. From that day, the development of Canada from the position of a British colony into that of a British nationality has gone on steadily. The colonial condition is one of incomplete political development, and Canada has passed through various stages, each of which marks a greater measure of self-government than the previous stage. The various Acts in the drama are indicated by successive civil conflicts always ending in constitutional changes that widened our liberties or by struggles against external enemies and influences that sought to interfere with our legitimate development. The making of Canada into a nation has been a long process, and the process is not yet ended. But to those who complain of the length of time, I would ask them to give an example of a nation or a tree that has been made in a day. Mushrooms grow in a night, but not cedars of Lebanon. It took Germany and Italy centuries to grow into their present stately strength and unity. The making of France and Britain into nations was in each case a long process. The United States of America — with all their immense advantages and with the aid of nineteenth century methods and speed — did not attain to that condition of stable political equilibrium which ensures permanence and prosperity till 1865, or almost a hundred years after their secession from Britain. With us the process of making Canada into a nation must end in one or other of two ways: — either clothing Canadians in a legitimate share in the supreme rights, privileges and responsibilities of the Empire to which they belong, that is in full citizenship, or in a Revolution which means the gradual disintegration or violent breaking up of the British Empire. Canada cannot continue long a mere dependency. Clearly, that is impossible. No living organism can continue long in a condition of arrested development. It must grow to its full stature or petrify. Even dwarfing means death. Besides, who wants to belong to a nation of dwarfs?

This brief sketch prepares us for a definition. Imperial Federation, then, may be defined as a union between the Mother Country and Canada that would give to Canada not only the present full management of its own affairs, but a fair share in the management and responsibilities of common affairs. As British citizens, ought we to ask for more? As Canadians and full-grown men, ought we to be satisfied with less?

In the meanwhile the object of the Imperial Federation League is to form branches all over Canada to discuss the question from every point of view, with the confident expectation that in due time our Parliament will feel itself warranted by public opinion to instruct the Government of the day to enter into negotiations with the British Government on the subject. Then will be the time to draw up a scheme.

Before forming a branch of the league, all that is necessary is that a number of people in the locality should have two principles rooted and grounded in them: 1. that Britain and Canada must continue to have one flag, in other words that the present union must be maintained; 2. that Canadians are prepared for full citizenship, in other words that they are determined to be the peers and not the dependents of their fellow-citizens in the British Islands. As to the particular form in which the movement may take shape, eventually, we are quite indifferent. We welcome the production of plans and of criticism on them, but we are committed to no scheme ...

... "What are the objections to Imperial Federation?"

It will not be necessary to dwell on the important objections that have been mentioned in some influential organs of public opinion — ... the objection that some vigorous writers have called Imperial Federation a fad. I may, however, note other arguments:

(a) It is said that "Imperial Federation would involve us in foreign relations." We are so involved already, from the fact every nation has neighbours, and that we in particular are a trading people; only, at present, we are without a voice as regards these relations. "We might be involved in European politics." We are so involved already, from the fact of our being united to Britain, only we cannot use any constitutional influence to detach the Empire from what is of less importance to what is of greater importance, from the affairs of Europe to the interests of an ever expanding Colonial Empire.

(b) "We might be involved in war." We may at any day now without our permission being asked. Ought we not to be in a position to give our voice for peace? Remember that democracy now rules in England, that its great interest is peace, and that we ought to reinforce it against any influence that might make for war. Ought we not to contribute our share towards securing the peace of the empire and even the peace of the world, instead of being selfishly satisfied that we ourselves are out of reach of war?

(c) "There would be expense." I have pointed out that Imperial Federation is simply the full development of self-government. Now, it is quite true that every development of self-government has brought with it additional expenses but would we on that account have been better off under tutelage or bondage? A Crown colony has usually little debt. In the old days of an irresponsible executive the debt of Canada was nominal. Now, our debt has attained to figures that are quite respectable. But, would we therefore go back to the old family compact regime? The sensible question to put is this: Are there corresponding advantages to the increase of expense? As regards the debt of Canada, no doubt mistakes have been made. Governments are not always wise and Government works are perhaps built and managed less economically than works under private management. But on the whole, we believe that we have got our money's worth and that no greater mistakes have been made in Canada than in other countries.

(d) "Our interests are different." Against whom, I ask. Not against enemies, for two are stronger than one. Canada and Britain must be stronger than either by itself. Not as against each other, for in almost every respect we are complementary ...

(e) "We would have little influence in the Federation." Well, in the first place, we would have more than we have now. We have none at all now, except that which is indirect and conceded by the generosity of Britain. We deserve to have none, for we have not shown that we value it, except by newspaper clamour when the inconvenience of our position is felt. It is humiliating to read articles in our papers calling on Britain to send *her* ships, for instance to Behring's Sea. I do not undertake to say whether ships of war should be sent there from Esquimault or not; but until we are able to change the pronoun and use the phrase *our* ships, we should have the grace to keep silent. Oh, but you say, think of the expense if we undertook to bear a share of the cost of the Imperial navy. Certainly, but if we go in for Independence, we shall have to build our own ships. Which will be the heavier burden, to build them at our own cost or in conjunction with the wealthiest Empire in the world? Again, if we go in for Annexation, we shall have to pay not only our share of the United States fleet, but our share of the pension fund. That of itself would be seven or eight millions a year, as the total is ninety millions — a good deal more, that one item, than our share in the British-Canadian fleet! Two or three years ago a Montreal newspaper made out that our connection with the Mother Country was only nominal, but when neighbours began to bully us for protecting our fisheries and to threaten war, the same paper pointed out that we were an integral part of the Empire, and that at the first movement in the direction of war the British fleet would destroy all the coastal cities of the United States. When the President threatened non-intercourse, the same paper pointed out clearly that he could not discriminate between one part of the Empire and another, and that non-intercourse with us meant commercial war with Great Britain too. In other words, the present union is nominal when it suits us, and real when it suits us. We run with the hare and hunt with the hounds. There is not much dignity in such a position. It has hardly the merit of impudence. It is simply childish. Is it too much to ask the gentlemen of the press who discuss this question to calmly consider these two questions: Ought we to ask for the service of a fleet for which we do not pay a cent? and is it not our right to ask for a share in the direction of the fleet which protects our coasts and our commerce? ...

The Empire to which we belong is admittedly the greatest the world has ever seen. In it, the rights of all men are sacred and the rights of the great men are also sacred. It is world-wide and therefore offers most opportunities for all kinds of noblest service to humanity, through the serving of fellow-citizens in every quarter of the globe. Let Canada ask for some emblem — let it be maple leaf or beaver — to represent it on the flag that represents so marvellous a past and present. Is it to be thought that we would separate from such a flag without cause, still less place our country in a position of antagonism to it? Think what it has always represented — personal and national freedom; civil and commercial, intellectual and religious freedom; righteousness in private and public affairs and the proclamation of eternal life to every son of Adam ...

What do I mean by our rightful place in the history of the world? This, to be the link shall bind into a world-wide brotherhood, into a moral — it may even be a political — unity the mother of nations and all her children, the great daughter in the south of us as well as the youngest born of the family. Mark it well, an independent Canada is out of the question. The days of small nations are over forever. Of the few great nations of the future the English-speaking people is destined if we are only true to ourselves, to be the greatest, simply because it represents most fully the highest political and spiritual life that humanity has yet realized. Break up the British Empire, and what prospect is there of a worthy place in history for any — even the greatest — of the parts? Bind the Empire into unity and we shall have solved the problem that Spain and her Colonies could not solve, though two centuries ago the future of the world seemed bound up with them. We have to choose between our rightful place in history or absorption, or a position somewhat like that of a South American Republic. Take your choice.

C) The French Canadian in the British Empire, 1902
Henri Bourassa

The present feeling of the French-Canadian is one of contentment. He is satisfied with his lot. He is anxious to preserve his liberty and his peace ... Upon any proposed modification of the constitutional system of Canada he is disposed to look with distrust, or at least with anxiety. He cannot forget that all changes in the past were directed against him, except those that were enacted under such peculiar circumstances as made it imperative for the British Government to conciliate him. He asks for no change — for a long time to come, at least. And should any change be contemplated, he is prepared to view it, to appreciate its prospective advantages and inconveniences, neither from a British point of view nor from his own racial standpoint, but to approach the problem as it may affect the exclusive interests of Canada. He has loyally accepted the present constitution; he has done his ample share of duty by the country; and he feels that he is entitled to be consulted before any change is effected.

How thoroughly and exclusively Canadian the French-Canadian is should never be forgotten by those who contemplate any change in the constitutional or national status of Canada. This is so patent a fact, so logical a consequence of historical developments, that nothing short of absolute ignorance or wilful blindness can justify the language of those who talk of drawing him either by persuasion or by force to a closer allegiance to the Empire. As a matter of fact, he constitutes the only exclusively Canadian racial group in the Dominion. A constant immigration from the British Isles has kept the English-speaking Canadians in close contact with their motherland; so that even now they still speak of the "Old Country" as their "home," thus keeping in their hearts a double allegiance. On the soil of Canada, his only home and country, all the national aspirations of the French-Canadian are concentrated. "Canadian" is the only national designation he ever claims; and when he calls himself "French-Canadian," he simply wants to differentiate his racial origin from that of his English, Scotch, or Irish fellow citizen, who, in his mind, are but partially *Canadianised.*

When he is told that Canada is a British country, and that he must abide by the will of the British majority, he replies that Canada has remained British through his own loyalty; that when his race constituted the overwhelming majority of the Canadian people, Canada was twice saved to the British Crown, thanks to him and to him only; that he has remained faithful to Great Britain because he was assured of certain rights and privileges; that his English-speaking fellow citizens have accepted the compact and should not now take advantage of their greater numerical strength to break the agreement; that when settling in Canada, newcomers from the British kingdom should understand that they become citizens of Canada, of a Confederacy where he has vested rights, and should not undertake to make the country and its people more British than Canadian ...

Independence is to his mind the most natural outcome of the ultimate destinies of Canada. But so long as the present ties are not strengthened he is in no hurry to sever British connection. He realises that time cannot but work in favour of Canada by bringing to her population and wealth, and that the later she starts on her own course the safer the journey ...

Now, apart from his instinctive reluctance to contemplate any political evolution, what are the feelings of the French-Canadian with regard to Imperial Federation or any form of British Imperialism?

First, as may be naturally expected, sentimental arguments in favour of British Imperialism cannot have any hold upon him. To his reason only must appeals on this ground be made. That the new Imperial policy will bring him, and Canada at large, advantages that will not be paid by any infringement on his long-struggled-for liberty, he must be clearly shown.

Towards Great Britain he knows that he has a duty of allegiance to perform. But he understands that duty to be what it has been so far, and nothing more. He has easily and generously forgotten the persecutions of the earlier and larger part of his national life under the British Crown. He is willing to acknowledge the good treatment which he has received later on, though he cannot forget that his own tenacity and the neighbourhood of the United States have had much to do with the improvement of his situation.

In short, his affection for Great Britain is one of reason, mixed with a certain amount of esteem and suspicion, the proportions of which vary according to time and circumstances, and also with his education, his temperament, and his social surroundings.

Towards the Empire he has no feelings whatever; and naturally so. The blood connection and the pride in Imperial power and glory having no claims upon him, what sentiment can he be expected to entertain for New Zealand or Australia, South Africa or India, for countries and populations entirely foreign to him, with which he has no relations, intellectual or political, and much less commercial intercourse than he has with the United States, France, Germany, or Belgium?

By the motherland he feels that he has done his full duty; by the Empire he does not feel that he has any duty to perform. He makes full allowance for the blood feelings of his English-speaking partner; but having himself, in the past, sacrificed much of his racial tendencies for the sake of Canadian unity, he thinks that the Anglo-Canadian should be prepared to study the problems of Imperialism from a purely Canadian standpoint. Moreover, this absence of racial feelings from his heart allows him to judge more impartially the question of the relations between Canada and the Empire.

He fully realises the benefits that Canada derives from her connection with a wealthy and mighty nation. He is satisfied with having the use of the British market. But this advantage he knows that Canada enjoys on the very same terms as any other country in the world, even the most inimical to Britain. From a mixed sense of justice and egotism he is less clamorous than the British Canadian in demanding any favour, commercial or other, from the motherland, because he has a notion that any favour received would have to be compensated by at least an equal favour given.

His ambition does not sway him to huge financial operations. Rather given to liberal professions, to agricultural life, or to local mercantile and industrial pursuits, he is more easily satisfied than the English-speaking Canadian with a moderate return for his work and efforts. He has been kept out of the frantic display of financial energy, of the feverish concentration of capital, of the international competition of industry, which have drawn his English-speaking fellow citizen to huge combinations of wealth or trade; and therefore, he is not anxious to participate in the organisation of the Empire on the basis of a gigantic co-operative association for trade. He would rather see Canada keep the full control of her commercial policy and enter into the best possible trade arrangements with any nation, British or foreign.

He is told that Canada has the free use of British diplomacy, and that such an advantage calls for sacrifices on her part when Britain is in distress. But considered in the light of past events, British diplomacy has, on the contrary, cost a good deal to Canada. So far the foreign relations of Canada, through British mediation, have been almost exclusively confined to America. That the influence and prestige of Great Britain were of great benefit to Canada in her relations with the United States is hardly conspicuous in the various Anglo-American treaties and conventions in which Canadian interests are concerned.

Not only did the American Republic secure the settlement of nearly all her claims according to her pretentions, but Canadian rights have been sacrificed by British plenipotentiaries in compensation for misdeeds or blunders of the British Government ...

It may be argued that all those concessions, made by Great Britain at the expense of Canada, were imposed by circumstances. It may be said also that by those same concessions Canada at large was affected, and that the French-Canadians had no greater cause of complaint than their English-speaking fellow citizens. But that exclusive Canadian sentiment which I have described makes the French-Canadian feel more deeply any encroachment upon the integrity of Canada. Unlike the Anglo-Canadian, he does not find in the glory of Empire a compensation and a solace for the losses suffered by Canada. That he entertains any rancour against Britain on that account would, however, be a false conclusion. For the international intricacies in which Great Britain has been and is still entangled he makes full allowance. With his strong sense of self-government, he does not expect the motherland to endanger her own position on behalf of Canada. But if Great Britain is either unable or unwilling to take risks for the sake of Canadian interests, he does not see why Canada should assume new obligations towards Great Britain and run risks on her behalf.

As far as war and defence are concerned, he is still less disposed to consent to any Imperial combination. First there is that aversion to militarism that I have mentioned. Then he has a notion that all the sacrifices he may make on this ground will be so much that Canada will give without any probable return.

When he turns towards the past, what does he find? He finds that for the hundred and forty years that he has been a British subject, no more than his English-speaking fellow citizen has he ever been the cause, near or distant, of any trouble to Great Britain. Never did Canada involve the Empire in any war or threat of war. But the policy, right or wrong, of the British Government did cause his country to be the battlefield of two Anglo-American struggles. Upon those two occasions Canada was saved to the British Crown, thanks to the loyalty of his own race. During the Secession war, the peace of Canada came very near being disturbed once more, and her territory was threatened with invasion because of the attitude of Great Britain. And if he has been spared this and other bloody contests, it was only by the granting to the United States of such concessions as are referred to above.

So much for the past. When he considers the present and the future, the French-Canadian does not see any reason why he should enter into a scheme of Imperial defence.

The argument that if Canada stands by the Empire, the Empire will stand by Canada, cannot have much weight with him; and his objections on that ground are founded both on past events and on prospective developments. In the South African War he has witnessed an application of the new doctrine. Of the expenditure of that war he has been called upon to pay his share — a small one if compared with that of the British Kingdom, but a large one when it is remembered that he had no interest whatever in the contest, and no control over the policy which preceded the conflict, or over its settlement. Should the principle of military Imperialism predominate, he foresees that he may find himself involved in wars occasioned by friction between Australia and Japan, between New Zealand and Germany, between Great Britain and France in Europe, or between Great Britain and Russia in Asia. He does not see any eventuality in which the Empire may be called upon to help Canada.

He is ready now, as he was in the past, to support a sufficient military force to maintain internal peace and to resist aggression on the territory of Canada. But these eventualities are most unlikely to occur in the near future. The enormous area as well as the vast resources of the country offer such opportunities to the care and activity of its population, that social struggles are almost impossible in Canada for many years to come. Foreign invasion, from the United States excepted, is most improbable. The Canadian territory is easy to defend against attacks on her sea borders, which would offer great difficulties and little benefit to any enemy of the Empire. Moreover, from a purely Canadian standpoint such occurrences are most unlikely to happen. Left to herself Canada has no possible cause of conflict with any other nation but the United States. On the other hand, by entering into a compact for Imperial defence, she may be involved in war with several of the strongest Powers. Therefore, as far as concerns any country outside America, the French-Canadian feels that the scheme of Imperial defence brings upon him new causes of conflict not to be compensated by any probable defensive requirement ...

From all those considerations the French-Canadian concludes that Canada has never been, and never will be, the cause of any display of Imperial strength, with the single exception of a possible encounter with a nation that he is not desirous of attacking, and against which, in his mind, the Empire would be either unwilling or incapable of defending him. He does not therefore feel bound to assume military obligations towards any other part of the Empire.

The stronger Canada grows in population and wealth, the slighter will be the dangers that may threaten her security, and the greater her contribution to the welfare and glory of the Empire. The French-Canadian thinks therefore that the best way in which he can play his part in the building up Empire is not by diverting the healthiest and strongest portion of its population from the pursuits of a peaceful and industrious life and sending them to fight in all parts of the world. He does not believe in fostering in Canada the spirit of militarism. He is only anxious to make his country attractive and prosperous by keeping aloof from all military adventures.

Indifferent as he is to commercial Imperialism, hostile as he is to military Imperialism, the French-Canadian cannot be expected to wish for any organic change in the constitution of Canada and to look favourably upon any scheme of Imperial Federation.

For years he fought to obtain full control of his laws, of his social system, of his public exchequer. With the principles of self-government, of self-taxation, of direct control over the legislative body, no other citizen of the British Empire is more thoroughly imbued than he is. His local organisation, in Church, educational or municipal matters, is still more decentralised and democratic than that of the English provinces of Canada. He likes to exercise his elective franchise and to keep as close as possible to the man, the law and the regulation that he votes for. He cannot view with favour a scheme by which any power that has heretofore been exercised by his own representative bodies may pass under the control of some Council sitting in London.

There remains to be considered the question of annexation to the United States.

As I have stated, left to himself, the French-Canadian is not eager for a change. He requires nothing but quietness and stability in order to grow and develop. He is satisfied with and proud of his Canadian citizenship. But should a change be forced upon him by those who aspire to a greater nationality, he would rather incline towards Pan-Americanism.

For a long time annexation to the United States was most abhorrent to the French-Canadian. In fact, when an agitation in that direction was started by several leading English-speaking Canadians, his resistance proved to be the best safeguard of the British connection. But should his past fidelity be now disregarded, and Canadian autonomy encroached upon in any way, should he be hurried into any Imperial scheme and forced to assume fresh obligations, he would prefer throwing in his lot with his powerful neighbour to the South. His present constitution he prizes far above the American system of Government; but if called upon to sacrifice anything of his Federal autonomy for the working of the Imperial machinery, he would rather do it in favour of the United States system, under which, at all events, he would preserve the self-government of his province. Should Imperial re-organisation be based on trade and financial grounds, he would see a greater future in joining the most powerful industrial nation of the world than in going into partnership with the British communities; and this sentiment is gaining greater force from the present influx of American capital into Canada. The fact that the union of Canada and the United States would bring again under the same flag the two groups, now separated, of his nationality has no doubt greatly contributed towards smoothing his aversion to annexation.

I have so far analysed the sentiments of the higher classes among the French-Canadian people, of those who control their feelings by historical knowledge or by a study of outside circumstances, political, military or financial. If I refer to the masses, mostly composed of farmers, I may say that they entertain similar feelings, but instinctively rather than from reflection. The French-Canadians of the popular class look upon Canada as their own country. They are ready to do their duty by Canada; but considering they owe nothing to Great Britain or any other country, they ask nothing from them. Imbued with a strong sense of liberty, they have no objection to their English-speaking fellow countrymen going to war anywhere they please; but they cannot conceive that Canada as a whole may be forced out of its present situation. They let people talk of any wise and wild proposal of Imperialism; but if any change were attempted to be imposed on them, they would resist the pressure, quietly but constantly.

To sum up, the French-Canadian is decidedly and exclusively Canadian by nationality and American by his ethnical temperament. People with world-wide aspirations may charge him with provincialism. But after all, this sentiment of exclusive attachment to one's land and one's nationality is to be found as one of the essential characteristics of all strong and growing peoples. On the other hand, the lust of abnormal expansion and Imperial pride have ever been the marked features of all nations on the verge of decadence.

D) Canadian Nationality: A Present-day Plea, 1880
William Norris

We are on the eve of startling events. Public opinion in Canada has come to the conclusion that something must be done, or some change made, to meet the crisis that is approaching. Half a continent cannot be settled and peopled by a colony; a nation may plant colonies, a colony never can. The Canadian people have assumed the responsibility of populating the North-West, and they must rise equal to the emergency ...

It is said there are two ways out of the difficulty — Canada must either assume nationality, or join the United States. The first is the legitimate and only solution. Generally speaking, England would never permit annexation, unless forced on her by a long and disastrous war, which would almost destroy Canada, for her soil would be the battle ground of the contending nations. Independence could be obtained without embittering the relations which now exist. But annexation would be no remedy for the evils from which we suffer. Politically, it would only be a change of masters; and, as a means of settling and developing our country, it would be more than doubtful. Indeed, it would be the sure means of killing all our projects. No one can believe that the Americans would build our Pacific Railway to the detriment of their own Northern Pacific and the one already in operation. Neither is it likely that our sea-board would be developed to the injury of Portland, Boston and New York. Hence, annexation would be of no use to further the projects upon which, for good or evil, the Canadian people have set their hearts.

Politically, annexation would surely render Canada tributary to the States. There are those who think, and say, that suitable enactments could be made to secure the liberties of Canada; but no enactments could make a dwarf equal to a giant; and we do not see that enactments, even among Americans themselves, have much force to protect their own people when the supposed interests of one of the parties require that any particular section should be oppressed ... The only valid ground which the advocates of annexation have to stand on, is that the measure would give us access to the markets of the United States — a very dear privilege if it would entail the loss of our liberties — and if this result could be obtained by a means which would not also bring with it the evils of annexation, then their only argument is gone ...

It would seem plain, then, that the present colonial position of Canada prevents her from obtaining a proper reciprocity treaty with the United States, and shuts up the markets of the world to her goods, while giving no possibility of securing any better position for her goods in British markets than that possessed by other countries. It would also seem that independence would enable us to make such a treaty with the United States, and treaties with other countries, as would enable us to gain access to their markets without lessening our present privileges in those of Britain. There is no question that access to these markets, especially to those of our own continent, would be to the great and lasting benefit of Canada: every one is agreed on that.

There is also no doubt that independence would elevate the character and status of our people. It would give Canada a national credit in the money markets of the world, and better enable it to raise money by borrowing, or, by the creation of a national currency, similar to that of the United States, for the purpose of building the Canadian Pacific Railway.

There is one more argument in favour of independence greater than all the others put together. Without population, a great North-West is useless to Canada. So is a Pacific Railway. If there be no one to use the railroad, the money required to build it may as well be thrown into the sea ... Leave Canada in her present condition, and the chief use of a Canadian Pacific Railway will be to carry food to starving Indians, or to serve the Americans. Who will use it? There is not much use of expecting the people of foreign countries to come hither and occupy our lands. Our emigration agents were arrested in Germany a few years ago as frauds and cheats, in trying to get the people to emigrate to a place where they would have no country, as Canada cannot make a British subject, and she has no citizenship of her own. Then look at the statistics of British emigration for the year 1878. One-half of all the people who left the United Kingdom went to the United States, and one-tenth only came to Canada. What else is to be expected? ... We never can expect to retain even our own Canadian population until we can give them the same advantages they can get in the United States — that is, a country with all that a nationality implies and manhood suffrage. As to obtaining the people of the old countries, we must remain content, as long as we are a colony, with the poorer classes of immigrants which charity and paid passages send to our shores.

Apart, however, from the advantages and disadvantages of independence, we must make up our minds to look the inevitable in the face. We have resolved not to cast in our own lot with the Americans, and their continual precarious political condition confirms our resolution. Coming events will surely force us shortly to take up the destiny which every one admits must necessarily ultimately be borne ...

It, therefore, behooves all true Canadians to be prepared for whatever may occur. There is but little to be done. A Governor elected every seven years by both our Houses of Parliament, the appointment of a small diplomatic body, and the adoption of a flag are all that is needful. Surely, a people who have an independent and final Supreme Court is equal to this. The flag may cause some difficulty, but not necessarily. We have the colours already — it is only necessary to place them. The red first, representing Englishmen and Scotchmen; the white, representing the French who first colonized Quebec and the French Canadian people who now inhabit it; and the green, though questioned by some, is acknowledged by all to represent the Irish. These colours, placed vertically, with the Union in the upper corner as now, would make a good Canadian flag and attract the regard of a majority of the people who inhabit the Dominion. The green, especially, would be worth 100,000 men to the Dominion in case of any difficulty with our neighbours, and would effectually Canadianize the Irish.

The near prospect here held out may frighten the timid, but timidity is one of the things nationality is intended to remove. "You are big enough and strong enough for independence," said the *Times*, "and if not, the education of self-reliance will soon make you so." But there is nothing to fear but weakness and cowardice. We shall have 5,000,000 of brave, hardy, industrious people, unused to luxuries and all enervating influences. We have a commercial marine second only to that of America to carry a fully developed national trade. We have 800,000 men between the ages of 16 and 45, should they be required to defend our liberties. We have resources in natural wealth — lumber, coal, iron, and gold — almost measureless, while our agricultural lands in the North-West give double the average of the yield of the North-Western States. We are already Confederated and bound together in one Dominion, having executive, legislative, and judicial bodies, the last of which is independent, and the other two nearly so. And, lastly, we shall have the good will of England and possibly her guarantee for our independence.

We can then look forward to the future with hope and confidence. In twenty years of Canadian independence, twelve or fourteen states will occupy what is now an unbroken solitude, whose trade, and that of the whole North-West of the continent, will flow in one stream through our territory, either through Lake Winnipeg and Nelson's River into Hudson Bay, or down the Great Lakes and the St. Lawrence to the Atlantic, fertilizing and enriching the country through which it passes. Political power follows in the steps of material wealth. Modern nations on this continent grow with prodigious strides. In one hundred years the United States have passed through all the phases of national life that took a thousand to mould Europe, and they are fast hastening to a premature old age. Our country has come into existence at a grand period of the world's history. Humanity, on this continent, has advanced beyond the evils of the old civilization. Feudalism, slavery, and extreme ignorance and poverty, have never been known to any extent among us, and we shall never be handicapped by them. Our great competitor and rival will never recover from the evils of one of them — slavery. Already she shows signs of dissolution. The evils of the old civilization amid which she was begotten, and the corruption engendered by the civil war, are doing their work. A hot-bed progress among alien and half-assimilated people will surely accelerate the end. They are in a dilemma either horn of which is fatal. They must either submit to the mob and the commune, and see their cities blaze as they did three years ago, or to a standing army and a general who will destroy their institutions and make himself dictator. In either event, disintegration is sure to follow. As power steps from the disorganized grasp of the United States, it will fall to Canada as her natural right, making her the first nation on this continent, as she is now the second. United closely, as we shall be from the Atlantic to the Pacific by a common nationality, our country will go on, increasing from age to age in wealth, in power and in glory; and it may not be too much of a stretch of the imagination to think, that as it is the latest developed portion of a new world — as it was the first, by millions of years, to nurse and cradle in her bosom the first spark of animal life in the eozoon, — it may be the country where a last great, and fully developed humanity may find its fitting habitation and abode.

6

"Malice and Bitterness"
Relations Between Church and State

DOCUMENTS

A) Pastoral Letter of the Bishops of the Ecclesiastical
   Province of Quebec, September 22, 1875
B) The Equal Rights Movement, 1890
   The Rev. William Caven
C) "Equal Rights", May 16, 1889
   The Brandon Sun
D) Education in Canada: The Encyclical Letter, 1897
   Pope Leo XIII
E) The Tragedy of Quebec, 1916
   Robert Sellars
F) And Our Dispersed Brethren ...?, 1922
   J.-M.-R. Villeneuve, O.M.I.

As a former British colony, Canada had strong constitutional, emotional, and cultural links to its motherland — a nation with an official Protestant church. Many Anglo-Canadian Protestants therefore assumed that Canada would also become predominantly Protestant. The Catholic element in Quebec, they mused, was an unhappy vestige of French colonial rule that would ultimately wither away.

Quebec Catholics did not see Canada's evolution in the same terms. Some, in fact, believed that it was their mission to spread the Catholic faith, not just to the rest of Canada, but throughout North America. The Catholic clergy, they believed, could best run all aspects of society. Other French Canadians clung to Catholicism for more temporal reasons, seeing it as the bulwark of French-Canadian cultural survival and the strongest bastion against creeping absorption into English culture.

Usually these differences of opinion between Anglophone Protestant and Francophone Catholics came into focus over the existence of separate, publicly funded Catholic schools. Whether it was in New Brunswick during the early 1870s, Manitoba in the 1890s, or Ontario after 1910, many Protestant newspapers, Protestant clergymen and politicians heaped abuse upon these institutions. Some of this activity coincided with the rise of French-Canadian nationalism in Quebec under Honoré Mercier. The Jesuit Estates Act passed by the Quebec legislature in 1888, offering funds to be used for Catholic education as compensation for the confiscation of Jesuit lands during the British Conquest, produced a frenzy of Protestant extremism in Ontario and resulted in the creation of an organization ironically called the Equal Rights Association, which commenced a bigoted assault upon the rights of French-speaking and Roman Catholic Canadians. John A. Macdonald referred to it as "one of those insane crazes." Yet outside Quebec the rights of Catholics to their own publicly funded schools slowly disappeared in one province after another.

Written at a time when the Catholic church feared liberal tendencies, not just in Canada but also in Europe, the central issue in *The Pastoral Letter of the Bishops of the Ecclesiastical Province of Quebec* was the question of civil or ecclesiastical supremacy in society. In his campaign to regenerate the faith, Pope Pius IX issued his 1864 *Syllabus of Errors*, which insisted on the precedence of ecclesiastical over civil authority. To the church, those who even suggested a division between spiritual and temporal power were wrong, as moral authority and moral cohesion originated with the Pope. In Quebec the Catholic church felt its exclusive prerogatives were at risk with the provincial government's establishment of a ministry of education and its intervention with burials in consecrated ground through the celebrated Guibord affair. Women taking up social and charitable work usually reserved for Catholic religious communities constituted another threat. In response, the Catholic church insisted that it should guide French Canada.

William Caven (1830–1904) came to Canada from Scotland in 1847 and worked as a Presbyterian minister until he, like Laflèche, became a college theology professor. He moderated the General Assembly of the Canadian Presbyterian Church and facilitated the union of the various Scottish Protestant branches. As a staunch anti-Jesuit, Caven fought the Jesuit Estates Act and organized an anti-Jesuit convention in Toronto. He served as president of the Equal Rights Association until 1890, but resigned over what he perceived as its intolerance. A tireless campaigner for stricter Sabbath observances through the Lord's Day Alliance, Caven also supported temperance via the Dominion Alliance.

The editorial in the Brandon, Manitoba, *Sun* appeared early in the campaign to remove public funds from separate schools.

Italian in origin, Pope Leo XIII (1810–1903) made substantial efforts to address contemporary issues such as the role of the church in increasingly secular and democratic nation states. His most ambitious plans for society appeared in his encyclical *Rerum Novarum* (1891), which dealt with the inadequacies of both capitalism and socialism. His commentary on the situation in Manitoba indicates just how significant and far-reaching the question of separate schools had become.

His critics dubbed Robert Sellars (1841–1919) "Fanatic Bob" for his strident Protestantism. He immigrated from Scotland to Toronto, working briefly there as a typesetter for the *Globe*. Moving to Quebec's Eastern Townships, Sellars founded the *Canadian Gleaner*, a rural newspaper based out of Huntington. Anglos in Quebec's Eastern Townships used to form the local majority, but French-Canadian farmers increasingly moved into the area, buying farms and creating much anxiety among the local English community. As a result, Sellars published his controversial *Tragedy of Quebec*, a passionate pro-Protestant book. Supporters dubbed it a timely warning to Canada's collapsing integrity, but opponents saw it as typically Anglo-Canadian Francophobia and Protestant bigotry. Sellars had a long history of anti-Catholicism, dedicating himself as early as 1864 to that cause. He opposed Confederation, arguing that new provincial boundaries abandoned the English of the Eastern Townships to the mercy of Quebec Catholics. Though a frequent target for attack, his figure regularly burned in effigy, Sellars continued railing against Catholic control of Quebec's politics, education, media, hospitals, and reformatories. Surprisingly, he rejected the adulation from more extremist groups like the Orange Order and the Protestant Protective Association, dismissing them as merely other versions of clerical control. He maintained that he was not against French Canadians, and believed a place existed for two equal languages and a distinct Quebecois culture; what he could not tolerate was the concept of "Providential Mission." Though he wrote other books, none gained the notoriety of *The Tragedy of Quebec*, which eventually went through four editions and became the anti-Catholic Ulster Unionists' blueprint for Northern Ireland.

Born in Montreal, Jean Marie Roderique Villeneuve, OMI (1883–1947), rose through Catholic ranks to become dean of theology at the University of Ottawa in 1930, bishop of Gravelbourg, Saskatchewan, archbishop of Quebec in 1931, and eventually a Cardinal in 1933. His 1922 article combines the idea of Catholic supremacy with Quebec nationalism and suggests that the French-Canadian nation had a special religious mission to spread throughout North America.

A) Pastoral Letter of the Bishops of the Ecclesiastical Province of Quebec, September 22, 1875

We, by the mercy of God and the favour of the Holy Apostolic See, Archbishop, Bishops, and administrator of the Dioceses of the Ecclesiastical Province of Quebec.

To the Clergy, Secular and Regular, and to all the Faithful of the said Province, Greeting and Benediction in Our Lord.

I. Powers of the Church

... To fulfil this sublime and difficult mission it was necessary that the Church be constituted by its Divine founder in the form of a Society perfect in itself, distinct and independent of civil society.

No society whatever can exist without laws, and consequently, without law-givers, judges and a power to make the laws respected; the Church has, therefore, necessarily received from its founder authority over its children to maintain order and unity. To deny this authority would be to deny the wisdom of the Son of God. To subordinate this authority to the civil power, would be to side with a Nero and a Diocletian against those millions of Christians who preferred death to betraying their faith; it would be to side with Pilate and Herod against Jesus Christ himself.

Not only is the Church independent of civil society, but it is superior to it by its origin, by its extent, and by its end.

Without doubt civil society has its root in the will of God, who has decreed that men would live in society; but the forms of civil society vary with times and places; the Church is born from the blood of a God on Calvary, has received direct from His mouth its unchangeable constitution, and no power on earth can alter it.

A civil society embraces but one people; the Church has received dominion over all the earth; Jesus Christ himself has given the mission 'to teach all nations', *docete omnes gentes* (Matt. xxviii, 20); the State, then, is in the Church, and not the Church in the State.

The aim of the Church is the eternal happiness of souls, the supreme and last aim of man; civil society has for its aim the temporal happiness of peoples. Even by the nature of things, civil society finds itself *indirectly* but in truth subordinate, for not only ought it to abstain from putting any obstacle in the way of that supreme and last aim of man, but it ought also to assist the Church in its divine mission and if need be to protect and defend it. And besides, is it not evident that even the temporal happiness of peoples depends on truth, justice and morality, and consequently, on all those truths the keeping of which is confided to the Church? The experience of the last hundred years teaches us there is no longer either peace or security for nations who have thrown off the yoke of religion, of which the Church is the only true guardian.

This subordination in no way prevents these societies [civil and religious] from being distinct, because of their aims, and independent, each in its proper sphere. But the moment a question touches on faith, morals or the divine constitution of the Church, on its independence or on what it needs to fulfil its spiritual mission, it is for the Church alone to judge, for Jesus Christ has said to it alone, 'All power is given me in heaven and on earth ... As my Father has sent me, so I send you ... Go then, teach all nations ... Who hears you hears me, and who contemns you contemns me, and who contemns me contemns Him that sent me ... Who does not listen to the Church deserves to be considered as a heathen and a publican', that is to say, as unworthy to be called His child. (Matt. xxviii, 18, 19; John xx, 21; [Luke x, 16;] Matt. xviii, 17.)

But in thus claiming the rights of the Catholic Church over its children, by no means do we intend to usurp or fetter the civil rights of our brothers who differ from us, with whom we will always be happy to be on the best of terms in the future as we have been in the past. The principles we expound are not new; they are as old as the Church itself. If we repeat them today, it is because certain Catholics appear to have forgotten them.

IV. Catholic Politics

... Far be it from us not to recognize the advantages of the constitutional regime considered in itself, and consequently, the usefulness of its distinctions of party, which hold one another in check, in order to signal and stop the errors of power. What we deplore, what we condemn, is the abuse of it; it is the pretension that politics, reduced to the mean and ridiculous proportions of party interests, becomes *the supreme rule* of every public administration, that *everything* may be *for the party* and nothing for *the common good;* nothing for *that society of which one has the charge.* What we condemn once again, is that one is allowed to say and to dare all that can tend to the triumph of a party. 'Listen to my words,' says the Holy Spirit (Wisdom of Solomon, vi), 'you who govern the people, consider you have received the power from the Most High, who will examine your works, scrutinize even your thoughts; because being the ministers of His kingdom, you have not guarded the law of justice nor walked according to His will. He will also come to you in a terrible manner to judge you with extreme severity.'

V. The Role of the Clergy in Politics

Men who would lead you astray, Our Dearly Beloved Brethren, tell you repeatedly that religion has nothing whatever to do with politics; that it is not necessary to take any account of religious principles in the discussion of public affairs; that the clergy have no functions except within the Church and the sacristy; and that the people should practice moral independence in politics.

Monstrous errors, Our Dearly Beloved Brethren; and woe to the country in which they take root. In excluding the clergy, the Church is excluded; and in putting aside the church, one is deprived of all that is salutary and unchangeable it contains — God, morality, justice, truth, and when one has swept away all the rest, one has nothing left to rely upon except force!

Every man who has his salvation at heart should govern his actions according to Divine law, of which religion is the expression and guardian. Who cannot understand what justice and rectitude would reign everywhere, if governments and peoples had always before their eyes that Divine law which is equity itself, and the formidable judgement which they will have to undergo one day before Him from whose hands no one can possibly escape? The greatest enemies of the people are, therefore, those who wish to banish religion from politics; for, under the pretext of freeing the people from what they call *the tyranny, the undue influence of the priest,* they are preparing for this people the heaviest chains and the ones that will be the most difficult to throw off; they place might above right, and take from the civil power the only moral check which can prevent it from degenerating into despotism and tyranny!

They wish to shut the priest up in the sacristy! Why? Is it because during his studies he has acquired certain and salutary knowledge of the rights and duties of each of the faithful confided to his care? Is it because he sacrifices his resources, his time, his health, even his life, for the benefit of his fellow creatures?

Is he not a citizen with the same rights as others? What! any newcomer may write, speak and act; you sometimes see an influx of strangers into a parish or a county, who came there to impose their own political opinions: and the priest alone will be unable to speak or to write! Any one who wishes will be permitted to come into a parish and to promulgate all sorts of principles and the priest, who in the midst of his parishioners is like a father amongst his children, will have no right to speak, no right to protest against the enormities which are submitted to them!

Those who today are shouting that the priest has nothing whatever to do in politics, not long ago were finding his influence salutary; those who now deny the competency of the clergy in these questions formerly used to praise the steadiness of principles that the study of Christian morality gives a man. Whence this change of mind, if not from sensing that this influence, which they are aware they no longer merit, now acts against them?

Without doubt, our Dearly Beloved Brethren, the exercise of all the rights of citizenship by a priest is not at all times opportune; it may even have its dangers and disadvantages: but it must not be forgotten that to the Church alone belongs the right to give to its ministers the instructions which she may deem appropriate, and to reprimand those who may go astray; and the Bishops of this Province have not failed to do their duty on this point.

Up to the present we have considered the priest as a citizen, and as speaking of politics in his own name, like any other member of civil society.

Are there questions in which the Bishop and the priest may, and sometimes even must, interfere in the name of religion?

We answer without hesitation: Yes, there are political questions in which the clergy may and even must interfere in the name of religion. The principle governing this right and duty is found in the very distinction we have already indicated, between the Church and the State.

There are, in effect, political questions which touch on the spiritual interests of souls, either because they relate to faith and morals, or because they can affect the liberty, independence or existence of the Church, even from a temporal point of view.

A candidate may present himself whose programme is hostile to the Church, or whose antecedents are such that his candidature threatens these same interests.

Likewise, a political party may be judged dangerous, not only because of its programme and antecedents, but also because of the particular programmes and antecedents of its leaders, of its principal members, and of the press which represents it, unless this party explicitly disavow them and separate itself from them, assuming they are persisting in their error after having been warned about it.

In this case a Catholic cannot, without denying his faith, show himself hostile to the Church of which he is a member, refuse to the Church the right of defending itself, or rather defending the spiritual interests of the souls confided to its safekeeping! But the Church speaks, acts, and fights through its clergy, and to refuse these rights to them is to refuse them to the Church.

Thus, the priest and the bishop may in all justice, and must in all conscience, raise their voices, point out the danger, declare authoritatively that to vote in a particular way is a sin, and that to do such a thing makes one liable to the censure of the Church. They may and must speak, not only to the electors and the candidates, but also to the constituted authorities, for the duty of every man who wishes to save his soul is traced out by divine law; and the Church, as a good Mother, owes to all her children, regardless of their station in life, love and, consequently, spiritual vigilance. It is not, therefore, converting the pulpit into a political platform [when the clergy] enlighten the conscience of the faithful on all those questions in which salvation is involved ...

Conclusion

Such, Our Dearly Beloved Brethren, is the important advice we deem it our duty to give you under the present circumstances.

Beware, above all, of this *liberalism* which hides itself under the beautiful name of *Catholic*, the more surely to accomplish its criminal work. You will easily recognize it from the picture the Sovereign Pontiff has so often drawn of it. 1st, Efforts to subjugate the Church to the State. 2nd, Incessant attempts to divide the bonds which unite the children of the Church amongst themselves and to the clergy. 3rd, Monstrous alliance of the truth with error under the pretence of resolving all differences and avoiding conflicts. 4th, Lastly, delusion and sometimes hypocrisy, which, under a religious exterior and fine protestations of submission to the Church, hide a boundless pride ...

B) The Equal Rights Movement, 1890
The Rev. William Caven

... [T]he Equal Rights Association may be opposed on two grounds; either that Equal Rights are already established so that there is nothing to complain of — nothing to reform, or that Equal Rights so-called are not Equal Rights but something else. The Equal Rights movement is certainly shown to be unnecessary and mischievous if either the one or the other proposition can be sustained.

The Equal Rights Association originated in the opposition offered to the Jesuits' Estates Act, passed by the Legislature of Quebec in 1888. In the correspondence with Rome, which is incorporated in the preamble of this famous Act, the Premier of Quebec asks permission of the Pope to sell certain Government properties, known as the Jesuit Estates, and the Pope grants permission to sell, under condition that the proceeds should be disposed of with his sanction. Large numbers of persons in Ontario, Quebec and other Provinces of the Dominion were shocked at legislation which not only recognized a moral claim on the part of the Jesuits to these estates, and endowed them with public funds, but placed, or seemed to place, the allegiance of a British Province at the feet of the Roman Curia — recognizing by implication, as it distinctly did, the superiority of the Canon Law to that of the Empire. The feeling of opposition to this Act of Quebec was greatly intensified by the unseemly haste with which the Dominion Government declared its allowance of it, and by the overwhelming vote by which the House of Commons refused to ask the Government to apply the veto.

Had this been the only instance in which the strong hand of Ultramontanism had been felt in Provincial or Dominion affairs, little more might have been heard of it, beyond the indignant protest which was raised in many quarters. But the Jesuits' Estates Act had the effect of bringing home to men more than anything which had recently occurred, the ascendancy which a powerful and well-organized ecclesiastical body had attained in the polities of Canada. It could hardly be disputed that the Church of Rome had it in her power to make or mar the fortunes of political parties, that she was ready on proper occasion to exercise this power, and that in consequence she was regarded by the parties with a subserviency which degraded not only them but the politics of the country, and even in some degree threatened its liberties. It was sufficient proof of this to remember that no election passed in the Protestant Provinces without the keenest competition for *the Catholic vote* — an expression which of itself bears witness to a disturbing element in the community; while in the Catholic Province of Quebec the parties were in equally keen competition for the especial favour of the Church. With the professional politicians it had become an instinct to court the Church of Rome.

The Equal Rights movement sees no adequate remedy for the evil referred to except in so defining the provinces of Church and State that the one shall be clearly discriminated from the other, that neither shall be under special temptation to seek favour from the other, and that the Church shall have to depend entirely upon its own resources in doing its own work. "We deem it essential to the peace and highest welfare of our country and to the maintenance of good government that the line between the civil and ecclesiastical authorities should be clearly defined and should be respected in all legislation and administration, both of the Dominion and the several Provinces thereof. While the Church is entitled to entire freedom and to protection in its own domain, which embraces all that is purely spiritual, the State must have full control in all temporal matters; and it cannot, without abrogating its just authority, ask or accept permission from any ecclesiastical person or organization, or from any extraneous body whatever, to exercise its own functions and perform its own duties." These words, which are the fourth article in the platform of the Equal Rights Association, express the central principle of the Association and of the movement which it represents. Churches must not under any pretext receive public moneys to aid them in their proper work; nor must they, under colour of doing work which is beneficial to the State, draw upon the public treasury. Their adherents must provide the means for carrying on all their operations. If the work for which in any case they claim assistance from the State is properly the business of the State, let the State attend to it, and if it is their own work let them do it on their own charges. To say that this work is beneficial to the State is no good argument for public aid, because all true work done by any class of people, in any connexion, is profitable to the whole community. The view here set forth is in no way allied to irreligion, and implies no failure to recognize the inestimable benefits which the Christian religion has conferred upon civil society ...

A word respecting the application of Equal Rights principles to Separate Schools. These schools are established in order that the Roman Catholic children may escape a danger to which it is alleged they are exposed in the Common School, and may be thoroughly indoctrinated in the tenets and observances of their faith. In our school law provision is made for the establishment in certain circumstances of Protestant Separate Schools also, but so little has advantage been taken of this provision that practically it is of no account. For the purposes of this argument Separate Schools may be identified with Roman Catholic Separate Schools. The objection, then, to such Schools from the Equal Rights point of view, is that they use public funds in the special service of a Church, and for teaching definitely and in detail, the peculiarities of a Church. The principle of the Equal Rights Association would not be more certainly violated by giving public money for the endowment of a church, or for its annual expenditure. This is so clear that it only needs to be stated, and to state it is, to Equal Rights men, to condemn it ...

C) "Equal Rights", May 16, 1889
The Brandon Sun

Nothing in the state can exceed the importance and value of our educational system and institutions. The health of the body politic is very largely regulated by the condition of these. If the educational policy of the country is confined in circumscribed limits, regulated by sectarian narrowness and petty jealousies, we cannot hope for the best results, and a distinct loss must be the consequence. If, however, liberal comprehensive ideas prevail in laying the foundations, and regard only for the general good is had, there will be ground to hope that the generous sympathies of the whole community will be enlisted in upbuilding an educational system that will promote the best interests of the state and of every citizen. No one can question these statements, and yet we are allowing separate schools to be maintained in our midst by public money and popular legislation. We are firmly of the opinion that this is a great injustice and great wrong.

In the first place, any one who knows anything of the country must admit that the best and undivided efforts of all are required — and will be for years to come — to put our educational affairs on anything like a satisfactory footing. To divide our efforts and money is to obtain less desirable results; to try to establish two separate systems is to squander money to gratify a sentiment or to promote the interests of a sect; to continue the separate school system is to promote divisions and dissensions, to place a barrier in the way of the development of one of our most important interests, and to create complications and distinctions, with resultant injury to the state and individual alike.

Every consideration argues the desirability of abolishing this useless and troublesome excrescence at the earliest possible date.

We have never yet heard a satisfactory argument advanced in favor of this extraordinary provision for one sect. Why a preference should be shown to Catholics more than to Baptists, Episcopalians or Methodists, we are at a loss to know. Why Catholics cannot obtain a satisfactory education at schools where Presbyterians, Congregationalists and Lutherans attend, we fail to understand. Why the public moneys should be handed over to such an institution as the convent in this city is quite puzzling. If a college or school under the control of any Protestant denomination were to ask a similar grant from the government, a very great amount of indignation would doubtless be raised, with the result that the grant would not be made. The fact is the continuance of these schools can only be defended on the ground of expediency, so far as we have yet learned. There should be no hesitation in doing equal justice to all classes. Unless some satisfactory reason can be advanced there should be no delay in demanding that no particular denomination should be preferred to all the rest, and thereby a distinct wrong be inflicted on the majority. We have no hesitation in stating — but we must be understood as only speaking for ourselves — that we consider the law that prefers the Catholics as a religious denomination to other religious denominations a great wrong. We demand the same rights for Methodists, Episcopalians, Presbyterians, and other Protestants, as for Catholics, and the same for the latter as the former. Let there be equality and justice in these matters. The Catholics now enjoy a preference to which they have no right, hence we desire the abolition of separate schools.

D) Education in Canada: The Encyclical Letter, 1897
Pope Leo XIII

To the Archbishops, Bishops, and other Ordinaries in the Federated States of Canada in grace and communion with the Holy See.

Venerable Brethren, health and apostolic benediction.

Education in Canada
... The Question at Issue

The question at issue is assuredly one of the highest and most serious importance. The decisions arrived at seven years ago on the school question by the Parliament of the province of Manitoba must be remembered. The Act of Union of the Confederation had secured to Catholics the right to be educated in the public schools according to their consciences; and yet this right the Parliament of Manitoba abolished by a contrary law. This is a noxious law. For our children cannot go for instruction to schools which either ignore or of set purpose combat the Catholic religion, or in which its teachings are despised and its fundamental principles repudiated. Wherever the

Church has allowed this to be done, it has only been with pain and through necessity, at the same time surrounding her children with many safeguards which, nevertheless, it has been too often recognized have been insufficient to cope successfully with the danger attending it. Similarly it is necessary to avoid at all costs, as most dangerous, those schools in which all beliefs are welcomed and treated as equal, as if, in what regards God and divine things, it makes no difference whether one believes rightly or wrongly, and takes up with truth or error. You know well, Venerable Brethren, that every school of this kind has been condemned by the Church, because nothing can be more harmful or better calculated to ruin the integrity of the faith and to turn aside the tender minds of the young from the way of truth.

The Need of Religious Education

There is another point upon which those will agree with us who differ from us in everything else; it is not by means of a purely scientific education and with vague and superficial notions of morality that Catholic children can quit school trained as the country desires and expects. Other serious and important teaching must be given to them if they are to turn out good Christians and upright and honest citizens; it is necessary that they should be formed on those principles which, deeply engraven on their consciences, they ought to follow and obey, because they naturally spring from their faith and religion. Without religion there can be no moral education deserving of the name, nor of any good, for the very nature and force of all duty comes from those special duties which bind to God, who commands, forbids, and determines what is good and evil. And so, to be desirous that minds should be imbued with good and at the same time to leave them without religion is as senseless as to invite people to virtue after having taken away the foundations on which it rests. For the Catholic there is only one true religion, the Catholic religion; and, therefore, when it is a question of the teaching of morality or religion, he can neither accept nor recognize any which is not drawn from Catholic doctrine.

Justice and reason then demand that the school shall supply our scholars not only with a scientific system of instruction, but also a body of moral teaching which, as we have said, is in harmony with the principles of their religion, without which, far from being of use, education can be nothing but harmful. From this comes the necessity of having Catholic masters and reading-books and textbooks approved by the bishops, of being free to regulate the school in a manner which shall be in full accord with the profession of the Catholic faith, as well as with all the duties which flow from it. Furthermore, it is the inherent right of a father's position to see in what institutions his children shall be educated, and what masters shall teach them moral precepts. When, therefore, Catholics demand, as it is their duty to demand, and work, that the teaching given by school-masters shall be in harmony with the religion of their children, they are contending justly. And nothing could be more unjust than to compel them to choose an alternative, or to allow their children to grow up in ignorance, or to throw them amid an environment which constitutes a manifest danger for the supreme interests of their souls. These principles of judgment and action, which are based upon truth and justice, and which form the safeguards of public, as well as private, interests, it is unlawful to call in question or in any way to abandon. And so, when the new legislation came to strike Catholic education in the province of Manitoba, it was your duty, Venerable Brethren, publicly to protest against injustice and the blow that had been dealt, and the way in which you fulfilled this duty has furnished a striking proof of your individual vigilance and of your true episcopal zeal. Although upon this point each one of you finds sufficient approbation in the witness of his own conscience: know, nevertheless, that we also join with it our assent and approval. For the things that you have sought and still seek to preserve and defend are most holy.

The Need of United Action

Moreover, the hardships of the law in question themselves plainly proved that there was need of complete union if any opportune remedy of the evil was to be found. So good was the Catholic cause that all fair and honest citizens without distinction of party ought to have taken common counsel and acted in concert to defend it. Unfortunately, however, and to the great detriment of the cause, just the contrary was done. And what is still more deplorable, Catholic Canadians themselves were unable to act in concert in the defence of interests which so closely touch the common good, and the importance and moment of which ought to have silenced the interests of political parties, which are on quite a lower plane of importance.

An Insufficient Remedy

We are not ignorant that something has been done to amend the law. The men who are at the head of the Federal Government and of the Government of the Province have already taken certain measures to diminish the grievances of which the Catholics of Manitoba rightly persist in complaining. We have no reason to doubt that these measures have been inspired by a love of fair dealing and by a good intention. But we cannot conceal the truth. The law made to remedy the evil is defective, imperfect, insufficient. Catholics demand, and have the right to demand, much more. Besides, the arrangements made may fail of their effect, owing to the variations in local circumstances; enough has not yet been done in Manitoba for the Catholic education of our children. The claims of justice demand that this question should be considered from every point of view, that those unchangeable and sacred principles which we have enunciated above should be protected and secured. This is what must be aimed at, and this the end which must be pursued with zeal and prudence. But there must not be discord; there must be union of mind and harmony of action. As the object does not impose a line of conduct determinate and exclusive, but, on the contrary, admits of several, as is usual in such matters, it follows that there may be on the line to be followed a certain number of opinions equally good and acceptable. Let none, then, lose sight of the value of moderation, gentleness and brotherly love. Let none forget the respect due to his neighbor, but let all, weighing the circumstances, determine what is best to be done, and act together after having taken counsel with you …

Given at St. Peter's, Rome, on the 18th day of December, 1897, in the twentieth year of Our pontificate.

Leo XIII, Pope

E) The Tragedy of Quebec, 1916
Robert Sellars

All French-Canadians are not Nationalists, there are thousands of them who have no sympathy with Nationalism, men who know what clericalism leads to and do not want Quebec to be like the South American States; men who would compel the priests to confine themselves to their spiritual duties and resent their interference in politics; men who consider it of vital importance that Quebec should apply itself to its development intellectually and commercially, and give up dreams of forming a separate nation that cannot be realized; men who are convinced and sincerely believe that government on British principles is a hundred-fold preferable to a government inspired and guided by the priesthood; men who desire a united Canada on the basis that the people shall rule and not the priests. The number who think thus is increasing, and they are the hope of that future Quebec which will cease to look backwards, not seeking isolation, not clinging to wornout ideals and naming it patriotism, but unite with the other peoples of the Dominion in building up a nation that will give opportunity to every man to earn a living without discrimination as to creed or origin. Against Nationalism, with its harking back to theocratic rule, let us set constitutional government as developed by the Motherland, and against the narrowness that would give a priestly caste influence to shape Canada's destiny, let us set the sovereignty of the people — the wideness that gives to all equal rights and knows naught of special privileges ...

The term Nationalist implies a man striving for another government than that he lives under. In Quebec it indicates one who is satisfied with the government of the province but who desires to change the federal government by bringing it into harmony with that of Quebec. In what regard is the Dominion at large not in harmony with Quebec? The answer is obvious — Quebec is obedient to the priesthood, the governments of the other provinces are not; a clerical government has been firmly established in Quebec ... The policy of isolation persistently followed for 150 years has put in the hands of the priesthood two million people who obey them and are the instrument by which they are resolved to win supremacy over all Canada ... Properly speaking, the Nationalist movement is not political, it is ecclesiastical. The idea as to when this Catholic nation is to be is vague; there is no hurry about it ...

Nationalism has produced a type of Canadian unknown thirty years ago, who shouts French when he knows he who asks him a question speaks only English, telephones in French, demands what he wants in French, persists in using his mother-tongue as an instrument to humiliate his English neighbor. Then there is a new air of superiority to make the English feel they are unwelcome intruders. When a Canadian of this sort is elected a representative he makes himself a nuisance in parliament. He lies in wait for fancied slights and omissions, yelling "En Francais," demands "une sou" be stamped on coppers, and French words on postage stamps; is loud in denouncing appointments of English to office ...

The idea fostered by the Nationalists, that the French-speaking people occupy a superior position to the English, and their insistent exhortation to boldly claim their alleged rights, is widening the cleavage between the two peoples. It is dangerous to foster in the minds of a section of our population that they are not receiving their due, that they are discriminated against, that they have wrongs that call for redress, and yet that is what the entire Nationalist press daily and weekly doing seconded by the exertions of the Nationalist members at Quebec and Ottawa.

The underlying idea of Nationalism is that the French have rights and privileges peculiar to themselves and which are not shared by others. The daily exhortations of their newspapers is, that they assert themselves and enter more fully into the enjoyment of those alleged rights and privileges. It is dangerous talk, ominous of serious trouble in the coming years. The Canadian who is discontented with his status as a British subject and who is preparing the way to replace the Union Jack with another flag, is a rebel. Nationalists repudiate being disloyal. They do not, many of them, realize it, but they are breeding a rebellion ...

Blot out your impression of priests, bishops, and cardinals as clergymen, and regard them as what they really are, members of a complete and highly organized society, whose master aim is to obtain power to rule whatever community in which they are placed. These priests, by years of skilful training, have had impressed upon their minds that they have been selected and set aside to win for their society the government of the world. Fresh from their ordination vows, they start to do what they can to establish the authority of their society as supreme over the rule of all laymen. The laws of their society are to be superior to all other laws, its mandates to go before those of kings and parliaments; the voice of the people to be a meaningless sound in their ears. Their years of training having left no doubt in their minds that the ruling of the people is committed to their hands, they believe that in striving to assert that rule they are only seeking what belongs to them. It is for them to mark out the limits wherein civil rulers are to act, to define what they are to do, and when they have given their orders all that is left for the civil authorities is to carry them into effect ... No more dangerous combination could attack the liberties of the people than a band of men aiming at supremacy under the guise of a church.

The Habitant Boy Who Becomes a Priest.

Here is a lad, one of a numerous family, who, by means of constant labor, earn a bare subsistence. The boy sees before him no better prospect than that his father had — to buy a farm with borrowed money, spend years in paying the mortgage, and live penuriously. It is the life of the habitants around him and he would like to do better. He sees how the priest of the parish is deferred to, how his word is law, how he lives in a style that seems to his eyes to be affluence. When the bishop comes on his yearly visit, he is met by a procession of habitants a mile long, the bells are rung and decorations appear. It is a high privilege to be introduced to him, do him reverence, and leave a donation with his secretary. In departing the bishop is again escorted until he meets the procession from the next parish. The boy is told the bishop is all-powerful at Quebec, that cabinet ministers and the premier himself drop on their knees to kiss his hand, and whatever he asks of them they are pleased to give. Yet this bishop was once like the boy who watches him, the son of a poor habitant, and so was also the priest of the parish. They escaped hard living by becoming priests: they emerged from being unknown to places of power and prominence. Why should he not do likewise? and his ambition is centred on becoming a member of that society which will change his home-spun into gorgeous robes, which will make his father drop on his knees to do him reverence, and give him the influence to dictate to his former neighbors who shall represent them, and to governments what laws they shall pass. By simply becoming a unit in the great secret society of Quebec the son of the habitant is transformed into a dictator. Were the head of one of our political parties to become possessed with the ambition of being a dictator and use all the means in his power to attain his object, the people of Canada would revolt, but a caste of men seeking the like end plan and work without hindrance because they do so in the character of ultra-pietists, asserting they are the sole authorized exponents of the one and only true faith, that the control of the solitary bridge which spans the gulf between earth and heaven has been committed to them by the Lord Jesus. Their claim is, they are extending the Kingdom of God, and millions believe it, when they are really engaged in adding to the strength of their society and preparing for the time when it shall have the supreme voice in the government of Canada. This may be said to be a vain dream of pious visionaries which, in our age, is impossible of fulfilment, were it not for the evidence of their success in the Province of Quebec.

What the Priests Have Accomplished.

1. Kept the French and English two separate peoples and thereby prevented Quebec becoming in reality as it is nominally — British;

2. Driven the English-speaking farmers out of the Townships;

3. Established schools which do not fit youth to act their part in a self-governing country;

4. Got the legislature to be its minister in whatever it desires, and is yearly entrusted by it with the spending of one-third of its income.

5. Established courts that administer foreign laws independent of and above those enacted by parliament;

6. The subserviency of the judges to their demands;

7. The suppression of free speech and of a free press;

8. The tacit acknowledgment by almost the entire Province of Quebec that there is a rule above that of the Crown and to which their first allegiance is due.

The marvellous success of the ecclesiastics in Quebec is their encouragement to assail the other provinces and seek to do in them what they have already done. Whoever claims there is no cause for fear, who denies that Quebec is a menace to the Dominion, that what the priests have accomplished in Quebec they cannot duplicate outside its limits, must demonstrate that these assertions of what they have accomplished in Quebec are fabulous.

Apart from Quebec, is there not evidence to be found in every corner of Canada? Is even British Columbia free from the demands of the priests for exceptional treatment? Are not separate schools and langauge the burning questions in the Maritime Provinces, in Ontario, and in the Northwest? So the original question asked stands, Is not Quebec a menace to every part of the Dominion? To master the answer to this question, get rid of prepossessions, such as that the first object of the priests is the conversion of Protestants. It is not a spiritual empire they aim at, but a political. They know that to bring the mass of Protestants into their fold is impossible, but it is not impossible, as Quebec has proved, to bring Protestants under their direction. To be the masters of Canada's political life, to dictate to Legislatures and Parliament what they shall do, is the goal aimed at. They have succeeded in Quebec in becoming masters, and from their entrenchment in Quebec they carry on their campaign to subjugate all Canada.

The Measures of Defence Called For.

If Canada is to continue to be a nation of freemen, it is necessary alike to demand that all interference by priests cease, and to repudiate the claim on which they base their pretension to interfere. It intensifies though it does not affect the merits of the situation, that these clerics assume their airs of superiority because of offices bestowed by a foreign power, and that a power repudiated by the Motherland and by a majority of Canadians. Apart from every other consideration, a government influenced by the agents of the Vatican would not be a free government ... The British North America Act had to be approved by the Pope before Quebec would accept Confederation. The constitutions of Saskatchewan and Alberta were drafted to suit his representative at Ottawa. The sovereign will of the people has to be vindicated in Canada — the battle of our fathers against ecclesiastical usurpation has to be fought over again and decided on the virgin soil of Canada. It is monstrous that such a contest should be forced on the people of a new country. It shall be to their everlasting shame if they evade it and do not repeat the victory of their fathers.

... The danger-centre of the Dominion is Quebec. A French Quebec, free in thought and action, would be no menace to the Dominion; a Papal Quebec is, for it stands for a power that is not working for the common good, but to place the reins of political power in the hands of an ecclesiastical caste. That caste seeks not to exalt our country by strengthening its unity, binding man to man in the bonds of common interests and of a common brotherhood. On the contrary, in order to advance its designs it schemes in every possible way to thrust wedges to keep our people apart ...

The Nature of Clericalism.

... Will the electors of Canada not arouse themselves to assert their manhood — are they going to continue to bow before a society of men who assume to be of different mould from the rest of mankind and pretend to have been given divine authority to govern them? This claim of the priests that they are members of a society to whom God has entrusted the rule of the world, is constantly overlooked ... That which makes the priesthood a menace to society and to free government, is their pretension that they are God's representatives, and as such have been given authority to dictate to mankind what they are to believe and do. Wherever there are a sufficient number of men who make this claim and are backed by a sufficient number of followers, it is vain to speak of liberty — of constitutional government, of a free Canada. The people are domineered, kept down, dictated to by a select body of men whose usurped authority is based on a claim of their own device, that they are the chosen and inspired representatives of Christ ...

The Claim to Divine Authority.

... The call to every Briton is to make a stand on behalf of British institutions, and to take it at once. Any plan of resistance will prove vain that does not comprehend that the menace is confined to the priests, that the French-Canadians are simply used as tools, and that the cry of a French nation is adopted to cover what is really aimed at, a nation subject to and controlled by Papal influence … Once the people outside Quebec realize the fact that a gigantic movement is in progress to enthrone the rule of priestcraft, they will proceed to deal with the men who shelter themselves under a cloak of divinity …

What is Your Choice?

… There shall be no peace known in Canada until the priest is made to understand he is not different from the ordinary citizen and is compelled to cease from interfering in public affairs. The struggle to vindicate the right of the people to be ruled by themselves and not by a clerical organization may be long and may be fierce, but it cannot be avoided, it must be fought, and on the result depends whether Canada is to be British or Papal.

The call to you, oh, reader, is to throw your influence on the side of rule by the people. Do not try to shirk. Give up calling yourself by a party name and determine you shall vote for the candidate who is to be depended upon to fight Clericalism. Your motive is no narrow one; it is, by destroying privilege, to bestow equality on all. Shall Canada be a land of equal rights, or shall it not? What say you?

F) And Our Dispersed Brethren ...?, 1922
J.-M.-R. Villeneuve, O.M.I.

The Objection

That a French and Catholic State should, during the course of the present century, be established in the St. Lawrence valley is, according to many people, no longer a utopian dream, but a viable ideal, a hope founded in reality. That, moreover, the French race in North America should thereby fulfil its supernatural vocation; that because of this long-awaited political independence our nationality should be granted the majestic role long destined for it by Providence; that its idealistic, generous civilization should thus become a flame to light the great complex of parts that is to be fused by our American future; that it should become, finally, a modern-day Israel in the midst of an emerging Babylon, a France of America, an apostolic nation, a nation of light: this is a divine grace that we would do well to request in our prayers and to become worthy of by meditation and by that courage that makes nations great.

To achieve such an end, however, our nation must preserve its soul, shield it from destructive contacts, escape from the pressures that could suffocate it, and parry the blows seeking to diminish it.

Otherwise, a future French State would have no reason to exist in this northern New World; worse still, it could never summon the kind of strength that engenders heroism and the victories it needs, nor could it be assured of the extraordinary help granted by the Almighty to those individuals or nations who are ambitious in their dreams for His greater glory and who risk all in their attempts to secure it.

It seems to me that such are, in substance, the conclusions to which we have been led by the inquiry into our political future conducted by *L'Action française* since its January issue.

Shall I be blunt? I know very well that this masterly program of political reorientation that is being proposed to the French race of Canada has been a source of profound concern to certain people, and not without considerable cause. The warning but electrifying trumpet-call that has stirred the blood of Quebec's sons with enthusiasm and hope has struck a melancholy, anxious note into many a soul: into the minds of our dispersed brethren — those who have remained true to themselves, that is, in communion with us, and those who meditate, searching the future, desiring their part in the French epic and their share of Christian glory.

There are a great number of these offshoots that have been scattered throughout the land according to the whim of our fecundity or spirit of adventure: scattered in the name of an ideal that was more generous than wise, sometimes because of necessity, but more often through a kind of patriotism that was too short-sighted, and far too bohemian. They went to the United States, spreading from east to west and even to the south, usually against their better judgment, and against the advice of our leaders and most prophetic minds. They went out to western Canada, drawn by urgent appeals from men who were serious and authoritative, but who could not foresee the course of subsequent events and could still adopt an optimism that it is no longer possible for us to affect. These men could not hear, as we do, the distant rumblings that presage the more or less imminent breaking up of a certain great, ostentatious empire, nor the significant creaking of a federation for which it would definitely be foolhardy to predict a very long existence; nor had they witnessed the land overrun, almost overnight, by European immigrants who settled for good, making themselves at home with their exotic ideals and interests, immigrants solicited by politicians who were certainly devoid of the qualities required of builders of nations.

The present anxiety of these, our kin, gives us, we must admit, food for thought.

'What about us?' they ask.

'If it is indeed the case that, to preserve our soul — this apostolic, exemplary soul that must be the supreme cause of the civilization we must build in the heart of America — we must be free from fatal contact with foreign influence, from the mortal pressures of a selfish, mercantile civilization: how can we achieve this if you abandon us?

'In order to realize an ideal which we share with you, must you take an axe and sever from the trunk all those branches that have sprung from your own life and spirit, branches that you yourself have nurtured? Must we suffocate so that you may be left in peace to meditate upon the uncertain hope of an independence that will be a heavy burden to carry and that may well prove to be a mere exchange of allegiance and servitude? While you prepare to sink into the quicksands of our great, neighbouring democracy, must we in the West be submerged by the rising tide of a foreign sea, like an island cut adrift from its continent?'

So will speak our French of the Diaspora. And so, I fear, will they all think.

And in fact, could we prepare our escape from the approaching storm with a dry eye and an unmoved heart before even, as families say, 'seeing to the children'? Could a shipwrecked mother seize a plank floating by or climb aboard an inviting raft if, all around her on precarious bits of wreckage or on isolated and barren crags surrounded by abysmal depths, the youngest children cried, with outstretched arms, for help?

In this inquiry into our political future are we really giving sufficiently serious consideration to the case of our brothers in the outposts, those whose fortune it is to succeed our great ancestors, the forerunners, heralds, discoverers, civilizers: Frenchmen whose taste was for vast horizons, whose gaze was bold and acute, whose ideal was ambitious; Frenchmen who cut out for us a new France larger than Europe, because it was a pleasure for them to work on such a large scale in creating both land and country?

Would not the severance of those colonial and federal ties that our own sense of loyalty does not consider unbreakable lead to more serious ruptures, much too cruel for the French family in Canada, too fatal to our permanent existence and our common mission?

Let us be precise. Some beginning of an answer has been made to the scruples of our national conscience as well as to the fears of our brothers outside our State. We need only to widen the perspective of this answer, and to analyse its elements.

'Our attitude does not imply desertion,' declared the program. 'We are not seeking any kind of separation, and will accept only that which is imposed upon us by necessity or the hazard of history, against which all of us are in any case powerless.

'When we speak of separation, we do not mean closed or, even less, hostile boundaries. For a long time it will be in our interest, and it will be our duty, to maintain relationships with our former associates to whom we will continue to be attached by many bonds.

'Our compatriots are quite aware, moreover, that our loyal friendship for them, and our ardent desire to share in their life, are in no way the result of actual political ties. Such feelings spring from a more spontaneous solidarity and a more profound sense of fraternity. They also realize that this solidarity and fraternity can only be strengthened if Quebec acquires a national personality.'

This logical and complete reasoning outlines the four parts of an answer to the above objections against the great project for the future that now haunts our masters of patriotism and national dignity, men who, in the eyes of the entire race, hold high the standard of the ideal.

1. Whether we like it or not, Canada is bound to split up. We do not have to bring it about, but merely to foresee it so that we can supervise the lines of fissure; and it would be inappropriate, indeed unjust, to blame us for it.

2. In any case, the political separation that could result for various French-Canadian groups would destroy neither our *duty* nor our *interests*, neither the *sentiments* nor the *ideal* that now lead us to maintain and strengthen our ethnic links with all French centres of America, and especially with those who are most desirous of remaining faithful to what we are in the schemes of history.

3. The breaking up of our present political structures could hardly diminish our ability to help our dispersed compatriots: that is a fact against which it would surely be difficult to argue. For, putting aside rhetoric and exaggeration, we may well ask what the fate of these compatriots has been under the federal régime during the half-century that has just elapsed, if not

to be shackled, weakened, annihilated by the letter of hypocritical laws perversely turned against them each time they tried to invoke them in their just appeals?

4. Quite the contrary, a strong French State, practically homogeneous and completely free in its activities, would be the surest guarantee of the survival and integrity of our people of the Diaspora, since they would, in a sense, be protected by the zeal of a powerful French and Catholic civilization, which would command the respect of, and finally triumph over, the always ephemeral forces of those civilizations rising to surround us, which are ambitious, but divergent and materialistic, in their aims.

And that is how, even from the point of view of French groups remaining outside Quebec, a French State of smaller but more sensible proportions would still continue to be, through its superiority, the best means of serving the universal interests of the entire race.

That is what we shall now attempt to demonstrate.

The Answer

We seek no separation. We see it coming, for it is indeed coming. It can be felt, glimpsed; there are indications, and even unequivocal signs. We must give it a great deal of thought.

Let us briefly recapitulate these premonitory symptoms. We need only mention, to refresh our memory, the present upheaval in the world, particularly detrimental to Europe, but the consequences of which we will surely have to share. We have greater cause to fear these fatal disturbances in Europe because the country most vulnerable to them is England, a country as proud and avid as always, but now destined, it seems, to drink deep of a vertiginous draught. Meanwhile, the Dominions, including our own, slowly progress by force of principle in their constant evolution toward self-government. This separation, added to the increasingly profound fissures in the Empire, does not bode well for its continued existence. 'Canada is moving toward total independence,' was the judgment of Marshal Fayolle in France last year. The time is past, if it ever existed, when our sole obligation to the metropolis consisted in drinking the Queen's health. Loyalty now involves us in subsidies, dreadnoughts, cannon fodder, all of which rather dampens our enthusiasm for it.

When the bonds of imperial nations are loosened, Canada, if it wishes to be a true nation, will surely not remain *one* country only. For, quite apart from the forces that undermine our bonds with the Empire, there are others at work preparing the dissolution of our federal ties. The United States has one hundred and ten million inhabitants. Canada has a total of seven or eight. Neither history nor our understanding of the psychology of our neighbours permits us to think that they never entertain the desire of Ahab for Naboth's vineyard. If, in our Canadian land, whole provinces are already Americanized, not only through the common language, but also through ideas, sentiments, and tastes; through interests, business, entertainment; through religious sects, schools, magazines and daily newspapers, the theatre; through equal licentiousness in their moral life: religious indifference, divorce, birth control, women's rights, libertarian democracy, social egalitarianism; through a similar materialism in their ideals, and an equally shameless paganism in their pleasures; in short, through a mentality tarred with the same brush, and a civilization as limited in its horizons; and if, in the four years from 1910 to 1914, over a million and a half American subjects have crossed into the Canadian West: is it possible to maintain that at the crucial moment these provinces would refuse the great honour of being annexed? That at this very moment, despite a superficial British surface, they are not more or less consciously promoting this permutation of imperialism?

In the long run will anything be able to resist the ogre next door? Yes. A province that has a civilization based on Catholicism and Gallo-Latin idealism will cultivate aversion for the new alliance. The element in our country that is concerned about rights superior to those of finance or pleasure to the extent of choosing to die rather than betray them, such an element alone will be able to stand up to the Colossus when negotiations begin. It is clear that, at that point, French Canada will no longer have the choice of breaking or not breaking with the rest of the Dominion if it wishes to remain at all faithful to its ideals and not deviate from the providential path its origins have traced.

God grant that the cancellation of the federal pact at least precede the political haggling over Canada that is bound to take place in the councils of the masters of the world! The French section would then be less likely to follow suit as a simple accessory. But could the disintegration of the Dominion occur independently of Americanizing pressures? Although some are still hesitant, we are not rash to consider an affirmative answer, without, of course, any need of trying to turn our predictions into reality. It would be enough to probe the Dominion in order to find, outside our own area, the symptoms of advanced dissolution.

Between the East and the West there is the great enemy, *distance*. Attempts to bridge this gap by the construction of interminable and costly railways have all been futile. Their only result will be the country's bankruptcy, unless those provinces that have no need of them pay for those that do, a state hardly calculated to cement unity. In any case, the natural divisions of a territory that has been called a 'geographical absurdity' impose a neat division of interests, making free trade imperative at the other end of the country, but requiring tariff protection at this end. I know very well that 'human geography' is not entirely dictated by rivers or mountains, and that the political boundaries that still exist derive from national spirit rather than survey demarcations. But only through close solidarity of interests and through a common spirit can geographical gaps be bridged. In the present case these are exactly the things we most lack.

The divergence of interests is obvious. The spiritual divergences are still more profound.

There is not the slightest meeting-point between our languages, social traditions, religious aims, habits of mind, spiritual formation, public institutions, or civil laws. The only way in which these could be closely united would be through the complete abdication of our Catholic and French personality. And these immigrants with whom it is 'criminally' desired to populate the West, these thousands of immigrants arriving from all over and spreading socialism and revolution, will certainly not help to strengthen interprovincial bonds! Their lack of assimilation to an effectively Canadian ideal will long retard the growth of the generous, faithful civic spirit that they would need in order to be helpful in this way. And when will Orangeism rise above itself and judge us fairly? When will it ever contribute to the organization of the country something other than malice and bitterness?

When will the English mind ever be able to conceive of a country effectively bilingual, with mutual respect between the races instead of abuse and the subordination of one to the profit of the other? To this add the religious fanaticism characteristic of any dissidents in matters of faith; the particular narrow-mindedness of a population that is completely unenlightened, that is not bound to the tradition of the great centuries by faith, or education, or purely human philosophy; a population whose science is mere mechanics, whose logic is numerical strength, whose unique standard for judging all things is number of dollars or weight in gold. Can we forget habits that consist entirely of sectarian chauvinism, or the reserve of virulence always ready to sally forth against 'French domination', 'the priest-ridden province', and 'Roman-Popism'? Can we altogether ignore the political passions that, at each new election, stir up to a frantic pitch the ambitions of conflicting parties whose fierce persistence is equalled only by the fanaticism that they provoke throughout the organized press and that sets province against province in shattering struggles. How much longer can this kind of 'clash' continue without the weaker side being crushed by the stronger?

Some people dream of 'bridging the chasm' that separates the two races. That would, indeed, require a new mechanism, and who is to invent it? Even if, through politics or interest, we desired to do so, it would become increasingly impossible to consolidate our part in Confederation. A nation is a moral organism, the fruit of nature: mathematics does not enter into it. Well might Joseph de Maistre scoff at the thought of a group of men putting themselves to the trouble of creating a nation. Any federation is by definition precarious. How much more so when there are hidden but increasingly strong forces working toward its disintegration!

We should perhaps be quiet about these apprehensions, since they are likely to cause anxiety. But what about our partners? 'A timely suggestion,' wrote one Westerner a short time ago in the Regina *Leader* reproduced in the Montreal *Gazette*, 'is that when the Prairie Provinces are conveniently grouped in their provincial Parliaments under the Progressive banner, these provinces, whose needs and development are diametrically opposed to those of the Eastern provinces, should themselves take steps to ensure their complete independence; such a demand could not easily be opposed if all the provinces were united in it. And this would open the way for reciprocal treaties with the United States.'

And so Canada will have its political hegemony. The consequence, unless it happens sooner, is almost bound to be the separation of its component parts. Even if we have, ourselves, tended to move in that direction, the separation would thus not result exclusively from our actions. We are, rather, witnesses of the trend. Our western compatriots may fear such a conclusion: they would perhaps suffer from it, particularly from a national point of view. But it would be a mistake for either of us not to think about it manfully and talk about it openly. From now on it becomes inevitable and will happen sooner or later.

For the moment it is not important to determine which of our brethren will be forced by future events to remain outside the boundaries of a broadened and liberated Quebec. In the first place, there will always be the part played by unforeseeable circumstances. But there will also be forces that can be brought freely into play and that others may need to define more precisely. The French-Canadian groups dispersed, for example, across the great prairie that constitutes the interior basin of the Canadian Northwest will inevitably be the ones most exposed to this severance from the mother province. And who is at fault? History, no doubt, for it sometimes acts without taking account of human wisdom or sentimental preferences. But Providence nevertheless weaves its mysterious designs, and its magnificent plan can be discovered later in the rise and fall of empires. We most warmly hope and wish that Quebec may hold on to all its offshoots; but we must not lull ourselves with chimerical hopes that are contradicted by the symptoms analysed above. When Canada's great skeleton is taken to pieces, French Canada will necessarily have to limit its power and territorial ambitions according to geographical indications, and especially according to the ethnic factors that are capable of being unified; otherwise the future state would lack stability: it could never last. To put it simply, it can never enter into any scheme not based upon reason.

Does this mean, however, that with no further ado we resign ourselves to abandoning our people who live, say, in provinces beyond Ontario? Not at all.

Four elements, as we have seen, combine to form a particular nationality: *origin, language, territory*, and *form of government*. These elements are of unequal importance: the first two are the soul, the last two the body, of a nation. As the soul by far transcends matter, so must unity of origin and community of language be much more important than the claims of territory or political forms. A family depends upon bonds of blood rather than mere physical proximity.

If individual charity is a duty, so is national charity. And if charity is judged by unity of hearts as well as need, it obviously follows that the disruption of political unity and the division of territories do not obviate the dictates of national duty, because they do not totally destroy its foundations. They leave the best part intact, the formal and spiritual links, those that ensure that the basic moral character remains the same; and an ideal community also remains: spirits and hearts are moulded in the same way by the influence of familiar words that carry the same connotations of superior thoughts and sovereign ambition. From this it is clear that even separated by legal boundaries our blood relationship would not be broken, but would continue to dictate the obligations of an effective fraternity.

It might be objected that our response to such a duty would be no more than platonic sympathy or short-term devotion. That would be to forget recent events which have revealed to both sides what our national fraternity makes us capable of accomplishing. The Ontario question, Green Valley, Gravelbourg, to mention only a few names, are eloquent testimony to it. Moreover, consider this fact: these public-minded acts did not spring from federal unity, but from a patriotism more alert, more fully conscious of its duty. In our opinion, any independence that gave us a country more completely ours would thereby develop our public spirit so that it became more enterprising and wider in scope. The dictates of duty would, in any case, be reinforced by our own interests.

Our French State, created through historical evolution, would not, we presume, be so puerile as to desire isolation and insularity. Fences do not prevent neighbourliness. Shunning our neighbours — former associates become competitors — would immediately spell ruin. Compromise would be necessary. Our politics, our trade, our social life would have to take theirs into account, for the separation of our governments would not of itself eliminate common problems deriving from similar needs or dangers. We would still need the water from their lakes, as they would that from our rivers. Our railways would end in their territory, and theirs in ours. To make us realize that all this would mean permanent relationships as close as those of today although more independent, we need only remember our necessary, but so imprudent, relations with our powerful neighbour, the United States. In addition, what an advantage it would be in our dealings with the other Canadian States of tomorrow to have, right there in those States, minds and intelligences fashioned in the same mould as ours, politicians, newspapermen, and men of our religion capable of understanding the situation within our country and of informing us about that of theirs. Obviously there would be shades of difference between our views and theirs, but would this prevent intimate affinities and profound understanding? Especially if we all tried, through an exchange of culture and customs, to safeguard our original temperament.

Then too, what is it that inspires our people in Quebec to fly to the rescue of our distant kin if it is not a religious and patriotic ideal unhampered by meridian lines? Our main ambition is that our Catholic faith be maintained and strengthened in every soul born of our race. The treasure of religion we consider a priceless one; whatever the cost, we intend to preserve it in those who received it at baptism, as well as to carry it to strangers still in the shadows of death. How much more strongly do we wish this for our brothers and nephews! I know that with time the bonds of consanguinity will be loosened. Others will be created by family alliances. And then we shall be stronger, and our distant compatriots as well. In any case they shall, if they wish it as we do, have remained our co-nationals. For since we know that language is the key to freedom and the guardian of faith; that ancestral traditions are as involucres protecting the flower of religion; that a nation's soul cannot be wounded in its individual, family, or social habits without also being wounded — and often fatally — in its religious sentiment; since we know this, we shall continue, through apostolic ideals and French proselytizing, to give our people beyond the 'lines' our vigilant interest and effective sympathy.

Why should not what happened to a certain extent for Franco-Americans — albeit largely through a kind of unreflecting, excessively naïve patriotism — why should it not occur for our Diaspora, and, indeed, for all those who, though stationed outside our political sphere, are nevertheless not insensitive to our moral attraction and the blaze of our genius? Comparisons, though they always falsify to some extent, confirm our ideas in this case. We have been neglected, forgotten, even despised, by political circles in France, because they were exclusively political; we have received very little attention from intellectual, literary, or social circles in France, and that little belated and awkward, because they were on another continent, separated from us for over two centuries, at a time when distance necessarily meant ignorance. But from the religious and most traditional circles we have received innumerable priests and religious persons. Through them has France not lent us its literature, preserved the memory of its history, which was ours as well in the beginning, inspired us with its enthusiasm? And has it not in some measure contributed to the survival of our nation? It would be unfair not to recognize all this. There were some indiscretions that could have been avoided, misunderstandings that should have been cleared up; but these are, at least partly, unavoidable human miseries. We shall never be so presumptuous as to cast doubt upon the continued influence that France has exerted, even during the English régime, upon our national mentality. And, in this age when visitors and tourists move about as easily as books or magazines, what would prevent our French charity from assuming a similar role, but magnifying it, fulfilling it with more determination, more wisdom, more results, with regard to all the miniature Canadas scattered throughout America? What was accomplished for our separated brothers, even under the federal régime, by a mere sister province hobbled by superstitious respect for provincial autonomy, will surely be multiplied tenfold in a State with a population comparable to that of Belgium or Portugal! Our civilization could fill this role the more easily were it to become, through its originality, through the transcendence of its traditions and the homogeneous nature of its religious spirit, a beacon for America, a shining example for everyone to see.

Furthermore, would it be legitimate to accuse us of betraying our fraternal obligations toward Canadians who have left the valleys of Quebec and Ontario, simply because we intend to withdraw, freely, from the political association of provinces? Let us ask a categorical question: what real profit, leaving aside some presumed comfort and some constant but futile hopes, can our French speaking brothers in English provinces have derived from the federal bond? Confederation has perhaps had the advantage of protecting us from our former bugbear, annexation. Today, as we have seen, the régime aggravates the peril for us: indeed it revives it. As for religious or national protection for French minorities outside Quebec, what assurances has Confederation really provided? At the beginning, and in the minds of the Fathers of Confederation, there were sincere, though relative, concessions of freedom. What has happened in practice? Has Orangeism faded, fanaticism waned? What about the Riel affair? And the *Ne Temere* decree? And the so-called 'troubles' in Quebec during the war? And the Despatie-Tremblay union, to mention only a few of the most unjustified crises? Was Confederation responsible for the concession of separate — that is to say Catholic — schools in Ontario, or the interests of the Protestant minority in Quebec and the excess of fanaticism in Upper Canada?

But was it not Confederation that prevented confessional schools in New Brunswick? And that also deprived us of them in Manitoba in 1896, in Alberta and Saskatchewan in 1905, in Keewatin in 1912? And was it not Confederation that refused to intervene on a federal level, and Confederation whose timid remedial bills were disdained when we tried to have recourse to them? Is it not Confederation that has always interpreted laws in the literal spirit that kills and has never understood that living, vital laws need a soul? Is it not Confederation that imposes upon us divorce, and women's suffrage, and imperial conscription, all principles of social dissolution fatal to a race? Is it not Confederation that gives us State schools, unilingual and neutral, and uniform laws in which perish the last traces of the French spirit that enlivened our civil and judicial institutions? Is it not Confederation that refuses to recognize the rights of our national, liberating unions, incapable as it is of judging the true meaning of order and the advantage of safeguarding sensible freedoms? And is it not Confederation that doles out our French language in the most parsimonious amounts in the public services; that keeps it from our youth in many provinces, and ostracizes it with insult and injury?

And finally, is it not Confederation that has anglicized the entire policies of our public representatives, subordinating them to the most risky naval, military, or imperialistic forces? It is impossible to calculate to what extent our morale and our political sense have been depressed by the role we have been fulfilling since 1867.

We must face the fact that Confederation by itself, as far as our national interests are concerned, has been nothing but a miserable bankruptcy, a bitter, humiliating deception. If we have progressed at all since its inception, it has been in spite of its framework; it has been entirely due to our natural growth, our Catholic institutions, our French vigour, the progress of the times, and not to a federal protection that has not proved to be the support we hoped it would be. I shall not mention the criticism that could be made, from a political point of view, of the work Confederation has done in developing a *Canadian* spirit in the largest sense of the word.

And that, in brief, is the kind of power we have received from Confederation to help our western brothers and friends in their survival and development.

Are they satisfied with it?

Let us now consider — without futile optimism, but in the light of our own hearts — the powers a State of Quebec would possess for the expansion of the French force in America.

The child who becomes a man, the teen-ager who comes of age, these constitute progress for the family and for the nation. The design of nature has reached maturity, and nature's aim, when not distorted, is good, its final result is good. The slave who is freed, the ward who is released from tutelage, the colonial who gains independence, the common man who is granted civil rights, all these, when they know the cost of freedom and the right way of using it, constitute a good for society and for human civilization. The same is true of a colony that becomes a nation or a province that becomes a State by the regular and judicial evolution of social factors; these are gains for humanity. Explicit confirmation of this was quoted recently: 'The autonomy of each adult race is not only its right and the normal condition of its proper life, but it is an advantage for all the others, since it is the most perfect form of order among humans.' (Etienne Lamy) And here is also the testimony of the great Bishop of Hippone: 'Everything would go much more smoothly in the world if all kingdoms were small ones, living side by side in joyful harmony. There would thus be many nations in the world, as there are many houses and families in a city. War and the subjugation of nations for the expansion of an empire are necessities that we bear ...'

Could it be claimed that the common advantage for human society that results from the independence of a nation would not be particularly great for those ethnic organizations similar in kind, I mean the French groups scattered outside our territory? A superficial notion, devoid of social psychology. Imagine this wonderful vision: a French race established on the shores of the Saint Lawrence, maintaining its traditions, remaining united in composition but liberal toward its temporary or permanent guests, a race that, through the crises of our contemporary age, would have gained the highest summit of freedom and there planted its banner for everyone to see, now and in future ages. It would present a model of autonomous government, steeped in wisdom because of the faith of its men and its institutions. With increased scope and brilliance, it would give examples of social responsibility and magnificent generosity, as outstanding as those that now have to be borrowed, for education, the arts and letters, religion, and public progress. Freed from its bonds, our Parliament would also shed its 'county council' atmosphere. It would inspire thinkers whose work would be elevated because Latinate, and gestures that would be civilizing because Catholic. Since it would control the main factors of the sociological problems that arise, the genius for political order and the chivalric nobility that form part of its heredity would find a field of action large enough to allow all the best instincts in our collective soul to be developed to the full. This would certainly not prove harmful to our remote brethren, and might indeed provide an ideal strong enough to strengthen resistance and eradicate weaknesses.

It may be objected that, according to many reports, our brothers in the United States are being lost to us. And what can we do for them?

Let us remember, first, that today our hands are tied; and that our people now living beyond the forty-fifth parallel left us at a time when our consciousness of nationhood was not well developed, and their own awareness of the possible alterations of a race living in a foreign nation less keen. From now on all these things could change considerably. We shall put aside modesty and ask whether all the priests we have sent them, the leaders we have trained for them, the attention and the esteem with which we have surrounded them, the fraternal friendship we have had and wish to continue having for them, the social ties they are free to keep with us, whether all these things have counted for nothing in their present French vitality? But we repeat, all this could be bettered.

There is not enough consideration given to the fact that ideas rule the world: *Mens molem agitat.* How strong our universities, our colleges, and our convents would become if their influence extended beyond our frontiers, if their doors were kept open for the sons and daughters of our brethren everywhere! They would be similar to those great schools that in past centuries formed a neo-Latin Europe and contributed so much to the extension of French influence. Would it not be possible to transplant our social institutions so that they grew and flourished under foreign skies, no doubt acquiring some native originality, but never losing any part of their own special personality? Would not the French-Canadian thought that fills our literature and our art, our customs and our experience flow outwards to fertilize our emigrated colonies? Then too, we would be a stronger country, free and independent: the exodus of our surplus population — this transfusion of new blood — would no longer present such grave risks. A glance at the geography of history, and the names of Ireland, Poland, Tyrol, Trentino, Latvia, Croatia, or the Balkans, would significantly confirm these views, which might otherwise be called over-hasty or optimistic. And this confirmation amply justifies the greatest hopes of all those who, like us, tend to believe that the day Quebec and its surrounding territories form a true State with complete mastery over its national personality, that day will see the dawning of a new era for all the French Canadians in America, those outside our State as well as those within, a dawn full of promise, heralding a beautiful day of hard work and glory in the history of nations.

And now to summarize the major conclusions to be drawn from the points we have just outlined.

In our humble opinion our distant brothers have little or no need to feel concern about the political system that links them to us at the moment, for heaven does not seem to smile upon it. What is of the foremost importance for them is to struggle along with us to preserve their soul; and what we owe them most is the Catholic faith and an authentic French civilization.

Let them not be unduly severe with those of us here who hesitate to send them new contingents: one would hesitate at less. Let them rather seek whatever will strengthen in them the desire to remain French and the awareness of belonging, in the words of Mgr Langevin, that great and blessed man of the West, to the most beautiful race in the world.

Let them import heroic priests who understand the value of the French school that stands beside the parish church. Let them train, or obtain from us if they wish, masters to teach their sons the harmony of our ancestral syllables and the lessons of enthusiastic patriotism to be derived from history.

Let them listen, as we do, to the teachings of our professors of national energy; let us all possess the uncompromising ambition always to continue our ascent toward superiority; let us remind one another that a race always has some call of duty and that, through its imminent energy and its desire to live, it weaves itself the mantle that envelops it in the gaze of human history. They, and we, will then have imposing destinies because we shall have used the ten or five talents given us. Equally, our tragedy would be to bury them in inertia or mediocrity.

7

"Throwing the Glass Aside"
Women's Roles

DOCUMENTS

A) The Woman Question, 1879
   Anonymous
B) Votes for Women, 1913
   Sonia Leathes
C) The Woman Question, 1916
   Stephen Leacock
D) The New Citizenship, 1913–1914
   Nellie L. McClung

S tatistical data clearly prove that Canadian women still struggle for equality as the twentieth century slips away — and some evidence suggests regression in certain areas. A glimpse at the House of Commons, any university engineering faculty, or a boardroom of a major company graphically illustrates that women still do not share power commensurate to their proportion of the population. And yet less than one hundred years ago, women could not even run for Parliament or venture into an engineering faculty, and could only enter boardrooms as decorous and silent stenographers.

Canadian feminism emerged in the second half of the nineteenth century. For much of its history the core of the movement remained in Toronto, which served as the headquarters for groups such as the Dominion Women's Emancipation Association, the Dominion Enfranchisement Association, and the Canadian Suffrage Association. While claiming to be national in outlook, these organizations had little impact outside Toronto. Most suffrage campaigns began as intensely provincial, not national, movements. What is now referred to as First Wave feminism declined by the 1920s, unable to sustain an attack on traditional male prerogatives. Today its limited agenda presently earns it dismissal or derision among some who argue that its motivation had little to do with emancipating Canadian women. It was, after all, thoroughly middle class, smug, and anti-immigration, and supported women as nurturing homemakers.

The Canadian feminist movement emerged simultaneously with those in the United States and Great Britain, but unlike the latter never became violent. First Wave feminism sprang from the ideological and social dilemmas posed by industrialization, urbanization, and a perceived decline of family values. As such, it shared ties with general Protestant reformist ideas challenging the ruthless and exploitive excesses of modern capitalism. But reform women did not speak as one, and deep divisions kept them divided and conquered. Some fought for complete gender equality across the socio-political spectrum. Most national organizations believed that women's voting and political participation would spread natural maternal qualities to the society at large. This "maternal" feminist agenda worried little about equality, believing instead that inasmuch as women perform different roles in society than men, they must champion those nurturing qualities from which the whole nation would benefit. For this group, achieving the vote was a means to social reform, not an end in itself. Thus it is hardly surprising that maternal feminists also formed the vanguard of the prohibition movement.

In the final analysis, because men wielded the legislative power, it was they who had to change, and they who had to accept the idea of women's suffrage for it to occur. Most men initially resented or feared the suffrage movement. Eventually, male farming associations in the prairies endorsed women's political rights — perhaps because prairie women so often worked as equals to their husbands as they struggled to hew new lives from the unyielding prairie. Manitoba granted women the franchise in 1916, the first province to do so. The other prairie legislatures soon followed. Quebec women, on the other hand, waited until 1940 before gaining the provincial vote, some twenty years after women earned the federal franchise!

The document entitled "The Woman Question" was published anonymously in the *Canadian Monthly and National Review*. Historians presently also know little about Sonia Leathes, whose article, "Votes for Women," appeared in *University Magazine*.

Stephen Leacock (1869–1944), on the other hand, is one of Canada's best known writers. Leacock's father uprooted young Stephen and his ten siblings from England, took them to South Africa, then Kansas, and finally to Ontario before abandoning them. Stephen went to Upper Canada College, then to the University of Toronto where he trained as a teacher, a vocation he described as "the most dreary, the most thankless and the worst paid profession in the world." He eventually received a Ph.D. from the University of Chicago in 1903, after which he joined the political science department at McGill University in Montreal. Leacock was a brilliant graduate student, writing numerous texts in political science as well as books on history and economics. He is, however, best known for his humour and social satire. And therein lies the problem for historians studying Leacock: he coaxes readers along masterfully developed and brilliantly written arguments that inevitably lead to outrageous conclusions blurring the distinction between irony and genuine beliefs. There is little doubt that he did not want higher education for women, but whether he really believed they found equality and freedom in the home, not the workforce, is open to debate.

Nellie McClung (née Mooney, 1873–1951) is so well known to Canadians through her books and articles that she is perhaps the personification of First Wave feminism. She grew up on farms in Ontario and Manitoba before becoming a school teacher, at age 16, and eventually marrying pharmacist Wesley McClung. Her efforts, particularly as writer and activist, earned her a reputation as a dogged but humorous activist for temperance and woman's suffrage, and her work went far to gain Manitoban women the vote. She and her family moved to Alberta in 1914, where she worked with equal diligence for the cause and eventually won a seat in the legislature in 1921. McClung's fame spread as one of the "Famous Five" women who tackled the Supreme Court of Canada's decision, in the 1928 Persons case, that women were not "persons." They won in 1929, but not before taking the appeal all the way to the Privy Council in London. She eventually retired to Vancouver Island, but continued as a social activist and critic, both as a governor of the CBC and as a delegate to the League of Nations. It was partly through her efforts that the United Church of Canada became the first Christian denomination to appoint female ministers.

A) The Woman Question, 1879
Anonymous

… Here then, is woman, a living, self-conscious, responsible, moral entity, endowed with all the instincts and faculties of her brother, man. Her's a bodily form, somewhat smaller upon the average, perhaps not less enduring, certainly more sensitive and more graceful than his. Her's every intellectual power, be it fancy or imagination, memory or hope, comparison or judgement. Her's too, every affectionate attribute, whether complacent benevolence or gentle pity, sublime enthusiasm or unselfish love. Her's likewise every spiritual capacity — impressibility to the unseen and invisible, longing after the divine and immortal. No matter, to the point I now make, whether she have all these powers and capacities in equal degree with man or not. It suffices that she has them.

And what is she to do with them? That is, What is the purpose of her being? Is it, essentially, any different from that of man's? ...

Is she not included in the generic term 'Man'? Is she not in the world to make the most of herself that her faculties will allow? Are not her life and culture intrinsically just as important, and provided for just as amply, in the nature of things, as her counterpart's? Is she not under just as imperative obligation to strive for the noblest goals of knowledge, wisdom, goodness, power, as is he? and does not her refusal or neglect to do so involve just as great guilt as his? Surely these questions carry their own answers.

But for the attainment of this end in any worthy degree, woman requires freedom of self-determination. Not freedom to do, or be, what idle caprice or blind passion may prompt; but, exercising her best faculties, and using such helps as she can command, to shape her own course and character, responsible only to her own conscience. This would seem to be the prerogative of every moral being, requiring only to be stated to be admitted. Of *man* it has never been denied, save in exceptional instances, and then only on the ground that the exceptions, though apparently, were not really, human beings — which was the stock justification of African slavery. Of *woman* it has not heretofore been, is not now fully, admitted. She has been the appendage of man; in savage and barbarous lands, his drudge and slave ...

But, with the remarkable development of civilization during the last few centuries, the condition of woman has steadily and greatly improved. One burden after another has been lifted from her shoulders. New and numerous avenues to usefulness and happiness have opened to her ...

I conclude then, that all the talk about 'woman's sphere,' as though it were something as accurately definable as a circle, or a triangle, is equally irrelevant and impertinent. I conclude that all fear that woman would fly off at a tangent, or describe an orbit as eccentric as a comet's, were all legal and social restrictions of her freedom removed, is equally idle and childish. I conclude that, spite of all the hindrances she has encountered, and is encountering, she is designed to be under the conditions of her own nature, a self-determining creature, shaping her own course, and working out for herself the problem of being.

And if a self-determining being, as she must be if a moral being, then all means and avenues of culture must be opened to her. To say the contrary is to say that her freedom is only nominal, and that her nature is unworthy a full development. Whether she will avail herself of all these means, and enter all these avenues is quite another question; and for a positive answer to which we have not yet perhaps, sufficient data. It is urged by many that she will not; that there are essential and uneffaceable mental and spiritual differences between woman and man; and that these differences if they do not actually disqualify her for the successful pursuit of certain kinds of culture, do cause her to turn away from them. It is said that she stands for beauty and grace, and man for strength and wisdom; and that therefore her physical frame is smaller, her brain lighter, her intellectual fibre less tough and enduring than man's; though it is admitted that her sense of fitness is finer, her instinct purer, her moral nature nobler. It is concluded accordingly, that if any do choose the educational course, and win distinction in the paths generally supposed to belong especially to man, they are exceptional persons from whom it is entirely unsafe to generalize for the sex ...

The theory of woman's intellectual inferiority is often based on the alleged smaller volume and lighter weight of her brain. But is it certain that her brain is smaller and lighter than man's? Absolutely, it doubtless is: relative to the size and weight of the body, there are reasons for believing there is a slight preponderance the other way. The average weight of man, the statisticians tell us, is 140 pounds; that of woman 124 pounds; making the ratio between them as 100 to 88.57. But the average weight of a woman's brain is said to be only ten per cent. less than man's, making the ratio between these organs as 100 to 90. Thus, proportionally to the weight of the body, there appears to be nearly $1\frac{1}{2}$ per cent. of brain-weight on the average in her favour. The authority for these statements also declares that, if we take the average *minimum* bodily weights of the sexes, the relative brainweight preponderance of the female is still greater, being nearly 4 per cent over man's brain.

Yet waiving this point, and conceding that possibly it may be demonstrable by existing, or yet to be collected statistics, that woman's brain is both absolutely and relatively smaller and lighter than man's, does that settle the question of his intellectual superiority? On the contrary how patent that some very large brains — that is, if they fill the cavities in which they are placed — are very dull and stupid brains; and that some, quite below the medium size are exceedingly active and vigorous ones! Is it not true here as elsewhere, that bulk and weight are no sure criterions of efficiency and value? 'It is curious to note,' says an author, 'the delight which Nature seems to take in iterating and reiterating the fact that a very large proportion of the great intellects of the age just passed, was lodged principally with men who fell short of the medium stature. Napoleon was so very short and slim in early life as to be nicknamed "Puss in Boots." Byron was no taller. Lord Jeffrey was not so tall; and Campbell and Moore were still shorter; while Wilberforce was a less man than any of them.' Size and weight of brain then, supposing these demonstrably in man's favour are not conclusive of his superiority; justify no theory of natural or essential differences between him and his sister …

Admitting, however, all that is urged by the most strenuous as to the essential difference between man and woman, and as to the latter's intellectual inferiority, what then? Are all, or any of the means of improvement and usefulness which man enjoys, and to which she may feel attracted, to be denied her? Is access to the same schools, pursuit of the same wide and varied culture to be prohibited her, if she yearn for it? Because weak and poorly able to cope with the world, is she to be made weaker still? or, if not that, to be hindered from putting forth to the utmost such powers as she has? Because she cannot rise into the empyrean with equal ease and speed with man, shall her wings be clipped, and her soul so heavily weighted as to hold her, an unwilling prisoner, in the dust? The justice of such a course I will not attempt to disprove. The magnanimity of it I will not endeavour to characterize! If woman be so unlike and so unequal to man, as is sometimes alleged, then all the more reason is there for removing every hindrance, and providing every help to her development. All the more reason for encouraging her to put forth every energy for the attainment of the worthiest goal, saying, Here is the wide world, the immeasurable universe, this mysterious life, with all their boundless wealth of knowledge, wisdom, and goodness: take what you can, assimilate what you may, become what your nature will admit.

From woman's right of self-determination follows also the correlative right to enter any employment or profession for which she has the taste and qualification. Within a half century probably not one person in a thousand would have listened to such a proposition with any other feeling than mingled indignation and contempt. But who thinks of questioning it now? A few, boldly entering on other vocations than public opinion had assigned their sex, and successfully discharging their functions, have conquered the right for all others. Whoso now wishes to follow any profession finds comparatively little hindrance outside herself. Talent, tact, devotion, enlarged and directed by sound culture, are all that are needed. With these she may till the soil, practise any handicraft, traffic in any merchandize. With these she may set free the divine image slumbering in the marble, thrill all beholders by the impersonations of genius, lift all listeners on wings of song to the gates of Paradise. With these she may practise the healing art, thread the mazes of legal lore, preach the unsearchable riches of the gospel of love. But as all this is so generally admitted, has been so frequently and clearly demonstrated, nothing more need be said of it here.

Still further, woman's right of self-determination involves the right of *suffrage*. She can never shape her own career, never be the arbiter of her own destiny, so long as she has no voice in framing the laws under which she lives, and to which she is amenable. At least so much is true of man. We cannot think of him as a self-directing being working out the high purpose of his existence, subject to the domination of another person or class. But if this be true of man, why not of woman? And why has she not the same natural right, as a free moral being, to the ballot, as has man? ...

Moreover, it seems to be universally admitted — is very often affirmed — that woman's moral instincts are purer and nobler than man's. If this be so, can the world afford to shut out their promptings and suggestions from all public affairs? Has it made such progress that it can safely trust all its political and civil interests, which are often intimately connected with its moral and religious interests, to the lower and coarser half of humanity?

It is said, however, and doubtless honestly thought by many, that the concession of the ballot to woman, instead of elevating public affairs, would injure herself. This has always been the argument against widening the sphere of her activity. Every change in her condition has been met the objection, "Take care, take care; you will harm instead of helping;" as though women were a delicate porcelain vase that any removal, if not the slightest touch, would shiver to atoms ...

Ask any, what gentleman would be willing to take his wife and daughter, supposing them willing to go, to the wretched places where elections are often held, and into the coarse, profane, and sometimes indecent crowd that clusters around? Evidently none; and there would be no need of it. The entrance of woman into any place, be it street-car, ferryboat, or political meeting, to which as a listener she is now sometimes invited, is a signal for every man to put himself on his good behaviour. Few are the men, on this continent at least, that in any mixed assembly would wish or dare insult, or show the least disrespect to, a woman who did not in some way invite it. Give woman the ballot, and the polling-place will soon be fit for her to enter. Even as it is, the man or the woman who does not shrink from many a public conveyance, with its filth, and vile air, and bad manners, need not be greatly shocked at the offensiveness of an ordinary election room.

But the concession of suffrage to woman, it is said, will beget different political convictions, and so endless bickering, in the family. Do differences in religion beget such discord? Between low and vulgar souls, Yes; and mainly because, amongst such, woman is not yet recognized as a self-determining being, having the right of independent convictions. Between noble and generous natures, No; and still less would different political opinions tend to domestic strife from the fact that the proposed change is based on woman's natural right to do her own thinking, and shape her own destiny. It is not found in business partnerships, the most common instance of voluntary association next to marriage, that political differences occasion serious troubles; and certainly no man would think of entering into such relationship where his freedom in this respect would be in the least danger. So, if there be any genuine respect of husband and wife for each other — if they *be* husband and wife — how much more conciliatory, and tolerant of each other's idiosyncrasies, will they be! If there be no such respect — if they be merely a couple of animals yoked together — it is doubtful if different political affiliations would render their condition any unhappier than it now is.

It may be said again, that the right to vote involves the right to hold office. Not necessarily. Many men now vote who have never been, who never expect to be, elected to any office; some of whom do not want to be, and others of whom are not fit to be so elected. But suppose no man voted, here for Mayor or Member of Parliament, or elsewhere for Governor or President, who is not qualified for, and might not properly aspire to, either of those positions, very few votes would be cast. Yet who, on that account, prizes any the less the sacred right of saying whom he prefers to have preside over the administration of city or country? Suppose, moreover, the right to vote does involve the right to hold office. What then? Have not many women already held office, one sort or another, and shown themselves fully equal to their duties! Were Maria Theresa, and Catharine, and Elizabeth, any the less rulers because they were women? Who for more than forty years has reigned over the vast British Empire, and reigned in the hearts of her subjects as well, but a woman? Have the women of England and the United States, appointed as school superintendents, members of charitable boards, post-mistresses, and clerks of various grades, proved themselves, as a class, either dishonest or incompetent? They have shown themselves just the opposite — able, efficient, upright administrators. Naturally enough, the women whose tastes will lead them to desire, whose relations will justify them in accepting, and whose qualifications will fit them for high office will be very few — certainly for no inconsiderable period. Nor is it fairly supposable, as some times seems to be feared, that, suffrage once conceded to women, both they and their brothers will instantly turn idiots, or act in an altogether idiotic manner in selecting candidates for public places, or that official position would not then, quite as often as now, seek out those most capable of discharging its functions.

But it may be asked, still further, Is not woman to be a wife and mother? Some women, whether from choice or necessity, sustain neither of these relations. Some of these — as Frances Cobbe, Florence Nightingale, Clara Barton — are amongst the ablest, most refined, and noble women of the world, whom it would be a gross insult to liken to the great majority of masculine voters. And there are few things that others of this class — numbering in some populous centres their tens of thousands — do so much need as the stimulus that this enlarged sphere of action, with its new ideas and purposes, would give. Besides, if every woman were to be a wife and mother — if every one were to aspire to these relations as intrinsically the most desirable for her, as in many respects they unquestionably are — I know not that those would be any reasons why she should be content with being a mere over-dressed doll on the one hand, or an abject slave, doing and thinking only what her master permits on the other ...

It is objected, finally, that women do not want the right of suffrage; that they are entirely content to remain without other influence on public affairs than they now have. Of many women — perhaps the majority — this is unquestionably true. How greatly to their praise it need not be said. Certainly it is not to their praise if they could, by their votes, help the industrial, educational, and moral interests of their country. Many persons are said to be wholly satisfied in very unnatural and pernicious relations ...

But it is very far from true that *no* women wish to vote. Thousands, and tens of thousands, and they will soon be hundreds of thousands wait impatiently to be invested with this right. And if there were but one woman in all the land who claimed the right, with what justice could it be withheld? Is there any better reason for wronging one or a few than for wronging many? It seems quite evident moreover, that the time is not far distant when this right will be conceded in all free countries; for how rapid has been the progress of public opinion in this direction during the last twenty-five years. That length of time ago, how few — and those counted as womanish men, or manish women, fanatics or lunatics — were willing to confess any leaning toward, or friendship for, the so-called 'Woman Movement'? Today, how many of the keenest politicians, quick to scent the coming breeze, are avowing themselves in its favour! Let us hope that it is not simply because they want votes. That there is a strong and growing feeling in England, and very considerable interest in certain circles in this Dominion, on the subject, is familiar to all intelligent persons. In the United States one territory has already placed woman, so far as the law is concerned on an entire equality with man; while many States have taken very decided steps in the same direction; among other things, endowing her with the right of suffrage on educational questions, as well as recognizing her eligibility to certain offices. During the last session of Congress a bill was passed authorizing her to practise in the Supreme Court on the same terms with man; while the Judiciary Committee of the Senate reported an amendment to the Constitution sweeping away all distinctions of sex in regard to political rights. It would seem that one risks little in predicting that another generation will see woman's claim to suffrage placed on the same basis with man's throughout the great Republic ...

B) Votes for Women, 1913
Sonia Leathes

... The problem of women suffrage which, though only a part of a general movement, is its culminating point, has its roots in, and grows directly out of these problems. It is indeed but a further, perhaps the last, chapter in the great history of the emancipation of the individual, black or white, rich or poor, male or female, from social and political disability imposed upon him or her on account of birth alone. This is the true meaning of democracy. It is not that all persons shall, or indeed ever can, be absolutely equal in intellect, moral power, influence, and wealth, and in the position among their fellows which is determined by the possession of these qualities. Democracy does not imply identity or equality in social status. The essence of democracy is the removal of all artificial restrictions which bar the way to the progress, development, and advancement, be it economic, social, or political, of any individual or of any class on account of birth, colour, religious creed, or sex alone. Democracy does not deal with people in herds or in sections. It says to each individual: "The road is clear. Go forth, and in your struggle onwards no one shall have the right to say to you, these are the limits of your sphere," or, "a further advance will injure your peculiar disposition and qualities, and I shall therefore take it upon myself to prevent your exceeding what I consider to be your limits." As one of the most eloquent preachers asked half a century ago: "Has God made woman capable, morally, physically, intellectually, of taking part in all human affairs? Then what God made her able to do, there is strong argument that He intended her to do. Our divine sense of justice tells us that the being who is to be governed by laws should first assent to them, that the being who is taxed shall have a voice in fixing the character and amount of the financial burden which it is to bear. Then, if woman is made responsible before the law, if she is admitted to the gallows, to the gaol, and to the tax lists, we have no right to debar her from the ballot box."

Practically all the arguments against women's suffrage fall under three categories: Some people say that they do not believe in women's suffrage, when really what they do not believe in is representative government. They observe the deficiencies created by our system of party government; they watch the abuse of electoral privileges; the comparative civil incompetency of a considerable portion of the existing electorate, the periodical occurrence of unseemly proceedings in the various parliaments, and they are disgusted. These persons will do well to study the probable conditions under which they themselves and the class to which they belong would have to live to-day if the three Reform Bills and the British North America Act had never been passed, and were the whole population of Great Britain, Ireland, and the Colonies still governed exclusively by the privileged class of land-owners of Great Britain, who until then controlled the election of the House of Commons, whilst they themselves then, as to-day, occupied a majority of the seats in the House of Lords.

The British Constitution allowed this state of things, but the people arose and claimed that the spirit of the British tradition of fair play, justice, and liberty was against it. They claimed that every class should have the right to protect its own interests directly instead of having to depend upon the sense of justice, generosity, or protection of another class. And they won on all points — where men were concerned. Women to-day still continue to live under conditions denounced as "a stigma" by Mr. Gladstone, when speaking of the then unenfranchised status of the agricultural labourer. "It is an intolerable injustice to inflict the stigma of electoral disfranchisement on any man," he exclaimed in 1884, yet, on the same occasion, he caused his supporters to abandon an amendment to the Bill which was to enfranchise women.

This brings us to the second category of the anti-suffrage arguments. Some people think that they do not believe in women's suffrage, when really what they do not believe is that women are persons. They have thought of women as "wives," "mothers," "daughters"; and though they have been obliged to admit the existence of the female stenographer, shop assistant, clerk, physician, even of the female mayor and city councillor, they cannot as yet fully grasp the fact that in addition to her private relationship to some man, a woman is still a social unit, a citizen, a subject, a person. The fact of her being somebody's wife, or daughter, or sister, has nothing to do with her being a tax-payer. She remains personally responsible for the observance or non-observance of the law of the land. She is equally affected by war, conditions of climate, finance, industry, national prosperity or adversity. All these matters affect women as well as men, and women should have the right to help decide all questions of policy for precisely the same reason that men possess this right. Yet how deeply rooted this androcentric view of society still is was illustrated again on the occasion when the Naval Bill was before the House of Commons. "Shall it be," said the premier on that occasion, "that we, contributing to that defence of the whole Empire, shall have absolutely, as citizens of this country, no voice whatever in the councils of the Empire? I do not think that such would be a tolerable condition." Unless the premier contemplated a measure for the enfranchisement of all the adult women of the Dominion, it is perfectly evident that he had, as many others had before him, entirely forgotten at the time, that women in Canada are one-half of the people and that the condition which he describes as "not tolerable" for the male half of the population of Canada is one under which the other, the female half, habitually has to live. "To exclude all Women, a whole sex, from representative government," said John Stuart Mill, "is tantamount to saying that women are not called upon to take an interest in the affairs of the nation." Yet, what nation can hope to possess public spirited men as long as it discourages its mothers from taking that interest in its collective concerns which only direct responsibility can create and keep up?

But, comes the great objection, woman must remain within her sphere, which is the home. If, by one's sphere is meant the place where one's daily occupation lies, then the place of those women who are wives and mothers, and have husbands who can, and will, support them and their children, will certainly be within the four walls of their home. In this same sense a man's place is the office or work-shop or farm or pulpit. Nobody's place is the polling booth. To be a voter does not mean sitting in parliament. Only a small number of voters are able or willing to stand for election to that august body and, if duly elected, parliament becomes their proper sphere. For the rest of the electors the recording of their ballots once every few years represents not so much the power to govern as the power to indict, to call to account those who govern them. This power to call the government to account, if it should fail to pursue a policy acceptable to a majority of its electors, an unenfranchised portion of the population does not possess. Where women are not electors, parliament is not responsible to women, and their interests and wishes are not directly represented. Even when legislation is passed affecting the special interests of women, — for instance, the hours and time of work in factories, their admission to, or exclusion from, certain trades and professions, and the minimum wage, — such laws are dealt with entirely as seems best to the representatives of the male electorate, and in no case are the women themselves consulted. This inability to control legislation brings with it hardships which increase with the advent of every newly enfranchised male section of the population. It becomes increasingly hard since, during this last century, the introduction of power-driven machinery has forced the woman of the working classes to the factory, in order to continue to do that share of her economically productive work which she used a century ago to do at home, by which she then, as now, contributed her share towards the support of herself and of the household to which she belongs, as wife, mother, or daughter. She has, thus, reluctantly in many cases, become the competitor and the rival of the working man.

And this brings us to the third category of arguments, which assumes that there is such a thing as a dividing line between the sphere properly belonging to men and the sphere belonging to women. There is no such thing in modern days. And if we make it our business to inquire into the exact circumstances relating to the obliteration of this dividing line, we cannot but come to the conclusion that the invasion of men into what was properly considered to be "woman's sphere" not only preceded but overwhelmingly exceeds the invasion of women into "man's sphere." It is, in fact, not too much to say that the former resulted in the latter.

A hundred years ago the home was not only a family but also an industrial unit. Woman was the spinner, the weaver, the provider of the food and of the clothing for the household; and the impelling motive behind these home industries was love and service. The linen that was "homespun," the cloth that was "home woven," the stockings which were "home knitted," were produced as strongly and as well made as it was possible to make them, in order that they might be of service as long as possible. The milk was pure and the butter sweet, for this was most profitable to the health of the household. There were no other profits to be considered.

Then it gradually began to dawn upon humanity, — and to be just, almost entirely upon its male half, — that it would be profitable to extend the principle of collective enterprise, a principle which had already been applied in matters of state and city defence and in the rudiments of public means of communication, to the feeding and to the clothing of society. Whilst the invention of power-driven machinery led to a rapid application of the principle to the latter needs, an improved system of the means of communication and transport soon revolutionized the principle of the former. Food, from being a thing to eat, became a thing to sell. It became more profitable to sell dirty and watered milk, cleanliness being a costly matter. It became profitable to sell adulterated food and adulterated cloth and shoddy articles of clothing, deliberately manufactured so as not to last and in order that the consumer might have to purchase again. It became profitable to carry on these collective industries by the sweated labour of men, and especially of women and children, and the most profitable forms of collective industrial enterprise left, and still leave, behind them a trail of broken health and broken lives and broken morals as inevitable by-products. "Let women attend to the work which still remains within their home-sphere," says the opponent, and leaves thereby entirely out of account that the remaining home industries of cooking and cleaning and washing to which he or she presumably alludes are already in the significant transition stage between individual, or private, and collective, or social, enterprise. "Laundry interests," and "baking interests," "canning interests," "jam and preserving interests," "dairy interests," have invaded the individual housewife's immemorial "sphere," and have wrenched from her hands her exclusive control and responsibility for the health and for the well-being of the household. And in all cases the "socializing" of a home industry meant the employment of many men where women used before to be exclusively employed. To sit at the domestic spinning wheel, to stand at the domestic wash tub or at the domestic kitchen-range we esteemed to be an exclusively female privilege and esteemed to be degrading to a man. To attend the powerdriven washing machines, spindles, and weaving loom, and bakeries is now not only "man's work," but the presence of female labour in this socialized form of female industries is condemned, in many cases successfully abolished, and in almost all cases discouraged by an arbitrary payment of a lower wage for an equivalent amount of work. Recently the London County Council established training classes for boys who wish to become cooks and waiters. To these classes no girls are admitted, the training which is offered to girls being of a "domestic" nature, for their own husbands and children, whilst the boys are trained to be specialists and social servants.

On all sides we hear this outcry that the inevitable advent of women into the socialized work of the world will react injuriously on the home. If the adaptation of the home to a new stage of social development is to be branded as injurious, it is the inoffensive looking baker's, dairy or laundry man's or department stores' delivery cart, stationed at our back door, that is the real offender against which the wrath should be directed with presumably as happy results. And let us remember that there is another side to the whole question. For centuries the home was almost the only humanizing centre where the spiritual ideals of love and service were kept alive and handed down from generation to generation. It was the inevitable result of the entrance of women into all the departments where the public business of the nation is carried on that there should steadily manifest itself a new but ever growing desire, peculiar to woman's nature, a desire to assist the weak, to make dirty places clean and crooked places straight. Those who attack this new phase of social development seem to be unable to comprehend that women will remain women whatever their occupation, and that if a woman's delicate feelings and susceptibilities have survived the realities and trials of a weekly "wash" for a family of six, they are likely to triumph in the face of her direct contact with any of the duties of her occupation in office, store, or factory. Women, instead of becoming unsexed, have a way of infusing their own home view into business, industry, and politics. Imperceptible at first, but increasing by degrees, this "indirect influence," though it cannot take the place of the direct power of the ballot, has yet placed its unmistakeable stamp on all the departments of social work to which it has been admitted. Hence the wave of reforms and enquiries into conditions which had previously been accepted with unquestioning acquiescence. It is this home-side, this human side, which has, wherever women have been granted the ballot, at once come to the forefront of politics.

The world is in a transition stage. Everywhere private and amateur service is being replaced by social and specialized service. We have discovered that it is more profitable and less wasteful for social purposes if the man who makes boots does not also kill pigs or build his own house. We have realized that, because a man is a good father or a woman is a good mother, they are neither of them necessarily able to instruct their children in mathematics, Latin, or art, or to remove their adenoids; and the employment of specialists to instruct their children and to treat their ailments is no longer a matter of privilege for the few but open to all classes. Our railways and mail service, our lighting and drainage, our press, our art collections, are for general use, and they are the results of collective enterprise and could never have existed but for it.

Our failure lies not in the replacement of private enterprise by collective and social enterprise, but in our slowness to grasp that just as private control and responsibility accompanied the former, collective control and collective responsibility must accompany the latter. And collective control is exercised through legislation, through the administration of laws, and through the control of public funds. From this collective control, in countries which do not possess women suffrage, women are completely excluded. They have no voice in the councils of the nation which decide whether a "pure milk bill" or a "housing bill" or a "mental deficiency bill" shall save the lives of millions of babies born and unborn, and mercifully protect the feeble-minded from society and society from the feeble-minded. They have not at their disposal the only effectual means of persuading a government that to offend the "dairy interests" or "the canning interests" will not mean disaster to the party in power. They have not the means of stamping upon the statutes and regulations referring to the meat trade the uncompromising point of view of all mothers and housekeepers, that meat which is not good enough for export purposes is not good enough for home consumption. At present the Canadian and American householder consumes, as is known to those familiar with blue books, a large proportion of the meat classified as "unfit for export." Unenfranchised women cannot effectually say to unscrupulous employers and slum landlords: you can make money, but you shall not make it at the expense of the physical, mental, and moral welfare of our children, or by excluding light and air and breathing space, and by causing the deadly perils of overcrowding. "The average man," as an eminent professor of political economy said, "thinks in terms of dollars, the average woman in terms of home, husband, and unborn babies." With the average man property interests come first. Man is the restless explorer, inventor, and conqueror. He roams the seas and the air. He bridles the forces of nature to do his bidding. He orders Niagara to grind his corn and to milk his cows, and he chains the lightning to his desk and to his toast rack. But there is just one industry from which he is forever excluded: it is the women who hold the monopoly of producing the people who are to benefit by all these great achievements, and without which the world within one generation would become a desert.

To be able to adequately protect human life from the onslaught of property interests, women must to-day have the ballot. The individual interests of yesterday have become collective interests to-day. The individual responsibilities of the home-maker of yesterday have become the collective interests of the home-maker of to-day. And collective interests are controlled by parliament, by legislation, and by the expenditure of public funds which are all in turn controlled by the elector's ballot.

It is on this account that women to-day say to the governments of all the world: You have usurped what used to be our authority, what used to be our responsibility. It is you who determine to-day the nature of the air which we breathe, of the food which we eat, of the clothing which we wear. It is you who determine when, and how long, and what our children are to be taught and what their prospects as future wage-earners are to be. It is you who can condone or stamp out the white slave traffic and the starvation wage. It is you who by granting or by refusing pensions to the mothers of young children can preserve or destroy the fatherless home. It is you who decide what action shall be considered a crime and how the offender, man, woman, or child, shall be dealt with. It is you who decide whether cannons and torpedoes are to blow to pieces the bodies of the sons which we bore. And since all these matters strike at the very heartstrings of the mothers of all nations, we shall not rest until we have secured the power vested in the ballot: to give or to withhold our consent, to encourage or to forbid any policy or course of action which concerns the people — our children every one.

C) The Woman Question, 1916
Stephen Leacock

… The great majority of women have no means of support of their own. This is true also of men. But the men can acquire means of support. They can hire themselves out and work. Better still, by the industrious process of intrigue rightly called 'busyness,' or business, they may presently get hold of enough of other people's things to live without working. Or again, men can, with a fair prospect of success, enter the criminal class, either in its lower ranks as a house breaker, or in its upper ranks, through politics. Take it all in all a man has a certain chance to get along in life.

A woman, on the other hand, has little or none. The world's work is open to her, but she cannot do it. She lacks the physical strength for laying bricks or digging coal. If put to work on a steel beam a hundred feet above the ground, she would fall off. For the pursuit of business her head is all wrong. Figures confuse her. She lacks sustained attention and in point of morals the average woman is, even for business, too crooked.

This last point is one that will merit a little emphasis. Men are queer creatures. They are able to set up a code of rules or a standard, often quite an artificial one, and stick to it. They have acquired the art of playing the game. Eleven men can put on white flannel trousers and call themselves a cricket team, on which an entirely new set of obligations, almost a new set of personalities, are wrapped about them. Women could never be a team of anything.

So it is in business. Men are able to maintain a sort of rough and ready code which prescribes the particular amount of cheating that a man may do under the rules. This is called business honesty, and many men adhere to it with a dog-like tenacity, growing old in it, till it is stamped on their grizzled faces, visibly. They can feel it inside them like a virtue. So much will they cheat and no more. Hence men are able to trust one another, knowing the exact degree of dishonesty they are entitled to expect.

With women it is entirely different. They bring to business an unimpaired vision. They see it as it is. It would be impossible to trust them. They refuse to play fair.

Thus it comes about that woman is excluded, to a great extent, from the world's work and the world's pay.

There is nothing really open to her except one thing — marriage. She must find a man who will be willing, in return for her society, to give her half of everything he has, allow her the sole use of his house during the daytime, pay her taxes, and provide her clothes.

This was, formerly and for many centuries, not such a bad solution of the question. The women did fairly well out of it. It was the habit to marry early and often. The 'house and home' was an important place. The great majority of people, high and low, lived on the land. The work of the wife and the work of the husband ran closely together. The two were complementary and fitted into one another. A woman who had to superintend the baking of bread and the brewing of beer, the spinning of yarn and the weaving of clothes, could not complain that her life was incomplete ...

But if the machine age has profoundly altered the position of the working man, it has done still more with woman. It has dispossessed her. Her work has been taken away. The machine does it. It makes the clothes and brews the beer. The roar of the vacuum cleaner has hushed the sound of the broom. The proud proportions of the old-time cook, are dwindled to the slim outline of the gas-stove expert operating on a beefsteak with the aid of a thermometer. And at the close of day the machine, wound with a little key, sings the modern infant to its sleep, with the faultless lullaby of the Victrola. The home has passed, or at least is passing out of existence. In place of it is the 'apartment' — an incomplete thing, a mere part of something, where children are an intrusion, where hospitality is done through a caterer, and where Christmas is only the twenty-fifth of December ...

Thus the unmarried woman, a quite distinct thing from the 'old maid' of ancient times, came into existence, and multiplied and increased till there were millions of her.

Then there rose up in our own time, or within call of it, a deliverer. It was the Awful Woman with the Spectacles, and the doctrine that she preached was Woman's Rights. She came as a new thing, a hatchet in her hand, breaking glass. But in reality she was no new thing at all, and had her lineal descent in history from age to age. The Romans knew her as a sybil and shuddered at her. The Middle Ages called her a witch and burnt her. The ancient law of England named her a scold and ducked her in a pond. But the men of the modern age, living indoors and losing something of their ruder fibre, grew afraid of her. The Awful Woman — meddlesome, vociferous, intrusive — came into her own.

Her softer sisters followed her. She became the leader of her sex. 'Things are all wrong,' she screamed, 'with the *status* of women.' Therein she was quite right. 'The remedy for it all,' she howled, 'is to make women "free," to give women the vote. When once women are free everything will be all right.' Therein the woman with the spectacles was, and is, utterly wrong.

The women's vote, when they get it, will leave women much as they were before ...

For when the vote is reached the woman question will not be solved but only begun. In and of itself, a vote is nothing. It neither warms the skin nor fills the stomach. Very often the privilege of a vote confers nothing but the right to express one's opinion as to which of two crooks is the crookeder.

But after the women have obtained the vote the question is, what are they going to do with it? The answer is, nothing, or at any rate nothing that men would not do without them. Their only visible use of it will be to elect men into office. Fortunately for us all they will not elect women. Here and there perhaps at the outset, it will be done as the result of a sort of spite, a kind of sex antagonism bred by the controversy itself. But, speaking broadly, the women's vote will not be used to elect women to office. Women do not think enough of one another to do that. If they want a lawyer they consult a man, and those who can afford it have their clothes made by men, and their cooking done by a chef. As for their money, no woman would entrust that to another woman's keeping. They are far too wise for that.

So the woman's vote will not result in the setting up of female prime ministers and of parliaments in which the occupants of the treasury bench cast languishing eyes across at the flushed faces of the opposition. From the utter ruin involved in such an attempt at mixed government, the women themselves will save us. They will elect men. They may even pick some good ones. It is a nice question and will stand thinking about.

But what else, or what further can they do, by means of their vote and their representatives to 'emancipate' and 'liberate' their sex?

Many feminists would tell us at once that if women had the vote they would, first and foremost, throw everything open to women on the same terms as men. Whole speeches are made on this point, and a fine fury thrown into it, often very beautiful to behold.

The entire idea is a delusion. Practically all of the world's work is open to women now, wide open. *The only trouble is that they can't do it.* There is nothing to prevent a woman from managing a bank, or organising a company, or running a department store, or floating a merger, or building a railway — except the simple fact that she can't. Here and there an odd woman does such things, but she is only the exception that proves the rule. Such women are merely — and here I am speaking in the most decorous biological sense — 'sports.' The ordinary woman cannot do the ordinary man's work. She never has and never will. The reasons why she can't are so many, that is, she *'can't'* in so many different ways, that it is not worthwhile to try to name them.

Here and there it is true there are things closed to women, not by their own inability but by the law. This is a gross injustice. There is no defence for it. The province in which I live, for example, refuses to allow women to practise as lawyers. This is wrong. Women have just as good a right to fail at being lawyers as they have at anything else. But even if all these legal disabilities, where they exist, were removed (as they will be under a woman's vote) the difference to women at large will be infinitesimal. A few gifted 'sports' will earn a handsome livelihood but the woman question in the larger sense will not move one inch nearer to solution.

The feminists, in fact, are haunted by the idea that it is possible for the average woman to have a life patterned after that of the ordinary man. They imagine her as having a career, a profession, a vocation — something which will be her 'life work' — just as selling coal is the life work of the coal merchant.

If this were so, the whole question would be solved. Women and men would become equal and independent. It is thus indeed that the feminist sees them, through the roseate mist created by imagination. Husband and wife appear as a couple of honourable partners who share a house together. Each is off to business in the morning. The husband is, let us say, a stock broker: the wife manufactures iron and steel. The wife is a Liberal, the husband a Conservative. At their dinner they have animated discussions over the tariff till it is time for them to go to their clubs.

These two impossible creatures haunt the brain of the feminist and disport them in the pages of the up-to-date novel.

The whole thing is mere fiction. It is quite impossible for women — the average and ordinary women — to go in for having a career. Nature has forbidden it. The average woman must necessarily have — I can only give the figures roughly — about three and a quarter children. She must replace in the population herself and her husband with something over to allow for the people who never marry and for the children that do not reach maturity. If she fails to do this the population comes to an end. Any scheme of social life must allow for these three and a quarter children and for the years of care that must be devoted to them. The vacuum cleaner can take the place of the housewife. It cannot replace the mother. No man ever said his prayers at the knees of a vacuum cleaner, or drew his first lessons in manliness and worth from the sweet old-fashioned stories that a vacuum cleaner told. Feminists of the enraged kind may talk as they will of the paid attendant and the expert baby minder. Fiddlesticks! These things are a mere supplement, useful enough but as far away from the realities of motherhood as the vacuum cleaner itself. But the point is one that need not be laboured. Sensible people understand it as soon as said. With fools it is not worth while to argue.

But, it may be urged, there are, even as it is, a great many women who are working. The wages that they receive are extremely low. They are lower in most cases than the wages for the same, or similar work, done by men. Cannot the woman's vote at least remedy this?

Here is something that deserves thinking about and that is far more nearly within the realm of what is actual and possible than wild talk of equalising and revolutionising the sexes.

It is quite true that women's work is underpaid. But this is only a part of a larger social injustice.

The case stands somewhat as follows: Women get low wages because low wages are all that they are worth. Taken by itself this is a brutal and misleading statement. What is meant is this. The rewards and punishments in the unequal and ill-adjusted world in which we live are most unfair. The price of anything — sugar, potatoes, labour, or anything else — varies according to the supply and demand: if many people want it and few can supply it the price goes up: if the contrary it goes down. If enough cabbages are brought to market they will not bring a cent a piece, no matter what it cost to raise them.

On these terms each of us sells his labour. The lucky ones, with some rare gift, or trained capacity, or some ability that by mere circumstance happens to be in a great demand, can sell high. If there were only one night plumber in a great city, and the water pipes in a dozen homes of a dozen millionaires should burst all at once, he might charge a fee like that of a consulting lawyer …

So it stands with women's wages. It is the sheer numbers of the women themselves, crowding after the few jobs that they can do, that brings them down. It has nothing to do with the attitude of men collectively towards women in the lump. It cannot be remedied by any form of woman's freedom. Its remedy is bound up with the general removal of social injustice, the general abolition of poverty, which is to prove the great question of the century before us. The question of women's wages is a part of the wages' question.

To my thinking the whole idea of making women free and equal (politically) with men as a way of improving their *status*, starts from a wrong basis and proceeds in a wrong direction.

Women need not more freedom but less. Social policy should proceed from the fundamental truth that women are and must be dependent. If they cannot be looked after by an individual (a thing on which they took their chance in earlier days) they must be looked after by the State. To expect a woman, for example, if left by the death of her husband with young children without support, to maintain herself by her own efforts, is the most absurd mockery of freedom ever devised. Earlier generations of mankind, for all that they lived in the jungle and wore cocoanut leaves, knew nothing of it. To turn a girl loose in the world to work for herself, when there is no work to be had, or none at a price that will support life, is a social crime …

I leave [readers] with the thought that perhaps in the modern age it is not the increased freedom of woman that is needed but the increased recognition of their dependence. Let the reader remain agonised over that till I write something else.

D) The New Citizenship, 1913–1914
Nellie L. McClung

Ideas are contagious and epidemic. They break out unexpectedly and without warning. Thought without expression is dynamic and gathers volume by repression. Evolution, when blocked and suppressed, becomes revolution.

At the present time there are many people seriously alarmed by the discontent among women. They say women are no longer contented with woman's work and woman's sphere. Women no longer find their highest joy in plain sewing and working in wool. The washboard has lost its charm and the days of the hair wreath are ended. Many people view this condition with alarm and believe that women are deserting the sacred sphere of home-making and the rearing of children; in short, that women are losing their usefulness. We may as well face the facts. We cannot drive women back to the spinning wheel and the mat hook. We do hear more of discontent among women than we once did. Labor saving devices have entered the home and women are saved the endless labor of days gone by, when a woman's hours of labor were: 5 a.m. to 5 a.m. The reason we hear of more discontent than formerly is that women have more time to be discontented. The horse on the tread-mill may be discontented, but he has to keep on going, he has no time to tell his troubles to the horse near him.

But discontent is not necessarily wicked. There is such a thing as criminal contentment and there is such a thing as divine discontent. Discontent means the stirring of ambition, the desire to spread out, to improve, to grow. Discontent is a sign of life corresponding to growing pains in a healthy child. The poor woman who is making a brave struggle for existence, whose every energy is bent to the task of making a living, is not saying much. She has not time. The women who are making the disturbance are women who have time of their own, who have time for observation. Women have more leisure than men now and the question is what are they going to do with it. Custom and conventionality recommends amusements, social functions intermixed with kindly deeds of charity, the making of strong and durable garments for the poor, visiting the sick, comforting the sad, advising the erring, all of which women are doing, but the trouble arises here, — is this, while women do these things they are thinking, they wonder about the causes, the underlying conditions, — must they always be.

Women have never yet lived in their own world. Man has assigned woman her sphere. Woman's sphere is anything a man does not wish to do himself. This is a simple distribution of labor and easily understood and very satisfactory to half the population. Men have given a great deal of attention to women. They have told us exactly what we are like. They have declared us to be illogical, hysterical, impulsive, loving, patient, forgiving, malicious, vindictive, bitter, not any too honest, not very reliable. They have given us credit for all the good in the world and yet blamed us for all the evil. They are very prone to speak of women, as a class, of women — women in bulk, making each individual woman responsible for the sins of all.

Recently when members of the W.C.T.U went before our law makers in Ottawa, pleading for a much needed reform, the prohibition of cigarettes, pleading in the name of our boys, who are every day being ruined in body and soul, one of the members of Parliament rose in his place and told these women to go home and reform their own sex before they came looking for any reforms from men. He said women were the slaves of fashion and should not look for any measure of reform from men until their own sex was emancipated. No one would have dared to speak so illogically to men. Think of telling half-a-dozen men to go home and reform all mankind! Quite a large order, too, — yet women have constantly to listen to such unjust and unreasonable criticism. This insult to womanhood passes unchallenged! The fault is not with the individual, but with the race. Our earliest writers spoke of women always in the mass. St. Augustine, one of the early writers of the Christian Church, described women as "a household menace, a daily peril, a necessary evil." St. Paul made his contribution, too, and although he was careful to say that in this matter he spoke on his own authority, yet this has not in any way obscured the faith of those who wish to believe as he did. "Wives obey your husbands." A woman must not speak in the Church but ask her husband quietly at home. St. Paul has made his commentary on the marriage question too, and advises all Christian workers to remain single "even as I am," but he goes on, "Marry if you must, only do not say 'I did not warn you'."

No wonder women have had a hard time living down these things. In our own day we have historians who undertake to state what we are like and just where we stand. Sir Almoth Wright has recently written a book which no doubt will be popular in some circles. He says there are no good women though there are some women who have come under the influence of good men. Women have never yet lived in their own world. Our world has been made for us; even the fashions for which we receive so much criticism are made by men. The feet of little girls in China are bound by the mother and the nurse, but it is not for their pleasure that this torture is practised, but that the little girl may be pleasing in the eyes of her father and in the eyes of a possible future husband. Missionaries tell us of the mother's grief and compassion for the little sufferer, yet the cruel fashion goes on. In our own civilization women have been taught that they must attract men. The attractive girl is the successful girl in the judgment of the world, and there is a deeper reason for this than appears, for the attractiveness of a girl often determines her social standing. A pretty girl marries a millionaire, is presented at court and travels in Europe; her plainer sister, though perhaps more intelligent and more unselfish, marries a boy from home, lives on a farm and works out in the harvest time. I am not comparing the two destinies as to which holds the greatest chances for usefulness or happiness, but merely showing how widely divergent two lives may be. A woman's social standing largely depends upon her ability to attract men and her chances of marriage are so directly in proportion to her personal charm that our girls have one definite problem which excludes all others. For this reason beauty parlors flourish and University extension lectures languish.

We blame girls for dressing foolishly, boldly and immodestly, yet we who uphold this system of women's economic and social dependence are responsible for it. It is perfectly true that men are attracted by the bold, foolish and frivolous girls, and that the girl who is quite independent and strong minded is matrimonially disqualified ...

Under our present social conditions many a woman has found that it pays to be foolish. Men like frivolity before marriage and yet all the sterner virtues after marriage. Men like frivolity and women have taken them at their word and given them too much of it.

The economic dependence of women, making it necessary that women must attract for a living, is one of the greatest injustices that has been done us.

Women are naturally the guardians of the race. Women know the cost of human life as no man can ever know it. Women learned to cook so that her children might be fed, learned to sew that her children might be clothed, learned to think that her children might be guided. Women no longer can be flattered or threatened into silence. For long years the old iniquitous lie has been told us that the hand that rocks the cradle rules the world, but it is no longer believed by thinking women. It is intended more as a bouquet than as a straight statement of facts. It is given as a sedative to soothe us if we grow restless. When driving with a small child we often let the little fellow hold the end of the reins, and if the child really believes he is driving we consider the game successful, but we cannot deceive the average child very long. So, too, the average woman refuses to be deceived when she is praised like an angel and treated like an idiot. The hand that rocks the cradle does not rule the world or the liquor traffic would have been outlawed many years ago. Would any mother accept money in return for her boy's soul, the purity of his mind and the health of his body? Would any liquor dealer dare to offer you money for the privilege of corrupting your son? "May your money perish with you!" you would cry in scorn, yet our Province does this, our Government does this and glorifies and justifies its action. If it is wrong for the individual to accept blood money, why is it not wrong for a State? The liquor traffic and the white slave traffic are kept up by men for men, women are the victims, women pay the price. Oh no, when the hand that rocks the cradle gets its chance at ruling the world, it will be a safer, sweeter, cleaner world for the occupant of the cradle. Women have kept silence a long time. They have religiously believed it their duty like charity to bear all things, believe all things, endure all things. Now a change has come. Women are awakening to a sense of citizenship. No longer is the ideal woman the one who never lifts her eyes higher than the top pantry shelf nor allows her sympathy to extend past her own family. Women who believed they must sit down and be resigned are now rising up and being indignant. The new womanhood is the new citizenship. Women are asking why should property be held more sacred than human life, why is a man punished more severely for stealing a fur coat or a gold watch than he is for stealing a woman's virtue, her happiness and her good name? Why is it that in the law of this Province a woman has no legal claim on either her home or her child? Why is a man liable to five years' imprisonment for stealing a young girl and fourteen years' imprisonment for stealing cattle? Why is a woman's virtue valued at only $25.00 in this Province? Why is not a woman factory inspector in this city, where there are so many more women employees than men? Why are women's petitions so regularly and systematically ignored? Why are women not given equal pay for equal work? Why are women debarred from taking up homesteads? Why are women, physically weaker than men, further handicapped in the race of life by political nonentity? Why are women on election day classed with idiots, lunatics and criminals? These are some of the questions women are asking in this Province and the wise politician is the one who listens. It is no use to try to hush us up, we refuse to be hushed. These questions cannot be smoothed over, they must be settled.

Politicians tell us it would never do to give women equal pay with men or let them take up homesteads, for that would make women even more independent of marriage than they are at the present time, and it is not independent women we want — it is population.

Granting that population is very desirable, would it not be a wise plan to try to save what we have? Six thousand boys are needed in Canada every year to take the place of the six thousand drunkards who drop out of the race. How would it be to save them? Thousands of babies die every year from preventable causes. Would it not be a good plan to try to save them? In the far West where women are beyond the reach of nurses and doctors, many mothers and babies die every year from lack of medical skill. How would it be to save them? Public spirited women, but alas, without votes, have interviewed august bodies on the subject of sending Government nurses to these brave women who pay the toll of colonization. These delegates have always been courteously received and complimented on their work, but up to date not one dollar of government money has been spent, notwithstanding the fact that when a prince or a duke comes to our country to visit, we can pour out money like water.

Women are beginning to think of these things and to talk of them, and the argument which is so often put forth — it would suit women better to go home and darn their children's stockings — does not exactly relieve the difficulty. It does not take all of woman's energy or brains to keep the stockings darned or the meals cooked. Women are cooks and housemaids and home makers and dressmakers and nurses, but they are something more, they are citizens. Already women have attained citizenship in ten states of the Union and Alaska, and instead of disaster to the homes, it has brought happiness and prosperity ...

But the dawn is breaking and the darkness flees away. Women who long have sat in their boudoirs like the Lady of Shallot, looking at life in a mirror, are now throwing the glass aside and coming down into the conflict. The awakened womanhood, the aroused motherhood is the New Citizenship.

8

"Dying for a Foreign Cause"
Military Service in World War I

DOCUMENTS

A) 123rd Battalion Recruiting Leaflet
   G.G. Starr
B) 'Country Recruits'
   Peter McArthur, Globe, *January 30, 1915*
C) To Henri Bourassa, March 21, 1916
   Talbot M. Papineau
D) Mr. Bourassa's Reply to Capt. Talbot Papineau's
   Letter, August 2, 1916
   Henri Bourassa
E) "No More Canadians For Overseas Service. This
   Young Dominion Has Sacrificed Enough"
   Sault Express, *June 23, 1916*
F) Speech, June 11, 1917
   Robert Borden
G) "Women's View of Conscription"
   Francis Marion Beynon, The Grain Growers' Guide,
   May 30, 1917

Northern France and Belgium are presently a peaceful mix of pastoral agriculturalism and humming industrial activity. Everything seems well orchestrated, functional, stable, and civilized. The war memorials and cemeteries dotting the landscape, however, dissipate at least some of the smug veneer of civilization permeating the region. Little signs point them out to travellers driving down the smoothly paved *Route Nationales*. There are cemeteries for Australians, British, South Africans, New Zealanders, Newfoundlanders, lots of German and French cemeteries, and some for Canadians. Each mark the final resting places for hundreds of thousands of young men slaughtered in the mud of the Western Front during the First World War. A contemplative walk between the orderly rows of headstones and flower beds cannot help but produce a profound sense of melancholy for the shattered ideals that slowly seeped from broken bodies into the poisoned local soil so many years ago.

Canada did not have a strong military tradition and was unprepared, psychologically and materially, for the Great War when it broke out in the summer of 1914. Just the same, the nation responded with aplomb to the British declaration of war. Some half million men and several thousand women actively served over the course of the war.

Modern mechanized warfare dehumanized combat to the point where the enemy became a faceless foe raining lethal shells upon them day after day. Living conditions at the front degenerated into pure survival in rat-infested, water-filled trenches. Soldiers were cold, hungry, flea-ridden, bored, terrified, and often deeply disillusioned. The landscape, said one disaffected Canadian infantryman, came to resemble nothing more than rich plum pudding after relentless bombardment.

Every November 11th, Canadians honour the more than sixty thousand men who died on the Western Front during the First World War. That enormous number, juxtaposed with a national population well below ten million in 1914, may tempt Canadians to believe that the nation gave a disproportionate number of its young to the bloody fields of battle in Northern France. Canada did indeed make an enormous sacrifice in the Great War but its efforts were, in fact, disproportionately small compared to some other parts of the British Empire.

Recruiting initially proceeded very successfully, with young men across Canada flocking to their nearest recruiting stations to volunteer for the cause. From there they filtered to basic training camps, then by rail to Halifax and troop ships bound for England. More training, then transshipment to northern France. There they entered the jaws of hell: the bloody, protracted, terrifying, and insane Western Front where officers bereft of innovation took turns hurling their men at each other across the putrid mud of no-man's-land.

Once young Canadian men back home heard of the horrors, the initial flood of volunteers turned to a trickle: patriotic enthusiasm dried up before the reality of trench warfare. The Federal government responded with an intense and relatively crude propaganda campaign geared to encourage recalcitrant young men to sign up. The essence of the campaign was simple: any young, able-bodied man not in uniform was presumably shirking his responsibility to Canada and the Empire, and must be "encouraged" to see the error of his ways. This could be done by humiliating him through "white-feathering," appealing to his sense of duty, warning him of the social stigma he would bear if he did not volunteer, and by any other means that the government thought might open the gates of recruitment. Propaganda posters glamorized the soldier's life and suggested that the war was a grand and noble adventure.

French-Canadians and pacifists came under an especially intense propaganda barrage. French-Canadian voluntarism, after all, lagged behind its Anglo-Canadian counterpart throughout the war. Why? Likely for as many reasons as there were young men who refused to sign up, but distinct trends also emerged. French Canada had few ties to France. French-Canadians were obliged to show patriotism toward England, the country that conquered them in 1763, but how realistic was that? Finally, the way in which Canadians fought guaranteed that French-Canadians would not show much enthusiasm. Few officers spoke French, chances of promotion remained very limited, an Anglican Minister headed official recruiting in Quebec, and there were no French-Canadian regiments until the Vandoos (Royal 22nd). Yet western Canada and the Maritimes also demonstrated a lack of commitment when compared to areas with large pockets of recent British immigrants.

Lack of recruits eventually led Prime Minister Robert Borden to introduce conscription, an Act of Parliament as contentious and divisive as anything since Confederation. It so badly divided the country that for the first and only time in Canadian history, the two main federal political parties split along ethnic lines: Quebec Members of Parliament rallied to Laurier's anti-conscription Liberals. Borden, meanwhile, created the new Union party made up of pro-conscriptionist Liberals and Conservatives. The ensuing election of 1917 was as bitter as any, with violence, unscrupulous political manipulation, intimidation, and propaganda on both sides. Borden won, and his Conscription Act led to clashes between troops and French-Canadians in Quebec that killed five civilians. In response the Quebec National Assembly discussed a resolution to secede from Canada.

Talbot Papineau (1883–1917) was a great-grandson of one of Quebec's most famous political reformers: Louis Joseph Papineau. He received a BA from Oxford in 1908, returned to Canada, and practiced law before volunteering for the Princess Patricia Canadian Light Infantry in August, 1914. Decorated and promoted to Major, Papineau died at Passchendaele in 1917.

In the years before the war, Henri Bourassa (1868–1952) believed that it was not Canada's duty to support its imperial mother whenever Britain found itself embroiled in some foreign conflagration. Thus it is perhaps surprising that Bourassa initially came out in support of Canada's participation in the First World War. In a *Le Devoir* editorial, he wrote that "Canada, an Anglo-French nation bound to England and to France by a thousand ethnic, social, intellectual and economic ties, has a vital interests in the maintenance of the prestige, power and world-wide action of France and England." He concluded that it was Canada's "national duty to contribute in the measure of her resources and by means of an appropriate action to the triumph, and above all, to the endurance of the combined efforts of France and England." But Bourassa's support was short-lived. By the end of that first year he passionately rejected any participation, concluding that the war would lead to the anglification of Quebec. In 1916 he stated that "the enemy, the permanent enemy is Anglo-saxonism." Thus Bourassa tackled the conscription issue with all his considerable intellectual strength, stating categorically: "No conscription, no enlistment: Canada has done enough." This did not sit well with most of the rest of the country, and some Ontario newspapers branded him a traitor.

Robert Borden (1854–1937) became Prime Minister of Canada in 1911 after a long struggle, first as a teacher, then lawyer, and finally leader of the Conservative Party. At the outbreak of war, he solemnly promised that conscription would not occur. The Department of Defense changed the rules as recruitment dwindled, making it ever easier to sign up. That was still insufficient, and so, after two major changes to the Elections Act, Borden reluctantly secured passage of his conscription bill with the 1917 election. The Act itself went through subsequent changes which allowed Ottawa to cast its net ever wider, conscripting younger men and farmers' sons who were initially exempted. Borden was alienated from much of rural Canada by war's end. He did, however, ensure that the country had at least a modicum of independence on the battlefield, and that Canada signed the Versailles treaty as an independent nation. Borden became a great champion of the League of Nations, and retired from active politics in 1921.

Francis Beynon (1884–1951) was a prominent Winnipeg journalist. As editor of the woman's section of the *Grain Growers' Guide* she achieved national recognition in the campaign for female political equality. However, her pacifist beliefs forced her to resign and move to the United States in 1917.

A)   123rd Battalion Recruiting Leaflet
G.G. Starr

To the Women of Canada

In addressing these few remarks exclusively to the women of the country, it is to be understood that we have arrived at that period in the struggle where we realize the utter futility of recruiting meetings.

The men who have as yet failed to join the colors will not be influenced by any eloquence from any platform.

The reason? The man we are trying to reach is the man who will never listen and the man who never for a moment considers the remarks as applicable to himself.

And so now we appeal to the women — the women who are the mainspring of all masculine action.

In the First Division of the C.E.F. we swept up the young manhood of the country in the first enthusiasm — we secured the cream of the country in the men who flocked to the colors taking thought of neither yesterday or to-morrow.

At the second call men were stopping to calculate and hesitate. Since then the hesitation has developed into stagnation. Men who see a desperate winter ahead are joining the colors, and a few others; the remainder are deadwood.

The reason? Firstly, the man who prefers to allow others to fight for him so that he may pursue a comfortable occupation, preserve his youth, be safe from danger, and explain to his friends that he would gladly join the colors could he obtain a commission — and yet take no steps towards that end.

Second. The man who is influenced by the selfish maternal appeal either from mother or wife.

Third. The man who claims his business would go to pieces without him, but is satisfied to let others throw away life and youth to sustain that business.

Fourth. The others — call them what you may.

And now my Appeal to Women

You entertain these wretched apologies in your homes. You accept their donations, their theatre tickets, their flowers, their cars. You go with them to watch the troops parade.

You foully wrong their manhood by encouraging them to perform their parlor tricks while Europe is burning up.

While Canada is in imminent danger of suffering the same were it not for the millions who are cheerfully enduring the horrors and privations of bloody warfare for the millions who stay at home watching the war pictures and drinking tea.

Bar them out, you women. Refuse their invitations, scorn their attentions. For the love of Heaven, if they won't be men, then you be women. Tell them to come in uniform, no matter how soiled or misfitting — bar out the able-bodied man who has no obligations, show that you despise him. Tell him to join the colors while he can do so with honor. And the day is not far off when he will have to go. The old mother has issued the last call to her sons.

Make your son, your husband, your lover, your brother, join now while he yet retains the remnants of honor. Compulsory training is in the offing.

Get the apologist, the weakling, the mother's pet, into the service. Weed out all, and we will find out who are the cowards. Analyze your friends — you women — refuse their attentions, and tell them why. Make them wake up.

GOD BLESS HIM THE KING CALLS! JOIN ROYAL GRENADIERS OVERSEAS BATTALION, 123rd C.E.F.

B) 'Country Recruits'
Peter McArthur, Globe, January 30, 1915

With all the papers lamenting the fact that the rural districts are not contributing a satisfactory number of recruits to the war, it is perhaps unsafe for me to point out a few facts about rural conditions, for the last time I did so I was accused in a section of the press of preparing a defence for people who lack patriotism. I have surely put myself on record often enough as believing that the war must be supported to the utmost, but I am not going to let that belief make me unjust. I have told you how scarce men of military age are in this district and that if they enlist there can be none of the increased production that is being urged as an expression of patriotism. The Department of Agriculture is proclaiming that the man who produces more foodstuffs is doing a man's work for the Empire, and the few young men who are on the farms are practically all producers. Each one who went to the front would leave a hundred acres untilled.

It is high time that the Department of Militia and the Department of Agriculture got together and decided on a definite policy. If a man is doing his duty by producing more, he should not be open to criticism if he does not enlist. To show you how shorthanded this district is it is only necessary to point out that during the past ten years the population of the county of Middlesex has been so greatly reduced that at the recent redistribution one riding was wiped out. I have not the figures by me, but I understand that the population has fallen off something over ten thousand. This decrease is largely due to the exodus of young men to the west and to the cities. If the country had been at war for the past ten years we could not have lost a greater proportion of our population. If every young man of military age enlisted, the county could hardly make a fair showing and it would fall behind in production. Will those who are condemning the rural districts for not sending more recruits kindly tell what should be done in the case of Middlesex county?

While the above paragraph was in course of preparation I received a letter from a correspondent in Castorville which reports a similar condition. The writer says

"While reading *The Globe* last evening I noticed a considerable complaint that the country districts are not responding very heartily to the call for volunteers to go to the war. In thinking the matter over I felt that there is a danger of not giving the country due consideration for this seeming shortcoming.

"I do not wish to excuse the country where it is lacking patriotism but I feel that the conditions of farmers are not fully comprehended which I will note briefly:

"(1) The smallness of families in farming districts these days is noticeable. There used to be five and six boys in a family on the farm. Today there are only one or two.

"(2) The spare boy that could be gotten along without has gone to the city or the west, and now not one farm in three has even one boy or man eligible to be a volunteer.

"(3) Help is scarce on the farms and in the farming districts. Most of the farmers are and have been running their farms with as little help as possible, and even when we feel we would like to have someone to help it is almost impossible to get it for there are no spare hands in the community.

"(4) If Canada is to provide bread, beef, horses, etc. for the war, the farmer must have sufficient help to do it.

"(5) The overflow of country population has gone to the cities or west. The congestion in the labour market at the present time is found in the cities, therefore it is not surprising that the majority of volunteers should come from that quarter."

This letter is of interest because it shows that conditions in other parts of the country are the same as I find them here in Middlesex. The farmers cannot both increase production and give volunteers to the army.

There is a thought that suggests itself in connection with this state of affairs. In the present national crisis we have a right to expect every man who is capable of rendering service to do so patriotically. The man who enlists to go to the front is making the supreme sacrifice that it is possible for a man to make. He is offering to give his life for his country. The man who is eligible to give similar service but feels that his call of duty is to stay at home and help his country with increased products should also be prepared to make many and great sacrifices. He is not offering his life, and therefore he should not stint in offering his means. If the young men who avoid military service do so because they think that during war times farming will yield them increased profits they must expect to take their profits with a share of public contempt. Never before has the call for unselfish service been so urgent and so great. Those who elect to serve their country as producers must be prepared to give to their full capacity. Even if they give all, they will not be giving so much as those who are offering their lives. As the war progresses public sentiment will probably be educated to a point where men in all walks of life who try to make profits from the unhappy condition of their country will be scorned for their selfishness. If we cannot serve at the front we must be prepared to serve unselfishly at home. As a matter of fact, I think it would be quite justifiable to ask the young married men of military age who are not enlisting what proportion of their products they will give for patriotic purposes over and beyond what they will have to pay in the form of taxes. When the survivors of those who volunteer for service at the front come back wounded and broken the young men who stay at home cannot feel much self-respect if they have spent the time in accumulating profits. This should show definitely whether their "patriotism of production" is real or only an excuse.

C) To Henri Bourassa, March 21, 1916
Talbot M. Papineau

In the Field, France, March 21, 1916.

My dear Cousin Henri,—

I was sorry before leaving Quebec in 1914 not to have had an opportunity of discussing with you the momentous issues which were raised in Canada by the outbreak of this war.

You and I have had some discussions in the past, and although we have not agreed upon all points, yet I am happy to think that our pleasant friendship, which indeed dates from the time of my birth, has hitherto continued uninjured by our differences of opinion. Nor would I be the first to make it otherwise, for however I may deplore the character of your views, I have always considered that you held them honestly and sincerely and that you were singularly free from purely selfish or personal ambitions.

Very possibly nothing that I could have said in August 1914 would have caused you to change your opinions, but I did hope that as events developed and as the great national opportunity of Canada became clearer to all her citizens, you would have been influenced to modify your views and to adopt a different attitude. In that hope I have been disappointed. Deeply involved as the honour and the very national existence of Canada has become, beautiful but terrible as her sacrifices have been, you and you alone of the leaders of Canadian thought appear to have remained unmoved, and your unhappy views unchanged.

Too occupied by immediate events in this country to formulate a protest or to frame a reasoned argument, I have nevertheless followed with intense feeling and deep regret the course of action which you have pursued. Consolation of course I have had in the fact that far from sharing in your views, the vast majority of Canadians, and even many of those who had formerly agreed with you, were now strongly and bitterly opposed to you. With this fact in mind, I would not take the time from my duties here to write you this letter did I not fear that the influence to which your talent, energy, and sincerity of purpose formerly entitled you, might still be exercised upon a small minority of your fellow countrymen, and that your attitude might still be considered by some as representative of the race to which we belong.

Nor can I altogether abandon the hope — presumptuous no doubt but friendly and well-intentioned — that I may so express myself here as to give you a new outlook and a different purpose, and perhaps even win you to the support of a principle which has been proved to be dearer to many Canadians than life itself.

I shall not consider the grounds upon which you base your opposition to Canadian participation in this more than European — in this World War. Rather I wish to begin by pointing out some reasons why on the contrary your whole-hearted support might have been expected.

And the first reason is this. By the declaration of war by Great Britain upon Germany, Canada became "ipso facto" a belligerent, subject to invasion and conquest, her property at sea subject to capture, her coasts subject to bombardment or attack, her citizens in enemy territory subject to imprisonment or detention. This is not a matter of opinion — it is a matter of fact — a question of international law. No arguments of yours at least could have persuaded the Kaiser to the contrary. Whatever your views or theories may be as to future constitutional development of Canada, and in those views I believe I coincide to a large extent, the fact remains that at the time of the outbreak of war Canada was a possession of the British Empire, and as such as much involved in the war as any country in England, and from the German point of view and the point of view of International Law equally subject to all its pains and penalties. Indeed proof may no doubt be made that one of the very purposes of Germany's aggression and German military preparedness was the ambition to secure a part if not the whole of the English possessions in North America.

That being so, surely it was idle and pernicious to continue an academic discussion as to whether the situation was a just one or not, as to whether Canada should or should not have had a voice in ante bellum English diplomacy or in the actual declaration of war. Such a discussion may very properly arise upon a successful conclusion of the war, but so long as national issues are being decided in Prussian fashion, that is, by an appeal to the Power of Might, the liberties of discussion which you enjoyed by virtue of British citizenship were necessarily curtailed and any resulting decisions utterly valueless. If ever there was a time for action and not for theories it was to be found in Canada upon the outbreak of war.

Let us presume for the sake of argument that your attitude had also been adopted by the Government and people of Canada and that we had declared our intention to abstain from active participation in the war until Canada herself was actually attacked. What would have resulted? One of two things. Either the Allies would have been defeated or they would not have been defeated. In the former case Canada would have been called upon either to surrender unconditionally to German domination or to have attempted a resistance against German arms.

You, I feel sure, would have preferred resistance, but as a proper corrective to such a preference I would prescribe a moderate dose of trench bombardment. I have known my own dogmas to be seriously disturbed in the midst of a German artillery concentration. I can assure you that the further you travel from Canada and the nearer you approach the great military power of Germany, the less do you value the unaided strength of Canada. By the time you are within fifteen yards of a German army and know yourself to be holding about one yard out of a line of five hundred miles or more, you are liable to be enquiring very anxiously about the presence and power of British and French forces. Your ideas about charging to Berlin or of ending the war would also have undergone some slight moderation.

No, my dear Cousin, I think you would shortly after the defeat of the Allies have been more worried over the mastery of the German consonants than you are even now over a conflict with the Ontario Anti-bi-linguists. Or I can imagine you an unhappy exile in Terra del Fuego eloquently comparing the wrongs of Quebec and Alsace.

But you will doubtless say we would have had the assistance of the Great American Republic! It is quite possible. I will admit that by the time the American fleet had been sunk and the principal buildings in New York destroyed the United States would have declared war upon Europe, but in the meantime Canada might very well have been paying tribute and learning to decline German verbs, probably the only thing German she *could* have declined ...

Nor disappointed as I am at the present inactivity of the States will I ever waiver in my loyal belief that in time to come, perhaps less distant than we realise, her actions will correspond with the lofty expression of her national and international ideals.

I shall continue to anticipate the day when with a clear understanding and a mutual trust we shall by virtue of our united strength and our common purposes be prepared to defend the rights of humanity not only upon the American Continent but throughout the civilised world.

Nevertheless we are not dealing with what may occur in the future but with the actual facts of yesterday and to-day, and I would feign know if you still think that a power which without protest witnesses the ruthless spoliation of Belgium and Servia, and without effective action the murder of her own citizens, would have interfered to protect the property or the liberties of Canadians. Surely you must at least admit an element of doubt, and even if such interference had been attempted, have we not the admission of the Americans themselves that it could not have been successful against the great naval and military organisations of the Central Powers?

May I be permitted to conclude that had the Allies been defeated Canada must afterwards necessarily have suffered a similar fate.

But there was the other alternative, namely, that the Allies even without the assistance of Canada would *not* have been defeated. What then? Presumably French and English would still have been the official languages of Canada. You might still have edited untrammelled your version of Duty ...

In fact Canada might still have retained her liberties and might with the same freedom from external influences have continued her progress to material and political strength.

But would you have been satisfied — you who have arrogated to yourself the high term of Nationalist? What of the Soul of Canada? Can a nation's pride or patriotism be built upon the blood and suffering of others or upon the wealth garnered from the coffers of those who in anguish and with blood-sweat are fighting the battles of freedom? If we accept our liberties, our national life, from the hands of the English soldiers, if without sacrifices of our own we profit by the sacrifices of the English citizen, can we hope to ever become a nation ourselves? How could we ever acquire that Soul or create that Pride without which a nation is a dead thing and doomed to speedy decay and disappearance.

If you were truly a Nationalist — if you loved our great country and without smallness longed to see her become the home of a good and united people — surely you would have recognised this as her moment of travail and tribulation. You would have felt that in the agony of her losses in Belgium and France, Canada was suffering the birth pains of her national life. There even more than in Canada herself, her citizens are being knit together into a new existence because when men stand side by side and endure a soldier's life and face together a soldier's death, they are united in bonds almost as strong as the closest of blood-ties.

There was the great opportunity for the true Nationalist! There was the great issue, the great sacrifice, which should have appealed equally to all true citizens of Canada, and should have served to cement them with indissoluble strength — Canada was at war! Canada was attacked! What mattered then internal dissentions and questions of home importance? What mattered the why and wherefore of the war, whether we owed anything to England or not, whether we were Imperialists or not, or whether we were French or English? The one simple commending fact to govern our conduct was that Canada was at war, and Canada and Canadian liberties had to be protected.

To you as a "Nationalist" this fact should have appealed more than to any others. Englishmen, as was natural, returned to fight for England, just as Germans and Austrians and Belgians and Italians returned to fight for their native lands.

But we, Canadians, had we no call just as insistent, just as compelling to fight for Canada? Did not the *Leipzig* and the *Gneisnau* possibly menace

Victoria and Vancouver, and did you not feel the patriotism to make sacrifices for the protection of British Columbia? How could you otherwise call yourself Canadian? It is true that Canada did not hear the roar of German guns nor were we visited at night by the murderous Zeppelins, but every shot that was fired in Belgium or France was aimed as much at the heart of Canada as at the bodies of our brave Allies. Could we then wait within the temporary safety of our distant shores until either the Central Powers flushed with victory should come to settle their account or until by the glorious death of millions of our fellowmen in Europe, Canada should remain in inglorious security and a shameful liberty?

I give thanks that that question has been answered not as you would have had it answered but as those Canadians who have already died or are about to die here in this gallant motherland of France have answered it.

It may have been difficult for you at first to have realised the full significance of the situation. You were steeped in your belief that Canada owed no debt to England, was merely a vassal state and entitled to protection without payment. You were deeply imbued with the principle that we should not partake in a war in the declaration of which we had had no say. You believed very sincerely that Canadian soldiers should not be called upon to fight beyond the frontier of Canada itself, and your vision was further obscured by your indignation at the apparent injustice to a French minority in Ontario.

It is conceivable that at first on account of this long held attitude of mind and because it seemed that Canadian aid was hardly necessary, for even we feared that the war would be over before the first Canadian regiment should land in France, you should have failed to adapt your mind to the new situation and should for a while have continued in your former views; — but now — now that Canada has pledged herself body and soul to the successful prosecution of this war — now that we know that only by the exerci[s]e of our full and united strength can we achieve a speedy and lasting victory — now that thousands of your fellow citizens have died, and alas! many more must yet be killed — how in the name of all that you hold most sacred can you still maintain your opposition? How can you refrain from using all your influence and your personal magnetism and eloquence to swell the great army of Canada and make it as representative of all classes of our citizens as possible?

Could you have been here yourself to witness in its horrible detail the cruelty of war — to have seen your comrades suddenly struck down in death and lie mangled at your side, even you could not have failed to wish to visit punishment upon those responsible. You too would now wish to see every ounce of our united strength instantly and relentlessly directed to that end. Afterwards, when that end has been accomplished, then and then only can there be honour or profit in the discussion of our domestic or imperial disputes.

And so my first reason for your support would be that you should assist in the defence of Canadian territory and Canadian liberties.

And my second would be this: —

Whatever criticism may to-day be properly directed against the Constitutional structure of the British Empire, we are compelled to admit that the *spiritual* union of the self governing portions of the Empire is a most necessary and desirable thing. Surely you will concede that the degree of civilisation which they represent and the standards of individual and national liberty for which they stand are the highest and noblest to which the human race has yet attained and jealously to be protected against destruction by less developed powers. All may not be perfection — grave and serious faults no doubt exist — vast progress must still be made — nevertheless that which has been achieved is good and must not be allowed to disappear. The bonds which unite us for certain great purposes and which have proved so powerful in this common struggle must not be loosened. They may indeed be readjusted, but the great communities which the British Empire has joined together must not be broken asunder. If I thought that the development of a national spirit in Canada meant antagonism to the "spirit" which unites the Empire today, I would utterly repudiate the idea of a Canadian nation and would gladly accept the most exacting of imperial organic unions.

Hitherto I have welcomed your nationalism because I thought it would only mean that you wished Canada to assume national responsibilities as well as to enjoy its privileges.

But your attitude in the present crisis will alienate and antagonise the support which you might otherwise have received. Can you not realise that if any worthy nationality is possible for Canada it must be sympathetic to and must co-operate with the fine spirit of imperial unity? That spirit was endangered by the outbreak of European war. It could only be preserved by loyal assistance from all those in whom that spirit dwelt.

And so I would also have had you support Canadian participation in the war, *not* in order to maintain a certain political organism of Empire, but to preserve and perpetuate that invaluable *spirit* which alone makes our union possible.

The third reason is this: You and I are so called French-Canadians. We belong to a race that began the conquest of this country long before the days of Wolfe. That race was in its turn conquered, but their personal liberties were not restricted. They were in fact increased. Ultimately as a minority in a great English speaking community we have preserved our racial identity, and we have had freedom to speak or to worship as we wished. I may not be, like yourself, "un pur sang," for I am by birth even more English than French, but I am proud of my French ancestors, I love the French language, and I am as determined as you are that we shall have full liberty to remain French as long as we like. But if we are to preserve this liberty we must recognise that we do not belong entirely to ourselves, but to a mixed population, we must rather seek to find points of contact and of common interest than points of friction and separation. We must make concessions and certain sacrifices of our distinct individuality if we mean to live on amicable terms with our fellow citizens or if we are to expect them to make similar concessions to us. There, in this moment of crisis, was the greatest opportunity which could ever have presented itself for us to show unity of purpose and to prove to our English fellow citizens that, whatever our respective histories may have been, we were actuated by a common love for our country and a mutual wish that in the future we should unite our distinctive talents and energies to create a proud and happy nation.

That was an opportunity which you, my cousin, have failed to grasp, and unfortunately, despite the heroic and able manner in which French Canadian battalions have distinguished themselves here, and despite the wholehearted support which so many leaders of French Canadian thought have given to the cause, yet the fact remains that the French in Canada have not responded in the same proportion as have other Canadian citizens, and the unhappy impression has been created that French Canadians are not bearing their full share in this great Canadian enterprise. For this fact and this impression you will be held largely responsible. Do you fully realise what such a responsibility will mean, not so much to you personally — for that I believe you would care little — but to the principles which you have advocated, and for many of which I have but the deepest regard. You will have brought them into a disrepute from which they may never recover. Already you have made the fine term of "Nationalist" to stink in the nostrils of our English fellow citizens. Have you caused them to respect your national views? Have you won their admiration or led them to consider with esteem, and toleration your ambitions for the French language? Have you shown your-self worthy of concessions or consideration?

After this war what influence will you enjoy — what good to your country will you be able to accomplish? Wherever you go you will stir up strife and enmity — you will bring disfavour and dishonour upon our race, so that whoever bears a French name in Canada will be an object of suspicion and possibly of hatred.

And so, in the third place, for the honour of French Canada and for the unity of our country, I would have had you favourable to our cause.

I have only two more reasons, and they but need to be mentioned, I think to be appreciated.

Here in this little French town I hear about all me the language I love so well and which recalls so vividly my happy childhood days in Montebello. I see types and faces that are like old friends. I see farm houses like those at home. I notice that our French Canadian soldiers have easy friendships wher-ever they go.

Can you make me believe that there must not always be a bond of blood relationship between the Old France and the New?

And France — more glorious than in all her history — is now in agony straining fearlessly and proudly in a struggle for life or death.

For Old France and French civilisation I would have had your support.

And in the last place, all other considerations aside and even supposing Canada had been a neutral country, I would have had you decide that she should enter the struggle for no other reason than that it is a fight for the freedom of the world — a fight in the result of which like every other country she is herself vitally interested. I will not further speak of the causes of this war, but I should like to think that even if Canada had been an independ-ent and neutral nation she of her own accord would have chosen to follow the same path of glory that she is following to-day.

Perhaps, my cousin, I have been overlong and tedious with my reasons, but I shall be shorter with my warning — and in closing I wish to say this to you.

Those of us in this great army, who may be so fortunate as to return to our Canada, will have faced the grimmest and sincerest issues of life and death — we will have experienced the unhappy strength of brute force — we will have seen our loved comrades die in blood and suffering. Beware lest we re-turn with revengeful feelings, for I say to you that for those who, while we fought and suffered here, remained in safety and comfort in Canada and failed to give us encouragement and support, as well as for those who grew fat with the wealth dishonourably gained by political graft and by dishonest business methods at our expense — we shall demand a heavy day of reckoning. We shall inflict upon them the punishment they deserve — not by physical violence — for we shall have had enough of that — nor by unconstitutional or illegal means — for we are fighting to protect not to destroy justice and freedom — but by the invincible power of our moral influence.

Can you ask us then for sympathy or concession? Will any listen when you speak of pride and patriotism? I think not.

Remember too that if Canada has become a nation respected and self-respecting she owes it to her citizens who have fought and died in this distant land and not to those self-styled Nationalists who have remained at home.

Can I hope that anything I have said here may influence you to consider the situation in a different light and that it is not yet too late for me to be made proud of our relationship?

At this moment, as I write, French and English-Canadians are fighting and dying side by side. Is their sacrifice to go for nothing or will it not cement a foundation for a true Canadian nation, a Canadian nation independent in thought, independent in action, independent even in its political organisation — but in spirit united for high international and humane purposes to the two Motherlands of England and France?

I think that is an ideal in which we shall all equally share. Can we not all play an equal part in its realisation?

I am, as long as may be possible,

Your affectionate Cousin,

TALBOT M. PAPINEAU.

D) Mr. Bourassa's Reply to Capt. Talbot Papineau's Letter, August 2, 1916
Henri Bourassa

Andrew R. McMaster, Esq., K.C.

189 St. James St., City.

Dear Sir,

On my return from an absence of several weeks, I found your letter of the 18th ult., and the copy of a letter apparently written to me by your partner, Capt. Talbot Papineau, on the 21st of March.

Capt. Papineau's letter, I am informed, appeared simultaneously, Friday last, in a number of papers, in Montreal, Quebec, Ottawa, and elsewhere. You have thus turned it into a kind of political manifesto and constituted yourself its publisher. Allow me therefore to send you my reply, requesting you to have it transmitted to Capt. Papineau, granting that he is the real author of that document. I can hardly believe it. A brave and active officer as he is has seldom the time to prepare and write such long pieces of political eloquence. Then, why should Capt. Papineau, who writes and speaks French elegantly, who claims so highly his French origin and professes with such ardour his love of France, have written in English to his "*dear cousin Henri*"? How is it that a letter written on the 21st of March has reached me but four months later, through your medium? For what purpose did you keep it so long in portfolio? and why do you send me a copy, instead of the letter itself?

It is, you say, an "open letter". It was, nevertheless, meant to reach me. It opens and ends with forms of language bearing the touch of intimate relationship — more so even than could be expected from the rare intercourse which, in spite of our blood connection, had so far existed between your partner and myself. The whole thing has the appearance of a political manoeuvre executed under the name of a young and gallant officer, who has the advantage or inconvenience of being my cousin. That Capt. Papineau has put his signature at the foot of that document, it is possible; but he would certainly not have written it in cool thought, after due reflexion. It not only expresses opinions radically opposed to those I heard from him before the war; it also contains inaccuracies of fact of which I believe him honourably incapable.

He mentions "some discussions in the past," "differences of opinion," which have left "uninjured" a "pleasant friendship," dating, he says, "from the time of [his] birth." From his childhood to his return from Oxford, I do not think we had ever met, and certainly never to exchange the slightest glimpse of thought or opinion. Of matters of national concern we talked but once in all my life. From that one conversation I gathered the impression that he was still more opposed than myself to any kind of imperial solidarity. He even seemed much disposed to hasten the day of the Independence of Canada. Since, I met him on two or three occasions. We talked of matters indifferent, totally foreign to the numerous questions treated with such eloquent profuseness and so little reasoning in his letter of the 21st of March.

How can he charge me with having expressed "unhappy views" "at the outstart of the war," in August 1914, and held them stubbornly "unchanged" till this day? In August 1914, I was abroad. My first pronouncement on the intervention of Canada in the war is dated September 8th, 1914. In that editorial, while repelling the principles of Imperial solidarity and their consequences, and maintaining the nationalist doctrine in which Capt. Papineau — and you as well — pretends to be still a believer, I pronounced myself in favour of the intervention of Canada, *as a nation*, for the defence of the superior interests uniting Canada with France and Britain. My "unhappy views" were thus analogous to those of your partner. It is but later, long after Capt. Papineau was gone, that my attitude was changed and brought me to condemn the participation of Canada in the war, — or rather the political inspiration of that participation and the many abuses which have resulted therefrom. The reasons of that change are well known to those who have read or heard with attention and good faith all my statements on the matter. To sum them up is now sufficient.

The free and independent participation of Canada — free for the nation and free for the individuals — I had accepted, provided it remained within reasonable bounds, in conformity with the conditions of the country. But the Government, the whole of Parliament, the press, and politicians of both parties all applied themselves systematically to obliterate the free character of Canada's intervention. "Free" enlistment is now carried on by means of blackmailing, intimidation, and threats of all sorts. Advantage has been taken of the emotion caused by the war to assert, with the utmost intensity and intolerance, the doctrine of Imperial solidarity, triumphantly opposed in the past by our statesmen and the whole Canadian people, up to the days of the infamous South African War, concocted by Chamberlain, Rhodes, and the British imperialists with the clear object of drawing the self-governing colonies into "the vortex of European militarism." That phrase of your political leader, Sir Wilfrid Laurier, is undoubtedly fresh in your mind. After having given way to the imperialistic current of 1899, Sir Wilfrid Laurier and the liberal party had come back to the nationalist doctrine. The naval scare of 1909 threw them again under the yoke of imperialism; the war has achieved their enslavement; they united with the tory-jingo imperialists of all shades to make of the participation of Canada in the war an immense political manoeuvre and thus assure the triumph of British imperialism. You and your partner, like many others, have followed your party through its various evolutions. I have remained firmly attached to the principles I laid down at the time of the South African war and maintained unswervingly ever since.

As early as the month of March 1900, I pointed out the possibility of a conflict between Great Britain and Germany and the danger of laying down in South Africa a precedent, the fatal consequence of which would be to draw Canada into all the wars undertaken by the United Kingdom. Sir Wilfrid Laurier and the liberal leaders laughed at my apprehensions; against my warnings they quoted the childish safeguard of the "no precedent clause" inserted in the Order in Council of the 14th of October 1899. For many years after, till 1912, and 1913, they kept singing the praises of the Kaiser and extolling the peaceful virtues of Germany. They now try to regain time by denouncing vociferously the "barbarity" of the "Huns." To-day, as in 1900, in 1911, and always, I believe that all the nations of Europe are the victims of their own mistakes, of the complacent servility with which they submitted to the dominance of all Imperialists and traders in human flesh, who, in England as in Germany, in France as in Russia, have brought the peoples to slaughter in order to increase their reapings of cursed gold. German Imperialism and British Imperialism, French Militarism and Russian Tsarism, I hate with equal detestation; and I believe as firmly today as in 1899 that Canada, a nation of America, has a nobler mission to fulfil than to bind herself to the fate of the nations of Europe or to any spoliating Empire — whether it be the spoliators of Belgium, Alsace, or Poland, or those of Ireland or the Transvaal, of Greece or the Balkans.

Politicians of both parties, your liberal friends as well as their conservative opponents, feign to be much scandalised at my "treasonable disloyalty." I could well afford to look upon them as a pack of knaves and hypocrites. In 1896, your liberal leaders and friends stumped the whole province of Quebec with the cry "WHY SHOULD WE FIGHT FOR ENGLAND?" From 1902 to 1911, Sir Wilfrid Laurier was acclaimed by them as the indomitable champion of Canada's autonomy against British Imperialism. His resisting attitude at the Imperial Conferences of 1902 and 1907 was praised to the skies. His famous phrase on the "vortex of European militarism", and his determination to keep Canada far from it, became the party's by-word — always in the Province of Quebec, of course. His Canadian Navy scheme was presented as a step towards the independence of Canada ...

By what right should those people hold me as a "traitor," because I remain consequent with the principles that I have never ceased to uphold and which both parties have exploited alternately, as long as it suited their purpose and kept them in power or brought them to office?

Let it not be pretended that those principles are out of place, pending the war. To prevent Canada from participating in the war, then foreseen and predicted, was their very object and *raison d'être*. To throw them aside and deny them when the time of test came, would have required a lack of courage and sincerity, of which I feel totally incapable. If this is what they mean by "British loyalty" and "superior civilisation," they had better hang me at once. I will never obey such dictates and will ever hold in deepest contempt the acrobats who lend themselves to all currents of blind popular passion in order to serve their personal or political ends.

This, let it be well understood, does not apply to your partner. His deeds have shown the sincerity of his political turn. Without agreeing with his new opinions, I admired his silent courage in running to the front at the first call. His verbose political manifesto — supposing he is really responsible for it — adds nothing to his merits. Still less does it enhance the dignity and moral worth of the politicians and pressmen of all kinds, who, after having denounced war and imperialism, and while taking great care not to risk their precious body, have become the apostles of war and the upholders of imperialism.

I will not undertake to answer every point of the dithyrambic plea of my gallant cousin. When he says that I am too far away from the trenches to judge of the real meaning of this war, he may be right. On the other hand, his long and diffuse piece of eloquence proves that the excitement of warfare and the distance from home have obliterated in his mind the fundamental realities of his native country. I content myself with touching upon one point, on which he unhappily lends credit to the most mischievous of the many anti-national opinions circulated by the jingo press. He takes the French-Canadians to task and challenges their patriotism, because they enlist in lesser number than the other elements of the population of Canada. Much could be said upon that. It is sufficient to signalise one patent fact: the number of recruits for the European war, in the various Provinces of Canada and from each component element of the population, is in inverse ratio of the enrootment in the soil and the traditional patriotism arising therefrom. The newcomers from the British Isles have enlisted in much larger proportion than English-speaking Canadians born in this country, while these have enlisted more than the French-Canadians. The Western Provinces have given more recruits than Ontario, and Ontario more than Quebec. In each Province, the floating population of the cities, the students, the labourers and clerks, either unemployed or threatened with dismissal, have supplied more soldiers than the farmers. Does it mean that the city dwellers are more patriotic than the country people? or that the newcomers from England are better Canadians than their fellow citizens of British origin, born in Canada? No; it simply means that in Canada, as in every other country, at all times, the citizens of the oldest origin are the least disposed to be stampeded into distant ventures of no direct concern to their native land. It proves also that military service is more repugnant to the rural than the urban populations.

There is among the French-Canadians a larger proportion of farmers, fathers of large families, than among any other ethnical element in Canada. Above all, the French-Canadians are the only group exclusively Canadian, in its whole and by each of the individuals of which it is composed. They look upon the perturbations of Europe, even those of England or France, as foreign events. Their sympathies naturally go to France against Germany; but they do not think they have an obligation to fight for France, no more than the French of Europe would hold themselves bound to fight for Canada against the United States or Japan, or even against Germany, in case Germany should attack Canada without threatening France.

English Canada, not counting the *blokes*, contains a considerable proportion of people still in the first period of national incubation. Under the sway of imperialism, a fair number have not yet decided whether their allegiance is to Canada or to the Empire, whether the United Kingdom or the Canadian Confederacy is their country.

As to the newcomers from the United Kingdom, they are not Canadian in any sense. England or Scotland is their sole fatherland. They have enlisted for the European war as naturally as Canadians, either French or English, would take arms to defend Canada against an aggression on the American continent.

Thus it is rigourously correct to say that recruiting has gone in inverse ratio of the development of Canadian patriotism. If English-speaking Canadians have a right to blame the French Canadians for the small number of their recruits, the newcomers from the United Kingdom, who have supplied a much larger proportion of recruits than any other element of the population, would be equally justified in branding the Anglo-Canadians with disloyalty and treason. Enlistment for the European war is supposed to be absolutely free and voluntary. This has been stated right and left from beginning to end. If that statement is honest and sincere, all provocations from one part of the population against the other, and exclusive attacks against the French-Canadians, should cease. Instead of reviling unjustly one-third of the Canadian people — a population so remarkably characterised by its constant loyalty to national institutions and its respect for public order, — those men who claim a right to enlighten and lead public opinion should have enough good faith and intelligence to see facts as they are and to respect the motives of those who persist in their determination to remain more Canadian than English or French.

In short, English-speaking Canadians enlist in much smaller number than the newcomers from England, because they are more Canadian; French-Canadians enlist less than English-Canadians because they are totally and exclusively Canadian. To claim that their abstention is due to the "baneful" influence of the Nationalists is a pure nonsense. Should I give way to the suggestion of my gallant cousin, I would be just as powerless as Sir Wilfrid Laurier to induce the French-Canadians to enlist. This is implicitly acknowledged in Capt. Papineau's letter: on the one hand, he asserts that my views on the participation of Canada in the war are denied by my own friends; on the other he charges the mass of the French-Canadian population with a refusal to answer the call of duty. The simple truth is, that the abstention of the French-Canadians is no more the result of the present attitude of the Nationalists than the consequence of the liberal campaign of 1896, or of the conservative appeals of 1911. It relates to deeper causes: hereditary instincts, social and economic conditions, a national tradition of three centuries. It is equally true, however, that those deep and far distant causes have been strengthened by the constant teaching of all our political and social leaders, from Lafontaine, Cartier, Macdonald, Mackenzie, to Laurier inclusively. The only virtue, or crime, of the Nationalists is to persist in believing and practising what they were taught by the men of the past, and even those of to-day. This is precisely what infuriates the politicians, either *blue* or *red.* To please the Imperialists, they have renounced all their traditions and undertaken to bring the French-Canadians under imperial command. Unable to succeed, they try to conceal their fruitless apostasy by denouncing to the hatred of the jingos the obtrusive witnesses of their past professions of faith.

The jingo press and politicians have also undertaken to persuade their gullible followers that the Nationalists hinder the work of recruiters *because* of the persecution meted out to the French minorities in Ontario and Manitoba. This is but another nonsense. My excellent cousin, I am sorry to say, — or his inspirer — has picked it up.

The two questions are essentially distinct, this we have never ceased to assert. One is purely internal; the other affects the international status of Canada and her relations with Great Britain. To the problem of the teaching of languages we ask for a solution in conformity with the spirit of the Federal agreement, the best interests of Confederation, and the principles of pedagogy as applied in civilised countries. Our attitude on the participation of Canada in the war is inspired exclusively by the constant tradition of the country and the agreements concluded half a century ago between Canada and Great Britain. Even if the irritating bilingual question was non-existent, our views on the war would be what they are. The most that can be said is, that the backward and essentially Prussian policy of the rulers of Ontario and Manitoba gives us an additional argument against the intervention of Canada in the European conflict. To speak of fighting for the preservation of French civilisation in Europe while endeavouring to destroy it in America, appears to us as an absurd piece of inconsistency. To preach Holy War for the liberties of the peoples overseas, and to oppress the national minorities in Canada, is, in our opinion, nothing but odious hypocrisy.

Is it necessary to add that, in spite of his name, Capt. Papineau is utterly unqualified to judge of the feelings of the French-Canadians? For most part American, he has inherited, with a few drops of French blood, the most *denationalised* instincts of his French origin. From those he calls his compatriots he is separated by his religious belief and his maternal language. Of their traditions, he knows but what he has read in a few books. He was brought up far away from close contact with French-Canadians. His higher studies he pursued in England. His elements of French culture he acquired in France. The complexity of his origin and the diversity of his training would be sufficient to explain his mental hesitations and the contradictions which appear in his letter ...

As to the scoundrels and bloodsuckers "who have grown fat with the wealth dishonourably gained" in war contracts, I give them up quite willingly to their just indignation. But those worthies are not to be found in nationalist ranks: they are all recruited among the noisiest preachers of the Holy War waged for "civilisation" against "barbarity," for the "protection of small nations," for the honour of England and the "salvation" of France.
Yours truly,
HENRI BOURASSA

P.S. — I hope this will reach you before you leave for the front: no doubt, you have been the first to respond to the pressing call of your partner. H.B.

E) "No More Canadians For Overseas Service. This Young Dominion Has Sacrificed Enough"
Sault Express, *June 23, 1916*

The Express in its limited sphere has been advocating peace among the warring nations of Europe, but save in the undercurrent of Canadian sentiment which we know exists in the heart of many of our people there appears to be no desire for a termination of hostilities until the Germanic power in Europe has been utterly destroyed and many of the old world wrongs have been made right. We fear that if Canada is to continue to shed her life blood until that day arrives there will not be many Canadians remaining to celebrate the conquest, and the high purposes for which our forefathers on this continent strove will all have been in vain. And more than that, we have grave fears that if this horrible conflict goes on for another two years we shall not have our United Empire to cheer for. These words are spoken in the fullest consciousness of their meaning. The destruction of the Teutonic race is quite as impossible as the destruction of the Anglo-Saxon race, and the destruction of either would be nothing short of a catastrophe handed down to posterity as an example of our present day higher civilization. What our empire needs right now and what Canada needs right now is PEACE. But we have drifted away from what we started out to say, which was that this Dominion should not send any more of her sons overseas to engage in this frightful cataclysm. The truth is that there has already been too much Canadian bloodletting and the cost of British connection has been away and beyond what our people counted on. We have less than eight millions of population as against three hundred millions in India. If, as we are told, the shedding of blood overseas is the silicon which binds the steel of Empire, then why does England not draw upon her three hundred millions in India as she has drawn upon her seven millions in Canada?

"The Canadian troops made a most gallant stand;" "the soldiers from Canada well upheld the traditions of the race;" "thousands of our brave Canadian soldiers fell with honour," "we can never forget the heroism of those grand Canadians." That kind of salve from London does not bind up the hearts of the thousands of Canadian mothers and sisters whose loved ones sleep in a foreign land after dying for a foreign cause.

It is about time for Canadians to wake up and realize that they are living in America and not Europe; that old world empires rise and fall; that we are the last great land to the west on this great planet and that the Lord has so ordained; that our neighbors and we are of the same faith, our language is the same and there is a comity of blood existing between us which makes us brothers in the truest human sense. A century of peace exemplifies the silicon in the steel.

Canada will contribute more to the future greatness of the Anglo-Saxon race by pursuing her own ideals and minding her own business on this side of the Atlantic then by spending "her last son and her last dollar" across the water in a futile effort to adjust the wrongs which most of our ancestors left the old world to escape ...

F) Speech, June 11, 1917
Robert Borden

... I announced to Parliament in the following terms the Government's conclusion that compulsory military service was necessary:

"I approached a subject of great gravity and seriousness, and, I hope, with a full sense of the responsibility that devolves upon myself and upon my colleagues, and not only upon us but upon the members of this Parliament and the people. We have four Canadian divisions at the front. For the immediate future there are sufficient reinforcements. But four divisions cannot be maintained without thorough provision for future requirements ... I think that no true Canadian, realizing all that is at stake in this war, can bring himself to consider with toleration or seriousness any suggestion for the relaxation of our efforts ... Hitherto we have depended upon voluntary enlistment. I myself stated to Parliament that nothing but voluntary enlistment was proposed by the Government. But I return to Canada impressed at once with the extreme gravity of the situation, and with a sense of responsibility for our further effort at the most critical period of the war. It is apparent to me that the voluntary system will not yield further substantial results. I hoped it would. The Government have made every effort within its power, so far a I can judge. If any effective effort to stimulate voluntary recruiting remains to be made, I should like to know what it is ...

"All citizens are liable to military service for the defence of their country, and I conceive that the battle for Canadian liberty and autonomy is being fought to-day on the plains of France and of Belgium. There are other places besides the soil of a country where the battle for its liberties and its institutions can be fought; and if this war should end in defeat, Canada, in all the years to come, would be under the shadow of German military domination. That is the very lowest at which we can put it ...

"Now the question arises as to what is our duty ... A great responsibility rests upon those who are entrusted with the administration of public affairs. But they are not fit to be trusted with that transcendent duty if they shrink from any responsibility which the occasion calls for ... The time has come when the authority of the state should be invoked to provide reinforcements necessary to maintain the gallant men at the front ... I bring back to the people of Canada from these men a message that they need our help, that they need to be sustained, that reinforcements must be sent to them. Thousands of them have made the supreme sacrifice for our liberty and preservation. Common gratitude, apart from all other considerations, should bring the whole force of this nation behind them. I have promised ... that this help shall be given. I should feel myself unworthy of the responsibility devolving upon me if I did not fulfil that pledge. I bring a message also from them, yes, a message also from the men in the hospitals, who have come back from the very valley of the shadow of death, many of them maimed for life ... But is there not some other message? Is there not a call to us from those who have passed beyond the shadow into the light of perfect day, from those who have fallen in France and in Belgium, from those who have died that Canada may live — is there not a call to us that their sacrifice shall not be in vain?

"I have had to take all these matters into consideration and I have given them my most earnest attention. The responsibility is a serious one, but I do not shrink from it. Therefore, it is my duty to announce to the House that early proposals will be made to provide by compulsory military enlistment on a selective basis, such reinforcements as may be necessary to maintain the Canadian army in the field ... The number of men required not be less than 50,000, and will probably be 100,000 ...

"It has been said of this Bill that it will induce disunion, discord and strife and that it will paralyze the national effort. I trust that this prophecy may prove unfounded. Why should strife be induced by the application of a principle which was adopted at the very inception of Confederation? ...

"It was my strong desire to bring about a union of all parties for the purpose of preventing any such disunion or strife as is apprehended. The effort was an absolutely sincere one, and I do not regret that it was made, although the delay which it occasioned may have given opportunity for increasing agitation and for excitement arising from misunderstanding. I went so far as to agree that this Bill should not become effective until after a general election, in the hope that by this means all apprehension would be allayed, and that there might be a united effort to fulfil the great national purpose of winning this war. What may be necessary or expedient in that regard, I am yet willing to consider, for ever since this war began I have had one constant aim and it was this: to throw the full power and effort of Canada into the scale of right, liberty and justice for the winning of this war, and to maintain the unity of the Canadian people in that effort ...

"God speed the day when the gallant men who are protecting and defending us will return to the land they love so well. Only those who have seen them at the front can realize how much they do love this dear land of Canada. If we do not pass this measure, if we do not provide reinforcements, if we do not keep our plighted faith, with what countenance shall we meet them on their return? ... They went forth splendid in their youth and confidence. They will come back silent, grim, determined men who, not once or twice, but fifty times, have gone over the parapet to seek their rendezvous with death. If what are left of 400,000 such men come back to Canada with fierce resentment and even rage in their hearts, conscious that they have been deserted or betrayed, how shall we meet them when they ask the reason? I am not so much concerned for the day when this Bill becomes law, as for the day when these men return if it is rejected."

G) "Women's View of Conscription"
Francis Marion Beynon, The Grain Growers' Guide, May 30, 1917

There are four objections to the government's announced intention of forcing conscription upon the people of Canada, the first and greatest being that the people have not been consulted about it, the second that it should include married as well as single men; third, that it should be accompanied by conscription of all wealth and all moneys invested in the war loans, and fourth, that the government of Great Britain no longer ago than last week closed out a motion saying that they were not fighting for imperialistic conquest or aggrandisement.

Before men are arbitrarily taken form their homes and put through the military machine, they and their mothers and fathers have a right to say that they are willing it should be done. More particularly is this the case since the killing or physical maiming of them is among the lesser evils that have befallen many of the Canadian boys who have gone to serve in the army. It was admitted in the British House of Commons the other day that in one Canadian camp alone there were seven thousand men suffering from venereal disease, and medical reports in Great Britain show that ten per cent of the forces are affected.

Of these thousands of men who have been ruined there are numbers who would not in any case have led a blameless life, but there are also thousands of clean-minded innocent young boys who would otherwise have been decent upright citizens who will now be nothing but a scourge to their country when they return and whose lives have been completely ruined. Their chances of marrying and having a happy home and healthy children have been taken away from them. Before any mother sees her son forcibly exposed to these temptations she has a right to say whether or not she is willing to have it so. When Everywoman's World took a vote of its women readers on the question of conscription recently it was defeated six to one. If this is any indication of public opinion it is certainly a minority decision the government has arrived at. If you feel at all strongly on this question, bombard Premier Borden with letters demanding a referendum, and write at once.

Although the government doubtless intends to follow the example of Great Britain of taking first the single men and then extending the principle to apply to the married men, as the demand increases, it seems fair to make it apply to both from the outset. If the good of the individual is to be set aside at the demands of the country, then the rights of the individual ought to be completely disregarded, and those men, married or single, left at home who are mostly useful to the country. There is nothing to be gained by deceiving ourselves, it means conscription for married men also, sooner or later, if the war goes on, as it seems likely to do, indefinitely. The Canadian government has followed so far, exactly the system that was followed in England at the beginning of the war, and it is likely that they will continue to follow it in every particular.

Then as regards the conscription of wealth. It has been said over and over again that this war will be won by the silver bullet, but instead of the government getting this silver bullet through war loans at five per cent and forever exempt from income tax, let them conscript the city houses and the bank accounts and the railways and the munition plants and the farms, and let all the citizens pay rent to the government. Then with this income pay a generous separation allowance to the wives of married men, and a liberal pension to their widows, and above all an especially generous pension to returned soldiers who are partially or completely disabled, so that these men who have faced death for their country may not need to be the objects of charity from people who have gotten rich out of war profits. Moreover it is obviously unjust to conscript the life of the poor working man, which is all that stands between his family and destitution, while another man can go to the front knowing that in the event of his complete disablement, neither he nor his family will have to eke out a miserable existence for years and years to come.

Finally, before men are compelled to go against their will to serve in the army they have a right to know what they are fighting for, whether it is indeed the principle of democracy, which they were assured at the beginning of the war it was, or whether it is for territory, the acquisition of which will lead to the shedding of the blood of hundreds of thousands of other men at a later date, as territory snatching almost invariably does ...

Now as has been pointed out in this column over and over again there is no territory in the world that is worth the slaughter of human beings, and, moreover, this snatching of territory is a positively bad and wicked thing, sowing the seeds of other wars for other men to be slaughtered in. It is utterly opposed to the principle of democracy for which the British Empire is supposed to stand and for which men believe they are dying in this war. No group of people have a right to be transferred from one government to another without their own consent, in a fair referendum, and they ought not so to be transferred at any time, whether in war time or peace. Therefore before conscription comes into force in Canada the British government should be compelled to repudiate any desire for territorial aggrandisement. Men have no right to be forcibly killed and maimed to acquire a few acres of land.

9

"Damming Up the Foul Streams of Degeneracy and Demoralization"

The Quest for Social Control

DOCUMENTS

A) "The Economics of the Drink Question",
   The Campaign Manual, 1912
   F.S. Spence

B) The Black Candle, 1922
   Emily Murphy

C) "Social Aspects of Mental Deficiency," 1926
   C.B. Farrar, M.D., Canadian Medical Association
   Journal

D) "Sterilization of the Feeble Minded," 1933
   H. A. Bruce, M.D., Canadian Medical Association
   Journal

D
emocracy is supposed to offer individual citizens greater levels of liberty than other forms of government. It is, after all, a political structure based upon the supremacy of the individual. Senior democracies
with stable and prosperous societies, such as Canada, tend to be smug about
their citizens' liberties and how little the state interferes in private lives. Ironically, however, reform-minded citizens and all levels of Canadian government have,
periodically, been at the vanguard of very repressive efforts at social control. Legislation limiting civil rights and freedoms invariably emerged as ways of ostensi-
bly protecting the wider social fabric from those who purportedly threatened it.
The crusaders set out, with a profound sense of righteousness on their side, to
limit the liberties of the few in order to safeguard the many. Most citizens either
did not object, or supported the new laws.

In the early twentieth century efforts at social control focused on three areas: saving society from the pernicious effects of alcohol, attacking the drug trade, and preventing the reproduction of the "feeble-minded." Though different, they all coalesced around a fundamentalist Anglo-Saxon and Protestant reform ethos.

Efforts to curb alcohol consumption in Canada went back as far as New France. The general trend, at least since the time of the British Conquest, was toward increasingly rigorous restrictions combining moral and practical rationales for suppressing drink. A new wave of evangelical Christianity surging across North America in the mid-nineteenth century swept up the cause, altering it to one of outright prohibition. Women, particularly middle-class suffragists and reformers, played crucial roles in the prohibition movement. They believed that alcohol was the scourge of families and a direct threat to the society. When individual responsibility through "taking the pledge" of total abstinence proved less than effective, the campaign shifted to controlling liquor distribution and distillation through government intervention. Innumerable anti-alcohol clubs and groups in Canada united under the banner of the Dominion Alliance and calling for the total suppression of the liquor traffic.

They were remarkably successful, convincing many municipalities to pass local laws outlawing alcohol. All provinces, except Quebec, had become dry even before the federal government passed national prohibition laws in 1918 under the guise of winning the war. Yet prohibition disappeared even more rapidly than it appeared. The tide turned in 1919 when British Columbia opted for government-controlled distribution centres rather than continuing outright prohibition. Province after province followed suit until, by 1930, only Prince Edward Island upheld the total ban. Many municipalities throughout Canada, however, remained dry under their local option. Though prohibition disappeared, liquor laws in Canada remained stricter than in most other western democracies.

Francis Stephens Spence (1850–1917) was an Irish-born journalist and teacher who became a devotee of prohibition. He lived in Ontario and worked his way through the ranks of the movement, eventually becoming honorary president of the Ontario branch of the Dominion Alliance in 1908. He is best known for his study *The Facts of the Case: A Summary of the Most Important Evidence and Argument Presented in the Report of the Royal Commission on the Liquor Traffic* (Toronto: Newton and Treloar, 1896).

Few Canadians realized that the country had an illicit drug problem in the 1920s, but Emily Murphy brought it to national prominence. It is impossible to say when non-medical drug use first began in Canada. Although a common accusation was that opium arrived with Chinese labourers working on the Canadian Pacific Railway in the 1880s, many studies disregard the high opiate content already found in numerous over-the-counter remedies produced and sold by Anglo-Canadian firms to cure a wide range of afflications from rheumatism to colic. Without consumer standards and content disclosure requirements, many Canadians undoubtedly consumed these substances in total ignorance. Smoking opium, which appeared risqué to mainstream Canadians, remained perfectly legal, the only restriction being import taxes. That changed after 1908 when Parliament passed the Opium Act, which prohibited the manufacture, sale, or import of opium for non-medical purposes. Controlling the trade, however, remained all but impossible.

Murphy (née Ferguson, 1868–1933) was one of the most prominent women in the suffrage and equal rights movement in Canada. A self-taught legal expert, she eventually rose to become Police Magistrate in Alberta in 1916, the first women judge in the British Empire. Unlike so many of her colleagues, Murphy became deeply involved in the lives of those standing accused in her docket. The results of drug abuse among her defendants caused her particular distress. Studying the problem turned her into a tireless anti-narcotics crusader, and she set out to educate Canadians about a problem that she feared could undermine the entire social fabric. This she did primarily through a series of articles in *Maclean's Magazine* during the early 1920s, exposing, in lurid detail, the evils of the drug trade. She eventually expanded the articles into a book, *The Black Candle.*

Murphy warned against "marahuana" and other non-medical drugs, and effectively lobbied to have their use declared illegal. Those caught, she argued, should pay a heavy price, including long jail sentences and whipping "when necessary." She also believed, however, that the state must establish addict rehabilitation clinics. Based largely upon Murphy's recommendations, the federal government passed the 1929 Opium and Narcotic Drug Act, which included marijuana as a banned substance.

Murphy and many of her fellow reformers also tackled the eugenics issue head on, generally giving the movement wholehearted support. Eugenics, the process of producing better human beings through selective breeding, gained popularity in Canada in the 1920s. Eugenicists offered a relatively simple argument for their cause: Societies must create the best citizens possible by excluding weak genetic strains from the gene pool. And according to these people it was in society's best interest to ensure that "feeble-minded" individuals not reproduce or the future net effect would be a "degraded" society. They believed that the easiest, cheapest, and most Christian way of achieving this was sterilizing those falling below "normal" intelligence. And there was no time for debate: most eugenicists held that the "feeble-minded" bred much more than "normal" citizens, so time was of the essence.

The problem became one of definition. What was "normal" and what constituted "feeble-mindedness"? Though Canadian scientists began categorizing, measuring, studying, and incarcerating the "feeble-minded," sterilization laws emerged more slowly. Professionals supporting it feared that the wider public might not concur with draconian measures limiting some citizens' reproductive capacity. Concentrated lobbying by pressure groups such as the National Council of Women, which publicly endorsed sterilization in 1925, eventually ensured that legislatures tackled the thorny issue. In 1928, Alberta was the first to pass laws allowing sterilization with parental or guardian consent, and British Columbia followed suit in 1933. While Manitoba and Ontario failed to produce legislation on the subject, doctors continued to recommend and practice sterilization. Provincial sterilization laws culminated in 1937 when the Alberta legislature passed amendments removing the consent clause. From then on it was solely at the state's behest whether to sterilize a mental patient, and thousands were.

Born in New York City, Dr. C.B. Farrar (1874–1970) attended and taught at Harvard and Johns Hopkins universities. Before immigating to Canada where he acted as chief psychiatrist at a number of institutions, he also held tenure as a professor at Princeton University. From 1931 to 1965 he edited the prestigious *American Journal of Psychiatry*.

Dr. H.A. Bruce (1868–1963) founded Wellesley Hospital in Toronto, acted as inspector general of the Canadian Medical Corps in the First World War, and served as Lieutenant Governor of Ontario from 1932 to 1937.

A) "The Economics of the Drink Question", The Campaign Manual, 1912
F.S. Spence

… It is well known that the drink habit and the drink traffic, working together, are responsible for much waste of wealth, and this waste not only involves the impoverishment of the liquor consumers, but the impoverishment of the country as a whole.

When attention is called to the great expenditure on strong drink it is sometimes said in reply that this amount of money is not destroyed, that it remains and circulates, and, therefore, if some are made poorer by the expenditure, others are made richer and the aggregate wealth of the community is not lessened.

It takes no deep knowledge of economics to demolish this absurdity. The liquor consumers have toiled for the production of the wealth which their money represents, or someone else has toiled for them. If they pay that money for clothing, food, furniture, fuel or other necessities or luxuries, they receive value for their toil. The producers of these articles have the money, the purchasers have the goods, and the community possesses the wealth represented by both, or double the amount which the purchases have invested.

If, on the other hand, the money is spent in drinking, while liquor vendors may have the amount of money named, the liquor consumers have absolutely nothing to show for their investment, and there is in the possession of consumers and dealers on the whole only one-half the wealth that existed when the money was otherwise invested.

What applies to the country at large applies also to a municipality. The money spent at the bar by people of a municipality leaves the local community that much poorer. Money cannot be spent on strong drink without being as really wasted, as absolutely destroyed, as if that amount of money or goods were buried in the bottom of the sea, or as if the money were spent in purchasing articles of value and committing them to the flames.

The actual spending of money in intoxicating liquor is not the only waste of wealth chargeable to the drink system. There is serious loss of wealth production, through idleness of men who are out of employment because of the drinking habits of themselves [or] of others. There is serious loss through the curtailment of the lives of citizens who, had they lived, might have been factors in the country's wealth production. There is loss through the practical destruction, in liquor manufacture, of large quantities of grain that would otherwise be among our surplus food products for export. There is loss through misdirection of the labor employed in this destruction. There is loss through the lessening of the market for products of all industries through the impoverishment of consumers. There is loss through the expenditure imposed upon the community in the custody and care of those who are morally, mentally and physically degraded through intemperance.

The business which causes all this waste is used by governmental institutions as a convenient method of raising revenue, because of the facilities it gives for imposing extra taxation on the consumers of drink. These consumers contribute to the direct loss that goes on, and also are required to make special and large contributions for public purposes.

These and some other aspects of the relation of the drink system to the individual and community wealth and poverty, will be presented in the following series of articles that will be found more suggestive than exhaustive by those who have time to study this important question ...

2. Drink Caused Idleness

The interference of the drinking habit with the country's wealth production is very great. The Royal Commission examined a great many employers of labor, and the general testimony of these men was that much time is lost by drinking employees, and that work is frequently interfered with, sometimes seriously by the absence or incapacity of drinking men.

The loss to the country is, of course, not at all represented by the mere loss of time by men who are regularly employed. The country loses through drink because of the prevention of the production of wealth on account of the persons in jails, in hospitals, in asylums out of employment or in any way idle when intemperance has caused the idleness.

It is also worthy of note, having been stated to the Commission by a number of witnesses, that the working of a gang of men in a factory or any set of persons who work to a certain extent dependent upon each other, is much interfered with by absence of some or even of one.

This is more and more the case as industrial development progresses, as machinery is being more generally used, and work more and more subdivided. In a highly-organized manufacturing industry, any interference with one part of the work affects the operation of the whole. So, not only those who drink lose time and possible earnings, but their fellow-employees who do not drink are also losers, and the industry which employs them suffers interference and loss.

There is also an important depreciation of wage-earning capacity on the part of men who habitually drink. They are less qualified for the performance of good work, and what they do is in both quality and quantity inferior to the work of men of sober habits.

The total loss in these various ways aggregates a very large percentage of the otherwise available working power of the community. There is some difficulty in estimating exactly how far this loss extends. The matter was inquired into some years ago by an English Parliamentary committee, the report of which contains the following statements:

> The loss of productive labor in every department of occupation, is to the extent of at least one day in six throughout the kingdom (as testified by witnesses engaged in various manufacturing operations), by which the wealth of the country created, as it is, chiefly by labor, is retarded or suppressed to the extent of one million of every six that is produced, to say nothing of the constant derangement, imperfection, and destruction in every agricultural and manufacturing process, occasioned by the intemperance and consequent unskilfulness, inattention and neglect of those affected by intoxication, and producing great injury in our domestic and foreign trade.

Canada suffers less in this way than do Old World countries. The people are more sober. Still the waste is very great. The Hon. Geo. E. Foster and the Hon. Geo. W. Ross both estimated that one-tenth the producing power of the country is destroyed by intemperance. If we fix it still lower, and say, to be safe, that only one-twelfth our working power is lost through intemperance, we shall have a basis from which a calculation may be made.

According to the estimate that the liquor traffic destroys one-twelfth of our country's wealth-producing power, the amount stated is only eleven-twelfths of what it would be if the liquor habit and the liquor traffic did not interfere with our workers and their work, and our country through loss of liquor-destroyed working power is kept poorer each year by $66,017,429.

3. Misdirected Labor

As far as enriching the country is concerned, the labor of the men engaged in the liquor business is absolutely thrown away.

The cabinet-maker takes some of the wood that is the raw material of his industry, and turns it into an article of furniture. He has added to the aggregate of the country's wealth the difference between the value of the material and the product.

A storekeeper takes the finished article of furniture, exhibits it for sale, delivers it at the home of its customer where it is of even more value than it was when the cabinet-maker had finished his work. The customer is better off in his ownership of the furniture than he was with the money which it represented.

The storekeeper and the cabinet-maker have added to their possessions the profits of the business done, and for years to come the whole community will be richer by the difference between the value of the raw material in the cabinet-maker's shop and the furniture in the customer's home.

We might illustrate the working out of the same principle in any line of industry. The supply of the community's needs means the benefiting of supplier and supplied, and the community enjoys the results of the work performed.

Now take the liquor makers and the liquor-sellers. Here is the grain fitted to furnish sustenance, and supply strength to man and beast. The liquor-maker destroys every particle of its value to the community, and turns it into a curse instead of a blessing. The liquor-seller stands behind his bar and hands out to his customers the distiller's product. When the whiskey is drunk, and the whole transaction is completed, we can examine the results. The customer has nothing. There is no sustenance or strength or property anywhere to represent the material taken for the liquor industry. The consumer's money is divided between the maker and the dealer and the government, but there is no furniture in the customer's home. He is poorer by the full amount that has been transferred to other parties.

The liquor business adds nothing to the sum of the commonwealth's common wealth. It may result in injured health, shortened lives, disease, poverty, insanity, remorse, or crime, but it has had no material result except the enrichment of some at the expense of others. The work of the liquor-maker and seller is worse than water as far as any wealth-producing effect is concerned.

Had the business energy, the judgment, the foresight, the physical power, the capital, and the time of these men been invested in almost any other occupation, they would have added to the country's wealth. As it is they are mere parasites, living on a community to which they give nothing in return. Were it not for this liquor system we would be better off by all that the capital and qualifications of the liquor-traffickers would have done for us if employed in some other way ...

4. Drink Caused Mortality

It is not practicable to ascertain accurately the extent to which the drink habit shortens life. Official reports of the causes of death are not of much help in solving this problem. Deaths are charged to diseases of many kinds, which diseases frequently grow out of intemperate habits.

The carelessness that leads to fatal accidents is often the result of the dulling by drink of the keenness of men's mental faculties.

Drink-caused poverty is the parent of a great mortality.

Recent investigations and deliverances by eminent medical men have given us knowledge of the fact that tuberculosis frequently finds its origin in drinking practices and facilities, and that its progress is accelerated by the same causes.

This applies to many other vital disturbances and weaknesses, which are not directly attributed to strong drink ...

In Canada, as a rule, the people drink less than in Great Britain and the United States, yet scarcely a day passes without some newspaper story of some terrible fatality directly attributed to strong drink. It is well known that diseases of many organs are caused or accelerated by intemperance. Everyone can think of some life which he is certain has been shortened because of the liquor evil, though no one would say it ended in a drink-caused death. We are probably well within the mark if we estimate the number of deaths from drink in Canada [as] being one-half the proportion calculated for Great Britain and the United States. This means that five per cent. of our mortality may be said to be the result of this evil.

The population of Canada in 1901 was 5,371,315, and in 1911 was 7,204,527, an increase of 34.12 per cent. The number of deaths reported for the former year in the census of 1901 was 81,201. Assuming that the death rate was still the same, there would be an increase of the total annual deaths to say 108,900.

Five per cent. of this number would be 5,445, and this is certainly a very low estimate of the number of lives that are cut short in Canada every year by strong drink.

Many of the persons whose lives are thus shortened would otherwise have been useful citizens for many years. If the untimely death of each one of them meant a loss on the average of ten years of participation in the activities of this young and progressive community, then our country was last year deprived because of this loss of the services of 54,450 persons who were in untimely graves, instead of being useful citizens, enjoying life and helping to build up the nation's prosperity ...

5. The Waste of Grain

Canada is a grain-growing country. Every year it produces vast quantities of wheat and other cereals more than the people of the country need. These products are shipped to other lands, and their value is represented by the product of other lands which our country is made able to buy. Every surplus bushel of Canadian grain is a national asset, an increase in the accumulating wealth of this prospering country.

In the year ending March 31st, 1911, the quantity of barley turned into malt for the production of beer and spirits was 125,546,514 pounds ...

6. Outlay Made Necessary by Drinking

The public expenditure incurred through intemperance is very great. It is universally admitted that much of the disease, insanity, idiocy, and other misfortunes which go to increase the dependent classes, is due to the liquor habit, and that a very large proportion of the pauperism and crime of the country is attributable directly or indirectly to the same cause.

The support of our great charities is, to a large extent, voluntary. Private benevolence supports homes, refuges, hospitals, and various other institutions for the maintenance of the destitute and other afflicted persons. There is no way of ascertaining what amount of money is expended in this way ...

The Hon. Sir Oliver Mowat, late Lieutenant-Governor of the Province of Ontario, was a man of cautious and conservative temperament, as well as of wide experience and close observation. He stated in the Ontario Legislature, when he was leader of the Provincial Government, that in his opinion, not less than three-fourths of the poverty, vice, disease and crime which afflicted the country was chargeable to the evil of intemperance. Let us be even more moderate in our reckoning than was Sir Oliver Mowat. Let us estimate that only one-half of the vast public outlay which we have detailed, results from the drinking habits of our people. Even then we have to face the formidable fact that in addition to all the suffering, the sorrow, the shame, and the sin that intemperance inflicts upon our fair Dominion, one year's cost of caring for those upon whom the liquor curse has fallen, which must be paid out of public funds, amounts to over $7,087,285 ...

CRIME AND DRUNKENNESS IN CANADA

It is true that during recent years there has been a rapid and regrettable increase in drunkenness and other crime in nearly every part of the Dominion of Canada. From the last published Government Criminal Returns, the following table is compiled, showing (1) the total number of convictions for all offences, including drunkenness, and (2) the total convictions for drunkenness alone:

Year	All Convictions	Convictions for Drunkenness
1898	38,206	11,259
1899	38,710	11,090
1900	41,653	12,215
1901	42,148	12,727
1902	43,536	13,324
1903	50,404	16,532
1904	54,946	18,895
1905	62,450	21,621
1906	70,903	25,110
1907	79,170	29,802
1908	88,633	31,089
1909	89,951	31,105
1910	102,903	34,068

The population has also increased during these years, but not at all in the same ratio as has the criminal record. The population, according to the census, in the year 1901 was 5,371,315, and in the year 1911, was 7,204,527.

Canada is a comparatively sober country. Its per capita consumption of intoxicating liquor is less than one-third that of the United States, and only about one-fifth that of England. A good deal of its territory is under prohibitory law, and the people, as a whole, are progressive, and have a reputation for sobriety and morality. What is the explanation of the increase in drunkenness and crime? ...

It required some time for the machinery of the federation of the original colonies and the subsequent addition of other areas to be adjusted to its work, and to develop effectiveness. Even in the matter of compiling statistics, time was needed to secure efficiency, and the records for early years were very defective. Recent returns are more accurate than those before obtained, and official statements come nearer to being a correct record of actual conditions. The thoroughness of law enforcement has also increased, so that for example the illicit manufacture of strong drink has been thoroughly suppressed, and crime, in general, now rarely escapes official recognition and action. No doubt, this change has had some influence in increasing the official figures of drink consumed, and crime punished. Their effect upon the record of the last ten years has, however, been very slight.

The three main factors or causes in the increased drinking and criminal record of Canada are: (1) A very large immigration; (2) unusual prosperity; (3) the concentration of population in large cities.

As is well known, there is now entering Canada a very large stream of the overflow of European population. England's per capita consumption of strong drink is over thirty gallons. Canada's is less than seven. It is easy to see that immigration tends to change the Canadian figures. Other European immigrants have grown up under conditions and customs in regard to strong drink very much like those of Great Britain. The rapid increase of Canadian population in this way tends to increase the record of both drinking and drunkenness. With an increase in drinking and drunkenness there always comes an increase in crime.

Police Court records register very fairly any change in the general material prosperity of the community. When men are well off, they develop luxurious habits. With a certain class of the population, increased earning power means increased drunkenness. Men who have money to pay police court fines put in more convictions than men who are compelled to serve terms of imprisonment which are imposed as alternative penalties. Here again, the increased drinking and drunkenness which comes with increasing prosperity are always accompanied by an increase in violations of law and order. So-called "good times" bring a history of bad conduct.

Improvements in agricultural machinery and the growing demand for manufactured articles have had the effect of concentrating a greater number of people in cities and large towns. The urban population of Canada has increased much more rapidly than the rural population, notwithstanding the vast agricultural possibilities which the country presents. Furthermore, the better class of immigration goes out on the land where drinking facilities and temptations are scarce, and the towns fill up with new-comers of a less desirable class. There is always more drinking and crime in congested centres than in sparsely-populated districts. Some Canadian cities are having a phenomenally rapid growth.

Certain industries, such as mining, attract a population that is not only large and congested, but made up to a certain extent of reckless people associating under conditions that do not promote order and morality.

There is another factor in Canadian conditions which tends to enlarge the criminal record. It is the stern and continuous operation of the machinery for the detection and punishment of offences against law and order. A high record of convictions may mean a high record of effective law inforcement. Therefore, comparisons between the criminal records of ldifferent countries are not of much value unless at the same time consideration is given to the thoroughness or laxity of law administration in the places compared.

The relations of the liquor traffic to crime is strikingly shown in the fact that, generally speaking, those Canadian provinces in which prohibition is most extensive have the lowest criminal record. There is one province, Prince Edward Island, under a prohibitory law throughout. The province of Nova Scotia comes next in the extent to which it has been brought under prohibition, by the Local Option plan. Then comes New Brunswick, and so on ...

Taking Canada as a whole, prohibition sentiment is growing, and the territory and population under prohibition is rapidly increasing. Because of immigration and concentration in urban centres, the population under license is still increasing more rapidly than the population under prohibition. As the prohibition area spreads, the relative proportions of increase will change and ultimately become reversed; but it is possible that for some time Canada may still present the apparent anomaly of development of prohibition sentiment and law, along with an increase in liquor consumption and crime. Yet the progress towards the general adoption of the prohibition plan is certain and rapid ...

B) The Black Candle, 1922
Emily Murphy

Chapter IV — The Drug Traffic in Canada

A while ago we said that America led the world in the narcotic drug traffic. This is quite true, but only during the past two years, for in 1919, before the Canadian Government recognized the necessity of taking immediate and drastic steps to remedy the condition, Canada held that direful distinction, if we will compute the population of this Dominion as thirteen times less than that of the United States.

The legitimate importations in narcotics for 1920 were reduced, in some instances, from 75% to 25% as against the previous year. This was due in a large measure to the establishing of the licensing system.

But, in spite of their bold and determined effort to grapple with the illicit or unlicensed traffic, and in spite of their large seizures of contraband narcotics, the Government have acknowledged that it is actually on the increase. The Department of Health says it would astound the people in this country, and the authorities in many towns and cities if the conditions as they exist were brought to light.

Indeed the unlicensed traffic has gained such a foothold in Canada that it has become most alarming. In one Western inland city with about thirty thousand of a population, the federal police found upon investigation that there were hundreds of young men and women, many of them not out of their teens, who were addicted to the drug habit.

This prairie town, which is typical of many others in the Dominion, would have indignantly denied this charge and there is no doubt the police, clergy, teachers and parents, not looking for addiction and not knowing the symptoms, would have said "Impossible! We do not know of any drug users, or not more than three or four."

Yet, before the federal police left this town they laid evidence before the local authorities which led to the conviction of nearly fifty persons, most of them pedlars.

The trouble in most cities appears to be that the police are untrained in the work, and, in some few instances, actually in league with the traffickers, thereby affording them a certain amount of indirect protection.

It is the opinion of the Government officials that this underground traffic continues to flourish in spite of the efforts which are being made by the Royal Canadian Mounted Police, and by the provincial and municipal police by reason of the fact that there are enormous quantities of these drugs available in European countries ...

For the twelve months ending March 31st, 1922, the Federal Government prosecuted, under the provisions of the Opium and Drugs Act, twenty-three doctors, eleven druggists, four veterinary surgeons, one hundred and sixty-five illicit dealers, and six hundred and thirty four Chinamen, making a total of eight hundred and thirty-five convictions. The fines imposed amounted to $127,947.00. These figures do not include provincial and municipal convictions.

The municipal drug convictions for Vancouver totalled 858 for the year 1921, having jumped from 293 in 1918. It is expected the convictions for 1922 will pass the one thousand mark.

By comparing these figures with those of the American cities on the Pacific Coast, it will be seen that in spite of their greater population, Vancouver leads San Francisco, Seattle and Los Angeles. Indeed with the exception of New York, and possibly Chicago, Vancouver leads all of the way.

Commenting on these convictions, a western editor says, "Some with the aid of purchased legal skill went scot free on pettifogging technicalities. A few of them went to jail, for the most part for pitifully insufficient periods. The vast majority of them were levied for a contribution to the city treasury in the form of a fine. All of them, in due course, became free to commit the same sin against society."

While undoubtedly seaport cities, like Vancouver and Montreal, have a greater incidence than the cities like Toronto and Winnipeg, still the difference is not as much as one might expect ...

The Kiwanis Club of Vancouver, in a report of its medical subcommittee, had this to say about the matter ... "In 1918, the late Chief of Police McLennan, who was brutally murdered by a drug-fiend, called attention to the prevalence of the drug habit in this city [Vancouver] which he stated was then becoming alarming. The police authorities claim that although the drug habit has been growing here, it has certainly not been growing any more rapidly than in other cities proportionately to population, but that greater prominence has been given to Vancouver on account of the publicity given to the subject in the daily press, and also on account of the great activity and success of the police department in prosecuting drug traffickers and seizing drugs." ...

It is generally held that breaches of the opium and liquor laws are proportionately more frequent in the cities that in the country. It is on this assumption that the special American Committee compute the numbers of their addicts, although they state that in the rural districts or smaller cities little or no attention has been given to this subject, and where decreases are reported, it is quite possible that the opinions expressed by the officials are at variance with the conditions as they actually exist.

If it could be shown that physicians, druggists, veterinarians and dentists who are responsible for a vast amount of the traffic were more honorable and less avaricious in the country districts than in the city, we might assume that New York was more deeply narcotised, proportionately, than the smaller places in Texas or Idaho, but such is not the case. The functioning of the Liquor Act in which prescriptions are freely distributed shows — in Canada anyway — that exactly the opposite condition prevails. In the Province of Ontario, which is thickly populated, for the year 1920, only 5% of the physicians wrote out their full quota of fifty prescriptions, while in Alberta where the population is less than one person to the square mile, 75% of the physicians wrote over 75 prescriptions per month.

It is well known by those who study the subject that drug runners are pushing out into the rural districts where there is comparatively little police supervision and where they can sell out their whole stock of contraband drugs to coal-miners, lumbermen, railway navvies, and even to the threshermen. It was also found that among those who took advantage of the harvest excursions from East and West to the Prairie Provinces were a number of addicts and pedlars …

At a meeting in March of this year, the following figures were presented to the Trades' and Labour Council of Vancouver showing the magnitude of the traffic: — "The amount of narcotic drugs legitimately sold in Canada in 1921 was valued at $182,484, including 2,416 ounces of cocaine, 5,286 ounces of morphine and 1,440 pounds of opium. Drug addicts known to Vancouver police are estimated at three thousand. The amount of drugs used per addict per day is from one to fifteen dollars' worth. If each addict used only one dollars' worth per day, then in Vancouver alone the traffic would amount to $912,516 a year. The total amount sold in the Dominion per year legitimately being $182,484, the balance of drugs used by addicts in Vancouver alone would be valued at $730,032. The estimated number of addicts in Canada and the United States is two million, on the basis of one dollar per day per addict, the traffic represents on the continent about $672,000,000 annually." …

Because they are more keenly awake to the menace, the city of Vancouver, in 1921 circularized one hundred cities and towns in Canada asking these to join with them in a drug war against the drug traffic, and proposing that the Dominion Government be requested to amend the penalty clause in the Opium and Drugs Act, so that a person guilty of an offence under the Act might be liable, on indictment, to imprisonment for seven years, or it convicted upon a summary proceeding, to a fine of from $200.00 to $1,000.00, or to imprisonment for eighteen months, or to both fine and imprisonment.

As a result of this campaign, a very distinct tightening was made in the

Act, although much better results would have been accomplished had it not been for the opposition of some few of the medical doctors who were members of the legislature ...

Heroin Slavery

... While insanity sometimes results in the advanced stages of drug-addiction, it is not nearly so common as the public suppose ...

While insanity within the meaning of the Criminal Code is not so frequent among addicts, it must be borne in mind that through excessive use of narcotics, or by means of sudden withdrawal, the victim undergoes what the French call "a crisis of the nerves" which amounts to insanity, but which is only temporary.

When a man is criminally inclined, cocaine and heroin produce delusions which actually make him "insane and dangerous to be at large." These drugs also give him courage without reason; make his vision more acute, and steady his hand so that he may commit murder with ease.

"I have noticed" says Dr. J.B. McConnell of Winnipeg, writing in this connection, "that the majority of petty thieves and hold-up men are usually addicts and they are very dangerous, and if ever they ask you to throw up your hands, I would advise you to do so at once, because they have to get the money in order to get the drugs."

When the four murderers of Herman Rosenthal were being tried, it was discovered that three of them were drug addicts who, before committing the deed, had to be "charged up" with cocaine, and it was under the leadership of "Dopey Benny," a slum addict, that a band of twelve dope-fiends hired out their services to "beat-up" or murder any individual, their regular fee for assassination being $200.00 ...

Persons suffering from cocaine-insanity have deep-seated delusions concerning electricity. Their nights become a termless hell when, because of their disordered perceptions, electric needles play over their skin or an enemy pours "the juice" into their head ...

During the year 1917, the cases which passed through the Vancouver jail numbered 3,863, and of these according to the Chief-Constable and others, a large proportion were drug addicts, and it is believed that the use of drugs is probably one of the chief contributors to crime in British Columbia, in that it diminishes the responsibility of those who are mentally or nervously subnormal or disordered.

It need scarcely be explained that a mentally abnormal person whose abnormality has been further augmented by the use of noxious drugs, can hardly be kept from committing crime. Indeed, one of the Western police magistrates in writing me on the subject says, "The taking of drugs is undoubtedly the cause of a great deal of crime because people under its influence have no more idea of responsibility of what is right or wrong than an animal."

Another says, "The spread of drug-addiction has been so insidious, and so rapid in its growth, that it is only within the last few years an enlightened public has begun to realize its menacing nature. People in every stratum of society are afflicted with this malady, which is a scourge so dreadful in its effects that it threatens the very foundations of civilization." ...

Crime and Narcotics

... Opium and morphine users seldom commit the more brutal crimes. The offences committed by these, in order of their frequency are: — larceny, burglary, vagrancy, forgery, assault, and violation of the drug laws.

Speaking of the effect of addiction on morals, a certain report has declared, however, that "the opium or morphine addict is not always a hopeless liar, a moral wreck, or a creature sunk in vice and lost to all sense of decency, but may often be an upright individual except under circumstances which involve his effection, or the procuring of the drug of addiction. He will usually lie as to the dose necessary to sustain a moderately comfortable existence, and he will stoop to any subterfuge, and even to theft to achieve relief from bodily agonies experienced as a result of the withdrawal of the drug."

A prominent Government official in a letter from Winnipeg, Manitoba, said recently, "Many crimes are to our knowledge committed by persons while under the influence of drugs, and we have good grounds for believing that the recent murder in the town of St. Boniface, whereby two Provincial police officers came to their death, was caused by a cocaine fiend." ...

Ways of the Traffickers

... While the Assyrians, Negroes and Greeks in Canada have become allies of the Chinese in carrying on the traffic, it is well known to the police and Government authorities that many Anglo Saxons, men prominent in social and business circles, as well as lawyers, physicians and druggists have also become engaged in the illicit sale, because of the enormous profits accruing therefrom. These profits range all the way from one hundred to ten thousand per cent ...

It is the habit of these peddlers to playfully shake some "snow" — that is to say a combination of cocaine and powdered borax — on the back of the hand of their friends and suggest that they sniff it up the nostrils. The friend is immediately stimulated, and if tired, loses his weariness and becomes mentally and physically alert. This is why the powder is sometimes described as "happy dust." The interest and curiosity of the recipients are aroused and if they enquire where they can get it, they are offered a package for a dollar. Presently, the new addicts pass on the discovery to their particular friends, with the information as to where the drug can be obtained ...

Older people falling victim to it, neglect all that life has held sweet to them in order that they may follow the trail of the scintillating powder. Fiends in human guise buy cocaine from certain quarters; it is then split into small quantities, wrapped in brown paper, each little package being sold for twenty-five cents.

"A dollar's worth of cocaine makes over one hundred such packages. The profit is therefore over two hundred and forty per cent. The sales are certain. The first samples are distributed to children free. The sample creates a demand and the children come again. It is refused unless they bind themselves to absolute secrecy. A few doses and the habit has grown. The children must have their dope. All moral sense is lost and in a few months our boys and girls are ruined."

A probation officer of the Children's Aid Society in one of our large cities has this to say of the subject: "So great has this evil become that one constable has on his book one hundred and forty cases in one district. I, personally, know at least fifty cases, all children, between the ages of twelve and eighteen. Little boys of eleven and fourteen have been caught peddling cocaine in houses of ill-fame.

"The physical aspect I can but liken to consumption. The deadly work of the drug is done before either the victim or the relatives perceive it. It is usually taken in powdered form and snuffed up the nostrils. The result, particularly in young people, is that the bones of the nose decay and they are subject to hemorrhages. It is the most diabolical of all drugs on this account, and for this reason, I am told by a physician, it directly attacks the lining of the nose and brain. The victim becomes emaciated, extremely irritable, nervous, suspicious, fearful of noise and darkness, depressed, without ambition and bad tempered to the extent of viciousness. Boys and girls lose all sense of moral responsibility, affection and respect for their parents, their one thought being to get the dope and be with their friends.

"So degenerate do they become that the public parks, roadside or shed, is the same to them as a home." ...

In both the Police and Juvenile Courts many young persons under eighteen are found to be suffering from the drug habit, and one, known to myself became violently insane. Most of these juveniles are brought for crime of some kind or other, and are found to be habituated to the use of deleterious drugs. Some of these have belonged to prominent families, but in all the cases their names are kept out of the papers in order that the children may have a chance to be restored to normality without the handicap of a bad reputation.

If these are well-advanced in addiction, we have no option but to send them to jail, there being no other place of detention where they may be kept away from the drug ...

Doctors and Magistrates

... From records in our possession — these being known to the police — we have the names of Canadian doctors who have, until the present, been prescribing, as high as 100 grains of cocaine in each prescription, or equal to four hundred quarter-grain tablets, or average adult doses.

In three months, this winter, it was found that a certain physician in a Western town, had issued fifty-two prescriptions for sixty grains of morphine and three thousand grains of cocaine. His extravagance is by no means peculiar, several other doctors having records approximately high.

In this same period of three months, one man not any considerable distance from where we write, was able to get from a drug company, by means of a doctor's prescription, nearly seven thousand grains of opium.

The doctors claim these prescriptions were given to cure the victim on the "gradual reduction" or "ambulatory method," and were without charge. Most of us will refuse to credit their claim. Men who are "yellow" enough to supply addicts, however much they suffered, with narcotics in such large bulk, ought for a certainty to be breaking stones in some jail yard ...

Forecast of Victory

... The medical, pharmaceutical, dental and veterinarian associations, in all parts of the continent, could do excellent service if, on their own initiative, they secured the evidence to prosecute those of their members who violate the federal, provincial or state narcotic enactments. Some associations are already performing this service although, up to the present, none can be charged as overly precipitate in action. There is no reason why these associations should not protect their own and the people's rights by prosecuting those renegade members of their profession — a minority, to be sure — who engage in so nefarious and disreputable a trade as poison vending.

Physicians could also help by drawing the attention of the public to the slum conditions which enable the Oriental pedlar to ply his business in comparative safety. Entering these places in his daily practice, the physician can speak with more authority than anyone else. It is a thousand pities they are so generally inarticulate on the subject. The unsanitary conditions prevailing should alone be sufficient cause for their taking the lead for better housing, with more sunlight and fresh air.

Physicians could also do much to prevent the acquiring of the drug habit by agitating for the examination of children in schools, by a specialist, whereby psychopathic tendencies could be detected and, if possible, corrected.

The system of medical inspection of schools being already established, this work would only be an adjunct thereto ...

In Canada, all persons who are arrested for trafficking in narcotics, whether convicted or not, in any city or town, should have their photograph and fingerprints taken by the police, and forwarded to a central bureau, preferably at Ottawa, where these could be copied and sent broadcast to all police officers throughout the Dominion.

In this way the police could be on the lookout for these traffickers and, as soon as they arrive in a city or town, if occasion warranted, apprehend them.

At the present time when a person is convicted of an offence against the Opium and Drugs Act and pays his fine, or serves a term in jail, he is released, and as a rule, leaves for some other locality to again ply his illegal trade, and the authorities of the city to which he goes have no information concerning him. He may, therefore, be able to operate for months or years before eventually being caught ...

The Traffic

... [I]t is plainly palpable that the illicit traffic in our Dominion has grown to menacing proportions and, as yet it remains to be grappled with ...

But, undoubtedly, Mr. W.L. MacKenzie King, in his report published in 1908 on "The Need for the Suppression of the Opium Traffic in Canada," struck the right note on this phase of the subject when he said: —

> "Other instances of legislative enactments to suppress the opium evil, and to protect individuals from the baneful effect of this drug might be given, if further examples were necessary. What is more important, however, than the example of other countries, is the good name of our own. To be indifferent to the growth of such an evil in Canada would be inconsistent with those principles of morality which ought to govern the conduct of a Christian nation."

Mr. King wrote these words in 1908, when the Chinese residents had presented claims to the Federal Government for losses occasioned by the anti-Asiatic riots during which seven of their opium factories were destroyed.

Mr. King, then the Minister of Labour, further said that the amount consumed in Canada, if known, would probably appall the ordinary citizen who is inclined to believe that the habit is confined to the Orientals. The Chinese with whom he had conversed assured him that almost as much opium was sold to white people as to Chinese, and that the habit was making headway, not only among white men and boys, but among women and girls.

This was eleven years ago, and no particular attention was paid Mr. King's warning, with the result that all the provinces of Western Canada are, today, suffering immensely from this evil. In referring to the traffic in drugs, the Editor of the *Edmonton Journal*, said in December 1919: —

> "It is known that vast forces are now engaged in peddling morphias, opiums, and lesser known and even more devilish narcotics and stimulants. A few days in the Edmonton police court would reveal the extent of the system here in the far north, and it is certain that a vast international organization is handling the importation and supply of huge quantities of every sort of vicious drug. Action cannot be taken too soon."

Anyone who has lived in British Columbia knows that where the Chinese have their own districts, much smoking is indulged in ...

The New Buccaneers

... While the drug habit affects all classes of society in Canada, there would seem to be more addicts, per capita, of the population, in some districts than in others.

Sometimes, one is inclined to think otherwise, and that the seeming difference is due to the various methods adopted in its detection.

In Edmonton, Alberta, our morality squad, or "plain-clothes men," who find inhibited drugs in the possession of any person are awarded half the fine by the magistrate. Indeed, any informant is awarded this if a conviction be made.

In Toronto, Winnipeg and other cities, this procedure is not pursued. It is claimed that if it were generally practised, the detectives would do no other work …

But apart from the sharpening of the official senses where the ferreting out of drugs is concerned, a moiety of the fines ought to be paid to the men who trail down the addicts and the illicit vendors. The traffic in drugs is carried on with such strict secrecy that the utmost caution and patience are required to secure information and evidence. This being secured, to force an entry to a drug den at two o'clock in the morning when the "dopers" are irresponsible either wholly or in part, is an unpleasant and often a dangerous task. A man needs to take his courage in both hands for, generally speaking, infuriated dopers are no herd of sheep.

In smoking, the Chinaman reclines on a mattress on the floor, having beside him a pan which contains the opium "lay-out." The cracks of the windows and doors are packed with wet cloths that the odor of the smoke may not escape. For the same reason, the keyhole of the door is plugged, thus preventing its being locked with a key. The door is secured with a butcher knife driven into the door-jamb.

Finally, the available furniture is piled against the door to guard against surprises. It is this butcher knife in the door-jamb, that constitutes the chiefest danger to the detectives who come with an order for search, although more than one officer has been killed by a bullet sent through the panel of the door. Two years ago, the Chief of Police at Vancouver and one of his men were murdered in this way while waiting in a hall-way for a dope-fiend to give entry.

In Toronto, they tell us that the Chinese used to smoke openly, but since 1911 when the Opium and Drug Act came into force, open smoking ceased and, as a result, there are fewer convictions.

Knowing the Chinese temperament and habits, one conjectures whether smoking is not as freely indulged in as formerly, but with probably more careful precautions and safeguards.

But if Toronto pays no *douceur* to the morality squad, still it has given considerable attention to the examination of the books and prescriptions of the druggists. If a druggist is selling more narcotics than other druggists he must render an accounting or lose his license ...

In Winnipeg, it is officially stated that the habit is growing rapidly, and that the police have on their lists the names and addresses of hundreds of persons who are inveterate users of narcotics.

It was recently declared by an investigating committee in California that the drug distribution centre for all America is in Western Canada. The evidence upon which this astounding assertion is based has not been made public but it is quite possible, even probable, that this assertion is true ...

It is claimed that less adroitness is required to land contraband in Canada than in the States, and that it is brought here daily in many and various containers, even in musical instruments.

Other than the assumption made by government officials at Ottawa that opium was being smuggled into the States from Montreal, it had occurred to few of us, if any, that an immensely greater traffic might have gained foothold in Western Canada. We took for granted that the commerce in drugs was directly between the United States and China, not dreaming that Canada might be the intermediary in the same ...

The Cure

... All drugs in Canada should be procured from the Government. What the Government does not prohibit, it must monopolize. There should be no profits on the products whatsoever.

If drugs were sold by the retailers on a system of triplicate order blanks, one of these going to the Federal Government, a complete check could be kept on sales, but, however managed, there should be a record on every grain from the time it leaves the importer till it reaches the ultimate consumer.

Illicit vendors in drugs should be handled sternly, whatever their status, and it would be well for the Government to consider whether or not these should be given the option of a fine. The profits from the traffic are so high that fines are not in any sense deterrent. Besides, these ruthless butchers of men and morals are entitled to no more delicate consideration than the white-slaver, the train-wrecker, house-breaker, or the perpetrator of any other headlong crime ...

C) "Social Aspects of Mental Deficiency," 1926
C.B. Farrar, M.D., Canadian Medical Association Journal

... It is now, to state a commonplace fact, correct to say that the great majority of delinquents and criminals, particularly the habitual types, are mentally subnormal or abnormal ...

Knowing these facts we are forced to conclude that the very circumstance that recidivism exists and bulks so large in our criminal procedure is a demonstration that we are not properly attacking the problem of crime. The career of many repeaters could readily be prophesied after the first conviction, if means were available to make an adequate study of their mental condition. The inevitable conclusion would be that many of those who have become criminal are mentally deficient or abnormal, and not only a dangerous element in society at the time the crime was committed, but remain a permanent menace and should be permanently segregated from society. Under ideal conditions recidivism should almost disappear. The recidivist by his repeated criminal acts testifies that society and the state have not recognized him for what he is.

A third problem of the mentally defective is that of marriage and parenthood. For some curious reason these two matters have quite commonly been regarded as one single problem. The scientific approach, however, is to reduce a problem to simpler terms and deal with them separately. The obvious intention of all those who have interested themselves in this question has been to prevent the propagation of mentally unfit individuals, and the methods hitherto commonly advocated have been to forbid the marriage of the mentally unfit, or, if necessary, to segregate them. In the latter case segregation throughout the entire reproductive period is of course necessary.

It is superfluous to remark that the prevention of marriage does not prevent reproduction; moreover, it is precisely in the group where the danger is greatest, namely among those of the upper levels of mental deficiency, the so-called morons, that the difficulties in carrying out the regulation of marriage would be greatest, if not insurmountable. Casual observation does not necessarily reveal the actual mental condition of these persons, and it is common knowledge that they find no difficulty in getting married under the existing laws, and it is most unlikely that any workable method could be devised to pick out unfit persons of this class from the community at large.

Even those who at one time or another may have been in an institution, or who may have come into conflict with the law, who may even have been convicted of crimes and served terms of imprisonment, are again easily lost in the social body. Their records do not necessarily follow them and there would be little chance of preventing their marriage if they found a willing partner. An effective marriage prohibition not only would be unenforcible, but would offer no prospect of preventing reproduction of the mentally unfit.

There are also convinced segregationists who insist upon the permanent custody of feeble-minded individuals for the purpose of preventing reproduction. They particularly insist upon this sort of imprisonment for feeble-minded girls and women of child-bearing age, although the unfairness of this kind of sex-discrimination is obvious.

Institutionalization of a permanent kind is self-evidently the only rational means of handling certain classes of defectives and abnormals. These classes are easily defined. Roughly they are those who are simply incapable of maintaining themselves satisfactorily in an independent existence, and those with dangerous or criminal tendencies which make them a menace to the public. There can be no reasonable argument about the necessity of placing such persons in safe keeping; but to order permanent custody of any individual for the main purpose of preventing propagation seems to me about as rational as to put the whole body in a plaster cast for the treatment of a broken finger.

Here, again, it would be necessary to lock up myriads of higher grade defectives, in other words, precisely those who are best able of all the subnormal types to carry on an independent life. In addition to the inherent unreasonableness of such a procedure the financial burden involved would be prohibitive.

There seems to be no very good reason why the questions of marriage and parenthood should not be considered as two separate matters, as they really are. In dealing with defectives the desired end is obviously to dam the stream, and to accomplish this there is only one method, namely by the operation of sterilization to make it impossible for the defective individual to reproduce his kind.

Once this end is attained the question of marriage might be left to take care of itself. In certain situations marriage between higher grade defectives might even be encouraged. The stabilizing influence of marriage is traditional, even if it is not always a fact, and it is easy to obtain family histories of the mating of defectives showing that it had been possible to maintain some sort of home life affording mutual satisfaction until the offspring began to arrive; but with an increasing family the burden became too great, and parents and children became public charges.

But as soon as the question of sterilization is raised public opinion shows a number of spontaneous and always more or less stereotyped reactions, and various objections are promptly brought forward. Some of these objections are based on sentimental or so-called humanitarian grounds against interfering with certain intimate personal rights. These objections are often based on a misunderstanding of the nature of the operation and of the fact that the only physiological function interfered with is that of begetting or conceiving as the case may be, all other aspects of the conjugal relationship being left untouched ...

Probably the chief obstacles to dispassionate consideration and rational action are the inertia of public opinion on the one hand, if we may so put it, and fear of public opinion on the other. Sterilization is something which has not been commonly done. To some people it at once suggests sinister motives. It seems in some vague way to subtract somewhat from the personal integrity of the individual. Moreover it is intimately bound up with the whole question of sex; and the hypocritical squeamishness of the public with regard to such matters is notorious.

And yet the procedure of sterilization is merely a surgical operation like other surgical operations; in the male, a minor one. Properly done it is not known to have ill effects, and no physiological effects not compatible with the end to be attained; and in the attainment of that end it is effective.

There are also those who speak from the scientific point of view, who assert that knowledge of the operations of heredity is incomplete, and that therefore the operation is unwarranted because perchance not every defective will necessarily always have defective children, and because not all cases of mental defect are hereditary in origin.

These contentions may be freely admitted, and yet it is a matter of experience that in general like mates with like, and that more often like begets like than the contrary. Along with ninety-nine potential defectives whose propagation is prevented by sterilization, possibly one potential genius will be lost to the world. Is that sufficient reason to authorize the reproduction of ninety-nine defectives? The fact that feeble-mindedness is sometimes due to conditions associated with birth or early post-natal life is hardly relevant to the question. It should be obvious that intelligent preventive measures would be directed primarily toward checking the transmission of defective inheritance.

There are also medical arguments and moral arguments. It is argued that under the protection of sterilization morals would relax, promiscuity be encouraged and the danger of the spread of venereal diseases be increased. Thses statements are made, however, without any basis in fact, do not rest on observations, and are merely the guesses of the objectors ...

The question of preventing by sterilization the reproduction of the mentally unfit has been discussed in this province (Ontario) from time to time, but has always been frowned down before it could make much headway. There is only one province in the Dominion of Canada in which a fair hearing on this question has so far been possible, namely British Columbia. In that province a Royal Commisson in Mental Hygiene sat during the month of April of this year to consider present resources and future needs in the treatment and disposal of the mentally handicapped in the province. The subject of sterilization received a very full consideration and from all quarters interested the proposal met with approval. It will not be surprising if a sterilization law is passed by the forthcoming legislature in British Columbia, which will thus set the example to the other provinces of an enlightened approach to a serious problem. It should be mentioned that there are also active advocates of sterilization of the mentally unfit in the Province of Alberta and that efforts are on foot to secure enabling legislation ...

In view of an experience such as that of California, extending now over a period of fifteen years, it is to be hoped that interest in this very valuable means of checking racial deterioration may receive more enlightened attention on the part of legislators and the public; and that similar measures may become available in our own country where the need is certainly no less.

D) "Sterilization of the Feeble Minded," 1933
H. A. Bruce, M.D., Canadian Medical Association Journal

... Like begets like, and so they propagate their kind at a rate which requires that every 20 months a new asylum be built at a cost of $2,000,000 and with an annual maintenance charge of $300,000. At the present rate of increase in mental defectives, we shall within 25 years be spending $8,000,000 annually in this Province for their maintenance and we shall have twice as many institutions as we have now devoted to their care. In the mental hospital at Orillia there are several groups of half a dozen — each group *from the same family*. You can in imagination trace the course of such unchecked propagation. The seeds of deficiency are transmitted from generation to generation continuously affecting an increasing number of unfortunates and imposing upon the shoulders of the mentally and physically fit a heavier burden, which, by its economic weight, discourages them from raising large families. Devastating as a forest fire, and all the more terrible that it rages unseen and undetected in our midst, race degenration takes its insidious toll here as everywhere else.

I cannot but feel that this is allowed to continue rather through ignorance than indifference. I feel sure that public opinion, once aware of the magnitude of this menace, will not be satisfied with less than thoroughly effective measures to make it in the course of time only a shameful memory, like the dungeons and torture chambers of the past. Between 1871 and 1931 our population little more than doubled, but the number of insane in our institutions multiplied sixfold and the cost of caring for them increased tenfold. I repeat the distressing figures — twice as many people, six times as many insane, ten times as heavy a burden of cost. Perhaps reference to one family history is all that is necessary to impress upon you the seriousness of the economic aspect of the problem. An immigrant tainted with mental deficiency entered this country. He, his son and two daughters and seven illegitimate offspring in the third generation are at this time costing a municipality $3,460 annually for support and care. Records have been kept of one Canadian family which has provided inmates for mental hospitals at New Westminster, London, Hamilton and Orillia. Of the four known branches, three are for the most part mentally defective. Ten Mongolian idiots have appeared in this family and twelve of its adult members were maniacs. Many other family histories could be cited; but why spend more time in the melancholy past and present? Our concern should be action that will mitigate this scourge in the future.

The remedy, the recourse which can save us from the horrors incidental to a continued spread of deficiency, is sterilization for individuals contemplating marriage when there exists that taint of insanity, mental deficiency or epilepsy in the family history. Such individuals should be subjected to thorough psychiatric examinations and sterilization advised if the dangers for their progeny seem great. It is, above all, desirable that we look to the possibility of social legislation which will prevent the marriage of mental defectives unless first of all they be sterilized.

Not only would sterilization curtail increasing demand for hospital accommodation for defectives, but it would permit of a restricted class of these defectives, who must now be confined, being allowed at large in the community. Thus it would relieve the pressure on public institutions. It would relieve the pressure on our penal institutions too ... Sterilization promotes both the health of the patient and the welfare of society. It is in no sense a punitive measure. It is protection to the individual, to the state and to posterity. It has no ill effects upon the individual. On the contrary, it results in a better physical and mental condition ...

May the day speedily come when Ontario will awake, as Alberta and British Columbia have awakened, and as 27 States in the American Union have awakened, to the enormity of this peril and the necessity for prompt action. Alberta and British Columbia and 27 American States have adopted legislation permitting the sterilization of mental defectives ...

I have said on a previous occasion, and I shall always be of the opinion, that moral and religious sense necessarily revolt against the destruction of human life at any stage. But sterilization contemplates no destruction of life. On the contrary, sterilization means the ennoblement of life by damming up the foul streams of degeneracy and demoralization which are pouring pollution into the nation's life blood. No reasonable man would countenance a diphtheria carrier going about communicating disease to many of those with whom he comes in contact. Yet the disease the diphtheria carrier tranmits is curable and is incidental only to the immediate period of a few weeks during which it runs its course. But the infection transmitted by mental defectives is incurable. Its victims are the unborn generations. Its potency for misery and for suffering is great beyond all powers of description.

... [W]hat could be more suicidal, what more destructive to any race than to permit degeneracy to increase at its present rate? It is indeed suicidal for a race, a nation or a province to cast its germ cells, its precious jewels of heredity, into the oblivious, bottomless sea of mental, moral and physical degradation. Let us pause for a moment and in a spirit not of intrusion but of sorrow and pity gaze into a home — there are many such hopeless homes in this country — where feeble-minded parents are being left to care for their young. You will never forget this sight. Terrible is the plight of these parents and their children, but even more shocking is the apathy of public opinion which has permitted them to reproduce their suffering, yet menacing, kind. Ontario is well to the fore of social legislation. I am sure that with a full understanding of the problem of race degeneration public opinion will not hesitate to demand action designed to relieve existing conditions and to crush the menace which the future holds in store ...

10

"This is My Last Chance"

Depression and Despair

DOCUMENTS

A) Thomas M. Gibbs, Sarnia, Ontario, December 1, 1930

B) A Nanaimoite, February 22

C) R.D., Ottawa, March 4, 1932

D) Mrs Ernest Ferguson, Ferguson, N.B., March 21, 1933

E) Brief Presented by the Unemployed of Edmonton to the Hon. R.B. Bennett, December 30, 1933

F) To Canadian Government, December 1934

G) P.R. Mulligan, Debden, Saskatchewan, March 3, 1934

H) Miss Elizabeth McCrae, Hamilton, Ontario April 6, 1934

I) L.M. Himmer, Blaine Lake, Saskatchewan, September 9, 1935

J) Dorothy Franklin, Brechin, Ontario, February 28, 1935

K) Mrs. Otto Brelgen, Dempster, Saskatchewan, April 15, 1935

L) Bruce Bass, Whiteway, N.B., October 7, 1935

M) A Mother

N) Experiences of a Depression Hobo

I n the early 1930s unemployment and distress appeared to exist on an unimagined scale. As other nations of the world aspired to economic self-sufficiency, Canada's export-based economy went into severe decline. The fortunes of resource- and export-based economies such as Canada's tend to swing more wildly than those of industrialized nations with strong secondary and tertiary economic sectors. When the Great Depression hit at the end of the 1920s, Canada was therefore among those nations worst affected, quickly skidding down the slippery slope toward insolvency and social catastrophe. The economic situation was bad enough, with some 20% of the population on relief over the worst years between 1933 and 1936. Environmental calamities on the southern prairies, however, exacerbated the problem by creating a dust bowl hell that thousands barely survived, and many did not. Drought conditions on the southern prairies made bad conditions so unbearable that the International Red Cross declared parts of Saskatchewan a disaster area. It is hardly surprising that survivors across the land subsequently developed "depression mentalities" that had them save bits of string and tin foil for the rest of their lives. Social assistance, inevitably inadequate, barely existed for those desperate people, and it came at a high psychological cost. Collecting relief, after all, collided with proud and independent souls who believed in self-reliance, not charity.

The depression, on the other hand, also offered unprecedented increases in the standard of living for employed people who did not suffer pay cuts, or for people enjoying independent means. Thus Canadians at the upper end of the socio-economic strata generally fared far better than the rest. The depression was, after all, a deflationary period where dollars, if one had them, bought more and more each day. Federal civil servants, for example, experienced a 25% increase in their standard of living over this period. Services, goods, food, entertainment — almost all became cheaper as the depression ground on, if you had cash at hand. The depression was anything but depressing for the minority with money and no social conscience.

The depression hit the aged, sick, marginalized, and young hardest — those least able to fend for themselves. Historians know how many Canadians sought relief, but statistics don't tell the whole story. They do not, for example, include those who eked out existences perched precariously just above the poverty line, and therefore not officially "poor," nor do compilations of facts include those thousands whose pride prevented them from seeking charity. Numbers cannot tell the human story. Statistics cannot show the humiliation of a father standing in front of a faceless bureaucrat, publicly avowing his failure to provide for his family in order to receive relief. Cold numbers do not show inspectors subsequently visiting his home looking for luxuries, such as telephones and drivers' licenses, which made the family ineligible. Numbers cannot show the paranoid requests from governments for people to inform on "relief cheats." Hard data cannot express the anguish a mother felt as she took her meagre food vouchers to the grocery store in her small community and traded them for equivalent goods.

Suspicious and cash-strapped governments in this era of liberal individualism assumed that relief recipients were actually masters of their own misfortune. They therefore made the relief process as humiliating and awkward as possible, and preferred vouchers in kind (redeemable for food, shelter, clothing) rather than cash, which untrustworthy poor people would presumably squander. Local governments, which often administered public relief, also preferred applicants to work for their assistance, as much on principle as anything, and created make-work schemes that contributed little more than further humiliation.

And for those without homes? Young men over 18 were ineligible for family relief. Many thus had to leave home and seek their fortunes elsewhere. But there weren't any jobs for unskilled young men, and relief was linked to long-term residency. So thousands of them wandered from town to town, city to city, riding boxcars with those in similar straits, increasingly marginalized by a nation that promised bright futures but delivered despair. No wonder they began to organize, to join organizations like the Communist Party of Canada, and to turn their backs on the mainstream society that had apparently betrayed their dreams. The Federal government feared this segment of society and enacted plans to contain them. Instead it further marginalized them by establishing work camps in remote areas where they worked for 20 cents per day at jobs with little social value, under the watchful gaze of the Department of National Defense, and without the right to vote.

Ironically, Canadians elected the nation's first millionaire prime minister in 1930. R.B. Bennett's annual income dropped considerably but never dipped below $150,000 per year during the depression, at a time when families could comfortably survive on $25 per week. He promised to end unemployment through increased tariffs, but his policies did more harm than good, especially in the agricultural sector. His administration, however, did provide extraordinary funds for destitute provincial coffers, and in fairness to Bennett, no world leader knew how to tackle a depression of this unprecedented depth and breadth.

Bennett hated the concept of "relief," fearing that it promoted "idleness" in people who should put their shoulder to the wheel and get to work. Yet the economy had all but ground to a halt, and even he had to admit that jobs were scarce. But Bennett was not heartless; he and his secretaries responded to virtually every letter they received. He also regularly dipped into his own funds after reading particularly heart-wrenching pleas for help. News of his philanthropic side spread quickly, and the volume of mail increased enormously. Bennett eventually established a special fund for his gifts, usually five dollars at a time. The number of gifts peaked around election time in 1935.

The historians who originally published these letters changed the senders' names and addresses in the interest of privacy. They also tended to choose the most poignant correspondence for publication and attempted to balance the regional, ethnic, and occupational balance reflected in the entire Bennett letter collection. Their analysis found that Bennett and his staff had a slight preference for sending cash to youth, westerners, and Anglophones.

A) Thomas M. Gibbs, Sarnia, Ontario, December 1, 1930

Hon. Mr. Bennet Ottawa Ont.
Dear Sir:

I am taking this priviledge in my own hands of writing you which a person of my class should be ashamed to take such athoraty. But I am down and out and do not know what to do. We have six children and I don't beleive it right to see them suffer for the want of food I tried everywhere to get things for them to eat this is Saturday and I must say we have to go all day Sunday with but one small meal that is dry bread and apple sauce which we have day after day the apples will soon run out then we will be out of luck. I asked for asistance from the township they never came near me. I was in the second Canadian infantry Battalion as a private. I wrote to London see if I could get releif there. Enclosed you will find a coppy which they sent me. I will not take up too much of your time just now. But in my case I am a good worker but the work is not to be had. My name has been in the employment office since June but there is no jobs comming in so I have to do something might soon I hate to go out and steal but the family can't starve to death. I am a butcher by trade and know cattle and understand them thourghly. Also farmed for twelve years. Am all willing to go anywhere to work if there is anything at all you can possible do for me this will be greatly appreciated if there is any dought these statements call Sarnia 1154 that will be Mr. A.E.Palmer Employment Bureau. Kindly over look the privledge Im taking I think this is my last chance to get help. If this fails I do not know what we will do.

Thanking you very kindly in advance.
Yours very Truly,
Thomas M. Gibbs

B) A Nanaimoite, February 22

Mr Bennett
Dear Sir

before we are much older there is going to be trouble in Nanaimo & Cumberland owing to the foreigners having jobs while the men & boys who are borne British subjects & who rightfully belong to these jobs have to go without jobs therefore they have to go without sufficient food & clothing, in Cumberland you have Japanese & Chinese working in & about the mines also other foreigners from other countrys who can neither read write or speak english & this is breaking the Coal Mines Rules and Regulation Act & they are a danger to both human life & property yet they hold the jobs which rightfully belong to us British although it is against the rules for these people to have jobs in the mines.

The same applied to Nanaimo only the Chinese are working on the surface here & not below but there are a very large number of foreigners working in the mines at Nanaimo who can neither read write nor speak English & apart from that besides having our jobs & getting the wages which is ours by right the money is not only going out of Nanaimo but it is going out of the country & that is not good for this country. I wish you could come yourself to the mines at Nanaimo & watch the ammount of foreigners who are employed at these mines & then look at the number of British men & boys who go to these same mines every day begging for a job only to be turned away & they have no money to buy bread & clothing while the foreigner has both the foreigners are also starting allkinds of stores & boarding houses & trying to buy beer parlours while the Britisher goes broke as there are not enough British men & boys in employment & the foreigner buys all from his own kind. It looks to me as though the chief Superintendent of these mines here is trying to cause a lot of trouble on this Island by employing as many foreigners as possible at the expense of the people who belong to this country if this is so he is going to see all the trouble & more than he wants before long as human nature can't stand for it much longer there is a lot of talk here (& men say they are prepared to prove it) that Robert Fox who is superintendent of these mines is accepting bribes from these foreigners for jobs. I hope government will take a hand in this before it is too late as there is so much money going out of this town & out of the country & our men & boys are asked to go to goverment camps & give up their homes to these foreigners the foreigner can come here and make a home while the men and boys who have a right to a home & a job have to get out to make room for the foreigner can you wonder that the Britisher is getting riled & again very many of these foreigners fought against our men & boys in the big war now they are given our jobs our bread & our homes if government does not take a hand in this at once I fear an uprising of all English speaking people on this Island & it may end in harm to the foreigner & also to property

Yours. A. Nanaimoite

C) R.D., Ottawa, March 4, 1932

Dear Sir,

I am just writing a few lines to you to see what can be done for us young men of Canada. We are the growing generation of Canada, but with no hopes of a future. Please tell me why is it a single man always gets a refusal when he looks for a job. A married man gets work, & if he does not get work, he gets relief. Yesterday I got a glimpse of a lot of the unemployed. It just made me feel downhearted to think there is no work for them, or in the future, & also no work for myself. Last year I was out of work three months. I received work with a local farm. I was told in the fall I could have the job for the winter; I was then a stable man. Now I am slacked off on account of no snow this winter. Now I am wandering the streets like a beggar, with no future ahead. There are lots of single men in Ottawa, who would rather walk the streets, & starve, than work on a farm. That is a true statement. Myself I work wherever I can get work, & get a good name wherever I go. There are plenty of young men like myself, who are in the same plight. I say again whats to be done for us single men? do we have to starve? or do we have to go round with our faces full of shame, to beg at the doors of the well to do citizen. I suppose you will say the married men come first; I certainly agree with you there. But have you a word or two to cheer us single men up a bit? The married man got word he was going to get relief. That took the weight of worry off his mind quite a bit. Did the single man here anything, how he was going to pull through? Did you ever feel the pangs of hunger? My idea is we shall all starve. I suppose you will say I cant help it, or I cant make things better. You have the power to make things better or worse. When you entered as Premier you promised a lot of things, you was going to do for the country I am waiting patiently to see the results. Will look for my answer in the paper.

Yours Truly R D Ottawa

D) Mrs. Ernest Ferguson, Ferguson, N.B., March 21, 1933

Hon. R. B. Bennett

Ottawa, Can.

Dear Sir,

The respectable people of this country are *fed up* on feeding the bums for that is all they can be called now. This "free" relief (free to the bums) has done more harm than we are altogether aware of. The cry of those who get it is "Bennett says he wont let anyone starve" They don't consider that the *people* (many poorer than themselves but with more spunk) have to foot the bill. The regulations (which are only a poor guide after all) were too loose from the start and *could be* and *were* easily side stepped many times.

Getting relief has become such a habit that the majority think only of how to get it regularly instead of trying to do without once in a while. Nearly all of them have dogs too which are fed by the country and are of no practical use. One family near me has three and another has two and others one and I know it is the same everywhere. I also know that food enough to keep one dog will keep at least four hens and keep them laying. The family that has the three dogs ate at least 550 pounds of meat from the second week in November until the first part of March. There are the parents, twins 10 years old and four children from one year to eight. Who but the dogs got a good part of that? Also dogs everywhere are chasing and catching deer but if a man tries to get one for the family he is either fined or jailed if found out. Or if he tries to get a few fish (he is mighty lucky if he succeeds above Newcastle on the Miramichi now) the wardens are right after him and he finds himself minus a net at the least.

Now the taxes are going to be forcibly collected to pay for the good-for-nothings for whom the debt was made. Those people should be made work and there wouldn't need to be much forcing for taxes. The taxpayers don't consider that they should keep people as well and sometimes better off than they are and their wives agree with them. We see plainly now that those being kept will not help themselves so long as they are fed for nothing.

Notice should be given at once to enable them to get crops in and so on and relief stopped altogether. The cost of that would pay for a good deal of work. Also please remember there are other people in the country who need your thought as well as those on relief as it is now though they are struggling along somehow. I think it only fair to state that if it continues or is considered for the future there will be a goodly number of Conservatives vote the other way for as I stated in the beginning we are sick and tired of being forced to keep the majority that are following the relief path. It hasn't been fair all through as any thoughtful man must know. I am not stating this idly because I have talked with many others many times and that is the general feeling. I think I can safely say too that the Liberals getting relief don't thank the Conservatives enough to give them a vote either because they nearly all say the country owes them a living and think no thanks are due.

I could write more but will let this suffice for this time but Please consider this question of relief as a very important one because a deal of trouble may brew from it.

Yours respectfully,

Mrs. Ernest Ferguson

E)   Brief Presented by the Unemployed of Edmonton to the Hon. R.B. Bennett, December 30, 1933

Mr. R.B.Bennett

Prime Minister of Canada

For three long, weary years you, Mr Bennett and your Conservative Party have held undisputed and unmolested sway in Canada. You and your coleagues were elected primarily because you gave the people two great promises, (1) you would end unemployment, (2) you would blast your way to foreign markets. As to the first of these promises, you Mr. Bennett as the chief Economic Doctor, have failed, miserable failed, not only to cure the dangerous disease, but even to give it an unbiased diagnosis; and the only blasting that has been apparent has been the inhuman wrecking of millions of once happy homes. You have repeatedly reminded us of the sacredness of our British Institutions. Mr. Bennett, is not the home an institution? Then why do you callously stand by while it is being wantonly destroyed by the Molloch of Big business? We have this to say Mr. Bennett. Even a yellow dog will resist, to the death, the ruthless destruction of his most priceless possession.

Surely, in three years of full political power you could have found, if you had tried, a better method of dealing with unemployment than the Direct Relief System. In view of the fact that you have not we hereby give you the only solution which is applicable in society as at present constituted. Non-contributary Unemployment Insurance. It must be non-contributary, otherwise the million and a half already unemployed will receive no benefit.

Pending the enactment of this Bill, Relief allowances must be raised. Seeing that we are not allowed to earn in wages sufficient to maintain us and our families, we demand adequate relief. The perpetual cry of Mayor Knott, and Premier Brownlee is "We can do nothing. We have no money". Without discussing the truthfulness of these statements, Mr. Bennett, we know that the contribution from the Federal Treasury must be doubled if it is designed to even remotely approach the need ... We have not words in our vocabulary sufficiently strong to properly condemn your method of dealing with unemployed single men. Those slave camps are a blot on the record of any civilized country. That young men, the very flower of the race, those who must make the next generation are forced, by economic necessity, to enter those isolated prisons, where there is neither proper physical food, nor mental stimulation, cries to Heaven for correction. What are you trying to do to our young men? Make a generation of physical wrecks and mental dolts? Or perhaps they will be used for cannon fodder? The militarization of those camps strongly points to this latter hypothesis as being the correct one ... placing the single men in camps under the control of the Department of National Defence is too apparent to be overlooked. We shall resist to the bitter end the slaughtering of those boys and young men in an Imperialist war. We demand that they be taken out of those camps and be given an opportunity to earn a civilized living, at a civilized wage, and live a normal life by taking a wife and raising a family. We protest against the increased appropriations for the National Defence. These monies should never be spent for these purposes, but instead, used to supplement the contribution to relief. The battleships and bombing planes, and big guns will never be used if it is left to the people to declare war. In this connection why has Japan been allowed to buy tremendous quantities of junk iron from Canada? Is it possible we shall again see and feel this iron in the form of bullets? If such a thing should come to pass, who is the butcher, the man behind the gun or the man who supplied him with the ammunition. We want it clearly understood that we consider the workers of Japan, Germany, France, Russia or any other country as nothing more nor less than brother workers and we strongly protest against the despicable and abominable part Canada is playing in hastening us toward another great Imperialist conflagration, the horrors of which were only too well forcast by the last World War.

Mr. Bennett, there was never a more damnable insult heaped upon a working class of any country than when armoured tanks and other highly perfected instruments of slaughter were sent into Stratford, Ontario. Are these the trying circumstances which will test the very best of our National fibre, which you mentioned upon your return from England? Why is it, that if our government is a Democratic institution, representing the whole people the armed forces of the nation is used to coerce the working class, who make up 95% of the population, and force them to submit to wage cuts and a general worsening of their living conditions? On the face of it, it appears that Big business, whose interest it is to force the working class into pauperism, is being protected and not we; that the minority is dictatorial machine, which our Democratic government allows to use the military power of the nation against the majority. Not only in Stratford does this phenomena manifest itself, but throughout the country, whenever the workers use the only economic weapon they have, the strike, the R.C.M.P. are rushed to the spot and club the workers into submission. We submit Mr. Bennett that we are a peaceful people. If you will send work at a living wage to strikers instead of tanks and machine guns your economic troubles will be considerably lessened. We protest against this Fascist terrorism, and demand the rights of free speech and free assemble. We protest against the policy of deporting foreign born workers simply because they can find no buyer for their labor power. The solidarity of the British Commonwealth of Nations is widely publicized, yet, we find workers born in the British Isles are subject to deportation. When a young and great country like Canada with only Ten million population finds itself in the position where it must deport labor power there must be something wrong with its economic system. Those workers, came to Canada in good faith, after being led to believe that this country was the land of their dreams. They did not come in order to get on Canada's Unemployed list. After promising them a Heaven. and then give them Hell is not a safe policy. The slightly lesser evil of the relief lists is, we feel, the worst that these people should be subject.

To sum up, Mr. Bennett, we are absolutely fed up with being on relief. The terrible waste that is implied in a million and a half idle man power is a crime against the human race. There is so much work to do, and here there are, unemployed. We don't know how the natural resources come to be where they are, but we do know, that neither you nor Big business created them. The material is here, land, lumber, iron, steel, etc. and so are we. If you can't supply the tokens of exchange that will bring us together, you had better resign and hand the country over to the workers. We may be ignorant uncouth men, belong to the lowest strata of a low society, but, and we don't boast, we will have enough sense to eat when there is food to eat, and work when there is work to be done and tools to work with.

F) To Canadian Government, December 1934

Canadian Govt. at Ottawa, Canada

Well Mr. R.B. Bennet, arnt you a *man* or are you? to be the cause of all this starvation and privation. You call us derelicts, then if we are derelicts *what else are you* but one too, only *a darn sight worse*. You said if you was elected, you would give us all work and wages, well you have been in the Prime Ministers shoes, now, for 4 years and we are *still looking for work and wages*. You took all our jobs away from us. We can't earn any money. You say a releif camp is good enough for us, then *its too good* for *you* Mr Bennet, you are on releif your own self. You put away your big govt salary, then ask the gov't. to pay for your big *feasts*, while *we* poor fellows starve. While *you* jazz around the hotel girls. You think people don't know any thing well, even if we are *"derelicts" "as you called us"* and which we consider you as the leader of the derelicts Band you have fooled us a lot, in the last four years. We have lived on your hot air, so you may know you had to expell a *lot*. But you can't fool *all* of us, *all* the time.

… Well now Mr. Bennet, I hope this sinks clear down to your toes, and gives you swelled feet, instead of a swelled head. You have had a swelled head ever since you had the "Eddy" Match Co. signed to you by Mrs. Eddy, don't think people don't know anything.

P.S. this will take my last 3 cents, but we hope it goes to the bottom of *you*, and that you will hand us out *both work* and *living wages*. You have caused *lots* of people to kill their families and themselves rather than to slowly starve to death, or freeze to death. Try it you prime minister, just try it.

Now you are trying to get war going to make yourself richer. Well R.B. Bennet, I hope you get your share of the bullets.

We are going to give you a chance, (which you don't deserve) either you will stop this war, now, and give us fellows work and living wages enough to stop such starving, and freezing, because we *can't* buy any clothes, the doukabours are jailed because they wont wear any clothing while *we* are jailed trying to get clothing to wear. You say we live too extravagance, then you shall be able to hand out $5.00 to anyone and everyone, then we wont live so extravagant. You have heaps of money laid away. Well, it wont do you a bit of good if we have another war.

We are giving you this chance. We say again you do not deserve it at all. If we dont get work or wages, and "living wages" to, we are going to tell the Canadian government they have a "murderer", in the house at Ottawa. You said a rich uncle left you your wealth, bah. We know better. We are not trying to scare you, but we are tired, of relief camps and going hungry and cold. no homes, or any thing else.

G) P.R. Mulligan, Debden, Saskatchewan, March 3, 1934

Hon. Mr. R. B. Bennet
Ottawa, Canada
Dear Sir —

I am writing to see if you could not give me a little help. I hear you are going to destroy some thousands of tons of wheat to get rid of it; while my family & stock are starving to death. There is lots of wheat and other things here but I have no money to buy them with. I have been farming in Central Sask. since 1909 until a yr ago when I was forced off my farm. So last yr I could not get a place for to farm so could only get what I could by working out on farms. Which was not near enough to keep my family in food. In the fall I moved to the North hoping to be able to keep my stock alive and to be able to get a homestead. I had applied to have my stock sent to Spiritwood but by some mistake somewhere I was sent to Debden instead so then I had neither buildings or feed in reach and dead broke in bitter cold weather. So could not buy feed or take a homestead either. As the relief officer for this part was in town here at the time I asked him for relief & for feed. I could not get any feed whatever out of him until my four horses and seven head of cattle (my two best cows included) 16 pigs (some of them weighed over 100 lbs) and most of my poultry had actually starved to death. All that was necessary was an order to get some feed from the relief officer, but though I asked him several times & did not get any until that many were dead. Since then I have had orders amounting to 1500 (fifteen hundred) oat sheaves but nothing to feed a pig or chicken. If I had been given sufficient feed in the first place my stock would be alive and most of those hogs would now be ready for market. We would then have some meat for our table and the rest would have repaid the relief I needed and most likely would have left something to take me off the relief list for a time at least. Now we cannot farm the land I had rented because I haven't a horse left to farm with. We kept off relief as long as we had a cent to buy food or a rag of clothes that would hang together. To date we have had $45.35 for food to feed ten of us from Dec 1st on until now, and I did relief bridge work to about that amount and was quite willing to do as much more as I would get the chance to do. But when I asked for a greater food allowance I was told that many were doing with much less as well as one insult upon another added thereto by the local relief officer. Yet I know several families right around here getting more relief according to the size of family and do not need relief at all but still they get it. I have 8 children ranging from 4 1/2 yrs to 14 1/2 yrs yet all we have had in the house for over a week has been dry bread and black tea and believe me Mr. Bennet it isn't very nice to listen hour after hr to young children pleading for a little butter or why can't we have some potatoes or meat or eggs. But how can I get it on what I have been getting when it takes most of it for flour alone. Because we were not sent where we asked to be sent to we have to live ten of us in cold one roomed shack instead of having a comfortable house to live in. We haven't a mattress or even a tick just simply have to sleep on a bit of straw and nearly every night we have to almost freeze because we haven't bed clothes. I did not ask relief to supply these but I did ask for pants, overalls and footwear for the children about two months ago, but to date we have had $15.95 of clothing (some of this had to be returned as it did not fit) and some of the children are at this time running barefooted & not one of them has either a pr. of pants or overalls to cover their nakedness. Neither can they go to school because they have no clothes and also because the local school board demand a tuition fee of $30 because we are not taxpayers as yet in this school and that after paying school taxes in this province for nearly 25 years. One result now is that the whole family have some kind of rash and running sores & I cannot take them to a Dr. as I have not the price to pay the Dr. or to buy the things that he would order. Also my wife has become badly ruptured and I can not have anything done about it for the same reason. I was born with one leg shorter than the other and am physically not a strong man but I have always done all I've been able to do and a lot more than many more able than I am and I am not in the habit of wasting any time or money on drinking, gambling or anything of the sort yet we have to sit here and see not only our stock starve but see my wife & children starve as well,

and do the same myself. So for God's sake give us an order to get a few bus. of wheat to help us live and to raise a few chickens and pigs to eat at least and if we ever make enough to do it with I'll return it with interest too.
Yours in need
P.R. Mulligan

H) Miss Elizabeth McCrae, Hamilton, Ontario, April 6, 1934

To His Excellency The Rt Hon. R B Bennett, Parliament Buildings, Ottawa Ontario.
Att: Mr.Bennett
Dear Sir:

I am writing you as a last resource to see if I cannot, through your aid, obtain a position and at last, after a period of more than two years, support myself and enjoy again a little independence.

The fact is: this day I am faced with starvation and I see no possible means of counteracting or even averting it temporarily!

If you require references of character or ability I would suggest that you write to T.M. Sanderson of Essex, Ontario. I worked as Stenographer and Bookkeeper with him for over three years in the office of the Sanderson-Marwick Co., Ltd., in Essex. I feel certain that you have made his acquaintance for he was President of the Conservative Association at the time of the Banquet held in your worshipful honour a few years ago.

I have received a high-school and Business-college education and I have had experience as a Librarian. My business career has been limited to Insurance, Hosiery, and Public Stenography, each time in the capacity of Bookkeeper and Stenographer — briefly, General Office work.

My father is a farmer at Pilot Mound, Manitoba and during the past years his income has been nil, so I cannot get any assistance from him. In fact, until I joined the list of unemployed I had been lending the folks at home my aid. To save my Mother from worry I have continually assured her that I am working and till the end I will save her from distress by sticking to this story.

When the Sanderson-Marwick Co., Ltd, went out of business I had saved a little money and there being no work there for me I came to Hamilton. Since then I have applied for every position that I heard about but there were always so many girls who applied that it was impossible to get work.

So time went on and my clothing became very shabby. I was afraid to spend the little I had to replenish my wardrobe. Always the fear was before me that I would fail to get the position and then I would be without food and a roof over my head in a short time. Many prospective employers just glanced at my attire and shook their heads and more times than I care to mention I was turned away without a trial. I began to cut down on my food and I obtained a poor, but respectable, room at $1. per week.

First I ate three very light meals a day; then two and then one. During the past two weeks I have eaten only toast and drunk a cup of tea every other day. In the past fortnight I have lost 20 pounds and the result of this deprivation is that I am so very nervous that could never stand a test along with one, two and three hundred girls. Through this very nervousness I was ruled out of a class yesterday. Today I went to an office for an examination and the examiner looked me over and said; "I am afraid Miss, you are so awfully shabby I could never have you in my office."

I was so worried and disappointed and frightened that I replied somewhat angrily: "Do you think clothes can be picked up in the streets?"

"Well," he replied with aggravating insolence, "lots of girls find them there these days."

Mr. Bennett, that almost broke my heart. Above everything else I have been very particular about my friends and since moving here I have never gone out in the evening. I know no one here personally and the loneliness is hard to bear, but oh, sir, the thought of starvation is driving me mad! I have endeavoured to be good and to do what is right and I am confident I have succeeded in that score but I can name more than ten girls here in Hamilton who I am sure are not doing right and yet they have nice clothes and positions. That is what seems so unfair. They never think of God nor do they pray and yet they seem so happy and have so many things I would like, while I, who pray every night and morning have nothing!

Day after day I pass a delicatessen and the food in the window looks oh, so good! So tempting and I'm so hungry!

Yes I am very hungry and the stamp which carries this letter to you will represent the last three cents I have in the world, yet before I will stoop to dishonour my family, my character or my God I will drown myself in the Lake. However, I do not hint that I have the slightest intention of doing this for I am confident that you will either be able to help me find employment or God will come to my aid.

But in the meantime my clothing is getting shabbier and I am faced with the prospect of wearing the same heavy winter dress, that has covered me all winter, during the coming summer.

Oh please sir, can you do something for me? Can you get me a job anywhere in the Dominion of Canada. I have not had to go on relief during this depression but I cannot get relief even here. Moreover it is a job I want and as long as I get enough to live I shall be happy again.

I have tried to get work at anything and everything from housework up but I have been unsuccessful and now I am going to starve and in debt to my landlady. I wouldn't mind if I could just lay down and die but to starve, oh its terrible to think about.

Mr. Bennett, even if you can do nothing for me I want to thank you for your kindness in reading this letter and if I were jobless and semi-hungry for a life-time I would still be a Conservative to the last, and fight for that Government.

Thanking you again for your very kind attention, I am,
Your humble servant,
(Miss) Elizabeth McCrae

l)   L.M. Himmer, Blaine Lake, Saskatchewan, September 9, 1935

Hon. R.B. Bennett
Ottawa, Ont.
Dear Sir:

For some time I have been thinking what this new country of ours was coming to. I had the pleasure of talking with Mr. F. R. MacMillan M.P. of Saskatoon and Senator Hornor of Blaine Lake. They both insisted that I write you a line.

I wish to give my opinion of relief. First it is a shame for a strong young man to ask for relief in this country. To my mind the relief has helped out the C.C.F. and Social Credit. When you give an inch they take a foot. There are men, who have been on relief, now sitting on the street asking $2.50 and 3.00 per day. Many of them would not be worth a $1.00 per day to stook 60 ct wheat.

To my mind the poet is right nine times out of ten. The best thing that can happen to a young man is toss him overboard and compel him to sink or swim, in all my acquaintance I have never known one to drown who was worth saving.

When I hear young men, with their head full of book knowledge, complaining about no money no work. They say they'll try for relief and they get it, then they spend two or three months around a lake shore rolling in the sand and splashing in the water. When winter comes they have no preparations of any kind. They say they'll try for relief and they get it.

I say again a man must have a purpose in life if he hasn't he will never amount to much. He will eat that which he has not earned, he will clog the wheels of industry and stand in the way of progress. Thoughts of this kind should be empressed on the pupils by the teachers, and ministers, instead of the C.C.F. doctrine, and athletic sports. The people have gone silly over nonsense and it is our leaders that are teaching the younger generations to be useless.

I asked a young man to help me thresh, he said he would not pitch sheaves for less than $5.00 per day, he can get relief, no doubt. I have four young men four harvest and threshing, they blow their wages every Saturday night, some of them will be on relief this winter, if not all.

It takes hardship to make real men and women so cut out relief …

Relief is like a sixteen year old boy getting money from dad, when the old man gets wise and tightens up the boy gets mad and cuts a shine just as the relief strikers did.

There are some people in this country who are in hard circumstances, but I can safely say there is no one having the hardships that we pioneers had 28 and 30 years ago

Yours turely

L. M. Himmer

J)   Dorothy Franklin, Brechin, Ontario, February 28, 1935

I hope you will pardon me for writing to you but I feel that, as the head of our country you should be made acquainted with some of the things we of the poorer class are up against. Oh, I know you have all kinds of this stuff thrown at you but today I just have to unload. You may recall that I wrote to you about three years ago and you very kindly interceded for a farm loan for us at Kent, but to no effect. We were refused the loan and the mortgage was foreclosed and we lost everything. We made a sale to pay the taxes and I reserved about thirty P. R. Hens that were laying and the only bit of money we had coming in. Well, the sale day was terribly stormy and along with other things on that day, there was a very poor turnout. The sale amounted to $220 for what we had paid $770. and the $220. was $24. less than the taxes. So my hens were sold at 80¢ each, which paid up the taxes and left us with nothing. When you wrote to me you said you hoped that year would be our best. Well, perhaps it was, It left us nothing but our experience and that has been dearly bought. We lost $3500. a mere nothing to some perhaps but our life's work. We moved to the front here hoping things might be better but since Dec. 10th, my man has been able to bring in $3.00. He is out every day looking for work and always the same results. Yesterday he came home and told me there is some road work starting next week but in order to get on, the men must sign up for relief. I wonder why men who are self-respecting have to be subjected to such humiliation and embarrassment when they are only too willing to work if possible. It isn't only the men who suffer but the families of these men. We have a pair of twin boys, sixteen years old. Both at school yet but those boys have gone all winter without underwear and no overcoats and do not even own a suit of clothes. They are wearing the same pants and sweaters week day and Sunday. I have to mend and wash their pullovers so they are presentable for Sunday School but they will not go to church because they are so shabby. We were taught to believe God put us women here for the noble cause of Motherhood. I wonder how many would have suffered what we have, had we known our children were not even going to have the necessities of life. This week we have bought just 1 lb of butter & 3 loaves of bread. I'm ashamed to ask the grocer for any more credit. We have been eating stew. First potatoes & carrots and then carrots and potatoes. I'm so discouraged. I wonder which requires the greater courage, to carry on knowing how much we are all needing and cannot have or to end it all as that poor woman did this week in Oakville by sticking her head in a pail of water and drowning. My last coat that I bought was eight years ago for the fabulous sum of $10.75 and my sunday dress is an old one of a cousin's made over. I wouldn't feel so badly if we only had our home but having no prospect of ever having anything is killing me. The people around this gritty hole are saying "Wait until the new government gets in". Its all bosh. No party alone can change things much. My idea is that all must work together to accomplish much good. In trouble such as the country is laboring under now, the partyism should be forgotten for the good of all mankind. Yes, I'm tory to my toes but just the same I have no hard feelings toward those who think differently from me. Some day things will turn out all right and I am very thankful that through it all I can truthfully say I can still maintain my faith and trust in God above.

Forgive me if I have taken too much of your time.
Yours respectfully,
Dorothy Franklin

K) Mrs. Otto Brelgen, Dempster, Saskatchewan, April 15, 1935

R.B. Bennett Esq
Ottawa, Ont
Dear Friend,

I just can not stand for our treatment any longer without getting it off our chest. We came out here in Aug 1932 from Saskatoon on the Government Relief Plan. So you will understand that we have practically nothing as we had very little to start on, and we have worked very hard but have had terrible bad luck. We have lost 3 horses since coming out here so now are stranded with one horse which is on last legs. So how is it possible to go ahead and farm without help from somewhere. Last spring we had a neighbor break some for us. We have 15 acres now broke here, and my husband was working nearly all summer to pay the neighbor back so that certainly isn't going to put us somewhere we are going back fast. Still we are working like slaves, never have enough to eat and very little to wear. We have 5 children and our 2 selves. My baby was born up here without help of doctor or help in the house. Only what the neighbors felt like helping out. Now she is 16 month old and doesn't walk mostly lack of proper food. The other children all boys have been sick this winter, but how would it be possible to be healthy in such a condition. Last August our relief was cut down to $8.25 a month, but since Jan have recieved $11.65 so you see it is impossible to give the children proper foods. We had no garden at all everything froze to the ground as soon as it was started growing. We have about 20 chicken 1 cow. no meat or potatoes only what we buy many a meal around here is dry bread and milk when our cow is milking otherwise its water, butter is an extra luxury which we cannot afford. None of us have proper footwear now its not fit to be outside unless clothed properly. Its is a sin and a shame to be in such circumstance as that. It sure does grieve one when there nothing to eat or wear. We loan settler from the city's do not seem to be treated as well as those that moved in from the dried-out areas as they are fully equiped with live stock and also machinery, where we have nothing. I sure would like to know why that is. You maybe able to understand how it would be possible to feed our family on less 2 1/2 cents each

person each meal it is quite impossible as I have tried every way of getting by. But cannot make it go. My family don't live anymore we only exist. I think if the situation was more clearly put to the right parties they could help us more some less, as there are people who have cattle, garden, and could get by without gov. help still they receive assitance which does only makes it worse for those who really need it. I am looking forward that you may be able to help us in some way. We most certainly would like to be on the upward road. Just think how many families in these north woods are starving, trying to make things go. Such hard work without food to supply body energy. So first the body fails then the mind. I know Im very near a nerbous wreck. If we were allowed supose the doctor would tell me I had a nervous breakdown as it is I have to keep trudging along trying to make the best, but don't think I can stand the strain much longer. We never get out amongst any kind of entertainment as relief people are not allowed any recreation of any kind. We would be so thankful to you if you could help us in some way. Today is only the 15th of the month and our flour is all gone already and the stores will not give any credit out. So we'll all be quite hungry until the first of the month. Please give this your personal consideration and send me an answer of what could be done we are practally at the end of our rope now. Thanking you again for your attention
Your Faithfull Servant
Mrs. Otto Brelgen

L)   Bruce Bass, Whiteway, N.B., October 7, 1935

Right Hon. R B Bennett,
Dear Sir: —
    I am writing to ask you if you could or would help me. As I have a big family and all are going to school at present, but I will soon have to keep them home as they have no clothes and very little to eat. I have been working nearly all summer but my pay was so small that I barley got enough to eat for them. There are six children, ages from 15 to 7, four of which are boys, one boy 13, and in Grade VIII. I would like for him to be in school till he get through. But with out help of some kind, I can't. I try every way to get work. There is no work and wages so small. All I can do is to get something to eat for my wife and children, and so many school books to buy, besides three of our children have one book between them. No way of

getting any more The times have been so hard around here that everything one had is all worn out. This very night we havn't a baking of flour in our house. I have order some whether we will get it I can't tell. No work nor no money I think it is a terrible thing for a man that is able and willing to work he has to see his little children go to school hungry and half enough cloth on them to keep them warm. I always support the Conservative Government, and intend to do the same next Monday if nothing happen.

I don't mind my self so bad, the children I am thinking most of now. I don't know How I am going to get cloth for them if your help me I would be very thankful to you.
I remain Your Truly,
Bruce Bass

M) A Mother

Hon. R.B. Bennett
Ottawa
Sir:

This is from a mother who's son is wandering somewhere in Ont. trying vainly to get work. What are you going to do for these thousands of young men? There is lots of work to be done if you would only start them at it. You have never had to sleep out in the snow and rain or go days without food. Just stop and think of these hungry boys when you are at your next banquet.

You have no children, so you cannot realize how parents feel with their sons wandering in this useless search for work.

You have only a short time now to try to help these men or it will be up to the other party to do it.
A Mother

N) Experiences of a Depression Hobo

I arrived in Toronto a week ago but have not got work yet. The trip down took 5 1/2 days and I did not visit any jails. My total expenses were 50 cents but I ate a [sic] slept well.

On the Saturday night of April 15 my friend and I took the last street car out to Sutherland having previously found out that a freight train was leaving for Winnipeg during the early hours of Sunday morning. We slunk around the yards till we came upon a brakeman and asked when the freight for the East was pulling out. Before he could reply a torch light beamed in our faces and the "bull" asked "Where are you guys going?" "East" — "Winnipeg." "Well that freight won't pull out till seven to-morrow morning." We thanked the policeman for this information and retired to the shadow of a nearby Pool Elevator, lighted cigarettes and attempted keep warm. Even I, with 2 pairs underclothing, 2 shirts, a sweater, my brown suit, overalls, overcoat, winter cap & 2 pairs sox was getting chilly. Presently we became restless & walked out onto the tracks to spy an ancient looking empty coach with a light in it. Prowling lower we observed a notice on the side telling us it was for the use of stockmen only. A brakeman informed us that the coach was to be put on the freight to Winnipeg for the use of some stockman travelling. We entered the coach, found a fire burning in the stove, wiped the dust off the seats, spread them out bed fashion & were soon asleep. We were suddenly awakened by the guard who informed us that the train was pulling out in 5 minutes and that a "bull" was going to travel with the train. Observing the "bull" walking down the side of the train we waited till he rounded the end before ourselves, hopping out, walked after him & inspected the box cars. All but one were sealed, this "one" being half full of coal. There were already about ten other travellers sprawling in various positions amongst the coal.

The first division stop was Wynyard and here my friend turned back. He had a warm bed in Saskatoon, a mother, a father and home — not work. He explained that he was a decent fellow, had never been in jail in his life &, didn't like freight riding. What would his mother say if he was arrested? Besides, supposing there was no work in Toronto what would we do? We'd be arrested, vagrants. He had never been in a big city before, our money would not last long, we might even starve to death! In other words, he'd had enough ... just chicken hearted.

The sun was warm and I rode on top of a box car all day. Towards evening the train pulled in at the next division stop, Bredenbury. I was hungry & made for the town semi-satisfying my appetite in a "Chinks". Returning to the train I fell in with two of my fellow passengers of the coal car who had been "bumming" the houses. They were lads of 23 also heading for Toronto — happy but broke. Arriving at the tracks we walked boldly towards the freight & walked right into the "bull" who instantly showed his ignorance.

"What the hell d'you fellows want here." We put him right as to our wants whilst he accompanied us to the entrance of the yards and the freight steamed out. He informed us that should he see us around again he would put us all in "clink". One of my new-found confederates thanked him very much and suggested that as we had lost the freight and had nowhere to sleep we should very much appreciate his hospitality. But the "bull" was not so hospitable & we slept in the C.P.R. round house beside a boiler. I slept well in spite of the sudden change from feather to concrete mattress. Following morning a pail & water from the boiler brightened our appearance & we made for town agreeing that the inhabitants should pay dearly for their ignorant railway cop. Meeting the oldest resident, I think he must have been, on "Main Street" we enquired as to the whereabouts of the local "town bull", the mayor, the residences of the station agent, the railway cop and the R.C.M.P. local. With this information we commenced our labours for breakfast. Seeing a man working in a garden we wondered whether he would like our aid or company. He was not impressed by either but gave us $1 for "eats". Entering the local hotel we explained our circumstances and gorged for 25 cents per head. During the morning we lay down on some open prairie & slept till roused by a crowd of children who had come to inspect us. One yelled "Hobo, hobo we've got some candy for you", but as I got up hopefully they took to their heals [sic] and ran for town. Our stomaches [sic] informed us dinner time had arrived, one of the boys set out for the mayors house and brought back a fine "hand out" which we consumed. The other set out for another of our addresses, split some wood & received a "sit-down". Then it was my turn to go "bumming". I set out for a large house set back from the town which looked hopeful. I tapped at the door nervously and a large man poked his head cautiously out of the door letting out an equally large dog as he did so. My knees knocked and I stuttered something about work & eat. The man told me he did not feed tramps & would set his dog on me. I moved toward the dog which instantly fled with its tail between its legs and the man slammed the door. As I was walking down the path the man popped his head out of an upstairs window and threatened to inform the police if I did not "get clear" immediately.

Towards evening the Winnipeg freight pulled in and we boarded it as it pulled out of the yards. There were no "empties" but a stock coach on the back, so we sat on the steps of this. As dusk fell we stopped for water at some place & the guard sighted us. He came up & inspected us, then unlocked the coach & told us to get in there for the night, we might go to sleep on the steps & fall off. Next morning we awoke to find our freight standing in the Portage La Prairie yards. Two "bulls" walked up the train, inspected the seals, glanced at the stock coach where we had assumed an attitude of sleep once more, walked off. We left the freight at a street crossing outside Winnipeg, yelled at a passing truck driver and were whirled into the city. The two lads I was with got a free shave at the Barber College and we learnt that the city was handing out meals to transients. After much walking and enquiring we obtained meal tickets and set out for the soup kitchens, which used to be the C.N.R. Immigration Hall where I stopped when first in Canada. The meal was awful! We walked down a counter gradually accumulating our ration which consisted of a piece of bread & square of butter, a small dish containing about a spoonful of sugar, a tin bowl containing a green fluid sometimes called soup, a tin plate on which had been dumped, dirty potatoes, two [sic] large hunks of fat, some carrots and thick gravy, and a mug contain -hot water the same colour as weak tea. We sat on a bench containing males of all types, nationalities and descriptions and attempted to eat. The gentleman on my right had developed a strange habit of wiping a running nose with the back of his hand between each mouthful which did not increase the flavour of my meal. A large bowl of rice was placed on the table for desert but as I had my plate already filled with leavings I did not try any.

We left the soup kitchens and made enquiries about the times of freight trains. There was one leaving from the C.N.R. Transcona yards at around midnight for Toronto. We commenced the 9 miles walk to Transcona.

On the way we passed over a bridge on the side of which some humorist had written with chalk "I'm fed up; for further information drag the river." Over the bridge is St. Boniface where there is a large catholic church, seminary, school, nuns home etc. etc. Whilst passing the seminary and admiring its size and beauty we espied the kitchen through a basement window. Thoughts concerning the higher arts vanished from our heads, we looked at each other, looked for the nearest door, and entered, coming upon a fat cook. I moved my hand over my chest and wore my most pious expression and one of the boys addressing the cook as "brother" explained that we were extremely undernourished and should be pleased with some bread. The cook prepared some sandwiches containing cold slabs of steak and we departed praising the Lord, the cook and ourselves.

Towards late afternoon we arrived at the yards, parked ourselves on the grass outside the fencing and built a fire of old ties — and commenced a 7 hour wait. We consumed our sandwiches which were delicious — I think I'll become a priest.

As time passed more "travellers" appeared and settled around our fire; soon we had about a dozen fellow "unionists" and grew to discussing "this world of ours" as men often do. In London there are cockney tales, in Scotland, Scotch tales and on the road, hobo tales. Hoboes also have quite a language of their own. The same as farmers but without the large variety of 'swear words' usually associated with the barnyard.

The depression, the railway companies and Bennett were our chief topics. We wisely listened to each others views on depression. Its due to tariffs, to immigration, the price of wheat, the U.S.A., Russia, war, their "big-bugs", religion, the "bohunks". Nothing but war will bring back prosperity; no cancellation of war debts; no socialism; no God; let's have the good old days; scrap machinery, to hell with motor cars, deport the Reds, deport the "bohunks", oust Bennett ...

Quite evidently there is no use for a penniless person in this land of opportunity; a person without work and money is considered an outcast, no town or city wants him but he can usually get two meals per day and exist because even Canadians do not usually let dogs starve. When a person has lost all his money and cannot get work he can either take to the road and become a bum or stop in his home town and get a free bed and two meals a day from the city relief for which he has to do as many hours work per week. I estimate that this scheme breaks the spirit of the average man within a year; hence I chose the road. My spirit is by no means broken I just feel angry and the harder Canada kicks me the more I'll retaliate. I do not consider myself an ordinary "bum". If there is any work to be done I'll do it providing I receive what I consider a decent living wage. I will certainly not work for my board and I will not work for the pittance many are receiving today.

Until such time as I get a decent job I intend to live well, dress respectably, eat all thats good for me, keep myself clean and have clean clothes. Canada generally will pay for this. I will obtain what I need by bumming and other comparatively honest methods. If such ways and means should fail I shall resort to thieving and other criminal ways of which I have some knowledge ...

11

"The Question of Loyalty"
Japanese Canadians and World War II

DOCUMENTS

A) Report and Recommendations of the Special Committee on Orientals in British Columbia, 1940

B) House of Commons, Debates, February 19, 1942
A.W. Neill

C) This Is My Own: Letters to Wes and Other Writings on Japanese Canadians, 1941–1948
Muriel Kitagawa

   i) To Wes December 21, 1941

   ii) To Wes January 21, 1942

   iii) To Wes February 19, 1942

   iv) To Wes March 2, 1942

   v) To Wes April 20, 1942

   vi) We'll Fight for Home, 1942

   vii) On Loyalty, 1942

   viii) Mr. and Mrs. Kitagawa to Custodian of Japanese Properties, Vancouver, B.C., July 1943

   ix) F.G. Shears, Department of the Secretary of State, Office of the Custodian, Japanese Evacuation Section, Vancouver, B.C., to Mr. and Mrs. Kitagawa, July 2, 1943

   x) T.M. Kitagawa to Mr. F.G. Shears, July 8, 1943

D) Government Policy Toward Japanese in Canada, August 4, 1944
Prime Minister W.L. Mackenzie King

National histories inevitably include certain closeted skeletons that most citizens prefer to keep firmly locked away. They are embarrassing to the collective psyche and threaten smug senses of righteous moral superiority. Canada too has its national skeletons, perhaps none larger than the story of the Japanese Canadians in British Columbia during the Second World War. Order-in-Council P.C. #1486, issued on February 24, 1942, called for the evacuation of all people of Japanese extraction living within a "protected area" of one hundred miles of the West Coast. This action took place, so Ottawa stated, in order to lessen the chance that *Nisei* (those born in Canada of Japanese ancestry), or *Issei* (naturalized Japanese immigrants) could act as fifth columnists for a Japanese naval attack upon British Columbia. Order-in-Council #1486 was not based on nationality: the majority of the 21,000 men, women, and children evacuated into British Columbia's interior, or Alberta, or Ontario, were Canadian citizens. Racial origin alone decided a person's fate because it apparently determined one's level of patriotism.

The question, of course, remains: was the evacuation based on genuine and legitimate fear, or was it polite racism masquerading as a national security issue? Was it an ugly but necessary defense measure, or did it simply make bigotry patriotic?

The former argument certainly held sway during and immediately after the war. The Japanese government, after all, had perpetrated a heinous surprise attack against Pearl Harbor in Hawaii — halfway to British Columbia. Though there were as yet no confirmed sightings of Japanese military activity on the coast, unconfirmed ones abounded, and they generated very genuine fears. Other issues, legitimate or not, heightened suspicion toward the community. Some perceived the Japanese-Canadians as relatively isolated from the rest of society, cloaked in the mantle of a radically different culture, language, religion, and appearance.

Currently, racism is widely believed to be the primary motivation behind the evacuation. The Canadian government recently acknowledged this by offering an apology and compensation to the Japanese-Canadian community. Canada did have a long history of racism, nowhere more so than along the West Coast and against "Orientals." Only racism could explain why evacuees were not permitted to return to British Columbia until four years after the war ended or why children and the aged — hardly security threats — were included in the evacuation order. Both the RCMP and military intelligence had agreed prior to the evacuation that the Japanese-Canadian community on the West Coast did not constitute a threat to national security. And Prime Minister MacKenzie King stated in 1948 that "no person of Japanese race born in Canada has been charged with any act of sabotage or disloyalty during the years of the war."

Order-in-Council #1486 astonished people like Muriel Kitagawa who probably did not really believe it until the knock at the door. They should have seen it coming. The Americans, after all, had passed legislation prohibiting the 120,000 Japanese-American community from living within one hundred miles of their west coast, and simultaneously seized their property. The new Canadian law allowed the RCMP to enter homes without warrants and to confiscate any property deemed a security risk. This included fishing boats, cameras, radios, and firearms. Vehicles had to be turned in, and the government imposed a dusk-to-dawn curfew. Japanese-Canadian newspapers and schools closed down. After the evacuation, the Custodian of Enemy Alien Property seized all unmoveable goods, such as businesses, homes and property, holding them in trust until January 1943 after which they disposed of them without their owners' consent. Money raised from auctions of Enemy Alien property alleviated the internment cost, using the official justification that "Canadian" taxpayers should not bear the financial burden of incarcerating their enemies. Selling off their possessions also ensured that Japanese-Canadians could not easily return to their former homes once hostilities ended.

The Special Committee on Orientals in British Columbia was formed by the federal cabinet just after Japan announced her alliance with the Axis powers and amidst protests against the prospect of Asian Canadians serving in Canada's armed forces. The committee's major recommendations were aimed at reducing public tensions in British Columbia.

A.W. Neill sat as an independent Member of Parliament for Comox-Alberni during the Second World War. A major street and a school in Port Alberni now carry his name.

Muriel Kitagawa (née Fujiwara) came from a humble family dogged by poverty and disintegration. Her father immigrated from Japan to Victoria, B.C., in 1890 where he worked in a saw mill before moving to Sidney and New Westminster. Kitagawa, born in Vancouver in 1912, excelled in English literature, and came in second for the Governor General's Award upon graduation from high school. She went to the University of British Columbia, but could not complete her studies for lack of money. She did, however, find an outlet for her writing talents in community newspapers such as the *New Canadian*. Like so many of her compatriots, she found her parents too old-fashioned and too Japanese, and she strove to integrate with mainstream Canadian culture. She kept in close touch with her brother Wes, a medical student in Toronto, and moved there when forced to relocate. She died in 1974, ever passionate about the Japanese experience in Canada.

Prime Minister William Lyon MacKenzie King (1874–1950) was not known as a racist and, in fact, regularly expressed his humanitarianism, especially toward those in "humble circumstances." King, though publicly a champion of human decency, integrity, and honour, regularly followed legislative paths that smacked more of opportunism and pragmatism than idealism. He ignored Quebec's infamous Padlock Law, for example, and refused to support either Ethiopia through the League of Nations, or the legitimate Republican government during the Spanish Civil War. In each case, his inaction stemmed from fear of stressing the Canadian national fabric, not from personal conviction. National harmony was paramount to King, and if achieving and maintaining that harmony required legislation that flew in the face of human rights, so be it. According to King, sometimes the ends justified the means. He publicly rationalized the internment by declaring that Japanese-Canadians were victims of a racism which they perpetrated upon themselves. Thus, he said that "the sound policy and the best policy for the Japanese-Canadians themselves is to distribute their numbers as widely as possible throughout the country where they will not create feelings of racial hostility."

A) Report and Recommendations of the Special Committee on Orientals in British Columbia, 1940

22. In the examining of witnesses the members of the Committee first directed their attention towards discovering whether, in fact, hostile feeling existed in any important degree. It became immediately apparent that there was in some quarters an active hostility towards the Japanese; and that, while many witnesses expressed a liking for them, or an admiration for their individual and national qualities, this was coupled with a greater or less degree of suspicion of the Japanese as a people and a feeling that their racial solidarity was likely in an emergency to override their loyalty to Canada and produce subversive or otherwise dangerous activities. No concrete evidence was adduced in support of this sentiment, and charges of disloyal conduct brought by witnesses against individual Japanese or groups of Japanese proved in every instance upon further examination to arise from unsubstantiated rumour and hearsay ...

... The police officers who appeared before the Committee, while in some cases they differed in their personal views on the questions at issue and in their attitude towards the Japanese as a people, all agreed that they formed one of the most law-abiding elements in the population of the Province and that they were in general industrious and inoffensive citizens.

24. Nevertheless, despite this favourable testimony, the Committee was obliged to recognize that, even granting the Japanese in British Columbia

to be innocent of acts or speech conducive to suspicion and hostility, they are in fact mistrusted and disliked by many people, particularly in those districts where they are most thickly congregated. It was, therefore, necessary to discover the true causes of this ill-feeling, and this point was put specifically to every witness examined. The almost invariable reply was to the effect that the chief cause of animosity was economic. The Japanese are disliked by those whom they injure (or who consider themselves injured) in competition with white Canadians as labourers, as fishermen, as farmers, as retail storekeepers or in other occupations, where they accept lower wages or subsist on a less expensive standard. This sentiment may sometimes be justified by the facts, since it is natural for a white competitor to resent the existence of a class which appears deliberately to depress standards of income, working hours, and living conditions. But even where it is not justified, it is easily rationalized by representing the Japanese as a community who, besides being economically undesirable, are politically dangerous.

25. It is doubtful whether these sentiments of dislike and mistrust would persist to any significant degree in times of normal economic activity and relatively full employment, unless they were kept alive and stimulated by other agencies. Unfortunately the Committee received ample evidence to show that hostility towards the Japanese has been deliberately inflamed by certain individuals for reasons which can only be ascribed to a desire for personal political advantage. While considering such practices to be objectionable at all times, and particularly dangerous in present circumstances, and, although not suggesting that to suppress those practices will remove the anti-Japanese sentiment which now exists, the members of the Committee are convinced that, as a first step towards diminishing the mutual antagonism between certain elements of the white population and the Japanese community, it is essential to prevent acts tending to create public suspicion and alarm. In this sense, the suppression of public statements arousing antagonism against the Japanese in British Columbia should be an integral part of plans for civil security and national defence ...

27. While there may be differences of opinion as to how far the charges levelled against the Japanese in respect of underselling and underliving their white competitors are justified, it is probable that many grievances could be removed by the proper enforcement of existing legislation, or the enactment of new laws or by-laws, which would prevent some forms of unfair competition, e.g., the custom of some Japanese food retailers of sleeping in their stores

and thus reducing overhead costs for rent. In general, any policy designed to raise the standard of living and the standard of income of the Japanese would tend to narrow their competitive margin and thus to remove causes of ill-feeling against them. In this connection it was brought out clearly by the evidence of many witnesses that it is the exclusion of Japanese from one occupation after another in British Columbia which has driven them into occupations of a different grade, e.g., when driven out of the fisheries they turned to small storekeeping, tailoring, dry-cleaning, where their inexpensive standards permit them to drive out white competitors. There is no doubt that the Japanese themselves have a sense of persecution when after being excluded from one occupation they are blamed for resorting to another. The animosity of the white population thus has its counterpart in the resentment of the Japanese; and it is obvious that such conditions make for neither loyalty nor harmony. It is indeed in some respects astonishing that the native born Japanese are not more vocal and active in their resistance to the discrimination to which they are subjected. This can partly be explained by the fact that, by and large, they are at least as well off, and in most cases are better off, materially than they would be in Japan. They are, moreover, a traditionally disciplined and obedient people, accustomed to thinking in terms of the interest of their community as a whole, so that any tendency toward imprudent action can be readily held in check by the leaders of their several groups.

28. While it is probable that, given patience and the lapse of time, the most serious economic causes of ill-feeling between white and Japanese could be modified, it was clear from the statements of many witnesses that most of the occidental population of British Columbia regard the Japanese as unassimilable because of their distinctive racial character. No doubt in the most favourable conditions racial animosity might, with the lapse of time, be expected to diminish, and it is possible that such conditions could be produced by legislation, good will and individual effort. But the chief problem before the Committee was the short-term problem. It was therefore obliged to recognize that, in addition to the economic factor, racial prejudice is an important element in producing dislike and mistrust of the Japanese. It does not matter whether this racial prejudice is reasonable or not. It exists and it has to be taken into account. Moreover, the present international situation, in which Japan has declared herself on the side of the enemies of the British Empire, has in itself intensified not only national feeling but also racial feeling.

29. It was very apparent, and in this the majority of the witnesses who appeared before the committee agreed, that this complex of economic, national and racial factors has produced a dangerous situation, but it was most significant that, with one exception, all the witnesses examined, even those most hostile to the Japanese, agreed that the greater danger was to be expected not from the Japanese themselves, but from the white population, who with only the slightest additional provocation, might suddenly resort to violence against Japanese individuals or groups. The Japanese themselves are alive to this hostility, and their fear and perplexity and their natural determination to protect themselves if attacked, are further elements of danger.

30. The committee recognized that the situation in British Columbia may be further complicated at any time by acts committed outside of Canada; acts which cannot be foreseen, but which may be intensely provocative. Any occurrence of that nature might not only provoke action against the Japanese in British Columbia, but, if there were Canadians of Japanese race serving at the time in the armed forces of Canada, they also might be in danger of attack by the less responsible element among their comrades.

31. In view of these considerations the members of the committee reached the conclusion that one of their main duties must be to point out that the first and perhaps the greatest potential source of danger is not disloyalty on the part of the Japanese in Canada but the animosity of white Canadians against the Japanese in general. The Committee's recommendations therefore deal principally with the measures which can be taken to prevent acts of hostility against Japanese resident in British Columbia. Among such measures must be included not only military and police precautions, but also the removal, so far as may be possible, of conditions likely to produce mistrust and anxiety among both the white and the Japanese populations.

32. ... While the committee is convinced that the investigation made by the Board of Review in 1938 indicated that these beliefs are, and for some years have been, unfounded, it is nevertheless true that some sections of popular opinion in British Columbia still accept the charges as true. For this and other reasons the demand for a complete registration of the Japanese population is still foremost in the minds of a considerable element in the population.

33. ... the General Officer Commanding in Chief, Pacific Command, was consulted, and stated that he was in full agreement with the Committee's view of the situation; that he had already taken, and would continue to

take, all possible military precautions against civil disturbance. With regard to police precautions it is believed, on the evidence of the witnesses examined, that all police authorities in the province are fully aware of the dangers to be guarded against and have laid plans accordingly.

34. An important aspect of the problem of protecting loyal Japanese against violence is the choice of methods to be used for the purpose of distinguishing potentially hostile elements from the loyal Japanese who are legally domiciled in Canada. For this purpose, it is, in the Committee's opinion, desirable to impress upon the responsible leaders of the various Japanese communities that the wrongful act of a single Japanese would, even in present circumstances, and *a fortiori* if the international situation were to deteriorate further, imperil the lives and property of *all* Japanese, whether loyal or otherwise; and that consequently it is their duty and in their interest to cooperate fully with the authorities by keeping a close watch on their own communities and reporting without delay any suspicious circumstances ...

37. Although the members of the Committee sympathize with this attitude, they are bound to consider the question in relation to other facts, and those facts are that opinion in British Columbia is on the whole against allowing persons of Japanese race to take military training or to serve in the armed forces. This opposition is based in part upon racial prejudice, as is shown by the statements of several witnesses who were offended by the prospect of white and Japanese youths being together in camp or in barracks. But what seems to the Committee to be a more valid objection was raised by those who urged that, particularly in the event of increased tension between Japan and the democratic states, the situation of Japanese Canadian youths in training or serving in military units with large numbers of white Canadians would be one of great danger should racial or national passion be aroused by some untoward incident at home or abroad. A quarrel in a canteen might lead to the gravest results to the Japanese directly concerned, and it might further set in motion currents of race hatred in other parts of the world, with the usual sequels of reprisals and counter-reprisals. Therefore, it has been decided to recommend, though most reluctantly and not unanimously, that at least for the present, Canadians of Japanese race should not be given military training (except of course the Basic Training provided for all students in public schools and universities) and should not be enlisted generally in the armed forces of Canada. Such exclusion will certainly give offence to a number of Japanese Canadians, and it would therefore be

prudent to explain the Government's decision to them in a sympathetic way, dwelling upon the fact ... that it is largely based upon a desire to protect and to ease the position of the Japanese themselves, and not upon any mistrust of their patriotism.

B) House of Commons, Debates, February 19, 1942
A.W. Neill

Mr. A.W. NEILL (Comox-Alberni): Mr. Speaker, I have listened to that appeasement talk for twenty years from the government benches, and I think the time has come to take a different stand. I believe we can best serve the interests of our country, and promote peace, by having plain talk, straightforward discussions and, I hope, definite action, with respect to the issues before us ...

In September, 1940, Japan signed the deal, agreement or whatever you call it with Italy and Germany. In plain English, they bound themselves to enter into war against us and the United States whenever it suited Germany or Hitler. Pressure was put upon the government by British Columbia, and I suppose some realization of the situation also led the government to take action. They appointed a hand-picked committee to investigate the subject, which... came back with a number of recommendations, I believe ten in all. There were only two of any importance, Nos. 5 and 7, and I shall deal with them. No. 5 recommended against allowing Japanese to enlist in our volunteer army then being raised. That was a very good idea, otherwise we would have had perhaps 1,500 Japanese training in our army, possibly in key positions, petty officers and the like. They would have been familiar with every detail of our army operations. Protests were made by the mayor of Nanaimo, and I think by other cities and by myself, and the recommendation of the committee carried. That was all right.

Recommendation No. 7 was that there should be a re-registration of the Japanese in Canada. It had been claimed by many people that the registration that had been taken was just a fake as regards the Japanese. Only those who felt like it registered, and there was a demand for a new registration. The recommendation was that they should be photographed at the same time. That was a good idea, but it had one fatal defect, if deception is regarded as a fatal defect. It was clearly understood that this registration was compulsory. We were told how well it was going on, how successful it was, and it was hoped that we malignants would now be satisfied and keep quiet. The whole thing turned on the point that it was compulsory.

If it had been voluntary, what use would it have been? ... Was it expected that Japanese who had entered the country illegally would come forward and say, "Yes, I came in illegally, take me." Of course they would not. A Jap is not a fool, any more than we are. The guilty ones did not register and the whole thing was a gigantic failure. It could not be otherwise if it were anything but compulsory.

Our main complaint was that many of them had come into the country illegally and this re-registration would have discovered that. Was it expected that those who had come in illegally would disclose that fact? The thing is ridiculous. When the war came on, after Pearl Harbour, it was discovered that it was not compulsory, that it was just a gesture to keep us quiet, just a farce. Then what happened? The war was on and the people know what war means; this government should know what it means. These same people were given two months in which to register; they were given until February 7 to get things fixed up, to get a fake birth certificate or a forged entry card. You can buy them in Vancouver. If they could not get either, they were given two months before they would be subject to the same action as that to which any other enemy alien would be exposed. Why give them two months? We were practically saying to them, "We are at war with you, but we will give you two months in which to get faked papers, or get out of the country." I never heard the like of it before, and I hope I never shall again ...

They were given two months in which to fix things up or get out. If that registration had been compulsory, we would have got the best of these Jap agents and the best of their spies. They have now gone home with their charts and plans and with a local knowledge that could not be bought for any money. Perhaps we shall see some of these Japs again peering over the side of the bridge of a German gunboat in Vancouver, Nanaimo or Port Alberni, because we now know that many of them were expert naval men ...

Paragraph 6 recommends that the government should seize immediately the Japanese fishing boats. That was done. It was done immediately war was declared, and for that action I have nothing but the utmost praise. It was done promptly and thoroughly ... At any rate it was done, and done well. While this is not part of the report, I may as well finish up that matter by saying that after they had 1,200 Japanese boats in their hands, the question arose, what to do with them? It was desirable to get them back into fishing again, so that white men could catch the fish so badly needed for the British market. Therefore they set up a committee to try to sell these boats ... Like all government offices, it is true that they were rather slow in going about their work, but they got started at last ...

I want to quote recommendation 7 in which was contained the policy of the cabinet. It reads: "For the same period — that is during the war — the sale of gasoline and explosives to persons of Japanese racial origin will be directly controlled under conditions prescribed by the Royal Canadian Mounted Police."

That is a good idea too, a very good idea, but unfortunately I read in the papers — I have to go to the press for information because I cannot get it anywhere else — that these sales are still going on.

Mr. HOMUTH: The sale of powder is still going on?

Mr. NEILL: Explosives. A man wrote to the Vancouver *Province* the other day and suggested that if this order was in effect, why was the Japanese station at the corner still selling gas the same as usual? That has been going on for two and a half months now, and I rather think permission has been extended to the 1st of April. The language is doubtful, but if it can be interpreted to the benefit of the Japanese, be sure it will be so interpreted. You are dealing with clever, subtle, unscrupulous enemies — and they are enemies — and when you say that you are not going to stop the sale for two months, that is just an invitation to them to accumulate as much gas and explosives as they can in the meantime. We say to them: "Remember, on the 7th of February or on the 1st of April we are going to shut down on you." Is that not an invitation to them to get explosives and gasoline against a rainy day? That time limit should never have been put in. The order should have been made applicable at once ...

There are three classes of Japanese we must deal with. There are the Japanese nationals, those born in Japan and never naturalized in Canada; they are Japanese nationals. Then there is the man born in Japan and naturalized in Canada. He is called a naturalized Japanese or a Canadian. Then there is the Japanese who was born in Canada, who can call himself a Japanese-Canadian if he likes. The government orders with regard to seizing the boats and the sale of gas and explosives applied to all three classes. That was all right.

Now I deal with paragraph 8. It says that Japanese nationals will be forbidden to possess or use short-wave receiving sets or radio transmitters in

Canada. A most excellent thing. Hon. members can all understand why it was necessary to do that. That was fine. But it does not come into effect until the 1st of April. Did the Japanese give us four months notice of what they were going to do at Pearl Harbour? Yet we say to them: "Go wandering about with your cameras and take pictures, and use your receiving sets to send word to Japan, and your receivers to get instructions from Japan. You can do this as much as you like until the 1st of April." Even if the order had been withheld, and they had been allowed to continue doing these things without being told of any date when they must stop, it would not have been so bad, because then they would never have known when the order was coming into force. But they were warned — you will not be interfered with until the 1st of April. The order was the equivalent of that. We told them: "Do your dirty work now. Use your radio and your receiving set but, remember, hide or bury them before the 1st of April, and then everything will be lovely." They told the Japanese nationals that they must not use these things in a protected area. But they can use them outside. I have a police order to that effect. It is signed by the police and says:

> "No enemy alien shall have in his possession or use while
> in such protected area any camera, radio transmitter, radio
> short-wave receiving set, firearm, ammunition or explosive."

... [Mr. NEILL:] Well, as I said, it is doubtful. There is, however, no question whatever that a man who is not a Japanese national can do these things any time, any place. The order applies only to nationals; that is, to men born in Japan and coming over here, and these are comparatively few in number, something like 1,700 out of 24,000, and only while they are in the area. The remaining 22,000 of naturalized Japanese are free to come and go, as I have said, anywhere. They can photograph what they like, radio what they like. They can do something else which I have not touched upon, and which is — not to make a joke — a burning question in British Columbia. Three, two, one of them can do endless damage in British Columbia with a box of matches. The most deadly enemy of the lumber industry in British Columbia is fire. Lumbermen are so afraid of it, it is so dangerous, that they shut their camps down in the middle of summer, as soon as the humidity reaches a certain point. A man can wander out in that bush, ten, fifty, a hundred miles from anywhere, and do more damage with a box of matches than it would take two armies to put out. The large number of forest rangers whom we have could not touch the fringe of the thing if these aliens were determined to commit sabotage. Some of the biggest lumbermen on the coast are much alarmed at this situation. If the Japanese were out of the area, they could not do this damage, because you can't do a thing if you are not there.

I have spoken of the freedom of Japanese to come and go with cameras, radios and matches. That is not restricted to two months or four months; that is for eternity, if the war lasts that long; it is for the duration of the war that the naturalized or Canadian-born Jap can go out and commit sabotage; he is free to do it the whole time, and he is the most dangerous of the lot. The naturalized Japanese speaks our language fluently, possibly he has been to college. He possesses far greater potentialities of trouble as a spy or an agent than if he had just come from Japan. The fellow dressed up like a white man, speaking our language glibly, is the one who should be interned. It is very hard for me to believe that the government are so remote from what is taking place or may take place as not to understand the situation ...

I should now like to make three charges against the government. The first is this, that, with the exception of seizing these boats they have been far too slow in handling the Japanese situation. They have let days go by when it should have been hours, and a month when it should have been days. Look at what was done in Mexico. There the government dealt with the whole lot as soon as war was declared, and ordered into the interior every Jap who was on the coast. They did it; they didn't talk about it. Cuba did the same thing. They arrested, I believe, eighteen Japanese, all but two of whom were naval officers. Nicaragua took the same course, and took it speedily ...

I note here that the council of the city of Vancouver has passed a resolution urging the government to get a move on. The report speaks of increasing irritation and criticism at the coast over the apparent failure of the government to implement its announced policy of removing Japanese.

The legislature of British Columbia, before adjourning a few days ago, passed unanimously a resolution urging the dominion government to strengthen Pacific defences. The feeling is very strong at the coast. I wish I could get the government to realize it.

Here is one incident I must quote, reported under a big headline in a leading Vancouver paper, the *Daily Province:*

"Japanese live undisturbed on dike adjoining airport.

There are 200 Japanese living a mile west of the airport. They are living on a dike. It would be very easy to blow up or open that dike, and the airport would be rendered useless for a long time to come. Yet they are living undisturbed within a mile of the airport; they are on a dike into which a gap could be blown with a few sticks of powder that would make the airport useless for a long time to come. Why does the government not take some action in this case?

The second charge is that even the small restrictions to which I have referred are applicable only to nationals, and I say it is inexcusable that they are not made applicable to all naturalized Japanese aliens in this country. To whom do you suppose they think they owe loyalty? If they were scattered all over Canada, the case might be different, but think what may happen when they are turned loose in a small area, when 25,000 are concentrated in an area where they could so readily combine to take action against Vancouver, or Victoria, as the case may be. It constitutes an unspeakable menace; I cannot understand why it is allowed to continue.

The third charge is that the government have shown indifference to British Columbia defence, also to air raid precautions work and the like of that. I am not blaming the government for preparations which they might have made six years ago. That is not their fault; I know that. We could not get the appropriation through the house ... But I do blame the government for not having taken the situation in hand since war was declared. They are too slack, they appear to adopt the attitude, "Oh, well, we have to take chances; we are doing the best we can; it will be all right." Well, they told us it would be all right about Hong Kong. But people make mistakes — even military men, even high military men. They told us it would be all right at Singapore. Yet we know that mistakes were made there. Here is the government's paper, the *Vancouver Sun*, expressing this opinion:

> "Canada obviously has not made its plan of defence on the assumption of any real attack on the Pacific coast ... That is the plan which must be reconsidered ... we do expect a well-equipped, mobile striking unit which could pounce upon any Japanese landing attempt from Alaska southwards.
>
> "No such force exists on our coast. No such force exists in Canada."

I am afraid that is too true. Perhaps in the secret session which is to be held we shall be given more information on this matter. I do not propose to blame the government for things which happened before they had control and knowledge of the situation, or for not having done what at the time was beyond their power. But the government must be ready at that secret session to give us genuine information, not general assurances and smooth-sounding platitudes. There has been too much of this in connection with the management of the war.

There is a certain place — I will not name names, I will call it *Y*. When the government began to think about building aerodromes I thought that *Y* would make a good site for one, and I said so. I put it up to the officials, and they said that they were experts and ought to know better than I did. Well, I accepted that decision — but they are building that aerodrome now with frantic haste. I fear we may have to paraphrase the hymn and say:

> Too late, too late will be the cry
> "The Japanese gunboats have gone by."

There was another aerodrome at a place we will call *X*. I wrote to the government in connection with this one, informing them that there were two things wrong about it. This was a year or two ago. I pointed out to the officials that there was a Jap village 200 yards from the mouth of it where the Japs could take photographs and keep a record of any aeroplanes leaving, with all the details, so that they could have it all recorded for the benefit of the Japanese: I have in my desk a letter in which some official tried to stall me off. I was told that they would expropriate the Japanese, but that they could not do it because there was some hitch. However, they said they would look into the matter. Imagine looking into the question of expropriating this particular property when other nations, as we know, take first what they require and then talk about expropriation. Again, I pointed out to the officials that there was a Jap who had been seen taking photographs from an aeroplane over the harbour, where the aerodrome was being built. It was a civilian aeroplane. I took this matter up with various bodies — I will not mention any names because I do not wish to give them away — and what was the answer? I was informed that the investigation was closed. They had ascertained the name of the man and had found that he had gone to Japan. I suppose he took photographs with him as a momento of us because he loved us so much. Well, he has gone back to Japan with whatever photographs he took — we do not know how many — and God knows how many more may have gone there. But the officials did not seem to think it was important. I was told that it would be difficult to take photographs through the glass of any aeroplane unless you had a particular sort of apparatus with which to do it. Well, would the Japanese not have that type of apparatus? I submitted all these matters to the department, and I have it all on record. One of the officials said to me, "There is nothing to this anyhow because it is not against the laws of the country to take photographs of an aerodrome."

I took it up with some of the higher officials, and they juggled with it and finally explained that they could get the Japs under the Official Secrets Act. The aerodrome is still there; the Japs are still staying there under their four months' lease of life, and doubtless they are still taking these photographs, which I have no doubt will be sent to the right place.

These men are not all Canadian nationals. Some of them may be the very best class of spies and foreign agents, and I contend that there has been too much sympathy for the Japanese viewpoint and Japanese interests. We must remember that we are at war with these people. Ottawa is 3,000 miles away from us out there ...

We who have taken the position that I am now taking have been called all sorts of names. We have been called agitators. It is said that we are willing to exploit the interests of Canada for our own political advantage; that we are rabble-rousers, Jap-baiters, and that we have a very dangerous influence ... I have heard that sort of thing, and hints of it even in this house, and certainly in the government press. You can get a man to write any letter you want; you can get a white man to make a tool of himself for a Jap if you pay him enough. There was a man who wrote to the papers saying what fine people the Japs are. I laid a trap for him and I discovered that he was a white man all right, but also a paid agent of a Japanese association, but he did not say that when he signed his name.

Yes, we are all bad because we want a white British Columbia and not a place like Hawaii! Fifty years from now, unless something is done to stop it, all west of the Rockies will be yellow. I submit, Mr. Speaker, that we want but little; we simply want to be left alone, like New Zealand and Australia, all white. I have no ill-will against the Japanese. Perhaps you may think I have been showing ill-will, but I assure you I have none towards the Japs. No Jap ever "did" me — I never gave him the chance. I wish to be fair to the Japanese, and I think that if we expatriated them, as we ought to do, they should be given full justice in regard to their property, because I am strongly in favour of a Japan controlled by the Japanese, just as I am in favour of a Canada controlled by Canadians. Let us continue to trade with them; let us do business with them across the ocean; but do not force into one nation two peoples separated by something that is wider than the ocean, two peoples who are different in race, in religion, in traditions and in their whole philosophy of life. This difference always has prevented assimilation and always will prevent it, between two nations so utterly divergent in every respect. The greatest path towards assimilation is marriage ... the Japs have been here fifty-eight years and there is no record of a single marriage, although there might be one. I asked a Japanese to produce the record of one marriage and he could not do so. We have heard of second generation Japanese born here going to Japanese schools here to learn Japanese, and that has been regarded as a small matter. We went into their textbooks and had them translated and we found that they were very anti-British. Yet there were people who thought that was a small matter — only the sort of thing that irresponsible people like myself would talk about. But when the war came, it was thought wise to shut down the Jap schools. There were fifty-nine in British Columbia, and leaving out small areas where they could not run a school, the great bulk of those children must have attended some Japanese school.

I have one more word ... we should make an arrangement that when peace time comes, we expatriate all the Japanese left in Canada; do it on fair terms, buy them out, pay them liberally ... it is much easier for us to move 25,000, and it is better to move them while their numbers are so small. Let us settle once and for all this canker in the life of Canada which prevents us from being a united white Canada. And that is what British Columbia wants.

C) This Is My Own: Letters to Wes and Other Writings on Japanese Canadians, 1941–1948
Muriel Kitagawa

i) December 21, 1941.

Dear Wes:

... So far as the new war affects us, I really haven't much to say. It is too early to estimate the effects. On the whole we are taking it in our stride. We are so used to wars and alarums, and we have been tempered for the anti-feelings these long years. It has only intensified into overt acts of unthinking hoodlumism like throwing flaming torches into rooming houses and bricks through plate glass ... only in the West End so far. What that goes to prove I don't know. We've had blackouts the first few nights but they have been lifted. Bad for the kids, because it frightens them so. Of course we have to be ready just in case and I sure hope there won't be any emergency ... not with the kids around. All three Japanese papers have been closed down. We never needed so many anyway. It is good for the *New Canadian* though, as it can now go ahead with full responsibility, though at first it is bound to be hard on the inexperienced staff. All Japanese schools have been closed too, and are the kids glad! Of course I have never intended my kids to go anyway so it doesn't affect us in the least. I am glad in a way that they have been closed down. I hope for good. But it is hard on the teachers who depended on them for a living.

There have been the usual anti-letters-to-the-editor in the papers. Some of them are rank nonsense, and some of the writers think like that anyhow, whatever the provocation. The majority of the people are decent and fair-minded and they say so in letters and editorials. The RCMP is our friend too, for they, more than anyone else, know how blameless and helpless we are, and they have already in one instance prevented tragedy when the City Fathers proposed cancelling all business licences, to say that we did not rate such harsh treatment. Now the North Vancouver Board of Trade goes on record to demand that all our autos be confiscated, but I hardly think that could be practical. What then would our doctors and businessmen do? Also, it is hard to take everything away from 22,000 people without the rest of B.C. feeling some of the bad effects. The dog salmon industry is already short-handed because the Japanese cannot fish any more. How they will make up the lack in the next season I don't know, though the 'white' fishermen seem to be confident, if they could use the fishing boats now tied up somewhere in New Westminster.

There was one letter in the *Province* protesting this confiscation of the right to earn a living from 1880 people ... said it wasn't democracy. Yes sir, when a people get panicky, democracy and humanity and Christian principles go by the board. Rather inconsistent, but human nature I guess. Some silly mothers even go so far as to say, what right have the black-haired kids to go to school with their own precious? One schoolteacher had the courage to say to one of the 'white' pupils who wanted all Japs to be kicked out of school — how they reflect their parents' attitude! — that there were no Japs, and in any case they were far better Canadians than the protester. Strange how these protesters are much more vehement against the Canadian-born Japanese than they are against German-born Germans, who might have a real loyalty to *their* land of birth, as we have for Canada. I guess it is just because we look different. Anyway it all boils down to racial antagonism which the democracies are fighting. Who said it was Woman ... or the Moon that was inconstant? Oh well, it is only the occasional one here and there. I personally have had no change in my relationship with my neighbours or my Egg-man, who told me not to worry. Most of the hakujin deplore the war but do not change to their known Japanese friends. It is the small businesses that are most affected ... like the dressmakers, the corner store, etc., because the clientele are rather shy of patronising in public such places, whatever their private thoughts may be. Powell Street is affected too, in that they have a slightly increased volume of sales to people who usually go to Woodwards etc. But so many have been fired from jobs that belts are tightening everywhere. I don't know yet how all this is going to affect Dad. Most of his patients are fishermen or farmers. So far the farmers haven't been touched.

Last Sunday, the national President of the IODE [Imperial Order of the Daughters of the Empire], who must live far from contact from the Nisei because she didn't seem to know the first thing about us, made a deliberate attempt to create fear and ill-will among her dominion-wide members by telling them that we were all spies and saboteurs, and that in 1931 there were 55,000 of us and that that number has doubled in the last ten years. Not only a biological absurdity, but the records of the RCMP give the lie to such round numbers. The trouble is that lots of women would like to believe their president rather than actual figures. Seems to me illogical that women who are the conservers and builders of the human race should be the ones to go all out for savagery and destruction and ill-will among fellow-humans. They are the ones who are expected to keep the peace with their neighbours in their particular block, but when it comes to blackballing some unfortunate people, they are the first to cast the stone. In times like this I always think of that line:

> "If there be any among you that is without sin, let him cast
> the first stone."

Or words to that effect. And certainly we Nisei are neither harlots nor criminals. We're just people.

But more to the point, how are you getting along, there? Is the feeling worse in Toronto where they don't know the Nisei as B.C. does? How does the war affect you personally? Can you get a loan to get through next year and the year after? After all, you are Canadian-born, and the Army needs MD's. How has it affected your living conditions at the Lethbridges? Or your acquaintance with Dent and others? Has it affected the wearing of your uniform? Your standing in class and lab? Have you heard from George Shimo? Please let me know fully. So far Doug hasn't let me know by word or line how he is, but he's never one to write, and he's carefree. I think he is all right. If he doesn't lose his job through this, I'll ask him to send you what he can every month. Dad and Nobi are getting along but I think Nobi's kind of sad that he won't see Mom again, and he does miss a home life. But I can't do a thing to help as Dad rejects every offer. I guess that when gas rationing starts Dad won't be able to use that darned car so often ... He has to report every month to the RCMP, just because when he first came to B.C., which was over forty years ago, and plenty of time to naturalize, he didn't look far enough ahead to know how it would have helped his children. That! for people who live only day to day. Politics never meant a thing to him, and doesn't yet. So long as he can eat and swank in his car he lets important things slide.

We're getting immune to the hitherto unused term 'Japs' on the radio and on the headlines of the papers. So long as they designate the enemy, and not us, it doesn't matter much. The Chinese here were indecently jubilant ... paraded and cheered in their quarters when the war was announced. They are rather childish that way. Of course, now they hope that both the U.S. and Canada will fork over a lot more help than they have so far. I think they are naive. War nowadays is too complicated and can't be compared simply to a street-fight. I am glad however that the Russian army is licking something out of Hitler's troops. The sooner Hitler stops his enslaving of conquered people ... you know, ship-loading them into Poland or into Germany proper to work for nothing in the fields and factories far from home and children; his way of stealing food from the conquered peoples; his system of captive labour; shooting hundreds in reprisal for one ... then the sooner will the little peoples have a chance at life again.

Ugh! I hate wars, and I've had one already, though I wasn't old enough to know anything then. Now I'm going through a worse one. War, active war, is easier to bear with courage than this surging up of mass hatred against us simply because we are of Japanese origin. I hope fervently that it will not affect the lives of Shirley and Meiko and the unborn son [Kitagawa's children], as the doctor believes. After all, my kids, as only proper being my kids, are so thoroughly Canadian they would never understand being persecuted by people they regard as one of themselves. Already Meiko came crying home once because some kid on the block whose father is anti, said something. Yet I try to rationalize things for them, so that they won't be inundated by self-consciousness. Children are so innocent, but they are savages too, and reflect faithfully their parents' attitudes. That was the one thing my doctor was worried about. Otherwise he, with most of the others, tells us not to worry. We're Canadians and can expect decent treatment from decent people ...

ii) January 21, 1942

Dear Wes:

... Since they are moving the unemployed Nisei first, I don't think Ed [Kitagawa's husband] will be affected. After all, they could hardly expect him to leave a good job for road work when he has a big family to feed. I have my fingers crossed — all ten of them. Of course, since I have been house-bound from October I haven't felt the full force of the changes since Dec. 7th.

[Alderman Halford] Wilson and his bunch are making political hay out of this. He does so with bland half-truths and falsehoods and hypocrisies enough to turn your stomach. So does the *Sun* paper. They are deliberately inflaming the mob instinct and inciting the irresponsible elements to a bloody riot — the kind they had in 1907, the one in which Wilson's father had a dirty hand. Once the flames catch, Powell Street will be in for a bad, bad time, not mentioning the scattered but large number of families in certain suburban districts. How that Wilson can square his conscience, eat three meals in peace, with his brand of patriotism that stinks to hell — I don't know.

The *Province* and *News-Herald* have been editorially condemning Wilson and his bunch and appealing to B.C. at large to give the local Japs a chance. Acts of vandalism make the headlines, and there has been one murder. Yoshiyuki Uno was shot to death by a 17 or 19 yr old bandit.

iii) February 19, 1942.

Dear Wes:

How's things? That was a good letter you wrote to the N.C. [*New Canadian*].

Well, I guess you've read in the papers that there isn't a province in Canada that will take the "Japs," and B.C. just has to have us whether she will or no. Ian Mackenzie has again come out with "Volunteer or else—." Vancouver City Fathers have petitioned Ottawa to put the OK on a ban of trade licences to Japanese here — 850 or so. Won't the Relief offices be flooded then! ... They don't care anyway — under their hypocritical Christian faces. It beats me how they can mouthe "Down with Hitler," and at the same time advocate a program against "Japs" (4-letter syllable in place of "Jews"). Now that attack on this coast is becoming more of a concrete threat, feeling is running pretty high — tho' the individuals in most cases are pretty decent. The rabble-rousers and the mob — haven't we learned about "mobs" in Roman days and in Shakespeare's works? — they are the ones to cause all the trouble. Even the Youth Congress has come out with a plea to move us all out someplace, anywhere except on the coast.

... Anyway I'm not sure what to believe these days. Dad takes no thought of his eventual transfer to a camp. (They're moving the over-45-year-olds after they get the first batch settled.) In fact, if the war comes any closer we'll all be kicked out.

Gosh, but hasn't 1941 been the awfullest year in our life?

Love,

Mur.

iv) March 2, 1942.

Dear Wes:

What a heavenly relief to get your letter. I was just about getting frantic with worry over you ... Oh Wes, the things that have been happening out here are beyond words, and though at times I thank goodness you're out of it, at other times I think we really need people like you around to keep us from getting too wrought up for our own good.

Eiko and Fumi [friends of Kitagawa] were here yesterday, crying, nearly hysterical with hurt and outrage and impotence. All student nurses have been fired from the [Vancouver] General.

They took our beautiful radio ... what does it matter that someone bought it off us for a song? ... it's the same thing because we had to do that or suffer the ignominy of having it taken forcibly from us by the RCMP. Not a single being of Japanese race in the protected area will escape. Our cameras, even Nobi's toy one, all are confiscated. They can search our homes without warrant.

As if all this trouble wasn't enough, prepare yourself for a shock. We are forced to move out from our homes, Wes, to where we don't know. Eddie was going to join the Civilian Corps but now will not go near it, as it smells of a daemonic, roundabout way of getting rid of us. There is the very suspicious clause 'within and *without*' Canada that has all the fellows leery.

The Bank is awfully worried about me and the twins, and the manager has said he will do what he can for us, but as he has to refer to the main office which in turn has to refer to the Head Office, he can't promise a thing, except a hope that surely the Bank won't let us down after all these years of faithful service. Who knows where we will be now tomorrow next week. It isn't as if we Nisei were aliens, technical or not. It breaks my heart to think of leaving this house and the little things around it that we have gathered through the years, all those numerous gadgets that have no material value but are irreplaceable ...

Oh Wes, the Nisei are bitter, too bitter for their own good or for Canada. How can cool heads like Tom's [Tom Shoyama, editor of the *New Canadian*] prevail when the general feeling is to stand up and fight.

Do you know what curfew means in actual practice? B.C. is falling all over itself in the scramble to be the first to kick us out from jobs and homes. So many night-workers have been fired out of hand. Now they sit at home, which is usually just a bed, or some cramped quarters, since they can't go out at night for even a consoling cup of coffee. Mr. Shimizu is working like mad with the Welfare society to look after the women and children that were left when their men were forced to volunteer to go to the work camps. Now those men are only in unheated bunk-cars, no latrines, no water, snow 15' deep, no work to keep warm with, little food if any. They had been shunted off with such inhuman speed that they got there before any facilities were prepared for them. Now men are afraid to go because they think they will be going to certain disaster ... anyway, too much uncertainty. After all, they have to think of their families. If snow is 15' deep there is no work, and if there is no work there is no pay, and if there is no pay no one eats. The *Province* reports that work on frames with tent-coverings is progressing to house the 2,000 expected.

Tent coverings where the snow is so deep! And this is Democracy! You should see the faces here, all pinched, grey, uncertain. If the Bank fails Eddie, do you know what the kids and I have to live on? $39. For everything ... food, clothing, rent, taxes, upkeep, insurance premiums, emergencies. They will allow for only two kids for the Nisei. $6 per., monthly. It has just boiled down to race persecution, and signs have been posted on all highways ... JAPS ... KEEP OUT. Mind you, you can't compare this sort of thing to anything that happens in Germany. That country is an avowed Jew-baiter, totalitarian. Canada is supposed to be a Democracy out to fight against just the sort of thing she's boosting at home.

And also, I'll get that $39 only if Eddie joins the Chain Gang, you know, *forced to volunteer* to let the authorities wash their hands of any responsibilities. All Nisei are liable to imprisonment I suppose if they refuse to volunteer ... that is the likeliest interpretation of Ian MacKenzie's "volunteer or else." Prisoners in wartime get short shrift ... and to hell with the wife and kids. Can you wonder that there is a deep bitterness among the Nisei who believe so gullibly in the democratic blah-blah that's been dished out. I am glad Kazuma [Uyeno] is not here.

There are a lot of decent people who feel for us, but they can't do a thing.

And the horrors that some young girls have already faced ... outraged by men in uniform ... in the hospital ... hysterical. Oh we are fair prey for the wolves in democratic clothing. Can you wonder the men are afraid to leave us behind and won't go unless their women go with them? I won't blame you if you can't believe this. It *is* incredible. Wes, you have to be here right in the middle of it to really know.

How can the hakujin face us without a sense of shame for their treachery to the principles they fight for? One man was so damned sorry, he came up to me, hat off, squirming like mad, stuttering how sorry he was. My butcher said he knew he could trust me with a side of meat even if I had no money ... Yet there are other people who, while they wouldn't go so far as to persecute us, are so ignorant, so indifferent they believe we are being very well treated for what we are. The irony of it all is enough to choke me. And we are tightening our belts for the starvation to come. The diseases ... the crippling ... the twisting of our souls ... death would be the easiest to bear.

The Chinese are forced to wear huge buttons and plates and even placards to tell the hakujin the difference between one yellow peril and another. Or else they would be beaten up. It's really ridiculous.

And Wes, we are among the fortunate ones, for above that $39 we may be able to fill it out by renting this house. Now I wish I hadn't given my clothes to Kath. We will need them badly. Uncle has been notified to get ready to move. Dad will be soon too.

There's too much to say and not enough time or words.

Can't send you pictures now unless some hakujin takes the snaps ... STRENG VERBOTEN [German for "strictly forbidden"] to use even little cameras to snap the twins ... STRENG VERBOTEN is the order of the day.
Love,
Mur.

v) April 20, 1942.

Dear Wes:

I went to the Pool yesterday to see Eiko who is working there as steno. I saw Sab too who is working in the baggage ... old Horseshow Building. Sab showed me his first paycheque as something he couldn't quite believe ... $11.75. He's been there for an awful long time. Eiko sleeps in a partitioned stall, she being on the staff, so to speak. This stall was the former home of a pair of stallions and boy oh boy, did they leave their odour behind. The whole place is impregnated with the smell of ancient manure and maggots. Every other day it is swept with dichloride of lime or something, but you can't disguise horse smell, cow smell, sheeps and pigs and rabbits and goats. And is it dusty! The toilets are just a sheet metal trough, and up till now they did not have partitions or seats. The women kicked so they put up partitions and a terribly makeshift seat. Twelve-year-old boys stay with the women too. The auto show building, where there was also the Indian exhibit, houses the new dining room and kitchens. Seats 3000. Looks awfully permanent. Brick stoves, 8 of them, shining new mugs ... very very barrack-y. As for the bunks, they were the most tragic things I saw there. Steel and wooden frames with a thin lumpy straw tick, a bolster, and three army blankets of army quality ... no sheets unless you bring your own. These are the 'homes' of the women I saw. They wouldn't let me into the men's building. There are constables at the doors ... no propagation of the species ... you know ... it was in the papers. These bunks were hung with sheets and blankets and clothes of every hue and variety, a regular gipsy tent of colours, age, and cleanliness, all hung with the pathetic attempt at privacy. Here and there I saw a child's doll and teddy bear ... I saw babies lying there beside a mother who was too weary to get up ... she had just thrown herself across the bed ... I felt my throat thicken ... an old old lady was crying, saying she would rather have died than have come to such a place ... she clung to Eiko and cried and cried. Eiko has taken the woes of the confinees on her thin shoulders and she took so much punishment she went to her former rooms and couldn't stop crying. Fumi was so worried about her. Eiko is really sick. The place has got her down. There are ten showers for 1500 women. Hot and cold water. The men looked so terribly at loose ends, wandering around the grounds, sticking their noses through the fence watching the golfers, lying on the grass. Going through the place I felt so depressed that I wanted to cry. I'm damned well not going there. They are going to move the Vancouver women first now and shove them into the Pool before sending them to the ghost towns.

   ... The other day at the Pool, someone dropped his key before a stall in the Livestock Building, and he fished for it with a long wire and brought to light rotted manure and maggots!!! He called the nurse and then they moved all the bunks from the stalls and pried up the wooden floors. It was the most stomach-turning nauseating thing. They got fumigators and tried to wash it all away and got most of it into the drains, but maggots still breed and turn up here and there. One woman with more guts than the others told the nurse (white) about it and protested. She replied: "Well, there's worms in the garden aren't there?" This particular nurse was a Jap-hater of the most virulent sort. She called them "filthy Japs" to their faces and Eiko gave her 'what-for' and Fumi had a terrible scrap with her, both girls saying: "What do you think we are? Are we cattle? Are we pigs you dirty-so-and-so!" You know how Fumi gets. The night the first bunch of Nisei were supposed to go to Schreiber and they wouldn't, the women and children at the Pool milled around in front of their cage, and one very handsome mountie came with his truncheon and started to hit them, yelling at them, "Get the hell back in there." Eiko's blood boiled over. She strode over to him and shouted at him: "You put that stick down! What do you think you're doing! Do you think these women and children are so many cows that you can beat them back into their place?" Eiko was shaking mad and raked him with fighting words. She has taken it on her to fight for the poor people there, and now she is on the black list and reputed to be a trouble-maker. Just like Tommy and Kunio. I wish I too could go in there and fight and slash around. It's people like us who are the most hurt . . . people like us, who have had faith in Canada, and who have been more politically minded than the others, who have a hearty contempt for the whites ...

By the way, we got a letter from Uncle ... or rather Auntie got it. He's the gardener, and has to grow vegetables and flowers on the side. Takashima is cook and gets $50 clear. Uncle only nets about $10. All cards and letters are censored, even to the Nisei camps. Not a word about sit-downs, gambaru-ing or anything makes the papers. It's been hushed. Good thing for us. I wondered why I didn't read about it. I haven't been to meetings so long now that I don't know what's going on. Uncle's camp is 8 miles from the station up into the hills. Men at the first camps all crowd down to the sta-tion every time a train passes with the Nationals and hang onto the win-dows asking for news from home. Uncle said he wept.

But the men are luckier than the women. They are fed, they work, they have no children to look after. Of course the fathers are awfully worried about their families. But it's the women who are burdened with all the re-sponsibility of keeping what's left of the family together. Frances went to Revelstoke, bag and baggage and baby. When I heard that I felt choked with envy, and felt more trapped than ever. Eiko tells me: "Don't you dare bring the kids into the Pool." And Mr. Maikawa says Greenwood is worse. They are propping up the old shacks near the mine shaft. Sab went through there and says it's awful. The United Church parson there says of the Japs: "Kick them all out." Sab knows his son who had the room next to him at Union College. Vic and George Saito and family went to the beet fields. Sadas are going tonight. They are going to hell on earth, and will be so contracted that they cannot leave the place or move. Whites will not go there.

I pray that Kath and Mom are safe. Mom's got to live through this. Now that Japan proper has been bombed they will come here.

Sab told me his father has applied to get to Winnipeg or to Toronto. Sab is hoping to get to Queens.

Eiko, Fumi and I, and all of us, have gotten to be so profane that Tom and the rest of them have given up being surprised. Eiko starts out with "what the hell" ... and Fumi comes out with worse. It sure relieves our pent-up feelings. Men are lucky they can swear with impunity. (Hell ... I can smell horse all of a sudden ...)

On account of those fool Nisei who have bucked the gov't, everything the JCCL fought for has been lost. Our name is mud. Why they don't arrest Fujikazu I don't know. I kind of feel that the RCMP are just letting us raise such a stink by ourselves ... that is fools like Fujikazu and his ilk ... that the rest of us who are really conscientious and loyal will never have a chance to become integrated with this country. It's damnable. All we have fought for and won inch by inch has gone down the drain. More than the Nationals, our name is mud. There's over 140 Nisei loose, and many Nationals. The Commission thinks the Nationals are cleared but oh boy there are a lot of them who have greased enough palms and are let alone.

By the way if you ever write anything for the NC write it to Tom personally.

How are things there? How are the Pannells and everybody? Three Nisei girls are going to Toronto for housework. Maybe you might get to see them, whoever they are. Aki Hyodo is in Hamilton. If Mrs. Pannell doesn't mind the typewriter, I think I shall write to her.

I'll write again soon.
With love,
Mur.

vi) We'll Fight for Home, 1942

The tide of panic, starting from irresponsible agitators, threatens to engulf the good sense of the people of British Columbia. The daily press is flooded with "letters to the editor" demanding the indiscriminate internment of all people of Japanese blood, alien or Canadian-born; demanding the immediate confiscation of our right to work as we like, our right to live like decent human beings. One and all, they add the height of sardonic cynicism: if we are as loyal as we say we are, then we ought to understand why we ought to be treated like poison.

If we were less Canadian, less steeped in the tradition of justice and fair play, perhaps we could understand and bow our heads before this strange, undemocratic baiting of thousands of innocent people.

For the very reason that our Grade School teachers, our High School teachers, and our environment have bred in us a love of country, a loyalty to one's native land, faith in the concepts of traditional British fair play, it is difficult to understand this expression of a mean narrow-mindedness, an unreasoning condemnation of a long suffering people. We cannot understand why our loyalty should be questioned.

After all, this is our only home, where by the sweat of our endeavours we have carved a bit of security for ourselves and our children. Would we sabotage our own home? Would we aid anyone who menaces our home, who would destroy the fruits of our labour and our love? People who talk glibly of moving us wholesale "East of the Rockies," who maintain that it is an easy task, overlook with supreme indifference the complex human character.

They do not think what it would mean to be ruthlessly, needlessly uprooted from a familiar homeground, from friends, and sent to a labour camp where most likely the decencies will be of the scantiest in spite of what is promised. They do not think that we are not cattle to be herded wherever it pleases our ill-wishers. They forget, or else it does not occur to them, that we have the same pride and self-respect as other Canadians, who can be hurt beyond repair. In short, they do not consider us as people, but as a nuisance to be rid of at the first opportunity. What excuse they use is immaterial to them. It just happens to be very opportune that Japan is now an active enemy.

We have often been accused of taking the bread out of "white" folks' mouths. Is there anything against the right to enjoy what one has earned? Our little trades and professions ... what golden loot for our would-be despoilers! No wonder they drool to get at them. These hard-earned, well-deserved small successes ... for out of the total of our enterprises, how many are there that can be classed as wealth? So few!

"Man's inhumanity to man makes countless thousands mourn."

Right here in British Columbia is a God-sent opportunity for the government and the people to practise democracy as it is preached. Not in panicky persecutions that do no one any good, but with sensible belief in our very real harmlessness, and consideration for us as a much-maligned people.

Ye gods! Can they not see that we love our home and would fight to protect it from the invader!

vii) On Loyalty, 1942

The quality of loyalty is difficult to define in exact terms. There is a oneness with one's country, just as there is the blood tie with one's mother. There is the fighting urge to defend that country should it be threatened in any way. There is a passionate, unquestioning, unqualified affinity with the land that excludes the pettiness of a manmade — and therefore imperfect — government. All this and active service for the country is loyalty.

Who can glibly say I am a Japanese National of Japan just because I am of the same race with black hair and yellow skin? Who can rightfully tell me where my heart lies, if I know better myself? Who can assume with omniscience that I am disloyal to Canada because I have not golden hair and blue eyes? What are these surface marks that must determine the quality of my loyalty? Nothing, nothing at all!

Yet because I am Canadian, must hate be a requisite for my patriotism? Must I hate vengefully, spitefully, pettily? Will not hate cloud my good sense, muddy the clean surge of willing sacrifice, the impulse to rally strongly to the flag of this country? Hate never fought as fiercely as love in the fight for one's country. Hate impedes, while love strengthens.

Therefore it is not hate for a country one has never known, but love for this familiar Canadian soil that makes me want to use my bare fists to uphold its honour, its integrity.

Who is there, unless he does not know the quality of loyalty, who will question mine?

viii) Mr. and Mrs. Kitagawa to Custodian of Japanese Properties, Vancouver, B.C., July 1943

Dear Sir:

This is to register with you our absolute opposition to the proposed liquidation of our house and lot at 2751 Pender Street East, Vancouver, B.C.

This house, bought out of slender earnings, represents our stake in this country of our birth, but sentiment alone is not for withholding our express and voluntary consent to sell.

Our present earnings are even more slender than before. You are doubtless aware, if you have a family of your own, what it costs in dollars and cents to feed, clothe, and house a family of six, excluding the other expenses incidental to schooling, medical services, etc. With four growing children, that $25 a week we receive from the rental of our house is more welcome than you could ever understand. Without that $25, meagre as it is, we could not meet all our monthly obligations. You know, too, that while cost of living rises, salaries do not. But now you [propose] to deprive us of that regular income on which we are desperately dependent. We are not among those who can afford the loss of their dear-bought investment.

Our house, a private residence belonging to a private citizen of this country, is in the capable hands of a trustworthy agent; the tenants are pleasant and punctual. They know they have a bargain, as the house is in good shape, with added improvements to the cost of many hundreds of dollars, boosting the saleable value of the house, too. This piece of real estate is not idle, either, housing as it does the family of a soldier, and also keeping poverty and hardship that much further away from the absent owners.

We cannot understand the official claim that it is necessary to sell over our heads the home from which we were forcibly ejected. We do not quarrel with military measure but this act can scarcely be in accordance with any war measure. Please hasten to assure us that our house is inviolate.

Thank you.

Yours truly,

Mr. and Mrs. E. Kitagawa.

ix) F.G. Shears, Department of the Secretary of State, Office of the Custodian, Japanese Evacuation Section, Vancouver, B.C., to Mr. and Mrs. Kitagawa, July 2, 1943

Dear Sir:

I am in receipt of your letter of the 26th instant in which you registered your disapproval of the sale of your property.

The proposed liquidation is of course a general one and not only applies to your particular property. The policy has been decided upon at Ottawa and this Office, acting under advice of an independent Advisory Committee, will endeavour to obtain the best possible results.

You are aware I hope that the proceeds of the liquidation will be available to you from time to time as you have need of same.

At the present moment tenders have not been called on your particular property but I am unable to give you the assurance asked for and it will be disposed of in due course if satisfactory offers are received.

Yours truly,

F.G. Shears,

Acting Director.

x) T.M. Kitagawa to Mr. F.G. Shears, July 8, 1943

Mr. F.G. Shears:

I received your letter of July 2nd, File No. 10004, yesterday and must say was not too greatly surprised. The reason for writing you at all was because the government had vested in you the final authority to sell or not to sell our homes, and perhaps I took a vain-hope gamble.

Would you give up a legitimate fight to defend what is yours though the odds are enough to overwhelm you? Britain didn't, did she? This war, for the common soldier, is a war for Principle: the rights and liberties and the pursuit of happiness for every man; and I'm on the side of the common soldier, giving his heart's blood that the oppressed may be free. Who would have thought that one day I would be unable to stand up for my country's government, out of sheer shame and disillusion, against the slurs of the scornful? The bitterness, the anguish is complete. You, who deal in lifeless figures, files, and statistics could never measure the depth of hurt and outrage dealt out to those of us who love this land. It is because we *are* Canadians, that we protest the violation of our birthright. If we were not we would not care one jot or tittle whatever you did, for then we could veil our eyes in contempt. You ... and by "you" I designate all those in authority who have piled indignity upon indignity on us ... have sought to sully and strain our loyalty but, I'm telling you, you can't do it. You can't undermine our faith in the principles of equal rights and justice for all, with "malice towards none, and charity for all."

Why can't you differentiate between those owners who don't care one way or the other what happens to their homes, and those who, born in this country, hate to lose their homes? If you are worried for our sakes about the depreciation of property values, then why will you not allow the owners a say in the sale price, the choice of prospective buyers? Can you, with a clear conscience, commit this breach of justice, and face the accusing eyes of all bereft and absent owners? Do you think it is logical, after what happened to the boats, the cars, and radios, that we have any faith in any promise of a fair price, which "proceeds of this liquidation will be available ... from time to time?" What will happen is the gradual dribbling away to nothing of the pitiful price, and then what shall we have left to show for our lifetime of struggling and saving and loving the bit of land we call our own? You may rightly say that wartime sacrifices are inevitable and honourable, but can you say with any truth that this sacrifice forced on us will be sanctified by a spirit of voluntary giving? What are platitudes against this humiliation!

Now you understand a little why I must contest the sale to the last bitter ditch, if we are to hold up our heads. You will concede us that, especially as this is the very principle for which the democracies are fighting.

However, if all fails and you are upheld in your purpose, then kindly send us our "proceeds" in one sum that we may personally reinvest it in something solid ... Victory Bonds, for instance.

There are still a few personal possessions in our home for which I shall send at once. You would not deny us that, I hope.

T.M. Kitagawa.

D) Government Policy Toward Japanese in Canada, August 4, 1944
Prime Minister W.L. Mackenzie King

... The government has had certain basic principles before it in formulating the policy which I wish to present to-day. In the first place, it recognizes the concern felt by British Columbia at the possibility of once again having within its borders virtually the entire Japanese population of Canada. In the past that situation has led to acrimony and bitterness. That the feeling is general in British Columbia has been made evident not only by the remarks of hon. members from that province but also through representations received from many west coast organizations and individuals. In view of the concern, it is felt that it must be accepted as a basic factor that it would be unwise and undesirable, not only from the point of view of the people of British Columbia, but also from that of persons of Japanese origin themselves, to allow the Japanese population to be concentrated in that province after the war.

Secondly, account should be taken of the fact that for the most part the people of Japanese race in the country have remained loyal and have refrained from acts of sabotage and obstruction during the war. It is a fact that no person of Japanese race born in Canada has been charged with any act of sabotage or disloyalty during the years of war. For the future protection of those who have remained loyal, as well as to eliminate those who have shown that their true allegiance is not to Canada but to Japan, the government is of the view that persons of Japanese race, whether Japanese nationals or British subjects by nationalization or birth, who have shown disloyalty to Canada during the war, should not have the privilege of remaining in Canada after the struggle is terminated. That is a second principle that is considered to be fundamental.

Thirdly, the government is of the view that, having regard to the strong feeling that has been aroused against the Japanese during the war and to the extreme difficulty of assimilating Japanese persons in Canada, no immigration of Japanese into this country should be allowed after the war. It is realized, of course, that no declaration of this type can or should be attempted which would be binding indefinitely into the future. Nevertheless, as a guiding principle in the years after the war, it is felt that Japanese immigrants should not be admitted.

Finally, the government considers that, while there are disloyal persons to be removed, and while immigration in future is undesirable, and while problems of assimilation undoubtedly do present themselves with respect even to the loyal Japanese in Canada, nevertheless they are persons who have been admitted here to settle and become citizens, or who have been born into this free country of ours, and that we cannot do less than treat such persons fairly and justly. The interests of Canada must be paramount, and its interests will be protected as the first duty of the government. It has not, however, at any stage of the war, been shown that the presence of a few thousand persons of Japanese race who have been guilty of no act of sabotage and who have manifested no disloyalty even during periods of utmost trial, constitutes a menace to a nation of almost twelve million people. Those who are disloyal must be removed. That is clear. Surely, however, it is not to be expected that the government will do other than deal justly with those who are guilty of no crime, or even of any ill intention. For the government to act otherwise would be an acceptance of the standards of our enemies and the negation of the purposes for which we are fighting ...

I should add that in handling the Japanese problem we shall attempt, in so far as it seems desirable, to maintain a policy that in a sense can be considered as part of a continental policy. The situation in the United States in a great many essentials, is the same as our own, and to the extent that it seems desirable we shall endeavour to ensure that our policy takes account of the policies which are being applied south of the border. There is no need for an identity of policy, but I believe there is merit in maintaining a substantial consistency of treatment in the two countries.

I might now mention the tentative measures which it is proposed to put into effect in order to carry out a policy based upon the principles I have indicated. The first and, in a sense, the fundamental task is to determine the loyal and the disloyal persons of Japanese race in Canada. The entire policy depends upon this being done. To some extent, of course, the task has been carried out through the examination and internment of suspicious or dangerous persons. It cannot be assumed, however, that all those who have been interned are disloyal. Some may have merely misunderstood their dispossession from their property in the protected zones, and, as peaceful and honest Canadian citizens, may have striven to protect and retain what they considered to be rightfully theirs. Undoubtedly some of these cases exist. Misunderstanding is not the same as traitorous intent, and a stubborn defence of one's own property is not necessarily disloyalty. On the other hand, there may be persons who have committed no act to justify their internment but who are in fact disloyal. What is clearly needed is the establishment of a quasi-judicial commission to examine the background, loyalties and attitudes of all persons of Japanese race in Canada to ascertain those who are not fit persons to be allowed to remain here. The commission I have referred to should, I think, be established in the fairly near future in order that it may begin what will be a large and important task. The result of the work of the commission would be to establish a list of disloyal Japanese persons, some of whom will be Japanese nationals, some British subjects by naturalization, and some British subjects by birth. The government's intention would be to have these disloyal persons deported to Japan as soon as that is physically possible. Prior to deportation, British subjects, falling within this class, would be deprived of their status as such. By the terms of the peace, Japan can be compelled, whether she wishes it or not, to accept these persons. There may also be some persons who will voluntarily indicate a desire to proceed to Japan. For these, no further examination would be necessary. Whatever their national status, they would be allowed and encouraged to go as soon as they can.

Once the examination has been carried out there will be established a list of Japanese persons who are loyal to Canada. These persons, if they have been properly admitted to this country, and wish to remain here, should be allowed to do so. However, as I have said, they should not be allowed once more to concentrate in British Columbia. To prevent such concentration, measures of two types can be taken — a maximum can be set on the number of persons of Japanese race to be allowed to return to British Columbia, and persons of Japanese race can be given encouragement to move and remain elsewhere. It would be most undesirable, I believe, to establish a permanent barrier to the movement within Canada of persons who have been lawfully admitted to Canada or who are nationals of Canada. That would raise the possibility of discrimination and restrictions on movement to and from provinces which might have most unfortunate consequences in the future. Even the establishment of a temporary limitation would be undesirable in principle, but as a practical question of policy it may well be inescapable.

There is little doubt that, with co-operation on the part of the provinces, it can be made possible to settle the Japanese more or less evenly throughout Canada. They will have to settle in such a way that they must be able to pursue the settled lives to which they are entitled, and that they do not present themselves as an unassimilable bloc or colony which might again give rise to distrust, fear and dislike. It is the fact of concentration that has given rise to the problem.

The sound policy and the best policy for the Japanese Canadians themselves is to distribute their numbers as widely as possible throughout the country where they will not create feelings of racial hostility.

… We must not permit in Canada the hateful doctrine of racialism, which is the basis of the Nazi system everywhere. Our aim is to resolve a difficult problem in a manner which will protect the people of British Columbia and the interests of the country as a whole, and at the same time preserve, in whatever we do, principles of fairness and justice.

12

"Cinderella of the Empire"
Newfoundland and Confederation

DOCUMENTS

A) To Norman Robertson, Canadian Under-Secretary of
   External Affairs, April 10, 1942
   C.J. Burchell, British High Commissioner

B) To Dominions Secretary, June 13, 1942
   *E. Machtig, Permanent Under-Secretary for
   Dominions Affairs of Great Britain*

C) Memorandum to Canadian Under-Secretary for
   External Affairs, January 8, 1944
   Special Assistant

D) Memorandum, n.d.
   *Assistant Under-Secretary of State for Dominions
   Affairs of Great Britain*

E) To Special Assistant to Canadian Under-Secretary of
   State for External Affairs, November 30, 1944
   *J.S. Macdonald, British High Commissioner in
   Newfoundland*

F) Memorandum to Prime Minister, September 25, 1945
   *N.A. Robertson, Under-Secretary of State for External
   Affairs*

G) Memorandum, October 17, 1946
   High Commissioner in Newfoundland

H) Memorandum by Second Political Division, n.d.
   P.A. Bridle

I) Speech to the National Convention, October 28, 1946
   Joseph Smallwood

J) To Canadian Secretary of State for External Affairs,
   January 9, 1948
   *J.S. Macdonald, British High Commissioner in
   Newfoundland*

K) Newfoundland National Convention:
Debates January 27, 1948
P. Cashin
L) *The Confederate*, May 31, 1948

To vote for entry into confederation with Canada, or stay as an English Crown Colony, that was the question that every adult Newfoundlander had to ponder when marking their ballots on July 22, 1949. The answer, as it emerged, proved more ambiguous than expected: 52.34% wanted Newfoundland to become Canada's tenth province, 47.66% voted against. That, in a democratic system, was enough for Newfoundland to take its ambivalent place in confederation.

This referendum was, in fact, a runoff, the second election to take place. The first, held the previous month, offered Newfoundlanders three choices: to regain responsible government; to join Canada as a province; or to continue the unhappy Commission of Government that then ruled Newfoundland through the Colonial Office in London. Voters overwhelmingly rejected the last choice, with only 23,311 supporting it. Confederationists, however, came out second best with 64,066 votes to 69,400 for responsible government. It looked as though Newfoundland would become an independent Dominion in the Gulf of St. Lawrence. In the end, however, most of those who had voted for the *status quo* became confederationists, which tipped the balance in Canada's favour in the final referendum.

Newfoundland's reticence to join Canada was hardly surprising considering its unique development. In fact, being part of the British Empire and sharing the same continent were arguably the only things most Newfoundlanders shared with Canada. If we must join somebody, many islanders proclaimed, let it be the United States with whom we have more in common.

From the time they first arrived on Newfoundland's craggy coast, most settlers, with their Gaelic and English roots, turned their backs to the North American continent, facing the rolling Atlantic instead. The islanders and the mainlanders developed along very different lines, and ended up with ever-diverging cultures.

The problem was, however, that Newfoundland had neither the population nor resource base to prosper. Britain provided most of the island's funding, and Newfoundland's standard of living languished as the rest of the continent's flourished. English voters, meanwhile, became resentful of the interminable bills, and called for their government to cast the island adrift. Newfoundlanders saw the writing on the wall well before the Second World War, particularly during the calamitous Depression era which cut a bitter swath of social deprivation through the colony. Something had to change. But Newfoundland suddenly found itself in a strategically critical location in 1939, jutting deep into the Atlantic where it served as a vital staging post for Atlantic convoys. All this led to a massive infusion of American and Canadian money and presence during the war. The United States leased huge military bases for 99-year terms, and thousands of Canadian troops milled about St. John's during World War II as they prepared to embark for Europe. The languishing Newfoundland economy found a new lease on life, and Newfoundlanders logically argued that they were, indeed, capable of standing on their own. Now was the time to cut a deal — or assert independence.

Islanders and their government administrators had regularly wrestled with Newfoundland's future, and the idea of federation with Canada was not new. While one after another of the other maritime provinces of British North America joined the Canadian federation in the late 1860s and 1870s, Newfoundland hesitated. The other colonies were not particularly interested in Newfoundland, and islanders wanted to steer their own course anyway. Canada's attitude did not help the confederation courtship. Most Canadians knew little about Newfoundland, and probably cared less. Newfoundland was, to most, a large rock in the Atlantic inhabited by vaguely odd fishers who spoke peculiar English and served as the butt of interminable jokes. Many Canadians also feared that Newfoundland's precarious financial situation would make it a future financial liability. Thus, the average person in the street thought that the disadvantages of inviting Newfoundland into the fold outweighed the advantages.

Newfoundlanders agreed. Islanders were aware of the condescending attitude Canadians had toward them, and it rankled their pride. They also feared that Canada, patronizing as it was, would absorb Newfoundland and use it however it saw fit, ignoring the wishes of the "lowly" islanders unless those wishes suited their own. The very democratic process that eventually brought Newfoundland into confederation also threatened it. Newfoundland's population, tiny in relation to the rest of Canada, ensured that it could easily be outvoted and ignored in future federal legislation. Thus they feared that the island's distinct culture, which islanders cherished, could be legislated out of existence once Newfoundland became part of Canada. This suspicion toward Ottawa deepened during the negotiation process when Newfoundlanders — with good reason — concluded that a conspiracy existed between Britain and Canada to bring the island into confederation without appropriate consultation.

In the end, and after a tumultuous and often dirty campaign, Newfoundland did join Canada. Newfoundland became part of Canada in 1949 with a very slim majority in favour, and Canadians were not polled. A simple majority among those directly involved apparently sufficed.

British High Commissioner to Newfoundland during much of the Second World War, C.J. Burchell administered most of the island's affairs in the critical period immediately before the referenda.

Sir Eric Machtig served as the permanent Under-Secretary of State for Dominion Affairs of Great Britain. As such, his responsibility included collecting and analyzing data on Newfoundland affairs, and interpreting them to the Colonial Office in London. He was Permanent Under-Secretary of State for Commonwealth Relations immediately prior to the Newfoundland referenda.

Counsellor to the Canadian Department of External Affairs from 1940 to 1944, J.S. Macdonald also became British High Commissioner to Newfoundland in May 1944, remaining in that post until 1948.

Norman A. Robertson was Under-Secretary of State for External Affairs in the Canadian government from 1941 through 1946. He then became Canada's High Commissioner to London from 1946 to 1949.

P.A. Bridle began his direct political involvement with Newfoundland as Canada's Third Secretary to the Canadian High Commission in St. John's in 1945. Though posted elsewhere in 1946-48, he returned to the Rock in May 1948, and rose to Acting High Commissioner, assuming that position from May to September 1948, and again in March 1949.

Journalist-turned-politician, Joseph R. "Joey" Smallwood fought tenaciously for confederation, believing it to be the only realistic solution to Newfoundland's woes. He was a member of the National Convention of Newfoundland from 1946-48, and a delegate to Ottawa in 1947. Smallwood managed the pro-confederation campaign, and deserves much of the credit for ultimately swaying enough Newfoundlanders toward Canada for it to occur. He subsequently played a major role in negotiating the terms of union with Canada. Smallwood, a Liberal, became Newfoundland's first premier and remained in power, virtually unopposed, for the next two decades. Joining Canada, he believed, could bring modernization and prosperity to his beloved land.

Major P.J. Cashin, as the driving force behind the Responsible Government side, was Smallwood's arch foe. He served in the National Convention from 1946–48 and went to London as a delegate in 1947.

Launched on April 7, 1948 by the Confederation Association, the *Confederate* newspaper provided a convenient means of counteracting arguments against union with Canada.

A) To Norman Robertson, Canadian Under-Secretary of External Affairs, April 10, 1942
C.J. Burchell, British High Commissioner

In one of my recent letters I mentioned the strength of the British tradition. I would say that in the City of St. John's, and particularly among certain sections of people, this is still very strong.

On the other hand, undoubtedly beneath the surface and among other sections of the people, there is quite a strong undercurrent running towards the U.S.A. This is particularly strong in the case of people who have made frequent visits to the United States or who have resided there and subsequently returned to Newfoundland. I am reliably informed also that in several of the outports there are a number of people — fishermen and others — who would strongly support Newfoundland going in with the U.S.A. instead of with Canada. These are people who lived in the United States for a period of years or whose sons or daughter went over there and did fairly well. I understand that in many of the better class of outports, the best houses are built with American money i.e. money earned either by the owner himself or some of his family who lived in the United States. A personal visit to some of these places would be necessary to get more exact information.

I think, however, that a general statement can be made that most thinking people in this country have decided that the future of Newfoundland lies with either one of the two countries in North America. If there was any break-up of the Empire, such, for example, as Australia pulling out and joining up with the U.S.A. so that the British tradition was weakened, I am afraid that the pull by Newfoundland would be towards the U.S.A. and not towards Canada ...

I would think that our policy in Canada at the present time should be to increase the number of links in the chain which now connects Newfoundland with Canada. The attitude of the present Commission of Government is to lean very heavily on Canada for support and I think that support should be given wherever this can reasonably be done ...

Yours faithfully,
C.J. Burchell

B) To Dominions Secretary, June 13, 1942
E. Machtig, Permanent Under-Secretary for Dominions Affairs of Great Britain

... The reason why, I think, we must actively consider the future after the war is that the immense efforts made by Newfoundlanders during the war in the Allied cause and the completely changed financial position, even if only temporary (they are now lending us money instead of our financing them), means that when the war ends there will be an overwhelming political move in favour of the restoration of self-government. This it will be difficult to resist and we ought to be prepared with our line of action ...

What we ought to make up our minds about is what future do we look for in Newfoundland after the war. As to this I find myself in very great agreement with Mr. Emrys-Evans' dictum that the aim of our policy should be to bring Newfoundland into the Canadian Federation if by any means this can be accomplished. The position, as I see it, is that the change which has taken place in the circumstances of Newfoundland will make it politically impossible to retain control from the United Kingdom through a Commission of Government. There will be great political pressure for the restoration of free Parliamentary institutions in Newfoundland. But a small country lacking in essential resources like Newfoundland is in fact unable to govern itself effectively and all recent experience has shown that small Governmental units are unable to exist effectively in the modern world. It follows that the only hope for the future within the British Empire is some union with Canada and the sooner this can be brought about the better.

It is clear that public opinion in Newfoundland has always been intensely against union with Canada but this largely due to the fact that the Canadians have regarded them as poor relations, have done in the main little to help them and have always taken the line that circumstances would force Newfoundland into Canada in due course on Canada's own terms. It might well be that if Canada were induced to take a more liberal view of the terms which she would offer Newfoundland for admission to the Canadian federation and if this could be backed by some attractive financial offer from ourselves, such as the acceptance by the British Exchequer of the existing Newfoundland debt charges, Newfoundland public opinion would move in the direction of union with Canada. At any rate it would be a constructive policy, which would be worth trying. I see little hope for Newfoundland's future if it is to consist of a series of changes from Government from Downing Street to self-government and intermediate variations ...   E. M[achtig]

C) Memorandum to Canadian Under-Secretary for External Affairs, January 8, 1944
Special Assistant

Part V. Canadian Policy

In view of Canada's vital interests in Newfoundland, a "Newfoundland Policy" would appear to be essential. There would appear to be three possible alternatives:

    (a) incorporation of Newfoundland as a tenth province of the Dominion;

    (b) continuation of Newfoundland as a joint military dependency of the United States, Canada and the United Kingdom;

    (c) Canada to assume complete responsibility for defence, Newfoundland remaining outside federation.

The last of these may be dismissed briefly — we should have freedom of action in defence but none of the benefits of effective control over Newfoundland in other respects. Moreover, complete responsibility for defence would entail heavy defence expenditures to cover our enormously extended Atlantic frontier.

Newfoundland as as a Tenth Province

Newfoundland could hardly be incorporated as a province unless the United States were prepared to surrender its bases, or unless we were prepared to compromise our political independence. It is probable that minimum terms would be assurance that the bases would be available in an emergency, but this would appear to be in line with joint defence arrangements for other air or naval bases in Canada. It is also possible that the general defensive rights of the United Kingdom which still extend to Newfoundland would also have to be extinguished or modified.

Advantages

    (a) Greater freedom of action in any crisis in the Atlantic.

    (b) Probably enhancement of our position as a world power if we maintained defence forces adequate for our new Atlantic commitments.

    (c) Possibly a better bargaining position in the matter of civil aviation, though the post-war pattern in civil aviation may be worked out before any decision is made about the status of Newfoundland.

(d) Possibly more effective control, or at least a better bargaining position in export fish markets.

(e) Control of iron ore deposits may conceivably be of future importance, politically and economically.

Disadvantages

(a) Newfoundland would certainly be a considerable financial liability. A very rough estimate of the net cost to the Dominion is from $5 to $6 millions annually, assuming cancellation of its sterling debt against United Kingdom account to Canada, and omitting costs of new Dominion services extended to Newfoundland such as, old age pensions, unemployment insurance and assistance for unemployment relief. The basic fact is that the productivity of Newfoundland is presently, and very probably will continue to be, substantially lower than the Canadian average. A rough calculation of the national income of Newfoundland for the period 1936–39 indicates a per capita average of about $150, whereas that of Prince Edward Island (then the lowest province) was $191, New Brunswick (next lowest) $225, and Nova Scotia $268.

(b) Newfoundland would probably be a political liability. It would not fit well into the Dominion's economy, since the fishing and pulp and paper industries would simply increase our present surplus production, while if trade were free between the provinces Newfoundland agriculture and manufacturing industries producing consumer's goods could scarcely survive. We might expect constant agitation for "better terms." Moreover, there would probably be a deep-seated opposition to union in many quarters from the outset which could be easily exploited afterwards.

(c) It would be extremely difficult to fit Newfoundland into the existing pattern of Dominion-Provincial relations. Since about three-quarters of its revenue is derived from customs taxes and since there are few alternative sources from which a "Provincial" revenue could be derived, it might even be necessary to permit Newfoundland to continue the existing customs tax, or to provide for "tapering off" in the customs tax over a period of years.

(d) Assuming withdrawal of the United States and the assumption of primary responsibility for the defence of all Newfoundland and

Labrador by Canada, Canada's defence establishment would have to be considerably larger in order to maintain effective defence of her greatly extended Atlantic frontier.

D) Memorandum, n.d.
Assistant Under-Secretary of State for Dominions Affairs of Great Britain

The approach to Canada

The general position in relation to Canada is as follows.

Although Newfoundlanders as individuals get on well with Canadians, and large numbers of them have settled in Canada, relations between the two countries have been marred by a long background of mutual suspicion and distrust — dating back to the 1860's when at a particularly bitter general election Newfoundland voted against entry into the Canadian confederation. Notwithstanding that over an ever-widening field the affairs of the two countries have tended to become increasingly mixed up together, the traditional Canadian attitude towards Newfoundland has been one of detachment, condescension and even contempt. In the background there has been the conviction that Newfoundland was too small and poor to be able to stand by herself in the modern world, and that one day, when it had tired of the struggle, the Island would fall into the Canadian lap; in the meantime, however, Canadians were in no hurry to add to their burdens by taking over the Island, with every prospect that it would prove more of a liability than an asset. Newfoundlanders on their side were well aware that this was the Canadian attitude, and the result over the years was merely to increase the jealousy and suspicion with which all Canada's actions in relation to the Island were regarded and to strengthen the determination of Newfoundlanders to hold on at all costs to their precious independence. Thus in turn a traditional attitude grew up in Newfoundland that whatever fate might hold in store for the Island, nothing could be so disastrous for Newfoundlanders as entry into the cold and comfortless Canadian fold.

The war has seen a marked change in the attitude of Canada; there has however been no change in the attitude of Newfoundlanders. Under the stress of war, Canadian official opinion has at last grasped what has always been evident for all to see, namely, that Newfoundland, situated as she is at the mouth of the St. Lawrence and commanding the gateway to Canada, is essential to Canada's defence, and that her full partnership is necessary not only for Canadian security but also for the proper rounding off of the Confederation, which would otherwise be incomplete. What has served to drive home this lesson has been the American entry into the Island, as a result of the grant to the U.S. Government of military, naval and air bases for 99 years. The Canadians have also been granted similar bases, but they fully realise that the Americans, if they wish to extend their influence in Newfoundland, can very readily outbid them. Even without any such intention on the part of the Americans the very fact that they are established in the Island will inevitably lead to closer and permanent links, commercial and otherwise, between Newfoundland and the U.S., and the lavish scale on which Americans habitually conduct their affairs coupled with the plain fact that assured entry to the huge and profitable U.S. market would revitalise Newfoundland's industries, may cause an increasing number of Newfoundlanders, notwithstanding their strong attachment to the Crown, to look upon union with the U.S. as their eventual destiny. The Canadians now realise that had they adopted a less parochial attitude towards Newfoundland in the past, there need never have been cause for the Americans to establish themselves in the Island. Now that the Americans are there, they must make the best of it; but it is not lost upon them that if the Island is not to swing into the U.S. orbit, Canadian policy must now become active instead of passive, and consciously designed to break down the old barriers of mistrust, to conciliate Newfoundland opinion and gradually to build up an atmosphere of comradeship and practical co-operation in which the union of the two countries could be seen to be in the common interest.

This, as is no doubt fully realised by the Canadians, will be a long process, for Newfoundlanders at present are as suspicious of Canada as ever. Indeed the experiences of the war have served to accentuate rather than diminish the traditional jealousies and dislikes, largely because the attitude of the Canadian forces towards the people of the Island has compared unfavourably with that of the Americans, who have proved excellent "mixers" and have won golden opinions. In this atmosphere the Canadians dare not make Newfoundland an offer, for fear that it would be rejected, as indeed it certainly would be: and they have therefore confined themselves to friendly expressions of interest, and assurances that if Newfoundlanders themselves should wish to turn to Canada they would be given a warm and sympathetic welcome. These assurances have cut no ice in Newfoundland, where indeed they have been received with something approaching derision.

The Canadian Government, who now have their own High Commissioner in the Island, will fully realise in these circumstances that there can be no prospect of Newfoundlanders, when they come to choose their course for themselves after the war, opting for political union with Canada. What would be the next best thing from the Canadian point of view? What the Canadians want is time, time to win over Newfoundland opinion and to bring home the advantages of the union of the two countries: what would suit them therefore would be something which was calculated to ensure reasonable stability in the Island until there had been opportunity for a policy of breaking down the barriers to take effect. This is exactly what our proposals are calculated to provide. If Newfoundland were to return to self-government, but without continued assistance from us, the result would almost certainly be chaos and a fresh crisis in a few years time; and the likelihood would be that this crisis would arrive *before* there had been any change of outlook towards Canada and while Newfoundlanders were still under the glamorous spell of the lavish American war-time expenditure in the Island, which has been the main factor in transforming them from an insolvent to a self-supporting community. Our proposals would relieve Canadians of this anxiety; for ten years at least the financial and economic position of the Island would be reasonably assured, and this would give them time to get to work on laying fresh foundations for the future. Moreover, in so far as the reconstruction schemes proposed would be calculated to add to the country's earning power, our proposals should be doubly welcome to the Canadians since the prospect would be that Canada, if and when she should take over Newfoundland in the future, would find herself relieved *pro tanto* of the expenditure which she would then otherwise be forced to incur ...

It should be added that it would of course be necessary to keep any discussions with the Canadians on a most secret basis, since any suspicion in Newfoundland that we were in touch with the Canadians regarding our policy in the Island would have the most damaging results.

E) To Special Assistant to Canadian Under-Secretary of State for External Affairs, November 30, 1944
J.S. Macdonald, British High Commissioner in Newfoundland

Dear Mr. Angus,

I appreciate very much your thoughtfulness in sending me an excerpt, dealing with Newfoundland, from the Memorandum on Post-War Plans of the United Kingdom Exchange Control prepared by Messrs. Turk and Tarr of our Foreign Exchange Control Board.

I find this information, supplementing as it does the material set forth in my despatch no. 401 of September 8th and subsequent communications dealing with the future form of government in Newfoundland, of very considerable interest. It helps, in particular, to clear up a point which had puzzled me a good deal, as to how, in view of its own financial situation, the United Kingdom expects to be in a position to give extensive financial aid to Newfoundland after the war.

I greatly doubt that the Dominions Office is receiving any information which would make it feel that "there is a real danger of Newfoundland electing to link up with the United States." It is quite true that there is not the long-established suspicion of the United States that there is, and has been for so long, with respect to Canada; that union with the United States would give Newfoundlanders an assured market for their fish which they could not hope to get by entering the Canadian Federation; that there is a large Irish element in Newfoundland that has no strong feeling of loyalty to the British connection; that Mr. H.M.S. Lewin, General Manager of Bowaters, Limited, and a very influential man on the West Coast, and a number of others have occasionally stressed the advantages of union with the United States; that a large number of Newfoundlanders have found a livelihood in the United States, particularly in the New England States; and that, undoubtedly, if the question ever arose, the attractions of tying-up with the powerful, rich and progressive American Union would have a very powerful appeal. I do not think, however, that the question has ever been seriously considered in Newfoundland and would rather be inclined to think that the United Kingdom officials were greatly exaggerating the possibility.

I would hope, also, that if the proposal outlined to borrow one hundred million dollars from Canada to be furnished to Newfoundland for road building and other development projects is made, it will receive scant consideration. If such a thing were agreed to, it would be a gift rather than a loan, would give rise to little gratitude and take away the meagre bargaining powers that we have.

Yours sincerely,

J.S. Macdonald

F) Memorandum to Prime Minister, September 25, 1945
N.A. Robertson, Under-Secretary of State for External Affairs

Top Secret

Policy Towards Newfoundland

... 6. There would be many advantages in bringing Newfoundland into Confederation at this time. It would solve at one stroke the difficult questions respecting title to the bases, permission to use them for civil aviation, and the right to maintain them for post-war defence. These objectives could probably be secured by negotiating with the Newfoundland Government but negotiation would be uncertain and probably not entirely satisfactory. In view of the United States decision not to withdraw, as was expected, but to maintain and enlarge its bases in Iceland the probability is that the post-war defence problem in Newfoundland will continue to be an important one and one in which Canada should, in its own interest, maintain a prime place. The accession of Newfoundland, with Labrador, moreover, would increase the Canadian population by 300,000 people and enlarge the Dominion by 192,000 square miles, an area nearly four times the size of the Maritime Provinces, possessing very considerable mineral and forest resources as well as the finest fishing grounds in the world. It would add materially to the richness and variety of Canada's resources, enhance her prestige and place in the world and would complete, in effect, the union of all British North America into the Canadian Dominion envisaged by the Fathers of Confederation.

7. It would, also, remove the danger that Newfoundland, if left to itself, will be driven to take measures to emphasize and strengthen its position as a separate political unit. Such measures though not directed specially against Canada would tend, because of your proximity, to affect us chiefly and to place a gradually increasing strain on good relations. Ultimately they might result in Newfoundland and Labrador coming under the United States.

8. There are, of course a number of considerations on the other side of the picture. The presence of the United States bases on the island at St. John's,

Stephenville and Argentia would constitute a limitation on Canada's sovereignty and the accession of Newfoundland to Confederation would tend to strengthen the centrifugal forces within the Dominion. Individualism, sensitiveness to criticism from outside, and a general backwardness of outlook are, moreover, strongly marked characteristics of the Islanders that would not make for tractability or their easy assimilation into the Dominion. Only the first of these conditions is of any real importance, however, and could probably be solved by some scheme for the internationalization of the bases.

9. If the financial arrangements with the Provinces proposed at the Dominion-Provincial Conference of last August are accepted, the process of union, if that be deemed desirable, would be greatly simplified. These new arrangements, together with the Dominion's programme of social security, should provide a basis to bring Newfoundland into Confederation on terms that would be favourable to her without at the same time necessitating very special treatment that is not extended to the other Provinces. In the past this has been one of the main obstacles to union from our point of view.

10. With respect to the cost to the Dominion it is very hazardous to forecast any figure in view of the many unknowns in the equation, as, for example, the degree of severity of Dominion taxation in the future; the effect of union on corporate earnings in Newfoundland; the possibilities of new industries (as, for example, development of the rich iron ore deposits recently discovered in Labrador); the future of world trade on which existing Newfoundland industries so largely depend; the increased markets, especially for consumers' goods, from the rest of Canada which union would bring about. A preliminary survey, however, indicates that exclusive of assistance on public works, the net cost to the Dominion might be of the order of from 5 to 8 millions annually at the outset, though this might well decline if prosperous conditions continued or new industries developed in Newfoundland following union.

11. The last pronouncement of the Canadian Government on the subject was your statement in Parliament on July 12th, 1943. The relevant portion reads as follows:

> "If the people of Newfoundland should ever decide that they wish to enter the Canadian federation and should make that decision clear beyond all possibility of misunderstanding, Canada would give most sympathetic consideration to the proposal."

This statement has usually been interpreted to mean that the initiative is left entirely to Newfoundland. But federation with Canada could not very well be discussed intelligently in the abstract ...

N.A.R[obertson]

G) Memorandum, October 17, 1946
High Commissioner in Newfoundland

The present position in Newfoundland with particular reference to the question of Confederation ...

The Question of Confederation

Interest in the question of Confederation has been growing since approaching termination of the war brought nearer the time that Newfoundlanders would be given an opportunity of expressing their views. It was born, I think, out of admiration for the Canadian war record and a growing realization of the increasing importance of Canada as a nation and was greatly stimulated by the progressive social legislation adopted by Canada in recent years and particularly by the passage of the Family Allowance Act. In considering the development of public opinion in Newfoundland in favour of Confederation we should, however, keep carefully in mind that there is little genuine sentiment in Newfoundland for union with Canada in the positive sense of desiring to be part of the Dominion and to work together for the building up of a great nation stretching from St. John's to Victoria. The sentiment that does exist is rather a negative one, based on the feeling that Newfoundland's economic position is rather precarious and that Newfoundlanders would enjoy greater prosperity and a more assured future in a turbulent world if they were part of the Dominion.

The present is not a particularly propitious time to discuss terms of union with Newfoundland for the tide of prosperity which came with the war shows as yet little sign of receding ...

But while economic conditions are not conducive to the growth of sentiment in favour of Confederation general political conditions are not unfavourable. A large section of the electorate is dubious about the wisdom of handing the country back to the control of the local politicians, whose regimes are still associated with the graft, favouritism and wide-spread misery that prevailed under them. The Commission of Government, it is true, has a wide measure of support among the people who recognize they are better off under it than they were under its predecessor Governments. The new Governor, Sir Gordon Macdonald, is undoubtedly increasing the popularity of the Commission both by the strong lead he is giving in the direction of more progressive administration and by the close contacts he is forming with the people in all parts of the Island. There is undoubtedly, however, a substantial body of opinion that feels so arbitrary a form of Government cannot be justified after a war fought for political freedom and democracy. Confederation with Canada on favourable terms would rally both those who are apprehensive of Newfoundland's ability to stand alone and those who genuinely desire an elected Government, but fear that, as of old, it would abuse its power if it possessed plenary authority. And it would run a better chance of being accepted in a referendum where voters were required to vote either for or against Confederation than if it were put forward, as a party question, in some future Assembly ...

It becomes desirable, therefore, that the Canadian Government consider carefully whether or not it desires to encourage Newfoundland to join the Dominion as the Tenth Province, and, if so, how far it is prepared to go in bringing it about.

Advantages and Disadvantages of Union

The more obvious factors which would require to be taken into consideration in coming to a decision may be set forth briefly as follows:

The accession of Newfoundland would increase the Canadian population by 312,889 people and enlarge the Dominion by 192,000 square miles, an area larger than Finland or Sweden and nearly four times the size of the Maritime Provinces, possessing very considerable mineral and forest resources as well as easy access to the finest fishing grounds in the world. It would solve, permanently, all questions of post-war military and civil aviation rights which are at present terminable after March 31st, 1949, on twelve months' notice. It would make possible a common jurisdiction over North Atlantic Fisheries. It would, in a sense, give Canada a frontage on the Atlantic and "a window towards Europe," and prevent the Dominion being shut off from the Atlantic as it is, to a considerable extent, from the Pacific. It would add materially to the extent and variety of Canada's resources and enhance her prestige and place in the world.

It should not be overlooked, in considering the advantages of Newfoundland to Canada, that those advantages are a good deal more substantial than in 1895 when the subject was last considered. Newfoundland is larger now by 110,000 square miles of territory commonly regarded at that time, in Canada at least, as forming part of the Canadian Labrador but since awarded to Newfoundland by the decision of the Judicial Committee of the Privy Council.

Moreover, the country is richer by the investment of at least $100,000,000 by Canada and at least $300,000,000 by the United States primarily for defence but much of which was spent on roads, wharfs, telephone lines, warehouses and similar buildings, radio ranges, airfields, the training of Newfoundlanders in various technical jobs, etc., and has redounded to the general development of the country.

On the debit side of the account consideration would have to be given to the following points:

On any terms that would be acceptable to Newfoundland the Island would undoubtedly receive from the Federal Treasury for many years a good many millions of dollars per annum more than it would produce in revenue. One important reason for this is that Newfoundland, as a Province, would not be able to raise any substantial amounts, as the existing Provinces do, by taxes on gasoline and motor vehicles. Another reason is that virtually the whole cost of administration falls on the central government of the Island, there being no general system of local taxation, and only a few municipalities all of which, except St. John's, have been established only within the last three years. Newfoundland would thus require a special grant from the Dominion to enable it to carry on as a Province. The crux of the problem of Confederation is to find a formula under which such a grant could be made without appearing to give Newfoundland more favourable terms than the existing Provinces enjoy or which they could make the basis of demands on the federal treasury.

The presence of the United States bases in the Island at St. John's, Stephenville and Argentia, on territory on which the leases have still ninety-five years to run, would constitute a limitation on Canadian sovereignty. Even if the United States would be prepared to hand over the bases to Canada, which is extremely unlikely, the investment involved amounting to more than $300,000,000 is clearly too large a sum to pay for a free hand in Newfoundland and Canada could not, in any case, take over the physical task for which the naval base at Argentia was constructed since it would require a powerful navy disposing of capital ships ...

There is a further point that should be considered. If nothing is done to encourage Newfoundland to come into Confederation the country will be driven, by the force of events, to take measures to emphasize and strengthen its position as a separate economic and political unit. Such measures would doubtless include, among other things, the appointment of Trade Agents to push the sale of Newfoundland fish in the United States, Cuba, the West Indies, Brazil, Spain, Portugal, Italy, Greece and other areas in which Canadian fish are also marketed; the negotiation of Trade Agreements with the countries who are the chief purchasers of Newfoundland products, offering them, in return, a market for their products to the detriment of our exports; the withdrawal of permission to Canadian fishing vessels to store fish and salt in bond while operating on the Banks; the raising of the royalties on iron and other minerals to buttress falling revenues; and the termination of defence rights except on payment of heavy rentals. The quest for diversification would be stimulated involving further development of local manufacturing which already includes paint, nails, rope, tobacco, biscuits, beer and soft drinks, oilskins, clothing, etc., cutting down our market and progressively adding to the vested interests that would be opposed to closer relations with Canada. Newfoundland might even, in view of the fact that it sells so largely to countries allied with sterling, be led to attach itself to the sterling bloc and terminate the special position accorded to Canadian financial institutions. Eventually it might be driven, as its finances became more strained, to offer Labrador, not to Canada, but to the highest bidder — which might well be the United States. Even though the measures taken were not directed specifically against Canada they would, in fact, react more heavily against Canada than against any other country and though we might, by exercising pressure at London and Washington, be able to counter or restrict such moves, obstructive action would inevitably arouse hostility in Newfoundland and permanently embitter relations with Canada.

We cannot, indeed, rule out altogether the possibility of a more far-reaching development — political union with the United States. Such a contingency, though unlikely at the moment, could easily take on great importance if the United States Government, influenced by strategic developments, should desire a freer hand in Newfoundland and Labrador. The immense economic advantages that would flow from the free entry of fish into the United States market; the already large and prosperous Newfoundland community in the new England States which still maintains many ties with its homeland; the large proportion of persons of Irish extraction in Newfoundland population; and the favourable impression created by lavish American spending in the Island, would give the United States powerful instruments with which to exert influence on the people of Newfoundland if it should desire to do so ...

Most of the considerations set forth above, for and against union, are rather intangible in character and are hard to measure or appraise in concrete terms. Generally, however, the conclusion seems clear that it would be in the best interests of Canada to encourage Newfoundland to join the Dominion as the Tenth Province now, provided the annual cost to the Federal Treasury is not too great a price for the advantages the accession of Newfoundland would bring ...

H) Memorandum by Second Political Division, n.d.
P.A. Bridle

1. The Chicago *Tribune* is continuing its campaign in favour of Newfoundland joining the United States. On October 11th it published an editorial, "The Way to Statehood." It makes three main points: (1) 80% of Newfoundlanders are in favour of becoming part of the American union; (2) their desires so far have been frustrated by their own politicians, by members of the "confederation with Canada" clique, as well as by the State Department, which considers Newfoundland a British Empire problem; (3) as a condition to applying for statehood Newfoundlanders must first achieve "independence."

2. The *Tribune* takes credit for having already influenced Newfoundland opinion and says that the Responsible Government League is urging a return to self-government as a preliminary to establishing sovereign relations with the U.S. ...

4. On October 19th the Chicago *Tribune* published an editorial which points [out] that, should Newfoundland wish to become a state of the American union, Americans would have good reason to favour the proposal, in order that they might retain possession of their strategic bases on the Island.

5. On October 22nd the New York *Daily News* and the Washington *Times Herald* carried a column by John O'Donnell which attacked U.S. policy with respect to Newfoundland. The column stated that the U.S. needs Green-

land and Newfoundland "to defend itself from an air bomb attack as vitally as a man needs his right fist in a slugging match." It said that, according to what it calls "the restrained, formal observations of Canada's Defence Minister Brooke Claxton," the situation, so far as United States bases are concerned, "would have to be looked at." It interprets this statement as meaning that, if Newfoundland becomes part of Canada, United States bases will come under the Canadian military control — the United States being allowed to staff them if they want to but taking "top orders" from Ottawa. The column claims that President Truman secretly approves this idea and says that Canadians believe that he has entered into "a secret agreement" with Prime Minister Mackenzie King to the effect that Canada has complete right to keep any foreign military establishment off its soil. The column asserts that "Newfoundlanders" have been told that President Truman would allow Canada to take over U.S. bases in Newfoundland in the event of Confederation ...

P.A. B[ridle]

I)   Speech to the National Convention, October 28, 1946
Joseph Smallwood

... I introduced my resolution [to the National Convention] on October 28, 1946... Then I launched into my speech.

"Our people's struggle to live commenced on the day they first landed here, four centuries and more ago, and has continued to this day. The struggle is more uneven now than it was then, and the people view the future now with more dread than they felt a century ago.

"The newer conceptions of what life can be, of what life should be, have widened our horizons and deepened our knowledge of the great gulf which separates what we have and are from what we feel we should have and be. We have been taught by newspapers, magazines, motion pictures, radios, and visitors something of the higher standards of well-being of the mainland of North America; we have become uncomfortably aware of the low standards of our country, and we are driven irresistibly to wonder whether our attempt to persist in isolation is the root-cause of our condition. We have often felt in the past, when we learned something of the higher standards of the mainland, that such things belonged to another world, that they were not for us. But today we are not so sure that two yardsticks were designed by the Almighty to measure the standards of well-being: one yard-stick for the mainland of the continent; another for this Island which lies beside it. Today we are not so sure, not so ready to take it for granted, that we Newfoundlanders are destined to accept much lower standards of life than our neighbours of Canada and the United States. Today we are more disposed to feel that our manhood, our very creation by God, entitles us to standards of life no lower than those of our brothers on the mainland.

"Our Newfoundland is known to possess natural wealth of considerable value and variety. Without at all exaggerating their extent, we know that our fisheries are in the front rank of the world's marine wealth. We have considerable forest, water power, and mineral resources. Our Newfoundland people are industrious, hard-working, frugal, ingenious, and sober. The combination of such natural resources and such people should spell a prosperous country enjoying high standards, Western World standards, of living. This combination should spell fine, modern, well-equipped homes; lots of health-giving food; ample clothing; the amenities of modern New World civilization; good roads, good schools, good hospitals, high levels of public and private health; it should spell a vital, prosperous, progressive country.

"It has not spelt any such things. Compared with the mainland of North America, we are fifty years, in some things a hundred years, behind the times. We live more poorly, more shabbily, more meanly. Our life is more a struggle. Our struggle is tougher, more naked, more hopeless. In the North American family, Newfoundland bears the reputation of having the lowest standards of life, of being the least progressive and advanced, of the whole family.

"We all love this land. It has a charm that warms our hearts, go where we will; a charm, a magic, a mystical tug on our emotion that never dies. With all her faults, we love her.

"But a metamorphosis steals over us the moment we cross the border that separates us from other lands. As we leave Newfoundland, our minds undergo a transformation: we expect, and we take for granted, a higher, a more modern, way of life such as it would have seemed ridiculous or even avaricious to expect at home. And as we return to Newfoundland, we leave that higher standard behind, and our minds undergo a reverse transformation: we have grown so accustomed to our own lower standards and more antiquated methods and old-fashioned conveniences that we readjust ourselves unconsciously to the meaner standards under which we grew up. We are so used to our railway and our coastal boats that we scarcely see them;

so used to our settlements, and roads, and homes, and schools, and hospitals and hotels and everything else that we do not even see their inadequacy, their backwardness, their seaminess.

"We have grown up in such an atmosphere of struggle, of adversity, of mean times that we are never surprised, never shocked, when we learn that we have one of the highest rates of tuberculosis in the world; one of highest maternity mortality rates in the world; one of the highest rates of beriberi and rickets in the world. We take these shocking facts for granted. We take for granted our lower standards, our poverty. We are not indignant about them. We save our indignation for those who publish such facts, for with all our complacency, with all our readiness to receive, to take for granted, and even to justify these things amongst ourselves, we are, strange to say, angry and hurt when these shocking facts become known to the outside world.

"We are all very proud of our Newfoundland people. We all admire their strength, their skill, their adaptability, their resourcefulness, their industry, their frugality, their sobriety, and their warm-hearted, simple generosity. We are proud of them; but are we indignant, does our blood boil, when we see the lack of common justice with which they are treated? When we see how they live? When we witness the long, grinding struggle they have? When we see the standards of their life? Have we compassion in our hearts for them? Or are we so engrossed, so absorbed, in our own struggle to live in this country that our social conscience has become toughened, even case-hardened? Has our own hard struggle to realize a modest competence so blinded us that we have little or no tenderness of conscience left to spare for the fate of the tens of thousands of our brothers so very much worse off than ourselves?

"Mr. Chairman, in the present and prospective world chaos, with all its terrible variety of uncertainty, it would be cruel and futile, now that that the choice is ours, to influence the handful of people who inhabit this small Island to attempt independent national existence. The earnings of our 65,000 families may be enough, in the years ahead, to support them half-decently and at the same time support the public services of a fair-sized municipality. But will those earnings support independent national government on an expanding, or even the present, scale? Except for a few years of this war and a few of the last, our people's earnings never supported them on a scale comparable with North American standards, and never maintained a government even on the pre-war scale of service. Our people never enjoyed a good standard of living, and never were able to yield enough taxes to maintain the government. The difference was made up by borrowing or grants-in-aid.

"We can indeed reduce our people's standard of living; we can force them to eat and wear and use and have much less than they have; and we can deliberately lower the level of governmental services. Thus we might manage precariously to maintain independent national status. We can resolutely decide to be poor but proud. But if such a decision is made, it must be made by the 60,000 families who would have to do the sacrificing, not the 5,000 families who are confident of getting along pretty well in any case.

"We have, I say, a perfect right to decide that we will turn away from North American standards of public services, and condemn ourselves as a people and government deliberately to long years of struggle to maintain even the little that we have. We may, if we wish, turn our backs upon the North American continent beside which God placed us, and resign ourselves to the meaner outlook and shabbier standards of Europe, 2,000 miles across the ocean. We can do this, or we can face the fact that the very logic of our situation on the surface of the globe impels us to draw close to the progressive outlook and dynamic living standards of this continent.

"Our danger, so it seems to me, is that of nursing delusions of grandeur. We remember the stories of small states that valiantly preserved their national independence and developed their own proud cultures, but we tend to overlook the fact that comparison of Newfoundland with them is ludicrous. We are not a nation. We are merely a medium-size municipality, a mere miniature borough of a large city. Dr. Carson, Patrick Morris, and John Kent were sound in the first decades of the nineteenth century when they advocated cutting the apron-strings that bound us to the Government of the United Kingdom; but the same love of Newfoundland, the same Newfoundland patriotism, that inspired their agitation then would now, if they lived, drive them to carry the agitation to its logical conclusion of taking the next step of linking Newfoundland closely to the democratic, developing mainland of the New World. There was indeed a time when tiny states lived gloriously. That time is now ancient European history. We are trying to live in the mid-twentieth-century, post-Hitler New World. We are living in a world in which small countries have less chance than ever before of surviving.

"We can, of course, persist in isolation, a dot on the shore of North America, ... struggling vainly to support ourselves and our greatly expanded public services. Reminded continually by radio, movie, and visitor of greatly higher standards of living across the Gulf, we can shrug incredulously or dope ourselves into the hopeless belief that such things are not for us. By our isolation from the throbbing vitality and expansion of the continent, we have been left far behind in the march of time, the "sport of historic misfortune" the "Cinderella of the Empire". Our choice now is to continue in blighting isolation or seize the opportunity that may beckon us to the wider horizons and higher standards of unity with the progressive mainland of America.

"I am not one of those, if any such there be, who would welcome federal union with Canada at any price. There are prices which I, as a Newfoundlander whose ancestry in this country reaches back for nearly two centuries, am not willing that Newfoundland should pay. I am agreeable to the idea that our country should link itself federally with that great British nation, but I am not agreeable that we should ever be expected to forget that we are Newfoundlanders with a great history and a great tradition of our own. I agree that there may be much to gain from linking our fortunes with that great nation. But I insist that as a self-governing province of the Dominion, we should continue to enjoy the right to our own distinctive culture. I do not deny that once we affiliated with the Canadian federal union, we should in all fairness be expected to extend the scope of our loyalty to embrace the federation as a whole. I do not deny this claim at all, but I insist that as a constituent part of the federation, we should continue to be quite free to hold to our love of our own dear land.

"Nor am I one of those, if there be any such, who would welcome union with Canada without regard for the price that the Dominion might be prepared to pay.

"I pledge myself to this House and to this country that I will base my ultimate stand in this whole question of Confederation upon the nature of the terms that are laid before the Convention and the country. If the terms are such as clearly to suggest a better Newfoundland for our people, I shall support and maintain them. If they are not of such a nature, I shall oppose them with all the means I can command.

"In the price we pay and the price we exact, my only standard of measurement is the welfare of the people. This is my approach to the whole question of federal union with Canada. It is in this spirit that I move this resolution today.

"Confederation I will support if it means a lower cost of living for our people. Confederation I will support if it means a higher standard of life for our people. Confederation I will support if it means strength, stability, and security for Newfoundland.

"I will support Confederation if it gives us democratic government. I will support Confederation if it rids us of Commission Government. I will support Confederation if it gives us responsible government under conditions that will give responsible government a real chance to succeed. Confederation I will support if it makes us a province enjoying privileges and rights no lower than any other province.

"These, then, are the conditions of my support of Confederation: that it must raise our people's standard of living, that it must give Newfoundlanders a better life, that is must give our country stability and security, and that it must give us full, democratic responsible government under circumstances that will ensure its success.

"Mr. Chairman, gentlemen, I have given a statement of my faith, but I do not expect members to support this motion for the reasons that impel me to do so.

"Members no doubt have a variety of reasons of their own, and their support of this resolution does not at all necessarily imply agreement with mine. There are many cases to be made for submitting and supporting this resolution quite apart from those I have given here today.

"In the name of the people of Bonavista Centre and of thousands of other Newfoundlanders throughout this Island, I move this resolution. I believe that this move will lead to a brighter and happier life for our Newfoundland people. If you adopt this resolution, and Canada offers us generous terms, as I believe she will, and Newfoundland decides to shake off her ancient isolation, I believe with all my heart and mind that the people will bless the day this resolution was moved. With God's grace, let us move forward for a brighter and happier Newfoundland."

J) To Canadian Secretary of State for External Affairs, January 9, 1948
J.S. Macdonald, British High Commissioner in Newfoundland

Despatch 13

Sir,

Referring to my despatch No. 9 of January 6th I have the honour to report that Major Cashin occupied the full time of the last two sessions of the National Convention with the continuation of his speech on the Canadian Proposals which he began on January 6th ...

2. Major Cashin at Wednesday's session resumed by claiming as unrealistic the figure of $20,000,000, mentioned in the Grey Book as the amount which Canada could expect to obtain from Newfoundland in the event of Union. In the first place, said the speaker, this country is now raising ten and a half million dollars annually from Personal Income Taxes, Corporation Taxes and Death Duties and it is ridiculous for the Canadian Government to anticipate a revenue of only about $11,000,000 from these sources. Under Confederation income tax rates would be higher and lower revenue groups would be subject to the tax, and the Major then quoted rates and revenues effected by Canadian income tax, also death duties and corporation taxes being higher in Canada it is logical to expect a greater revenue from these sources. Emphasis was put on the fact that in Newfoundland no death duties are attached to life insurance policies made payable to beneficiaries.

3. Major Cashin declared that the figure of $2,000,000 anticipated from customs duties in the event of Confederation was incorrect. "Does it mean," said the Major, "that we won't be allowed to trade with the United States, Great Britain or anywhere else except Canada under Confederation? Last year alone on imports of $25,000,000 from the United States customs duties of $3,000,000 were collected."

4. The question of revenue from liquor and tobacco sales was then taken up. The speaker claimed that last year Newfoundland collected $1,500,000 from liquor sales and $2,000,000 from tobacco and cigarette sales. He thought that the customs revenues from these sources of $400,000 and $500,000 respectively, given in the Grey Book, [were] ridiculously low taking into account the higher rate of taxes in Canada. "Today," said Major Cashin, "we pay thirty-five cents for a package of Lucky Strikes, under Confederation we would pay fifty-two cents."

5. In the final analysis the Major contended that the Canadian Government would collect revenue of $30,0000,000 from Newfoundland and not $20,000,000 as anticipated in the Proposals. We would be smothered under all sorts of taxes, namely, Income Tax, Sales Tax, Poll Tax, Federal Tax, Provincial Tax, Municipal Tax, Luxury Tax, School Tax, Hospital Tax and goodness knows how many more taxes.

6. Under Confederation, continued the speaker, the Agreements with the operating Companies for the exclusive employment of Newfoundland workmen would cease to exist and all Canadians would be eligible for these jobs.

7. Major Cashin alleged that there was a connection between the pressure which at the present time was being brought to bear on Newfoundland to enter Confederation and the visit made several years ago of Professor R.A. MacKay to Newfoundland and the appointment of a Canadian High Commissioner in 1941.

8. The Major attacked the Family Allowance Act as the most immoral and corrupt enactment which had ever stained the pages of the Statutes of Canada. An enactment, said he, brought into force to bribe the French-speaking population of Canada into supporting conscription. The people seem to forget, said the Major, that the money for these allowances comes from the taxpayer after all.

9. The Canadian Old Age Pensions Act then bore the brunt of the Major's remarks. He said that to become eligible for a pension the applicant must practically be a pauper and must assign to the Government any property or assets he may have and which, when he dies, are taken over by the Government and sold to reimburse it for the pensions paid.

10. In so far as Unemployment Insurance is concerned the Major stated that it would not apply to fishermen, loggers, miners, farmers or longshoremen, the bulk of the Newfoundland labour class.

11. The speaker asked whether Canada was, after all, such a prosperous and solvent country. A few months ago it had to seek a loan of $700,000,000 from the United States Government and was only granted $300,000,000.

12. The Federal Government offered to take over the operation of the Railway and general transportation system but, said the Major, did not guarantee to maintain the present schedules or keep the present employees with their pension scheme. Canada contemplated spending $30,0000,000 annually in Newfoundland and in return would take over approximately $120,000,000 in assets without taking into account any profits which may accrue from the development of the Labrador properties and under Confederation Newfoundland would, of course, lose any bargaining power for economic concessions from the United States from the presence on her soil of United States bases.

13. Speaking on the subject of Newfoundland's surplus Major Cashin pointed out that $10,000,000 is to be placed on deposit with the Federal Government, nearly $10,000,000 is now to the credit of Newfoundland in London in the form of interest-free loans and this amount would have to be converted to dollars, $6,000,000 must be held in abeyance for the payment

of last year's fish contracts which leaves in dollar currency a cash surplus of $4,000,000 instead of around $30,000,000.

14. At Thursday's session Major Cashin resumed his remarks by considering the question of the sales tax from which source according to the proposals the Federal Government could expect to obtain from Newfoundland revenue amounting to $4,000,000. The amount should be $8,000,000 for Newfoundland's population, said the speaker, because the 1946-47 returns from this tax in Canada showed that Canadians paid an average of $25.00 per head under this form of taxation for the period.

15. Major Cashin then turned to Mr. Smallwood's estimate of a provincial budget which, according to the Major, was the most glaring and high-flying attempt at frenzied finance that he had ever witnessed and which provided for an annual provincial expenditure of fifteen and a half million dollars. Reviewing the provisions of Mr. Smallwood's budget for each department and commenting that they were completely inadequate, the speaker then gave his idea of the financial needs of Newfoundland as a province as amounting to a minimum of $19,275,000 the breakdown being as follows: Finance (administration) $200,000; Pensions $200,000; Interest and sinking fund $375,000; Provincial legislature $200,000; Assessor of Taxes $10,500; Home Affairs $300,000; Education $3,750,000; Justice $1,100,000; Natural Resources $2,500,000; Public Works $4,000,000; Public Health and Welfare $6,500,000; Liquor Control $35,000.

16. Turning to revenues the Major arrived at a total of $9,762,000. To this figure should be added the transitional grant of three and a half millions yearly for the first three years of union thereafter reducing itself by $350,000 a year while the grant would totally disappear after the twelfth year of union. Eight years' revenue would amount to approximately $77,000,000 which with $23,000,000 of transitional grants would amount to about $100,000,000. Eight years' expenditure would total around $156,000,000 or a deficit of nearly $56,000,000. This deficit could only be met from the $10,000,000 Trust Fund set up at the beginning of union while additional taxation of $46,000,000 would have to be imposed on the people to meet the balance. Even if the $16,000,000 held in sterling were converted to dollars and the $4,000,000 cash surplus were applied against the deficit, the Government would still have to find $20,000,000 in taxation. The proposed Royal Commission would then recommend either increased taxation or the sale or lease of Labrador either to Quebec Province or the Federal Government.

17. The only reason Canada wants Newfoundland, said the Major, is for the iron ore and the fifty or sixty million cords of wood in Labrador. By the inclusion of Newfoundland into the federation Canada would be in the position of controlling the entire steel industry of the entire North American Continent. He then compared the present situation to the sale of Alaska by Russia to the United States for a mere pittance.

18. Summing up the Major said that the terms were fraudulent, not equitable and did not constitute a fair basis of union ...

I have etc.

J.S. Macdonald

K) Newfoundland National Convention: Debates January 27, 1948
P. Cashin

Mr. Cashin: Mr. Chairman, ... is this convention ... of the opinion that union with Canada should be recommended to our people as a possible form of government in the forthcoming referendum? On this we are, as representatives of the Newfoundland people, asked to make a decision. For myself, my conclusion in the light of all the information at my disposal is, that it would be neither wise or profitable for us to recommend such a form of government to our people; and I propose in my remarks to give my reasons for saying so. I will as best I can explain to you why I believe that the so-called proposals are not alone without the virtue of being properly negotiated terms, but that they fail to present either a true or complete picture of the real position. Indeed, for myself, I find them more remarkable for what they conceal than for what they actually tell us; that instead of being possessed of the dignity or standing of a legitimate contractual agreement between two countries, they resemble more the brief of a slick salesman trying to sell a defective bill of goods to a gullible people. In short, Mr. Chairman, I regard them as an insult to the intelligence of this Convention, and a reflection on the sound common sense of all the people of Newfoundland...

I do realise, as everyone with intelligence must realise, the value of free enterprise. All democratic peoples know that capital and labour depend upon each other for existence. I know and you know, that without the so-called capitalists the great United States would not be where she is today. Canada, the much vaunted Canada, had her resources developed and her railways constructed, and their country opened up only through and with the driving power of capitalism, and the same thing applies to the British Empire, and if we look at our history we find that the same thing applies to this country. I know and you know, that today the country which is the envy of all the world, whose people enjoy the highest standard of living, is also the country which has the greatest number of rich individuals per square mile than any country on earth. Must we put two and two together? Do we not also know what happened to those countries in which agitators arose to turn the people of the country against those possessing money? Yes, these people destroyed the capitalists, but at the same time they destroyed their own country — a Hitler, a Mussolini, and a Stalin replaced the banker and industrialist and the merchant. Would anyone want that sort of thing to happen here? Listening to the heated abuse which Mr. Smallwood directed at the successful business organisations of this country, and the businessmen, the same businessmen who furnished the fishermen with their ships, the men who built the factories, the men who started new industries, the men who employ thousands of our people at union wages, the men who, [it] is estimated, pay large annual sums to our treasury by way of annual taxation. Listening to his unreasonable attacks on these people on Friday, I somehow got the idea that for the first time a new and unsavory and even alien note had been injected into the proceedings of this Convention. It seemed to me that a foreign influence was loose: the spirit of Trotsky, the virulent harangue of the soapbox orator playing on the discontent of an unthinking and innocent people. If patriotism, it has been said, is the last refuge of a scoundrel, then it seems to me to be equally true that the setting of class against class is the last refuge of the political demagogue. When all else fails, when his case can't be won on its merits, there is always available the red banner with the words inscribed upon it, "Down with the rich."

Political history shows that there is only one worse thing, and that is the setting of creed against creed. Let us hope that such a thing will never be allowed, as I am sure it will not be, to raise its ugly head in this country. The people of Newfoundland, in spite of Mr. Smallwood's words, were always ready to put their trust in our businessmen. It has always been so in the past and it is just as true today, for have we not here in this very chamber many of them — prominent and well-known businessmen, some of them even representing Mr. Smallwood's hated corporations? These men were selected by the people to represent them and to protect their interests, and I know, and our people themselves know, that these men will do their jobs as best they know how. Certainly, I admit that our businessmen and our New-foundland corporations have made money, just as similar businessmen all over the North American continent have made money, and this applies, as I will show later on, even in that place of perfection, the Dominion of Canada. Many Newfoundlanders were well aware of that because we send them each year some $40 million. But let us be fair about this matter. Let us see if our wealthy men are the evil characters that Mr. Smallwood would have us believe. Is it not to these same individuals that a great portion of our people must look for wages? Union wages, sir, based on a mutual agreement between the worker and the employer. Must we not also give them credit for keeping money in this country, circulating it amongst our people instead of it being drained off by foreign corporations? ...

I repeat that the deficit on the proposed provincial budget would be not less than $9 million annually, and that in order to balance that account increased taxes would have to be placed on our people in the way of further sales tax, hospital tax, property tax, educational tax, municipal tax, and God knows how many other kinds of taxes.

I know that the advocates of confederation do not look at this matter in the light of what would accrue for provincial administration. Their sole ambition is to stress to our people the advantages to our people that would accrue from the payment of baby bonuses, and the vilification of our merchants, etc. I know that is their policy, but I tell them now that knowingly or unknowingly they are traitors to their country. Some of us have been accused of national treachery ...

I would throw that back at the faces of those who so accuse us, and tell them that the proposals contained in the Grey Book sent us by His Excellency the Governor by Prime Minister King are not such as would constitute an equitable basis of union of our two countries, and should not be submitted to the people at the coming national referendum. I tell those that would accuse us of national treachery, and who would advocate such proposals, they themselves can by their very own actions claim the first right and title to this dishonourable name. To me sir, it seems that any Newfoundlander, or group of Newfoundlanders, who deliberately set out to pass all that they are and have across the traitor's counter, I say such people owe an explanation of their attitude.

I have yet to hear them give us that explanation. To trifle with a people and a country, to compromise the lives of future generations, are no small things. Yet that is the very thing that is now being attempted, to the end that we shall cease to exist as an independent country, and that Newfoundlanders shall be no longer Newfoundlanders. I would go on at much greater length than the time allotted to me in showing why this country of ours should not and must not allow itself and its nationhood to be absorbed by the dominion to the west it, but I think that I should avail of the short time left to me in attempting to boil this whole thing down to its broad outlines, and see the thing at its proper worth. Does not all this confederation business come down to a matter of a cold, commercial business deal, whereby we were asked to sell out our country and our future to Canada for a certain sum of money? And speaking of this attitude, I confess it seems to me to be a terribly serious thing for any country or any people to place themselves in the balance against the pull of Canadian dollars. What is the price, or shall I say the bribe, they offer us? The prize bait seems to be that a certain number of our people will get this thing called the baby bonus. But do they tell us that this baby bonus is an unsubstantial thing, that it is something that we cannot depend upon? That it may vanish overnight, and that in the event of a depression in Canada it will die a quick death? Indeed, my own personal opinion is that it will not exist longer than two years. Do they tell us that when our babies reach the age of 16 they will spend the rest of their lives paying back to the Canadian government the amount of their bonus? Do they tell us that when our babies reach military age they will almost certainly be conscripted into the Canadian military forces? Do they tell us that in the event of confederation a big percentage of these young people will have to emigrate from this country to seek employment which cannot be found at home? Of course they do not tell us those things, because they know, and know well, that if we saw the truth of these things this baby bonus would be no longer able to bluff and deceive us...

Soon I trust, Mr. Chairman, our people will be called upon to once again mark their cross upon a national ballot paper ... That "X" will be written by every real Newfoundlander on a day not too far distant. It too will indicate, if correctly placed, our love and our affection for the land of our birth. I ask you gentlemen to ponder and hesitate before you make that little mark by which you, your children, and your children's children can be blessed or blasted. That cross must be the kiss of love given by every loyal citizen to our own mother—Newfoundland. Take care, I say, that it is placed with zeal and loyalty just where it belongs, just where she wishes it, and tremble like Iscariot ere you place it on your own shame and future despair, in the place that means your traitorous denial of your mother country's best interests ... once done it cannot be undone. It is final, irrevocable and unchangeable...

In closing, I can think of no more appropriate words to say than that which I regard as having been prostituted for another purpose in this Assembly a couple of weeks ago, for this is the time, this is the hour, this is the moment when from the hearts of every one of us who love this country who wish her, well the prayer should go forth: "God guard thee, Newfoundland."

L) *The Confederate*, May 31, 1948
Are You In This List?

To all mothers: Confederation would mean that NEVER AGAIN would there be a hungry child in Newfoundland. If you have children under the age of 16, you will receive EVERY MONTH a cash allowance for every child you have or may have.

To all war veterans: Canada treats her Veterans better than ANY OTHER COUNTRY in the world. She has just increased their War Pensions 25%. Under Confederation you will be BETTER TREATED than under any other form of government.

To all wage workers: All wage-workers will be protected by Unemployment Insurance. Newfoundland, under Confederation, will be opened up and developed. Your country will be prosperous. Your condition will be better.

To all over 65: You would have something to look forward to at the age of 70. The Old Age Pension of $30 a month for yourself, and $30 a month for your wife ($60 a month between you) will protect you against need in your old age.

To all railroaders: You will become employees of the biggest railway in the world, the C.N.R. You will have SECURITY and STABILITY as C.N.R. employees. Your wages and working conditions will be the same as on the C.N.R. Under Responsible or Commission you face sure and certain wage-cuts and lay-offs. You, your wives and sons and daughters and other relatives should flock out on June 3 and vote for Confederation.

To all building workers: Under Confederation Newfoundland will share fully in the Canadian Government Housing Plan, under which cities and towns are financed to build houses, 1,000 new houses will be built in St. John's under this Plan.

To all light-keepers: You will become employees of the Government of Canada. Your wages and working conditions will be greatly improved. You will be treated just the same as the light-keepers in the 5 Canadian lighthouses already in Newfoundland.

To all postal-telegraph workers: You will all become employees of the Government of Canada, at higher salaries and much better working conditions.

To all customs officials: You will become employees of the Government of Canada, at better salaries and much better working conditions.

To all Gander workers: You who are now employed by the Newfoundland Government will become employees of the Government of Canada. The Department of Transport of the Government of Canada will operate Gander. They will not try to make Gander pay by cutting you down and trying to make you pay the costs of operating the Airport. Everybody on Gander will be better off under Confederation.

To all fishermen: The cost of living will come down. The cost of producing fish will come down. The Government of Canada will stand back of our fisheries. The Fish Prices Support Board of Canada, backed by Canada's millions, will protect the price of your fish.

To all Newfoundlanders: The cost of living will come down. The 120,000 children in our country will live better. The 10,000 Senior Citizens of our country will be protected in their old age. Newfoundland will be linked up with a strong, rich British nation. Newfoundland will go ahead with Canada.

GIVE YOURSELF A CHANCE. GIVE THE CHILDREN A CHANCE. GIVE NEWFOUNDLAND A CHANCE. VOTE FOR CONFEDERATION AND A HEALTHIER, HAPPIER NEWFOUNDLAND.

13

"Ignorant, Lazy and Unaware"

The Debate over Progressive Education

Documents

A) "Is Alberta Education a Failure? No...", Alberta Teachers' Association Magazine, December, 1947
   A.L. Doucette, Faculty of Education, University of Alberta

B) Report of the Superintendent of Winnipeg Schools, 1937–8
   Manitoba Department of Education

C) Programme of Studies for the Intermediate School (Grades VII, VIII, IX), 1935
   Alberta Department of Education

D) "New Schools for Democracy," Behind the Headlines, 1944
   C.E. Phillips

E) So Little for the Mind, 1950
   Hilda Neatby

F) "Culture? Liberal Education? Education For Democracy? ... Does Anybody Know?", The Teachers' Magazine, February, 1954
   J.M. Paton

G) "Dr. Neatby's 'Doctored' Diatribe: An Unblushingly Biased Review of an Unblushingly Biased Book", The Teachers' Magazine, February, 1954
   J.M. Paton

W hat function do schools serve in the twentieth century? Society and technology, after all, change so rapidly that years of accumulated knowledge sometimes seems entirely irrelevant in the brutal reality of the real world beyond the school yard. No wonder many students feel cynical about their education as they launch themselves out the school door for the last time, tentatively clutching their sacred diplomas. On the other hand, few go as far as Pink Floyd, suggesting that "We don't need no education."

This confusion over the role of education is not solely a phenomenon of the late twentieth century. Canadian students, parents, and educators regularly wrestled over the role and purpose of schools in Canada, and never more so than during the 1950s. The answer initially seemed straightforward: teach people what they need to know after they graduate. But does everyone need the same thing? And what about society's requirements? Should schools limit themselves to transmitting factual knowledge, or should they act as socializing agents for the nation? Should they inculcate young Canadians with a sense of their heritage, or look exclusively toward society's occupational demands?

It was easier in pre-industrial society. Then, education was not "public," limited instead to practical skills children absorbed in the family environment. Only the lucky few went to formal educational institutions beyond the primary level, and there, education remained largely limited to the classics. The state remained virtually uninvolved in the process, instead allowing religious institutions or private individuals to create schools and establish curricula. Thus it is hardly surprising that standards varied wildly from one part of the nation to the next.

The advent of the industrial revolution and the nineteenth-century philosophy of positivism changed that. Society became far more diverse, complex, and demanding. Suddenly nations needed citizens who could do far more than plough a perfect furrow. Nineteenth-century positivists believed it possible to accurately quantify and measure human behaviour and calculate how it fitted society's needs. Thus, if one wanted public education, as increasing numbers of Canadians did, the form and function it took could be codified based upon scientific investigation.

As schooling expanded, the old methods based upon rote memorization of supposedly useful facts absorbed under threat of corporal punishment slowly gave way to "progressive education." Based on psychological studies, the new approach concluded that children go through phases of development and must be inspired to learn relevant information, rather than absorb anachronistic classics that only served the tiny minority who went on to universities.

This new progressive education expanded, but did so only after a considerable battle with conservatives who feared that child-centred learning put too much emphasis on the student's enjoyment to the detriment of knowledge. The old guard argued that school must serve the nation by producing loyal graduates exposed to the great works of western civilization and by enabling students to develop and follow a logical argument in fluid prose. Education, they said, was the gradual attainment of intellectual power, not some nebulous "how-to" process. The world, after all, was a difficult place, and stressing a comfortable environment would do more harm than good in the long run.

The progressives struggled on, backed by the latest scientific studies that proved that the old ways did not create citizens capable of taking their places in modern mass participation democracies. They set out to replace the old formalism with a new kind of learning based on individual students' interests, abilities, and experiences, not upon obscure Greek paradigms. Children learned practical skills, such as co-operation, at the primary level, because it related more directly to their lives beyond the schoolyard. Progressive educators streamed high school students according to ability and aptitude: less cerebral youth were shuffled off to vocational programs while those destined for university focussed on academic subjects.

Massive post-war reconstruction plus a soaring population ensured that Canada boomed in the 1950s. Huge immigration and a marked increase in the birthrate put enormous pressure on school systems from Newfoundland to British Columbia. Simultaneously, it became increasingly obvious that modern governments had to take a role in how and what their children are taught. This, of course, required major expenditures of public money, and voters increasingly insisted upon knowing whether they received appropriate bang from their school-tax buck. The old argument between the "new pedagogy" and the more conservative approach to education once again boiled over. The root of the debate, however, remained essentially the same, gaining urgency because of the enormous number of children and the astronomical costs involved.

Detractors of progressive education railed that students now graduated feeling positive about themselves, but unable to mount a reasonable argument, write cogent sentences, or comprehend their cultural roots. That, said critics like Hilda Neatby, served neither the student nor society. Supporters, on the other hand, argued that an ability to regurgitate a list of early Canadian explorers served no purpose, but that healthy and happy children who liked working together grew into mature citizens capable of contributing to the dynamic growth of the nation.

Little is known about the authors of the first three documents in this chapter, but C.E. Phillips of the Ontario College of Education published the first major historical survey of education in this country, *The Development of Education in Canada*, in 1957. Widely read, it is still considered a monumental pioneering study.

Hilda Neatby (1904–1975) was perhaps the most articulate of the "back to basics" movement in the 1950s. Her book *So Little for the Mind*, published in

1953, established her as a virulent critic of what she saw as a degenerative school system leveling students to the lowest common denominator, and eliminating the pursuit of intellectual rigour. Her detractors, mainly educators and educational bureaucrats, dismissed her as an elitist. Neatby's book, however, struck a chord among Canadians, and it certainly encouraged wide debate. Born in England, Neatby went to the universities of Saskatchewan and Minnesota, and finally to the Sorbonne in Paris. She was a long-time history professor at the University of Saskatchewan, specializing in early Quebec.

James M. Paton spent a lifetime in education. In the 1930s he taught history and English in Hamilton and Toronto secondary schools. He then moved to Quebec where, as a professor, he taught English in what is now the faculty of education at McGill University. From there he became, from 1949–63, General Secretary of the Provincial Association of Protestant Teachers of Quebec, and finally, Professor of Education in the Department of Education at the University of Toronto. Paton researched and wrote widely on education, producing textbooks for secondary school English and numerous articles on educational philosophy, and editing two teachers' professional journals. He retired in 1972.

A) "Is Alberta Education a Failure? No...", Alberta Teachers' Association Magazine, December, 1947
A.L. Doucette, Faculty of Education, University of Alberta

Any adequate educational program must assist the individual child to mature from his initial state of independence to a participation in rich group life, which in a democracy includes full sharing in group living as a responsible member of society. The good life should be made available to all, both privileged and underprivileged, and one aim of a democratic society should be the elimination of an underprivileged state of existence.

Knowledge is acquired in human experience in the process of living in a culture of social groups. Living is the process of interaction between the organism and the environment.

For the *experimentalist* thinker, ideas are the result of consequences in experience ... Life experience and life expectations are the result of studying how the *human* being behaves in *human* experience.

Such moral behavior as regard for others, tolerance, even the simple experience of "taking turns", grows out of practice and experience. The test of good music is in the hearing of it, and as a result we place our stamp of approval or disapproval on it. Alternatives generally are decided in the light of tested experience. Such decisions represent the habit of weighing our thoughts or of acting thoughtfully. For the *experimentalist*, human values are the result of tested choice.

Let us list some of the principles which the experimentalist holds dear, and which are related to progressive education and to the democratic way of life:

1. Experimentalism stresses the supreme worth of the individual.

2. Experimentalism stands by the golden rule of conduct because it has been found to be practical and the result of tested experience.

3. Experimentalism advocates mutual respect between individuals, co-operation, and an active sharing of responsibility on the part of the individual in his group interaction.

4. Experimentalism stresses the freeing of intelligence and is opposed to the curbing of intelligence by a dictator or by state control.

5. Experimentalism cannot accept absolute values because they are out of the realm of tested experience.

6. Experimentalism accepts goals within experience, such goals being continuously modified by subsequent experience.

7. Experimentalism aims to train for democratic living by educating its members to manage society cooperatively.

Progressive education is a means of implementing the philosophy of experimentalism. Thinking is not limited to the intellectual. The effective use of intelligence applies to all and any phase of life, be it physical, mental, emotional or social.

But thinking must be based on data and this calls for a careful study and interpretation of facts — not the memory of facts, but rather the use of reason in the interpretation of facts. If we wish to evaluate a given social theory, for example, it is necessary to have all the facts before we are in a position to know fully the significance of such a theory. If we lack sufficient evidence, or if we are biased because of prejudice, then we are unable to give a sound judgment. Even after passing judgment on the theory, the latter must stand the pragmatic test of application in experience.

A child growing up in a culture must learn the essential elements of the culture. The function of the school is threefold: (i) it must transmit the culture, (ii) it must maintain the culture, and (iii) it must improve the culture. Our modern culture, based as it is on science and industry, is characterized by rapid change. Our schools, our curricula, and our educational methods must change in order to keep pace with the rapid development in the material, social, and spiritual phases of the culture. If our curriculum and methods are static, then we shall intensify the present cultural lag of our social and spiritual institutions behind our material institutions. The school, as a social institution, must not contribute to this social lag by its own lag in methods and functions. Our material and scientific achievements are far behind our man-to-man and man-to-spirit relations. We have an atom bomb, but we lack the social control to make it serve mankind profitably. We have a newer psychology of child growth and development, but our educational practices lag far behind the findings of organismic psychology, with the result that outmoded methods of faculty training and mental discipline persist in our schools of today.

Those who object to the modern school with its activities of excursions, community study, projects, problem studies, its methods of personality development and character building, are simply not up-to-date because they fail to face the educational issues demanded by a rapidly changing civilization. Our schools must prepare youth for life in a real world and not for life in the past. It is as important a function of the school to train in personality adjustment as it is to train him in abstract mathematics — probably a more important function. The school must accept the responsibility for developing social and moral attitudes, such as a regard for the rights and feelings of others and an acceptance of responsibility for the good of all. Inasmuch as our changing civilization brings ever new and challenging social problems, children must be taught to face issues, to solve problems, and to think about social issues of group living.

Such is the task which progressive educators set for themselves, and surely it is no mean task. Children must learn by living and acting. No one can learn in any other way. Learning is significant to the child if it has meaning to him and if he accepts that meaning. His learnings, his attitudes, his appreciations, his knowledge, his understanding — these build character through group activity and through individual responsibility to the group.

Such is the spirit of the classroom pervading the progressive schools. The curriculum starts where the child is.

Aims of the Progressive School

The progressive school aims to develop the social intelligence of the child in order to assist him to come to grips with the social problems of adult living, provincially, nationally, or internationally. Children should work at current problems and controversial issues in order to develop independent thinking in preparation for citizenship.

Experimentalism and progressive education utilize the scientific method and both are rooted in experience. Learning must be related to living. So, too, character is built up in living. The curriculum must be related to real life.

Experimentalism and progressive education aim at democratic education which should produce responsible, self-directed citizens who are to live in a rapidly changing world. Since such a world will always be a problem-solving world, the progressive educator upholds the experimental method and an experimentally directed curriculum.

The Curriculum

The curriculum should be based on lessons learned from a study of child behavior. The psychology of learning appropriate to progressive education will then be based on maturational growth and development of the child. Teaching procedures will recognize all aspects of the human personality as requiring development, not merely the intellectual skills, but also manual skills, bodily skills, social skills and emotional well-being.

Education

Education is co-extensive with life and includes the countless contacts with people and things in and out of school. Hence the importance of organizing the curriculum in terms of areas of living rather than in terms of rigid subject-planned zones. A progressive curriculum lays emphasis on the maintenance of health, recreation, making a living, getting an education, carrying out civic responsibilities, making a home. The curriculum aims at a broad experience in order to assist the child to later participate in all important phases of living.

B) Report of the Superintendent of Winnipeg Schools, 1937–8
Manitoba Department of Education

During the past few years schoolroom practice in the Elementary classes of the Winnipeg Public Schools, in common with that in progressive centres everywhere, has given much attention to projects, activity programmes and similar methods for obtaining results which were formerly obtained by direct drill, by definite teaching and by constant practice.

The tendency in education today is towards greater informality. Natural free expression is encouraged, developed and directed, so that every talent or interest of each child has some opportunity for expression and improvement. The happiness of the child is of paramount importance and any child is happy when interested. It is recognized that with the passing on to the school of the vastly greater part of all child training, the school has become responsible for the building of character and the development of personality in the basic essentials of social living and in the ability to meet life situations.

The teacher of beginning pupils today develops in her pupils a desire to learn to read by interesting them in some project such as the building of a "Health House," the construction of a model of a farm, or the illustration of some simple story. In this way, concrete conceptions of words and language are built up and the translation of the word concepts to the word symbols is relatively easy because the child is thoroughly interested in the translation.

Practice and drill in reading are obtained by the use of mimeographed sheets giving directions to pupils to do things in which they are interested rather than by assigning a lesson to be read which may be entirely remote from the interests of the children.

In the upper grades of the Elementary schools the "activity method" is being used to advantage. For example in the teaching of Geography, "Transportation in Canada" may be the immediate subject of study. In place simply reading about transportation and reproducing what has been read, orally or in writing, the class undertakes the study as a project. Some of the class will search for information as to transportation during the days of the explorers and fur traders. This will lead to the drawings of maps showing routes taken; the calculation of distances of journeys and the time taken to make them; the making of birch-bark canoes; models of York boats, forts, Red River carts, etc. Another group will take railroad development; another transportation by river, lake, canal, and ocean; still another the development of motor car traffic including construction of highways. Lastly a group will study transportation by air naturally leading to a study of Canada's great mineral resources in the north. In this way the whole class working together will assemble models, maps, pictures and written work of their own which makes the whole study vital and real.

An activity programme of this kind is in itself so fascinating to pupils and teacher alike that a possible danger arises of losing sight of the objective to be reached by means of the activity which from the standpoint of the teacher is not an end in itself but a means to an end. It must always remain the fundamental task of the Elementary schools to provide young people with the tools of learning, proficiency in the use of which is so essential to later learning and to life. There is also a further point that must not be overlooked. Society has not reached and probably will never reach a point at which the individual is able to do only that in which he is interested or only what he would select to do from choice. Life requirements still demand obedience at times to externally imposed authority and one requires to be able to face unpleasant tasks and conquer difficult situations ...

Notwithstanding, therefore, the allure of activity programmes with their projects and other methods of undoubted value and interest, the Winnipeg Elementary schools are endeavoring to preserve a reasonable balance between the so-called "old" and the so-called "new". While trying to use what is good in the "new", they are not overlooking the "old". While using what is felt to be the best in the activity approach they are demanding the high standard of the past in the basic skills and are still doing what they can in strengthening the fibre of the young people in facing the difficult and in obedience to discipline which may at times run counter to the immediate desires and interests of the pupil.

C) Programme of Studies for the Intermediate School (Grades VII, VIII, IX), 1935
Alberta Department of Education

Many pupils complete their education as citizens in the Intermediate School, and all complete there the period of compulsory school attendance. There is a special connection, therefore, between the Programme of the Intermediate School and the subsistence of democracy ...

Writers on education make a practice of setting forth many aims of education. In reality, there are as many aims of education in any given society as there are patterns of behaviour in that society. Every culture pattern is a legitimate aim of education in some society. Some aims, however, are more important than others at a given stage of the learner's development. Some aims, moreover, are so important at all stages that they cannot safely be left to haphazard or unduly time-consuming modes of learning. Schools were established in the first instance to facilitate the learning of things which must be learned anyway sooner or later, but which can be learned more economically and expeditiously through the specialized procedures of formal instruction than in any other way. In pioneer days it was the main function of schools to inculcate the three R's because this was the only educative function that could not be performed equally well by other social institutions such as the home and the church. Through the change from a simple agrarian to a complex industrialized economy, the pattern of society and social relationships has become exceedingly intricate, with the result that the schools are now called upon to do many other things than merely to train for literacy. The schools of today have been compelled through economic and social developments to take over, in a large measure, the educative functions of other social institutions. Schools now provide a social environment for the learner in which he must react to social situations. The learner develops his capacities as an individual. He also acquires, through the attitudes and relationships induced by social behaviour, a personality that reaches out and enfolds society. The learner is part of society, and society becomes part of the learner.

In general, one may say that the following educational trends of the present day will be found in the up-to-date school programme:

1. A broad perspective in education, with recognition not only of knowledge, but also of skills, habits, appreciations, attitudes and ideals as valid objectives. Training for literacy is not enough. The traditional view that education is book-learning still prevails, however, in socially backward communities.

2. A reaction against the mechanized routine of formal instruction, with the consequent adoption of project or enterprise procedures, and the substitution of pupil for teacher activity.

3. Recognition in the programme of training for personal and social efficiency, emotional control, and integration of personality.

4. General acceptance of the principle that the purpose of education is fundamentally social, and that an understanding of the social environment is quite as necessary as an understanding of the physical environment.

5. Belief in the ideals of democracy, and in the possibility of maintaining them through education.

The General Aim of the Intermediate School

The Intermediate School is a school for pupils of the "between ages" — pupils from eleven to fifteen years of age. It offers a distinctive programme of studies and activities specially suited to pupils who have attained the status of early adolescence. Like the elementary school, it represents an attempt to adjust the school programme and environment to the needs of an age group. Like the high school, it offers a programme of liberal-cultured studies, but with the difference that its programme is not primarily concerned with preparation for advanced academic instruction.

It is difficult for most adolescents to make a wise choice from the adult occupations. Some will later go to the farm; some will go into the trades, some into business; some will find clerical or civil service positions; and some will enter the professions. But the intermediate school cannot segregate these groups. It must offer a sound "core" of instruction that is of value to all pupils, and, by way of enriching the programme, make provisions for individual interests and aptitudes through elective and more or less exploratory courses. The intermediate school must be a preparatory school for pupils who will proceed to the high school; but at the same time it must serve as a "finishing school" for pupils who, for one reason or another, are unable to advance beyond Grade IX.

Many pupils who have no aptitude for academic training drop out of Grade VII or VIII with a sense of inadequacy and failure, when they could still profit from further education if it were of a kind suited to their needs. It is the proper function of the intermediate school to offer a programme that will appeal to all pupils of the adolescent group; a programme that is complete in itself and valuable in its own right, without regard to preparation for the high school; a programme that will, in effect, enable pupils who leave school to do so with a sense of accomplishment.

The intermediate school must accept responsibility for completing the education of many young citizens. It should, therefore, inculcate loyalty to the democratic ideal, and exemplify in its programme, procedures and government, the value and efficacy of that ideal. It should continue the programme, begun in the elementary school, of teaching the pupil how to examine both sides of a question, how and where to find facts, and how to use the evidence of authorities in reaching a conclusion. It should preserve and foster the spirit of personal freedom, evoked in the elementary school by the enterprise procedure.

D) "New Schools for Democracy," Behind the Headlines, 1944
C.E. Phillips

How can we get high schools which will educate everybody, or at least the majority of our citizens?

Fortunately we have come a long way towards achieving the first of two steps in the solution of the problem. We have high school accommodation for nearly everybody now.

The growth of the high school is the most notable educational achievement of the present century. Observe the gain in secondary school enrolment over a forty-year period in Ontario, the most populous province of Canada. In a period during which the population increased by roughly 60%, and elementary school enrolment by less than 20%, secondary school enrolment increased nearly 500%. If all factors were taken into account — including post-secondary classes in the public schools — the proportion of the population who received some secondary education would be found to be three times as great in 1940 as it was when the century began. For the whole of English-speaking Canada it would be close to the truth to say that in 1900 about one person in five went on to high school, whereas about three persons in five do so now.

As far as the provision of schools is concerned, we have therefore a record of which we may be proud. True, there remains the problem of establishing high schools in the less populous rural section of Canada; but although it is a big problem … it will be solved in the period of post war reconstruction. Even then, however — even when rural children have the same advantages in secondary schools that city children have now — even if there are literally high schools for everybody and if everybody is made attend them — we will not have reached the millennium …

Secondary education used to be a monopoly of the privileged few in the aristocratic type of society which prevailed a hundred or more years ago. These few were being prepared to assume positions of leadership, and they were given a distinctive type of education which marked them off from the common people … This secondary, or "higher class", education was of the type required for admission to university — consisting then exclusively of classical languages and mathematics, and now including modern languages, science, and history as well. It is the type of distinctive education — distinctive in the sense of being removed from the lives of ordinary people — that the great majority of our high schools continue to offer. And that in spite of the fact that high schools are now attended by the general public, and in spite of the fact that not one high school student in ten has any real intention of proceeding to university.

During the present century an attempt has been made to remedy this condition by providing boys and girls in urban centres with schools of an entirely different type. These are the vocational schools — commercial, technical, and, in a few cases, agricultural — which train pupils for particular jobs. Since we live in a world where making a living and getting money are matters of great concern to young people, attendance in these schools has increased tremendously and will undoubtedly continue to increase after the war. To refer again to Ontario, we find that nearly one third of all high school pupils are enrolled in vocational courses.

But strange as it may appear, even these schools fail to hold the interest of a great many boys and girls, with the result that a great many drop out before completing a three or four years' course of training. Indeed, statistics for Ontario show that the vocational schools are even less successful than the academic schools in retaining their pupils. In 1940 there were in Ontario only 2/3 as many children enrolled in Grade XI in academic secondary schools as in Grade IX, and only 3/5 as many in Grade XI in vocational schools as in Grade IX.

Of course one reason that so many pupils leave the vocational schools before completing their course is that they have more than their share of boys and girls who are simply filling in time until they have reached the age (16 in Ontario) when the law permits them to leave school. But the very fact that many parents and teachers send these restless pupils into vocational schools shows a popular belief that vocational training is something less than a complete education and suitable for pupils of inferior ability.

Hence the plan we now follow of retaining the academic type of secondary education for some pupils and providing vocational training for other pupils has the effect of dividing young people into sheep and goats. It is a carry-over from the old aristocratic idea that only a few need be educated for leadership, while the many are given a training which fits them to be merely workers in society ...

Of course the vocational schools do offer so-called cultural subjects in addition to vocational training — but the focus of the pupils' attention is on the job for which he is preparing. Similarly the academic schools do offer some education of a practical nature, but most of what the pupil studies has little bearing on his life in the twentieth century ...

Such are the schools we have.

So far we have fixed our attention on the faults of two different types of school. It is time now to recognize that each type has its own distinctive merits. If we can discover the merits of each and combine them, without the faults, in a single programme for one new type of school, we shall have gone a long way towards the solution of the problem.

The merit of the vocational school is its contact with reality — its concern for at least one important aspect of life in the world today. This fact needs no enlargement.

The merit of the academic school is more difficult to explain, but educationally no less vital. The old way of putting it was to say that an academic education trains the mind. Actually this is, or should be, the truth. But this worthy purpose has been defeated by superstitious faith in discredited formulae and insistence on the use of antiquated curriculum content, so that many people today laugh at the very idea to scorn. It is therefore essential to clear the grounds by renouncing any such notion as that the school study of Latin, or French, or algebra, or geometry necessarily enables young people to think more clearly when they are faced with the problems of life, and similarily to reject the corresponding notion that an education without these particular subjects necessarily fails to educate in this sense. But it is true that intellectual content can be presented in such a way as to broaden a young person's interests and accustom him to thinking in important fields left untouched by the technical skills and narrowly practical knowledge of vocational training.

The school we need … is a school for making people. Like the vocational school it will offer a programme related to the needs of today — but to broad needs of people as individuals and citizens, and not merely as workers. Like the academic school, it will aim at teaching to think — but it will do this successfully by using any and every means for its purpose instead of limiting itself to the traditional content of traditional subjects. Unlike either of these schools it will be a many-sided institution offering a well-rounded education adapted to the needs of all pupils. It will not turn out sheep or goats because there will be no fanatical insistence on either a completely academic or preponderantly vocational curriculum. It will be able to produce educated persons because it will not be hampered by having to teach unwanted subject matter and being compelled to forego desirable types of guidance and instruction for lack of time …

E) So Little for the Mind, 1950
Hilda Neatby

… The average progressive school is not, as certainly many traditional schools were, an abode of darkness and cruelty, or, at best, of dull and meaningless fact grinding. Rather it is a place where all children find sympathy, under-standing and encouragement. There are no terrors for the dunce, there is demand for no feverish application from the good scholar. Learning is free and unforced because it is believed that children work best when they are happy and retain most firmly what they learn gladly. "The whole child goes to school" and when he arrives he is accepted as an individual of the first importance. "The school is child centred."

Happiness and cheerful learning are promoted and the new attitude of sympathy is expressed first, by much attention to health, physical comfort, and pleasure through suitable and properly constructed school buildings, good lighting, comfortable seats, facilities for recreation and, in general, cheerful and attractive surroundings …

The healthy child in cheerful surroundings is presented not with a load of tasks that must be done but rather with "activities" physical and mental which can be readily related to his life outside of the school. His need for variety and change, movement and action, is understood and met with sym-pathy and encouragement. In other words, he meets people who know he cannot sit still and who find a way of teaching him that suits his physical and emotional needs, in defiance of previous "traditional" notions of how teaching ought to be done. He is confronted, it is said, not with synthetic but with "real" situations and problems, and is encouraged to meet them by means suitable to the particular stage of his development.

It is further claimed that he is led to grapple with his problems by means of "real" as opposed to formal discipline, externally applied. He is to be trained for democracy, that is for cooperation in a society of free and equal indi-viduals. He must have guidance, not harshness. He is led by discussion, not driven by dictation. He is led by natural means to self-discipline, the object of all moral training.

This sympathetic and understanding attention to the child as an individual, to his physical well-being, to his interests, and to his moral growth must win the approval of all who are interested in children or in education. It is not, of course, entirely new. But progressivists are right in maintaining that the foundation of general and nationwide systems of education on such principles is new. Neglect of health and comfort, lack of sympathy, and harshness, drill and discipline for their own sakes are as unfashionable today as their opposites were a generation or two ago. The educational system which undertakes to care adequately for all, the dull, the lazy and the misfits, as well as for the bright and the industrious is indeed a new and notable achievement ...

But in English-speaking Canada, as in the United States, there are signs of unrest and dissatisfaction which go beyond the normal grumbling ...

The bored "graduates" of elementary and high schools often seem, in progressive language, to be "incompletely socialized". Ignorant even of things that they might be expected to know, they do not care to learn. They lack an object in life, they are unaware of the joy of achievement. They have been allowed to assume that happiness is a goal, rather than a by-product ...

These intellectual leaders of the future literally cannot read, write, or think. They are good at word recognition, but to "read, mark, learn and inwardly digest" even simple material is beyond them. They can write, and often type, but too often they cannot construct a grammatical sentence. They can emit platitudes, but they can neither explain nor defend them. They are often as incapable of the use of logic as they are ignorant of its very name. Yet those high school "graduates" are not stupid, or ill-intentioned, or incurably indifferent to what they have never learned to call their duty. They are only ignorant, lazy, and unaware of the exacting demands of a society from the realities of which they have been carefully insulated ...

Our schools seem to have missed the challenge of a brutal and dangerous but stimulating age. Somehow educators for all their talk of the world of today are still dreaming the simple philosophic dreams of the eighteenth century, that men are all naturally intelligent, reasonable and moral, needing only the opportunity for a free and full development of their faculties. This dreaming has been only slightly modified by the psychologists, who seldom know any philosophy, and who would cope with mankind, not by the old-fashioned "development of faculties", but by manipulation and socialization. Progressivists, true to the revolutionary tradition, read no history. They have not perceived that all societies, civilized and otherwise, no matter what their ultimate ideals, have adapted the education of children to the kind of world they must live and die in. If they had grasped this important truth they would surely have realized what progressivism and pragmatism alike demand, in the hard world of today, a hard and selective discipline that will fit every individual to make his utmost contribution to a society in which, with all our effort, life for many will probably still be "nasty, brutish and short".

The twentieth century school is faced with a tremendous threefold task.

First it must accept, and afford some sort of training for every child above a very low intellectual level. This has meant an enormous and rapid increase in numbers in all schools, and a vast increase in the numbers of intellectually incompetent in the high schools. Somehow all these future citizens must receive education or training appropriate to their capacities.

Secondly, the school must convey to these swollen numbers a mass of information useful and even essential to them, information of which their grandparents never dreamed. They must learn the rules of health, the principles of a balanced diet, safety regulations, traffic laws, the operations of public services and utilities, the use and hazards of modern domestic equipment, and literally hundreds of other matters. Much of this practical instruction may be unnecessary and even absurd. Most of it should be learned in the home. But some school instruction in these matters is probably inescapable, time consuming though it may be.

Thirdly, the school should, in addition, convey to all, insofar as they are capable of receiving it, the intellectual, cultural and moral training which represents the best in a long and honourable tradition of Western civilization. On the proper performance of this task depends the future of our society. Informed individuals outside the progressive schools speak of the crisis in civilization with seriousness and intelligence. Progressive educators have apparently not even heard of it; they continue blandly to socialize for a society which threatens every moment to cease to exist.

Looking back over the past generation or two, it seems obvious that the true "pragmatist", that is the really practical and forward looking man or woman, would have used the great resources of the schools, public interest, increasing wealth, improved buildings, up-to-date equipment, adequate teacher training, more effective methods of teaching, to fulfil this threefold obligation. They would have realized that all the new resources and all the new enthusiasm would be barely enough to meet the heavy new responsibility of teaching the multiudes and of imparting an ever-increasing mass of useful, practical information, without neglecting the task, now more essential than ever, of offering mental discipline and intellectual and spiritual enrichment. They did not see either the challenge or the opportunity. They took the easy way out. Instead of using their enormous new resources in material equipment, knowledge and skill to cope with their tremendous task, they frittered them away in making school life easy and pleasant, concentrating on the obvious, the practical, and the immediate. Democratic equalitarianism encouraged the idea of a uniform low standard easily obtainable by almost all. Special attention was given to all physical, emotional, and mental abnormalities, but the old-fashioned things called the mind, the imagination and the conscience of the average and of the better than average child, if not exactly forgotten, slipped into the background ...

Progressivism is anti-cultural. This is quite in keeping with the revolutionary, pseudo-scientific materialist fashions of the day. In this scientific age we find that everything, not just educational methods, but everything, is better than it used to be. It is the pride of the machine age that we can now understand, manipulate and control men as we do machines. Why should we look at the evidence of human joys, sorrows, failures, and achievements in the past? It would almost be an admission of defeat. We manage everything better now ... But the result of progressivism has been effectively to cut off many if not most of our pupils from any real enjoyment or understanding of the inheritance of western civilization; and certainly from any sense that the achievements and values of the past are a trust to be preserved and enriched for the future. Culture in its traditional sense of intellectual and moral cultivation is as unfashionable as is scholarship.

Finally, progressive education is, or has been amoral. ... [F]or a generation it has been unfashionable, to say the least, to speak openly of right and wrong actions. Teachers take cover instead under "desirable" and "undesirable" "attitudes" or "responses". But these are not enough. The pupil soon learns the meaning of desirable and thinks, quite rightly, that in a democratic society he has as much right to desire as anyone else. Even the elementary discipline of establishing rules which the child required to keep was questioned. True, rules certainly existed in practice; but pragmatic theory frowned on all external control and therefore rules were enforced uneasily and with a bad conscience. The general tendency of the progressive approach has been to weaken respect for the law and authority as such, and to dull discrimination between right and wrong, by the teaching, implied if not expressed, that "desirable" actions on the part of the child (actions pleasing to others) will bring "desirable" responses (actions pleasing to him). It is no doubt often true that honesty is the best policy, but no one ever learned honesty from that maxim ... The progressive school has added to the intellectual confusion without establishing any clear moral principles ...

The sensible and fair thing is surely to let children know by experience in school that life may be difficult and disagreeable as well as delightful and simple; that theirs is a world for workers, and that work demands their best effort; and to help them to acquire in school such firm habits and such clear principles as will enable them, whether they gain or lose the world, to do their duty in it with diligence and with intelligence ...

F) "Culture? Liberal Education? Education For Democracy? ... Does Anybody Know?", The Teachers' Magazine, February, 1954
J.M. Paton

So Little for the Mind by Dr. Hilda Neatby, Professor of History at the University of Saskatchewan — a book which is reviewed, not too sympathetically, in this issue of the magazine — will have performed a very useful function in this New Year of 1954 if it compels school administrators, classroom teachers, and community leaders in Canada to re-examine their basic assumptions regarding the aims of education, and, at the same time, to assess critically the implications of these assumptions for many educational theories that are currently popular.

Everyone, for example, likes to think that our schools are producing good democratic citizens, without having too clear an idea of the meaning of democratic in this context. Most people believe in the democratic principle of equality of educational opportunity for all Canadian youth, but not too many worry about whether or not the schools are developing our best intellects to their capacity or, of equal importance, obtaining from the majority of pupils the best efforts of which they are capable.

Is Dr. Neatby right when she accuses our schools of being anti-intellectual and anti-cultural? Have we in reality misinterpreted or misapplied such presumably sound theories as "teach the child, not the subject," "prepare the pupil for life, not for written examinations," "motivation for learning should be found in co-operation and group participation rather than in competition and individual success"? Are teachers generally (including the "experts" in normal schools and provincial departments of education) guilty of watering down course content and examination standards, of belittling academic distinction and exalting social success, of emphasizing occupational training at the expense of liberal education?

This writer is not prepared to answer any of these questions with a categorical affirmative, but does think there is merit in Dr. Neatby's recommendation that some national body in this country be given plenty of time and money to consider the whole problem of education and of its relation to the past and to the future of our society. We need a "clear and precise statement of a Canadian philosophy of education" in place of what we have now, which is not unfairly described by Miss Neatby as "an awkward synthesis of three or four mutually exclusive American schools of thought."

Four Important Questions

This authoritative statement of a philosophy of education for Canadian schools will avail us little if it fails to answer the crucial questions which, I believe, must be answered if we are not to make the grave error of swinging the pendulum of educational change too far in the contrary direction merely because a number of university professors, some employers, not a few chronic complainers of advancing years, and the worshippers of tradition for its own sake happen at the moment to be the most articulate critics of our schools at a time when professional educators are themselves beginning (with war and post-war problems either solved or less demanding) to call for a critical assessment of school courses and teaching methods.

The crucial questions awaiting an answer include these: (1) What kind of person do we want young Canadians to become? (2) What course content and teaching methods are the best for the purpose? (3) Can the job possibly be done in Grades 1 to 12 alone? If not, what is to be expected of the home, the church, the community, the employer, the university, and of each adult citizen, and to what extent can society (or "the state") require that these duties be performed? (4) Is it reasonable to insist that all desirable qualities be acquired by all persons and to the same degree? If not, who or what is to decide the level of attainment expected of the individual, and in which of the many desirable areas of knowledge, skill, and attitude?

The proponents of liberal education in the traditional sense can usually, by ignoring the details which inevitably concern the school administrator, answer all these questions very briefly. Education, they say, should produce a person acquainted with our cultural heritage, one who has in addition a trained or disciplined mind, mature emotions, and a sound system of values. He will be able to think critically, to weigh evidence impartially, to view problems with some historical perspective, to appreciate beauty in the arts and letters, and to distinguish clearly between good and evil. In short, he will be a wise man, or at the least one who loves wisdom and pursues it.

The trouble with all this is that it seems to apply exclusively to an intellectual elite or, as so often happened in the past, to a few people with enough money and leisure to live the contemplative life of Socrates and Plato ...

Are the Humanities Enough? ...

... Why is it that a considerable number of teachers, particularly in the academic classes of the secondary school, applaud the views of Hutchins, Neatby, and the rest? Surely it is because they are rebelling against the modern emphasis on practical subjects, on occupational preparation, on results that "show." They may feel, too, that quality is sacrificed to numbers and that the humanities are running a poor second to applied science and mathematics. The answer, it seems to me, is not a return to the aristocratic schools of the last century, but a critical re-examination of our educational system in the light of the world as it is and of people as they are and as we would (within reason) like them to be.

... It will be strange indeed if the commission of inquiry advocated by Dr. Neatby concludes that this "improvement" and "fulfilment" leave no place for vocational preparation. It has been well said that man does not live by bread alone; it was also truly said that by the sweat of his brow shall he eat bread. An education which liberates a man's intelligence for further learning, searching, and thinking is surely none the less liberal if the motive for learning happens to be the need to earn his living as well as to occupy his leisure time.

Which brings us right back to where we started, without a satisfactory answer to the question of the right kind of education for the citizens of a democracy. Is culture enough? Will liberal education suffice? Will education for work and for leisure make a satisfactory definition of aims?

Does anybody know?

G) "Dr. Neatby's 'Doctored' Diatribe: An Unblushingly Biased Review of an Unblushingly Biased Book", The Teachers' Magazine, February, 1954
J.M. Paton

Hilda Neatby's *So Little for the Mind* (Clarke Irwin, Toronto, 1953) is rapidly becoming the most discussed non-fiction book published recently in Canada. That is not surprising, since it more than lives up to the promise of its sub-title "an indictment of Canadian education," and most people like controversy, especially when the subject is one on which everybody is an authority of sorts.

It is devoutly to be hoped, however, that those who are waxing ecstatic over the book's onslaught upon progressive education in large capital letters will take the trouble to read it carefully, including the thirty-four pages of notes; because this is much more than a lively brochure poking a finger of ridicule at a few stock figures among educators and psychiatrists. It is a full-length book with a pretentious apparatus of annotated quotations and references, which deliberately creates the impression that most of the ills of our society may justly be laid at the door of a group of educational experts in nine provinces (Newfoundland and Catholic Quebec are excluded from the survey) who have embraced the materialistic philosophy of John Dewey and have at the same time succeeded in bamboozling or in silencing the teachers ...

Some Shafts Strike Home

... I also agree with much that she says in ridicule of the lengths to which some educators have gone in requiring that the interest of the learner be aroused before teaching can begin, with the result that teachers have frequently felt constrained to invent a whole battery of devices by which to persuade the pupil to "identify himself" with the aim of every lesson.

Miss Neatby has more important criticisms than these. Her insistence on facts and on memorized propositions as furnishing the raw material of thought, should be carefully considered in the light of the prevailing notion that pupils must always "understand" what they are required to "learn." Her chief indictment of today's schooling — that it is anti-intellectual, that it leaves to little for the mind to work on — should not be ignored merely because she has, in my view, placed the wrong prisoner in the dock. Less urgent but not unimportant would be an inquiry into the validity of the assertion that brilliant students are not welcome in education faculties, and that most of our career educators come not from the top but from the second or third ten per cent of university graduates.

Misleading Documentation

This is not an opinion capable of easy proof, and the book offers none. It does, however, attempt to establish another opinion — that the majority of Canadian education experts have come under American, and in particular, Dewey influence. As happens too often in this book, the documentation is completely misleading. The author merely takes a small and unrepresentative sampling of educators and notes the source of their degrees. When she finds the total of American degrees higher that the Canadian and British combined, she feels that her conclusion is justified. Had she made a respectable effort to take an adequate sampling of school principals, superintendents, inspectors, etc., across Canada, she might have had to modify her thesis, but at least the reader would have had his confidence in her sincerity strengthened.

For example, Miss Neatby frequently refers to our "largest college of education" as a stronghold of Deweyism where many of the "experts" she dislikes received their pedagogical training. I can personally testify from an experience extending over ten years and ending about six years ago that American textbooks and Teachers' College philosophies were not at that time given the slightest priority. Indeed it was largely the other way. The only textbooks I recall buying in educational philosophy and psychology were published in England, and while the courses required wide reading and some acquaintance with most schools of educational thought, the bias was most certainly towards a critical and somewhat skeptical evaluation of the views of Dewey, Kilpatrick, *et al.* ...

Some Threats to Culture

On the other hand, this book is on much stronger ground when it seriously questions the modern over-emphasis on social adjustment, on individual satisfaction, on the complete avoidance of frustration, and on every kind of manipulation to eliminate pupil experience with failure. While more aware of the practical difficulties than Dr. Neatby seems to be, teachers should give serious thought to her insistence that we teach "a firm and fixed moral law, rendered flexible only through the operation of grace and a total renunciation of self"; in short, that we substitute Christian morality for amoral pragmatism in our educational philosophy and practice. Some of these difficulties, as the historian Dr. Neatby must appreciate, are inherent in modern society: the decline of religion (or rather of organized religion), the growth of materialism, and the worship of Success as an end in itself. Had Miss Neatby directed her main attack on everyone responsible for these cultural evils, including, surely, some of her university colleagues in arts faculties and history departments, her book might have been more warmly received by school people, because it would have had the great virtue of a humble striving after truth.

It is difficult to understand why the author devoted so much time and space to a one-sided attack on a small group of educators whose influence for evil she has ludicrously exaggerated, when her conclusion is an excellent plea for a truly Canadian philosophy of education and for a national inquiry into the whole question of education and for a national inquiry into the whole question of education and its relation to the past and the future of our society ...

By this time the reader may have guessed the reason for the quotation marks in the title of this article. Miss Neatby does indeed "punch the pedagogues" with a skill worthy of the holder of a Ph.D. But she is also guilty of unfair manipulation of arguments and references which amounts to a kind of doctoring of the evidence.

Specific Defects

... Much of the evidence in the book is unreliable: to wit, the opinions of a few disgruntled education students, the writer of "an unpublished master's thesis," one or two letters to the editor, and isolated excerpts from provincial courses of study. Surely an historian of Dr. Neatby's standing should have been able to devise a satisfactory method of obtaining representative opinions of Canadian parents and teachers (students also) concerning teaching methods and classroom procedures. Her assumption that statements in courses of study are a reliable indication of classroom practice is naïve in the extreme. Common sense might have suggested to her that most people, including teachers, resist change and are suspicious of new ideas; therefore, that Deweyism has not transformed the schoolrooms of Canada ...

Many pages of this book exude the odour of intellectual snobbery, perhaps better described more kindly as an ivory tower myopia. Mediocre academic achievement, narrow specialization, anti-cultural and illiberal tastes, and the like, are cited as characteristics of the staff, the students, and the graduates of colleges of education, with never a hint that other university faculties and departments, including history, might occasionally harbour a few specimens. This inability to see the beam in one's own eye is further illustrated by Miss Neatby's remarks on objective testing, in which it appears not to have occurred to her that many college tests of the essay type leave room for improvement in content validity and in accuracy of marking.

... At another place in the book there is the astonishing statement (from an historian) that the one thing needful in history courses is to "teach the facts accurately and honestly" from a good textbook, as if "fact" and "truth" were as readily ascertainable as today's weather report.

Other weaknesses are the result of ignorance of the Canadian school system … She concludes, for instance, that normal school courses on teaching method preclude any solid teaching of the content of the subject. She thinks that the composite school and the typical vocational school (as in Ontario) are trade schools which provide little or no academic instruction. She assumes that the modern emphasis on pupil taste and interest in the teaching of literature is but another weak concession to the soft pedagogy of the day; whereas a better case could be made out for the claim that it arose from the shortcoming of traditional content and methods, particularly as regards the 90 per cent of pupils who will never attend a university.

The Author's "Solution"

So much for details. The crowning evidence that this book is not the unanswerable indictment of education in Canada that some people have apparently been waiting for lies in the chief solution offered by Dr. Neatby … [I]t means a return to the exclusive aristocratic schools of the nineteenth century.

Her answer, however, does have the virtue of simplicity. First of all, the schools should restore the rigorous entrance examination to high school and thus eliminate about 40 percent of the academic misfits at one stroke. Thereafter, a series of strict academic tests, plus permission to potential drop-outs to leave school whenever they are so inclined, will ensure that the upper grades of the secondary school contain only the top 5 to 10 percent who are of university calibre. These students will, presumably, be able to "read, write, and think" and the troubles of college professors will be over.

What is to happen to the other 90 percent? Dr. Neatby does not appear to care. Let them go, she says. They were allowed to go in the good old days, so why worry about them now? In another place, she is not quite so ruthless and suggests that some "other type of institution" may have to be provided. It must not be called a secondary school, however, and the reader is left to draw his own conclusions as to whether employers are to provide parttime education or the state to establish evening classes. Where all these young people are to find employment, what the reaction of labour will be to the glutting of the market with unskilled hands, what parents and taxpayers will think of a provision of secondary schools and colleges only for an academic elite, Dr. Neatby does not say. She is too intelligent not to realize that she has presented her much despised school administrator with a terrific problem. She has, in fact, proposed the implementation of a revolutionary interpretation of the democratic concept of equality of educational opportunity, but there is no hint of this in the brief, precise utterance from her ivory tower ...

14

"Ingested into the Eagle's Gut"
Canadian-American Relations

DOCUMENTS

A) The Massey Report, 1951

B) Letter to My Son, 1968
Farley Mowat

C) Their America and Mine, 1968
Robert Fulford

D) Canada-U.S. Relations: Options for the Future, 1972
Mitchell Sharp

A sk someone to define a Canadian. The answer inevitably takes time as the individual considers the question that has haunted Canada since its inception. The eventual response? "I'm not an American". That, for better or for worse, epitomizes the relentless nationalistic struggle, and sense of insecurity, Canadians have long suffered. This is not surprising. Before 1867 British North America regularly winced at American might. They attacked Quebec during the American revolution and returned for more prolonged offensives during the War of 1812. Later, Americans actively assisted Canadian rebels intent on overthrowing British rule during the 1830s. Although Lincoln knew better than to engage the British in North America during the American Civil War, Canadians feared he would. By the mid-1860s rumours spread that the incursions of the Irish-American Fenians into New Brunswick and central Canada were actually undertaken with the tacit approval of the American government.

Those were merely the most blatant examples of American aggression. There were other, and arguably more subtle, ways in which the United States has penetrated Canadian sovereignty. John A. Macdonald's National Policy ironically opened the doors for American branch plants to establish themselves from coast to coast, buying up so much of Canada's industrial infrastructure that they eventually owned most of it. During the Second World War, U.S. president Franklin

Roosevelt and Canadian prime minister William Lyon Mackenzie King integrated the two economies still further, and American soldiers guarded parts of Canada. Then, during the Cold War, the NORAD defense agreement ensured that Canada took shelter under an American umbrella.

To some, the most insidious invasion of all, however, came not from military or political maneuvres, but from an unparalleled cultural juggernaut rolling north. American literature, sports, art, movies, music, and clothing inundated Canadians, leaving them insecure and feeling inferior. The huge American population, some ten times greater than Canada's, also ensured that their cultural economies of scale allowed them to produce far more glamorous versions of virtually everything, often at lower prices. America was Canada's cultural brother, biggest trading partner, and the new-world friend with whom Canada shared a continent and to whom she looked for guidance. Many Canadians enjoyed cross-border family ties, and many Canadians regularly vacationed in the United States. Sales of Levis, Buicks, and *Sports Illustrated* remained buoyant in Canada, and every kid still wanted G.I. Joe or Barbie's latest accoutrements. Canadians bought in and became, according to Canadian nationalists like George Grant, just so many second-rate Americans.

Grant, in his scathing *Lament for a Nation*, argued that Canadians quietly loved being American, and our last hope of sovereignty died with Diefenbaker's defeat. Others, however, especially academics, people in the arts, and those on the political left, still held out hope. They called for immediate remedial action. American cultural supremacy north of the 49th parallel could be curtailed or at least limited, they said, if Canadians had the will. Nationalists argued that Canada needed an independent foreign policy, freed from Uncle Sam. Branch plants, in their minds, had to be brought under Canadian control, and promoting Canadian culture was absolutely vital.

This smoldering Canadian nationalism burst into flame during the 1960s, not just because American control and ownership reached unprecedented levels, but as a result of American foreign policy forays. The end of the '60s was the height of the Vietnam war, and many Canadians eventually believed that it was an unjustified war promoting American imperialism in the name of peace and security.

The war demonstrated Canada's ambivalence toward the United States. Though not directly involved, Canada played a role in Vietnam. Many Canadian manufacturers provided the U.S. military with war material, and the Canadian government refused to condemn most American actions in Southeast Asia. Some fifty thousand Canadian volunteers fought for the United States, and legions of

Canadians fervently believed that the United States was the only bulwark against creeping communism. Yet Canada also opened its doors to thousands of American draft-dodgers. Prime Minister Lester Pearson raised the ire of President Lyndon Johnson, who apparently bellowed "you've pissed on my carpet" when Pearson opposed the American bombing of North Vietnam during a speech at an American university.

Canadian nationalism did not burst from a vacuum in the 1960s. The Canadian government, for example, expressed deep concern over encroaching Americana immediately after the Second World War. That led to the 1951 "Massey Report," officially called the Royal Commission on National Development in the Arts, Letters and Sciences. It stemmed from the debate about private versus public control over broadcasting in Canada, but was equally a result of a funding crisis in the CBC. It also tackled the divisive issue of public subsidies for Canadian universities. Members of the Commission ultimately recommended that Canadian taxpayers secure the nation's culture and identity by funding organs such as the CBC, the National Film Board, and the university system.

Farley Mowat (1921–) is reputedly Canada's best-read author with almost three dozen books translated into many languages to his credit. Most deal with naturalist subjects and are often autobiographical, but Mowat also used them as vehicles for his passionate environmentalism. He is a strident Canadian nationalist and opponent of American imperialism, and has locked horns with the U.S. State Department, which refused him entry into the United States.

A self-taught journalist, Robert Fulford (1932–) joined the Toronto *Globe and Mail* as a copy boy in 1949. He became editor and contributor to various magazines, notably *Maclean's*, before joining the *Toronto Star* in 1958. There he gained a reputation as a lucid art, jazz, and ideas critic. His article "Their America, and Mine" appeared in 1968, the year he became editor of *Saturday Night,* a post he held until resigning over Conrad Black's acquisition of the magazine in 1987. His early continentalist ideas slowly gave way to an increasing sense of Canadian nationalism.

Mitchell Sharp (1911–) entered politics through the civil service. There he came to the attention of Trade and Commerce minister C.D. Howe, who promoted him through the various ranks of the department where he actively encouraged business between Canada and the United States. His Liberal ties led to his departure from government during the Diefenbaker administration, and entry into business. He won a seat in the House of Commons in 1963 and, because of his considerable experience, became Liberal Prime Minister Pearson's Trade and

Commerce minister. There he gained a reputation as the cabinet's leading antinationalist. Sharp ran for the leadership of the Liberal party in 1968 but waves of "Trudeaumania" swept him away. He was, by the time of "Options for the Future," Canada's Minister of External Affairs.

A) The Massey Report, 1951

The Forces of Geography

… Canadians, with their customary optimism, may think that the fate of their civilization is in their own hands. So it is. But this young nation, struggling to be itself, must shape its course with an eye to three conditions so familiar that their significance can too easily be ignored. Canada has a small and scattered population in a vast area; this population is clustered along the rim of another country many times more populous and of far greater economic strength; a majority of Canadians share their mother tongue with that neighbour, which leads to peculiarly close and intimate relations. One or two of these conditions will be found in many modern countries. But Canada alone possesses all three. What is their effect, good or bad, on what we call Canadianism? …

8. From these influences, pervasive and friendly as they are, much that is valuable has come to us, as we shall have occasion to observe repeatedly in this chapter and indeed throughout this entire survey: gifts of money spent in Canada, grants offered to Canadians for study abroad, the free enjoyment of all the facilities of many institutions which we cannot afford, and the importation of many valuable things which we could not easily produce for ourselves. We have gained much. In this preliminary stock taking of Canadian cultural life it may be fair to inquire whether we have gained a little too much.

9. We are thus deeply indebted to American generosity. Money has flowed across the border from such groups as the Carnegie Corporation, which has spent $7,346,188 in Canada since 1911 and the Rockefeller Foundation, to which we are indebted for the sum of $11,817,707 since 1914. There are other institutions from whose operations we benefit such as the Guggenheim Foundation and the American Association for the Advancement of Science. Through their generosity countless individuals have enjoyed opportunities for creative work or for further cultivation of their particular field of study. Applied with wisdom and imagination, these gifts have helped Canadians to live their own life and to develop a better Canadianism. Libraries given

to remote rural areas or to poorly endowed educational institutions are another example of the great diversity of our neighbour's broad benevolence. Many institutions in Canada essential to the equipment of a modern nation could not have been established or maintained without money provided from the United States. In addition, the scholarships and fellowships awarded to Canadian students in American universities without any discrimination, represent an impressive contribution to the advanced training of our young men and women of promise ...

11. Finally, we benefit from vast importations of what might be familiarly called the American cultural output. We import newspapers, periodicals, books, maps and endless educational equipment. We also import artistic talent, either personally in the travelling artist or company, or on the screen, in recordings and over the air. Every Sunday, tens of thousands tacitly acknowledge their cultural indebtedness as they turn off the radio at the close of the Sunday symphony from New York and settled down to the latest American Book of the Month.

12. Granted that most of these American donations are good in themselves, it does not follow that they have always been good for Canadians. We have not much right to be proud of our record as patrons of the arts. Is it possible that, beside the munificence of a Carnegie or a Rockefeller, Canadian contributions look so small that it seems hardly worthwhile making them? Or have we learned, wrongly, from our neighbour an unnecessary dependence on the contributions of the rich? A similar unworthy reliance on others appears in another field. Canada sends a number of students abroad, many of them on fellowships provided by other countries; Canada offers very few of her own fellowships to non-Canadians, none at all until very recently. Perhaps we have been tempted by a too easy benevolence, but this leaves us in an undignified position, unworthy of our real power and prestige.

13. Canada has, moreover, paid a heavy price for this easy dependence on charity and especially on American charity. First, many of our best students, on completing their studies at American institutions, accept positions there and do not return. The United States wisely relaxes its rigid immigration laws for all members of "learned professions" and profits accordingly. Our neighbours, able to take their choice of the foreign students attracted to their universities by far-seeing generosity, naturally choose many Canadians, partly because they are there in such numbers, partly because they fit in more readily with American ways than do others.

14. In consideration of American generosity in educating her citizens Canada "sells down south" as many as 2500 professional men and women in a year. Moreover, Canada by her too great dependence on American fellowships for advanced study, particularly in the humanities and social studies, has starved her own universities which lack not only money but the community of scholarship essential to the best work. "... American generosity has blinded our eyes to our own necessities. Culturally we have feasted on the bounty of our neighbours, and then we ask plaintively what is wrong with our progress in the arts." So runs a comment in the brief of the National Conference of Canadian Universities.

15. This impoverishment of Canadian universities for want of effort to keep our scholars at home, brings us to the whole question of our dependence on the United States for the satisfaction of so many non-material needs. Few Canadians realize the extent of this dependence. We know that if some disaster were to cut off our ready access to our neighbours, our whole economic life would be dislocated; but do we realize our lack of self-reliance in other matters?

16. Such a catastrophe for instance would no doubt hasten the establishment of the National Library so long overdue, but without many bibliographical aids now coming to us from the United States this would be very difficult, and the library would be deprived of countless invaluable Canadian books now available only in the United States. Moreover, it would be difficult to staff it properly without the facilities for advanced library training not found in Canada. The National Conference of Canadian Universities would no doubt make hasty plans for developing and expanding the few adequate schools of graduate studies which we now possess in view of the expense of sending large numbers of students to England or France. The development of many various specialized schools in the arts would be essential. Extensive provision would have to be made also for advanced study, research, and publication in the humanities and social studies as these are now almost wholly supported by American bounty. One Canadian body in this field indeed derives its entire support from the United States.

17. In this general picture of American influence on our cultural life it is perhaps permissible to mention that it extends to an extraordinary degree into an area beyond the limits of our inquiry, but closely related to it. Teachers from English-speaking Canada who wish to improve their talents or raise their professional status almost automatically make their pilgrimage to Teach-

ers' College at Columbia University or to one of half a dozen similar institutions. They return to occupy senior positions in elementary and high schools and to staff our normal schools and colleges of education. How many Canadians realize that over a large part of Canada the schools are accepting tacit direction from New York that they would not think of taking from Ottawa? On the quality of this direction it is not our place to pronounce, but we may make two general observations: first, Americans themselves are becoming restive under the regime; second, our use of American institutions, or our lazy, even abject, imitation of them has caused an uncritical acceptance of ideas and assumptions which are alien to our tradition. But for American hospitality we might, in Canada, have been led to develop educational ideas and practices more in keeping with our own way of life.

18. It may be added that we should also have been forced to produce our own educational materials — books, maps, pictures and so forth. As it is, the dependence of English-speaking Canada on the United States for these publications is excessive. In the elementary schools and high schools the actual texts may be produced in Canada, but teachers complain that far too much of the supplementary material is American with an emphasis and direction appropriate for American children but unsuitable for Canadian. As an illustration of the unsuitability of even the best American material, the statement was made in one of our briefs that out of thirty-four children in a Grade VIII class in a Canadian school, nineteen knew all about the significance of July 4 and only seven could explain that of July 1.

19. In our universities the situation is very much more serious. The comparative smallness of the Canadian university population, and the accessibility of American publishing houses with their huge markets has resulted in an almost universal dependence on the American product. It is interesting that a vigorous complaint of American text books should come from a scientist:

> "Where personalities and priorities are in question, American writings are very much biased in favour of the American. This is not to suggest that the facts will be distorted, but by mentioning the American names and industries and omitting mention of any others, a very unbalanced picture can be given. To subject Canadian students year in and year out to these influences are not particularly good for the growth of a wholesome Canadianism."

20. In other fields, the complaint may be not so much one of bias as of emphasis. In history, for example, dependence on the United States for source books and text books makes it difficult for history departments to plan any courses not generally taught in American universities. Junior courses in Canadian history present particular problems because American publishers do not find an adequate market for books and maps in that field. It must be emphasized that we have benefited greatly from many American productions; but because we have left the whole field to our neighbour our own special needs are not supplied.

21. Although in French-speaking Canada the difference in language offers some measure of protection, elsewhere in Canada the uncritical use of American training institutions, and therefore of American educational philosophy and what are referred to as teaching aids, has certainly tended to make our educational systems less Canadian, less suited to our traditions, less appreciative of the resources of our two cultures. It has also meant — and this is a matter with which we have a direct concern — that a large number of our leading teachers who are not only teachers but community leaders have received the final and often the most influential part of their training in the United States. This training may be excellent in itself, but it is surely permissible to wish that men and women who are going to exercise such a powerful influence on Canadian life should meet and work in some institution which, however international its staff may be, could put Canadian interests and problems in the first place.

22. The problem of text books just mentioned shows how American imports may harm as well as help us. But this is only part of the larger problem of vast cultural importations. Elsewhere in this Report we refer to concert tours in Canada organized beyond our borders. These are good in so far as they enable Canadians to hear artists eminent in the musical world. But, to hear the recognized artists, subscribers must also support many who are unknown and who, we are told, could not compete with Canadian talent if they were not supported by these powerful organizations. The unfortunate Canadian artist to get placed must go across the line, not the most happy solution for him or for his community.

23. Every intelligent Canadian acknowledges his debt to the United State for excellent films, radio programmes and periodicals. But the price may be excessive. Of films and radio we shall speak in more detail later, but it may be noted in passing that our national radio which carries the Sunday sym-

phony from New York also carries the soap-opera. In the periodical press we receive indeed many admirable American journals but also a flood of others much less admirable which, as we have been clearly told, is threatening to submerge completely our national product:

> "A Canadian culture with an English-French background,"so runs the brief of the *Société des Ecrivains Canadiens*, "will never reach the level which we desire so long as suitable measures are not taken against the invasion of the Canadian press by one of the most detestable products of the American press, so long as thousands of pages *Made in the United States* are slavishly reproduced by English language papers or translated for French-speaking readers, so long as pulp magazines and other works of the same nature enter or are distributed in Canada without any restriction, as is now the case."

24. The Canadian Periodical Press Association tells the same tale. Although during the last generation our periodicals have maintained and greatly strengthened their position, the competition they face has been almost overwhelming. Canadian magazines with much difficulty have achieved a circulation of nearly forty-two millions a year as against an American circulation in Canada of over eighty-six millions. "Canada ... is the only country of any size in the world," one of their members has observed, "whose people read more foreign periodicals than they do periodicals published in their own land, local newspapers excluded." The Canadian periodical cannot in its turn invade the American market; for Americans, it seems, simply do not know enough about Canada to appreciate Canadian material. Our periodicals cannot hold their own except in their limited and unprotected market, nine million English-speaking readers. These must be set against the one hundred and sixty millions served by their competitors in the whole North American continent.

25. The American invasion by film, radio and periodical is formidable. Much of what comes to us is good and of this we shall be speaking presently. It has, however, been represented to us that many of the radio programmes have in fact no particular application to Canada or to Canadian conditions and that some of them, including certain children's programmes of the "crime" and "horror" type, are positively harmful. News commentar-

ies too, and even live broadcasts from American sources, are designed for American ears and are almost certain to have an American slant and emphasis by reason of that they include or omit, as well as because of the opinions expressed. We think it permissible to record these comments on American radio since we observe that in the United States many radio programmes and American broadcasting in general have recently been severely criticized. It will, we think, be readily agreed that we in Canada should take measures to avoid in our radio, and in our television, at least those aspects of American broadcasting which have provoked in the United States the most outspoken and the sharpest opposition.

26. American influences on Canadian life to say the least are impressive. There should be no thought of interfering with the liberty of all Canadians to enjoy them. Cultural exchanges are excellent in themselves. They widen the choice of the consumer and provide stimulating competition for the producer. It cannot be denied, however, that a vast and disproportionate amount of material coming from a single alien source may stifle rather than stimulate our own creative effort; and, passively accepted without any standard of comparison, this may weaken critical faculties. We are now spending millions to maintain a national independence which would be nothing but an empty shell without a vigorous and distinctive cultural life. We have seen that we have its elements in our traditions and in our history; we have made important progress, often aided by American generosity. We must not be blind, however, to the very present danger of permanent dependence ...

B) Letter to My Son, 1968
Farley Mowat

My dear Sandy:

A couple of months ago you asked me whether I thought it had been worthwhile to have spent so much of my time and energy tilting against American windmills. Feeling that there was a certain measure of condescension in the question, I replied with one of my facile, TV-type answers: to wit, that there can be no other real choice open to a Canadian except to resist the Yanks and all their works so that we, as a people and a nation, may escape being ingested into the Eagle's gut, never to emerge again except — maybe — as a patch of excrement upon the pages of world history.

That should have disposed of your question — but it didn't, and the damned thing has been festering within me ever since. It has finally forced me, very reluctantly you can believe, to make a new evaluation of the belief which has sustained me through some twenty years of waging verbal warfare against the encroachments of Uncle Sam. Have I indeed been wasting my time? I'm afraid, God help me, that I have. I can no longer convince myself that we have even a snowball's chance in hell of escaping ultimate ravishment at the hands of the Yankee succubus. And what really hurts is the belated recognition on my part that there never *was* much chance; that Canadians have become so fatally infected with a compulsive desire to be screwed, blued, and tattooed as minions of the U.S.A.; that they not only do not wish to be saved — they are willing to fight against salvation with all the ferocity of cornered rats.

So wipe that smug smile off your face. You knew it all along, eh? Well, I should have known it too. God wot, enough people have tried to put me straight. There was Joey Smallwood for one (as smart a promoter as ever hustled a vote), who gave me a fatherly lecture about a year ago. "What the U.S. wants, it will get," he told me. "And if we don't *give* them what they want, they'll take it anyway. And what they want — is most of what we've got."

That was about as clear an expression of *Realpolitik* as one can expect from the political animal, even if it was primarily a rationalization intended to excuse our political masters for having *already* given the Yanks almost everything of any value in this country. Nevertheless, Joey's point was well taken since those who rule us (they do not "govern" — that word implies statesmanship combined with honourable intentions) have, for their own reasons, long since sold us out. Or maybe they just saw the light a long way back and, in keeping with their dubious professional practices, took the line of least resistance. Some of them, that is. Others sold out with deliberate intent. One day I must tell you the full and stirring story of one of the greatest of all such salesmen — C. D. Howe — and of how *he* put us on the block. Of course, Howe's plan was to sell us down the river on the national scale, and we've progressed since then. Now every single province is trying to conduct its own sellout, in direct competition with the Ottawa salesmen, and it wouldn't surprise me much to see the game, which is called "who'll sell out the mostest, the soonest," reach right down to the municipal level before too long. Hell, what am I saying? It is past that point already. Witness the almost frantic rush of businessmen and owners of Canadian resources to sell themselves and their holdings ("*their* holdings"? I mean *ours*, of course) for a quick handful of Yankee bucks.

Joey wasn't the only one to point me in the direction of acute aware-ness, and I must add, in my own defense, that I wasn't as stupid as you may think. I realized what the politicians, at least, were up to ages ago. My na-ivety — if such it was — lay in my continuing conviction that the people of this land would not forever continue to acquiesce in this piecemeal be-trayal of themselves and of their country. I was much influenced by what took place in Cuba and, before that, in Mexico. I believed that if such small, relatively powerless serf states could muster the guts to really kick Big Uncle in the backside, the people of Canada might be goaded into an equivalent demonstration of courage. Alas, Canadians are not Mexicans or Cubans, and I realize now that I miscalculated on a horrendous scale in ever thinking that Canadians would risk cutting off rich Uncle's dole by assuming the pos-ture of a Man.

This is a fact that I am going to have to learn to live with. We have become a prostrate people — by our own volition. Actually the only time Canadians even raise themselves on their elbows these days is to *defend* their chosen masters and to attack, with the bitter hostility only known to turncoats, those who dare reproach them for their spineless espousal of slave status ...

But there is no point in running on about what's past. My concern is for the future, because the future contains the world in which you'll have to live. So I have a few words of wisdom for you. Here speaks the hoary elder, and if I belabour the obvious a bit, bear with me.

Despite poor old Lester Pearson's recent statement in *Maclean's* that "the Americans are the least imperialistic people in history" (honest to God — that's what he said!), the Yanks now control the largest empire the world has ever known. Its citizens have, as Henry R. Luce (founder of Canada's two favourite magazines — *Life* and *Time*) once put it, now risen to the chal-lenge: "to accept wholeheartedly the duty and opportunity as the most pow-erful and vital nation in the world and in consequence to exert upon the world the full impact of our influence, *for such purposes as we see fit and by such means as we see fit*". In this delightfully frank statement, combined with one by John Foster Dulles — "There are two ways of conquering a foreign nation. One is to gain control of its people by force of arms. The other is to gain control of its economy by financial means." — you have the essential dogma subscribed to by the military-political-economic hegemony that runs the U.S.A. Once you understand this dogma you will have no difficulty understanding the true significance of current events in Spain, Korea, Greece, Formosa, the Philippines, Venezuela, Dominica; and all the rest of the sixty-odd serf states which are euphemistically referred to as U.S. "client" states. Note with particular attention that most of these U.S. "client" states are run by military, aristocratic, or political juntas of a totalitarian nature — juntas whose prime allegiance is to the hungry Eagle, rather than to their own peoples: juntas, many of which are maintained in power *by* the United States through classic applications of the principles of bribery, blackmail, subversion ... and armed force.

Or, if you find such a mass of evidence too complex for easy assimilation, take a long look at Vietnam instead. Observe, if you dare, the fantastic, and fearful similarities between the way the United States is behaving in that small and benighted country and the way Hitler behaved in *his* heyday.

Having done one or the other — preferably both — I ask you to consider the reality behind the American claims ... to being the world's greatest defenders of democracy. Democracy? My God, it is to laugh ... but bitter laughter it must be since demonstrably the United States is currently engaged in almost every form of domestic and external brutality, aggrandizement, degradation of the individual, and destruction of freedom which, so the U.S.A. maintains with a straight face, are the *singular* hallmarks of the beast called communism.

And what, you say, is this tirade in aid of? Well, it is intended to ensure that you harbour no further illusions about living in a democracy or of being protected by one. You, my son, are a helot, born and bred under the aegis of the United States, and you had damned well better come to terms with this inescapable fact. The illusion of democracy is one that you and your generation can ill afford to nurture. You must recognize that hard reality which not all the cherry-flavoured words of all the hucksters in the world can adequately conceal — you are a serf, no more than that . . . and Massa lives away down south.

You must rid yourself of this delusion because, as I see things, there is no guarantee that the privileged position presently enjoyed by Canadians as "most-favoured serfs" will last. The day is near when the Yankees will see no further need to pamper us — they'll own us outright. And then we may expect to be subjected to the same forms of direct oppression that have been

inflicted on most of the other peoples inhabiting the two American conti-
nents. The steady growth of overt totalitarianism within the Master State
itself brings ominous intimations that the good, fat days for the people who
sold themselves into bondage may even now be drawing to a close. And
remember — a man who sells *himself* into slavery does not earn the gratitude of his master: instead he earns a deep contempt. We Canadians have
well earned such contempt — and a wise slave knows that a contemptuous
master is more to be feared, in the long run, than an angry one.

Which leads me to an aside I think worth making. Not *all* Canadians
have sold themselves. As you are well aware, the French-Canadians in Quebec don't share our desire for self-immolation. They are resisting and thereby
rousing our particular hatred and resentment. Why so? It is not because we
really fear the development of a true federation of two nations (many other
countries live with such federations, and live well); it is because we are deathly
afraid that the intransigence of Quebec will draw the cold and hooded stare
of the Eagle and thereby expose *us*, by implication, to the furies meted out
to helots who revolt.

What I am trying to tell you is that nobody can, at this late stage, reverse the tide. Quebec, bravely as she may struggle, will fail. And so your
own survival now depends on your becoming as selfishly inclined, as amoral
as the men who have brought you and this country to its present sorry pass.
You must needs become one of them, and you might as well become one of
the overseer class, if you can make the grade. I recommend that you enter
politics. Although you have not yet displayed the requisite capabilities for
duplicity, cowardice, self-serving, and betrayal which pass for morality in
high places, you might improve with practice. It is at least certain that a
political career is one of the few available that will permit you to enjoy, with
any security of tenure, the benefits accrued by renegades and sycophants ...

Time is running out for your fellow slaves who, complacent and my-
opic as they are, believe they have made a splendid bargain with a kindly
master. The cold and brutal hour when they learn the truth, and when they
learn the price of their betrayal of themselves and of their land, lies close at
hand. God help them then, for no one else will wish to, if they could.

C) Their America and Mine, 1968
Robert Fulford

Once I spent a golden week in America. It seemed to me that within six magic days I went almost everywhere in the United States I could want to go. I was in Washington, New York, Cleveland, Pittsburgh. I was in Kentucky, Maryland, Delaware, Iowa. I was even in Oshkosh, Wisconsin. And everywhere it was beautiful: the sun was bright and the air bracing, the crops were good, the people were happy and prosperous. It was like a holiday, and I woke every morning full of joyful expectancy. ...

For anyone who loves the United States, the years since 1964 have been torture. I am, to state a fairly vital point, pro-American. Some good friends of mine are basically suspicious of the American idea, and many Canadians who are otherwise sensible are given to the view that Americans as a class are "immature" or "irresponsible" or just plain obnoxious. Not me. I like America and Americans. I admire them. I've always been profoundly grateful that Canada shares this continent with the American people: God bless America, as I think both Frank Underhill and Marshall McLuhan have said, for saving us from the fate of Australia.

This affection, like most affection, proceeds not from a conscious decision but from my personal history and from the nature of what might be called my interior design. For the fact is that some large part of the furniture of my mind and imagination has always been clearly stamped "Made in U.S.A." My first heroes were American musicians: Ellington, Armstrong, Peewee Russell, later Charlie Parker and Miles Davis. The novelists I first took seriously — Mark Twain, Hemingway, Fitzgerald, Salinger, eventually Bellow — were all American. The painters of my lifetime who have meant most to me have been those same painters who made New York the centre of their world: Pollock, de Kooning, Kline. And in my own trade, literary journalism, my heroes (with two major exceptions, Shaw and Orwell) have all been American: Lionel Trilling and Clement Greenberg, Leslie Fiedler and Edmund Wilson, Dwight Macdonald and Murray Kempton. Why, even my favourite English poet, W.H. Auden, has been an American citizen for a long time.

These people, more than any Englishmen or Frenchmen or Canadians, have taught me what art is, what is going on in the world out there, and who I am. I would not, looking at it objectively, recommend them to anyone else, nor would I suggest them as the basis of a course in civilization. They are merely the basis of *my* sense of civilization, such as it is. Heroes and models, I discovered only a few years ago, *happen* to you; as with parents, you don't choose them. You wake up one morning and discover they are there. You can hardly defend them or explain them, any more than you can defend or explain your parents. Most of mine are American, and that's all there is to it.

Still, I confess to an even deeper pro-Americanism than all this suggests. In the early 1950s, when I was in my twenties, I came to realize — "believe", perhaps, would be a more objective and defensible way to say it, but even now I'll stick with "realize" — that the world was involved in a basic conflict of values and that this conflict involved me. Some people in Moscow, whom I had every reason to despise, were trying to take over the world — *they* said this was so, and I for one believed them. And some people in Washington, whom I had no reason to despise, were opposing them. The issues were complicated, as all issues are, but that was the basic point. Ottawa had little to do with it. London was involved rather more, but was not important. Moscow versus Washington: this was what counted. I knew what side I was on, and through the 1950s, indeed up to (and past) President Kennedy's death in 1963, I had few doubts.

Now, of course, doubts swarm around me. I find myself susceptible to even the most tenuous arguments of the Cold War revisionist historians, not because their view of the past is so persuasive but because the present in which I read them is so poisoned. Vietnam is a terrible disaster for everyone involved; the Vietnamese suffer horribly, but what may finally be even worse is that the American spirit, on which so much of the future of mankind depends, is buckling under the strain. ...

D) Canada-U.S. Relations: Options for the Future, 1972
Mitchell Sharp

... In the review of Canadian foreign policy which the Canadian Government published in 1970 under the title *Foreign Policy for Canadians*, the challenge of "living distinct from, but in harmony with, the world's most powerful and dynamic nation, the United States" was described as one of two "inescapable realities, both crucial to Canada's continuing existence" in the context of which Canadian policy needs — domestic and external — must be assessed. The other was the "multi-faceted problem of maintaining national unit."

If the importance of this unique relationship is such as to affect the whole of Canada's foreign policy, it is in turn influenced by the nature of the world environment, and of the relations the United States and Canada have with other countries. As was recognized in the foreign policy review, and has been dramatically illustrated by more recent developments, the postwar international order is giving way to a new pattern of power relations. The preponderant position of the two super-powers, the United States and the U.S.S.R., is being reduced by the emergence of other major power centres. China, with its vast population and immense potential, has emerged from its long isolation, achieved the status of an important nuclear power, and taken its place in the community of nations. Western Europe is making historic strides towards unity through the enlargement and development of the European Economic Community. Japan has developed as a modern, industrial giant in Asia. Confrontation is giving way to negotiation and accommodation in East-West relations and major progress has been achieved on the road toward a political settlement in Europe.

In this evolving new world situation, enlarged opportunities are opening up for Canada and the United States to extend and broaden their relations with Communist countries and with the developing world, while continuing to develop their ties with their more traditional political and trading partners. These major changes will undoubtedly have a bearing on Canada-U.S. relations in the years ahead and on the option that may be open to Canada in particular.

The Canada-U.S. relationship, as it has evolved since the end of the Second World War, is in many respects a unique phenomenon. It is by far our most important external relationship, but it is more than an external relationship. It impinges on virtually every aspect of the Canadian national interest, and thus of Canadian domestic concerns.

Because of the vast disparity in power and population, it is also inevitably a relationship of profoundly unequal dependence; the impact of the United States on Canada is far greater than Canada's impact on the United States.

Some two decades ago, Lester B. Pearson warned that, as the two countries became more interdependent, relations between them would become more, not less, difficult. As interactions increased, conflicts of interest and differences of views were also bound to increase. Preserving harmony in the relationship would require careful and sensitive management.

In recent years, however, the occasional strains and difficulties that have affected relations between the two countries have also had a more basic and deep-seated source. In a Canada undergoing profound and rapid changes associated with industrialization, urbanization, improved education, cultural development, and a major reassessment of values, there has been a growing and widely felt concern about the extent of economic, military and cultural dependence on the United States, and the implications for Canadian independence.

Apart from the relationship itself, which has become more complex, public attitudes in Canada have also changed. In the past, Canadians have generally supported an easy-going, pragmatic approach to our relations with the United States in the belief that Canada's separate national existence and development were fully compatible with an unfolding, increasingly close economic, cultural and military relationship between the two countries. Many Canadians no longer accept this view, or at least do not regard it as self-evident. It is widely believed that the continental pull, especially economic and cultural, has gained momentum. In this on-going national debate, the fundamental question for Canada is whether and to what extent interdependence with the United States impairs the reality of Canada's independence. How strong has the continental pull become? Can it be resisted and controlled and, if so, at what price? ...

Perhaps more than ever before, the Canada-U.S. relationship is becoming an absorbing focus of much Canadian thinking about the Canadian condition. This is nowhere more evident than in the foreign policy review, which attributes its own genesis in part to "frustration ... about having to live in the shadow of the United States and its foreign policy, about the heavy dependence of Canada's economy on continuing American prosperity, and about the marked influence of that large and dynamic society on Canadian life in general."

This is a relatively new set of perceptions. In fact, one of the most dramatic aspects of such evidence as is provided by the public opinion polls has been the change in Canadian attitudes over the past two decades. In the 1950s and early 1960s, most Canadians were firm in their support for U.S. policies and certainly gave no evidence of perceiving a U.S. threat to Canada. In 1956 as many as 68 percent of those polled supported the idea of free trade with the United States. On the more general issue of dependence, the polls taken between 1948 and 1963 indicated that at least half of those polled did not think Canadian life was being unduly influenced by the United States. Indeed, a 1963 poll recorded 50 percent as believing that dependence on the United States was beneficial to Canada. All in all, attitudes during that period appeared to be much more congenial to close Canadian involvement with the United States than is the case today.

The evidence suggests that the overriding issue to emerge from the Canada-U.S. relationship for most Canadians today is that of economic independence. For example, a cross-section of various polls indicates that 88.5 percent of Canadians think it important for Canada to have more control over its own economy; that two of every three Canadians view the current level of American investment in Canada as being too high; that, while seven out of every ten Canadians are prepared to acknowledge that American investment has given them a higher standard of living than they might otherwise have had, almost half of them would be willing to accept a lower living standard if that were the price to be paid for controlling or reducing the level of American investment. These are admittedly national averages. They do not necessarily do justice to pronounced regional variations.

If the national mood is to be comprehended in one sentence, it would appear that Canadians remain aware of the benefits of the American connection but that, today more than at any other time since the Second World War they are concerned about the trend of the relationship and seem willing to contemplate and support reasonable measures to assure greater Canadian independence.

It is a matter of more than passing interest that the movement of people between Canada and the United States runs in remarkable parallel with the attitudes reflected in the public opinion polls. The 1950s, for example, saw an average of some thirty thousand Canadians a year moving to the United States, against a reverse flow of only about eleven thousand. These were the years of the "brain drain," when doctors, engineers, teachers, artists, writers and musicians comprised the largest group of Canadian emigrants. By the 1960s, the net flow of Canadians moving across the border started to level off dramatically until, in 1969, for the first time in the postwar period, the movement of Americans to Canada actually exceeded that of Canadians to the United States by a small margin.

The trend may prove temporary. It probably reflects, to some extent at least, U.S. restrictions on Canadian immigration and the impact of the Vietnam war. Nevertheless, the trend is not without significance. It cannot easily be explained by the normal quantitative factors. The difference in per capita gross national product between the two countries has not varied widely on either side of the 25 percent mark and the gap in real per capita income has stayed about the same since the war. The skilled Canadian can still command a significantly higher salary in the United States. The sunny climates of California and Florida as places of retirement have also not changed. Indeed, the eighteen thousand Canadians who emigrated to the United States in 1969 obviously felt all the old pulls. But something evidently had changed.

Canada had matured. The outlines of a more distinct national profile were emerging. An increasingly industrial economy had taken shape. The revolution in communications gave promise of knitting the country more closely together. A quieter revolution had transformed the face of French Canada. The flow of immigrants from Europe and elsewhere was adding new dimensions to Canadian life. The foundations of Canada's cultural personality were being strengthened.

Inevitably, Canadians became more aware of themselves, of the kind of society they were intent on shaping, of the particular problems that lay ahead for them. They were concerned about maintaining national unity; about equalizing economic opportunities as between the different regions of the country; about the best ways of meeting the challenges of a bilingual and multicultural society. They were concerned about their future prosperity; about the problem of providing employment for the most rapidly expanding labour force of any industrialized country; about the management of the resources with which their country had been so richly endowed. They were concerned about the quality of their life; about the risks of blight brought about by unplanned urban growth; about the threat to the environment represented by industrial and technological growth; about the fragile balance of nature in the Arctic and the quality of the waters off Canada's coasts.

If these concerns can be brought within a single focus, it is that of Canada's distinctness. And for Canada distinctness could, in recent years, have only one meaning: distinctness from the United States. What more and more Canadians were brought to realize was that, with all the affinities and all the similarities they shared with the United States, Canada was a distinct country with distinct problems that demanded Canadian solutions. It was not and is not that Canadians underrate the tremendous achievements of American society or its unbounded capacity for self-renewal. It is simply that more and more Canadians have come to conclude that the American model does not, when all is said and done, fit the Canadian condition. Such a conclusion has led, not unnaturally, to the assertion of the right of Canadians to fashion their national environment according to their own perceptions.

In this changing context, what is to be done about the continental pull and the internal momentum with which it is thought by many to be endowed? It is probably useful to start out by acknowledging that there are immutable factors that cannot be changed. Our history, our geography, our demographic structure have imposed and will continue to impose limitations on Canada's freedom of action. Whether we defend it or not, there will be three thousand miles of common frontier with the United States. Chinese Walls, Maginot Lines or Iron Curtains have never lived up to the claims of impermeability that were made for them. We could conceivably keep out American products but not American ideas, tastes or life styles. We could theoretically have one hundred percent Canadian content in our broadcasting but could hardly ban the airwaves to American stations. We could prohibit the migration of people but not eliminate the strong interpersonal relationships on each side of the border. Canadian independence can be realistic only within some measure of interdependence in the world. Canadian energies should not be wasted or efforts misspent on policies that give little promise of being achievable.

In examining the options before us, therefore, we must necessarily focus on those areas of the Canada-U.S. relationship where movement is not foreclosed by factors about which nothing can be done.

This is not the first time Canadians have asked themselves which way they should go. The factor of geography remains a constant element in the equation. The disproportion between Canada and the United States in terms of power has not changed all that much. The continental pull itself has historical antecedents. The pursuit of distinctive identity runs through the process of Canadian nation-building.

But if the signposts are familiar, the landscape is undoubtedly different. Many of the old countervailing forces have disappeared. The links across the common border have increased in number, impact and complexity. New dimensions are being added to the Canada-US relationship all the time. On both sides, there is now difficulty in looking upon the relationship as being wholly external in character.

The world trend is not helpful to Canada in resolving this dilemma. For the trend is discernibly in the direction of interdependence. In the economic realm, in science, in technology, that is the direction in which the logic of events is pointing. In Canada's case, inevitably, interdependence is likely to mean interdependence mainly with the United States. This is a simple statement of the facts. It does not pretend to be a value judgment. In point of fact, the balance of benefits of such a trend for Canada may well be substantial.

But this evades the real question that looms ahead for Canada. And this is whether interdependence with a big, powerful, dynamic country like the United States is not bound, beyond a certain level of tolerance, to impose an unmanageable strain on the concept of a separate Canadian identity, if not on the elements of Canadian independence.

To pose these questions is simple enough. To propound answers to them is more difficult because any answer is likely to touch on the central ambiguity of our relationship with the United States. The temper of the times, nevertheless, suggests that Canadians are looking for answers. It is also apparent that many of the answers are in Canadian hands. This is because few of the problems engendered by the relationship are, in fact, problems of deliberate creation on the U.S. side. They are problems arising out of contiguity and disparity in wealth and power and, not least, out of the many affinities that make it more difficult for Canadians to stake out an identity of their own.

The real question facing Canadians is one of direction. In practice, three broad options are open to us:

a) We can seek to maintain more or less our present relationship with the United States with a minimum of policy adjustments;

b) We can move deliberately toward closer integration with the United States;

c) We can pursue a comprehensive, long-term strategy to develop and strengthen the Canadian economy and other aspects of our national life and in the process to reduce the present Canadian vulnerability.

Such a statement of options may err on the side of oversimplification. The options are intended merely to delineate general directions of policy. Each option clearly covers a spectrum of possibilities and could be supported by a varied assortment of policy instruments. Nevertheless, the importance of the options notion is not to be discounted. For, in adopting one of the options, Canadians would be making a conscious choice of the continental environment that, in their view, was most likely to be responsive to their interests and aspirations over the next decade or two. Conversely, no single option is likely to prove tenable unless it commands a broad national consensus.

The first option would be to aim at maintaining more or less the present pattern of our economic and political relationship with the United States with a minimum of policy change either generally or in the Canada-United States context.

The formulation notwithstanding, this is not an option meaning no change. In the present climate, any option that did not provide for change would clearly be unrealistic. The realities of power in the world are changing. Some of the international systems that have provided the context for our monetary and trading relations in the postwar period are in the process of reshaping. The United States is embarked on a basic reappraisal of its position and policies. The Canadian situation is itself changing and new perceptions are being brought to bear on the Canada-U.S. relationship. All this suggests that some adjustments in Canadian policy are unavoidable.

The first option would neither discount the fact of change nor deny the need to accommodate to it. But it would imply a judgment that, at least on the present evidence, the changes that have occurred or are foreseeable are not of a nature or magnitude to call for a basic reorientation of Canadian policies, particularly as they relate to the United States.

In practical terms, this would mean maintaining the general thrust of our trade and industrial policies, including a large degree of laissez faire in economic policy, a multilateral, most-favoured-nation approach as the guiding principle of our trade policy, emphasis on securing improved access to the U.S. market, the vigorous export of commodities and semi-processed goods, and continuing efforts to industrialize domestically by rationalizing production, in large part for export. Presumably, little or no change would be made in the present way of handling matters at issue with the United States, which is one of dealing with each problem as it arises and seeking to maintain something of a "special relationship."

But there is another side to the coin. The changes that are taking place on both sides of the border point to new opportunities and new constraints emerging for Canada. We would aim at seizing the opportunities and managing the constraints to the best of our ability. In the process we would be concerned about the balance of benefits for Canada, but we would be less concerned about how any given transaction or act of policy fitted into some overall conception of our relationship with the United States.

Nevertheless, other things being equal, we would seek to avoid any further significant increase in our dependence on the United States and our vulnerability to the vicissitudes of the U.S. market and to changes in U.S. economic policy. An effort to diversify our export markets would not be incompatible with the first option; nor would a policy to take advantage of accelerating demand for our mineral and energy resources to secure more processing and employment in Canada and, generally, to reap greater benefits from this major national asset; nor would some further moderate Canadian action to achieve greater control over the domestic economic and cultural environment.

In sum, this is essentially a pragmatic option. It would not, by definition, involve radical policy departures. It would deal with issues as they arose on the basis of judgments made in relation to each issue. It is not a static option because it would address itself to the solution of problems generated by an environment which is itself dynamic. One of its main attractions is that, we trust, it would not foreclose other options.

The precise implications and costs of this option are difficult to predict because they would vary significantly depending on developments over the short and medium term. Accommodation of current U.S. preoccupations, however limited, would entail some costs and could involve an increase in our dependence on the United States. If U.S. difficulties proved more durable, and if significant improvements in access to other markets did not materialize, pressures might develop in the United States and in Canada for further special bilateral arrangements. Alternatively, if protectionist attitudes in the United States were to find reflection in official policy, we might be forced to seek other markets on whatever terms we could and perhaps to make painful adjustments in order to reorient our industry to serve mainly the domestic market.

On more optimistic assumptions about the course of U.S. policy and the future of the international trading system, the first option might be followed for some time with ostensible success. The real question is whether it comes fully to grips with the basic Canadian situation or with the underlying continental pull. There is a risk that, in pursuing a purely pragmatic course, we may find ourselves drawn more closely into the U.S. orbit. At the end of the day, therefore, it may be difficult for the present position to be maintained, let alone improved, without more fundamental shifts in Canadian policy.

The second option is to accept that, in a world where economies of scale are dictating an increasing polarization of trade and in the face of intensified integrating pressures within North America, the continuation of the existing relationship, based on the economic separation of Canada and the United States, does not make good sense, and to proceed from that conclusion deliberately to prepare the ground for an arrangement with the United States involving closer economic ties.

The option spans a considerable range of possibilities. At the lower end of the scale, it might involve no more than the pursuit of sectoral or other limited arrangements with the United States based on an assessment of mutual interest. In effect, this would represent an extension of past practices except to the extent that such arrangements would be pursued more as a matter of deliberate policy. We might seek, for example, to adapt to other industries the approach reflected in the Automotive Products Agreement. The chemical industry is one such industry that could lend itself to rationalization on a North-South basis. The aerospace industry might well be another. We might also endeavour to negotiate a continental arrangement with the United States covering energy resources. Under such an arrangement, U.S. access to Canadian energy supplies might be traded in exchange for unimpeded access to the U.S. market for Canadian uranium, petroleum, and petrochemical products (to be produced by a much expanded and developed industry within Canada).

This more limited form of integration has a certain logic to it and, indeed, warrants careful examination. It may be expected, however, to generate pressures for more and more continental arrangements of this kind that would be increasingly difficult to resist. Experience with the Automotive Products Agreement suggests that, in any such sectoral arrangements, there may be difficulty in maintaining an equal voice with the United States over time. Nor could we be sure that the concept of formal symmetry, on which the United States has lately insisted, is one that can easily be built into a sectoral arrangement without impairing the interets of the economically weaker partner. In the energy field, by dealing continentally with the United States, we would almost certainly limit our capacity to come to an arrangement with other potential purchasers, in Europe or Japan, quite apart from possibly impinging upon future Canadian needs. In sum, we might well be driven to the conclusion that partial or sectoral arrangements are less likely to afford us the protection we seek than a more comprehensive regime of free trade.

A free trade area or a customs union arrangement with the United States would, to all intents and purposes, be irreversible for Canada once embarked upon. It would, theoretically, protect us against future changes in U.S. trade policy towards the rest of the world, though not against changes in U.S. domestic economic policy. This option has been rejected in the past because it was judged to be inconsistent with Canada's desire to preserve a maximum degree of independence, not because it lacked economic sense in terms of Canadian living standards and the stability of the Canadian economy.

A free trade area permits greater freedom that a customs or economic union, which calls for a unified external tariff and considerable harmonization of fiscal and other domestic economic policies. It might enable us, for example, to continue to protect our energy resources by limiting exports to the surpluses available after meeting present and prospective Canadian requirements and to ensure against harmful pricing practices. It would not debar us from continuing to bargain with third countries for improved access to their markets or from protecting ourselves against low-cost imports. Yet it must be accepted that the integration of the Canadian and U.S. economies would proceed apace and we should be bound to be more affected than ever by decisions taken in Washington with only limited and indirect means of influencing them.

Internationally, there is a real risk that the conclusion of a free trade arrangement between Canada and the United States would be taken as setting the seal upon the polarization of world trade. To the extent that it was, our room for bargaining with third countries would inevitably be reduced and our economic fortunes become more closely linked with those of the United States.

The experience of free trade areas (such as the European Free Trade Association) suggests, in any case, that they tend to evolve toward more organic arrangements and the harmonization of internal economic policies. More specifically, they tend towards a full customs and economic union as a matter of internal logic. A Canada-U.S. free trade area would be almost certain to do likewise. Indeed, such a course could be argued to be in the Canadian interest because, to compete, we would probably require some harmonization of social and economic costs.

If a free trade area or customs union is a well nigh irreversible option for Canada, this cannot necessarily be assumed to be the case for the United States. A situation could easily be imagined in which difficulties arose in certain economic sectors or regions of the United States when the Congress might feel constrained to seek to halt or reverse the process. The central problem, here as elsewhere, is the enormous disparity in power between the United States and Canada.

It is arguable, therefore, that in the end the only really safe way to guard against reversal and to obtain essential safeguards for Canadian industry and other Canadian economic interests might be to move to some form of political union at the same time. The object would be to obtain for Canadians a genuine and usable voice in decisions affecting our integrated economies.

At first glance this might look like pursuing the argument to an unwarranted conclusion. The Europeans, it could be argued, have, after all, found it possible to operate a customs union without substantial derogations from their sovereignty. Even if this changes to some extent as they progress towards economic and monetary union, the prospects for full political union or confederation continue to look relatively remote.

But the configuration of power in Europe is different. The European countries are more recognizably different from one another; their identities are older and more deeply anchored; and they are much more nearly equal in resources and power. There is a certain balance in the decision-making system of the European Economic Community that would not be conceivable in a bilateral Canada-U.S. arrangement. For the Europeans, moreover, the problem has been one of transcending historical conflicts. For Canada, on the contrary, the problem has been one of asserting its separate identity and developing its character distinctive from that of the United States in the face of similarities, affinities and a whole host of common denominators.

Throughout this discussion it has been assumed that proposals for free trade or a customs union with Canada would be welcomed in the United States. This is not an unreasonable assumption, taking account of the substantial interpenetration that already exists between the two economies and the vested interests that have been created in the process on the part of U.S. business and labour. It is, nevertheless, an assumption that remains to be tested against changing attitudes in the United States and the implications for U.S. trade and other policies that, like Canada's, have been global rather than regional in their general thrust. Congressional reaction, in particular, would be a matter of conjecture until the issue was on the table. Political union would presumably raise issues of a different order of complexity, although it has from time to time had respectable support in some circles in the United States.

If we were to opt for integration, deliberate and coherent policies and programs would be required, both before and after an arrangement was achieved, to cope with the difficult adjustments that would be entailed for Canada. An adequate transitional period would be essential: Some safeguards for production and continued industrial growth in Canada would have to be negotiated. Agriculture might emerge as another problem sector. In practice, any safeguards would probably be limited largely to a transitional period and could not be expected to cushion the impact of integration for an indefinite future. A tendency for the centres of production — and population — to move south might, in the long run, be difficult to stem. But the more relaxed environment Canada has to offer and the lesser prominence of pressures in Canadian society might also, over time, exert a countervailing influence on any purely economic trend.

The probable economic costs and benefits of this option would require careful calculation. The more fundamental issues, however, are clearly political. In fact, it is a moot question whether this option, or any part of it, is politically tenable in the present or any foreseeable climate of Canadian public opinion.

Reactions and attitudes would no doubt differ across the country. The cleavage of interest between the central, industrialized region and the Western provinces on this issue has become apparent in recent years. Attitudes rooted in historical tradition could be expected to play their part in the Atlantic Provinces. The reaction in the French-speaking areas is more difficult to predict. On the one hand, they tend not to draw a very sharp distinction between the impact of economic control of local enterprise whether exercised from the United States or from elsewhere in Canada. But it is not unlikely that among many French-speaking Canadians the prospect of union with the United States would be viewed as risking their eventual submergence in a sea of some two hundred million English-speaking North Americans and as a reversal of the efforts made in Canada over the last ten years to create a favourable climate for the survival and development of the French language and culture in North America.

There is a real question, therefore, whether the whole of Canada could be brought into union with the United States. Of course, full-fledged political union is not the basic intent of this option. But, to the extent that the logic of events may impel us in that direction, almost any form of closer integration with the United States may be expected to generate opposition in Canada. If it is true, moreover, as appears to be the case, that a more vigorous sense of identity has been taking root among Canadians in recent years, it is unlikely that opposition to this option would be confined to particular parts of the country.

The basic aim of the third option would be, over time, to lessen the vulnerability of the Canadian economy to external factors, including, in particular, the impact of the United States and, in the process, to strengthen our capacity to advance basic Canadian goals and develop a more confident sense of national identity. If it is to be successfully pursued, the approach implicit in this option would clearly have to be carried over into other areas of national endeavour and supported by appropriate policies. But the main thrust of the option would be towards the development of a balanced and efficient economy to be achieved by means of a deliberate, comprehensive and long-term strategy.

The accent of the option is on Canada. It tries to come to grips with one of the unanswered questions that runs through so much of the Canada-U.S. relationship, and which is what kind of Canada it is that Canadians actually want. It is thus in no sense an anti-American option. On the contrary, it is the one option of all those presented that recognizes that, in the final analysis, it may be for the Canadian physician to heal himself.

The option is subject to two qualifications. "Over time" recognizes that the full benefits will take time to materialize, but that a conscious and deliberate effort will be required to put and maintain the Canadian economy on such a course. "To lessen" acknowledges that there are limits to the process because it is unrealistic to think that any economy, however structured, let alone Canada's, can be made substantially immune to developments in the world around us in an era of growing interdependence.

The option is one that can have validity on most assumptions about the external environment. A basically multilateral environment, of course, in which trade is governed by the most-favoured-nation principle, would enhance its chances of success. But it would not be invalidated by other premises. That is because the option relates basically to the Canadian economy. Its purpose is to recast that economy in such a way as to make it more rational and more efficient as a basis for Canada's trade abroad.

The present may be an auspicious time for embarking on this option. Our trading position is strong. We are regarded as a stable and affluent country with a significant market and much to offer to our global customers in the way of resources and other products. Our balance of payments has been improving in relative terms. We are no longer as dependent on large capital inflows as we once were. A new round of comprehensive trade negotiations is in prospect during 1973. Above all, there is a greater sense of urgency within Canada and greater recognition abroad of Canada's right to chart its own economic course.

The option assumes that the basic nature of our economy will continue unchanged. That is to say that, given the existing ratio of resources to population, Canada will continue to have to depend for a large proportion of its national wealth on the ability to export goods and services to external markets on secure terms of access. The object is essentially to create a sounder, less vulnerable economic base for competing in the domestic and world markets and deliberately to broaden the spectrum of markets in which Canadians can and will compete.

In terms of policy, it would be necessary to encourage the specialization and rationalization of production and the emergence of strong Canadian-controlled firms. It is sometimes argued that a market of the size of Canada's may not provide an adequate base for the economies of scale that are a basic ingredient of international efficiency. The argument is valid only up to a point. The scale of efficiency is different for different industries and there is no reason why a market of twenty-two million people with relatively high incomes should prove inadequate for many industries which are not the complex or capital-intensive.

The close co-operation of government, business and labour would be essential through all phases of the implementation of such an industrial strategy. So would government efforts to provide a climate conducive to the expansion of Canadian entrepreneurial activity. It may be desirable, and possible, in the process to foster the development of large, efficient multinationally-operating Canadian firms that could effectively compete in world markets. It may also be possible, as a consequence of greater efficiencies, for Canadian firms to meet a higher proportion of the domestic requirement for goods and services. But that would be a natural result of the enhanced level of competitiveness which the option is designed to promote; it is not in the spirit of the option to foster import substitution as an end in itself with all the risks that would entail of carrying us beyond the margins of efficiency.

The option has been variously described as involving a deliberate, comprehensive, and long-term strategy. It is bound to be long-term because some substantial recasting of economic structures may be involved. It is comprehensive in the sense that it will entail the mutually-reinforcing use and adaptation of a wide variety of policy instruments. Fiscal policy, monetary policy, the tariff, the rules of competition, government procurement, foreign investment regulations, and science policy may all have to be brought to bear on the objectives associated with this option. The choice and combination of policy instruments will depend on the precise goals to be attained. The implications, costs, and benefits of the option will vary accordingly.

In saying that the strategy must be deliberate, it is accepted that it must involve some degree of planning, indicative or otherwise, and that there must be at least a modicum of consistency in applying it. One implication of the conception of deliberateness is that the strategy may have to entail a somewhat greater measure of government involvement than has been the case in the past. The whole issue of government involvement, however, needs to be kept in proper perspective. The Government is now and will continue to be involved in the operation of the economy in a substantial way. This is a function of the responsibility which the Canadian Government shares with other sovereign governments for ensuring the well-being and prosperity of its citizens in a context of social justice. A wide variety of policy instruments and incentives is already being deployed to that end, largely with the support and often at the insistence of those who are more directly concerned with the running of different segments of the economy. It is not expected that the pursuit of this particular option will radically alter the relation between Government and the business community, even if the Government were to concern itself more closely with the direction in which the economy was evolving.

Much the same considerations apply to the relationship between the federal and provincial jurisdictions. It is true that, in the diverse circumstances that are bound to prevail in a country like Canada, the task of aggregating the national interest is not always easy. There may be a problem, therefore, in achieving the kind of broad consensus on objectives, priorities and instrumentalities on which the successful pursuit of anything on the lines of the present option is likely to hinge. Part of the problem may derive from a divergent assessment of short-term interests. In terms of longer-range goals, it is much less apparent why federal and provincial interests should not be largely compatible or why the elaboration of this option should not enhance and enlarge the opportunities for co-operation with the provinces. Indeed, there are many areas, such as the upgrading of Canada's natural resource exports, where the implications of this option are likely to coincide closely with provincial objectives.

What of the impact on the United States, which could be critical to the success of the option? There again, it is necessary to keep matters in perspective. There is no basic change envisaged in Canada's multilateral trade policy. On the contrary, we could expect to be working closely with the United States in promoting a more liberal world-trading environment. Nor does the option imply any intention artificially to distort our traditional trading patterns. The United States would almost certainly remain Canada's most important market and source of supply by a very considerable margin.

The fact remains, nevertheless, that the option is directed towards reducing Canada's vulnerability, particularly in relation to the United States. A good deal of this vulnerability derives from an underlying continental pull, which is inadvertent. To that extent, the risk of friction at the governmental level is lessened, although it would be unrealistic to discount it altogether. Much would depend on what policy instruments were selected in support of this option and how we deployed them. The state of the U.S. economy could be another factor determining U.S. reactions at any given time. On any reasonable assumptions, however, such impact as the option may unavoidably have on U.S. interests would be cushioned by the time-frame over which it is being projected and should be relatively easy to absorb in a period of general growth and prosperity. When all is said and done, the option aims at a relative decline in our dependence on the United States, not at a drastic change in our bilateral relationship. As such, it is not incompatible with the view, recently advanced by President Nixon in his address to the House of Commons, that "no self-respecting nation can or should accept the proposition that it should always be economically dependent upon any other nation."

The continental pull appears to be operating most strongly in the economic and cultural sectors. There are those who, like Professor John Kenneth Galbraith, argue that U.S. economic influence can be disregarded so long as Canada manages to maintain a distinct culture of its own. Many Canadians would disagree with him. Nevertheless, no prescription for Canada is likely to be complete that did not attempt to cover the cultural sector.

There are differences between the economic and the cultural forces that are at work in the Canada-U.S. relationship. In the first place, culture has more than one dimension; it means different things to different Canadians. Second, the cultural interaction between Canada and the United States is, if anything, even less a matter of governmental policy than the interaction between the two economies. Third, it is much harder to influence the movement of ideas than it is to influence the movement of goods. Finally, it is evidently not a threat about which the public at large feels anything like the concern that, according to the opinion polls, it feels about the threat to Canadian control of the domestic economic environment.

This is one reason why the cultural scene requires separate discussion. But there is another. In the economic sector, it is clear, Canadians do face difficult choices. It is a moot question whether this is really true when it comes to the cultural sector. This is not to discount the importance of a healthy cultural environment to the Canadian sense of identity and national confidence. It is merely to suggest that in this sector the essential choices may, in fact, already have been made.

Domestically, two prescriptions have, by and large, been applied. The first is regulatory. It recognizes that some of the means of cultural expression are subject to the competition of the marketplace in the same way as the offer of other services. The purpose of regulation in these instances is simply to ensure that, where the standards of the product are equal, the Canadian offering is not ruled out by terms of competition that are unequal. This is the general philosophy that has guided the efforts of the Canadian Radio and Television Commission. It is probably applicable in other areas where the Canadian product — whether film, record, or publication — is held back because the requisite measure of control of the distribution system is not in Canadian hands.

The other prescription has been to give direct support to cultural activity in Canada. This role has, on the whole, fallen to government. Support has taken the form of financial assistance, but also of institutions that have been established to encourage the expression of Canadian creative talent. The Massey Commission judged in 1951 that money spent on cultural defences was, in the end, no less important than money spent on defence so-called. In the eyes of most Canadians, this remains a valid judgment.

As in the economic sector, any policy aimed at lessening the impact of U.S. influences on the Canadian cultural scene should presumably have an external dimension. This is not simply a matter of diversification for its own sake. Canada's cultural roots are, after all, widely ramified. International projection will enable Canada to reaffirm its distinctive linguistic and cultural complexion. But it will also give Canadians the opportunity to test their product in a wider market and to draw, in turn, on the currents of cross-fertilization.

In sum, Canadians will not be able to take their cultural environment for granted. It is on the cultural front, as on the economic front, that the impact on Canada of the dynamic society to the south finds its strongest expression. The impact has no doubt been magnified by the development of the mass media and their counterpart: the mass market. French-speaking Canadians may be less exposed to it for reasons of language, but they are not immune. Canadians generally appear to find it more difficult to focus on it than on the U.S. impact on the Canadian economy, perhaps because the many affinities between Canadians and Americans tend to make any concept of a threat unreal. On the whole, the general directions of Canadian policy in the cultural sector have been set and they have been pursued with reasonable success. Perhaps we have already turned the corner. But it remains for these policies to be extended to other vulnerable areas and to take account of the further impetus that the new technologies may give to the cultural thrust of the United States as it affects Canada.

This is, fortunately, an area in which there is broad convergence between the perceptions and goals of the federal and provincial governments. It would not be unrealistic, therefore, to look to a high degree of co-operation between the two levels of government in creating the kind of climate we shall need over the next decade or two if Canadian themes are to find their distinctive expression.

It is also one of the areas in which Canadians can act with the least risk of external repercussion. It has been said that culture is imported rather than exported. This is not wholly true. But to the extent that cultural influences are brought in willingly, they can be shaped domestically without affront to the exporter ...

The foreign policy review speaks of living distinct from but in harmony with the United States. There is no anomaly in this proposition. The concept of distinctness is taken for granted as the natural context for international relations and no qualitative inferences should be drawn from it one way or the other. There are many countries in the world that certainly regard themselves as being distinct and have no difficulty in living in the closest harmony of purpose and endeavour with other countries. There is no intrinsic reason, therefore, why Canadian distinctness should in any way inhibit the continued existence of a fundamentally harmonious relationship between Canada and the United States.

It is fair to assume that, in the 1970s and 1980s, Canadian-American relations may become more complex than they have been in the past. It is part of the trend toward increasing complexity in the relationship that a larger number of issues may arise between us that engage the national interest on each side. It is also to be assumed that, if the national interest were interpreted in a new and possibly narrower focus, the issues arising between us would, on occasion, be judged to bear more critically on it than when the relationship was more relaxed. Finally, as governments on both sides of the border are more and more being drawn by their various domestic constituencies into areas of social and economic activity that involve the shaping of national goals, the nature of the issues between us and the means of resolving them may change.

There is nothing in all this that should be thought to imply a scenario for greater contention. Far from it. There will, of course, be issues, such as Canada's policies on foreign ownership and perhaps in relation to energy and other resources — and in many other areas — where perceptions will differ. The same will almost certainly be true of United States policies as that country continues to grapple with secular and strutural problems of economic adjustment. On occasion, as [U.S.] Secretary of State Rogers recently put it, each government "may be required to take hard decisions in which the other cannot readily concur." In the main, however, we should expect both countries to manage change in a spirit of harmony and without doing unnecessary damage to interests on the other side. Above all, it is in Canada's interest to work closely with a dynamic and outward-looking United States whose influence and the leverage it can bring into play will continue to be critical to the achievement of some of Canada's principal objectives in the international environment.

In the final analysis, harmony is not an extraneous factor in the Canada-United States relationship because it is based on a broad array of shared interests, perceptions and goals. It also reflects the many affinities that have linked Canadians and Americans traditionally and that continue to link them as members of changing but still broadly compatible societies. What is at issue at the moment is, as someone has aptly defined it, "the optimum range of interdependence" between Canada and the United States. All the evidence suggests that the issue is being reviewed on both sides of the border. But, understandably, it is of immensely greater significance for Canada. If the outcome is a Canada more confident in its identity, stronger in its capacity to satisfy the aspirations of Canadians and better equipped to play its part in the world, it is an outcome that is bound to make Canada a better neighbour and partner of the United States. Above all, it is an outcome that should buttress the continuation of a harmonious relationship between the two countries.

15

"The Hard Knocks of History"

Natives and the Federal Government

DOCUMENTS

A) Speech, August 8, 1969
   Pierre E. Trudeau
B) Citizens Plus: The Red Paper, 1970
   Indian Association of Alberta
C) The Unjust Society, 1969
   Harold Cardinal
D) Ruffled Feathers, 1971
   William Wuttunee

To what extent must subsequent generations honour their ancestors' actions? Must they uphold agreements signed more than a century ago in a world radically different from their own? What if current social values no longer reflect those of the signatories? Must they maintain covenants that defy present sensibilities? And what if two parties created a contract but each interpreted it differently? Could their descendants renegotiate it long after the original signatories died? What if some future generation wants to change a document that was flawed from inception, but others insist on maintaining it intact? Finally, if treaties must be honoured, are they obeyed in their precise terms or in their intent? When, for example, the federal government in 1879 promised to supply and stock a Native band's medicine chest in perpetuity, does that now imply providing it with universal health care or simply satisfying its pharmaceutical needs? Does it refer to holistic care or licensed medical practices?

These contentious issues continue to percolate through Canadian society, periodically bubbling over as one side or the other re-examines the troubled story of the relationship between the federal government and Canada's indigenous population. Native people often contend that successive white governments cheated and abused them from first contact to the present. Many indigenous people see their post-contact history as a period of brutal colonization by a ruthless and duplicitous culture that sucked everything it needed from Canada's first people. The dominant white culture left the dregs for the Natives, and in the process marginalized and destroyed a once proud culture and people.

Angry Natives argue that indigenous leaders in the nineteenth century did not fully understand the implications of the treaties they signed. They also suggest that only Native people kept their side of the bargain in the various treaties that robbed them of their lands and futures. More radical and frustrated adherents of this interpretation increasingly take Canadian law, which they see as foreign and imposed, into their own hands in an effort to gain back what they believe is rightfully theirs. They argue that they have certain inalienable rights setting them apart from other Canadians — rights agreed to by the federal government when it signed the treaties. Those claims are sacred and must be protected in whatever way necessary, regardless of human or monetary cost.

At the other end of the spectrum are those who believe that Natives and the federal government signed agreements in good faith: there was no conspiratorial agenda to assimilate or eliminate Natives from the Canadian social fabric. But times have changed. Now, so the argument goes, Canadian aboriginal people should integrate into the mainstream mosaic and take their rightful place as equals — which means no special treatment. What was true of 1879 is not necessarily so of the late twentieth century, and Canadians must deal with the reality that was both created and inherited. This school of thought calls for abrogating or ignoring old treaty rights.

One of the most contentious pieces of legislation designed by the federal government for Canada's first nations was the nineteenth-century Indian Act that brought aboriginal people under Ottawa's jurisdiction. As such, Status Indians became wards of the state, a position radically different from that enjoyed by non-Natives. In a positive light, the act guaranteed indigenous people certain rights and privileges, as well as affording them promises of protection and developmental assistance. The negative impact was that the Act and its various amendments can be interpreted as profoundly paternalistic legislation that prevented Native people from achieving opportunities equal to other non-Native citizens.

Successive Native and non-Native leaders, with their own agendas and perspectives, periodically attempted to evaluate the Indian Act, usually seeing it as a well-intentioned folly that presently serves no other purpose than subjugating Canada's first people while providing comfortable jobs for legions of faceless bureaucrats. Many from both sides interpret the Indian Act as the main culprit in ensuring that Native Canadians remain unable to enjoy as high a standard of living as other Canadians.

In 1969, then-Federal Minister of Indian Affairs Jean Chrétien introduced the infamous "White Paper," which called for the abolition of both the Department of Indian Affairs and the Indian Act. Prime Minister Pierre Trudeau argued that both were patronizing anachronisms that had no place in a modern democracy where everyone enjoyed equal rights regardless of ethnic origin. The White Paper recommended an end to all laws offering differential treatment for Natives. Reserves, the Paper further stated, should revert to indigenous control "to enable the Indian people to be free — free to develop Indian cultures in an environment of legal, social and economic equality with other Canadians." The American Indian Movement, influential among more radical Canadian Natives, certainly encouraged this shift, one that the U.S. government had made years previously.

Much to the federal government's surprise, Native reaction to the Paper was swift and condemnatory. Ten chiefs from across the nation rejected it the day after its release. Though they did not question the government's good will and appreciated the consultative process, they believed the Department of Indian Affairs remained deaf to Native needs. The Paper, they said, was "a policy designed to divest us of our aboriginal residual rights. If we accept this policy and in the process lose those rights and our lands, we become willing partners in cultural genocide." The federal government's proposal, they said, amounted to nothing less than the traditional assimilationist policy practiced by successive administrations since first contact. Not that Native leaders necessarily liked the Indian Act. As Harold Cardinal stated: "We do not want the Indian Act retained because it is a good piece of legislation; it isn't ... [but] we would rather continue to live in bondage under the Indian Act than surrender our sacred rights." This interpretation ironically shifted the Act from being one of oppression to one of protection.

Although there was some support for the White Paper in the Native community, most Natives rejected it. Trudeau and Chrétien acquiesced, and the Paper officially died on March 17, 1971. This, of course, meant continuation of the *status quo* — something that satisfied few, either in or outside the Native community.

Harold Cardinal (1945–) was one of the most eloquent and vociferous opponents to the White Paper. Born and raised on the Sucker Creek Reserve in Alberta, Cardinal attended residential schools before studying sociology at Carleton University. He became the youngest president of the Indian Association of Alberta, and eventually rose to be Alberta's first Native regional director of Indian Affairs. There he generated considerable opposition and consequently lasted less than a year. He returned briefly to national politics in 1983 as vice chief of the Assembly of First Nations. Cardinal wrote two seminal books on the plight of Canada's indigenous people, both of which found a receptive audience among Canadians.

William Wuttunee grew up on the Red Pheasant Reserve in Saskatchewan. He graduated in law from the University of Saskatchewan and joined the provincial government's legal department. Later he worked for the Canadian Citizenship Branch and practiced law in Alberta and the Northwest Territories. Eventually he became Chief of the National Indian Council of Canada. Then the federal government hired him to promote the White Paper among Natives. This proved very unpopular, most Natives seeing him as a traitor. Vilified, Wuttunee was even banned from his own reserve by his tribe. Though he quickly disassociated himself from the White Paper, he continued to support integration of Natives into "the white man's society." Wuttunee's 1971 book, *Ruffled Feathers*, was considered far outside the mainstream of Native thought.

Pierre Elliot Trudeau (1919-) had a long history of fighting reactionary elitism and, although branded a socialist in his early life, he was, in fact, more a liberal-democrat. He entered the political arena in Quebec during the 1950s under Maurice Duplessis' repressive regime. There, aided by other young intellectuals, he challenged the status quo through his influential journal *Cité Libre*. He had impeccable credentials for the job. Trudeau shifted to the federal scene during the 1960s, lured to Ottawa by Lester Pearson's Liberal regime that hoped to quash separatist rumblings by including prominent Quebecers in cabinet. Trudeau always emphasized equality rights and opposed any legislation that segregated or limited peaceful individual expression. Thus, as Justice Minister, he repealed laws against homosexuality, and it was he who insisted upon a charter of rights and freedoms in the 1982 constitution. Special status for Quebec was unacceptable, he believed, because every Canadian is equal. The obviously second-class status of Canada's indigenous people was grist for his mill, and he logically hoped to change this by repealing the Indian Act — legislation that clearly denoted Natives as different from other Canadians. Hence the 1969 White Paper.

A) Speech, August 8, 1969
Pierre E. Trudeau

... I think Canadians are not too proud about their past in the way in which they treated the Indian population of Canada and I don't think we have very great cause to be proud.

We have set the Indians apart as a race. We've set them apart in our laws. We've set them apart in the ways the governments will deal with them. They're not citizens of the province as the rest of us are. They are wards of the federal government. They get their services from the federal government rather than from the provincial or municipal governments. They have been set apart in law. They have been set apart in the relations with government and they've been set apart socially too.

So this year we came up with a proposal. It's a policy paper on the Indian problem. It proposes a set of solutions. It doesn't impose them on anybody. It proposes them — not only to the Indians but to all Canadians — not only to their federal representatives but to the provincial representatives too and it says we're at the crossroads. We can go on treating the Indians as having a special status. We can go on adding bricks of discrimination around the ghetto in which they live and at the same time perhaps helping them preserve certain cultural traits and certain ancestral rights. Or we can say you're at a crossroads — the time is now to decide whether the Indians will be a race apart in Canada or whether they will be Canadians of full status. And this is a difficult choice. It must be a very agonizing choice to the Indian peoples themselves because, on the one hand, they realize that if they come into the society as total citizens they will be equal under the law but they risk losing certain of their traditions, certain aspects of a culture and perhaps even certain of their basic rights and this is a very difficult choice for them to make and I don't think we want to try and force the pace on them any more than we can force it on the rest of Canadians but here again is a choice which is in our minds whether Canadians as a whole want to continue treating the Indian population as something outside, a group of Canadians with which we have treaties, a group of Canadians who have as the Indians, many of them claim, aboriginal rights or whether we will say well forget the past and begin today and this is a tremendously difficult choice because, if — well one of the things the Indian bands often refer to are their aboriginal rights and in our policy, the way we propose it, we say we won't recognize aboriginal rights. We will recognize treaty rights. We will recognize forms of contract which have been made with the Indian people by the Crown and we will try to bring justice in that area and this will mean that perhaps the treaties shouldn't go on forever. It's inconceivable, I think, that in a given society one section of the society have a treaty with the other section of the society. We must be all equal under the laws and we must not sign treaties amongst ourselves and many of these treaties, indeed, would have less and less significance in the future anyhow but things that in the past were covered by treaties like things like so much twine or so much gun powder and which haven't been paid this must be paid. But I don't think that we should encourage the Indians to feel that their treaties should last forever within Canada so that they be able to receive their twine or their gun powder. They should become Canadians as all other Canadians and if they are prosperous and wealthy they will be treated like the prosperous and wealthy and they will be paying taxes for the other Canadians who are not so prosperous and not so wealthy whether they be Indians or English Canadians or French or Maritimers and this is the only basis on which I see our society can develop as equals. But aboriginal rights, this really means saying, "We were here before you. You came and took the land from us and perhaps you cheated us by giving us some worthless things in return for vast expanses of land and we want to re-open this question. We want you to preserve our aboriginal rights and to restore them to us". And our answer — it may not be the right one and may not be one which is accepted but it will be up to all of you people to make your minds up and to choose for or against it and to discuss with the Indians — our answer is "no".

If we think of restoring aboriginal rights to the Indians well what about the French who were defeated at the Plains of Abraham? Shouldn't we restore rights to them? And what about though the Acadians who were deported — shouldn't we compensate for this? And what about the other Canadians, the Immigrants? What about the Japanese Canadians who were so badly treated at the end or during the last war? What can we do to redeem the past? I can only say as President Kennedy said when he was asked about what he would do to compensate for the injustices that the Negroes had received in American society. We will be just in our time. This is all we can do. We must be just today ...

B) Citizens Plus: The Red Paper, 1970
Indian Association of Alberta

INDIAN STATUS

The White Paper policy said "that the legislative and constitutional bases of discrimination should be removed".

We reject this policy. We say that the recognition of Indian status is essential for justice.

Retaining the legal status of Indians is necessary if Indians are to be treated justly. Justice requires that the special history, rights and circumstances of Indian people be recognized. The Chrétien policy says, "Canada cannot seek the just society and keep discriminatory legislation on its statute books". That statement covers a faulty understanding of fairness. [A study done by a] Professor L.C. Green found that in other countries minorities were given special status ...

The legal definition of registered Indians must remain. If one of our registered brothers chooses, he may renounce his Indian status, become "en-franchised", receive his share of the fund of the tribe, and seek admission to ordinary Canadian society. But most Indians prefer to remain Indians. We believe that to be a good useful Canadian he must first be a good, happy and productive Indian.

THE UNIQUE INDIAN CULTURE AND CONTRIBUTION

The White Paper Policy said "that there should be positive recognition by everyone of the unique contribution of Indian culture to Canadian life".

We say that these are nice-sounding words which are intended to mis-lead everybody. The only way to maintain our culture is for us to remain as Indians. To preserve our culture it is necessary to preserve our status, rights, lands and traditions. Our treaties are the bases of our rights.

There is room in Canada for diversity. Our leaders say that Canada should preserve her "pluralism", and encourage the culture of all her peoples. The culture of the Indian peoples are old and colorful strands in that Canadian fabric of diversity. We want our children to learn our ways, our history, our customs, and our traditions.

Everyone should recognize that Indians have contributed much to the Canadian community. When we signed the treaties we promised to be good and loyal subjects of the Queen. The record is clear — we kept our prom-ises. We were assured we would not be required to serve in foreign wars: nevertheless many Indians volunteered in greater proportion than non-Indian Canadians for service in two world wars. We live and are agreeable to live within the framework of Canadian civil and criminal law. We pay the same indirect and sales taxes that other Canadians pay. Our treaty rights cost Canada very little in relation to the Gross National Product or to the value of the lands ceded, but they are essential to us.

CHANNELS FOR SERVICES

The White Paper Policy says "that services should come through the same channels and from the same government agencies for all Canadians".

We say that the federal government is bound by the British North America Act, Section 9k, Head 24, to accept legislative responsibility for "Indians and Indian lands". Moreover in exchange for the lands which the Indian people surrendered to the Crown the treaties ensure the following benefits:

(a) To have and to hold certain lands called "reserves" for the sole use and benefit of the Indian people forever and assistance in the social, economic, and cultural development of the reserves.

(b) The provision of health services to the Indian people on the reserve or off the reserve at the expense of the federal government anywhere in Canada.

(c) The provision of education of all types and levels to all Indian people at the expense of the federal government.

(d) The right of the Indian people to hunt, trap, and fish for their livelihood free of governmental interferences and regulation and subject only to the proviso that the exercise of this right must not interfere with the use and enjoyment of private property.

These benefits are not "handouts" because the Indian people paid for them by surrendering their lands. The federal government is bound to provide the actual services relating to education, welfare, health, and economic development.

ENRICHED SERVICES

The White Paper policy says "that those who are furthest behind should be helped most". The policy also promises "enriched services".

We do not want different treatment for different tribes. These promises of enriched services are bribes to get us to accept the rest of the policy. The federal government is trying to divide us Indian people so it can conquer us by saying that poorer reserves will be helped most.

All reserves and tribes need help in the economic, social, recreational, and cultural development.

LAWFUL OBLIGATIONS

The White Paper policy says "that lawful obligations should be recognized". If the Government meant what it said we would be happy. But it is obvious that the Government has never bothered to learn what the treaties are and has a distorted picture of them.

The Government shows that it is willfully ignorant of the bargains that were made between the Indians and the Queen's commissioners.

The Government must admit its mistakes, and recognize that the treaties are historic, moral and legal obligations. The Red men signed them in good faith, and lived up to the treaties. The treaties were solemn agreements. Indian lands were exchanged for the promises of the Indian commissioners who represented the Queen. Many missionaries of many faiths brought the authority and prestige of the White man's religion in encouraging Indians to sign.

In our treaties of 1876, 1877 and 1899, certain promises were made to our people: some of these are contained in the text of the treaties, some in the negotiations, and some in the memories of our people. Our basic view is that all these promises are part of the treaties and must be honored.

The intent and spirit of the treaties must be our guide, and not the precise letter of a foreign language. Treaties that run forever must have room for the changes in the conditions of life. The understanding of the government to provide teachers was a commitment to provide Indian children the educational opportunity equal to their White neighbors. The machinery and livestock symbolized economic development.

The White Paper policy says "a plain reading of the words used in the treaties reveals the limited and minimal promises which were included in them ... and in one treaty only a medicine chest". But we know from the commissioners' report that they told the Indians that medicine chests were included in all three.

Indians have the right to receive, without payment, all health-care services without exception and paid by the Government of Canada.

The "medicine chests" that we know were mentioned in the negotiations for Treaties Six, Seven and Eight, mean that Indians should now receive free medical, hospital and dental care ...

The Indian people see the treaties as the basis of all their rights and status. If the Government expects the cooperation of Indians in any new policy, it must accept the Indian viewpoint on treaties. This would require the Government to start all over on its new policy.

INDIAN CONTROL OF INDIAN LANDS

The White Paper policy says "that control of Indian lands should be transferred to Indian people".

We agree with this intent but we find that the Government is ignorant of two basic points. The Government wrongly thinks that Indian reserve lands are owned by the Crown. The Government is of course, in error. These lands are held in trust by the Crown but they are Indian lands.

The Indians are the beneficial (actual) owners of the lands. The legal title has been held for us by the Crown to prevent the sale or breaking up of our land. We are opposed to any system of allotment that would give individuals ownership of rights to sell.

According to the Indian Act, R.S.C. 1952, the land is safe and secure, held in trust for the common use and benefit of the tribe. The land must never be sold, mortgaged or taxed.

The second error the Government commits is making the assumption that Indians can have control of the land only if they take ownership in the way that ordinary property is owned. The Government should either get some legal advice or get some brighter legal advisers. The advice we have received is that the Indian Act could be changed to give Indians control of lands without changing the fact that the title is now held in trust.

Indian lands must continue to be regarded in a different manner than other lands in Canada. It must be held forever in trust of the Crown because as we say, "The true owners of the land are not yet born".

C) The Unjust Society, 1969
Harold Cardinal

The history of Canada's Indians is a shameful chronicle of the white man's disinterest, his deliberate trampling of Indian rights and his repeated betrayal of our trust. Generations of Indians have grown up behind a buckskin curtain of indifference, ignorance and, all too often, plain bigotry. Now, at a time when our fellow Canadians consider the promise of the Just Society, once more the Indians of Canada are betrayed by a programme which offers nothing better than cultural genocide …

Torrents of words have been spoken and written about Indians since the arrival of the white man on the North American continent. Endless columns of statistics have been compiled. Countless programmes have been prepared for Indians by non-Indians. Faced with society's general indifference and a massive accumulation of misdirected, often insincere efforts, the greatest mistake the Indian has made has been to remain so long silent.

... We do question how sincere or how deep such concern may be when Canadians ignore the plight of the Indian or Métis or Eskimo in their own country. There is little knowledge of native circumstances in Canada and even less interest. To the native one fact is apparent — the average Canadian does not give a damn.

The facts are available, dutifully compiled and clucked over by a handful of government civil servants year after year. Over half the Indians of Canada are jobless year after year. Thousands upon thousands of native people live in housing which would be condemned in any advanced society on the globe. Much of the housing has no inside plumbing, no running water, no electricity. A high percentage of the native peoples of Canada never get off welfare. This is the way it is, not in Asia or Africa but here in Canada. The facts are available; a Sunday drive to the nearest reserve will confirm them as shocking reality ...

Many Canadians, however, have always claimed and continue to assert that Canada has little racial difficulty. Statements of this nature are just so much uninformed nonsense.

In any area where there is a concentration of native people there exists racial tension. Urban centres with their multiplicity of attractions and opportunities are drawing more and more natives who come in hope and stay in misery. These migrants, with little financial security, all too often with insufficient job training and nearly always with terribly inadequate knowledge of white mores, inevitably jam into ghettos, increasing not only their own problems but those of the city. The people of the city answer with bigotry, wrongly attributing the problem to colour or race rather than to any inadequacy of opportunity and social response ...

Ignorance? It thrives on the incestuous mating of indifference and bigotry and in turn breeds more of the same. Ignorance is irretrievably locked in with prejudice. How often have you heard a white man say, "Indians are lousy workers" or, "Indian are shiftless" or "dirty" or "lazy" or, "Indians are drunken bums?" I have seen in numerous cities across the country non-Indians engaged in excessive drinking, making drunken fools of themselves. In these circumstances, what do you hear? "Well, isn't he having a ball," or "He's just letting his hair down," or perhaps, "Boy, isn't he a real swinger!" Let native people be seen in similar conditions and what do you get? The comments are more in the nature of epithets" "Worthless drunks!" or "Drunken bums!" ...

However, even more reprehensible than the man who does not act because he is ignorant is the man who *does* know the situation but fails to act. I can only label this type of performance *gutless*. When I talk of a gutless person, I am talking about a human being who does not have the courage to try to change an unjust situation. I call gutless a person who, rather than change an indefensible state of affairs, tries to sweep the mess under a rug. I call gutless the politician who stalls, procrastinates and tries to perpetuate the antiquated systems and attitudes which have produced injustice, in order to try to maintain his own positive image. When I look at the existing situation among the natives of Canada, I cannot help but assume we must have a hell of a lot of gutless politicians in this country ...

The white man's government has allowed (worse, urged) its representatives to usurp from Indian peoples our right to make our own decisions and our authority to implement the goals we have set for ourselves. In fact, the real power, the decision-making process and the policy-implementing group, has always resided in Ottawa, in the Department of Indian Affairs and Northern Development. To ensure the complete disorganization of native peoples, Indian leadership over the past years and yet today has been discredited and destroyed. Where this was not possible, the bureaucrats have maintained the upper hand by subjecting durable native leaders to endless exercises in futility, to repeated, pointless reorganizations, to endless barrages of verbal diarrhoea promising never-coming changes ...

These faceless people in Ottawa, a comparatively small group, perpetually virtually unknown, have sat at their desks eight hours a day, five days a week, for over a century, and decided just about everything that will ever happen to a Canadian Indian. They have laid down the policy, the rules, the regulations on all matters affecting native peoples. They have decided where our sons will go to school, near home or hopelessly far from home; they have decided what houses will be built on what reserves for what Indians and whether they may have inside or outside toilets; they have decided what types of social or economic development will take place and where and how it will be controlled. If you are a treaty Indian, you've never made a move without these guys, these bureaucrats, these civil servants at their desks in their new office tower in Ottawa saying "yes" ... or "no." ...

Through generations of justifying their positions to the Canadian public and to Canada's political leaders, the bureaucrats within the department have come to believe their own propaganda. They have fostered an image of Indians as a helpless people, an incompetent people and an apathetic people in order to increase their own importance and to stress the need for their own continued presence.

Most of their action stems from their naiveté and a genuine belief that their solutions are necessary to ensure the survival of Indians. For the most part they are not really evil men. They have evolved no vicious plots intentionally to subjugate the Indian people. The situation for the Indian people, as bad as it is, has resulted largely from good intentions, however perverted, of civil servants within the Department of Indian Affairs. However, one cannot forget the direction usually taken by roads paved with nothing but good intentions.

... Talking and listening have been one-way streets with white men and Indians. Until very recently white men have expected Indians to do all the listening. Indians, on the other hand, have felt that the white man just couldn't shut up long enough to listen. For many years now our people have talked about what concerned them most, have suggested solutions to our problems as we see them, have talked generally about our hopes for a better future. Some have talked articulately and with eloquence, some less lucidly; some have spoken with great intensity and emotion, others with objectivity and almost passively. But all talk, brilliant or dull, visionary or cautiously realistic, remains futile when the people you talk to simply won't listen. We want the white man to shut up and listen to us, really listen for a change. Some Canadians listen but they wish to hear Indians say only what white people want to hear. They like to hear an Indian tell them what a good job government is doing and how the lowly Indian would have vanished if not for the white man's help. Such people quit listening when an Indian tries to tell them the hard facts of Indian life in Canada ...

We listen when Canadian political leaders talk endlessly about strength in diversity for Canada, but we understand they are talking primarily about the French Canadian fact in Canada. Canadian Indians feel, along with other minorities, that there is a purpose and a place for us in a Canada which accepts and encourages diversified human resources. We like the idea of a Canada where all cultures are encouraged to develop in harmony with one another, to become part of the great mosaic. We are impatient for the day when other Canadians will accord the Indian the recognition implied in this vision of Canada ...

The language barrier has isolated our people as truly as the geographical barrier. There are eleven different major language groups among the Indians of Canada with scores of dialects changing from band to band. Only recently has English become universal enough among Indians to serve as a medium of communication. And, even today, the most articulate (in English) Indian will confess readily that he still feels more at home in his mother tongue.

Nationwide Indian unity represents a dream long held by Indian leaders well aware of the divisive influence of the emphasis upon individual bands and tribes. Only recently, with the growth of strong provincial organizations in turn leading to the creation for the first time of a viable national organization, the National Indian Brotherhood, has this dream shown signs of realization. When our people begin to call themselves Indians instead of Crees or Saulteaux or Mohawks, when intertribal cooperation no longer allows the government to threaten our individual treaties, then we will have the strength of unity, the power to help make some of our other dreams come true.

Canada is an enormous country. Even within a single province such as Alberta, conditions vary so widely from reserve to reserve that common needs, aspirations and goals that can be attributed to the entire Indian people are often difficult to determine.

... Indians gladly accept the challenge — to become participating Canadians, to take a meaningful place in the mainstream of Canadian society. But we remain acutely aware of the threat — the loss of our Indian identity, our place as distinct, identifiable Canadians.

However idealistic some Indian dreams may be, there remain everyday hopes that come right down to earth. Indians are like anyone else. We look around and see a very affluent society. Just like our non-Indian neighbours, we want a share, a new car, a well-built home, television. These represent surface things, but it hurts deeply to see the affluence of our country and not be allowed to benefit from it. We want better education, a better chance for our children and the option to choose our own pathway in life. If we are to be part of the Canadian mosaic, then we want to be colourful red tiles, taking our place where red is both needed and appreciated.

... There have been sporadic indications of the growth of a red power faction in Canada, paralleling to a degree the rise of black power in the United States. Some individual Indians and some Indian organizations have suggested that more adroit use of political power or the even uglier use of physical strength (both to be achieved through more effective organization and evidenced by protest demonstrations) would be more effective than continued efforts to talk to a government which refuses to listen. Students of Indian affairs have noted that one finds many indications among Indians of an appreciation of the principle of sovereignty, and note the recurrence of such phraseology as "We are sovereign nations." Some government officials have even suggested that financial assistance to native organizations would foster separation among the Indian people in Canada.

People who think this adds up to leanings toward separatism among Indians do not know and have not even begun to understand the basic concerns of our people. However, as long as the government persists in denying to our people the legislation necessary for the protection of our rights, our people must be expected to look for alternatives. Who can say at what point such alternatives may become viable? ...

The Indian people cannot be blamed for feeling that not until the sun ceases to shine, the rivers cease to flow and the grasses to grow or, wonder of wonders, the government decides to honour its treaties, will the white man cease to speak with forked tongue.

The way it stands now, the much laughed-at American Indians who sold all of Manhattan Island for twenty-four dollars' worth of beads and trinkets got a better deal than Canadian Indians. The white man has never conducted such a clearly defined exchange with our people. There are precedents for the present government's betrayal; the white man took what we gave him, and more, but we never received payment. It was planned that way.

The truth of the matter is that Canadian Indians simply got swindled. Our forefathers got taken by slick-talking, fork-tongued cheats. It wasn't their fault. Our forefathers, with possibly a few cynical exceptions, never understood the white man. They had fought battles, known victory and defeat, but treachery was new to them. They were accustomed to trusting another man's word, even an enemy's.

The Indian leaders who signed our treaties with the representatives of the government of Canada came to the signatory negotiations and meetings with honourable intent and laudable purpose. Their gravest mistake was to give the white man the benefit of the doubt and attribute to him the same high principles. He didn't have them. He, the white man, talked one way and wrote another.

... Yes, the prime minister roused our hopes with his talk of a compassionate and just society. Then his minister for Indian Affairs told us our problems would vanish if we would become nice, manageable white men like all other Canadians. Just recently, the prime minister himself flicked the other fork of his tongue. In a speech in Vancouver, Mr. Trudeau, said, "The federal government is not prepared to guarantee the aboriginal rights of Canada's Indians." Mr. Trudeau said, "It is inconceivable that one section of a society should have a treaty with another section of a society. The Indians should become Canadians as have all other Canadians."

Have other Canadians been led to this citizenship over a path of broken promises and dishonoured treaties?

To the Indians of Canada, the treaties represent an Indian Magna Carta. The treaties are important to us, because we entered into these negotiations with faith, with hope for a better life with honour. We have survived for over a century on little but that hope. Did the white man enter into them with something less in mind? Or have the heirs of the men who signed in honour somehow disavowed the obligation passed down to them? The Indians entered into the treaty negotiations as honourable men who came to deal as equals with the queen's representatives. Our leaders of that time thought they were dealing with an equally honourable people. Our leaders pledged themselves, their people and their heirs to honour what was done then ...

Our people talked with the government representatives, not as beggars pleading for handouts, but as men with something to offer in return for rights they expected. To our people, this was the beginning of a contractual relationship whereby the representatives of the queen would have lasting responsibilities to the Indian people in return for the valuable lands that were ceded to them ...

We cannot give up our rights without destroying ourselves as people. If our rights are meaningless, if it is inconceivable that our society have treaties with the white society even though those treaties were signed by honourable men on both sides, in good faith, long before the present government decided to tear them up as worthless scraps of paper, then we as a people are meaningless. We cannot and we will not accept this. We know that as long as we fight for our rights we will survive. If we surrender, we die ...

D) Ruffled Feathers, 1971
William Wuttunee

... There have been veiled threats by Red Power advocates against the establishment in Canada. Negative attitudes against white society are prevalent across Canada and they do untold damage. Many young Indians who are struggling to gain an education get caught up in the rat race of condemning Canadian society. The advocacy of an administration which is to be run by Indians for Indians, without the participation of the white man, destroys the initiative of those young Indians who are trying to educate themselves and trying to fit into Canadian society as a whole. The over-all effect of the anti-white bombardment is for the young Indians to drop out of Canadian society and suffer the usual affliction of excessive use of alcohol ...

Too often Indians spend their time criticizing and blaming the white man for their problems. Is it not possible that they are themselves responsible for the creation and the perpetuation of these problems? Is it not possible that they, too, can do something about them?

... There is certainly something good to be said about the value of people living together peacefully, mutually, for the benefit of one another. It is time to blast the arguments against integration and to speak in favour of it ...

The proposal to repeal the Indian Act was a great step forward. For many years both Indians and non-Indians had criticized the Indian Act as being discriminatory. In fact, the Indian Act is one of the most discriminatory pieces of legislation which exists in either the provincial or federal Statutes. Parliament has exclusive jurisdiction over Indians and lands reserved for Indians by reason of The British North America Act. The Act applies only to Indians who are registered under the Act.

The provisions of the Indian Act do not give native people equality. They are saddled with disadvantages which hound them continually in their daily lives. It cannot be said that an Indian has equality before the law if he cannot enjoy his property and if he has to depend on a Minister in Ottawa to exercise and make decisions on his behalf ...

The Indian Act promotes a spirit of inferiority and dependence and, coupled with the treaty mentality, is one of the main reasons for the current difficult situation. Canada will continue to have this problem unless definite steps are taken to change the provisions of the Indian Act or to repeal the Act completely.

INDIAN LANDS

It was proposed in the White Paper that legislative steps would be taken to enable Indians to control their lands and to acquire title to them ...

PHASING OUT OF THE DEPARTMENT OF INDIAN AFFAIRS

The White Paper proposed that the Branch would be phased out within a period of five years, and that programs in the field of Indian affairs would be transferred to other appropriate federal departments. This recommendation, if carried out, would have a profound effect on the Indian people. The removal of the Indian Affairs Branch would be a big step forward, for its very existence has caused a great deal of the administrative discrimination which now exists. Indian people have reached a standard of education which enables them to administer their own affairs ...

The treaty mentality of dependence is being prolonged by some Indian leaders today who are encouraging it among their people. It is unlikely that the government is going to renegotiate these treaties or to read more into them than was actually provided for. It is time that the Indian leaders recognized this principle. Nothing has been taken away from the Indian that was rightfully his, even though it is hard to acknowledge that the Indian at the time of the negotiation of the treaties was not in a strong bargaining position to maintain his national independence.

The Indians have built up the treaties to such an extent that nearly everything in their lives hinges upon them. They have developed a mentality which, like the treaties, is dependent. The treaties were negotiated at a time when the Indians were no longer strong and powerful; they were peaceful and wanted good relations with the white man. They wanted the assistance which the white man was prepared to give to them and which they eventually received ...

One cannot overstress the significance of ending these treaties and of ending the treaty mentality which has spread throughout the country. It has embedded itself so firmly in the Indian mind that it clouds all his thinking and he cannot seem to see his way clearly, for his feelings work more strongly than his mind on this subject. The Indian people cannot keep living in the past. They can never rewrite what actually transpired at the signing of the treaties because the cold facts of history have indelibly written themselves in the hearts and minds of the people. We cannot re-interpret them; we cannot give more significance to either the one side or the other; we cannot improve the bargaining position of either side, and neither can we take away. We can realistically look at the past, the present and the future, and learn from the hard lessons of history those truths which will assist us in facing the problems of the day.

The people who negotiated the treaties have died and we should leave them in peace. They did the very best they could in the circumstances and they left to us a commission to fight new battles for a new era. It is our responsibility to settle this land peacefully and to look to the new boundaries. Let us then gather the old treaties, the Queen Victoria medals, the flags and the chiefs' uniforms and put them in the museums of our land, so that they can forever remind our children that this land was built and created out of the hopes and frustrations of ancestors who earnestly desired the peaceful development of Canada. Let us consider them hereafter without frustration, and regard the treaty period as a necessary development in the process of fusing together the red and the white ...

Reservations are now completely out of date. We no longer need reservations; their function has changed and it is time to change them. If we were to put any group of people on reserves and leave them there for a century without giving them medical attention, education facilities or the necessary nourishment to keep body and soul together, they would undoubtedly become a pretty helpless group. Since there is absolutely nothing to do on some reserves, the people spend their time travelling back and forth to the nearest town. Because so many of them spend so much time in town, it is therefore evident that these Indians really wish to be integrated and to be with the mainstream of society, rather than stuck back on the reserve. The figures of the Indian Affairs Branch indicate that nearly one-third of the registered natives are now living in urban areas. This means that only two-thirds of the residents remain on the poor reserves, usually only the very old and the very young ...

It comes as no surprise that so many Indians are leaving the reserves. The conditions which exist on most reserves are deplorable. Usually there is no electricity and no running water, and the houses are mostly shacks. The poverty is depressing, and there is an obvious lack of motivation. The residents of a reserve seem to always carry with them an air of failure ...

Young people should be encouraged to leave the reserve as early as possible, and they should be helped to fit into the Canadian way of life. They don't have to give up their culture; if they wish to maintain their culture off the reserve they can probably more easily do so by living in better surroundings.

At present the federal government is making every effort to assist in the development of Indian culture. For many years there had been a lack of any interest at all in this area. National conferences have been sponsored by the Indian Affairs Branch in order to take positive steps toward the preservation and promotion of Indian culture, but in the long run it is going to be a losing battle to try to maintain the Indian culture which was throttled for so many years. The process of integration and assimilation is far more rapid than the increase or maintenance of Indian culture.

This is not a bad sign — it means that a new culture will develop in which they will maintain some of their own culture and also adopt something different. Just because a culture dies does not mean that something good has died. People do not exist for culture's sake. Culture must be malleable to the wants and tastes of its living participants. Real Indian culture is just about dead on the reserves. To maintain Indian culture does not mean wearing feathers and hopping around on one foot; it means the belief in the Great Spirit who inhabits the sun, the stars, the wind and all of nature. It means that one is honourable, brave, generous and kind. It means that one has a sense of responsibility to his immediate family and to the other members of the community with whom he is in contact ...

Reserves as presently constituted are a hindrance to integration and assimilation. Although the Indians leave the reserves to live and work in the cities, they always have one foot behind them in the reserve, to which they run as soon as they encounter any difficulty in the cities. The reserve gives them a sense of security, of belonging somewhere, even if it is a poor place. Very few people have succeeded by remaining on the reserve. The opportunities live off the reserves in the towns and cities. It is there that they can get away from the long arm of the band council and the chief. It is there they can seek the agencies which serve the ordinary Canadian without distinction. Reserves are destined to become municipalities or suburban areas of larger cities ...

Old attitudes toward Indian people have to be changed. Some of these attitudes and statements which have caused a great deal of damage are statements like "The Indian is the only true Canadian." This implies that the Indian is a better type of Canadian than newly-arrived immigrants, and this is not true. The further ideas that "Indians were the first owners of this country" and "the land was taken from them" are again misconceptions. At the time of the arrival of the white man, the Indian did not occupy all of the country; therefore it cannot be said that the land was taken away from him. Those areas which were unoccupied were never taken away from anyone. Indians never owned Canada; they do not own it now, and they never will. Once this concept is clearly understood, there will be less torment in the hearts of Indians in assessing their relationship with the dominant society.

The Indian people will never regain this country from the white man. They can, however, effectively participate with the white man in its full development. Indians can work with the white men in partnership to develop a country which will provide for each of our children a legacy of great value. It is not necessary to separate from the white man, either physically or spiritually. The long period of separation of the two races has now ended ...

The hard knocks of history are pushing the Indian into a new way of life, and he must learn to accept this new challenge with faith and with hope. History has taught a hard lesson, but history will vindicate itself one day when the Indian finally finds his place in Canadian society ...

16

"Turn On, Tune In, Take Over"

The Georgia Straight and Counterculture

DOCUMENTS

Has adolescent behaviour always irked the older generation? Did Neanderthal mothers wring their hairy hands in despair at sons and daughters who challenged their authority? It's doubtful. Modern mass youth culture and the teenager were products of the post-Second World War era. In the United States and Canada the 1950s were boom times, a period when most adolescents no longer had to contribute to family coffers and could instead remain in school through graduation and possibly enter university as well. This, for the majority of working-class North Americans, was something entirely new. The economy also generated enough wealth for teenagers to hold jobs that had been the domain of adults in previous generations: waitressing, gardening, errands, babysitting, gas jockeys, and the like.

With money and time to spare, these new "teens" created a culture distinctly their own — one based upon a rejection of what they perceived as their parents' stuffy conservatism. It did not take long for Madison Avenue to discover this untapped market, and by the late '50s, a whole industry — from fan magazines to records, clothing, and films — focused directly at teenagers' hearts and wallets. Heartthrobs like Pat Boone, though marketed to teens as their own creation, were, in fact, generated in boardrooms by the old capitalist establishment.

The problem for this new generation was its lack of rules. There were no previous teenagers to tell them how to rebel: to offer them codes of behaviour. Thus it is hardly surprising that James Dean rebelled without a cause. He knew something was amiss, but couldn't put a finger on it and consequently limited himself to a great deal of melancholy pouting. Nor is it surprising that his father ranted against his disrespectful behaviour — young men didn't used to be that way! Despite the generation gap, fifties teenagers were, however, decidedly apolitical, unthreatening to the social fabric, and quite naïve.

That changed by the late '60s. Youth culture entered a new phase, and this time it did menace the establishment. The hippy generation threatened to tear down the old order by tuning in, turning on, and dropping out. Their musicians sang about revolutions, not sock-hops. The image of the parental generation was transformed into something quite different from James Dean's stodgy father who wouldn't let the kids stay out past ten o'clock. Youths saw the older generation as their political enemies who had created the Vietnam war, environmental degradation, enslavement of women and minority groups, and an unfeeling capitalist economy. No wonder the flower children cried: "Don't trust anyone over thirty!"

The *Georgia Straight* once touted itself as Canada's premier underground newspaper specifically geared to rebellious youth. Born in May of 1967, the year of the "summer of love", the *Straight* came into being in the counterculture's heyday. It immediately set out to challenge the establishment and its press organs, the *Vancouver Sun* and *Province*. Contributors directly tackled those issues that the mainstream papers either ignored or interpreted through "bourgeois" eyes. The *Straight* favored decriminalizing homosexuality, supported "appropriate" drug use, fought for women's rights and abortion on demand, tackled environmental issues long before it was politically correct to do so, challenged the role of public education, and promoted love and left-wing revolution. And, unlike most newspapers, which offered mere snippets of news with limited analysis, the *Straight* dug deeply into its stories and often carried articles over 3000 words long. They may have used primitive publishing equipment, but the writing was at least semi-professional.

Not that the *Georgia Straight* maintained a consistent editorial policy. Feminists once shut it down, accusing it of sexism, particularly in its cartoons, which often depicted optimistic pubescent boyhood fantasies rather than sympathetic feminist ideology. The editors responded with an abject apology and had women produce several issues before they returned to a milder version of their old ways. Did the *Straight* really support bra burning on ideological grounds? Some of their writers saw social redemption in the deeds of Marxist revolutionaries like Ché Guevara, and slammed American imperialism while myopically ignoring Soviet foreign policy forays. Other contributors argued that the route to salvation was eliminating all "isms," including communism. There were those columnists who saw liberty in dropping out, taking consciousness altering drugs, and proclaiming peace and love. Others wanted to fight the "pigs" and Vancouver mayor Tom Campbell. The *Straight* arguably had only two consistent editorial themes: a witty irreverence that loved nothing better than challenging established middle class values, and a deep suspicion of the United States and all America symbolized.

The *Georgia Straight* repeatedly courted trouble. Vancouver mayor Tom Campbell revoked its business license after its premier issue, and its editors faced frequent arrest and court appearances on obscenity charges. When the paper printed instructions on marijuana cultivation, its staff faced charges of "inciting to commit an indictable offense." Newspaper vendors selling the *Straight* had their supplies confiscated and met regular "establishment" harassment in the form of the Vancouver Police Department. The editors, however, rose to each attack, deftly deflecting them to their advantage. They challenged obscenity charges under free speech and freedom of the press guarantees. Witty and sarcastic "Guerilla Theater" performances played on the sidewalk outside the Vancouver courthouse as editors paraded before magistrates inside. The *Straight* parried every establishment thrust, and along the way gained a sizable following from those disillusioned or feeling marginalized by modern Canadian society.

A)   "Turn On, Tune In, Take Over" September 8, 1967

If you drop out of school, you'll probably have to get a job. You'll hate *that*, too. The pay will be low, and it'll be even more boring than school was.

If you don't get a job, your parents will do all they can to make life rough for you.

You could leave home, but what happens then? It's getting too cold for sleeping outside, or hitch-hiking around the country. Staying with friends can be fun — for a while. But you'll find it impossible to *do* anything. You'll soon grow tired of 'making the scene', and living on somebody else's terms.

ACTION is the answer. When you close yourself up in your own little world, you're just avoiding questions that will have to be answered, sooner or later. If school is a drag, it's up to you to make it better. If you're thinking of leaving school anyway, what's wrong with getting 'KICKED OUT'?

Nobody has the right to tell you how to run your life. You know more than the 'elders' do, about the things that are really important today. *Make school interesting by taking it over.* How can [you] begin? Here are some ideas:

**Organize a union, to put pressure on the teachers and principals, so they'll give you what you want.

*petitions can be circulated, to get rid of bad teachers and principals.

*a delegation can be sent to every PTA meeting, to present student demands. Don't ask for permission; tell them what you intend to do.

**Fight against all age restrictions. If you want to do something, go ahead. If you get caught, call the *GEORGIA STRAIGHT* Defense Fund. The "laws" are so bad that, nowadays, it is dishonorable *not to* have a criminal record. Just forget about building a future in *their* society. *You* can do better.

**Organize love-ins in schoolyards, perhaps every noon-hour.

**During fire drills, act as if there were a real fire. Once you get outside, keep going.

**If you don't like a textbook, lose it.

TAKE OVER!

****Stamp out corporal punishment. If any teacher or principal hits you, charge him with assault. One student actually hit back, when a teacher attacked him. This is not recommended, however, except in extreme emergencies.

**Insist that schools be left open at night, so you can have a place to sleep, in case conditions at home become unbearable.

****Plan out your own courses, and teach them yourselves. Ask sympathetic teachers to help you.

**Start up school newspapers. *GEORGIA STRAIGHT* will help in any way possible. If you are interested, come and watch us in action(?). Also, send us anything you think we can use.

**Let your imagination run wild. Each day should bring new ideas. Once you get started, nothing can stop you. All ideas and questions will be gladly received and personally dealt with. Write to: *Project X, GEORGIA STRAIGHT.*

B) "Grass in Class" February 17–24, 1971

Lucky students in King George and several other Vancouver high schools yesterday (Tuesday) received a free marijuana cigarette, says the Vancouver High School Underground, an organization of revolutionary high school students.

One was even mailed to the Vancouver Sun, taped to a copy of their program and plans for future actions. Their statement reads as follows:

Taped to this sheet of paper is a joint of Marijuana. The Vancouver High School Underground is placing ten letters, containing ten joints, in this prison today.

The jailers who run this school (prison) say that grass is dangerous and heads to heroin, etc. They are lying. Grass is a harmless herb. It is not habit-forming, it's less dangerous than aspirin, and it makes you feel good. Try it. You'll like it.

We are revolutionary High School students (prisoners) who believe that the time has come for a jail break. We are going to break FREE. We're going to toke up in the halls, we're going to dance in the classrooms, we're going to neck or make love wherever we please.

We're going to start turning our schools, which parents and principals and pigs make us go to, into OUR SCHOOLS. Places where we can laugh.

Places where we can live. Places where we can learn. Places where we have a SAY in what goes on.

We are giving you this joint to turn you on to yourself, to conditions in this prison, and to a revolutionary five point program for making this school a place where we decide what happens to us — instead of being herded into classes every day and having stuff crammed down our throats whether we like it or not. Here is the five point program of the Vancouver High School Underground.

1. Freedom to smoke grass in school. No narks in the schools. No lies about grass being bad for you.

2. Freedom of appearance. Whatever clothes we want. Whatever hair length we want. Whatever make up or face paint we want.

3. Freedom to plan our own courses. We demand the right for each class to decide what it will do, how it will learn, and what teachers it will work with. We are forced to attend this school whether we like it or not. We have every right and more to decide what we will do here. You can't learn very much in a prison.

4. Freedom to skip classes, for any reason, at any time if all you're getting out of a class is boredom, why the hell should you go there? There are some pretty boring classes in this school. Maybe some of the teachers would smarten up and maybe we'd learn a bit more if we didn't have to be there.

5. Freedom from grades. The whole idea of grades is sick. It makes us compete against each other. It makes us go after grades instead of knowledge. Down with grades, up with learning.

Giving away grass is the first action of the Vancouver High School Underground. It won't be the last!!!

C) "Education — For What?" May 28–June 1, 1968
Dara

U.B.C. Convocation

… As the graduates were lining up waiting to march in "an orderly, quiet manner (no chewing gum please)" to Memorial Gym to receive their useless scraps of paper (otherwise known as diplomas). (I wonder how many trees McMillan-Blodel ripped off to print the diplomas), the A.M.S. information booth posted signs reading "WELFARE INFORMATION" and "MAN-POWER RETRAINING INFORMATION" and spread out pamphlets explaining how to apply for assistance. Most people smiled wryly as they passed the booth and some stopped to pick up literature.

Human government and A.M.S. also distributed a sheet entitled "EDU-CATION — FOR WHAT???" and "CONVOCATION: CIRCUMCISION OR CASTRATION" which gave statistics such as 10% of B.A.s and 10% of M.A.s are unemployed, 26% of Ph.D.s from UBC in the past two years are unemployed. It also pointed out how difficult it is to get a job in B.C. with an Arts or Science degree since the economy is geared to primary re-source give-away. University education does not help you understand the real problems of society or how to deal with them. It is geared rather to training one to be a robot who can fit into the machine. But even robots are unemployed these days.

The cost of a university education is five times the median expected life earnings of the majority of human beings.

I walked around handing out the A.M.S. sheet and asking people what they thought of it. Most said, "Yeah, it's all true but what do you want me to do about it?" Some said they did it all for their parents. No one, except the few who had jobs lined up, seemed very optimistic about getting unem-ployment. Some said they were going to graduate school for lack of any-thing else to do, a few more monied graduates were planning to travel. One woman said she was lucky and didn't need or care about a job because she was getting married. (I fail to see how being an unpaid house slave is "luck.") One philosophy major said he thought the facts on the sheet were true but, after all, "What is truth?"

What is education???????

A Law Professor gave instructions about how to go through the convo-cation ceremonies. Line up by number, come to the platform, hand in your card (if your name is difficult to pronounce whisper it so they'll get it right), kneel down in front of Chancellor McGavin (on your left knee, please), McGavin will then tap your head and "admit you." Dean Gage may shake your hand ("He always shakes hands with pretty girls" — *giggle, giggle* — up yours, buddy). His little talk was the culmination of at least four years of similar bullshit ...

All in all, it was pretty heart-breaking. So much wasted time, work, en-ergy and pride. And for what? If you're really lucky you get to spend your life serving a few monopoly capitalists.

D) "Learning to Live Without Schools" October 8–15, 1969
Chris MacLeod

Do you fancy education is some thing that you can get? Do you hope to become a great teacher or creator by pursuing some particular course, by assiduously studying the irrelevant in a "high" school? Ah, dreamer … Why, in order to discover that there exists a world of mind and spirit, "must" one attend a university? As a grade-school graduate, you assume your thoughts are first-rate, but they're not even first-grade. Art cannot be taught, yet must be learned: the key is love, which takes no time, as graduating does. Of school-marms you've been told there is a dearth; but it is learners are in short supply. Compulsory education is not education, and in classes lives no learning and less wisdom. Schools teach how to compare and conform successfully, but how to live is left in the laps of the devils. Lecture rooms display more science fiction than news stands do. Mastering a language means far more than putting the first two letters of the alphabet after your name. The pedagogue to whom the classics are closed books and impertinent to everyday life is himself closed and impertinent, not a Bachelor but a pimp of Arts. By all means earn your Master's degree in the multiversity of the underworld: then you can enroll in the one-room kindergarten of heaven, wherein degrees do not count. Where's the topnotch Alma Mater offering credits for leaving erudition, forebrain chatter, canned knowledge, alone? What true teacher is paid for his services, save with mockery? The Nazarene lacked the latest diplomas, but he probably could and would take any of your "greatest" doctors to the cleaners. Normal schools expel the supernormal, since in salmon runs there's scarcely room for kraken. Petty civil services that chiefly serve in perpetuating affluent and indigent classes cannot specialize in courage, independence or imagination. Inferior minds feels most at home among inferiors. Fear-ridden souls with little self-respect and little reason for it by and large choose to become teachers; their hostility towards rebellion, inquiry and free spirits is practically second nature, and understandably they do their best to ensure that their pupils' mentalities are also thickly insulated from reality. It is the character of master and of man, not the school's reputation, that determines the value of the time they spend "together." Should not every "normal" student be obliged to undergo psychoanalysis, in order to weed out the deformed majority that might be better, less harmfully employed tending a factory conveyor belt? The modern school conditions its thumb-twiddling prisoners for society's not the individual's alleged good; for a "life" time of undisturbed banality on a treadmill swallowing saccharine barf. Are you pleasant, passive, well-liked, easy-going, cute, co-operative, good-natured, uninquiring, amiable, a regular fellow, in like Flynn, well trained to play ball with your owners? There's a good lad. Behind the idealistic, camouflaging blah-blah of Good Citizenship, the system is strictly geared to producing a steady outgo of cheap labour questioning nothing but its income — perish the possibility of enriching impoverished person-alities. Custodial care is provided creatures branded undesirable elsewhere if only by the fact that fences have been set up to contain them: cattle cannot be allowed to wander wild in a sensible, sophisticated society. Amazing as it may seem, among the primitive Greeks *skhole* meant leisure for the pursuit of insight. Textbooks may enable your pencil-pushing self to reach its ob-jects in passing many subjects, but they won't help you one iota in the ex-amination of yourself, which is simple as simple can be, covering neither subjects nor objects. The last test is not final, though in it the student stips *(sic)*. Intelligence quotients have not measured intelligence, which is immeas-urable. True learning is sheer play, and yet the most arduous of sports. Read what you want to read, not what you ought to read. Talk gibberish if you wish, so long as it's uncopied, straight from the horse's mouth, no worse-hipped wiseacre's. Have you a mind of your own, or only a well-recorded tape of some articulate dolt? Write what you think but do not think what you will write. Calculation kills invention. You think that you can procreate with your *head*? That is amusing. Listen, you fathead: to create, you need not brains but guts.

E) "Homosexuality" December 15, 1967
Bob Cummings

… Under present Canadian laws, the penalty for murder is "life", which usually means twenty years. Under the same legal system, a homosexual, even with a consenting partner over the age of consent, can be sentenced to "preventive detention", which could mean literally the rest of his life. Re-cently the press carried a story of a man who is serving this sentence, even though he was arrested originally on another charge and cleared. The Su-preme Court of Canada Appeal Court upheld the conviction and sentence, fully knowing that the man had no history of violence and that his sex part-ner was over the age of consent.

The law does not contend that a convicted homosexual may be violent, a menace to normal people or that he may molest children. It is satisfied that if he may continue to indulge in homosexual acts then he is liable to the full severity of the law. According to this ludicrous law, being 'different' may, at the questionable discretion of the courts, be more serious than murder.

For most convicted homosexuals, 'preventive detention' is more of an extreme potential danger than a reality. The usual charge laid against a homosexual with a consenting partner is 'Gross Indecency in a Public Place' even though the arrest might be made in a hotel room or private residence. That a private room with a closed door can be deemed a 'public place' is a stunning indictment of our "system of Justice". Justice, if it is to be respected, must above all be just.

In ancient Sparta, homosexuality was considered a way of life and accepted, in modern Britain, it is considered a private act between private consenting individuals. Aside from these and other notable exceptions, the homosexual has, over the centuries, been subjected to hatred, ridicule, persecution and humiliation. The 'where', 'when' and 'how' of this persecution can be affirmed in any library, the 'why' is a question that has never been answered. If this 'why' is ever answered, it may give us an insight into mankind's traditional violent attitude towards peaceful minorities.

Even in our "enlightened" society, to most people, the homosexual is the subject of sick joke. To others, he is a justifiable excuse for violence to such an extent that the man who speaks of "kicking the shit out of a queer" is more likely to be condemned for his language than for his intentions. A third segment of our populace feels that he should be locked up in a mental institution to be 'cured' as would a raving lunatic. A growing percentage see him as a human being that should be left alone to live his life in the only way that he can find happiness.

This persecution by society and the law puts the homosexual in a shadow class apart from his fellow citizens and makes him extremely vulnerable to the criminal element. Many are blackmailed with the threat of exposure which would lose them their jobs if not put them in jail. There is no real estimate of how many robberies and thefts are perpetrated with the knowledge that these people are afraid to complain to the police. A large percentage of the murders every year leave a homosexual dead from a robbery that went too far. The term "rolling a queer" is so widespread and so common that in many circles it is barely considered a crime for young hoodlums to rob a homosexual, even where violence is used.

Aside from the law, society and the criminal element, the homosexual's greatest problem is learning to live with himself. We of the heterosexual world can only imagine the terrible mental anguish that must beset a growing boy when he realizes that his sexual drives are different than most. Who does he turn to for help? How does a teenage boy tell a father, or school counsellor, or church minister, that through some twist of fate he has feelings that run against society's norm? And how does the father, or school counsellor or church minister react to such a confession? We can only imagine how much damage and pain must be caused by a reaction of violence, shock or visible repulsion. Any of these could add a guilt complex to an already serious emotional problem of adjustment. The most important thing with the growing homosexual, as with any person, is gaining the self-acceptance that will allow him to live at peace with himself. Guilt feelings added to society's rejection of him could easily lead to insanity or suicide.

With homosexuals, as with any group, there is a small percentage who attempt to inflict their way of life on others. These are the ones who frequent public washrooms, beer parlours and parks in search of a pick-up. Another variety is the type that cruises the highways looking for young hitchhikers to pick up. It is this percentage that does the average homosexual the most harm by trying to take advantage of helpless young boys. The vast majority of homosexuals prefer to frequent their own clubs, bars and beer parlours and associate with their own kind.

Other than their sexual urges, most homosexuals are little different in their needs from the average person. They want friendship, acceptance, warmth and the amenities that make for a more comfortable life. Often they need these more than most people because of the general rejection faced by their kind. But most of all, they want to be left to live their own lives in their own way without prejudice or harassment.

The contribution of the homosexual to the theatre and arts is considerable. Writers, poets, artists, film makers, ballet dancers, composers, fashion designers, in fact in almost every facet of the arts you will find a high percentage of homosexuals creatively involved. The direct beneficiary of this talent is the same general public that condemns the homosexual.

By his nature, the homosexual tends to make a good employee, especially in creative fields such as hair-dressing or design or in anything dealing with the general public. They are considered to be good workers and extremely affable to fellow employees and customers. It is rare that they ever make a homosexual advance to anyone they work with or come into contact with on the job. They can't afford an indiscretion.

It may be symbolic of the ruling establishment that while the Law declares homosexuality a crime, and society deems it a social evil, most doctors and psychiatrists prefer to see it as a 'variation' of sexual behaviour rather than a disease or sickness. The consensus of those interviewed believe that homosexuality is caused by a combination of genetics and environment, although they differed on the relative importance of each. It was explained that each person, whatever their sex, has both male and female hormones. An imbalance of the genetic qualities could produce a man who is genetically more feminine than masculine. Most of these people still manage to lead 'normal' lives although a man with a high female hormone count may choose a wife with latent masculine tendencies. However, if such a person lives in an environment conducive to homosexuality in any way, the two factors may combine to firmly establish the person as a homosexual. As almost every person requires sexual release, this person would naturally seek it with members of his own sex. For him there would be no alternative except frustration and unhappiness.

Those interviewed (who asked that their names not be mentioned) agreed that in borderline or bisexual cases, it was advisable to make every attempt to guide the person to a 'normal' male-female relationship. The better able a person is to adjust to the society around him, the less likely he is to develop serious mental problems.

The case of the confirmed, deep rooted homosexual poses other problems. An attempt at a 'cure' could cause problems of self adjustment that might lead to a mental breakdown or even suicide. It was stressed that the most important thing is for a person to able to live with himself.

All of those interviewed emphasized that too little is known about homosexuality, either from the medical or psychiatric standpoints, for any definite conclusions to be drawn.

At present, there is no 'cure' for homosexuality. And if a 'cure' is found, it is highly unlikely that it will involve "kicking the shit out of them" or locking them up in a prison. The time has come for us to accept the homosexual as a human being with human rights and human needs. Until we do, the real perversion will be less with the homosexual than with the law and society that persecute him for living the only way that he can.

F) "Atomic Roulette" September 17–23, 1969
Bob Cummings

Amchitka Island is an unimpressive link in the Aleutian chain of volcanic islands which jut out from the tip of Alaska like the tail vertebrae of a dog. Thirty-five miles long and three wide, it is inhabited by sea otters, emperor geese, bald eagles and sundry other wild life. Amchitka, however, has two other features which, if combined, could make it one of the most infamous islands in the world! It lies within a natural earthquake zone AND it is about to become a test site for underground nuclear explosions …

Code named Milrow, the test series will begin with an experimental blast sometime NEXT MONTH that A.E.C. [Atomic Energy Commission] officials … who are not prone to exaggerating the possible harmful effects of their nuclear Frankensteins … predict will produce a shock wave of 6.5 on the ten-point Richter scale. Although they refuse to divulge the force of the explosion, it is expected to be in the 1.1 to 1.2 megaton range … at least fifty times larger than the blasts which devastated Hiroshima and Nagasaki.

The OCTOBER test … which could be described as a form of nuclear Russian roulette … is designed to determine if Amchitka has the geological stability necessary to withstand the strain of underground atomic detonations. It will also be used to calibrate measuring and recording instruments for later — and more powerful — tests to develop warheads for the misnamed "Safeguard" ABM system.

Aside from the earthquake gamble … if anything can be called 'aside from' when it endangers thousands of human lives … is the threat to the ecology of the region. Conservationists feel that the shock of the blast alone will upset the wildlife on the island to such an extent that it might be permanently altered …

Another leading opponent to the Milrow project is Democratic Senator Mike Gravel of Alaska who is concerned that the tests might seriously affect commercial fishing in the area. His fears are based both on the island location and the fact that the detonations will be set off at the bottom of a four thousand foot shaft well below sea level. Should the blast find or create, a horizontal fissure, radiation poisoning would be released directly into the ocean …

The danger of a radiation leak, however, is not confined to the ocean. As recently as August 14th, the A.E.C. admitted that a low yield blast —

under 20 kilotons — at its Nevada Test Site has spilled "small amounts" of radioactive material into the atmosphere. Previous tests at the same site have occasionally produced radiation readings up to 20 times normal in eastern Canadian sampling stations. While those leaks are an exception rather than a rule, they indicate that the A.E.C.'s nuclear alchemists are unable to accurately predict or control the effects of underground explosions.

Another prediction that is now being questioned is the so-called "safety level" of atomic contamination. According to Dr. Ernest Sternglass, a physics professor in the University of Pittsburgh's Department of Radiology, radiation poisoning may have caused genetic defects resulting in a 1% increase in the infant mortality rate in the U.S. since 1950 …

Equally unconvincing was the Atomic Energy Commission's statement on the Amchitka project. According to a story carried by AP, A.E.C. officials said that while results "cannot be exactly predicted", there is "good assurance" that the first in the series of at least three tests "can be conducted safely as planned". Almost as useless was their reminder that a previous test had been conducted in the Aleutians in 1965 without apparently harmful effects. That blast was in the 80 kiloton range, only one-thirteenth as powerful as the Milrow experimental shot.

If the public is indeed becoming frightened by the military-industrial-scientific establishment's tampering with the environment, it is mainly due to the proven incompetence and past mistakes of these organizations. Radiation leakage, atomic fallout, thousands of sheep killed by a nerve-gas accident and a proposal to dump hundreds of cannisters of poison-gas into the sea are hardly a basis for public confidence. Possibly if people become a little more frightened and a little less complacent, they might apply enough pressure to avert the major tragedy that is bound to happen if things continue as they are.

Another objection to the Milrow tests is that Amchitka Island is only 700 miles from the Kamchatka Peninsula in the U.S.S.R. While the main danger is a worsening of east-west tensions should there be an earthquake or radiation leak, there is also the possibility of the Soviets using the American tests as an excuse for intensifying their own underground nuclear program which, in turn, would 'justify' an increase in the American tests. This could easily negate any chance for ending the nuclear game.

Ironically, it may have been the fear of radiation spillage and seismic disturbance that prompted the move of underground tests to Amchitka. When the location was announced, the A.E.C. said it was to permit tests "with yields higher than are considered desirable in Nevada". The decision coincided with objections by billionaire Howard Hughes to subterranean blasts near his extensive holdings in the state. In the U.S., even more than in Canada, wealth is the common-law wife of political influence. There are no Aleutian Eskimo billionaires.

Because of the proximity of Amchitka Island to Canada — and B.C. in particular — the Milrow project can, and should, be considered an issue of vital concern to this country. If the fears of Dr. Twenhofel become a reality, the west coast could be devastated by a tidal wave. A massive radiation leak, if Dr. Sternglass' theory is correct, would be even more tragic.

So far, the only comment by a government official was made by B.C. Conservation Minister Ken Kiernan, who said, "Our position has to be that we can not interfere in what is U.S. jurisdiction." From its silence, Ottawa seems to be totally unaware of either the tests or their possible consequences.

While experience has shown that nothing short of God changing the power output in Bennett's plug will move the Victoria government, there is a chance that public concern could get 'swinging' Pierre Trudeau to shift his butt into action. As the Amchitka tests are scheduled to begin as early as October ... two or three weeks from now ... anyone opposed to them, whatever their reason, must begin to fight NOW.

Organize protest demonstrations ... circulate petitions ... but above all write letters to:
Prime Minister P.E. Trudeau ...
Sen. Mike Gravel ...
U Thant. Sec.-General, United Nations ...
and even:
Premier W.A.C. Bennett ...

Editors, writers and columnists in the 'other' press can, if they are concerned about the Amchitka project, bring the issue to the attention of their readers and invite them to write to any or all of the above people.

Each of us is a part of the ecology of this planet and, as such, have a born right to fight for the preservation of its environment. Each of us is a human being and, as such, have an obligation to fight for the right of survival for those species threatened by mankind's greed and insanity. No individual, group, or nation has the right to desecrate this world or destroy any of its life giving qualities.

G) "Cherry Point vs Life" February 10–17, 1971
Jeannine Mitchell

Ah … Cherry Point. A name that may go down in Ripley's Believe it or Not. Mark it well.

Massive oil spills are just a part of the total threat to the west coast ecology and economy. The pipeline through Alaska that will bring oil from the North Slopes to Valdez for loading into the supertankers may turn out to be an equal threat.

Canadians have shown little interest in this angle because it would appear to be threatening to American territory only. But wildlife and rivers aren't hung up on border concepts.

The pipeline will contain hot oil — between 158 and 176 degrees Fahrenheit. For the most part it will cross permafrost. The hot pipe will melt the permafrost, causing possible ruptures of the pipe as a result.

The pipeline also cuts through wildlife migration and breeding grounds. If it was buried underground to avoid obstruction, the permafrost would turn into sloughs in some places and would continually shift and buckle hence the likelihood of rupture and massive oil spill.

If placed on top of the permafrost, it would create a barrier over four feet high, effectively blocking migration of land animals like elk into their feeding grounds. And it would still cause melting and buckling of the permafrost.

A large section of the pipeline crosses through the centre of a major earthquake belt. Alaska, you may recall, suffered a disastrous quake in 1964. And this natural vulnerability to quakes is greatly increased with the Amchitka nuclear tests which are still going on.

After the last Amchitka test, a flood of tremors ranging to 6.5 on the Richter scale were picked up along the west coast. And the Queen Charlotte Islands have been hit by several tremors since the last test. (Note: each mile of pipeline will carry 500,000 gallons of hot oil.)

Water Pollution

Furthermore, the Cherry Point refinery has requested permission to dump 4 million gallons of alkaline effluent every day into surrounding waters.

The effluent will contain oil and grease (which will probably contain toxic petroleum distillates), ammonia, phosphates, phenols (which cause fish and shellfish to taste foul), sulfide and mercaptans (which stink), several metals, and sulfate (expected to combine into sulfuric acid — which is harmful to fish life.)

At the same time 4 million gallons of clean fresh water will be taken in each day by the plant. This will be made unusable by effluent.

If you like math, you might be interested to know that this translates into:

1 1/2 BILLION gallons of alkaline effluent each year dumped into the Strait of Georgia, and 1 1/2 BILLION gallons of fresh water made unusable each year.

Thus, the land ecosystem will suffer from the resulting loss of water and greenery, as well as from the emission of possible toxic fumes.

Local sea life, and the multi-million dollar sea-related economy that goes with it, will thus be at the mercy of:

a) massive amounts of effluent discharged at Cherry Point

b) practically inevitable oil spills at the loading areas

c) possible massive oil spills along the B.C. coast.

It appears that the permit to dump the effluent will be granted (by the U.S. Corps of Engineers), unless last minute public actions holds it up. Atlantic Richfield has already got a permit from the State of Washington Department of Ecology to dump it until 1975, subject to renewal. It is apparently not subject to cancellation.

Approval from the Corps is necessary as well, however. The Engineers are accepting arguments from the public until February 17. Unless an unusual number of letters are received the permit will undoubtedly be granted.

Spill threat

... [Supertankers] hold more and they're relatively fragile — a bad combination.

Further, the route from Valdez, Alaska to Cherry Point is not the most favourable for safe shipping. The coast is rocky throughout and tides are strong on the west side of Vancouver Island and around the Queen Charlottes.

To make things worse, the proposed routes through the Juan de Fuca Strait are unusually tricky ones. Juan de Fuca is a hazardous run — rocky, narrow and requiring great navigational skill.

And supertankers are themselves hard to handle. They cannot stop quickly to avoid collision, and they are awkward to steer. Supertankers and Juan de Fuca, then, are another bad combination.

More than 1,000 tankers will be plying the B.C. coast each year when the system reaches full capacity. Of these, over 300 will be heading through Juan de Fuca to Cherry Point.

What would happen if a tanker did run aground or collide on the route? The Queen Charlottes are not near enough to urban areas to be highly valued for recreation, but the area is beautiful and unspoiled, and is a gathering place for large numbers of marine animals and birds. It is also a vital fishing ground.

Long Beach is just now being developed as an important tourist and recreational area. Wildlife abounds along the coast, which is famous for its lonely beauty. The same goes for most of Vancouver Island's west coast.

But the most vulnerable and most precious area that could be affected is the Gulf Islands–San Juan Islands and lower mainland region. In terms of financial loss alone, a spill in this lovely recreational area would be disastrous. And Vancouver beaches are bad enough already, without crude oil and carcasses.

There are two tentative routes through the Strait. One would pass within about two miles of the Gulf Islands, and the other would skirt them by ten miles. Unfortunately for us, the area involved is in international waters. Thus, Canadians have no say in the matter.

Boundary Bay, Goodbye

The refinery itself, which is bound to be the site of smaller loading spills at some points of the operation, is about 12 miles from Boundary Bay.

Boundary Bay is now being viewed as an important potential recreation centre. It is also an unofficial sanctuary for waterfowl.

Over 100,000 birds spend their winters at Boundary Bay and at no time in the year does the population go below 20,000 birds. If a spill was to affect the Bay most of these birds would die, unless research comes up with a more effective way of rescuing oil-soaked birds than is used now.

In both the Santa Barbara and the recent San Francisco spills, scarcely any birds survived, despite careful treatment by volunteers. The percentage of survivors in these cases was roughly 3 to 4%.

Upon spilling the oil releases toxins that paralyze nearby wildlife, and life thus affected usually dies, after much suffering ...

Industry Aims its Gun

Right now, the Amerikan government is hold a hearing on the environmental aspects of the pipeline. This is only because conservationists took the case to court and got an injunction against construction until a hearing was held.

But the picture here is bleak. Henry Jackson and Warren Magnussen, the senators of Washington State are both pro-pipeline and pro-Cherry Point. Unemployment is high in the area, and the U.S. government is trying to get more oil from U.S. sources for security reasons. This is largely a result of the shaky situation in the Mid-East.

However, 1985 estimates of oil consumption in the U.S. suggest that without the pipeline, the U.S. will have to get 34% of its oil from the Mid-East. And WITH the pipeline, they will be able to get 23%. So much for security.

And employment resulting from the refinery and pipeline operations will look very very thin and small indeed if the multi-million dollar tourist and fishing industries of B.C. and Washington are endangered by a spill of the effluent.

But the scheme marches on. Washington senators are for it. Alaskan senators are for it. (They too are thinking about their high unemployment, plus such goodies as the free superhighway that the oil industry will build along the oil route.)

Canadians don't seem to count. And Atlantic Richfield has invested heavily in the project in hopes of pulling a Utah Mines act and getting through by default. In fact, Liberal MP, David Anderson of Esquimault, has claimed that "the private oil companies now are holding a gun to the heads of all officials involved" (in the environmental hearings).

Reportedly, official reaction to the conservationists has been quite hostile, and it seems likely that the hearing (due to end this month) will go in favor of the pipeline. (Incidentally, the oil companies involved in the venture have invested $900 million in gas and oil leases alone on the North Slope, from where the oil will be drawn.)

Indians or Spacemen

There appear to be two [solutions] left. One is that Arco refinery be magically pulverized into dust by spacemen, witches or other funny characters, an occurrence which would possibly also hold back the building of the pipeline.

The other is that the Alaskan Indians win their land claims. The Indians are taking on the powerful oil industry for a number of reasons. Their livelihood as hunters would be destroyed if wildlife was cut off from feeding and breeding grounds by the line.

They would suffer if the disruption of the delicate balance of the permafrost caused ecological damage to the area, or if spilled oil flooded into a river or poured over the surrounding land.

And they claim it is their land, and it is up to them what is to be done with it. Some observers think a settlement of the claims may take at least another year. In the meantime Cherry Point would operate on Canadian and Washington oil, at partial capacity.

If the settlement promises to take years to work out, the industry may start working on a slower route, one less valuable in terms of Amerikan security. This route would involve a lengthy all-land pipeline from the North Slope to the Mackenzie Delta and down (over permafrost) to Edmonton, Alberta.

Does all this frustrate you, tie you into little knots and whimpers? You may, in this case, like to join in on a demonstration against the scheme on February 21, 2 p.m. The address is the Peach Arch, by Blaine. Then again, maybe you'd like to become a witch …

H) "Cocaine: Ain't It a Shame" April 27–30, 1971
Doug Long

Apropos

Time misused, Energy misdirected, and Knowledge misinterpreted has wrought for man a causeless death — slow death by State-enforced conformity, progressive death by the poisons of industrial "progress", or moment-flash death by atomic bomb. Twentieth-century civilization, eclipsing inevitable death with its own form of death-in-life.

In opposition to established society's adverse "death" style, an alternate society has evolved which heralds itself as generating and living a "life"-style. A sound and well-grounded assertion, shown by its expanding awareness, energetic actions and sincere concern of earth ecology, human dignities, individual freedoms, creative communications, peace, love — all conditions for POSITIVE EXISTENCE.

It was the alternate society's profuse use of drugs that first set its people on this road toward "life". Drugs were initial aides in transcending this society's collective consciousness through and above death-in-life and closer to real death; closer to a knowledge and understanding of inevitable death. Thus, the alternate society has come to accept the terms of death, enabling it to divorce itself from dallying on Death's doorstep and to continue on down the road, utilizing Time, Energy and Knowledge in re-establishing meaningful life — indeed, in living a "life"-style.

But to everything, always, there is a light realm (plus) and a dark realm (minus). And a large portion of our "life"-style's dark realm lies in its drug culture.

Associated with the culture is a large number of people who have misinterpreted the objective of drug use; who have misapplied drugs, missed the benefits and got screwed up in over-indulgence or in the consumption of the "hard-core" chemicals. These people are flag-rings in the mainline of the drug culture. They exist within what Allen Ginsberg calls a "Crystal Universe". They don't traverse toward any enlightened understanding of death; however, they do have an awareness of death—they must, living a death of their own! Deadweights of the underground community, restraining its rise from within.

In the summer of 1968, the dope that plagued the underground was "the real horror monster Frankenstein" SPEED. Destructo-zombie speed demons racing around burning and bad-rapping everyone. A bummer scene. A heavier, death-lier, more perfidious scene in 1970 was ... the comeback of that "heroic" drug HEROIN. And now another death trip drug is making its debut in the dope industry: COCAINE.

Although not yet "popular" (not in Vancouver, anyway — such organizations as the Narcotics Addictions Foundation and X-Kalay have not encountered a "problem") a switch to coke is happening. From October through December of last year, over two hundred kilos of cocaine were confiscated by "authorities" in its chief import cities, New York and Miami, and a 40-kilo bust was reported in San Francisco in mid-February of this year. Underground rags report Washington is watching the South American cocaine trade "with deep interest and local agents".

Many of our more affluent and industrious local dealers are handling coke, and (sadly) many close acquaintances of mine are getting fucked up on it — the cause of my concern and the motivation behind the writing of this article.

The reasons for the switch: On the dealers' part: hard drugs are more compact and easier to transport than, say, bulky odourous marijuana, and profits are fantastic (around 3000 per cent in the long run). And so the people lost in their "Crystal Universe" it's another kind of lovin' spoonful (variety adds spice to death!) to those riding the nova express it's another brief-shining bright star to be guided by ...

Applicatios

The greatest gamble in the use of cocaine is, of course, addiction — a psychic dependence which is strong and followed by a deep depression. Addiction can develop in a startlingly short time (although there is no record of poisoning or addiction among the conqueros of the Andes, perhaps because the minute amounts of cocaine alkaloid found in the coca leaf taken at the altitude at which the Indians live is adequate for their stimulation; Indians who come down from the "high country" and enter "civilization" find it easy to give up the "habit") and is commonest in the mentally unstable and psychotic person (this statement remains open to moral argument). An acquaintance of mine who is in to cocaine, in order to check addiction, indulges on the first three days of every month only, and plans an occupied fourth day to avoid to entailing depression. For him it seems to work (so far).

Coke is usually taken in the nose, sniffed and absorbed from the nasal mucosa, producing a pronounced stimulation on the central nervous system, causing pupil dilation, elation, false confidence ("it makes heroes out of cowards!"), rapid pulse, insomnia, enhanced reflexes, and visual, auditory and tactile (touch) hallucinations. A lot of people take cocaine because of its lauded aphrodisiacal quality. If these people require a chemical to get their mojos working, then they certainly do have a problem! (To the side: in an interview with Richard G. Stern in 1958, novelist Norman Mailer hypothesized that the drug-taker is perhaps receiving love from God, and in doing so he is draining God, exhausting Him, thus doing "an extraordinary evil the instant he is filled with God and good and a beautiful mystic".) (More meat for a moral discussion.)

But back to our article-main:

Prolonged sniffing of cocaine eventually creates ulcerations in the nasal cavity and the deterioration of the lining of the nose — ultimately it eats the bone.

When taken orally it causes anesthesia of the stomach, so that hunger and thirst are not felt, and you tend not to eat well enough to nourish your body, along with leading yourself to digestive system damage, nausea and convulsions.

If administered intravenously (1.2 grams is the lethal dose and remains constant), cocaine rushes to the cortex of the brain. Mental power increases, the want for sleep disappears, you become excited, restless, garrulous, confused. You don't get your necessary sleep and your unconscious dreamworld rises to a state of conscious reality — you become a hyperneurotic hallucinating zombie. Gradually and increasingly a paranoic psychosis develops that may render the user dangerous.

In the long run, brain-cell damage and mental deterioration result, and if you are fortunate enough to escape death by paralysis of the brain's breathing centre, or cardiac failure, you may only end up as a babbling inmate in a mental institution.

Or perhaps you may turn to seeking sedatives or morphine-like drugs (e. g. heroin) to counter the hyper-excitability. Here you run the double risk of physical dependence added to psychic craving.

Cocaine is an anesthetic, not an aesthetic. It becomes an asthenic. It is pernicio-social, paranoid producing, bad for your body, bad for your mind. Bad for the whole underground community, if only for the fact that it is uncreative.

The answer to this new plague on the underground? I suppose the same cure Allen Ginsberg fashioned for the speed-freak: quiet farms in the mountain wilderness, a getting back to clean nature, where the addict could sleep and work off his depression until he finally feels like building a bridge back.

In the meantime, heed the warnings: "coke is for horses and not for men", so "you had better watch your speed".

l) "Come, All Ye Women" March 8–21, 1968
Bob Cummings

… The social position of women over the centuries has ranged very little from the common conception of them as a piece of valuable property or a protected house-pet. Sexually, the men used their once virgin brides as masturbating machines, neither knowing or caring if the woman received any pleasure from it. The value of virginal weddings and moral codes so restrictive that sexual matters were never discussed among decent women, was that the average female was unaware of the pleasure she was capable of receiving. This prevented the clumsy and lazy husbands from losing their wives to lovers with a knowledge of the sensual arts.

We now admit as fact that women should have the right to vote, to become involved in civic affairs and to freely express opinions. What many people cannot concede is that the female has an equal right to search for sexual and emotional satisfaction. This is gradually changing in the only way that it can ... through a fundamental evolution in the thinking of females that over-rides all the training and indoctrination of thousands of years of traditional inferior classification.

The greatest threat of sexual equality is not to the establishment or to the old system. They were dying before it began with the demise of belief in the church and other morality enforcing institutions. The ones in greatest peril from the sexual emancipation of women are the men. While it is true that they are now enjoying a greater frequency and selection of the once forbidden fruit, they may soon find themselves with problems undreamed of by their fathers. Under the old system, the competition was between the male seducer and the female resisting his "charms". Now and in the future the focus will be on what happens after they get into bed. Where sexual intercourse was once the prize, sexual satisfaction now becomes the challenge.

The man who felt his ego slighted because he failed to entice a coy female into bed was nothing compared to the crushing defeat of the man who is freely given the opportunity and then fails to draw his partner to an orgasm. In the future, sexual compatibility and the ability to satisfy will be essential parts in the selection of a mate. Women will reject the inadequate lover as they now reject the drunkard, the bully and the fool. The crux of masculinity and femininity have always been where they are most pertinent ... in sex itself.

In sex, the female is under a double handicap. Generally, her sexual demand is greater than the male's, both in frequency and duration. Added to this is the fact that it takes the average female longer to get sexually aroused and reach an orgasm. Medical experts disagree on whether this is a result of a natural female trait or the product of generations accustomed to sexual satisfaction as an accidental occurrence. Whatever the cause, it is up the male to favorably alter the results. The only way he can do this is to become adept in the art of lovemaking. Compatible sex is a science, an art, a philosophy and a basic instinct ... but is not a clumsy accident.

Women were expected to be in a state of almost constant pregnancy. While helping to populate the tribe, city or state, this also ensured fidelity. The quality of womanhood was directly equated to fertility. These beliefs were strongest among the lower classes and actively encouraged by the authorities.

As housekeepers, women were confined to a world of trivia. It is only recently that automatic appliances and smaller families have given married women the time to gain a knowledge of the world outside their kitchen. Unfortunately, most of them were conditioned from birth to seek marriage and motherhood as their highest goal. Having achieved this, they have neither the incentive nor the encouragement to strive for self improvement. Society still strives to rush the "weaker sex" from the protection of the family to the protection of marriage with as little transition time as possible. Her equality is limited to what she can achieve within these sanctities. To many of these women, sexual equality means withholding sex from their husbands rather than a mutual orgasm. If they were truly equals, they would realize that denial of sex meant a denial of their own pleasure and satisfaction.

Sexual freedom has produced a new species of female that might be called the subtle aggressor. Denied the right to openly pursue her choice of sexual and emotional partners, she is forced to gentle subterfuge to attain this goal. While women have always been skilled at this, the modern female is free to take her enticement into the open and he no longer feels obligated to pretend shock when he reacts. Once he approaches, she is at liberty to suggest dates, invite both him and his attentions, and to admit her desire for a social or sexual relationship. In bed, the female is longer confined to a passive role. She can use her hands, lips and body to actively pursue pleasure. Having achieved sexual freedom, the modern female will no longer be denied it.

What separates sexual freedom from sexual equality is the right of active pursuit. The she-sex is getting tired of quietly sitting at home waiting for the male to call at his pleasure. She wants to be able to go out and stalk him with the same freedom he can stalk her. Each female has a body that needs the satisfaction of being touched, kissed and made love to. She has emotions that must be fed on affection and very real charms that must be accepted. She is a human being, not a pawn in a social game.

Modern females have carried subtle pursuit to its limitations and are now beginning to reach beyond it. A high percentage of these female hunters are women whose beauty and charm would ensure them a date under any circumstances. In active pursuit they are not merely searching for men but are seeking particular men whose masculine qualities best suit the individual needs of these women. Confinement within a social group, hoping that the right men will somehow find their way into it is no longer satisfactory.

The today-female is highly curious about the opposite sex. She wants to know men of many types, not necessarily sexually although this is a matter of strictly personal choice, but at least enough to help her choose her own type of mate. She may not be a lady by the old standards, but she is far more a woman in every meaningful sense.

Sexual equality presages a complete breakdown of the established system and its replacement by standards based on human values and happiness rather than an artificially contrived moral code.

The emancipation of women, like any liberation in history, is only as complete as the mental freedom of the individuals involved. Until she can learn to be free of the restrictions that demand that she deny her desires and instincts as a woman, she will remain under the domination of sex, not because she is forced to it, but because she is denied the right to express herself as a sexual being.

J) "On Abortion" May 14–18, 1971

What's been did and what's been hid

A year ago last Sunday 1,000 women stormed the parliament buildings in Ottawa declaring war on the Canadian government for its treatment of women who need or want abortions. As Women's Liberation said at that time: "more than 2,000 Canadian women are killed or wounded each year by bungled abortions. If any foreign government killed that many Canadians we would declare war on them. Since the government has done this to us — we as women are declaring war on the Canadian Government."

35 women disrupted parliament for an hour, chaining themselves to the gallery, demanding that the MPs listen to our demands. We forced the session to close.

Peter Trudeau's re-formed abortion law of '68 said that an abortion could be performed if the life OR HEALTH of the mother was endangered. It also set up a bureaucratic machinery (a hospital board, minimum 3 doctors — the physician and the specialist are not allowed on the board). This setup excludes most rural areas which do not have large hospitals and a minimum of 5–6 doctors none of whom are Catholic. Robert Stanfield, in response to a question last April, stated that his information indicated that there were LESS abortions performed in Canada then (April '70) than BEFORE the supposed liberalized law. This is because the practice in small towns previously to the changed law had allowed some women informally to get abortions in the hospital and those abortions were often not reported.

Not only does the federal law exclude large rural areas, but it also in practice excludes cities where there is not a large active women's liberation movement. Because Vancouver Women's Caucus initiated the National Abortion Cavalcade ('70) because we disrupted both federal and provincial parliament, and meetings of the BC Medical Association and the BC College of Physicians and Surgeons, because of the militancy of our fight, abortions are available to Vancouver women.

The law stated that if the life OR HEALTH of a mother is endangered an abortion can be performed. We argued that the World Health Organization of the UN defines health as complete mental, physical and SOCIAL well-being. We argued that we, as women, are the best judge of our own social well-being, (rather than some social worker, or welfare agent or teacher or shrink or parent) and therefore our demand for an abortion was sufficient "social grounds".

It was this legalistic loophole that some hospitals have grabbed hold of in order to "get us off their back" as one doctor put it. That is how VGH explains itself to the "powers that be".

That is what they say now — now that they have been faced with the anger and power of Vancouver women and have made a "strategic retreat". (Isn't that what the Amerrikans said when they were trashed in LAOS?) It is significant to look at a Vancouver Sun editorial when we invaded parliament last spring. They spent 9/10 of the article attacking women's liberation, our "lack of understanding and disrespect for the demokratik process", our unladylike behaviour. But in the final paragraph they said that what was most pathetic was that the cause we were fighting for had "merit" — certainly the law should be changed, they said. But that was the first time the Sun had taken an editorial position in favour of a changed law. At that time Trudeau told us that we "should form an Abortion Party" ... that the 2,000 women (the number that die) constitute about one constituency and that we didn't understand the "demokratic process".

But our militancy, action on behalf of Canadian women, changed the real conditions for each of you reading this article, each of you who want to make love with your brothers and sisters without fear, each us who want to have children that we choose to have ...

Women needing abortions face the same horrid hospital conditions as all people seeking medical care. The waiting period has been up to 3 weeks at points which becomes critical for some women.

In the action of last year, we coupled the demand for free abortion with the demand for women's clinics under community control. Because of the pressure on the gynecology operating rooms by approximately 60 abortions per week the government may set up "women's clinics" (not at VGH) to perform abortions. We must make sure that these clinics continue to be free (i.e. covered by medical plans or welfare). Community control is essential to prevent institutional control over reproduction as well as most other aspects of our lives. If they attempt to make us pay at their new abortion clinics, it will be seen by women as a further move of control. Free medical care is the right of all people.

Up until 12 weeks (approximately) the operation is a D & C (dilation of the cervix and scraping of the womb). It takes 20 minutes and is less dangerous than having your tonsils out. VGH does not have a vacuum aspirator (they can't afford one), but Royal Columbian does. From 12 weeks to 20 the operation is called a saline injection. This involves the injection of a salt solution into the uterus. Within 8 to 15 hours after injection, one has a natural miscarriage.

For women who do not have medical plans and who earn less that $150 per month there is a free women's clinic at VGH. For more information call Janis ... or D-J ... This information indicates fairly clearly that we have won the battle for abortion in this city. But have we won the war (which we declared) for the right to control over our own bodies?

Stop hey what's that sound
Everybody look what's coming down

In a society in which production and social organisation is controlled by a very few rich, the dangers of those pigs having control over reproductions are enormous. The Chinese after liberation '48 held off for quite a few years the introduction of birth control and abortion because the revolutionaries feared the control that might be placed in the hand of bureaucratic officials. It was only as socialism was strengthened in China that it could not be used in an inhuman way that massive BC programs were introduced. By contrast in Alaska native women are forced to have abortions or their welfare cheques are cut off. In Amerika — a campaign of population genocide is being waged by the pig power structure (welfare agents, courts) against Black, Puerto Rican and Mexican peoples, against the right to have their children. John D. Rockefeller (head of Planned Parenthood), who makes the majority of his money from the exploitation of Latin America (where many revolutionary movements are growing) attempts to limit the number of the "underprivileged" because he know the strength of numbers, because he fears that Third World people are rising up.

Women's Liberation sees counselling as a serve the people project — a survival program for Vancouver women. Our militant actions have won us a measure of control over our lives. We must not win that battle only to lose the war. We must be conscious that the power structure will try to use abortion against us. If they will take Grace Bisson's children away, will they not try to stop us from having the children we want? We must struggle for control over our bodies. We must struggle for control over our lives! NOUS VAINCRONS!

K) "Off with Bras and Girdles" February 1–22, 1968
Bob Cummings

A walk through the Chamber of Horrors past such chilling relics of sadism as the rack, thumbscrew, bustle, iron-maiden, corset, bed of nails and the uplift brassiere. The twenty-first Century tourists shuddered that such cruel devices could ever be inflicted on human flesh. The last visitor left and the lights dimmed. A single shaft of moonlight through the windows cast its glow on a hideous apparatus called the 'panty-girdle'.

If the above description seems whimsical it is no more than an extension of the modern opinion of foot binding in China and the whalebone corset. Despite "light, lovable Lycra", these is no reason why our attempts at beauty through constriction should be considered any different by future generations.

By any standards, brassieres and girdles must be considered among the most ugly creations ever to defile a human body, both in appearance and function. Their intended purpose is to create an artificial, sexless, motionless shape catering to drab conformity. By implication they contend that the image is more important than the reality, conformity preferable to individuality. If a woman has small breasts, she is told to pad them or use falsies ... if she has large breasts, she is instructed to constrict them. Her hips and upper legs must be bound into an immovable lump, devoid of any signs of life.

Until recently, girdles and brassieres were considered fundamental truths of fashion. Clothing was designed on the premise that it would be covering a stereotyped shape. Women were expected to suit the clothing instead of the clothing suiting them. For proof, watch some old movie re-runs and try to tell one woman from another without a close examination.

With advent of the natural-line fashions, including mini-skirts and see-through blouses, bras and girdles not only became superfluous but actually detracted from the basic theme. In fact, many modern designers insist that their creations are ruined if worn with constrictive underwear. The idea is that the clothes should compliment and accent the natural line and motion of the female body including the sway of the breasts and hips. Panty-hose have eliminated the questionable need of girdles, especially panty-girdles to hold up stockings. Any female lithe enough to wear a mini-skirt doesn't need a girdle.

A more difficult illusion to dispell is the great brassiere myth. Young girls are given training bras before there is any thing to put in them. In truth, with the exception of obesity and physical deformity, no female should need anything to support her breasts until maternity or age breaks down their ability to support themselves. With moderate exercise, a woman can keep her breasts, as well as the rest of her body, firm and healthy. One of the most damaging aspects of wearing bras and girdles is that they are used as a substitute for exercise and sensible diet. When Playtex advertises that their panty-girdle can trim five pounds, it just means that it conceals it. The five pounds is still there and the wearer is tempted to ignore diet and exercise until there is another five pounds to go with it. The same ad says that the girdle holds you in like "firm young muscles". True, and what's more it's doing the job in place of the muscles. With the girdle holding in the stomach, the muscles will turn to fat, the same as chest muscles when a bra is supporting the breasts. Within a few years, Playtex has a customer for life and even their heavy duty bras and girdles can't make middle age fat-collapse look attractive.

The strongest opposition to the elimination of bras and girdles can be expected from the $500 million a year industry that produces them. These companies are heavy advertisers and it is impossible to determine how much heavy pressure will be put on fashion writers to come out against the elimination of these products. Establishment newspapers and magazines are not in the habit of ignoring their advertisers.

The trend towards eliminating bras and girdles is in full swing. Fashion designers openly advocate it, avant-garde pacesetters are practicing it and it is quickly spreading to the masses of women who are sick of being bound in any respect. The greatest deterrents are the inbred inhibitions fostered on young people by the past generations. Many girls are afraid that they will appear cheap or look foolish. Neither of the fears are true. The best advice is for a girl to start by going without a bra and girdle at home for a few months until she becomes accustomed to the feel of being natural. Any man who thinks that a bra-less girl is an easy lay will be in for a surprise. They are striving for a natural honesty in themselves and they will demand it in the men they date.

L) "Obscenity: Who Really Cares, All is Phoney" January 12–25, 1968
Bob Cummings

The way they manage to stir people up, they should be packaged and sold as 'pep' pills. They are usually short and of simple construction, but the way they affect some people makes them a potent force. Users most often render their intended purpose meaningless through improper usage, but even then they are so powerful as to render the non-immunized to a state of shock. Science can find no cure, theology tried and failed to crush them, and society long ago gave up the fight to eliminate them. They are, of course, those infamous four letter words. They are of the sub specie obscenity and can also be called 'dirty words' and 'bad language'. At times they contain more than four letter[s] and longshoremen, taxi-drivers and editors of the GEORGIA STRAIGHT have been known to string them in almost poetic chains to emphasize a point where mere words fail. (The latter use them when articles like this appear in place of regular assignments.)

The mere presence of them have gotten books, plays and magazines banned, thus insuring a fortune for the author. Harry Crankshaw uses them to describe a sticky bathroom faucet and Norman Mailer finds them indispensable to describe the war in Vietnam. They live best on toilet walls, daily conversation and in great literature where the hero, who has just lost his wife, his job and his sexual capacity, needs a world stronger than "drat" to express his feelings.

They are listed in most dictionaries (with the remark 'not in polite use') which may explain why the average prude gets screwed up while doing a crossword puzzle. There is an unconfirmed rumour that Education Minister Les Peterson wants the Oxford Concise banned from school usage to be replaced with the Armenian Unabridged Dictionary (Same words, but nobody can pronounce them ... including the Armenians).

What? Some idiot just asked 'What is a "dirty" word?' Why, that's simple. A dirty word is a .... It's a collection of letters that .... It's a damn good question?

Let's start at the basics. A word is made of letters. Letters in themselves can't be dirty. Soooo, it must be the combination of letters that is dirty. Fine! Let's take an 'f', a 'u', a 'c', and a 'k', and put them together in a pronounceable order. Then we have "CUFK" ... Sounds Armenian?

Never mind the composition. Let's take the words themselves. (We are grateful to the office girls at the local cafe for the following and apologize for eavesdropping on their conversation.) A cursory examination of the words shows that they are only made up of letters, and we've already been through that shot.

If the obscenity has nothing to do with the letters, or combination, it must be the meaning that is dirty. So, here they are, obscene words with their approximate meanings:

FUCK: sexual intercourse — usually warm and most often accompanied by another four letter word, "Love". What's obscene about love?

FART: heavenly release — only obscene in a closed room when done by somebody else. The only available single word for the act.

SHIT: people droppings — not overly pleasant, but hardly a secret to anyone over the age of toilet training. Dirty only when the toilet seat is faulty or broken.

CUNT: female sex organ — a giver and receiver of enjoyment, a gift of love to husbands or lovers. The only non-latin word available ... and everybody knows all about those old Italians.

Something is wrong. Every word there concerns a natural function or an act of love or both. Only a pervert could consider them obscene. Either that or the P.T.A. Ladies who defined them for us were putting us on.

We seem to have flopped in finding four-letter words, so let's try three-letter four-letter words. Ready?

SEX: male, female, or act of -?????? bit loose in the interpretation but hardly obscene.

ASS: buttocks — a much better word. Can you imagine saying 'My, she has a lovely buttocks', or 'Look at Jose leading his buttocks into Vera Cruz, loaded down with fresh Tamales'.?????? This is getting discouraging. We'll give it one more try.

WAR: organized murder usually for political gain — AaaaaaaHaaaaaaa, now we've got one. Definitely obscene. Must crush it before it gets out and begins to multiply. What's that? You say it's too late? It already dominates the press, radio and TV. Lives in the minds of all decent establishment type people who want to educate other peoples to our way of purity even if it kills them? Oh come on ... You must be joking? It's only a little three letter word. Here. I'll open the dictionary for a better look ... Oh my God, it's getting out ... There's a whole cesspool of dirty words in there ... here they come ... Forget me, save yourself ... "INJUSTICE ... HATRED ... IN-TOLERANCE ... BOMBS ... PREJUDICE ... NAPALM ... TORTURE ... GUNS ... KILLING ... INFANTICIDE ... " They're all over ... They're reaching for me ... I'm going ... fast! Make up some new censorship laws before it's too late. Wipe them out start a new society where they will die of malnutrition. Make them a part of the past. Destroy them, for the sake of humanity.

M) "Beautify Vancouver: Get a Haircut" September 13–19, 1968
Bob Cummings

According to the reaction, it would appear to be one of the greatest enemies ever to confront the civilized world. Nations have declared it illegal, men of God have decried it as immoral, educators believe that it breeds mental re-tardation and political leaders find in it the onslaught of anarchy.

The Communist hierarchy of Bulgaria have used armed border guards to keep it from entering their country and destroying Marxism. Western courts of law are often unable to function if it enters their hallowed doors. And once it appears on any university campus in any country at any time — the word education becomes a sordid synonym for revolution.

This super international composite threat to the entire human species is — hair! Deceptively described as an inert group of cylindrical filaments of cornified epidermal nature in medical books, it is actually a virulent social evil that is unceasing in its attempts to conquer the world. Proof of the insidious qualities of "hair" is evidenced each time a dissident group of anti-status-quos attempts to disrupt the peaceful tranquility of a police state or a dictatorship.

Photographs from Prague show "hair" enslaved youths impeding the lawful progress of visiting Soviet tanks through that city. Films from Chicago portray "hair" corrupted people littering the streets with their bodies. Contrasting this long tressed evil in both cities were the clean, smooth hairless domes of police and army helmets.

To anyone with half a mind — such as Mayor Daley, Alexei Kosygin, George Wallace and Mayor Campbell — the connection between "hair" and anti-authority behavior is obvious. To them, and the millions of others with equal perception, it is self-evident that the man who shuns the barber shop today could be mixing Molotov cocktails by tomorrow. The route from respectability to the barricades is often marked by a pair of rusted clippers.

These stalwart leaders, each in his own inimitable way, have worked towards the curtailing of the ever-growing enemy — "hair". Mayor Daley's solution was to order his men to knock it off with nightsticks ... Premier Kosygin, with the thoroughness of a dedicated Marxist, had the offensive locks clipped off by tank fire. George Wallace solved the problem by eliminating the need for a head among those joining his American Independence Party. Less forceful, but equally dedicated was Vancouver's Mayor Tom Campbell who tried to bribe the evil substance off the heads of local hippies.

However, the enemy is not so easily thwarted. Even as these guardians of "short back and sides and trim the sideburns" were clipping the frontal assault, "hairs" in their countless billions, were creeping out of head and chin holes to fill the gap. Soon they would begin encroaching on decently bare ears and necks, forming themselves into waves and tresses and moustaches and beards. And soon, the hoards of "hair" would again be carried into battle by willing collaborators such as student activists, hippies, artists, writers and other enemies of the state.

Of course, it's not the "hair" itself that's the problem, it's the troublemakers that encourage it to get out of hand. As long as it keeps its place, doesn't cause any trouble and doesn't try to get uppity, no decent folks are going to complain about the presence of "hair". In fact, most people will tell you that some of their best friends have "hair".

But when "hair" goes beyond the length allowed by decent people, the line has to be drawn. If "hair" was just allowed to grow anywhere, unchecked and unshorn, the result would be a cranial anarchy that could destroy civilization as we know it. From ungoverned hair length, society would be plunged deeper into nonconformity. The ultimate result could be free thought in the streets and complete breakdown in the blind obedience that has consistently kept religions, laws and moral codes a century behind the times.

Aside from the moral aspects, the uninhibited growth of "hair" could have serious economic effects. Unemployed barbers obviously cannot buy groceries and soon the grocers would become unemployed and, obviously, unemployed grocers could not afford to pay their rent which, obviously, would lead to the landlords going broke which, obviously, would flood the market with unsaleable property which, obviously, would lead to a slump in the market which, obviously, would mean unpaid taxes which, obviously, could cause a depression. This, in turn, could be an ideal situation for the rise of Communism which would destroy the freedom of democracy.

An equal fiscal disaster could occur with a reduction of the facefuzz removal industry. Every time "hair" takes over a chin, it strikes a blow at labour, management, free-enterprise and "our way of life". Each morning, millions of square inches of stubble across the country help to create a healthy economy. First, each face must be lathered — from an aerosol can with a touch of menthol to give a cool shave; then finally an after-shave — with a man's scent ... either musty or leather or fresh limes, depending on whether one wishes to smell like a shoe shine boy or a fruit picker.

There can be little doubt that the elimination of "hair" is the vital concern of all freedom-loving, Christian patriots and that those who oppose this battle are an enemy that must be met and defeated. Today, the front line is occupied; not by youth, but by those veterans of a thousand broken combs — the establishment generation. The proof of their dedication to the defeat of "hair" is self-evident in the gleaming domes of head skin from which "hair" had been abolished forever.

The crisis of the hour calls for bold action and a new leader — seed the clouds with "hair" remover and elect Yul Brynner as President of the World.

N) "Easter Be-In" April 11–17, 1969
Bill Tait

Good, good, good vibrations ... The Easter Be In in Stanley Park freed the heads of 5000 people from the bring down karma of the city for a few hours, and hopefully has set in motion the spring and summer offensive of love and peach against the plastic and dead culture of the insane city of Vancouver. On the beautiful earth of Prospect Point picnic area, surrounded by tall majestic trees, and just a hop, skip, and jump from the ocean, tribes of free people from Vancouver, Seattle, and surrounding areas gathering to BE IN together on the day of rebirth for worship of the earth and sun, and to purify themselves of the bad karma of plastic, turned off commercial industrial minds which has for too long been destroying the earth and its inhabitants.

The Be In began at 10 am when about 500 people showed up to be greeted with free joints which had been specially rolled for the Easter Be In. By noon, when the first band began blasting out the good cheer, everyone was stoned out of their egos, and for the rest of the day the good vibrations created kept everyone up. Seven bands played the seven hours to sunset on the giant Deyong sound system provided: Seeds of Time, Mother Tucker's Yellow Duck, Mock Duck, Billy Joe Bottom Band, Canned Head, a Seattle band, and Genesis.

A beautiful chick passed out a poem telling everyone that today everyone was free and it was okay to lose yourself so that you could be free.

Throughout the day prophylactic balloons containing joints were burst providing manna for all. Thanks to the two way radios and "nark" spotters it was possible to keep tabs on the narks. Crowds of people surrounded the identified narks and offered them pot, which some broke down and took. Only two were busted, Bob Hill and Bob Hyde, by the RCMP.

A purifying turn on ritual happened in the center of the picnic area, lasting until near sunset. Wood drums, bottles, hand clapping, and chanting made rhythmic vibrations for dancers in the purifying ecstatic ritual. It created a tribe of beautiful people, who did their thing. People met each other and turned each other on just by their good vibrations. All in all, everyone just did what they wanted, which was to turn on.

17

"Merely a Province Among Others"
Quebec and Independence

DOCUMENTS
A) Quebec-Canada: A New Deal, 1979
    The Parti Québécois
B) A New Canadian Federation, 1980
    The Liberal Party of Quebec

erhaps Terry Mosher, drawing as cartoonist "Aislin," best captured Canada's mood on the morning of November 16, 1976, the day after the Parti Québécois came to power in Quebec. His predictably scabrous editorial cartoon depicted a disheveled René Lévesque, ubiquitous cigarette in hand, against an unusually plain black background. The caption: "Okay, everybody take a Valium." Canada, awakened from its post-war complacent slumber, discovered to its horror that one of the country's provincial governments and some 30% of the nation's population apparently wished to leave. "Sovereignty-association," the Parti's blueprint for a new Quebec, called for a politically sovereign Quebec with an economic association featuring a common currency, free trade and movement between the two nations, and a structure to jointly administer the whole thing.

The Parti Québécois kept its promise to hold a referendum on sovereignty-association within its first term in office, doing so in 1980 after postponing it for as long as politically feasible. Polls taken early in the Parti's mandate proved that separatist support was far from unanimous, and that made all but diehards nervous. The PQ also knew, however, that a large percentage of Quebecers were unhappy with the present federal-provincial arrangement. Thus Lévesque and his team spent four years carefully cultivating the idea of separatism; slowly and gently nurturing it as a logical, safe, and advantageous route for the province. Gentle persuasion was the order of the day, for they knew that being either too cavalier or too dogmatic about their central agenda risked alienating vital support. Lévesque de-emphasized independence in favour of simple good government, thereby hoping to gain credibility and support among "soft separatists" and un-decided voters. Claude Morin, one of the architects of separatism and the *oui* side of the referendum campaign, logically pointed out that "you don't make a flower grow by pulling at it."

The referendum campaign officially began on April 15, 1980, after which the gloves came off between separatist and federalist forces as they fought for the hearts and minds of Quebecers. The Parti Québécois authorized strict referen-dum guidelines for the two sides, clearly trying to establish rules for a fair fight. Fairness, stated Pierre Trudeau's federal government, was impossible when the rest of the country was not consulted in a matter that clearly concerned all Cana-dians. Thus the federal government refused to play by the rules and fought a strong anti-separatist campaign according to its own strategy.

Besides histrionics, both sides also offered reasonable and logical arguments in support of their positions during the referendum campaign. Neither attempted the futile exercise of persuading hard-liners from the opposite camp. Lévesque, knowing he had to proceed cautiously without spooking undecided voters, sof-tened his view of sovereignty. A solid "yes" on May 20th, he reminded Quebecers, did not mean a separate Quebec on the 21st. It merely gave the Parti Québécois the mandate to begin negotiations with the federal government for a future inde-pendent Quebec. A yes vote essentially guaranteed another referendum, at which time Quebecers would have a second chance to vote for independence. This, ar-gued Lévesque, gave non-independentists unhappy with the present federal-pro-vincial relationship an opportunity to express their disapproval of the *status quo* without radically changing it. Though Lévesque could not say as much, the impli-cation was clear: a strong yes vote held out the possibility of a new relationship between Quebec and Ottawa within Canada.

The federalist forces, led by Prime Minister Pierre Trudeau and Quebec pro-vincial Liberal leader Claude Ryan, argued that a yes vote was a vote for inde-pendence. "Sovereignty-association" was a contradiction in terms, they said, like being "sort of" pregnant. You either were or you weren't. They, and other provin-cial premiers, also stated that the federal government would not negotiate sover-eignty, regardless of the referendum outcome.

The federal side, however, pledged to renegotiate existing federal-provincial relationships to more accurately reflect the wishes of Quebec's people. Trudeau rightly recognized the long history of alienation and disaffection between Que-bec and the federal government, largely centred on perceived arrogance on the latter's part. This, promised Trudeau, would change if the people of Quebec rejected sovereignty. Canada would, he guaranteed, create its own constitution reflecting the needs of provinces like Quebec. By implication, a strong no vote offered Quebec power and rights in jurisdictions that were hitherto part of the federal bailiwick. It might not be sovereignty, but it was an appealing deal that avoided locking horns with an angry federal government and stepping into the abyss of independence. A no vote apparently meant Quebec getting its cake and eating it too.

Not surprisingly, the referendum campaign left Quebecers deeply perplexed and exhausted. Thousands remained undecided right up until they signed their names and entered the voting booths. Commentators at the scene remarked how many people tarried long over simple "Xs" on their ballots. Part of the reason, of course, was the impossibly long-winded referendum question which said in English and French:

> The government of Québec has made public its proposal to negotiate a new agreement with the rest of Canada, based on the equality of nations; this agreement would enable Québec to acquire the exclusive power to make its laws, levy its taxes and establish relations abroad — in other words, sovereignty — and at the same time, to maintain with Canada an economic association including a common currency; no change in political status resulting from these negotiations will be affected without approval by the people through another referendum; on these terms, do you give the government of Québec the mandate to negotiate the proposed agreement between Québec and Canada?

Several weeks of nervous nail biting came to an end shortly after 8:00pm on May 20th. The vote in favour of a mandate to negotiate sovereignty-association was 40.4%; opposed, 59.6%. While separatists wept over their seemingly catastrophic defeat, federalists from British Columbia to Newfoundland vented a collective sigh of relief. This surely forestalled future separatist ambitions. The people of Quebec had spoken. It was over. Done. Or was it? Closer examination of the referendum results allowed sovereignists to dry their tears and draw comfort from a result that was far more ambiguous than simple numbers initially suggested. Federalists also had no cause for smugness.

The sizable non-Québécois community in Quebec, for example, predictably voted overwhelming "no" to sovereignty-association. Native French speakers, however, voted almost 50-50 *"oui,"* and young secular urbanites, the next generation of leaders, supported independence by a reasonably wide margin. The next provincial election, held April 13, 1981, saw the Parti Québécois, still dedicated to a sovereign Quebec, swept back into power, winning 80 out of the 122 seats—a two-thirds majority. These facts, plus subsequent developments in the 1980s and '90s, clearly demonstrated that the dream of an independent Quebec did not die with the 1980 referendum.

A) Quebec-Canada: A New Deal, 1979
The Parti Québécois

Our ancestors put down their roots in American soil at the beginning of the 17th century, cleared the land of the St. Lawrence Valley and ... by 1760 they already formed a distinct society which would sooner or later have freed itself of the colonial yoke as did the United States in 1776. But in 1763 they came under British rule.

They chose to remain faithful; they withdrew to the countryside and patiently rebuilt their country. The 60,000 Francophones of the time gradually strengthened their institutions ... They also made good the numbers they had lacked in 1760; doubling their population every 25 years, they totalled 500,000 by about 1835 ...

The 1867 Confederation was a federation in name only; the central government, far from being a reflection of the provinces, dominated them in fact, even to the point of deciding on the direction they were to take, thanks to the power it held.

The federal Parliament had exclusive jurisdiction in all the fields deemed essential to the development of a State: transportation, criminal law, money, banking, fisheries, excise and customs duties, interprovincial and international trade; the federal government could also tax and spend as it pleased, make laws on all questions of "national" interest, disallow any provincial statute which appeared to encroach upon its authority, and exercise jurisdiction in any field not covered by the constitution. In other words, it had all the powers it needed to ensure its ascendancy, and that of English Canada.

The provinces had jurisdiction in fields considered at that time to be of purely local interest. And in every respect, Quebec was merely a province like all the others ...

As a minority within the federal system, Quebecers could no longer make their voices heard, or at any rate heeded; even less were they able to obtain satisfaction. What Quebecers wanted in 1867 was to be able to manage their own affairs and build their own future. Not only were they unsuccessful, but they even had to submit to interference by the central government in the fields under Quebec's jurisdiction, to look on while its rights and powers were continually eroded. From the outset our federal system has manifested an implacable tendency to centralize ...

Quebec has, of course, constantly attempted to resist this centralizing trend, particularly in recent years. Duplessis, Sauvé, Lesage, Johnson, Bertrand and Bourassa all struggled to safeguard or even repatriate our powers and fiscal resources. But they were barely able to slow down the centralization, a situation which produced increasingly pronounced overlapping and duplication in almost every area of government activity. The citizen finally loses his bearings; he pays double income tax; he suffers from the administrative confusion resulting from this unacceptable situation, and he must foot the bill for wasted time, energy and money, the total cost of which is difficult to calculate.

In an attempt to settle virtually insoluble problems, committees are set up ...

And while precious time is lost running from committee meeting to conference and back, we men and women of Quebec are becoming an ever-dwindling minority; accounting for 36 per cent of the population in 1851, we made up only 28 per cent in 1971; in 2001, we shall represent only 23 per cent ...

It is illusory to believe that under such circumstances Quebecers can play a decisive role within the Government of Canada. On the contrary, they will become a smaller and smaller minority, and it will become increasingly easier for the rest of Canada to govern without them. In this respect the Clark government is far from being an anomaly: it is a sign of the future.

Under the terms of the British North America Act Quebec is not the homeland of a nation, but merely a province among others. Nowhere in the British North America Act is there talk of an alliance between two founding peoples, or of a pact between two nations; on the contrary, there is talk of political and territorial unity, and of a national government which essentially dictates the direction the regional governments are to take. The English provinces know the score since, despite regional differences, they have always considered the central government to be the "senior government," the one that takes precedence over the others — from the point of view of the heart as well as the mind — and the one to which one owes allegiance.

It appears certain that in 1867, the Anglophones of Canada saw the British North America Act as simply a British law, not a pact between two nations.

Though federalism is not necessarily synonymous with poverty and political domination, neither is it a guarantee of freedom or a high standard of living; and it is no more the formula of the future than the unitary state is the formula of the past. In fact there are several kinds of federalism: some are found in rich countries, others in poor countries; some in democratic regimes, others in dictatorships ...

An insurmountable obstacle blocks the way to "renewed federalism." In order to strengthen Quebec, to build it, Quebecers must, as the system now stands, ask English Canadians to undermine and dismantle their national institutions. To respond to Quebec's needs and ensure its development, it would indeed be necessary to transfer to all the provinces so many powers that now belong to Ottawa that it would add up, in the eyes of English Canadians, to the almost total disappearance of the central government.

Logic of the system

Of course English Canadians say they are ready to improve the system. But we must be wary of words: the expression "renewed federalism," very much in fashion these days, can have many meanings.

Certain Quebecers, when they talk of "renewed federalism" because they are dissatisfied with the status quo, think of a serious and substantial transformation of the system, not a cosmetic job.

English Canadians, on the other hand, give quite a different meaning to the term: it is a "touched up" federalism that they want, since they feel that any reform must totally respect the role and the prerogatives of the central government, seen as the "national government" of all Canadians ...

The very balance of the system, as the Canadian majority wants it, requires that Quebec remain a province — or perhaps a territory — among ten others, and forbids the formal and concrete recognition of a Quebec nation. The fact that it is impossible, in the present federal framework, for Quebec to become a nation, constitutes the very basis of the Canada-Quebec political problem.

Special status

Some Quebecers believe in good faith that the answer to the problem is to give Quebec a special status. The idea, fashionable during the sixties ... seems to have the advantage of answering a good many of Quebec's aspirations without forcing other provinces into constitutional rearrangements they do not want. But this solution is rejected out of hand by English Canada, which has always been opposed to Quebec's possible acquisition of powers denied to the other provinces ...

One simple conclusion can be drawn from all these observations. If we want both to save the present system and to renew federalism, we will have to resign ourselves to giving up to the central government, in which Quebecers will always be a minority, an impressive number of prerogatives and decision-making centres that to date Quebec has been demanding for itself. For Quebecers that would mean implicitly accepting the fact that control over some of their most vital affairs would go to a government over which they could never exert more than an indirect or passing influence; it would mean entrusting their interests and their future to others. Very few nations in the world would be satisfied with such an arrangement ...

The recent history of international relations shows that federalism can no longer be regarded as the only formula capable of reconciling the objectives of autonomy and interdependence. Although it was fashionable in the past century, the federal formula must now give way to associations between sovereign countries. While no new federations are being created, economic associations are on the increase on every continent.

Basing itself firmly on the historical trend of Quebec thinking, which has always sought to redefine relations between Quebec and the rest of Canada on a more egalitarian basis, the Government of Quebec proposes this type of modern formula of association between sovereign countries to ensure for Quebecers a better control of their own affairs, without shattering the Canadian economic framework ... The Quebec government wants to propose to the rest of Canada that the two communities remain in association, not only in a customs union and a common market but in a monetary union as well ...

Through sovereignty, Quebec would acquire, in addition to the political powers it already has, those now exercised by Ottawa.

Sovereign powers

Sovereignty is the power to levy all taxes, to make all laws and to be present on the international scene; it is also the possibility of sharing freely, with one or more states, certain national powers. Sovereignty for Quebec, then, will have a legal impact on the power to make laws and to levy taxes, on territorial integrity, on citizenship and minorities, on the courts and various other institutions, and on the relations of Quebec with other countries.

The only laws applying on Quebec's territory will be those adopted by the National Assembly, and the only taxes levied will be those decreed by Quebec law. In this way, there will be an end to the overlapping of federal and Quebec services ...

Existing federal laws will continue to apply as Quebec laws, as long as they are not amended, repealed or replaced by the National Assembly.

Quebec has an inalienable right over its territory, recognized even in the present Constitution, which states that the territory of a province cannot be modified without the consent of that province. In becoming sovereign, Quebec, as is the rule in international law, will thus maintain its territorial integrity.

The Quebec government gives its solemn commitment that every Canadian who, at the time sovereignty is achieved, is a resident of Quebec, or any person who was born there, will have an automatic right to Quebec citizenship; the landed immigrant will be able to complete residency requirements and obtain citizenship.

Quebec citizenship will be recognized by a distinct passport, which does not rule out the possibility of an agreement with Canada on a common passport.

The government pledges that Quebec's Anglophone minority will continue to enjoy the rights now accorded it by law, and that other communities in Quebec will be given the means to develop their cultural resources.

The Amerindian and Inuit communities, if they so desire, will be in full possession on their territory of institutions that maintain the integrity of their societies and enable them to develop freely, according to their own culture and spirit.

Interdependence

Quebec has never wanted to live in isolation; from the start it has accepted interdependence. However, it wishes to ensure that it will be directly involved in determining the terms of this interdependence.

To this end, the Quebec government intends to offer to negotiate with the rest of Canada a treaty of community association, whose aim will be, notably, to maintain the present Canadian economic entity by ensuring continuity of exchange and by favouring, in the long run, a more rapid and better balanced development of each of the two partners.

This treaty will have an international status and will bind the parties in a manner and for a term to be determined. It will define the partners' areas of common activity and confirm the maintenance of an economic and monetary union between Quebec and the rest of Canada. It will also determine the areas where agreement on goals is considered desirable. Finally, it will establish the rules and institutions to ensure the proper functioning of the Quebec-Canada community, and determine its methods of financing.

Common Action

Areas of common action will include:

FREE CIRCULATION OF GOODS
In order to ensure the free circulation of goods, the present situation in Quebec and Canada will be maintained, and each party will renounce any right to customs barriers at common borders. With regard to foreign countries, the partners will jointly establish the tariff protection they deem necessary, taking into account the short and long-term interests of each of the parties, and multilateral agreements in the areas of trade and customs tariffs.

MONETARY UNION
The dollar will be maintained as the only currency having legal tender, and real or liquid assets as well as letters of credit will continue to be expressed in dollars. Circulation of capital will be free, but each party will be entitled to proclaim an investment code or to adopt, if need be, particular regulations applicable to certain financial institutions.

FREE MOVEMENT OF PEOPLE
In order to ensure the free movement of people from one territory to the other, the two States will give up their right to impose a regular police control at their common border. It goes without saying that no passport will be required between Quebec and Canada.

In one of the outstanding documents of our time, the Club of Rome clearly identified the essential conditions for progress in modern societies: according to this prestigious body, the future belongs to countries whose population is young and well educated, which have abundant natural resources and which specialize in international exchanges.

We, in Quebec, have the resources, the talent and the knowledge enabling us to assume, quite calmly, control of our own affairs and to meet the challenges of our general growth, notably in the economic area. For this, we hold trump cards, which might even be called exceptional.

Why then should we be content with an inferior political status?

We are already a rich country. In 1978, our per capita Gross Domestic Product ranked Quebec 14th among 150 countries in the world. This is not a matter of chance, the result of some political system or some magnanimous gift from outside; our standard of living is based essentially on our wealth of resources, on our advantageous geographical position, close to rich markets, and on the stimulating effect of the North American environment.

And our country is vast; Quebec ranks 16th in area among the 150-odd countries in the world. It is true that it has only six million inhabitants, but standard of living has nothing to do with the size of a population. Some highly populated countries, such as the United States, France and the Federal Republic of Germany, enjoy high standards of living, but it is striking and noteworthy that five of the six richest countries in the world, Switzerland, Denmark, Sweden, Norway and Belgium, have a population of less than ten million, as does Quebec. On the other hand, countries with the largest populations are often the poorest ...

Respect for diversity

Sovereignty will not change the policy Quebec has always followed regarding the various cultural communities that make up its people and reflect the cultural riches of our planet. It is in the interest of those communities, as well as of Quebec, that they assert and develop that part of themselves which is essential to their heritage ...

As for Francophones living outside Quebec, the government promises them the support and solidarity of Quebecers. In an association between equals with the rest of Canada, Quebec will be able to give them the financial and technical help it already provides, and make it easier for those who so wish to settle on its territory. Moreover, reciprocity agreements that would give them the same advantages now enjoyed by Anglophone Quebecers could preserve many of them from assimilation, which in their present conditions they rightly fear ...

Quebec will be in a better position to take advantage of its major assets if, as a community, it has new instruments in hand, instruments such as it has never had before. The assumption is that in any society that wants to progress, the impetus must come first and foremost from within — from that society itself. Sweden, Japan, France and Germany, whose performances are remarkable, owe almost nothing to outside help: they owe what they have to the resources and know-how of their own people. Quebec too will follow that fundamental rule: its future rests primarily on Quebecers' increased sense of responsibility and their determination to help themselves.

Mutual areas

To ensure the proper functioning of the monetary and economic community, the two parties will agree on certain goals and types of legislation. This will be the case, notably, in the area of transportation, where it will be possible to make special agreements for railways, air transportation, and inland shipping; such agreements could also provide for joint management of public carriers, Air Canada and Canadian National, for example. Such efforts could be extended to several other areas, in particular defence ...

In association between two partners, some fundamental subjects must naturally be subjected to parity, otherwise one of the parties would be at the mercy of the other. That does not mean, however, that in everyday practice everything will be subject to a double veto. Certain institutions of the union (the monetary authority, for instance) would, on the contrary, enjoy a large measure of autonomy of management ...

The Referendum

The Referendum, by directly involving citizens in a debate that has always been the preserve of politicians, will add to the Quebec-Ottawa dispute an element of greater consequence, more decisive than all the files and protest meetings and public statements which so far have brought no results: the democratically expressed will of Quebecers.

This is the main objective of the Referendum. Opponents of the Referendum, aware that a positive answer, democratically expressed under the eyes of the international community, would force Ottawa and the rest of Canada to react in the same democratic way in an attempt to avoid embarrassment, have devoted themselves to convincing Quebecers that a positive answer would be useless since, in their opinion, the rest of Canada would never agree to negotiate the implementation of sovereignty-association.

Many English-Canadian personalities, politicians and others, tell anyone who will listen that they will categorically refuse to negotiate. This is quite fair, though rather crude. We must not be taken in by it but must, on the contrary, stand firm in our conviction that if the majority of Quebecers say YES in the Referendum, Ottawa and the rest of Canada, though they will be disappointed, will have no choice: they will negotiate.

Those Canadian citizens and leaders are realists; they recognize, among other things, the importance of the economic links between Quebec and the rest of Canada, and that it is much better to maintain them than to break and split up markets. Quebec proposes specifically to maintain the existing economic entity rather than break it up.

Economic association, which some English-Canadian spokesmen say will automatically be rejected should there be a YES in the Referendum, already exists insofar as its essentials are concerned, as explained above, and the Quebec government does not challenge it. What it does propose, quite firmly, is to negotiate its structures and its decision-making processes. Under these circumstances, stating that there will be no economic association is tantamount to saying that English Canada is ready to get along without the Quebec market, that it will create its own separate currency to avoid sharing one with Quebec, and that the Maritimes will agree to having a customs barrier put up between them and Ontario! It would then be the rest of Canada that would reject the advantages of economic union ...

If statements about the possibility of a refusal to negotiate cannot, as we have just seen, justify a negative answer in the Referendum, it is still appropriate to ask what the consequences of such an answer would be for Quebec's future ...

If they get the NO they want, Ottawa and the rest of Canada, buoyed up by a sense of relief and a bit of simplification, would inevitably conclude that, although somewhat late in the game, Quebecers are resigned and prepared to embrace the present federal system with no special demands, that they have finally chosen the status quo.

The Mandate

By giving a positive answer in the Referendum, Quebecers will express their desire to reach a new political agreement with the rest of Canada based, this time, on the legal equality of the two peoples. A YES vote by Quebecers would thus be, in fact, a mandate given the Quebec government to make this new agreement a reality through negotiation. By its vote, the Quebec people will have clearly established the negotiations on the principle of Quebec's accession, in law and in fact, to the status of sovereign state, and association with Canada. Sovereignty is inseparable from association ...

The Quebec government has always believed that it would take time to achieve the orderly and democratic constitutional change proposed. The transformation of the present federal system into an association between sovereign states can occur only through successive stages. The process proposed thus includes four major phases:

REFLECTION

Publication of this document is a decisive step in the phase of reflection and consultation to which all citizens are invited, so that they will know the exact content of what they will be asked to decide upon ...

REFERENDUM

Early in February 1980, the National Assembly should begin the debate on a motion by the Prime Minister proposing the adoption of the text of the question to be submitted to the voters. The text of this question, as the government has pledged, will be revealed before the end of this year, so that no one will be taken by surprise at the time of the debate, at the end of which it will be adopted.

Once the question is approved, the referendum writs will be issued in April or May, so that the vote can be held in May or June 1980.

(Note: The text of the question will be bilingual).

NEGOTIATION

If the result of the Referendum is positive, there will be a period of negotiation with Ottawa and the rest of Canada. Then Quebec will have unprecedented power at its disposal, based for the first time on the clearly expressed will of the Quebec population. These negotiations should bear first on the repatriation to Quebec of those powers exercised by the federal Parliament, and on the transfer of the corresponding resources.

Negotiations will also bear on the nature of the Quebec-Canada association, its content (the powers to be shared), institutions, rules of procedure and financing; other questions to be dealt with include territory, the protection of minorities, citizenship, the transfer of federal civil servants, the armed forces, etc.

All these negotiations will lead to the preparation of a treaty of association creating the Quebec-Canada community.

IMPLEMENTATION

It is necessary to ensure that during the period of transfer of powers the population does not ... suffer any decrease in government services. The transition must be planned in the preceding phase so as to avoid upsetting the operation of the administration. That will require agreement on a schedule for the transfers and a gradual establishment of the various services involved.

ACQUIRED RIGHTS

The Government of Quebec, not wanting any individual to be deprived of his or her rights as a result of this constitutional change, pledges to maintain acquired rights — allowances, pensions, services or jobs. The government also promises federal civil servants, if they are residents of Quebec and so wish, that they will be integrated into the Quebec civil service, without financial loss to them, as powers and resources are transferred from Ottawa to Quebec.

B) A New Canadian Federation, 1980
The Liberal Party of Quebec

At a moment when Quebecers are preparing to make an historic decision on their collective future, they have every right to ask that the major options competing for their loyalty be presented to them honestly and clearly.

The government of Quebec, led by the Parti Québécois, has already made public the broad outline of its option, sovereignty-association, in the white paper entitled "Quebec-Canada: A New Deal."

One objective emerges clearly from the white paper. The Parti Québécois and the present government, propose to make Quebec a fully sovereign state.

It is true the government's white paper also proposes an economic association between the future sovereign state of Quebec and whatever remains of Canada.

But such an economic association, even in the event of a "yes" vote in the referendum, appears highly improbable. It would depend upon the consent of the other partner, without which it could not come into being.

The Péquiste view of our collective future is new in terms of the radical solution proposed. However, their resolutely pessimistic view of our past history and our present situation is all too familiar.

In this frame of mind, they perpetuate an attitude which was held by the opponents of Confederation in the last century.

During the years which preceded the proclamation of the BNA Act, the enemies of this new constitution pronounced it to be a suicidal adventure for the people of Quebec. They predicted freely that Quebec and its traditions would be devoured by the Canadian federation, that it would mark the end of our culture and our own institutions.

It is this same theme, with a few variations, which forms the basis of the Péquiste refrain.

But alongside this negative attitude, there has always existed in Quebec another viewpoint, resolutely open to a more optimistic perspective of confidence and co-operation.

Those who hold this vision have always defended the existence in Quebec of a distinct and unique society, with all the attributes of a national community. Far from denigrating the Quebec government's key role in the development of this community, they are its very architects, the ones who have built and strengthened it.

The exponents of this larger vision unhesitatingly affirm the right of the people of Quebec to choose their own future.

But today, as in 1867, they believe profoundly that the best future for Quebec lies in a freely-made decision to remain within the Canadian federation.

In their eyes, the Canadian federal framework provides Quebec with two major advantages: the chance to develop freely, in accordance with its own nature, and at the same time to participate, without renouncing its own identity, in the benefits and challenges of a larger and much richer society.

The Quebec Fathers of Confederation did not fear the assimilation of Quebec in 1867. They believed that the federal challenge presented a unique occasion for the disparate colonies of that day to form a great country, one in which Quebec would be called upon to play a major role.

Those who defend the federal tie today are the true inheritors of that vision.

It is certainly necessary to review in depth the constitutional arrangements bequeathed to us in 1867. The venture has become urgent in the light of current tensions which have been generated not only in Quebec but elsewhere, and particularly in Western Canada.

But a realistic and honest evaluation of the Canadian federation can lead to only one conclusion — the assets far outweigh the liabilities.

In the short run, however, the primary and most urgent source of anxiety for the future of Canada comes from a problem as old as the federation itself; the relationship between the two founding peoples. The problem has never been resolved and is today more urgent than ever before.

It is evident that the only reasonably satisfactory relationship is one which is based on equality, an equality accepted by both parties.

However, in the past, francophones, because they were less numerous and much too frequently excluded from important decisions, came to the conclusion that equality worked in only one direction and remained, for them, a platitude, void of content.

For many years the problem presented itself in terms of the linguistic rights of francophones outside Quebec.

In 1867, the French believed that the new constitution guaranteed, at least in principle, the equality of French and English across the new Canadian territory. But the reality was quite different.

Almost everywhere outside of Quebec, the French language was relegated to second-class status.

Since throughout this period the minority language rights of anglophone Quebecers were scrupulously respected, francophones had every right to complain about the disregard in which their rights were held in the federal government, in the other provinces, and indeed, in important sectors of activity within Quebec itself.

It was one hundred years before Parliament began to resolve the situation. The federal Official Languages Act came into effect in 1969. And only in the course of the last twenty years have other provinces begun to redress injustices accumulated over a century.

Yet at a time when new measures have just begun to bear fruit, Quebec has toughened its language policy and oriented it in the direction of French unilingualism.

And at the same time that Quebec has been restricting the rights of the anglophone minority, it has been manifesting a reduced interest in the objective of achieving linguistic equality across the whole country.

So the question of linguistic rights remains critical. Recently some elements of a solution have begun to surface, but a just and durable constitutional resolution remains to be developed.

Before making a start on the project of constitutional reform, agreement should be reached on the objectives which are to be pursued.

We would establish the following as our fundamental goals:

1. We must aim at providing the people of this country with a written constitutional document, modern and Canadian. The document must be solemn and formal in character. It will define the commitment we have made to live together.

2. We must affirm the fundamental equality of the two founding peoples who have given, and still provide, this country its unique place in the family of nations.

3. We must ensure the judicial primacy of the rights and fundamental liberties of individual citizens in the Canadian political system.

4. We must affirm and give faithful recognition to the fundamental rights of the first inhabitants of this country.

5. We must acknowledge the richness of the cultural heritages of the different regions, and affirm Canada's interest in their preservation and development. We must also note the wealth of cultural, economic and social experience contributed by the ethnic groups, and assert their right to preserve their culture and heritage.

6. We must aim to provide equal access to economic, social and cultural development for all individuals, regions and provinces.

Keeping in mind provincial responsibilities in this area, we must, nevertheless, state clearly the federal government's fundamental role in the redistribution of wealth, and see that it is granted the necessary means for the efficient discharge of this responsibility.

7. We must maintain in Canada a federal system of government.

8. We must ensure the existence of a central power strong enough to serve the whole country in the face of whatever new challenges the modern world presents, whether internally or externally.

9. We must ensure the existence of provincial powers strong enough to take charge, in their respective territories, of the tasks related to the development of their physical and human resources.

This implies, among other things, the management of their natural resources, land use, local and provincial commerce, regional economic development, education and culture, social and sanitary services, the administration of justice, and social insurance schemes.

10. We must aim at establishing a clear division of legislative and fiscal responsibilities between the two orders of government. We must also aim at eliminating powers which are too general in nature, which allow almost limitless extension and therefore lead to abuse.

11. We must aim to ensure that the very great disproportion in size among the member-states of the federation can be corrected by the eventual amalgamation of some services, while still respecting the acquired rights of each province.

12. We must establish a system of arbitration for constitutional disputes which recognizes the fundamental dualism of the population and the judicial institutions of this country, and which is above all suspicion.

13. We must aim to recognize in the text of the constitution the fact that in almost all fields, any governmental action has international repercussions, a reality which has been magnified by the communications revolution.

We must affirm [the]need to harmonize provincial initiatives with the broad orientation of federal foreign policy. But we must draft this part of the constitutional text so that the province's role in those international activities relating to its areas of jurisdiction is recognized ...

Recommendations

1. The constitution should preserve the parliamentary system and responsible government as the form by which the new federation and the provinces will be governed.

2. Constitutional usages and customs basic to the rules of procedure of the House of Commons and of the legislatures should be entrenched in the constitution.

3. The constitution should state that the House of Commons and the legislatures will meet annually, and that the duration of their mandate be no more than four years.

In emergency situations, the mandate could be prolonged for a period not to exceed one year by a two-thirds vote of the members of the House or the legislature.

4. The constitution should oblige the House of Commons and the legislatures to hold at least one session a year.

5. The constitution should recognize the principle of universal suffrage and of free elections to both the House of Commons and the legislatures.

THE PROVINCES
The provinces must be sovereign and autonomous in their fields of jurisdiction. This implies that the provinces' exclusive fields of jurisdiction must remain inviolable, except by constitutional amendment or by their approval expressed at the level of the Federal Council.

The provinces are also equal in law to each other. They all have the same powers, the same rights and the same obligations.

The provinces are administered today by legislatures composed of a lieutenant-governor and a legislative assembly. We propose to maintain this regime ...

THE SENATE

Under the present constitution, the Canadian Senate has powers comparable to those of the House of Commons. It must approve all federal laws.

However, laws pertaining to taxation and to the use of public funds must first be presented in the House of Commons.

The Senate we have today was conceived at a time when it was deemed necessary to curb the democratic "excesses" of the members of Parliament elected through universal suffrage.

The Pépin-Robarts Report described numerous tasks which could have been carried out by the Senate.

They include the critical evaluation of the central government's bills, and their improvement, the protection of minority rights, the holding of enquiries, the encouragement of federal-provincial consultations in fields of common interest, and representation of the provinces on a basis fairer than that of a House elected through universal suffrage.

In practice, however, principally because of the nomination process which has been employed, the Senate has never been able to use all of the powers entrusted to it by the constitution.

For example, it has never played a significant role in federal-provincial relations.

Because this institution no longer seems to us to be adapted to the needs of a modern federal system, we propose that the Senate be abolished and that, henceforth, the federal Parliament be made up of only one body, the House of Commons ...

THE FEDERAL COUNCIL

It would have been difficult to imagine in 1867 the complex and vast operation which the governing of Canada was to become 100 years later. It was, at the time, easy to conceive of two levels of government, central and provincial, working more or less independently. Intergovernmental relations involved only a few isolated subjects and except for these special cases, it was unnecessary to establish a formal delineation of federal-provincial relations. Furthermore, the central government was equipped with extraordinary powers which transcended the division of jurisdictions and which would enable it to ensure the cohesion needed to preserve and unify the federation.

However, particularly in the last thirty years, there has been an uninterrupted and explosive growth in government activity.

Tensions have developed because of the expansion of provincial governments combined with frequent incursions by the federal government into their exclusive jurisdictions.

The imbalance between the responsibilities of each level of government and their fiscal resources has also caused many frustrations. Legislative and administrative overlapping and duplication have multiplied.

It has become more and more evident that federal-provincial relations are not sufficiently defined and are often based on confrontation rather than consultation and cooperation.

It has become more evident too, that in a modern federal system it is impossible to grant absolute jurisdiction to one or the other level of government in fields as complex as energy, industrial development, transport and social policy.

Constitutional reform will thus be inadequate if it simply improves the existing division of jurisdictions.

It is now imperative to invent an institution which will allow the provinces, which have become senior governments, to participate directly in the government of the federation itself, and to verify or influence, as the case may be, the federal government's actions in matters where consultation between the two levels of government is vital to the health of the federation.

The aim of such an institution is certainly not to prevent the central government from exercising sovereignty in the fields granted to it by the constitution.

Its aim is, rather, to ensure a better cohesion in Canadian policies, by allowing the provinces a say in the development of those federal initiatives which are so far-ranging that they affect the whole country and which, therefore, have implications for provincial jurisdictions.

COMPOSITION

This new institution would be known as the "Federal Council", to emphasize the fact that it is conceived as a special intergovernmental institution and not as a legislative assembly controlled by the central government.

The Federal Council would be formed by delegations from the provinces acting on the instructions of their respective governments. These provincial delegates would express the political policies of their governments and the length of their mandate would be determined in accordance with this principle.

The constitution would provide that the provincial premiers or their representatives would be ex officio members of their provinces' delegations.

There would be no delegates of the central government with a right to vote in the Federal Council.

THE DELEGATIONS AND THEIR VOTING PROCEDURE

In keeping with the nature of the Federal Council, provincial delegations would vote "en bloc" *according* to the instructions of their respective governments.

For example, a Federal Council of eighty members might be composed of the following delegations:

Prince Edward Island, 2 delegates; Newfoundland, 3 delegates; New Brunswick, 4 delegates; Nova Scotia, 4 delegates; Saskatchewan, 5 delegates; Manitoba, 5 delegates; Alberta, 8 delegates; British Columbia, 9 delegates; Ontario, 20 delegates; Quebec, 20 delegates.

Those territories which do not have the status of provinces, such as the Northwest Territories and the Yukon, nevertheless have important interests and issues which are their own and should enjoy full participation and voting rights at the Federal Council ...

The Federal Council's jurisdiction should be limited to predetermined subjects and should be exercised in the following way:

a) the council will ratify:
- the use of the federal emergency power;
- the use of federal spending power in fields of provincial jurisdiction;
- any intergovernmental delegation of legislative powers;
- treaties concluded by the federal government ... in fields of provincial jurisdiction;
- international and interprovincial marketing programs of agricultural products;
- the appointment of judges of the Supreme Court and of its chief justice, and their destitution when required;

- the appointment of presidents and chief executive officers of those federal and Crown corporations of major importance;

b) the council will give its advice on the following questions:
- the monetary, budgetary and fiscal policies of the federal government;
- mechanisms and operating formulas used for equalization; and
- in general, on all matters having, in its opinion, substantial regional or provincial impact.

The council should reflect Canada's duality by means of a permanent committee half of which will be made up of francophone delegates, which will be convened whenever this dimension of the Canadian reality is likely to be affected by federal proposals submitted for the council's consideration.

The constitution will contain a provision ensuring the Federal Council the necessary human, physical and financial resources, while protecting its independence from the House of Commons and from the federal government ...

Recommendations

1. The provinces should retain complete jurisdiction in matters of education and development of human resources.
2. The extent of this jurisdiction should be defined so as to cover the following matters:
   a) all levels of education;
   b) matters relating to the language of education, but subject to entrenched language rights;
   c) subsidies and bursaries;
   d) matters relating to social readaptation;
   e) manpower training;
   f) the training and control of trade associations and professional corporations; and
   g) the reception and integration of immigrants.
3. Research should not be considered as a separate head of jurisdiction but as a means of action to achieve objectives under the authority of either order of government.
4. The constitution should grant authority to the provinces in cultural matters including the arts, literature, leisure activities, cinema, theatre, plastic arts, radio and television programming, music, libraries, museums, archives, cultural exchanges, publishing and sports.

5. The federal government should be granted the specific powers necessary for the protection and development of the cultural heritage of all Canadians, including the power to create or maintain national institutions such as the Canadian Broadcasting Corporation, the national archives, a national library, the National Gallery and the National Film Board.

6. Aside from these specific jurisdictions, the federal government should be empowered to intervene in cultural matters on the basis of its spending powers. Such interventions should be subject to two-thirds approval by the Federal Council ...

Other Recommendations

1. The constitution should be repatriated within the framework of an over-all agreement on the content and procedure for adoption of a new constitution.

2. The provincial governments and the federal government should assume the political responsibility for constitutional reform.

3. The mechanism for achieving the reform of the constitution should be a special federal-provincial conference.

4. Such a conference should be preceded by a commitment on the part of all the provincial legislatures and of Parliament to:

   a) endow Canada with a new constitution and to repatriate the BNA Act;

   b) devote themselves without interruption to the project until it is completed;

   c) agree to increase representation by participating governments so that members of the opposition parties can be included, without voting rights.

5. When the project is completed, the new constitution should be submitted to the provincial legislatures and to Parliament for their approval ...

Sources

Introduction

Excerpt from Al Purdy, "A Walk on Wellington Street," 1968. Reprinted with permission.

Chapter 1. "Our Hands are Poor But Our Heads are Rich"

A. Morris, *The Treaties of Canada with the Indians of Manitoba and the North West-Territories* (Toronto: Belfords, Clarke and Co., 1880), pp. 55, 58–76, 321–324.

Chapter 2. "Not an Ordinary Criminal"

Alexander Campbell, "Memorandum Respecting the Case of The Queen v. Riel, prepared at the Request of the Committee of the Privy Council, November 25, 1885," Canada Sessional Papers 1886, Vol. 19, No. 43a. Honoré Mercier, "Speech, Champ de mars, November 22, 1885," in J.O. Pelland (ed.), *Biographie Discours Conferences, etc. de l'Hon. Honore Mercier* (Montreal: 1890). Wilfrid Laurier, House of Commons Debates, March 16, 1886. Joseph Adolphe Chapleau, House of Commons Debates, March 11, 1886. Charles A. Boulton, *Reminiscences of the North West Rebellion* (Toronto: Grip Printing & Publishing Co., 1886).

Chapter 3. "Hopeless Degradation of the Toiling Masses"

Canada, *The Royal Commission on the Relations of Labor and Capital in Canada*, 1889. "Fourth Annual Report of the Inspector of Factories," *Ontario, Sessional Papers*, XXIV (1892), v, no. 25, 6–7. "Preamble and declaration of principles of the Knights of Labor," in the Appendix, G. Kealey and B. Palmer, *Dreaming of What Might Be: The Knights of Labour in Ontario, 1880-1900* (Toronto: New Hogtown Press, 1987), pp. 399–400. Reprinted with the permission of New Hogtown Press. Many thanks for the research and invaluable collection of documents provided by M. Cross (ed.) in *The Workingman in the Nineteenth Century* (Toronto: Oxford University Press, 1974): "The Labour Question," *The Mail* (Toronto), April 25, 1872; "The Sweating System: The 'People's Press' Reports," from *The Daily Mail and Empire* (Toronto), October 9, 1897; "There is a Reason For It," *Industrial Banner* (London, Ontario), February, 1897; "Labour Demands Equal Rights,"

Industrial Banner (London, Ontario), October, 1897; "The Rise of Social-ism," *Labour Advocate* (Toronto), September 4, 1891; and "The Curse of Chinese Immigration: What It Has Done for Other Countries and What It is Doing for Canada," *Industrial Banner* (London, Ontario), October, 1897.

Chapter 4. "Let Someone Else Have a Taste of Our Good Life"

W.D. Scott, "The Immigration by Races," in A. Short and A.C. Doughty (eds.), *Canada and Its Provinces*, vol. 7 (Toronto: Glascow, 1914). Maria Adamowska's account is found in H. Piniuta (ed. and transl.), *Land of Pain, Land of Promise* (Saskatoon: Western Producer Prairie Books, 1978). Georgina Binnie-Clark, "Conditions of Life for Women in Canada" (1913).

Chapter 5. "Our Rightful Place"

Goldwin Smith, *Canada and the Canadian Question* (Toronto: Hunter Rose, 1891). George Grant, *On Imperial Federation* (1889). Henri Bourassa, "The French Canadian in the British Empire," *The Monthly Review*, IX, October 1902. W. Norris, "Canadian Nationality: A Present-day Plea," *The Canadian Monthly and National Review*, vol. IV, February 1880.

Chapter 6. "Malice and Bitterness"

"Pastoral Letter of the Bishops of the Ecclesiastical Province of Quebec, Sep-tember 22, 1875." W. Caven, "The Equal Rights Movement," University Quarterly Review, 1, 1890. Editorial, "Equal Rights," *The Brandon Sun*, May 16, 1889. Excerpt from "The Encyclical Letter of Pope Leo XIII," from *The American Catholic Quarterly Review*, vol. XXIII, no. 2, 1897, pp. 189–195, on the topic of "Education in Canada." R. Sellars, *The Tragedy of Quebec*, 1916 edition. J.M.R. Villeneuve, "And Our Dispersed Brethren..." in R. Cook (ed.), *French Canadian Nationalism* (Toronto: Macmillan, 1971), pp. 202-214. Translated from "Et nos Freres de la Dispersion," Notre Avenir Politique: Enquéte de l'Action Française (Montréal: Bibliothèque de l'Action Française). Reprinted with permission.

Chapter 7. "Throwing the Glass Aside"

"The Woman Question," *The Canadian Monthly and National Review*, May 1879, vol. II, pp. 568–70. Sonia Leathes, "Votes for Women," speech given to National Council of Women of Canada, Montreal, 1913, reprinted in *University Magazine*, February 1914, vol. XIII. S. Leacock, "The Woman

Question," in *Essays and Literary Studies* (New York: John Lane, 1916). Nellie McClung, from *The New Citizenship* (Political Equality League of Manitoba, n.d.), pp. 2–8. Reprinted with permission of the estate of Nellie McClung.

Chapter 8. "Dying for a Foreign Cause"

123rd Battalion Recruiting Leaflet, "Royal Grenadiers. Extracts from letter which appeared in the *Evening Telegram*, December 3rd, over the name of G.G. Starr:-", in B. Wilson (ed.), *Ontario and the First World War 1914–1918* (Toronto: University of Toronto Press, 1977), pp. 19–21. Reprinted with permission of the Champlain Society. Globe Editorial, 30th January 1915, p. 13, Peter McArthur's "Country Recruits," in B. Wilson (ed.), *Ontario and the First World War 1914–1918* (Toronto: University of Toronto Press, 1977), pp. 7–8. Reprinted with permission of the Champlain Society. Editorial, "No More Canadians For Overseas Service. This Young Dominion Has Sacrificed Enough," *Sault Express*, 23 June 1916, in B. Wilson (ed.), *Ontario and the First World War 1914–1918* (Toronto: University of Toronto Press, 1977), pp. 36–37. Reprinted with permission of the Champlain Society. "An Open Letter from Capt. Talbot Papineau to Mr. Henri Bourassa," in *Canadian Nationalism and the War* (Montreal: 1916). "Mr. Bourassa's Reply to Capt. Talbot Papineau's Letter," in *Canadian Nationalism and the War* (Montreal: 1916). Robert Laird Borden's speech on conscription is found in H. Borden (ed.), *Robert Laird Borden: His Memoirs*, vol. II (Toronto: Macmillan, 1938), pp. 698–701. Reprinted with permission. Francis Marion Beynon, "Conscription," *The Grain Grower's Guide*, 30 May 1917, vol. x, 934. Reprinted with permission.

Chapter 9. "Damming Up the Foul Streams of Degeneracy and Demoralization"

F.S. Spence, "The Economics of the Drink Question," *The Campaign Manual for Prohibition 1912* (Toronto: 1912). Excerpts from Emily Murphy, *The Black Candle* (1922). C.B. Farrar, "Social Aspects of Mental Deficiency," *Canadian Medical Association Journal*, 1926. H. A. Bruce, "Sterilization of the Feeble Minded," *Canadian Medical Association Journal*, September 1933.

Chapter 10. "This Is My Last Chance"

Selected letters from L. M. Grayson and M. Bliss (eds.), *The Wretched of Canada: Letters to R. B. Bennett 1930-1935* (Toronto: University of Toronto

Press, 1971). Reprinted with permission. "Experiences of a Depression Hobo," *Saskatchewan History*, 22, Spring 1969. Reprinted with the permission of the Saskatchewan Archives Board.

Chapter 11. "The Question of Loyalty"

"The Situation in 1940," *Report and Recommendations of the Special Committee on Orientals in British Columbia*, December 1940. A.W. Neill, *House of Commons Debates*, February 19, 1942. Muriel Kitagawa, excerpts from *This Is My Own: Letters to Wes and Other Writings on Japanese Canadians, 1941-1948* (Vancouver: Talonbooks, 1985). Reprinted with permission. W.L. Mackenzie King, *House of Commons Debates*, August 4, 1944.

Chapter 12. "Cinderella of the Empire"

Extract from Letter from High Commissioner in Newfoundland to Under-Secretary of State for External Affairs, in P. Bridle (ed.), *Documents on Relations Between Canada and Newfoundland* (Ottawa: Department of External Affairs, 1984), pp. 12–14. Memorandum from Permanent Under-Secretary of State for Dominions Affairs of Great Britain to Dominions Secretary, *ibid.*, pp. 26–29. Memorandum by Special Assistant to Under-Secretary of State for External Affairs, *ibid.*, pp. 98–99. Memorandum by Assistant Under-Secretary of State for Dominions Affairs of Great Britain, *ibid.*, pp. 130–133. High Commissioner in Newfoundland to Special Assistant to Under-Secretary of State for External Affairs, *ibid.*, p. 136. Memorandum from Under-Secretary of State for External Affairs to Prime Minister, *ibid.*, pp. 169–171. Extracts from Memorandum by High Commissioner in Newfoundland, January 9, 1948, *ibid.*, pp. 295–299. Extracts from Memorandum by High Commissioner in Newfoundland to Special Assistant to Under-Secretary of State for External Affairs, November 30, 1944, *ibid.*, p. 136. Memorandum by Second Political Division, *ibid.*, pp. 674–675. J. Smallwood, excerpts from *I Chose Canada* (Toronto: Macmillan, 1973). Reprinted with permission. P. Cashin's speech of January 27, 1948, in J. K. Hiler and M. F. Harrington (eds.), *Newfoundland National Convention 1946–48* (Montreal: McGill-Queens University Press, 1995). Reprinted with permission. "Are You In This List?" *The Confederate*, May 31, 1948.

Chapter 13. "Ignorant, Lazy and Unaware"

A.L. Doucette, Faculty of Education, University of Alberta, "Is Alberta Education A Failure? No...," *A.T.A. Magazine*, vol. 23, no. 3 (December, 1947), pp. 8–10. Report of the Superintendent of Winnipeg Schools, in Manitoba, Department of Education, *Report, 1937-38*, pp. 112–113. Alberta, Department of Education, Programme of Studies for the Intermediate School (Grades VII, VIII, IX) (Edmonton: 1935), pp. 5–9. C.E. Phillips, "New Schools for Democracy," *Behind the Headlines*, vol. 4, no. 6, published jointly by the Canadian Association for Adult Education and the Canadian Institute of Internal Affairs, 1944. Hilda Neatby, excerpts from *So Little for the Mind* (Toronto: Clarke, Irwin and Company, 1953), pp. 8–19. Reprinted with the permission of Stoddart Publishing Co. Limited. J.M. Paton, "Culture? Liberal Education? Education For Democracy? ... Does Anybody Know?" *The Teachers' Magazine, The Official Organ of The Provincial Association of Protestant Teachers of Quebec*, February, 1954, pp. 5–6. Reprinted with permission. J.M. Paton, "Dr. Neatby's 'Doctored' Diatribe: An unblushingly biased review of an unblushingly biased book," *The Teachers' Magazine, The Official Organ of The Provincial Association of Protestant Teachers of Quebec*, February, 1954, pp. 15–21. Reprinted with permission.

Chapter 14. "Ingested into the Eagle's Gut"

Canada, *Report of the Royal Commission on National Development in the Arts, Letters and Sciences* (Ottawa: King's Printer, 1951). Farley Mowat, "A Letter to My Son," in Al Purdy (ed.), *The New Romans* (Edmonton: Hurtig, 1968), pp. 1–6. Reprinted with permission. Robert Fulford, "Their America, and Mine," in T. Axworthy (ed.), *Our American Cousins* (Toronto: James Lorimer and Company, 1987), pp. 223–226. Reprinted with the author's permission. Mitchell Sharp, excerpted from "Canada-U.S. Relations: Options for the Future," *International Perspectives*, special volume (Autumn 1972), pp. 1–24. Reprinted with permission.

Chapter 15. "The Hard Knocks of History"

Pierre Trudeau, "Speech," August 8, 1969, Vancouver. Indian Association of Alberta, *Citizens Plus*, a brief presented to the federal government in response to "The Statement of the Government of Canada on Indian Policy" (i.e., "The White Paper"), June 1970. Harold Cardinal, excerpts from *The Unjust Society: The Tragedy of Canada's Indians* (Edmonton: M. G. Hurtig, 1969). W. Wuttunee, excerpts from *Ruffled Feathers: Indians in Canadian Society* (Calgary: Bell Books Ltd., 1971). Reprinted with permission.

Chapter 16. *"Turn On, Tune In, Take Over"*

"Turn On, Tune In, Take Over," *Georgia Straight*, Vancouver Free Press, vol. 1, September 8, 1967. "Grass in Class," *Georgia Straight*, Feb. 17–24, 1971. Chris MacLeod, "Learning to Live Without Schools," *Georgia Straight*, Oct. 8–15, 1969. Bob Cummings, excerpt from "Homosexuality," *Georgia Straight*, Dec. 15, 1967, p. 13. Bob Cummings, excerpt from "Atomic Roulette," *Georgia Straight*, Sept. 17–23, 1969. Jeannine Mitchell, "Cherry Point vs Life," *Georgia Straight*, Feb. 10–17, 1971. Doug Long, excerpt from "Cocaine: Ain't It a Shame," *Georgia Straight*, April 27–30, 1971. Bob Cummings, excerpt from "Come, All Ye Women," *Georgia Straight*, March 8–21, 1968. "On Abortion," *Georgia Straight*, May 14–18, 1971. Bob Cummings, "Off With Bras and Girdles," *Georgia Straight*, Feb. 2–22, 1968. Bob Cummings, "Obscenity: Who Really Cares, All is Phoney," *Georgia Straight*, Jan. 12–25, 1968. Bob Cummings, "Beautify Vancouver: Get a Haircut," *Georgia Straight*, Sept. 13–19, 1968. Bill Tait, "Easter Be-In," *Georgia Straight*, April 11–13, 1969. Reprinted with permission of the publisher. Dara Culhane, "Education — For What?" *Georgia Straight*, May 28–June 1, 1971. Reprinted with permission of the author.

Chapter 17. *"Merely a Province Among Others"*

Excerpts from *Quebec-Canada: A New Deal*, published by the Parti Québécois in 1979. Reprinted with the permission of the Parti Québécois. Excerpts from *A New Canadian Federalism*, published by the Liberal Party of Quebec in 1980. Reprinted with the permission of the Liberal Party of Quebec.

Note: All excerpts from government documents have been reprinted with the permission of the Ministry of Supplies and Services, Ottawa.

Every attempt has been made to acquire permission to reprint articles in this book. We would be grateful for information that would allow us to correct any errors or omissions in a subsequent edition of the work.